Python Cookbook™

Other resources from O'Reilly

Related titles
Python in a Nutshell   Programming Python
Python Pocket Reference   Python Standard Library
Learning Python

oreilly.com
oreilly.com is more than a complete catalog of O'Reilly books. You'll also find links to news, events, articles, weblogs, sample chapters, and code examples.

oreillynet.com is the essential portal for developers interested in open and emerging technologies, including new platforms, programming languages, and operating systems.

Conferences
O'Reilly brings diverse innovators together to nurture the ideas that spark revolutionary industries. We specialize in documenting the latest tools and systems, translating the innovator's knowledge into useful skills for those in the trenches. Visit *conferences.oreilly.com* for our upcoming events.

Safari Bookshelf (*safari.oreilly.com*) is the premier online reference library for programmers and IT professionals. Conduct searches across more than 1,000 books. Subscribers can zero in on answers to time-critical questions in a matter of seconds. Read the books on your Bookshelf from cover to cover or simply flip to the page you need. Try it today with a free trial.

SECOND EDITION

Python Cookbook™

Edited by Alex Martelli,
Anna Martelli Ravenscroft, and David Ascher

O'REILLY®

Beijing · Cambridge · Farnham · Köln · Paris · Sebastopol · Taipei · Tokyo

Python Cookbook™, Second Edition
Edited by Alex Martelli, Anna Martelli Ravenscroft, and David Ascher

Compilation copyright © 2005, 2002 O'Reilly Media, Inc. All rights reserved.
Printed in the United States of America.

Copyright of original recipes is retained by the individual authors.

Published by O'Reilly Media, Inc., 1005 Gravenstein Highway North, Sebastopol, CA 95472.

O'Reilly books may be purchased for educational, business, or sales promotional use. Online editions are also available for most titles (*safari.oreilly.com*). For more information, contact our corporate/institutional sales department: (800) 998-9938 or *corporate@oreilly.com*.

Editor:	Jonathan Gennick
Production Editor:	Darren Kelly
Cover Designer:	Emma Colby
Interior Designer:	David Futato
Production Services:	Nancy Crumpton

Printing History:

July 2002:	First Edition.
March 2005:	Second Edition.

Nutshell Handbook, the Nutshell Handbook logo, and the O'Reilly logo are registered trademarks of O'Reilly Media, Inc. The *Cookbook* series designations, *Python Cookbook*, the image of a springhaas, and related trade dress are trademarks of O'Reilly Media, Inc.

Many of the designations used by manufacturers and sellers to distinguish their products are claimed as trademarks. Where those designations appear in this book, and O'Reilly Media, Inc. was aware of a trademark claim, the designations have been printed in caps or initial caps.

While every precaution has been taken in the preparation of this book, the publisher and authors assume no responsibility for errors or omissions, or for damages resulting from the use of the information contained herein.

 This book uses RepKover™, a durable and flexible lay-flat binding.

ISBN-10: 0-596-00797-3
ISBN-13: 978-0-596-00797-3
[M]

Table of Contents

Preface

This book is not a typical O'Reilly book, written as a cohesive manuscript by one or two authors. Instead, it is a new kind of book—a bold attempt at applying some principles of open source development to book authoring. Over 300 members of the Python community contributed materials to this book. In this Preface, we, the editors, want to give you, the reader, some background regarding how this book came about and the processes and people involved, and some thoughts about the implications of this new form.

The Design of the Book

In early 2000, Frank Willison, then Editor-in-Chief of O'Reilly & Associates, contacted me (David Ascher) to find out if I wanted to write a book. Frank had been the editor for *Learning Python*, which I cowrote with Mark Lutz. Since I had just taken a job at what was then considered a Perl shop (ActiveState), I didn't have the bandwidth necessary to write another book, and plans for the project were gently shelved. Periodically, however, Frank would send me an email or chat with me at a conference regarding some of the book topics we had discussed. One of Frank's ideas was to create a *Python Cookbook*, based on the concept first used by Tom Christiansen and Nathan Torkington with the *Perl Cookbook*. Frank wanted to replicate the success of the *Perl Cookbook*, but he wanted a broader set of people to provide input. He thought that, much as in a real cookbook, a larger set of authors would provide for a greater range of tastes. The quality, in his vision, would be ensured by the oversight of a technical editor, combined with O'Reilly's editorial review process.

Frank and Dick Hardt, ActiveState's CEO, realized that Frank's goal could be combined with ActiveState's goal of creating a community site for open source programmers, called the ActiveState Programmer's Network (ASPN). ActiveState had a popular web site, with the infrastructure required to host a wide variety of content, but it wasn't in the business of creating original content. ActiveState always felt that the open source communities were the best sources of accurate and up-to-date content, even if sometimes that content was hard to find.

The O'Reilly and ActiveState teams quickly realized that the two goals were aligned and that a joint venture would be the best way to achieve the following key objectives:

- Creating an online repository of Python recipes by Python programmers for Python programmers
- Publishing a book containing the best of those recipes, accompanied by overviews and background material written by key Python figures
- Learning what it would take to create a book with a different authoring model

At the same time, two other activities were happening. First, those of us at ActiveState, including Paul Prescod, were actively looking for "stars" to join ActiveState's development team. One of the candidates being recruited was the famous (but unknown to us, at the time) Alex Martelli. Alex was famous because of his numerous and exhaustive postings on the Python mailing list, where he exhibited an unending patience for explaining Python's subtleties and joys to the increasing audience of Python programmers. He was unknown because he lived in Italy and, since he was a relative newcomer to the Python community, none of the old Python hands had ever met him—their paths had not happened to cross back in the 1980s when Alex lived in the United States, working for IBM Research and enthusiastically using and promoting other high-level languages (at the time, mostly IBM's Rexx).

ActiveState wooed Alex, trying to convince him to move to Vancouver. We came quite close, but his employer put some golden handcuffs on him, and somehow Vancouver's weather couldn't compete with Italy's. Alex stayed in Italy, much to my disappointment. As it happened, Alex was also at that time negotiating with O'Reilly about writing a book. Alex wanted to write a cookbook, but O'Reilly explained that the cookbook was already signed. Later, Alex and O'Reilly signed a contract for *Python in Nutshell*.

The second ongoing activity was the creation of the Python Software Foundation. For a variety of reasons, best left to discussion over beers at a conference, everyone in the Python community wanted to create a non-profit organization that would be the holder of Python's intellectual property, to ensure that Python would be on a legally strong footing. However, such an organization needed both financial support and buy-in from the Python community to be successful.

Given all these parameters, the various parties agreed to the following plan:

- ActiveState would build an online cookbook, a mechanism by which anyone could submit a recipe (i.e., a snippet of Python code addressing a particular problem, accompanied by a discussion of the recipe, much like a description of why one should use cream of tartar when whipping egg whites). To foster a community of authors and encourage peer review, the web site would also let readers of the recipes suggest changes, ask questions, and so on.

- As part of my ActiveState job, I would edit and ensure the quality of the recipes. Alex Martelli joined the project as a co-editor when the material was being prepared for publication, and, with Anna Martelli Ravenscroft, took over as primary editor for the second edition.

- O'Reilly would publish the best recipes as the *Python Cookbook*.

- In lieu of author royalties for the recipes, a portion of the proceeds from the book sales would be donated to the Python Software Foundation.

The Implementation of the Book

The online cookbook (at *http://aspn.activestate.com/ASPN/Cookbook/Python/*) was the entry point for the recipes. Users got free accounts, filled in a form, and presto, their recipes became part of the cookbook. Thousands of people read the recipes, and some added comments, and so, in the publishing equivalent of peer review, the recipes matured and grew. While it was predictable that the chance of getting your name in print would get people attracted to the online cookbook, the ongoing success of the cookbook, with dozens of recipes added monthly and more and more references to it on the newsgroups, is a testament to the value it brings to the readers—value which is provided by the recipe authors.

Starting from the materials available on the site, the implementation of the book was mostly a question of selecting, merging, ordering, and editing the materials. A few more details about this part of the work are in the "Organization" section of this Preface.

Using the Code from This Book

This book is here to help you get your job done. In general, you may use the code in this book in your programs and documentation. You do not need to contact us for permission unless you're reproducing a significant portion of the code. For example, writing a program that uses several chunks of code from this book does not require permission. Selling or distributing a CD-ROM of code taken from O'Reilly books does require permission. Answering a question by citing this book and quoting example code does not require permission. Incorporating a significant amount of code from this book into your product's documentation does require permission. We appreciate, but do not require, attribution. An attribution usually includes the title, author, publisher, and ISBN. For example: "Python Cookbook, 2d ed., by Alex Martelli, Anna Martelli Ravenscroft, and David Ascher (O'Reilly Media, 2005) 0-596-00797-3." If you feel your use of code from this book falls outside fair use or the permission given above, feel free to contact us at *permissions@oreilly.com*.

Audience

We expect that you know at least some Python. This book does not attempt to teach Python as a whole; rather, it presents some specific techniques and concepts (and occasionally tricks) for dealing with particular tasks. If you are looking for an introduction to Python, consider some of the books described in the "Further Reading" section of this Preface. However, you don't need to know a lot of Python to find this book helpful. Chapters include recipes demonstrating the best techniques for accomplishing some elementary and general tasks, as well as more complex or specialized ones. We have also added sidebars, here and there, to clarify certain concepts which are used in the book and which you may have heard of, but which might still be unclear to you. However, this is definitely not a book *just* for beginners. The main target audience is the whole Python community, mostly made up of pretty good programmers, neither newbies nor wizards. And if you *do* already know a lot about Python, you may be in for a pleasant surprise! We've included recipes that explore some the newest and least well-known areas of Python. You might very well learn a few things—we did! Regardless of where you fall along the spectrum of Python expertise, and more generally of programming skill, we believe you will get something valuable from this book.

If you already own the first edition, you may be wondering whether you need this second edition, too. We think the answer is "yes." The first edition had 245 recipes; we kept 146 of those (with lots of editing in almost all cases), and added 192 new ones, for a total of 338 recipes in this second edition. So, over half of the recipes in this edition are completely new, and all the recipes are updated to apply to today's Python—releases 2.3 and 2.4. Indeed, this update is the main factor which lets us have almost 100 more recipes in a book of about the same size. The first edition covered all versions from 1.5.2 (and sometimes earlier) to 2.2; this one focuses firmly on 2.3 and 2.4. Thanks to the greater power of today's Python, and, even more, thanks to the fact that this edition avoids the "historical" treatises about how you had to do things in Python versions released 5 or more years ago, we were able to provide substantially more currently relevant recipes and information in roughly the same amount of space.

Organization

This book has 20 chapters. Each chapter is devoted to a particular kind of recipe, such as algorithms, text processing, databases, and so on. The 1st edition had 17 chapters. There have been improvements to Python, both language and library, and to the corpus of recipes the Python community has posted to the cookbook site, that convinced us to add three entirely new chapters: on the iterators and generators introduced in Python 2.3; on Python's support for time and money operations, both old and new; and on new, advanced tools introduced in Python 2.2 and following releases (custom descriptors, decorators, metaclasses). Each chapter contains an introduction, written by an expert in the field, followed by recipes selected from the online cookbook (in some cases—about 5% of this book's recipes—a few new recipes were specially written for this volume) and edited to fit the book's formatting and style requirements. Alex (with some help from Anna) did the vast majority of the selection—determining which recipes from the first edition to keep and update, and selecting new recipes to add, or merge with others, from the nearly 1,000 available on the site (so, if a recipe you posted to the cookbook site didn't get into this printed edition, it's *his* fault!). He also decided which subjects just *had* to be covered and thus might need specially written recipes—although he couldn't manage to get quite *all* of the specially written recipes he wanted, so anything that's missing, and wasn't on the cookbook site, might not be entirely his fault.

Once the selection was complete, the work turned to editing the recipes, and to merging multiple recipes, as well as incorporating important contents from many significant comments posted about the recipes. This proved to be quite a challenge, just as it had been for the first edition, but even more so. The recipes varied widely in their organization, level of completeness, and sophistication. With over 300 authors involved, over 300 different "voices" were included in the text. We have striven to maintain a variety of styles to reflect the true nature of this book, the book written by the entire Python community. However, we edited each recipe, sometimes quite considerably, to make it as accessible and useful as possible, ensuring enough uniformity in structure and presentation to maximize the usability of the book as a whole. Most recipes, both from the first edition and from the online site, had to be updated, sometimes heavily, to take advantage of new tools and better approaches developed since those recipes were originally posted. We also carefully reconsidered (and slightly altered) the ordering of chapters, and the placement and ordering of recipes within chapters; our goal in this reordering was to maximize the book's usefulness for both newcomers to Python and seasoned veterans, and, also, for both readers tackling the book sequentially, cover to cover, and ones just dipping in, in "random access" fashion, to look for help on some specific area.

While the book should thus definitely be accessible "by hops and jumps," we nevertheless believe a first sequential skim will amply repay the modest time you, the reader, invest in it. On such a skim, skip every recipe that you have trouble following or that is of no current interest to you. Despite the skipping, you'll still get a sense of how the whole book hangs together and of where certain subjects are covered, which will stand you in good stead both for later in-depth sequential reading, if that's your choice, and for "random access" reading. To further help you get a sense of what's where in the book, here's a capsule summary of each chapter's contents, and equally capsule bios of the Python experts who were so kind as to take on the task of writing the chapters' "Introduction" sections.

Chapter 1, *Text*, introduction by Fred L. Drake, Jr.

This chapter contains recipes for manipulating text in a variety of ways, including combining, filtering, and formatting strings, substituting variables throughout a text document, and dealing with Unicode.

Fred Drake is a member of the PythonLabs group, working on Python development. A father of three, Fred is best known in the Python community for single-handedly maintaining the official documentation. Fred is a co-author of *Python & XML* (O'Reilly).

Chapter 2, *Files*, introduction by Mark Lutz

This chapter presents techniques for working with data in files and for manipulating files and directories within the filesystem, including specific file formats and archive formats such as *tar* and *zip*.

Mark Lutz is well known to most Python users as the most prolific author of Python books, including *Programming Python*, *Python Pocket Reference*, and *Learning Python* (all from O'Reilly), which he co-authored with David Ascher. Mark is also a leading Python trainer, spreading the Python gospel throughout the world.

Chapter 3, *Time and Money*, introduction by Gustavo Niemeyer and Facundo Batista

This chapter (new in this edition) presents tools and techniques for working with dates, times, decimal numbers, and some other money-related issues.

Gustavo Niemeyer is the author of the third-party dateutil module, as well as a variety of other Python extensions and projects. Gustavo lives in Brazil. Facundo Batista is the author of the Decimal PEP 327, and of the standard library module decimal, which brought floating-point decimal support to Python 2.4. He lives in Argentina. The editors were delighted to bring them together for this introduction.

Chapter 4, *Python Shortcuts*, introduction by David Ascher

This chapter includes recipes for many common techniques that can be used anywhere, or that don't really fit into any of the other, more specific recipe categories.

David Ascher is a co-editor of this volume. David's background spans physics, vision research, scientific visualization, computer graphics, a variety of programming languages, co-authoring *Learning Python* (O'Reilly), teaching Python, and these days, a slew of technical and nontechnical tasks such as managing the ActiveState team. David also gets roped into organizing Python conferences on a regular basis.

Chapter 5, *Searching and Sorting*, introduction by Tim Peters

This chapter covers techniques for searching and sorting in Python. Many of the recipes explore creative uses of the stable and fast list.sort in conjunction with the decorate-sort-undecorate (DSU) idiom (newly built in with Python 2.4), while others demonstrate the power of heapq, bisect, and other Python searching and sorting tools.

Tim Peters, also known as *the tim-bot*, is one of the mythological figures of the Python world. He is the oracle, channeling Guido van Rossum when Guido is busy, channeling the IEEE-754 floating-point committee when anyone asks anything remotely relevant, and appearing conservative while pushing for a constant evolution in the language. Tim is a member of the PythonLabs team.

Chapter 6, *Object-Oriented Programming*, introduction by Alex Martelli
This chapter offers a wide range of recipes that demonstrate the power of object-oriented programming with Python, including fundamental techniques such as delegating and controlling attribute access via special methods, intermediate ones such as the implementation of various design patterns, and some simple but useful applications of advanced concepts, such as custom metaclasses, which are covered in greater depth in Chapter 20.

Alex Martelli, also known as *the martelli-bot*, is a co-editor of this volume. After almost a decade with IBM Research, then a bit more than that with think3, inc., Alex now works as a freelance consultant, most recently for AB Strakt, a Swedish Python-centered firm. He also edits and writes Python articles and books, including *Python in a Nutshell* (O'Reilly) and, occasionally, research works on the game of contract bridge.

Chapter 7, *Persistence and Databases*, introduction by Aaron Watters
This chapter presents Python techniques for persistence, including serialization approaches and interaction with various databases.

Aaron Watters was one of the earliest advocates of Python and is an expert in databases. He's known for having been the lead author on the first book on Python (*Internet Programming with Python*, M&T Books, now out of print), and he has authored many widely used Python extensions, such as kjBuckets and kwParsing. Aaron currently works as a freelance consultant.

Chapter 8, *Debugging and Testing*, introduction by Mark Hammond
This chapter includes a collection of recipes that assist with the debugging and testing process, from customizing error logging and traceback information, to unit testing with custom modules, unittest and doctest.

Mark Hammond is best known for his work supporting Python on the Windows platform. With Greg Stein, he built an incredible library of modules interfacing Python to a wide variety of APIs, libraries, and component models such as COM. He is also an expert designer and builder of developer tools, most notably Pythonwin and Komodo. Finally, Mark is an expert at debugging even the most messy systems—during Komodo development, for example, Mark was often called upon to debug problems that spanned three languages (Python, C++, JavaScript), multiple threads, and multiple processes. Mark is also co-author, with Andy Robinson, of *Python Programming on Win32* (O'Reilly).

Chapter 9, *Processes, Threads, and Synchronization*, introduction by Greg Wilson
This chapter covers a variety of techniques for concurrent programming, including threads, queues, and multiple processes.

Greg Wilson writes children's books, as well as books on parallel programming and data crunching. When he's not doing that, he's a contributing editor with *Doctor Dobb's Journal*, an adjunct professor in Computer Science at the University of Toronto, and a freelance software developer. Greg was the original driving force behind the Software Carpentry project, and he recently received a grant from the Python Software Foundation to develop Pythonic course material for computational scientists and engineers.

Chapter 10, *System Administration*, introduction by Donn Cave
This chapter includes recipes for a number of common system administration tasks, from generating passwords and interacting with the Windows registry, to handling mailbox and web server issues.

Donn Cave is a software engineer at the University of Washington's central computer site. Over the years, Donn has proven to be a fount of information on *comp.lang.python* on all matters related to system calls, Unix, system administration, files, signals, and the like.

Chapter 11, *User Interfaces*, introduction by Fredrik Lundh
This chapter contains recipes for common GUI tasks, mostly with Tkinter, but also a smattering of wxPython, Qt, image processing, and GUI recipes specific to Jython (for JVM—Java Virtual Machine), Mac OS X, and IronPython (for dotNET).

Fredrik Lundh, also known as *the eff-bot*, is the CTO of Secret Labs AB, a Swedish Python-focused company providing a variety of products and technologies. Fredrik is the world's leading expert on Tkinter (the most popular GUI toolkit for Python), as well as the main author of the Python Imaging Library (PIL). He is also the author of *Python Standard Library* (O'Reilly), which is a good complement to this volume and focuses on the modules in the standard Python library. Finally, he is a prolific contributor to *comp.lang.python*, helping novices and experts alike.

Chapter 12, *Processing XML*, introduction by Paul Prescod
This chapter offers techniques for parsing, processing, and generating XML using a variety of Python tools.

Paul Prescod is an expert in three technologies: Python, which he need not justify; XML, which makes sense in a pragmatic world (Paul is co-author of the *XML Handbook*, with Charles Goldfarb, published by Prentice Hall); and Unicode, which somehow must address some deep-seated desire for pain and confusion that neither of the other two technologies satisfies. Paul is currently a product manager at Blast Radius.

Chapter 13, *Network Programming*, introduction by Guido van Rossum

This chapter covers a variety of network programming techniques, from writing basic TCP clients and servers to manipulating MIME messages.

Guido created Python, nurtured it throughout its infancy, and is shepherding its growth. Need we say more?

Chapter 14, *Web Programming*, introduction by Andy McKay

This chapter presents a variety of web-related recipes, including ones for CGI scripting, running a Java servlet with Jython, and accessing the content of web pages.

Andy McKay is the co-founder and vice president of Enfold Systems. In the last few years, Andy went from being a happy Perl user to a fanatical Python, Zope, and Plone expert. He wrote the *Definitive Guide to Plone* (Apress) and runs the popular Zope discussion site, *http://www.zopezen.org*.

Chapter 15, *Distributed Programming*, introduction by Jeremy Hylton

This chapter provides recipes for using Python in simple distributed systems, including XML-RPC, CORBA, and Twisted's Perspective Broker.

Jeremy Hylton works for Google. In addition to young twins, Jeremy's interests including programming language theory, parsers, and the like. As part of his work for CNRI, Jeremy worked on a variety of distributed systems.

Chapter 16, *Programs About Programs*, introduction by Paul F. Dubois

This chapter contains Python techniques that involve program introspection, currying, dynamic importing, distributing programs, lexing and parsing.

Paul Dubois has been working at the Lawrence Livermore National Laboratory for many years, building software systems for scientists working on everything from nuclear simulations to climate modeling. He has considerable experience with a wide range of scientific computing problems, as well as experience with language design and advanced object-oriented programming techniques.

Chapter 17, *Extending and Embedding*, introduction by David Beazley

This chapter offers techniques for extending Python and recipes that assist in the development of extensions.

David Beazley's chief claim to fame is SWIG, an amazingly powerful hack that lets one quickly wrap C and other libraries and use them from Python, Tcl, Perl, and myriad other languages. Behind this seemingly language-neutral tool lies a Python supporter of the first order, as evidenced by his book, *Python Essential Reference* (New Riders). David Beazley is a fairly sick man (in a good way), leading us to believe that more scarily useful tools are likely to emerge from his brain. He's currently inflicting his sense of humor on computer science students at the University of Chicago.

Chapter 18, *Algorithms*, introduction by Tim Peters

> This chapter provides a collection of fascinating and useful algorithms and data structures implemented in Python.

> See the discussion of Chapter 5 for information about Tim Peters.

Chapter 19, *Iterators and Generators*, introduction by Raymond Hettinger

> This chapter (new in this edition) contains recipes demonstrating the variety and power of iterators and generators—how Python makes your loops' structures simpler, faster, and reusable.

> Raymond Hettinger is the creator of the `itertools` package, original proposer of generator expressions, and has become a major contributor to the development of Python—if you don't know who originated and implemented some major novelty or important optimization in the 2.3 and 2.4 releases of Python, our advice is to bet it was Raymond!

Chapter 20, *Descriptors, Decorators, and Metaclasses*, introduction by Raymond Hettinger

> This chapter (new in this edition) provides an in-depth look into the infrastructural elements which make Python's OOP so powerful and smooth, and how you can exploit and customize them for fun and profit. From handy idioms for building properties, to aliasing and caching attributes, all the way to decorators which optimize your functions by hacking their bytecode and to a factory of custom metaclasses to solve metatype conflicts, this chapter shows how, while surely "there be dragons here," they're the wise, powerful and beneficent Chinese variety thereof...!

> See the discussion of Chapter 19 for information about Raymond Hettinger.

Further Reading

There are many texts available to help you learn Python or refine your Python knowledge, from introductory texts all the way to quite formal language descriptions.

We recommend the following books for general information about Python (all these books cover at least Python 2.2, unless otherwise noted):

- *Python Programming for the Absolute Beginner*, by Michael Dawson (Thomson Course Technology), is a hands-on, highly accessible introduction to Python for people who have never programmed.

- *Learning Python*, by Mark Lutz and David Ascher (O'Reilly), is a thorough introduction to the fundamentals of Python.

- *Practical Python*, by Magnus Lie Hetland (APress), is an introduction to Python which also develops, in detail, ten fully worked out, substantial programs in many different areas.

- *Dive into Python*, by Mark Pilgrim (APress), is a fast-paced introduction to Python for experienced programmers, and it is also freely available for online reading and downloading (*http://diveintopython.org/*).
- *Python Standard Library*, by Fredrik Lundh (O'Reilly), provides a use case for each module in the rich library that comes with every standard Python distribution (in the current first edition, the book only covers Python up to 2.0).
- *Programming Python*, by Mark Lutz (O'Reilly), is a thorough rundown of Python programming techniques (in the current second edition, the book only covers Python up to 2.0).
- *Python Essential Reference*, by David Beazley (New Riders), is a quick reference that focuses on the Python language and the core Python libraries (in the current second edition, the book only covers Python up to 2.1).
- *Python in a Nutshell*, by Alex Martelli (O'Reilly), is a comprehensive quick reference to the Python language and the key libraries used by most Python programmers.

In addition, several more special-purpose books can help you explore particular aspects of Python programming. Which books you will like best depends a lot on your areas of interest. From personal experience, the editors can recommend at least the following:

- *Python and XML*, by Christopher A. Jones and Fred L. Drake, Jr. (O'Reilly), offers thorough coverage of using Python to read, process, and transform XML.
- *Jython Essentials*, by Samuele Pedroni and Noel Rappin (O'Reilly), is the authoritative book on Jython, the port of Python to the JVM. Particularly useful if you already know some (or a lot of) Java.
- *Game Programming with Python*, by Sean Riley (Charles River Media), covers programming computer games with Python, all the way from advanced graphics to moderate amounts of "artificial intelligence."
- *Python Web Programming*, by Steve Holden (New Riders), covers building networked systems using Python, with introductions to many other related technologies (databases, HTTP, HTML, etc.). Very suitable for readers with none to medium experience with these fields, but has something to teach everyone.

In addition to these books, other important sources of information can help explain some of the code in the recipes in this book. We've pointed out the information that seemed particularly relevant in the "See Also" sections of each recipe. In these sections, we often refer to the standard Python documentation: most often the *Library Reference*, sometimes the *Reference Manual*, and occasionally the *Tutorial*. This documentation is freely available in a variety of forms:

- On the *python.org* web site (at *http://www.python.org/doc/*), which always contains the most up-to-date documentation about Python.

- On the *pydoc.org* web site (at *http://pydoc.org/*), accompanied by module-by-module documentation of the standard library automatically generated by the very useful pydoc tool.

- In Python itself. Recent versions of Python boast a nice online help system, which is worth exploring if you've never used it. Just type help( ) at the interactive Python interpreter prompt to start exploring.

- As part of the online help in your Python installation. ActivePython's installer, for example, includes a searchable Windows help file. The standard Python distribution currently includes HTML pages, but there are plans to include a similar Windows Help file in future releases.

We have not included specific section numbers in our references to the standard Python documentation, since the organization of these manuals can change from release to release. You should be able to use the table of contents and indexes to find the relevant material. For the *Library Reference*, in particular, the Module Index (an alphabetical list of all standard library modules, each module name being a hyperlink to the *Library Reference* documentation for that module) is invaluable. Similarly, we have not given specific pointers in our references to *Python in a Nutshell*: that book is still in its first edition (covering Python up to 2.2) at the time of this writing, but by the time you're reading, a second edition (covering Python 2.3 and 2.4) is likely to be forthcoming, if not already published.

Conventions Used in This Book

Pronouns: the first person singular is meant to convey that the recipe's or chapter introduction's author is speaking (when multiple credits are given for a recipe, the author is the first person credited); however, even such remarks have at times had to be edited enough that they may not reflect the original author's intended meaning (we, the editors, tried hard to avoid that, but we know we must have failed in some cases, since there were so many remarks, and authorial intent was often not entirely clear). The second person is meant to refer to you, the reader. The first person plural collectively indicates you, the reader, plus the recipe's author and co-authors, the editors, and my friend Joe (hi Joe!)—in other words, it's a very inclusive "we" or "us."

Code: each block of code may indicate a complete module or script (or, often, a Python source file that is usable both as a script and as a module), an isolated snippet from some hypothetical module or script, or part of a Python interactive interpreter session (indicated by the prompt >>>).

The following typographical conventions are used throughout this book:

Italic for commands, filenames, for emphasis, and for first use of a term.

Constant width for general code fragments and keywords (mostly Python ones, but also other languages, such as C or HTML, where they occur). Constant width is also used for all names defined in Python's library and third-party modules.

Constant width bold is used to emphasize particular lines within code listings and show output that is produced.

How to Contact Us

We have tested and verified all the information in this book to the best of our abilities, but you may find that some features have changed, or that we have let errors slip through the production of the book. Please let us know of any errors that you find, as well as any suggestions for future editions, by writing to:

O'Reilly Media
1005 Gravenstein Highway North
Sebastopol, CA 95472
(800) 998-9938 (in the United States or Canada)
(707) 829-0515 (international/local)
(707) 829-0104 (fax)

We have a web site for the book, where we'll list examples, errata, and any plans for future editions. You can access this page at:

http://www.oreilly.com/catalog/pythoncook2

To ask technical questions or comment on the book, send email to:

bookquestions@oreilly.com

For more information about our books, conferences, Resource Centers, and the O'Reilly Network, see our web site at:

http://www.oreilly.com/

The online cookbook from which most of the recipes for this book were taken is available at:

http://aspn.activestate.com/ASPN/Cookbook/Python

Safari® Enabled

When you see a Safari Enabled icon on the cover of your favorite technology book, that means the book is available online through the O'Reilly Network Safari Bookshelf.

Safari offers a solution that's better than e-books. It's a virtual library that lets you easily search thousands of top tech books, cut and paste code samples, download chapters, and find quick answers when you need the most accurate, current information. Try it for free at *http://safari.oreilly.com*.

Acknowledgments

Most publications, from mysteries to scientific papers to computer books, claim that the work being published would not have been possible without the collaboration of many others, typically including local forensic scientists, colleagues, and children, respectively. This book makes this claim to an extreme degree. Most of the words, code, and ideas in this volume were contributed by people not listed on the front cover. The original recipe authors, readers who submitted useful and insightful comments to the cookbook web site, and the authors of the chapter introductions, are the true authors of the book, and they deserve the credit.

David Ascher

The software that runs the online cookbook was the product of Andy McKay's constant and diligent effort. Andy was ActiveState's key Zope developer during the online data-collection phase of this project, and one of the key developers behind ASPN (*http://aspn.activestate.com*), ActiveState's content site, which serves a wide variety of information for and by programmers of open source languages such as Python, Perl, PHP, Tcl, and XSLT. Andy McKay used to be a Perl developer, by the way. At about the same time that I started at ActiveState, the company decided to use Zope to build what would become ASPN. In the years that followed, Andy has become a Zope master and somewhat of a Python fanatic (without any advocacy from me!), and is currently a Zope and Plone author, consultant and entrepreneur. Based on an original design that I put together with Diane Mueller, also of ActiveState, Andy single-handedly implemented ASPN in record time, then proceeded to adjust it to ever-changing requirements for new features that we hadn't anticipated in the early design phase, staying cheerful and professional throughout. It's a pleasure to have him as the author of the introduction to the chapter on web recipes. Since Andy's departure, James McGill has taken over as caretaker of the online cookbook—he makes sure that the cookbook is live at all hours of the day or night, ready to serve Pythonistas worldwide.

Paul Prescod, then also of ActiveState, was a kindred spirit throughout the project, helping with the online editorial process, suggesting changes, and encouraging readers of *comp.lang.python* to visit the web site and submit recipes. Paul also helped with some of his considerable XML knowledge when it came to figuring out how to take the data out of Zope and get it ready for the publication process.

The last activator I'd like to thank, for two different reasons, is Dick Hardt, founder and CEO of ActiveState. The first is that Dick agreed to let me work on the cookbook as part of my job. Had he not, I wouldn't have been able to participate in it. The second reason I'd like to thank Dick is for suggesting at the outset that a share of the book royalties go to the Python Software Foundation. This decision not only made it easier to enlist Python users into becoming contributors but has also resulted in some long-term revenue to an organization that I believe needs and deserves financial support. All Python users will benefit.

Writing a software system a second time is dangerous; the "second-system" syndrome is a well-known engineering scenario in which teams that are allowed to rebuild systems "right" often end up with interminable, over-engineered projects. I'm pleased to say that this didn't happen in the case of this second edition, for two primary reasons. The first was the decision to trim the scope of the cookbook to cover only truly modern Python—that made the content more manageable and the book much more interesting to contemporary audiences. The second factor was that everyone realized with hindsight that I would have no time to contribute to the day-to-day editing of this second edition. I'm as glad as ever to have been associated with this book, and pleased that I have no guilt regarding the amount of work I didn't contribute. When people like Alex and Anna are willing to take on the work, it's much better for everyone else to get out of the way.

Finally, I'd like to thank the O'Reilly editors who have had a big hand in shaping the cookbook. Laura Lewin was the original editor for the first edition, and she helped make sure that the project moved along, securing and coordinating the contributions of the introduction authors. Paula Ferguson then took the baton, provided a huge amount of precious feedback, and copyedited the final manuscript, ensuring that the prose was as readable as possible given the multiplicity of voices in the book. Jonathan Gennick was the editor for the second edition, and as far as I can tell, he basically let Alex and Anna drive, which was the right thing to do. Another editor I forgot to mention last time was Tim O'Reilly, who got more involved in this book than in most, in its early (rough) phases, and provided very useful input.

Each time I review this acknowledgments section, I can't help but remember O'Reilly's Editor-in-Chief at the inception of the project, Frank Willison. Frank died suddenly on a black day, July 30, 2001. He was the person who most wanted to see this book happen, for the simple reason that he believed the Python community deserved it. Frank was always willing to explore new ideas, and he was generous to a fault. The idea of a book with over a hundred authors would have terrified most editors. Frank saw it as a challenge and an experiment. I still miss Frank.

Alex Martelli

I first met Python thanks to the gentle insistence of a former colleague, Alessandro Bottoni. He kept courteously repeating that I really should give Python a try, in spite of my claims that I already knew more programming languages than I knew what to do with. If I hadn't trusted his technical and aesthetic judgment enough to invest the needed time and energy on the basis of his suggestion, I most definitely wouldn't be writing and editing Python books today. Thanks for your well-placed stubbornness, Alessandro!

Of course, once I tasted Python, I was irretrievably hooked—my lifelong taste for very high-level (often mis-named "scripting") languages at last congealed into one superb synthesis. Here, at long last, was a language with the syntactic ease of Rexx (and then some), the semantic simplicity of Tcl (and then some), the intellectual rigor of Scheme (and other Lisp variants), and the awesome power of Perl (and then some). How could I resist? Still, I do owe a debt to Mike Cowlishaw (inventor of Rexx), who I had the pleasure of having as a colleague when I worked for IBM Research, for first getting me hooked on scripting. I must also thank John Ousterhout and Larry Wall, the inventors of Tcl and Perl, respectively, for later reinforcing my addiction through their brainchildren.

Greg Wilson first introduced me to O'Reilly, so he must get his share of thanks, too—and I'm overjoyed at having him as one of the introduction authors. I am also grateful to David Ascher, and several people at O'Reilly, for signing me up as co-editor of the first edition of this book and supporting so immediately and enthusiastically my idea that, hmmm, the time had sure come for a second edition (in dazed retrospect, I suspect what I meant was mostly that I had forgotten how deuced much *work* it had been to do the first one...and failed to realize that, with all the new materials heaped on ActiveState's site, as well as Python's wonderful progress over three years, the second edition would take *more* work than the first one...!).

I couldn't possibly have done the job without an impressive array of technology to help me. I don't know the names of all the people I should thank for the Internet, ADSL, and Google's search engines, which, together, let me look things up so easily—or for many of the other hardware and software technologies cooperating to amplify my productivity. But, I do know I couldn't have made it without Theo de Raadt's OpenBSD operating system, Steve Jobs' inspiration behind Mac OS X and the iBook G4 on which I did most of the work, Bram Moolenaar's VIM editor, and, of course, Guido van Rossum's Python language. So, I'll single out Theo, Steve, Bram, and Guido for special thanks!

Nor, as any book author will surely confirm, could I have done it without patience and moral support from friends and family—chiefly my children Lucio and Flavia, my sister Elisabetta, my father Lanfranco. But the one person who was truly indispensable to this second edition was my wife and co-editor Anna. Having reconnected (after many years apart) thanks to Python, taken our honeymoon at the Open Source Convention, given a joint Lightning Talk about our "Pythonic Marriage," maybe I should have surmised how wonderful it would be to work so closely with her, day in and day out, on such a large and complex joint project. It was truly incredible, all the way through, fully including the heated debates about this or that technical or organizational point or exact choice of wording in delicate cases. Throughout the effort and the stress, her skill, her love, her joy, always shined through, sustained me, and constantly renewed my energies and my determination. *Thanks*, Anna!

Anna Martelli Ravenscroft

I discovered Python about two years ago. I fell in love, both with Python and (concurrently) with *the martelli-bot*. Python is a language that is near to my heart, primarily because it is so quickly usable. It doesn't require you to become a hermit for the next four years in order to do anything with the language. Thank you to Guido. And thanks to the amazing Python community for providing such a welcoming atmosphere to newcomers.

Working on this book was quite the learning experience for me. Besides all the Python code, I also learned both XML and VI, as well as reacquainting myself with Subversion. Thanks go to Holger Krekel and codespeak, for hosting our subversion repository while we travelled. Which brings us to a group of people who deserve special thanks: our reviewers. Holger Krekel, again, was exceptionally thorough, and ensured, among other things, that we had solid Unicode support. Raymond Hettinger gave us a huge amount of valuable, detailed insight throughout, particularly where iterators and generators were concerned. Both Raymond and Holger often offered alternatives to the presented "solutions" when warranted. Valentino Volonghi pointed out programming style issues as well as formatting issues and brought an incredible amount of enthusiasm to his reviews. Ryan Alexander, a newcomer to Python with a background in Java, provided extremely detailed recommendations on ordering and presenting materials (recipes and chapters), as well as pointing out explanations that were weak or missing altogether. His perspective was invaluable in making this book more accessible and useful to new Pythonistas. Several other individuals provided feedback on specific chapters or recipes, too numerous to list here. Your work, however, is greatly appreciated.

Of course, thanks go to my husband. I am amazed at Alex's patience with questions (and I questioned a lot). His dedication to excellence is a co-author's dream. When presented with feedback, he consistently responded with appreciation and focus on making the book better. He's one of the least ego-istical writers I've ever met.

Thank you to Dan, for encouraging my geekiness by starting me on Linux, teaching me proper terminology for the stuff I was doing, and for getting me hooked on the Internet. And finally, an extra special thanks to my children, Inanna and Graeme, for their hugs, understanding, and support when I was in geekmode, particularly during the final push to complete the book. You guys are the best kids a mother could wish for.

## CHAPTER 1

Text

1.0 Introduction

Credit: Fred L. Drake, Jr., PythonLabs

Text-processing applications form a substantial part of the application space for any scripting language, if only because everyone can agree that text processing is useful. Everyone has bits of text that need to be reformatted or transformed in various ways. The catch, of course, is that every application is just a little bit different from every other application, so it can be difficult to find just the right reusable code to work with different file formats, no matter how similar they are.

What Is Text?

Sounds like an easy question, doesn't it? After all, we know it when we see it, don't we? Text is a sequence of characters, and it is distinguished from binary data by that very fact. Binary data, after all, is a sequence of bytes.

Unfortunately, all data enters our applications as a sequence of bytes. There's no library function we can call that will tell us whether a particular sequence of bytes represents text, although we can create some useful heuristics that tell us whether data can safely (not necessarily correctly) be handled as text. Recipe 1.11 "Checking Whether a String Is Text or Binary" shows just such a heuristic.

Python strings are immutable sequences of bytes or characters. Most of the ways we create and process strings treat them as sequences of characters, but many are just as applicable to sequences of bytes. Unicode strings are immutable sequences of Unicode characters: transformations of Unicode strings into and from plain strings use *codecs* (coder-decoders) objects that embody knowledge about the many standard ways in which sequences of characters can be represented by sequences of bytes (also known as *encodings* and *character sets*). Note that Unicode strings do *not* serve double duty as sequences of bytes. Recipe 1.20 "Handling International Text with Unicode," recipe 1.21 "Converting Between Unicode and Plain Strings," and recipe 1.22 "Printing Unicode Characters to Standard Output" illustrate the fundamentals of Unicode in Python.

Okay, let's assume that our application knows from the context that it's looking at text. That's usually the best approach because that's where external input comes into play. We're looking at a file either because it has a well-known name and defined format (common in the "Unix" world) or because it has a well-known filename extension that indicates the format of the contents (common on Windows). But now we have a problem: we had to use the word *format* to make the previous paragraph meaningful. Wasn't text supposed to be simple?

Let's face it: there's no such thing as "pure" text, and if there were, we probably wouldn't care about it (with the possible exception of applications in the field of computational linguistics, where pure text may indeed sometimes be studied for its own sake). What we want to deal with in our applications is information contained in text. The text we care about may contain configuration data, commands to control or define processes, documents for human consumption, or even tabular data. Text that contains configuration data or a series of commands usually can be expected to conform to a fairly strict syntax that can be checked before relying on the information in the text. Informing the user of an error in the input text is typically sufficient to deal with things that aren't what we were expecting.

Documents intended for humans tend to be simple, but they vary widely in detail. Since they are usually written in a natural language, their syntax and grammar can be difficult to check, at best. Different texts may use different character sets or encodings, and it can be difficult or even impossible to tell which character set or encoding was used to create a text if that information is not available in addition to the text itself. It is, however, necessary to support proper representation of natural-language documents. Natural-language text has structure as well, but the structures are often less explicit in the text and require at least some understanding of the language in which the text was written. Characters make up words, which make up sentences, which make up paragraphs, and still larger structures may be present as well. Paragraphs alone can be particularly difficult to locate unless you know what typographical conventions were used for a document: is each line a paragraph, or can multiple lines make up a paragraph? If the latter, how do we tell which lines are grouped together to make a paragraph? Paragraphs may be separated by blank lines, indentation, or some other special mark. See recipe 19.10 "Reading a Text File by Paragraphs" for an example of reading a text file as a sequence of paragraphs separated by blank lines.

Tabular data has many issues that are similar to the problems associated with natural-language text, but it adds a second dimension to the input format: the text is no longer linear—it is no longer a sequence of characters, but rather a matrix of characters from which individual blocks of text must be identified and organized.

Basic Textual Operations

As with any other data format, we need to do different things with text at different times. However, there are still three basic operations:

- Parsing the data into a structure internal to our application
- Transforming the input into something similar in some way, but with changes of some kind
- Generating completely new data

Parsing can be performed in a variety of ways, and many formats can be suitably handled by ad hoc parsers that deal effectively with a very constrained format. Examples of this approach include parsers for RFC 2822-style email headers (see the rfc822 module in Python's standard library) and the configuration files handled by the ConfigParser module. The netrc module offers another example of a parser for an application-specific file format, this one based on the shlex module. shlex offers a fairly typical tokenizer for basic languages, useful in creating readable configuration files or allowing users to enter commands to an interactive prompt. These sorts of ad hoc parsers are abundant in Python's standard library, and recipes using them can be found in Chapter 2 and Chapter 13. More formal parsing tools are also available for Python; they depend on larger add-on packages and are surveyed in the introduction to Chapter 16.

Transforming text from one format to another is more interesting when viewed as text processing, which is what we usually think of first when we talk about text. In this chapter, we'll take a look at some ways to approach transformations that can be applied for different purposes. Sometimes we'll work with text stored in external files, and other times we'll simply work with it as strings in memory.

The generation of textual data from application-specific data structures is most easily performed using Python's print statement or the write method of a file or file-like object. This is often done using a method of the application object or a function, which takes the output file as a parameter. The function can then use statements such as these:

```
print >>thefile, sometext
thefile.write(sometext)
```

which generate output to the appropriate file. However, this isn't generally thought of as text processing, as here there is no input text to be processed. Examples of using both print and write can of course be found throughout this book.

Sources of Text

Working with text stored as a string in memory can be easy when the text is not too large. Operations that search the text can operate over multiple lines very easily and quickly, and there's no need to worry about searching for something that might cross a buffer boundary. Being able to keep the text in memory as a simple string makes it very easy to take advantage of the built-in string operations available as methods of the string object.

File-based transformations deserve special treatment, because there can be substantial overhead related to I/O performance and the amount of data that must actually be stored in memory. When working with data stored on disk, we often want to avoid loading entire files into memory, due to the size of the data: loading an 80 MB file into memory should not be done too casually! When our application needs only part of the data at a time, working on smaller segments of the data can yield substantial performance improvements, simply because we've allowed enough space for our program to run. If we are careful about buffer management, we can still maintain the performance advantage of using a small number of relatively large disk read and write operations by working on large chunks of data at a time. File-related recipes are found in Chapter 2.

Another interesting source for textual data comes to light when we consider the network. Text is often retrieved from the network using a socket. While we can always view a socket as a file (using the makefile method of the socket object), the data that is retrieved over a socket may come in chunks, or we may have to wait for more data to arrive. The textual data may not consist of all data until the end of the data stream, so a file object created with makefile may not be entirely appropriate to pass to text-processing code. When working with text from a network connection, we often need to read the data from the connection before passing it along for further processing. If the data is large, it can be handled by saving it to a file as it arrives and then using that file when performing text-processing operations. More elaborate solutions can be built when the text processing needs to be started before all the data is available. Examples of parsers that are useful in such situations may be found in the htmllib and HTMLParser modules in the standard library.

String Basics

The main tool Python gives us to process text is strings—immutable sequences of characters. There are actually two kinds of strings: plain strings, which contain 8-bit (ASCII) characters; and Unicode strings, which contain Unicode characters. We won't deal much with Unicode strings here: their functionality is similar to that of plain strings, except each character takes up 2 (or 4) bytes, so that the number of different characters is in the tens of thousands (or even billions), as opposed to the 256 different characters that make up plain strings. Unicode strings are important if you must deal with text in many different alphabets, particularly Asian ideographs. Plain strings are sufficient to deal with English or any of a limited set of non-Asian languages. For example, all western European alphabets can be encoded in plain strings, typically using the international standard encoding known as ISO-8859-1 (or ISO-8859-15, if you need the Euro currency symbol as well).

In Python, you express a literal string (curiously more often known as a *string literal*) as:

```
'this is a literal string'
"this is another string"
```

String values can be enclosed in either single or double quotes. The two different kinds of quotes work the same way, but having both allows you to include one kind of quotes inside of a string specified with the other kind of quotes, without needing to escape them with the backslash character:

```
'isn\'t that grand'
"isn't that grand"
```

To have a string literal span multiple lines, you can use a backslash as the last character on the line, which indicates that the next line is a continuation:

```
big = "This is a long string\
that spans two lines."
```

You must embed newlines in the string if you want the string to output on two lines:

```
big = "This is a long string\n\
that prints on two lines."
```

Another approach is to enclose the string in a pair of matching triple quotes (either single or double):

```
bigger = """
This is an even
bigger string that
spans three lines.
"""
```

Using triple quotes, you don't need to use the continuation character, and line breaks in the string literal are preserved as newline characters in the resulting Python string object. You can also make a string literal "*raw*" string by preceding it with an r or R:

```
big = r"This is a long string\
with a backslash and a newline in it"
```

With a raw string, backslash escape sequences are left alone, rather than being interpreted. Finally, you can precede a string literal with a u or U to make it a Unicode string:

```
hello = u'Hello\u0020World'
```

Strings are immutable, which means that no matter what operation you do on a string, you will always produce a new string object, rather than mutating the existing string. A string is a sequence of characters, which means that you can access a single character by indexing:

```
mystr = "my string"
mystr[0]        # 'm'
mystr[-2]       # 'n'
```

You can also access a portion of the string with a slice:

```
mystr[1:4]      # 'y s'
mystr[3:]       # 'string'
mystr[-3:]      # 'ing'
```

Slices can be extended, that is, include a third parameter that is known as the *stride* or *step* of the slice:

```
mystr[:3:-1]    # 'gnirt'
mystr[1::2]     # 'ysrn'
```

You can loop on a string's characters:

```
for c in mystr:
```

This binds c to each of the characters in mystr in turn. You can form another sequence:

```
list(mystr)     # returns ['m','y',' ','s','t','r','i','n','g']
```

You can concatenate strings by addition:

```
mystr+'oid'     # 'my stringoid'
```

You can also repeat strings by multiplication:

```
'xo'*3          # 'xoxoxo'
```

In general, you can do anything to a string that you can do to any other sequence, as long as it doesn't require changing the sequence, since strings are immutable.

String objects have many useful methods. For example, you can test a string's contents with s.isdigit( ), which returns True if s is not empty and all of the characters in s are digits (otherwise, it returns False). You can produce a new modified string with a method call such as s.upper( ), which returns a new string that is like s, but with every letter changed into its uppercase equivalent. You can search for a string inside another with haystack.count('needle'), which returns the number of times the substring 'needle' appears in the string haystack. When you have a large string that spans multiple lines, you can split it into a list of single-line strings with splitlines:

```
list_of_lines = one_large_string.splitlines( )
```

You can produce the single large string again with join:

```
one_large_string = '\n'.join(list_of_lines)
```

The recipes in this chapter show off many methods of the string object. You can find complete documentation in Python's *Library Reference* and *Python in a Nutshell*.

Strings in Python can also be manipulated with regular expressions, via the re module. Regular expressions are a powerful (but complicated) set of tools that you may already be familiar with from another language (such as Perl), or from the use of tools such as the vi editor and text-mode commands such as grep. You'll find a number of uses of regular expressions in recipes in the second half of this chapter.

For complete documentation, see the *Library Reference* and *Python in a Nutshell*. J.E.F. Friedl, *Mastering Regular Expressions* (O'Reilly) is also recommended if you need to master this subject—Python's regular expressions are basically the same as Perl's, which Friedl covers thoroughly.

Python's standard module `string` offers much of the same functionality that is available from string methods, packaged up as functions instead of methods. The `string` module also offers a few additional functions, such as the useful `string.maketrans` function that is demonstrated in a few recipes in this chapter; several helpful string constants (`string.digits`, for example, is `'0123456789'`) and, in Python 2.4, the new class `Template`, for simple yet flexible formatting of strings with embedded variables, which as you'll see features in one of this chapter's recipes. The string-formatting operator, `%`, provides a handy way to put strings together and to obtain precisely formatted strings from such objects as floating-point numbers. Again, you'll find recipes in this chapter that show how to use `%` for your purposes. Python also has lots of standard and extension modules that perform special processing on strings of many kinds. This chapter doesn't cover such specialized resources, but Chapter 12 is, for example, entirely devoted to the important specialized subject of processing XML.

1.1 Processing a String One Character at a Time

Credit: Luther Blissett

Problem

You want to process a string one character at a time.

Solution

You can build a list whose items are the string's characters (meaning that the items are strings, each of length of one—Python doesn't have a special type for "characters" as distinct from strings). Just call the built-in `list`, with the string as its argument:

```
thelist = list(thestring)
```

You may not even need to build the list, since you can loop directly on the string with a `for` statement:

```
for c in thestring:
    do_something_with(c)
```

or in the `for` clause of a list comprehension:

```
results = [do_something_with(c) for c in thestring]
```

or, with exactly the same effects as this list comprehension, you can call a function on each character with the `map` built-in function:

```
results = map(do_something, thestring)
```

Discussion

In Python, characters are just strings of length one. You can loop over a string to access each of its characters, one by one. You can use map for much the same purpose, as long as what you need to do with each character is call a function on it. Finally, you can call the built-in type list to obtain a list of the length-one substrings of the string (i.e., the string's characters). If what you want is a set whose elements are the string's characters, you can call sets.Set with the string as the argument (in Python 2.4, you can also call the built-in set in just the same way):

```
import sets
magic_chars = sets.Set('abracadabra')
poppins_chars = sets.Set('supercalifragilisticexpialidocious')
print ''.join(magic_chars & poppins_chars)    # set intersection
acrd
```

See Also

The *Library Reference* section on sequences; *Perl Cookbook* Recipe 1.5.

1.2 Converting Between Characters and Numeric Codes

Credit: Luther Blissett

Problem

You need to turn a character into its numeric ASCII (ISO) or Unicode code, and vice versa.

Solution

That's what the built-in functions ord and chr are for:

```
>>> print ord('a')
97
>>> print chr(97)
a
```

The built-in function ord also accepts as its argument a Unicode string of length one, in which case it returns a Unicode code value, up to 65536. To make a Unicode string of length one from a numeric Unicode code value, use the built-in function unichr:

```
>>> print ord(u'\u2020')
8224
>>> print repr(unichr(8224))
u'\u2020'
```

Discussion

It's a mundane task, to be sure, but it is sometimes useful to turn a character (which in Python just means a string of length one) into its ASCII or Unicode code, and vice versa. The built-in functions ord, chr, and unichr cover all the related needs. Note, in particular, the huge difference between chr(n) and str(n), which beginners sometimes confuse...:

```
>>> print repr(chr(97))
'a'
>>> print repr(str(97))
'97'
```

chr takes as its argument a small integer and returns the corresponding single-character string according to ASCII, while str, called with any integer, returns the string that is the decimal representation of that integer.

To turn a string into a list of character value codes, use the built-in functions map and ord together, as follows:

```
>>> print map(ord, 'ciao')
[99, 105, 97, 111]
```

To build a string from a list of character codes, use ''.join, map and chr; for example:

```
>>> print ''.join(map(chr, range(97, 100)))
abc
```

See Also

Documentation for the built-in functions chr, ord, and unichr in the *Library Reference* and *Python in a Nutshell*.

1.3 Testing Whether an Object Is String-like

Credit: Luther Blissett

Problem

You need to test if an object, typically an argument to a function or method you're writing, is a string (or more precisely, whether the object is string-like).

Solution

A simple and fast way to check whether something is a string or Unicode object is to use the built-ins isinstance and basestring, as follows:

```
def isAString(anobj):
    return isinstance(anobj, basestring)
```

Discussion

The first approach to solving this recipe's problem that comes to many programmers' minds is type-testing:

```
def isExactlyAString(anobj):
    return type(anobj) is type('')
```

However, this approach is pretty bad, as it willfully destroys one of Python's greatest
strengths—smooth, signature-based polymorphism. This kind of test would reject
Unicode objects, instances of user-coded subclasses of str, and instances of any user-
coded type that is meant to be "string-like".

Using the isinstance built-in function, as recommended in this recipe's Solution, is
much better. The built-in type basestring exists exactly to enable this approach.
basestring is a common base class for the str and unicode types, and any string-like
type that user code might define should also subclass basestring, just to make sure
that such isinstance testing works as intended. basestring is essentially an "empty"
type, just like object, so no cost is involved in subclassing it.

Unfortunately, the canonical isinstance checking fails to accept such clearly string-
like objects as instances of the UserString class from Python Standard Library module UserString, since that class, alas, does *not* inherit from basestring. If you need to
support such types, you can check directly whether an object behaves like a string—
for example:

```
def isStringLike(anobj):
    try: anobj + ''
    except: return False
    else: return True
```

This isStringLike function is slower and more complicated than the isAString function presented in the "Solution", but it does accept instances of UserString (and
other string-like types) as well as instances of str and unicode.

The general Python approach to type-checking is known as *duck typing*: if it walks
like a duck and quacks like a duck, it's duck-like enough for our purposes. The
isStringLike function in this recipe goes only as far as the quacks-like part, but that
may be enough. If and when you need to check for more string-like features of the
object anobj, it's easy to test a few more properties by using a richer expression in
the try clause—for example, changing the clause to:

```
try: anobj.lower() + anobj + ''
```

In my experience, however, the simple test shown in the isStringLike function usually does what I need.

The most Pythonic approach to type validation (or any validation task, really) is just
to try to perform whatever task you need to do, detecting and handling any errors or
exceptions that might result if the situation is somehow invalid—an approach
known as "it's easier to ask forgiveness than permission" (EAFP). try/except is the

key tool in enabling the EAFP style. Sometimes, as in this recipe, you may choose some simple task, such as concatenation to the empty string, as a stand-in for a much richer set of properties (such as, all the wealth of operations and methods that string objects make available).

See Also

Documentation for the built-ins isinstance and basestring in the *Library Reference* and *Python in a Nutshell*.

1.4   Aligning Strings

Credit: Luther Blissett

Problem

You want to align strings: left, right, or center.

Solution

That's what the ljust, rjust, and center methods of string objects are for. Each takes a single argument, the width of the string you want as a result, and returns a copy of the starting string with spaces added on either or both sides:

```
>>> print '|', 'hej'.ljust(20), '|', 'hej'.rjust(20), '|', 'hej'.center(20), '|'
| hej                 |                  hej |         hej          |
```

Discussion

Centering, left-justifying, or right-justifying text comes up surprisingly often—for example, when you want to print a simple report with centered page numbers in a monospaced font. Because of this, Python string objects supply this functionality through three of their many methods. In Python 2.3, the padding character is always a space. In Python 2.4, however, while space-padding is still the default, you may optionally call any of these methods with a second argument, a single character to be used for the padding:

```
>>> print 'hej'.center(20, '+')
++++++++hej+++++++++
```

See Also

The *Library Reference* section on string methods; *Java Cookbook* recipe 3.5.

1.5 Trimming Space from the Ends of a String

Credit: Luther Blissett

Problem

You need to work on a string without regard for any extra leading or trailing spaces a user may have typed.

Solution

That's what the lstrip, rstrip, and strip methods of string objects are for. Each takes no argument and returns a copy of the starting string, shorn of whitespace on either or both sides:

```
>>> x = '   hej   '
>>> print '|', x.lstrip(), '|', x.rstrip(), '|', x.strip(), '|'
| hej    |      hej | hej |
```

Discussion

Just as you may need to add space to either end of a string to align that string left, right, or center in a field of fixed width (as covered previously in recipe 1.4 "Aligning Strings"), so may you need to remove all whitespace (blanks, tabs, newlines, etc.) from either or both ends. Because this need is frequent, Python string objects supply this functionality through three of their many methods. Optionally, you may call each of these methods with an argument, a string composed of all the characters you want to trim from either or both ends instead of trimming whitespace characters:

```
>>> x = 'xyxxyy hejyx  yyx'
>>> print '|'+x.strip('xy')+'|'
| hejyx  |
```

Note that in these cases the leading and trailing spaces have been left in the resulting string, as have the 'yx' that are followed by spaces: only all the occurrences of 'x' and 'y' at either end of the string have been removed from the resulting string.

See Also

The *Library Reference* section on string methods; Recipe 1.4 "Aligning Strings"; *Java Cookbook* recipe 3.12.

1.6 Combining Strings

Credit: Luther Blissett

Problem

You have several small strings that you need to combine into one larger string.

Solution

To join a sequence of small strings into one large string, use the string operator join.
Say that pieces is a list whose items are strings, and you want one big string with all
the items concatenated in order; then, you should code:

```
largeString = ''.join(pieces)
```

To put together pieces stored in a few variables, the string-formatting operator % can
often be even handier:

```
largeString = '%s%s something %s yet more' % (small1, small2, small3)
```

Discussion

In Python, the + operator concatenates strings and therefore offers seemingly obvious solutions for putting small strings together into a larger one. For example, when
you have pieces stored in a few variables, it seems quite natural to code something
like:

```
largeString = small1 + small2 + ' something ' + small3 + ' yet more'
```

And similarly, when you have a sequence of small strings named pieces, it seems
quite natural to code something like:

```
largeString = ''
for piece in pieces:
    largeString += piece
```

Or, equivalently, but more fancifully and compactly:

```
import operator
largeString = reduce(operator.add, pieces, '')
```

However, it's very important to realize that none of these seemingly obvious solution is good—the approaches shown in the "Solution" are *vastly* superior.

In Python, string objects are immutable. Therefore, any operation on a string, including string concatenation, produces a new string object, rather than modifying an
existing one. Concatenating N strings thus involves building and then immediately
throwing away each of N-1 intermediate results. Performance is therefore vastly better for operations that build no intermediate results, but rather produce the desired
end result at once.

Python's string-formatting operator % is one such operation, particularly suitable
when you have a few pieces (e.g., each bound to a different variable) that you want
to put together, perhaps with some constant text in addition. Performance is not a
major issue for this specific kind of task. However, the % operator also has other
potential advantages, when compared to an expression that uses multiple + operations on strings. % is more readable, once you get used to it. Also, you don't have to
call str on pieces that aren't already strings (e.g., numbers), because the format specifier %s does so implicitly. Another advantage is that you can use format specifiers

other than %s, so that, for example, you can control how many significant digits the string form of a floating-point number should display.

What Is "a Sequence?"

Python does not have a specific type called sequence, but *sequence* is still an often-used term in Python. *sequence*, strictly speaking, means: a container that can be iterated on, to get a finite number of items, one at a time, *and* that also supports indexing, slicing, and being passed to the built-in function len (which gives the number of items in a container). Python lists are the "sequences" you'll meet most often, but there are many others (strings, unicode objects, tuples, array.arrays, etc.).

Often, one does not need indexing, slicing, and len—the ability to iterate, one item at a time, suffices. In that case, one should speak of an *iterable* (or, to focus on the finite number of items issue, a *bounded* iterable). Iterables that are not sequences include dictionaries (iteration gives the *keys* of the dictionary, one at a time in arbitrary order), file objects (iteration gives the *lines* of the text file, one at a time), and many more, including iterators and generators. Any iterable can be used in a for loop statement and in many equivalent contexts (the for clause of a list comprehension or Python 2.4 generator expression, and also many built-ins such as min, max, zip, sum, str.join, etc.).

At *http://www.python.org/moin/PythonGlossary*, you can find a *Python Glossary* that can help you with these and several other terms. However, while the editors of this cookbook have tried to adhere to the word usage that the glossary describes, you will still find many places where this book says *a sequence* or *an iterable* or even *a list*, where, by strict terminology, one should always say *a bounded iterable*. For example, at the start of this recipe's Solution, we say "a sequence of small strings" where, in fact, any bounded iterable of strings suffices. The problem with using "bounded iterable" all over the place is that it would make this book read more like a mathematics textbook than a practical programming book! So, we have deviated from terminological rigor where readability, and maintaining in the book a variety of "voices", were better served by slightly imprecise terminology that is nevertheless entirely clear in context.

When you have many small string pieces in a sequence, performance can become a truly important issue. The time needed to execute a loop using + or += (or a fancier but equivalent approach using the built-in function reduce) grows with the square of the number of characters you are accumulating, since the time to allocate and fill a large string is roughly proportional to the length of that string. Fortunately, Python offers an excellent alternative. The join method of a string object s takes as its only argument a sequence of strings and produces a string result obtained by concatenating all items in the sequence, with a copy of s joining each item to its neighbors. For example, ''.join(pieces) concatenates all the items of pieces in a single gulp, without interposing anything between them, and ', '.join(pieces) concatenates the items putting a comma and a space between each pair of them. It's the fastest, neatest, and most elegant and readable way to put a large string together.

When the pieces are not all available at the same time, but rather come in sequentially from input or computation, use a list as an intermediate data structure to hold the pieces (to add items at the end of a list, you can call the append or extend methods of the list). At the end, when the list of pieces is complete, call `''.join(thelist)` to obtain the big string that's the concatenation of all pieces. Of all the many handy tips and tricks I could give you about Python strings, I consider this one *by far* the most significant: the most frequent reason some Python programs are too slow is that they build up big strings with + or +=. So, train yourself never to do that. Use, instead, the `''.join` approach recommented in this recipe.

Python 2.4 makes a heroic attempt to ameliorate the issue, reducing a little the performance penalty due to such erroneous use of +=. While `''.join` is still way faster and in all ways preferable, at least some newbie or careless programmer gets to waste somewhat fewer machine cycles. Similarly, psyco (a specializing just-in-time [JIT] Python compiler found at *http://psyco.sourceforge.net/*), can reduce the += penalty even further. Nevertheless, `''.join` remains the best approach in all cases.

See Also

The *Library Reference* and *Python in a Nutshell* sections on string methods, string-formatting operations, and the `operator` module.

1.7   Reversing a String by Words or Characters

Credit: Alex Martelli

Problem

You want to reverse the characters or words in a string.

Solution

Strings are immutable, so, to reverse one, we need to make a copy. The simplest approach for reversing is to take an extended slice with a "step" of -1, so that the slicing proceeds backwards:

```
revchars = astring[::-1]
```

To flip words, we need to make a list of words, reverse it, and join it back into a string with a space as the joiner:

```
revwords = astring.split()      # string -> list of words
revwords.reverse()              # reverse the list in place
revwords = ' '.join(revwords)   # list of strings -> string
```

or, if you prefer terse and compact "one-liners":

```
revwords = ' '.join(astring.split( )[::-1])
```

If you need to reverse by words while preserving untouched the intermediate whitespace, you can split by a regular expression:

```
import re
revwords = re.split(r'(\s+)', astring)    # separators too, since '(...)'
revwords.reverse( )                        # reverse the list in place
revwords = ''.join(revwords)               # list of strings -> string
```

Note that the joiner must be the empty string in this case, because the whitespace separators are kept in the revwords list (by using re.split with a regular expression that includes a parenthesized group). Again, you could make a one-liner, if you wished:

```
revwords = ''.join(re.split(r'(\s+)', astring)[::-1])
```

but this is getting too dense and unreadable to be good Python code!

Discussion

In Python 2.4, you may make the by-word one-liners more readable by using the new built-in function reversed instead of the less readable extended-slicing indicator [::-1]:

```
revwords = ' '.join(reversed(astring.split( )))
revwords = ''.join(reversed(re.split(r'(\s+)', astring)))
```

For the by-character case, though, astring[::-1] remains best, even in 2.4, because to use reversed, you'd have to introduce a call to ''.join as well:

```
revchars = ''.join(reversed(astring))
```

The new reversed built-in returns an *iterator*, suitable for looping on or for passing to some "accumulator" callable such as ''.join—it does not return a ready-made string!

See Also

Library Reference and *Python in a Nutshell* docs on sequence types and slicing, and (2.4 only) the reversed built-in; *Perl Cookbook* recipe 1.6.

1.8   Checking Whether a String Contains a Set of Characters

Credit: Jürgen Hermann, Horst Hansen

Problem

You need to check for the occurrence of any of a set of characters in a string.

Solution

The simplest approach is clear, fast, and general (it works for any sequence, not just strings, and for any container on which you can test for membership, not just sets):

```
def containsAny(seq, aset):
    """ Check whether sequence seq contains ANY of the items in aset. """
    for c in seq:
        if c in aset: return True
    return False
```

You can gain a little speed by moving to a higher-level, more sophisticated approach, based on the itertools standard library module, essentially expressing the same approach in a different way:

```
import itertools
def containsAny(seq, aset):
    for item in itertools.ifilter(aset.__contains__, seq):
        return True
    return False
```

Discussion

Most problems related to sets are best handled by using the set built-in type introduced in Python 2.4 (if you're using Python 2.3, you can use the equivalent sets.Set type from the Python Standard Library). However, there are exceptions. Here, for example, a pure set-based approach would be something like:

```
def containsAny(seq, aset):
    return bool(set(aset).intersection(seq))
```

However, with this approach, every item in seq inevitably has to be examined. The functions in this recipe's Solution, on the other hand, "short-circuit": they return as soon as they know the answer. They must still check every item in seq when the answer is False—we could never affirm that no item in seq is a member of aset without examining all the items, of course. But when the answer is True, we often learn about that very soon, namely as soon as we examine one item that *is* a member of aset. Whether this matters at all is very data-dependent, of course. It will make no practical difference when seq is short, or when the answer is typically False, but it may be extremely important for a very long seq (when the answer can typically be soon determined to be True).

The first version of containsAny presented in the recipe has the advantage of simplicity and clarity: it expresses the fundamental idea with total transparency. The second version may appear to be "clever", and that is not a complimentary adjective in the Python world, where simplicity and clarity are core values. However, the second version is well worth considering, because it shows a higher-level approach, based on the itertools module of the standard library. Higher-level approaches are most often preferable to lower-level ones (although the issue is moot in this particular case). itertools.ifilter takes a predicate and an iterable, and yields the items in that iterable that satisfy the "predicate". Here, as the "predicate", we use aset.__contains__, the bound method that is internally called when we code in aset for membership testing. So, if ifilter yields anything at all, it yields an item of seq that is also a member of aset, so we can return True as soon as this happens. If we get to the statement following the for, it must mean the return True never executed, because no items of seq are members of aset, so we can return False.

What Is "a Predicate?"

A term you can see often in discussions about programming is *predicate*: it just means a function (or other callable object) that returns True or False as its result. A predicate is said to be *satisfied* when it returns True.

If your application needs some function such as containsAny to check whether a string (or other sequence) contains any members of a set, you may also need such variants as:

```
def containsOnly(seq, aset):
    """ Check whether sequence seq contains ONLY items in aset. """
    for c in seq:
        if c not in aset: return False
    return True
```

containsOnly is the same function as containsAny, but with the logic turned upside-down. Other apparently similar tasks don't lend themselves to short-circuiting (they intrinsically need to examine all items) and so are best tackled by using the built-in type set (in Python 2.4; in 2.3, you can use sets.Set in the same way):

```
def containsAll(seq, aset):
    """ Check whether sequence seq contains ALL the items in aset. """
    return not set(aset).difference(seq)
```

If you're not accustomed to using the set (or sets.Set) method difference, be aware of its semantics: for any set a, a.difference(b) (just like a-set(b)) returns the set of all elements of a that are not in b. For example:

```
>>> L1 = [1, 2, 3, 3]
>>> L2 = [1, 2, 3, 4]
>>> set(L1).difference(L2)
set([ ])
>>> set(L2).difference(L1)
set([4])
```

which hopefully helps explain why:

```
>>> containsAll(L1, L2)
False
>>> containsAll(L2, L1)
True
```

(In other words, don't confuse difference with another method of set, symmetric_ difference, which returns the set of all items that are in *either* argument and not in the other.)

When you're dealing specifically with (plain, *not* Unicode) strings for both seq and aset, you may not need the full generality of the functions presented in this recipe, and may want to try the more specialized approach explained in recipe 1.10 "Filtering a String for a Set of Characters" based on strings' method translate and the string.maketrans function from the Python Standard Library. For example:

```
import string
notrans = string.maketrans('', '')          # identity "translation"
def containsAny(astr, strset):
    return len(strset) != len(strset.translate(notrans, astr))
def containsAll(astr, strset):
    return not strset.translate(notrans, astr)
```

This somewhat tricky approach relies on strset.translate(notrans, astr) being the subsequence of strset that is made of characters not in astr. When that subsequence has the same length as strset, no characters have been removed by strset.translate, therefore no characters of strset are in astr. Conversely, when the subsequence is empty, all characters have been removed, so all characters of strset are in astr. The translate method keeps coming up naturally when one wants to treat strings as sets of characters, because it's speedy as well as handy and flexible; see recipe 1.10 "Filtering a String for a Set of Characters" for more details.

These two sets of approaches to the recipe's tasks have very different levels of generality. The earlier approaches are very general: not at all limited to string processing, they make rather minimal demands on the objects you apply them to. The approach based on the translate method, on the other hand, works only when both astr and strset are strings, or *very* closely mimic plain strings' functionality. Not even Unicode strings suffice, because the translate method of Unicode strings has a signature that is different from that of plain strings—a single argument (a dict mapping code numbers to Unicode strings or None) instead of two (both strings).

See Also

Recipe 1.10 "Filtering a String for a Set of Characters"; documentation for the translate method of strings and Unicode objects, and maketrans function in the string module, in the *Library Reference* and *Python in a Nutshell*; ditto for documentation of built-in set (Python 2.4 only), modules sets and itertools, and the special method __contains__.

1.9   Simplifying Usage of Strings' translate Method

Credit: Chris Perkins, Raymond Hettinger

Problem

You often want to use the fast code in strings' translate method, but find it hard to remember in detail how that method and the function string.maketrans work, so you want a handy *facade* to simplify their use in typical cases.

Solution

The translate method of strings is quite powerful and flexible, as detailed in recipe 1.10 "Filtering a String for a Set of Characters." However, exactly because of that power and flexibility, it may be a nice idea to front it with a "facade" that simplifies its *typical* use. A little factory function, returning a closure, can do wonders for this kind of task:

```
import string
def translator(frm='', to='', delete='', keep=None):
    if len(to) == 1:
        to = to * len(frm)
    trans = string.maketrans(frm, to)
    if keep is not None:
        allchars = string.maketrans('', '')
        delete = allchars.translate(allchars, keep.translate(allchars, delete))
    def translate(s):
        return s.translate(trans, delete)
    return translate
```

Discussion

I often find myself wanting to use strings' translate method for any one of a few purposes, but each time I have to stop and think about the details (see recipe 1.10 "Filtering a String for a Set of Characters" for more information about those details). So, I wrote myself a class (later remade into the factory closure presented in this recipe's Solution) to encapsulate various possibilities behind a simpler-to-use facade. Now, when I want a function that keeps only characters from a given set, I can easily build and use that function:

```
>>> digits_only = translator(keep=string.digits)
>>> digits_only('Chris Perkins : 224-7992')
'2247992'
```

It's similarly simple when I want to *remove* a set of characters:

```
>>> no_digits = translator(delete=string.digits)
>>> no_digits('Chris Perkins : 224-7992')
'Chris Perkins : -'
```

and when I want to replace a set of characters with a single character:

```
>>> digits_to_hash = translator(from=string.digits, to='#')
>>> digits_to_hash('Chris Perkins : 224-7992')
'Chris Perkins : ###-####'
```

While the latter may appear to be a bit of a special case, it is a task that keeps coming up for me every once in a while.

I had to make one arbitrary design decision in this recipe—namely, I decided that the delete parameter "trumps" the keep parameter if they overlap:

```
>>> trans = translator(delete='abcd', keep='cdef')
>>> trans('abcdefg')
'ef'
```

For your applications it might be preferable to ignore delete if keep is specified, or, perhaps better, to raise an exception if they are both specified, since it may not make much sense to let them both be given in the same call to translator, anyway. Also: as noted in recipe 1.8 "Checking Whether a String Contains a Set of Characters" and recipe 1.10 "Filtering a String for a Set of Characters," the code in this recipe works only for normal strings, not for *Unicode* strings. See recipe 1.10 "Filtering a String for a Set of Characters" to learn how to code this kind of functionality for Unicode strings, whose translate method is different from that of plain (i.e., byte) strings.

Closures

A *closure* is nothing terribly complicated: just an "inner" function that refers to names (variables) that are local to an "outer" function containing it. Canonical toy-level example:

```
def make_adder(addend):
    def adder(augend): return augend+addend
    return adder
```

Executing p = make_adder(23) makes a closure of inner function adder internally referring to a name addend that is bound to the value 23. Then, q = make_adder(42) makes *another* closure, for which, internally, name addend is instead bound to the value 42. Making *q* in no way interferes with *p*, they can happily and independently coexist. So we can now execute, say, print p(100), q(100) and enjoy the output 123 142.

In practice, you may often see make_adder referred to as a *closure* rather than by the pedantic, ponderous periphrasis "a function that returns a closure"—fortunately, context often clarifies the situation. Calling make_adder a *factory* (or *factory function*) is both accurate and concise; you may also say it's a *closure factory* to specify it builds and returns closures, rather than, say, classes or class instances.

See Also

Recipe 1.10 "Filtering a String for a Set of Characters" for a direct equivalent of this recipe's translator(keep=...), more information on the translate method, and an equivalent approach for Unicode strings; documentation for strings' translate method, and for the maketrans function in the string module, in the *Library Reference* and *Python in a Nutshell*.

1.10   Filtering a String for a Set of Characters

Credit: Jürgen Hermann, Nick Perkins, Peter Cogolo

Problem

Given a set of characters to keep, you need to build a filtering function that, applied to any string s, returns a copy of s that contains only characters in the set.

Solution

The translate method of string objects is fast and handy for all tasks of this ilk. However, to call translate effectively to solve this recipe's task, we must do some advance preparation. The first argument to translate is a translation table: in this recipe, we do not want to do any translation, so we must prepare a first argument that specifies "no translation". The second argument to translate specifies which characters we want to *delete*: since the task here says that we're given, instead, a set of characters to *keep* (i.e., to *not* delete), we must prepare a second argument that gives the *set complement*—deleting all characters we must not keep. A closure is the best way to do this advance preparation just once, obtaining a fast filtering function tailored to our exact needs:

```
import string
# Make a reusable string of all characters, which does double duty
# as a translation table specifying "no translation whatsoever"
allchars = string.maketrans('', '')
def makefilter(keep):
    """ Return a function that takes a string and returns a partial copy
        of that string consisting of only the characters in 'keep'.
        Note that `keep' must be a plain string.
    """
    # Make a string of all characters that are not in 'keep': the "set
    # complement" of keep, meaning the string of characters we must delete
    delchars = allchars.translate(allchars, keep)
    # Make and return the desired filtering function (as a closure)
    def thefilter(s):
        return s.translate(allchars, delchars)
    return thefilter
if __name__ == '__main__':
    just_vowels = makefilter('aeiouy')
    print just_vowels('four score and seven years ago')
```

```
# emits: ouoeaeeyeaao
    print just_vowels('tiger, tiger burning bright')
# emits: ieieuii
```

Discussion

The key to understanding this recipe lies in the definitions of the maketrans function in the string module of the Python Standard Library and in the translate method of string objects. translate returns a copy of the string you call it on, replacing each character in it with the corresponding character in the translation table passed in as the first argument and deleting the characters specified in the second argument. maketrans is a utility function to create translation tables. (A translation table is a string t of exactly 256 characters: when you pass t as the first argument of a translate method, each character c of the string on which you call the method is translated in the resulting string into the character t[ord(c)].)

In this recipe, efficiency is maximized by splitting the filtering task into preparation and execution phases. The string of all characters is clearly reusable, so we build it once and for all as a global variable when this module is imported. That way, we ensure that each filtering function uses the same string-of-all-characters object, not wasting any memory. The string of characters to delete, which we need to pass as the second argument to the translate method, depends on the set of characters to keep, because it must be built as the "set complement" of the latter: we must tell translate to delete every character that we do not want to keep. So, we build the delete-these-characters string in the makefilter factory function. This building is done quite rapidly by using the translate method to delete the "characters to keep" from the string of all characters. The translate method is very fast, as are the construction and execution of these useful little resulting functions. The test code that executes when this recipe runs as a main script shows how to build a filtering function by calling makefilter, bind a name to the filtering function (by simply assigning the result of calling makefilter to a name), then call the filtering function on some strings and print the results.

Incidentally, calling a filtering function with allchars as the argument puts the set of characters being kept into a canonic string form, alphabetically sorted and without duplicates. You can use this idea to code a very simple function to return the canonic form of any set of characters presented as an arbitrary string:

```
def canonicform(s):
    """ Given a string s, return s's characters as a canonic-form string:
        alphabetized and without duplicates. """
    return makefilter(s)(allchars)
```

The Solution uses a def statement to make the nested function (closure) it returns, because def is the most normal, general, and clear way to make functions. If you prefer, you could use lambda instead, changing the def and return statements in function makefilter into just one return lambda statement:

```
    return lambda s: s.translate(allchars, delchars)
```

Most Pythonistas, but not all, consider using def clearer and more readable than using lambda.

Since this recipe deals with strings seen as sets of characters, you could alternatively use the sets.Set type (or, in Python 2.4, the new built-in set type) to perform the same tasks. Thanks to the translate method's power and speed, it's often faster to work directly on strings, rather than go through sets, for tasks of this ilk. However, just as noted in recipe 1.8 "Checking Whether a String Contains a Set of Characters," the functions in this recipe only work for normal strings, not for *Unicode* strings.

To solve this recipe's task for Unicode strings, we must do some very different preparation. A Unicode string's translate method takes only one argument: a mapping or sequence, which is indexed with the code number of each character in the string. Characters whose codes are not keys in the mapping (or indices in the sequence) are just copied over to the output string. Otherwise, the value corresponding to each character's code must be either a Unicode string (which is substituted for the character) or None (in which case the character is deleted). A very nice and powerful arrangement, but unfortunately not one that's identical to the way plain strings work, so we must recode.

Normally, we use either a dict or a list as the argument to a Unicode string's translate method to translate some characters and/or delete some. But for the specific task of this recipe (i.e., *keep* just some characters, delete all others), we might need an inordinately large dict or string, just mapping all other characters to None. It's better to code, instead, a little class that appropriately implements a __getitem__ method (the special method that gets called in indexing operations). Once we're going to the (slight) trouble of coding a little class, we might as well make its instances callable and have makefilter be just a synonym for the class itself:

```
import sets
class Keeper(object):
    def __init__(self, keep):
        self.keep = sets.Set(map(ord, keep))
    def __getitem__(self, n):
        if n not in self.keep:
            return None
        return unichr(n)
    def __call__(self, s):
        return unicode(s).translate(self)
makefilter = Keeper
if __name__ == '__main__':
    just_vowels = makefilter('aeiouy')
    print just_vowels(u'four score and seven years ago')
# emits: ouoeaeeyeaao
    print just_vowels(u'tiger, tiger burning bright')
# emits: ieieuii
```

We might name the class itself `makefilter`, but, by convention, one normally names classes with an uppercase initial; there is essentially no cost in following that convention here, too, so we did.

See Also

Recipe 1.8 "Checking Whether a String Contains a Set of Characters"; documentation for the `translate` method of strings and Unicode objects, and `maketrans` function in the `string` module, in the *Library Reference* and *Python in a Nutshell*.

1.11 Checking Whether a String Is Text or Binary

Credit: Andrew Dalke

Problem

Python can use a plain string to hold either text or arbitrary bytes, and you need to determine (heuristically, of course: there can be no precise algorithm for this) which of the two cases holds for a certain string.

Solution

We can use the same heuristic criteria as Perl does, deeming a string binary if it contains any nulls or if more than 30% of its characters have the high bit set (i.e., codes greater than 126) or are strange control codes. We have to code this ourselves, but this also means we easily get to tweak the heuristics for special application needs:

```python
from __future__ import division          # ensure / does NOT truncate
import string
text_characters = "".join(map(chr, range(32, 127))) + "\n\r\t\b"
_null_trans = string.maketrans("", "")
def istext(s, text_characters=text_characters, threshold=0.30):
    # if s contains any null, it's not text:
    if "\0" in s:
        return False
    # an "empty" string is "text" (arbitrary but reasonable choice):
    if not s:
        return True
    # Get the substring of s made up of non-text characters
    t = s.translate(_null_trans, text_characters)
    # s is 'text' if less than 30% of its characters are non-text ones:
    return len(t)/len(s) <= threshold
```

Discussion

You can easily do minor customizations to the heuristics used by function `istext` by passing in specific values for the `threshold`, which defaults to 0.30 (30%), or for the string of those characters that are to be deemed "text" (which defaults to normal ASCII characters plus the four "normal" control characters, meaning ones that are often found in text). For example, if you expected Italian text encoded as ISO-8859-

1, you could add the accented letters used in Italian, "àèéìòù", to the text_ characters argument.

Often, what you need to check as being either binary or text is not a string, but a file. Again, we can use the same heuristics as Perl, checking just the first block of the file with the istext function shown in this recipe's Solution:

```
def istextfile(filename, blocksize=512, **kwds):
    return istext(open(filename).read(blocksize), **kwds)
```

Note that, by default, the expression len(t)/len(s) used in the body of function istext would truncate the result to 0, since it is a division between integer numbers. In some future version (probably Python 3.0, a few years away), Python will change the meaning of the / operator so that it performs division without truncation—if you really do want truncation, you should use the truncating-division operator, //.

However, Python has not yet changed the semantics of division, keeping the old one by default in order to ensure backwards compatibility. It's important that the millions of lines of code of Python programs and modules that already exist keep running smoothly under all new 2.x versions of Python—only upon a change of major language version number, no more often than every decade or so, is Python allowed to change in ways that aren't backwards-compatible.

Since, in the small module containing this recipe's Solution, it's handy for us to get the division behavior that is scheduled for introduction in some future release, we start our module with the statement:

```
from __future__ import division
```

This statement doesn't affect the rest of the program, only the specific module that starts with this statement; throughout this module, / performs "true division" (without truncation). As of Python 2.3 and 2.4, division is the only thing you may want to import from __future__. Other features that used to be scheduled for the future, nested_scopes and generators, are now part of the language and cannot be turned off—it's innocuous to import them, but it makes sense to do so only if your program also needs to run under some older version of Python.

See Also

Recipe 1.10 "Filtering a String for a Set of Characters" for more details about function maketrans and string method translate; *Language Reference* for details about true versus truncating division.

1.12 Controlling Case

Credit: Luther Blissett

Problem

You need to convert a string from uppercase to lowercase, or vice versa.

Solution

That's what the upper and lower methods of string objects are for. Each takes no arguments and returns a copy of the string in which each letter has been changed to upper- or lowercase, respectively.

```
big = little.upper( )
little = big.lower( )
```

Characters that are not letters are copied unchanged.

s.capitalize is similar to s[:1].upper( )+s[1:].lower( ): the first character is changed to uppercase, and all others are changed to lowercase. s.title is again similar, but it capitalizes the first letter of each word (where a "word" is a sequence of letters) and uses lowercase for all other letters:

```
>>> print 'one tWo thrEe'.capitalize( )
One two three
>>> print 'one tWo thrEe'.title( )
One Two Three
```

Discussion

Case manipulation of strings is a very frequent need. Because of this, several string methods let you produce case-altered copies of strings. Moreover, you can also check whether a string object is already in a given case form, with the methods isupper, islower, and istitle, which all return True if the string is not empty, contains at least one letter, and already meets the uppercase, lowercase, or titlecase constraints. There is no analogous iscapitalized method, and coding it is not trivial, if we want behavior that's strictly similar to strings' is... methods. Those methods all return False for an "empty" string, and the three case-checking ones also return False for strings that, while not empty, contain no letters at all.

The simplest and clearest way to code iscapitalized is clearly:

```
def iscapitalized(s):
    return s == s.capitalize( )
```

However, this version deviates from the boundary-case semantics of the analogous is... methods, since it also returns True for strings that are empty or contain no letters. Here's a stricter one:

```
import string
notrans = string.maketrans('', '')  # identity "translation"
def containsAny(str, strset):
    return len(strset) != len(strset.translate(notrans, str))
def iscapitalized(s):
    return s == s.capitalize( ) and containsAny(s, string.letters)
```

Here, we use the function shown in recipe 1.8 "Checking Whether a String Contains a Set of Characters" to ensure we return False if s is empty or contains no letters. As noted in recipe 1.8 "Checking Whether a String Contains a Set of Characters," this means that this specific version works only for plain strings, not for Unicode ones.

See Also

Library Reference and *Python in a Nutshell* docs on string methods; *Perl Cookbook* recipe 1.9; recipe 1.8 "Checking Whether a String Contains a Set of Characters."

1.13 Accessing Substrings

Credit: Alex Martelli

Problem

You want to access portions of a string. For example, you've read a fixed-width record and want to extract the record's fields.

Solution

Slicing is great, but it only does one field at a time:

```
afield = theline[3:8]
```

If you need to think in terms of field lengths, `struct.unpack` may be appropriate. For example:

```
import struct
# Get a 5-byte string, skip 3, get two 8-byte strings, then all the rest:
baseformat = "5s 3x 8s 8s"
# by how many bytes does theline exceed the length implied by this
# base-format (24 bytes in this case, but struct.calcsize is general)
numremain = len(theline) - struct.calcsize(baseformat)
# complete the format with the appropriate 's' field, then unpack
format = "%s %ds" % (baseformat, numremain)
l, s1, s2, t = struct.unpack(format, theline)
```

If you want to skip rather than get "all the rest", then just unpack the initial part of theline with the right length:

```
l, s1, s2 = struct.unpack(baseformat, theline[:struct.calcsize(baseformat)])
```

If you need to split at five-byte boundaries, you can easily code a list comprehension (LC) of slices:

```
fivers = [theline[k:k+5] for k in xrange(0, len(theline), 5)]
```

Chopping a string into individual characters is of course easier:

```
chars = list(theline)
```

If you prefer to think of your data as being cut up at specific columns, slicing with LCs is generally handier:

```
cuts = [8, 14, 20, 26, 30]
pieces = [ theline[i:j] for i, j in zip([0]+cuts, cuts+[None]) ]
```

The call to zip in this LC returns a list of pairs of the form (cuts[k], cuts[k+1]), except that the first pair is (0, cuts[0]), and the last one is (cuts[len(cuts)-1], None). In other words, each pair gives the right (i, j) for slicing between each cut and the next, except that the first one is for the slice before the first cut, and the last one is for the slice from the last cut to the end of the string. The rest of the LC just uses these pairs to cut up the appropriate slices of theline.

Discussion

This recipe was inspired by recipe 1.1 in the *Perl Cookbook*. Python's slicing takes the place of Perl's substr. Perl's built-in unpack and Python's struct.unpack are similar. Perl's is slightly richer, since it accepts a field length of * for the last field to mean all the rest. In Python, we have to compute and insert the exact length for either extraction or skipping. This isn't a major issue because such extraction tasks will usually be encapsulated into small functions. *Memoizing*, also known as *automatic caching*, may help with performance if the function is called repeatedly, since it allows you to avoid redoing the preparation of the format for the struct unpacking. See recipe 18.5 "Memoizing (Caching) the Return Values of Functions" for details about memoizing.

In a purely Python context, the point of this recipe is to remind you that struct.unpack is often viable, and sometimes preferable, as an alternative to string slicing (not quite as often as unpack versus substr in Perl, given the lack of a *-valued field length, but often enough to be worth keeping in mind).

Each of these snippets is, of course, best encapsulated in a function. Among other advantages, encapsulation ensures we don't have to work out the computation of the last field's length on each and every use. This function is the equivalent of the first snippet using struct.unpack in the "Solution":

```
def fields(baseformat, theline, lastfield=False):
    # by how many bytes does theline exceed the length implied by
    # base-format (struct.calcsize computes exactly that length)
    numremain = len(theline)-struct.calcsize(baseformat)
    # complete the format with the appropriate 's' or 'x' field, then unpack
    format = "%s %d%s" % (baseformat, numremain, lastfield and "s" or "x")
    return struct.unpack(format, theline)
```

A design decision worth noticing (and, perhaps, worth criticizing) is that of having a lastfield=False optional parameter. This reflects the observation that, while we often want to skip the last, unknown-length subfield, sometimes we want to retain it instead. The use of lastfield in the expression lastfield and s or x (equivalent to C's ternary operator lastfield?"s":"c") saves an if/else, but it's unclear whether the saving is worth the obscurity. See recipe 18.9 "Simulating the Ternary Operator in Python" for more about simulating ternary operators in Python.

If function `fields` is called in a loop, memoizing (caching) with a key that is the tuple (`baseformat`, `len(theline)`, `lastfield`) may offer faster performance. Here's a version of `fields` with memoizing:

```
def fields(baseformat, theline, lastfield=False, _cache={ }):
    # build the key and try getting the cached format string
    key = baseformat, len(theline), lastfield
    format = _cache.get(key)
    if format is None:
        # no format string was cached, build and cache it
        numremain = len(theline)-struct.calcsize(baseformat)
        _cache[key] = format = "%s %d%s" % (
            baseformat, numremain, lastfield and "s" or "x")
    return struct.unpack(format, theline)
```

The idea behind this memoizing is to perform the somewhat costly preparation of format only once for each set of arguments requiring that preparation, thereafter storing it in the _cache dictionary. Of course, like all optimizations, memoizing needs to be validated by measuring performance to check that each given optimization does actually speed things up. In this case, I measure an increase in speed of approximately 30% to 40% for the memoized version, meaning that the optimization is probably not worth the bother unless the function is part of a performance bottleneck for your program.

The function equivalent of the next LC snippet in the solution is:

```
def split_by(theline, n, lastfield=False):
    # cut up all the needed pieces
    pieces = [theline[k:k+n] for k in xrange(0, len(theline), n)]
    # drop the last piece if too short and not required
    if not lastfield and len(pieces[-1]) < n:
        pieces.pop( )
    return pieces
```

And for the last snippet:

```
def split_at(theline, cuts, lastfield=False):
    # cut up all the needed pieces
    pieces = [ theline[i:j] for i, j in zip([0]+cuts, cuts+[None]) ]
    # drop the last piece if not required
    if not lastfield:
        pieces.pop( )
    return pieces
```

In both of these cases, a list comprehension doing slicing turns out to be slightly preferable to the use of `struct.unpack`.

A completely different approach is to use generators, such as:

```
def split_at(the_line, cuts, lastfield=False):
    last = 0
    for cut in cuts:
        yield the_line[last:cut]
        last = cut
    if lastfield:
        yield the_line[last:]
```

```
def split_by(the_line, n, lastfield=False):
    return split_at(the_line, xrange(n, len(the_line), n), lastfield)
```

Generator-based approaches are particularly appropriate when all you need to do on the sequence of resulting fields is loop over it, either explicitly, or implicitly by calling on it some "accumulator" callable such as `''.join`. If you do need to materialize a list of the fields, and what you have available is a generator instead, you only need to call the built-in `list` on the generator, as in:

```
list_of_fields = list(split_by(the_line, 5))
```

See Also

Recipe 18.9 "Simulating the Ternary Operator in Python" and recipe 18.5 "Memoizing (Caching) the Return Values of Functions"; *Perl Cookbook* recipe 1.1.

1.14 Changing the Indentation of a Multiline String

Credit: Tom Good

Problem

You have a string made up of multiple lines, and you need to build another string from it, adding or removing leading spaces on each line so that the indentation of each line is some absolute number of spaces.

Solution

The methods of string objects are quite handy, and let us write a simple function to perform this task:

```
def reindent(s, numSpaces):
    leading_space = numSpaces * ' '
    lines = [ leading_space + line.strip()
              for line in s.splitlines() ]
    return '\n'.join(lines)
```

Discussion

When working with text, it may be necessary to change the indentation level of a block. This recipe's code adds leading spaces to or removes them from each line of a multiline string so that the indentation level of each line matches some absolute number of spaces. For example:

```
>>> x = """   line one
...     line two
...   and line three
...   """
>>> print x
line one
```

```
    line two
  and line three
>>> print reindent(x, 4)
    line one
    line two
    and line three
```

Even if the lines in s are initially indented differently, this recipe makes their indentation homogeneous, which is sometimes what we want, and sometimes not. A frequent need is to adjust the amount of leading spaces in each line, so that the relative indentation of each line in the block is preserved. This is not difficult for either positive or negative values of the adjustment. However, negative values need a check to ensure that no nonspace characters are snipped from the start of the lines. Thus, we may as well split the functionality into two functions to perform the transformations, plus one to measure the number of leading spaces of each line and return the result as a list:

```
def addSpaces(s, numAdd):
    white = " "*numAdd
    return white + white.join(s.splitlines(True))
def numSpaces(s):
    return [len(line)-len(line.lstrip()) for line in s.splitlines()]
def delSpaces(s, numDel):
    if numDel > min(numSpaces(s)):
        raise ValueError, "removing more spaces than there are!"
    return '\n'.join([ line[numDel:] for line in s.splitlines() ])
```

All of these functions rely on the string method splitlines, which is similar to a split on '\n'. splitlines has the extra ability to leave the trailing newline on each line (when you call it with True as its argument). Sometimes this turns out to be handy: addSpaces could not be quite as short and sweet without this ability of the splitlines string method.

Here's how we can combine these functions to build another function to delete just enough leading spaces from each line to ensure that the least-indented line of the block becomes flush left, while preserving the relative indentation of the lines:

```
def unIndentBlock(s):
    return delSpaces(s, min(numSpaces(s)))
```

See Also

Library Reference and *Python in a Nutshell* docs on sequence types.

1.15   Expanding and Compressing Tabs

Credit: Alex Martelli, David Ascher

Problem

You want to convert tabs in a string to the appropriate number of spaces, or vice versa.

Solution

Changing tabs to the appropriate number of spaces is a reasonably frequent task, easily accomplished with Python strings' expandtabs method. Because strings are immutable, the method returns a new string object, a modified copy of the original one. However, it's easy to rebind a string variable name from the original to the modified-copy value:

```
mystring = mystring.expandtabs()
```

This doesn't change the string object to which mystring originally referred, but it does rebind the name mystring to a newly created string object, a modified copy of mystring in which tabs are expanded into runs of spaces. expandtabs, by default, uses a tab length of 8; you can pass expandtabs an integer argument to use as the tab length.

Changing spaces into tabs is a rare and peculiar need. Compression, if that's what you're after, is far better performed in other ways, so Python doesn't offer a built-in way to "unexpand" spaces into tabs. We can, of course, write our own function for the purpose. String processing tends to be fastest in a split/process/rejoin approach, rather than with repeated overall string transformations:

```
def unexpand(astring, tablen=8):
    import re
    # split into alternating space and non-space sequences
    pieces = re.split(r'( +)', astring.expandtabs(tablen))
    # keep track of the total length of the string so far
    lensofar = 0
    for i, piece in enumerate(pieces):
        thislen = len(piece)
        lensofar += thislen
        if piece.isspace():
            # change each space sequences into tabs+spaces
            numblanks = lensofar % tablen
            numtabs = (thislen-numblanks+tablen-1)/tablen
            pieces[i] = '\t'*numtabs + ' '*numblanks
    return ''.join(pieces)
```

Function unexpand, as written in this example, works only for a single-line string; to deal with a multi-line string, use ''.join([unexpand(s) for s in astring.splitlines(True)]).

Discussion

While regular expressions are never indispensable for the purpose of manipulating strings in Python, they are occasionally quite handy. Function unexpand, as presented in the recipe, for example, takes advantage of one extra feature of re.split with respect to string's split method: when the regular expression contains a (parenthesized) *group*, re.split returns a list where the split pieces are interleaved with the "splitter" pieces. So, here, we get alternate runs of nonblanks and blanks as items of list pieces; the for loop keeps track of the length of string it has seen so far, and changes pieces that are made of blanks to as many tabs as possible, plus as many blanks are needed to maintain the overall length.

Some programming tasks that could still be described as *expanding tabs* are unfortunately not quite as easy as just calling the expandtabs method. A category that does happen with some regularity is to fix Python source files, which use a mix of tabs and spaces for indentation (a very bad idea), so that they instead use spaces only (which is the best approach). This could entail extra complications, for example, when you need to guess the tab length (and want to end up with the standard four spaces per indentation level, which is strongly advisable). It can also happen when you need to preserve tabs that are inside strings, rather than tabs being used for indentation (because somebody erroneously used actual tabs, rather than '\t', to indicate tabs in strings), or even because you're asked to treat docstrings differently from other strings. Some cases are not too bad—for example, when you want to expand tabs that occur only within runs of whitespace at the start of each line, leaving any other tab alone. A little function using a regular expression suffices:

```
def expand_at_linestart(P, tablen=8):
    import re
    def exp(mo):
        return mo.group( ).expandtabs(tablen)
    return ''.join([ re.sub(r'^\s+', exp, s) for s in P.splitlines(True) ])
```

This function expand_at_linestart exploits the re.sub function, which looks for a regular expression in a string and, each time it gets a match, calls a function, passing the match object as the argument, to obtain the string to substitute in place of the match. For convenience, expand_at_linestart is coded to deal with a multiline string argument P, performing the list comprehension over the results of the splitlines call, and the '\n'.join of the whole. Of course, this convenience does not stop the function from being able to deal with a single-line P.

If your specifications regarding which tabs are to be expanded are even more complex, such as needing to deal differently with tabs depending on whether they're inside or outside of strings, and on whether or not strings are docstrings, at the very least, you need to perform a tokenization. In addition, you may also have to perform a full parse of the source code you're dealing with, rather than using simple string or regular-expression operations. If this is the case, you can expect a substantial amount of work. Some beginning pointers to help you get started may be found in Chapter 16.

If you ever find yourself sweating out this kind of task, you will no doubt get excellent motivation in the future for following the normal and recommended Python style in the source code you write or edit: only spaces, four per indentation level, no tabs, and always '\t', never an actual tab character, to include a tab in a string literal. Your favorite editor can no doubt be told to enforce all of these conventions whenever a Python source file is saved; the editor that comes with IDLE (the free integrated development environment that comes with Python), for example, supports these conventions. It *is* much easier to arrange your editor so that the problem never arises, rather than striving to fix it after the fact!

See Also

Documentation for the expandtabs method of strings in the "Sequence Types" section of the *Library Reference*; *Perl Cookbook* recipe 1.7; *Library Reference* and *Python in a Nutshell* documentation of module re.

1.16   Interpolating Variables in a String

Credit: Scott David Daniels

Problem

You need a simple way to get a copy of a string where specially marked substrings are replaced with the results of looking up the substrings in a dictionary.

Solution

Here is a solution that works in Python 2.3 as well as in 2.4:

```
def expand(format, d, marker='"', safe=False):
    if safe:
        def lookup(w): return d.get(w, w.join(marker*2))
    else:
        def lookup(w): return d[w]
    parts = format.split(marker)
    parts[1::2] = map(lookup, parts[1::2])
    return ''.join(parts)
if __name__ == '__main__':
    print expand('just "a" test', {'a': 'one'})
# emits: just one test
```

When the parameter safe is False, the default, every marked substring must be found in dictionary d, otherwise expand terminates with a KeyError exception. When parameter safe is explicitly passed as True, marked substrings that are not found in the dictionary are just left intact in the output string.

Discussion

The code in the body of the expand function has some points of interest. It defines one of two different nested functions (with the name of lookup either way), depending on whether the expansion is required to be *safe*. Safe means no KeyError exception gets raised for marked strings not found in the dictionary. If not required to be safe (the default), lookup just indexes into dictionary d and raises an error if the substring is not found. But, if lookup is required to be "safe", it uses d's method get and supplies as the default the substring being looked up, with a marker on either side. In this way, by passing safe as True, you may choose to have unknown formatting markers come right through to the output rather than raising exceptions. marker+w+marker would be an obvious alternative to the chosen w.join(marker*2), but I've chosen the latter exactly to display a non-obvious but interesting way to construct such a quoted string.

With either version of lookup, expand operates according to the split/modify/join idiom that is so important for Python string processing. The *modify* part, in expand's case, makes use of the possibility of accessing and modifying a list's slice with a "step" or "stride". Specifically, expand accesses and rebinds all of those items of parts that lie at an odd index, because those items are exactly the ones that were enclosed between a pair of markers in the original format string. Therefore, they are the marked substrings that may be looked up in the dictionary.

The syntax of format strings accepted by this recipe's function expand is more flexible than the $-based syntax of string.Template. You can specify a different marker when you want your format string to contain double quotes, for example. There is no constraint for each specially marked substring to be an identifier, so you can easily interpolate Python expressions (with a d whose __getitem__ performs an eval) or any other kind of placeholder. Moreover, you can easily get slightly different, useful effects. For example:

```
print expand('just "a" ""little"" test', {'a' : 'one', '' : '"'})
```

emits just one "little" test. Advanced users can customize Python 2.4's string.Template class, by inheritance, to match all of these capabilities, and more, but this recipe's little expand function is still simpler to use in some flexible ways.

See Also

Library Reference docs for string.Template (Python 2.4, only), the section on sequence types (for string methods split and join, and for slicing operations), and the section on dictionaries (for indexing and the get method). For more information on Python 2.4's string.Template class, see recipe 1.17 "Interpolating Variables in a String in Python 2.4."

1.17 Interpolating Variables in a String in Python 2.4

Credit: John Nielsen, Lawrence Oluyede, Nick Coghlan

Problem

Using Python 2.4, you need a simple way to get a copy of a string where specially marked identifiers are replaced with the results of looking up the identifiers in a dictionary.

Solution

Python 2.4 offers the new `string.Template` class for this purpose. Here is a snippet of code showing how to use that class:

```
import string
# make a template from a string where some identifiers are marked with $
new_style = string.Template('this is $thing')
# use the substitute method of the template with a dictionary argument:
print new_style.substitute({'thing':5})    # emits: this is 5
print new_style.substitute({'thing':'test'}) # emits: this is test
# alternatively, you can pass keyword-arguments to 'substitute':
print new_style.substitute(thing=5)         # emits: this is 5
print new_style.substitute(thing='test')    # emits: this is test
```

Discussion

In Python 2.3, a format string for identifier-substitution has to be expressed in a less simple format:

```
old_style = 'this is %(thing)s'
```

with the identifier in parentheses after a %, and an s right after the closed parenthesis. Then, you use the % operator, with the format string on the left of the operator, and a dictionary on the right:

```
print old_style % {'thing':5}     # emits: this is 5
print old_style % {'thing':'test'} # emits: this is test
```

Of course, this code keeps working in Python 2.4, too. However, the new `string.Template` class offers a simpler alternative.

When you build a `string.Template` instance, you may include a dollar sign ($) by doubling it, and you may have the interpolated identifier immediately followed by letters or digits by enclosing it in curly braces ({ }). Here is an example that requires both of these refinements:

```
form_letter = '''Dear $customer,
I hope you are having a great time.
If you do not find Room $room to your satisfaction,
let us know. Please accept this $$5 coupon.
          Sincerely,
          $manager
          ${name}Inn'''
letter_template = string.Template(form_letter)
print letter_template.substitute({'name':'Sleepy', 'customer':'Fred Smith',
                                  'manager':'Barney Mills', 'room':307,
                                  })
```

This snippet emits the following output:

```
Dear Fred Smith,
I hope you are having a great time.
If you do not find Room 307 to your satisfaction,
let us know. Please accept this $5 coupon.
```

```
                 Sincerely,
                 Barney Mills
                 SleepyInn
```

Sometimes, the handiest way to prepare a dictionary to be used as the argument to the substitute method is to set local variables, and then pass as the argument locals() (the artificial dictionary whose keys are the local variables, each with its value associated):

```
msg = string.Template('the square of $number is $square')
for number in range(10):
    square = number * number
    print msg.substitute(locals())
```

Another handy alternative is to pass the values to substitute using keyword argument syntax rather than a dictionary:

```
msg = string.Template('the square of $number is $square')
for i in range(10):
    print msg.substitute(number=i, square=i*i)
```

You can even pass both a dictionary *and* keyword arguments:

```
msg = string.Template('the square of $number is $square')
for number in range(10):
    print msg.substitute(locals(), square=number*number)
```

In case of any conflict between entries in the dictionary and the values explicitly passed as keyword arguments, the keyword arguments take precedence. For example:

```
msg = string.Template('an $adj $msg')
adj = 'interesting'
print msg.substitute(locals(), msg='message')
# emits an interesting message
```

See Also

Library Reference docs for string.Template (2.4 only) and the locals built-in function.

1.18   Replacing Multiple Patterns in a Single Pass

Credit: Xavier Defrang, Alex Martelli

Problem

You need to perform several string substitutions on a string.

Solution

Sometimes regular expressions afford the fastest solution even in cases where their applicability is not obvious. The powerful sub method of re objects (from the re module in the standard library) makes regular expressions particularly good at performing string substitutions. Here is a function returning a modified copy of an input string, where each occurrence of any string that's a key in a given dictionary is replaced by the corresponding value in the dictionary:

```
import re
def multiple_replace(text, adict):
    rx = re.compile('|'.join(map(re.escape, adict)))
    def one_xlat(match):
        return adict[match.group(0)]
    return rx.sub(one_xlat, text)
```

Discussion

This recipe shows how to use the Python standard re module to perform single-pass multiple-string substitution using a dictionary. Let's say you have a dictionary-based mapping between strings. The keys are the set of strings you want to replace, and the corresponding values are the strings with which to replace them. You could perform the substitution by calling the string method replace for each key/value pair in the dictionary, thus processing and creating a new copy of the entire text several times, but it is clearly better and faster to do all the changes in a single pass, processing and creating a copy of the text only once. re.sub's callback facility makes this better approach quite easy.

First, we have to build a regular expression from the set of keys we want to match. Such a regular expression has a pattern of the form a1|a2|...|aN, made up of the N strings to be substituted, joined by vertical bars, and it can easily be generated using a one-liner, as shown in the recipe. Then, instead of giving re.sub a replacement string, we pass it a callback argument. re.sub then calls this object for each match, with a re.MatchObject instance as its only argument, and it expects the replacement string for that match as the call's result. In our case, the callback just has to look up the matched text in the dictionary and return the corresponding value.

The function multiple_replace presented in the recipe recomputes the regular expression and redefines the one_xlat auxiliary function each time you call it. Often, you must perform substitutions on multiple strings based on the same, unchanging translation dictionary and would prefer to pay these setup prices only once. For such needs, you may prefer the following closure-based approach:

```
import re
def make_xlat(*args, **kwds):
    adict = dict(*args, **kwds)
    rx = re.compile('|'.join(map(re.escape, adict)))
    def one_xlat(match):
        return adict[match.group(0)]
    def xlat(text):
        return rx.sub(one_xlat, text)
    return xlat
```

You can call make_xlat, passing as its argument a dictionary, or any other combination of arguments you could pass to built-in dict in order to construct a dictionary; make_xlat returns a xlat closure that takes as its only argument text the string on which the substitutions are desired and returns a copy of text with all the substitutions performed.

Here's a usage example for each half of this recipe. We would normally have such an example as a part of the same *.py* source file as the functions in the recipe, so it is guarded by the traditional Python idiom that runs it if and only if the module is called as a main script:

```
if __name__ == "__main__":
    text = "Larry Wall is the creator of Perl"
    adict = {
      "Larry Wall" : "Guido van Rossum",
      "creator" : "Benevolent Dictator for Life",
      "Perl" : "Python",
    }
    print multiple_replace(text, adict)
    translate = make_xlat(adict)
    print translate(text)
```

Substitutions such as those performed by this recipe are often intended to operate on entire words, rather than on arbitrary substrings. Regular expressions are good at picking up the beginnings and endings of words, thanks to the special sequence r'\b'. We can easily make customized versions of either multiple_replace or make_xlat by simply changing the one line in which each of them builds and assigns the regular expression object rx into a slightly different form:

```
rx = re.compile(r'\b%s\b' % r'\b|\b'.join(map(re.escape, adict)))
```

The rest of the code is just the same as shown earlier in this recipe. However, this sameness is not necessarily good news: it suggests that if we need many similarly customized versions, each building the regular expression in slightly different ways, we'll end up doing a lot of copy-and-paste coding, which is the worst form of code reuse, likely to lead to high maintenance costs in the future.

A key rule of good coding is: "once, and only once!" When we notice that we are duplicating code, we should notice this symptom as a "code smell," and refactor our code for better reuse. In this case, for ease of customization, we need a class rather than a function or closure. For example, here's how to write a class that works very similarly to make_xlat but can be customized by subclassing and overriding:

```
class make_xlat:
    def __init__(self, *args, **kwds):
        self.adict = dict(*args, **kwds)
        self.rx = self.make_rx()
    def make_rx(self):
        return re.compile('|'.join(map(re.escape, self.adict)))
    def one_xlat(self, match):
        return self.adict[match.group(0)]
```

```
def __call__(self, text):
    return self.rx.sub(self.one_xlat, text)
```

This is a "drop-in replacement" for the function of the same name: in other words, a snippet such as the one we showed, with the if __name__ == '__main__' guard, works identically when make_xlat is this class rather than the previously shown function. The function is simpler and faster, but the class' important advantage is that it can easily be customized in the usual object-oriented way—subclassing it, and overriding some method. To translate by whole words, for example, all we need to code is:

```
class make_xlat_by_whole_words(make_xlat):
    def make_rx(self):
        return re.compile(r'\b%s\b' % r'\b|\b'.join(map(re.escape, self.adict)))
```

Ease of customization by subclassing and overriding helps you avoid copy-and-paste coding, and this is sometimes an excellent reason to prefer object-oriented structures over simpler functional structures, such as closures. Of course, just because some functionality is packaged as a class doesn't magically make it customizable in just the way you want. Customizability also requires some foresight in dividing the functionality into separately overridable methods that correspond to the right pieces of overall functionality. Fortunately, you don't have to get it right the first time; when code does not have the optimal internal structure for the task at hand (in this specific example, for reuse by subclassing and selective overriding), you can and should refactor the code so that its internal structure serves your needs. Just make sure you have a suitable battery of tests ready to run to ensure that your refactoring hasn't broken anything, and then you can refactor to your heart's content. See *http://www.refactoring.com* for more information on the important art and practice of refactoring.

See Also

Documentation for the re module in the *Library Reference* and *Python in a Nutshell*; the Refactoring home page (*http://www.refactoring.com*).

1.19 Checking a String
for Any of Multiple Endings

Credit: Michele Simionato

Problem

For a certain string s, you must check whether s has any of several endings; in other words, you need a handy, elegant equivalent of s.endswith(end1) or s.endswith(end2) or s.endswith(end3) and so on.

Solution

The `itertools.imap` function is just as handy for this task as for many of a similar nature:

```
import itertools
def anyTrue(predicate, sequence):
    return True in itertools.imap(predicate, sequence)
def endsWith(s, *endings):
    return anyTrue(s.endswith, endings)
```

Discussion

A typical use for `endsWith` might be to print all names of image files in the current directory:

```
import os
for filename in os.listdir('.'):
    if endsWith(filename, '.jpg', '.jpeg', '.gif'):
        print filename
```

The same general idea shown in this recipe's Solution is easily applied to other tasks related to checking a string for any of several possibilities. The auxiliary function anyTrue is general and fast, and you can pass it as its first argument (the *predicate*) other bound methods, such as `s.startswith` or `s.__contains__`. Indeed, perhaps it would be better to do without the helper function endsWith—after all, directly coding

```
if anyTrue(filename.endswith, (".jpg", ".gif", ".png")):
```

seems to be already readable enough.

Bound Methods

Whenever a Python object supplies a method, you can get the method, already *bound* to the object, by just *accessing* the method on the object. (For example, you can assign it, pass it as an argument, return it as a function's result, etc.) For example:

```
L = ['fee', 'fie', 'foo']
x = L.append
```

Now, name x refers to a *bound method* of list object L. Calling, say, x('fum') is the same as calling L.append('fum'): either call mutates object L into ['fee', 'fie', 'foo', 'fum'].

If you access a method on a type or class, rather than an instance of the type or class, you get an *unbound* method, not "attached" to any particular instance of the type or class: when you call it, you need to pass as its first argument an instance of that type or class. For example, if you set y = list.append, you cannot just call y('I')—Python couldn't possibly guess *which* list you want to append I to! You can, however, call y(L, 'I'), and that is just the same as calling L.append('I') (as long as isinstance(L, list)).

This recipe originates from a discussion on *news:comp.lang.python.* and summarizes inputs from many people, including Raymond Hettinger, Chris Perkins, Bengt Richter and others.

See Also

Library Reference and *Python in a Nutshell* docs for `itertools` and string methods.

1.20 Handling International Text with Unicode

Credit: Holger Krekel

Problem

You need to deal with text strings that include non-ASCII characters.

Solution

Python has a first class unicode type that you can use in place of the plain bytestring str type. It's easy, once you accept the need to explicitly convert between a bytestring and a Unicode string:

```
>>> german_ae = unicode('\xc3\xa4', 'utf8')
```

Here german_ae is a unicode string representing the German lowercase a with umlaut (i.e., diaeresis) character "ä". It has been constructed from interpreting the bytestring '\xc3\xa4' according to the specified UTF-8 encoding. There are many encodings, but UTF-8 is often used because it is universal (UTF-8 can encode any Unicode string) and yet fully compatible with the 7-bit ASCII set (any ASCII bytestring is a correct UTF-8–encoded string).

Once you cross this barrier, life is easy! You can manipulate this Unicode string in practically the same way as a plain str string:

```
>>> sentence = "This is a " + german_ae
>>> sentence2 = "Easy!"
>>> para = ". ".join([sentence, sentence2])
```

Note that para is a Unicode string, because operations between a unicode string and a bytestring always result in a unicode string—unless they fail and raise an exception:

```
>>> bytestring = '\xc3\xa4'      # Uuh, some non-ASCII bytestring!
>>> german_ae += bytestring
UnicodeDecodeError: 'ascii' codec can't decode byte 0xc3 in
position 0: ordinal not in range(128)
```

The byte '0xc3' is not a valid character in the 7-bit ASCII encoding, and Python refuses to guess an encoding. So, being explicit about encodings is the crucial point for successfully using Unicode strings with Python.

Discussion

Unicode is easy to handle in Python, if you respect a few guidelines and learn to deal with common problems. This is not to say that an efficient implementation of Unicode is an easy task. Luckily, as with other hard problems, you don't have to care much: you can just use the efficient implementation of Unicode that Python provides.

The most important issue is to fully accept the distinction between a bytestring and a unicode string. As exemplified in this recipe's solution, you often need to explicitly construct a unicode string by providing a bytestring and an encoding. Without an encoding, a bytestring is basically meaningless, unless you happen to be lucky and can just assume that the bytestring is text in ASCII.

The most common problem with using Unicode in Python arises when you are doing some text manipulation where only some of your strings are unicode objects and others are bytestrings. Python makes a shallow attempt to implicitly convert your bytestrings to Unicode. It usually assumes an ASCII encoding, though, which gives you UnicodeDecodeError exceptions if you actually have non-ASCII bytes somewhere. UnicodeDecodeError tells you that you mixed Unicode and bytestrings in such a way that Python cannot (doesn't even try to) guess the text your bytestring might represent.

Developers from many big Python projects have come up with simple rules of thumb to prevent such runtime UnicodeDecodeErrors, and the rules may be summarized into one sentence: always do the conversion at IO barriers. To express this same concept a bit more extensively:

- Whenever your program receives text data "from the outside" (from the network, from a file, from user input, etc.), construct unicode objects immediately. Find out the appropriate encoding, for example, from an HTTP header, or look for an appropriate convention to determine the encoding to use.

- Whenever your program sends text data "to the outside" (to the network, to some file, to the user, etc.), determine the correct encoding, and convert your text to a bytestring with that encoding. (Otherwise, Python attempts to convert Unicode to an ASCII bytestring, likely producing UnicodeEncodeErrors, which are just the converse of the UnicodeDecodeErrors previously mentioned).

With these two rules, you will solve most Unicode problems. If you still get UnicodeErrors of either kind, look for where you forgot to properly construct a unicode object, forgot to properly convert back to an encoded bytestring, or ended up using an inappropriate encoding due to some mistake. (It is quite possible that such encoding mistakes are due to the user, or some other program that is interacting with yours, not following the proper encoding rules or conventions.)

In order to convert a Unicode string back to an encoded bytestring, you usually do something like:

```
>>> bytestring = german_ae.decode('latin1')
>>> bytestring
'\xe4'
```

Now bytestring is a German ae character in the 'latin1' encoding. Note how '\xe4' (in Latin1) and the previously shown '\xc3\xa4' (in UTF-8) represent the same German character, but in different encodings.

By now, you can probably imagine why Python refuses to guess among the hundreds of possible encodings. It's a crucial design choice, based on one of the *Zen of Python* principles: "In the face of ambiguity, resist the temptation to guess." At any interactive Python shell prompt, enter the statement import this to read all of the important principles that make up the *Zen of Python*.

See Also

Unicode is a huge topic, but a recommended book is *Unicode: A Primer*, by Tony Graham (Hungry Minds, Inc.)—details are available at *http://www.menteith.com/unicode/primer/*; and a short but complete article from Joel Spolsky, "The Absolute Minimum Every Software Developer Absolutely, Positively Must Know About Unicode and Character Sets (No Excuses)!," located at *http://www.joelonsoftware.com/articles/Unicode.html*. See also the *Library Reference* and *Python in a Nutshell* documentation about the built-in str and unicode types and modules unidata and codecs; also, recipe 1.21 "Converting Between Unicode and Plain Strings" and recipe 1.22 "Printing Unicode Characters to Standard Output."

1.21 Converting Between Unicode and Plain Strings

Credit: David Ascher, Paul Prescod

Problem

You need to deal with textual data that doesn't necessarily fit in the ASCII character set.

Solution

Unicode strings can be encoded in plain strings in a variety of ways, according to whichever encoding you choose:

```
unicodestring = u"Hello world"
# Convert Unicode to plain Python string: "encode"
utf8string = unicodestring.encode("utf-8")
asciistring = unicodestring.encode("ascii")
```

```
isostring = unicodestring.encode("ISO-8859-1")
utf16string = unicodestring.encode("utf-16")
# Convert plain Python string to Unicode: "decode"
plainstring1 = unicode(utf8string, "utf-8")
plainstring2 = unicode(asciistring, "ascii")
plainstring3 = unicode(isostring, "ISO-8859-1")
plainstring4 = unicode(utf16string, "utf-16")
assert plainstring1 == plainstring2 == plainstring3 == plainstring4
```

Discussion

If you find yourself dealing with text that contains non-ASCII characters, you have to learn about Unicode—what it is, how it works, and how Python uses it. The preceding recipe 1.20 "Handling International Text with Unicode" offers minimal but crucial practical tips, and this recipe tries to offer more perspective.

You don't need to know everything about Unicode to be able to solve real-world problems with it, but a few basic tidbits of knowledge are indispensable. First, you must understand the difference between bytes and characters. In older, ASCII-centric languages and environments, bytes and characters are treated as if they were the same thing. A byte can hold up to 256 different values, so these environments are limited to dealing with no more than 256 distinct characters. Unicode, on the other hand, has tens of thousands of characters, which means that each Unicode character takes more than one byte; thus you need to make the distinction between characters and bytes.

Standard Python strings are really bytestrings, and a Python character, being such a string of length 1, is really a byte. Other terms for an instance of the standard Python string type are *8-bit string* and *plain string*. In this recipe we call such instances bytestrings, to remind you of their byte orientation.

A Python Unicode character is an abstract object big enough to hold any character, analogous to Python's long integers. You don't have to worry about the internal representation; the representation of Unicode characters becomes an issue only when you are trying to send them to some byte-oriented function, such as the write method of files or the send method of network sockets. At that point, you must choose how to represent the characters as bytes. Converting from Unicode to a bytestring is called *encoding* the string. Similarly, when you load Unicode strings from a file, socket, or other byte-oriented object, you need to *decode* the strings from bytes to characters.

Converting Unicode objects to bytestrings can be achieved in many ways, each of which is called an *encoding*. For a variety of historical, political, and technical reasons, there is no one "right" encoding. Every encoding has a case-insensitive name, and that name is passed to the encode and decode methods as a parameter. Here are a few encodings you should know about:

- The UTF-8 encoding can handle any Unicode character. It is also backwards compatible with ASCII, so that a pure ASCII file can also be considered a UTF-8 file, and a UTF-8 file that happens to use only ASCII characters is identical to an ASCII file with the same characters. This property makes UTF-8 very backwards-compatible, especially with older Unix tools. UTF-8 is by far the dominant encoding on Unix, as well as the default encoding for XML documents. UTF-8's primary weakness is that it is fairly inefficient for eastern-language texts.

- The UTF-16 encoding is favored by Microsoft operating systems and the Java environment. It is less efficient for western languages but more efficient for eastern ones. A variant of UTF-16 is sometimes known as UCS-2.

- The ISO-8859 series of encodings are supersets of ASCII, each able to deal with 256 distinct characters. These encodings cannot support all of the Unicode characters; they support only some particular language or family of languages. ISO-8859-1, also known as "Latin-1", covers most western European and African languages, but not Arabic. ISO-8859-2, also known as "Latin-2", covers many eastern European languages such as Hungarian and Polish. ISO-8859-15, very popular in Europe these days, is basically the same as ISO-8859-1 with the addition of the Euro currency symbol as a character.

If you want to be able to encode all Unicode characters, you'll probably want to use UTF-8. You will need to deal with the other encodings only when you are handed data in those encodings created by some other application or input device, or vice versa, when you need to prepare data in a specified encoding to accommodate another application downstream of yours, or an output device. In particular, recipe 1.22 "Printing Unicode Characters to Standard Output" shows how to handle the case in which the downstream application or device is driven from your program's standard output stream.

See Also

Unicode is a huge topic, but a recommended book is Tony Graham, *Unicode: A Primer* (Hungry Minds)—details are available at *http://www.menteith.com/unicode/primer/*; and a short, but complete article from Joel Spolsky, "The Absolute Minimum Every Software Developer Absolutely, Positively Must Know About Unicode and Character Sets (No Excuses)!" is located at *http://www.joelonsoftware.com/articles/Unicode.html*. See also the *Library Reference* and *Python in a Nutshell* documentation about the built-in str and unicode types, and modules unidata and codecs; also, recipe 1.20 "Handling International Text with Unicode" and recipe 1.22 "Printing Unicode Characters to Standard Output."

1.22 Printing Unicode Characters to Standard Output

Credit: David Ascher

Problem

You want to print Unicode strings to standard output (e.g., for debugging), but they don't fit in the default encoding.

Solution

Wrap the sys.stdout stream with a converter, using the codecs module of Python's standard library. For example, if you know your output is going to a terminal that displays characters according to the ISO-8859-1 encoding, you can code:

```
import codecs, sys
sys.stdout = codecs.lookup('iso8859-1')[-1](sys.stdout)
```

Discussion

Unicode strings live in a large space, big enough for all of the characters in every language worldwide, but thankfully the internal representation of Unicode strings is irrelevant for users of Unicode. Alas, a file stream, such as sys.stdout, deals with bytes and has an encoding associated with it. You can change the default encoding that is used for new files by modifying the site module. That, however, requires changing your entire Python installation, which is likely to confuse other applications that may expect the encoding you originally configured Python to use (typically the Python standard encoding, which is ASCII). Therefore, this kind of modification is *not* to be recommended.

This recipe takes a sounder approach: it rebinds sys.stdout as a stream that expects Unicode input and outputs it in ISO-8859-1 (also known as "Latin-1"). This approach doesn't change the encoding of any previous references to sys.stdout, as illustrated here. First, we keep a reference to the original, ASCII-encoded sys.stdout:

```
>>> old = sys.stdout
```

Then, we create a Unicode string that wouldn't normally be able to go through sys.stdout:

```
>>> char = u"\N{LATIN SMALL LETTER A WITH DIAERESIS}"
>>> print char
Traceback (most recent call last):
  File "<stdin>", line 1, in ?
UnicodeError: ASCII encoding error: ordinal not in range(128)
```

If you don't get an error from this operation, it's because Python thinks it knows which encoding your "terminal" is using (in particular, Python is likely to use the right encoding if your "terminal" is IDLE, the free development environment that comes with Python). But, suppose you do get this error, or get no error but the output is not the character you expected, because your "terminal" uses UTF-8 encoding and Python does not know about it. When that is the case, we can just wrap sys.stdout in the codecs stream writer for UTF-8, which is a much richer encoding, then rebind sys.stdout to it and try again:

```
>>> sys.stdout = codecs.lookup('utf-8')[-1](sys.stdout)
>>> print char
ä
```

This approach works only if your "terminal", terminal emulator, or other window in which you're running the interactive Python interpreter supports the UTF-8 encoding, with a font rich enough to display all the characters you need to output. If you don't have such a program or device available, you may be able to find a suitable one for your platform in the form of a free program downloadable from the Internet.

Python tries to determine which encoding your "terminal" is using and sets that encoding's name as attribute sys.stdout.encoding. Sometimes (alas, not always) it even manages to get it right. IDLE already wraps your sys.stdout, as suggested in this recipe, so, within the environment's interactive Python shell, you can directly print Unicode strings.

See Also

Documentation for the codecs and site modules, and setdefaultencoding in module sys, in the *Library Reference* and *Python in a Nutshell*; recipe 1.20 "Handling International Text with Unicode" and recipe 1.21 "Converting Between Unicode and Plain Strings."

1.23 Encoding Unicode Data for XML and HTML

Credit: David Goodger, Peter Cogolo

Problem

You want to encode Unicode text for output in HTML, or some other XML application, using a limited but popular encoding such as ASCII or Latin-1.

Solution

Python provides an encoding error handler named xmlcharrefreplace, which replaces all characters outside of the chosen encoding with XML numeric character references:

```
def encode_for_xml(unicode_data, encoding='ascii'):
    return unicode_data.encode(encoding, 'xmlcharrefreplace')
```

You could use this approach for HTML output, too, but you might prefer to use HTML's *symbolic* entity references instead. For this purpose, you need to define and register a customized encoding error handler. Implementing that handler is made easier by the fact that the Python Standard Library includes a module named htmlentitydefs that holds HTML entity definitions:

```
import codecs
from htmlentitydefs import codepoint2name
def html_replace(exc):
    if isinstance(exc, (UnicodeEncodeError, UnicodeTranslateError)):
        s = [ u'&%s;' % codepoint2name[ord(c)]
                for c in exc.object[exc.start:exc.end] ]
        return ''.join(s), exc.end
    else:
        raise TypeError("can't handle %s" % exc.__name__)
codecs.register_error('html_replace', html_replace)
```

After registering this error handler, you can optionally write a function to wrap its use:

```
def encode_for_html(unicode_data, encoding='ascii'):
    return unicode_data.encode(encoding, 'html_replace')
```

Discussion

As with any good Python module, this module would normally proceed with an example of its use, guarded by an if __name__ == '__main__' test:

```
if __name__ == '__main__':
    # demo
    data = u'''\
<html>
<head>
<title>Encoding Test</title>
</head>
<body>
<p>accented characters:
<ul>
<li>\xe0 (a + grave)
<li>\xe7 (c + cedilla)
<li>\xe9 (e + acute)
</ul>
<p>symbols:
<ul>
<li>\xa3 (British pound)
<li>\u20ac (Euro)
<li>\u221e (infinity)
</ul>
</body></html>
'''
    print encode_for_xml(data)
    print encode_for_html(data)
```

If you run this module as a main script, you will then see such output as (from function encode_for_xml):

```
<li>&#224; (a + grave)
<li>&#231; (c + cedilla)
<li>&#233; (e + acute)
    ...
<li>&#163; (British pound)
<li>&#8364; (Euro)
<li>&#8734; (infinity)
```

as well as (from function encode_for_html):

```
<li>&agrave; (a + grave)
<li>&ccedil; (c + cedilla)
<li>&eacute; (e + acute)
    ...
<li>&pound; (British pound)
<li>&euro; (Euro)
<li>&infin; (infinity)
```

There is clearly a niche for each case, since encode_for_xml is more general (you can use it for any XML application, not just HTML), but encode_for_html may produce output that's easier to read—should you ever need to look at it directly, edit it further, and so on. If you feed either form to a browser, you should view it in exactly the same way. To visualize both forms of encoding in a browser, run this recipe's module as a main script, redirect the output to a disk file, and use a text editor to separate the two halves before you view them with a browser. (Alternatively, run the script twice, once commenting out the call to encode_for_xml, and once commenting out the call to encode_for_html.)

Remember that Unicode data must always be encoded before being printed or written out to a file. UTF-8 is an ideal encoding, since it can handle any Unicode character. But for many users and applications, ASCII or Latin-1 encodings are often preferred over UTF-8. When the Unicode data contains characters that are outside of the given encoding (e.g., accented characters and most symbols are not encodable in ASCII, and the "infinity" symbol is not encodable in Latin-1), these encodings cannot handle the data on their own. Python supports a built-in encoding error handler called xmlcharrefreplace, which replaces unencodable characters with XML numeric character references, such as ∞ for the "infinity" symbol. This recipe shows how to write and register another similar error handler, html_replace, specifically for producing HTML output. html_replace replaces unencodable characters with more readable HTML symbolic entity references, such as ∞ for the "infinity" symbol. html_replace is less general than xmlcharrefreplace, since it does not support *all* Unicode characters and cannot be used with non-HTML applications; however, it can still be useful if you want HTML output that is as readable as possible in a "view page source" context.

Neither of these error handlers makes sense for output that is neither HTML nor some other form of XML. For example, TeX and other markup languages do not recognize XML numeric character references. However, if you know how to build an arbitrary character reference for such a markup language, you may modify the example error handler html_replace shown in this recipe's Solution to code and register your own encoding error handler.

An alternative (and very effective!) way to perform encoding of Unicode data into a file, with a given encoding and error handler of your choice, is offered by the codecs module in Python's standard library:

```
outfile = codecs.open('out.html', mode='w', encoding='ascii',
                      errors='html_replace')
```

You can now use outfile.write(unicode_data) for any arbitrary Unicode string unicode_data, and all the encoding and error handling will be taken care of transparently. When your output is finished, of course, you should call outfile.close( ).

See Also

Library Reference and *Python in a Nutshell* docs for modules codecs and htmlentitydefs.

1.24 Making Some Strings Case-Insensitive

Credit: Dale Strickland-Clark, Peter Cogolo, Mark McMahon

Problem

You want to treat some strings so that all comparisons and lookups are case-insensitive, while all other uses of the strings preserve the original case.

Solution

The best solution is to wrap the specific strings in question into a suitable subclass of str:

```
class iStr(str):
    """
    Case insensitive string class.
    Behaves just like str, except that all comparisons and lookups
    are case insensitive.
    """
    def __init__(self, *args):
        self._lowered = str.lower(self)
    def __repr__(self):
        return '%s(%s)' % (type(self).__name__, str.__repr__(self))
    def __hash__(self):
        return hash(self._lowered)
    def lower(self):
```

```
            return self._lowered
    def _make_case_insensitive(name):
        ''' wrap one method of str into an iStr one, case-insensitive '''
        str_meth = getattr(str, name)
        def x(self, other, *args):
            ''' try lowercasing 'other', which is typically a string, but
                be prepared to use it as-is if lowering gives problems,
                since strings CAN be correctly compared with non-strings.
            '''
            try: other = other.lower( )
            except (TypeError, AttributeError, ValueError): pass
            return str_meth(self._lowered, other, *args)
        # in Python 2.4, only, add the statement: x.func_name = name
        setattr(iStr, name, x)
    # apply the _make_case_insensitive function to specified methods
    for name in 'eq lt le gt gt ne cmp contains'.split( ):
        _make_case_insensitive('__%s__' % name)
    for name in 'count endswith find index rfind rindex startswith'.split( ):
        _make_case_insensitive(name)
    # note that we don't modify methods 'replace', 'split', 'strip', ...
    # of course, you can add modifications to them, too, if you prefer that.
    del _make_case_insensitive    # remove helper function, not needed any more
```

Discussion

Some implementation choices in class iStr are worthy of notice. First, we choose to generate the lowercase version once and for all, in method __init__, since we envision that in typical uses of iStr instances, this version will be required repeatedly. We hold that version in an attribute that is private, but not overly so (i.e., has a name that begins with one underscore, not two), because if iStr gets subclassed (e.g., to make a more extensive version that also offers case-insensitive splitting, replacing, etc., as the comment in the "Solution" suggests), iStr's subclasses are quite likely to want to access this crucial "implementation detail" of superclass iStr!

We do not offer "case-insensitive" versions of such methods as replace, because it's anything but clear what kind of input-output relation we might want to establish in the general case. Application-specific subclasses may therefore be the way to provide this functionality in ways appropriate to a given application. For example, since the replace method is not wrapped, calling replace on an instance of iStr returns an instance of str, *not* of iStr. If that is a problem in your application, you may want to wrap all iStr methods that return strings, simply to ensure that the results are made into instances of iStr. For that purpose, you need another, separate helper function, similar but not identical to the _make_case_insensitive one shown in the "Solution":

```
    def _make_return_iStr(name):
        str_meth = getattr(str, name)
        def x(*args):
            return iStr(str_meth(*args))
        setattr(iStr, name, x)
```

and you need to call this helper function _make_return_iStr on all the names of relevant string methods returning strings such as:

```
for name in 'center ljust rjust strip lstrip rstrip'.split():
    _make_return_iStr(name)
```

Strings have about 20 methods (including special methods such as __add__ and __mul__) that you should consider wrapping in this way. You can also wrap in this way some additional methods, such as split and join, which may require special handling, and others, such as encode and decode, that you cannot deal with unless you also define a case-insensitive unicode subtype. In practice, one can hope that not every single one of these methods will prove problematic in a typical application. However, as you can see, the very functional richness of Python strings makes it a bit of work to customize string subtypes fully, in a general way without depending on the needs of a specific application.

The implementation of iStr is careful to avoid the boilerplate code (meaning repetitious and therefore bug-prone code) that we'd need if we just overrode each needed method of str in the normal way, with def statements in the class body. A custom metaclass or other such advanced technique would offer no special advantage in this case, so the boilerplate avoidance is simply obtained with one helper function that generates and installs wrapper closures, and two loops using that function, one for normal methods and one for special ones. The loops need to be placed *after* the class statement, as we do in this recipe's Solution, because they need to modify the class object iStr, and the class object doesn't exist yet (and thus cannot be modified) until the class statement has completed.

In Python 2.4, you can reassign the func_name attribute of a function object, and in this case, you should do so to get clearer and more readable results when introspection (e.g., the help function in an interactive interpreter session) is applied to an iStr instance. However, Python 2.3 considers attribute func_name of function objects to be read-only; therefore, in this recipe's Solution, we have indicated this possibility only in a comment, to avoid losing Python 2.3 compatibility over such a minor issue.

Case-insensitive (but case-preserving) strings have many uses, from more tolerant parsing of user input, to filename matching on filesystems that share this characteristic, such as all of Windows filesystems and the Macintosh default filesystem. You might easily find yourself creating a variety of "case-insensitive" container types, such as dictionaries, lists, sets, and so on—meaning containers that go out of their way to treat string-valued keys or items as if they were case-insensitive. Clearly a better architecture is to factor out the functionality of "case-insensitive" comparisons and lookups once and for all; with this recipe in your toolbox, you can just add the required wrapping of strings into iStr instances wherever you may need it, including those times when you're making case-insensitive container types.

For example, a list whose items are basically strings, but are to be treated case-insensitively (for sorting purposes and in such methods as count and index), is reasonably easy to build on top of iStr:

```
class iList(list):
    def __init__(self, *args):
        list.__init__(self, *args)
        # rely on __setitem__ to wrap each item into iStr...
        self[:] = self
    wrap_each_item = iStr
    def __setitem__(self, i, v):
        if isinstance(i, slice): v = map(self.wrap_each_item, v)
        else: v = self.wrap_each_item(v)
        list.__setitem__(self, i, v)
    def append(self, item):
        list.append(self, self.wrap_each_item(item))
    def extend(self, seq):
        list.extend(self, map(self.wrap_each_item, seq))
```

Essentially, all we're doing is ensuring that every item that gets into an instance of iList gets wrapped by a call to iStr, and everything else takes care of itself.

Incidentally, this example class iList is accurately coded so that you can easily make customized subclasses of iList to accommodate application-specific subclasses of iStr: all such a customized subclass of iList needs to do is override the single class-level member named wrap_each_item.

See Also

Library Reference and *Python in a Nutshell* sections on str, string methods, and special methods used in comparisons and hashing.

1.25 Converting HTML Documents to Text on a Unix Terminal

Credit: Brent Burley, Mark Moraes

Problem

You need to visualize HTML documents as text, with support for bold and underlined display on your Unix terminal.

Solution

The simplest approach is to code a *filter* script, taking HTML on standard input and emitting text and terminal control sequences on standard output. Since this recipe only targets Unix, we can get the needed terminal control sequences from the "Unix" command tput, via the function popen of the Python Standard Library module os:

```
#!/usr/bin/env python
import sys, os, htmllib, formatter
# use Unix tput to get the escape sequences for bold, underline, reset
set_bold = os.popen('tput bold').read()
set_underline = os.popen('tput smul').read()
perform_reset = os.popen('tput sgr0').read()
class TtyFormatter(formatter.AbstractFormatter):
    ''' a formatter that keeps track of bold and italic font states, and
        emits terminal control sequences accordingly.
    '''
    def __init__(self, writer):
        # first, as usual, initialize the superclass
        formatter.AbstractFormatter.__init__(self, writer)
        # start with neither bold nor italic, and no saved font state
        self.fontState = False, False
        self.fontStack = []
    def push_font(self, font):
        # the `font' tuple has four items, we only track the two flags
        # about whether italic and bold are active or not
        size, is_italic, is_bold, is_tt = font
        self.fontStack.append((is_italic, is_bold))
        self._updateFontState()
    def pop_font(self, *args):
        # go back to previous font state
        try:
            self.fontStack.pop()
        except IndexError:
            pass
        self._updateFontState()
    def updateFontState(self):
        # emit appropriate terminal control sequences if the state of
        # bold and/or italic(==underline) has just changed
        try:
            newState = self.fontStack[-1]
        except IndexError:
            newState = False, False
        if self.fontState != newState:
            # relevant state change: reset terminal
            print perform_reset,
            # set underine and/or bold if needed
            if newState[0]:
                print set_underline,
            if newState[1]:
                print set_bold,
            # remember the two flags as our current font-state
            self.fontState = newState
# make writer, formatter and parser objects, connecting them as needed
myWriter = formatter.DumbWriter()
if sys.stdout.isatty():
    myFormatter = TtyFormatter(myWriter)
else:
    myFormatter = formatter.AbstractFormatter(myWriter)
myParser = htmllib.HTMLParser(myFormatter)
# feed all of standard input to the parser, then terminate operations
```

```
myParser.feed(sys.stdin.read( ))
myParser.close( )
```

Discussion

The basic `formatter.AbstractFormatter` class, offered by the Python Standard Library, should work just about anywhere. On the other hand, the refinements in the `TtyFormatter` subclass that's the focus of this recipe depend on using a Unix-like terminal, and more specifically on the availability of the `tput` Unix command to obtain information on the escape sequences used to get bold or underlined output and to reset the terminal to its base state.

Many systems that do not have Unix certification, such as Linux and Mac OS X, do have a perfectly workable `tput` command and therefore can use this recipe's `TtyFormatter` subclass just fine. In other words, you can take the use of the word "Unix" in this recipe just as loosely as you can take it in just about every normal discussion: take it as meaning "*ix," if you will.

If your "terminal" emulator supports other escape sequences for controlling output appearance, you should be able to adapt this `TtyFormatter` class accordingly. For example, on Windows, a `cmd.exe` command window should, I'm told, support standard ANSI escape sequences, so you could choose to hard-code those sequences if Windows is the platform on which you want to run your version of this script.

In many cases, you may prefer to use other existing Unix commands, such as `lynx -dump -`, to get richer formatting than this recipe provides. However, this recipe comes in quite handy when you find yourself on a system that has a Python installation but lacks such other helpful commands as `lynx`.

See Also

Library Reference and *Python in a Nutshell* docs on the `formatter` and `htmllib` modules; `man tput` on a Unix or Unix-like system for more information about the `tput` command.

CHAPTER 2

Files

2.0 Introduction

Credit: Mark Lutz, author of Programming Python *and* Python Quick Reference, *co-author of* Learning Python

Behold the file—one of the first things that any reasonably pragmatic programmer reaches for in a programming language's toolbox. Because processing external files is a very real, tangible task, the quality of file-processing interfaces is a good way to assess the practicality of a programming tool.

As the recipes in this chapter attest, Python shines in this task. Files in Python are supported in a variety of layers: from the built-in open function (a synonym for the standard file object type), to specialized tools in standard library modules such as os, to third-party utilities available on the Web. All told, Python's arsenal of file tools provides several powerful ways to access files in your scripts.

File Basics

In Python, a file object is an instance of built-in type file. The built-in function open creates and returns a file object. The first argument, a string, specifies the file's path (i.e., the filename preceded by an optional directory path). The second argument to open, also a string, specifies the mode in which to open the file. For example:

```
input = open('data', 'r')
output = open('/tmp/spam', 'w')
```

open accepts a file path in which directories and files are separated by slash characters (/), regardless of the proclivities of the underlying operating system. On systems that don't use slashes, you can use a backslash character (\) instead, but there's no real reason to do so. Backslashes are harder to fit nicely in string literals, since you have to double them up or use "raw" strings. If the file path argument does not include the file's directory name, the file is assumed to reside in the current working directory (which is a disjoint concept from the Python module search path).

For the mode argument, use 'r' to read the file in text mode; this is the default value and is commonly omitted, so that open is called with just one argument. Other common modes are 'rb' to read the file in binary mode, 'w' to create and write to the file in text mode, and 'wb' to create and write to the file in binary mode. A variant of 'r' that is sometimes precious is 'rU', which tells Python to read the file in text mode with "universal newlines": mode 'rU' can read text files independently of the line-termination convention the files are using, be it the Unix way, the Windows way, or even the (old) Mac way. (Mac OS X today is a Unix for all intents and purposes, but releases of Mac OS 9 and earlier, just a few years ago, were quite different.)

The distinction between text mode and binary mode is important on non-Unix-like platforms because of the line-termination characters used on these systems. When you open a file in binary mode, Python knows that it doesn't need to worry about line-termination characters; it just moves bytes between the file and in-memory strings without any kind of translation. When you open a file in text mode on a non-Unix-like system, however, Python knows it must translate between the '\n' line-termination characters used in strings and whatever the current platform uses in the file itself. All of your Python code can always rely on '\n' as the line-termination character, as long as you properly indicate text or binary mode when you open the file.

Once you have a file object, you perform all file I/O by calling methods of this object, as we'll discuss in a moment. When you're done with the file, you should finish by calling the close method on the object, to close the connection to the file:

```
input.close( )
```

In short scripts, people often omit this step, as Python automatically closes the file when a file object is reclaimed during garbage collection (which in mainstream Python means the file is closed just about at once, although other important Python implementations, such as Jython and IronPython, have other, more relaxed garbage-collection strategies). Nevertheless, it is good programming practice to close your files as soon as possible, and it is especially a good idea in larger programs, which otherwise may be at more risk of having excessive numbers of uselessly open files lying about. Note that try/finally is particularly well suited to ensuring that a file gets closed, even when a function terminates due to an uncaught exception.

To write to a file, use the write method:

```
output.write(s)
```

where s is a string. Think of s as a string of characters if output is open for text-mode writing, and as a string of bytes if output is open for binary-mode writing. Files have other writing-related methods, such as flush, to send any data being buffered, and writelines, to write a sequence of strings in a single call. However, write is by far the most commonly used method.

Reading from a file is more common than writing to a file, and more issues are involved, so file objects have more reading methods than writing ones. The readline method reads and returns the next line from a text file. Consider the following loop:

```
while True:
    line = input.readline( )
    if not line: break
    process(line)
```

This was once idiomatic Python but it is no longer the best way to read and process all of the lines from a file. Another dated alternative is to use the readlines method, which reads the whole file and returns a list of lines:

```
for line in input.readlines( ):
    process(line)
```

readlines is useful only for files that fit comfortably in physical memory. If the file is truly huge, readlines can fail or at least slow things down quite drastically (virtual memory fills up and the operating system has to start copying parts of physical memory to disk). In today's Python, just loop on the file object itself to get a line at a time with excellent memory and performance characteristics:

```
for line in input:
    process(line)
```

Of course, you don't always want to read a file line by line. You may instead want to read some or all of the bytes in the file, particularly if you've opened the file for binary-mode reading, where lines are unlikely to be an applicable concept. In this case, you can use the read method. When called without arguments, read reads and returns all the remaining bytes from the file. When read is called with an integer argument N, it reads and returns the next N bytes (or all the remaining bytes, if less than N bytes remain). Other methods worth mentioning are seek and tell, which support random access to files. These methods are normally used with binary files made up of fixed-length records.

Portability and Flexibility

On the surface, Python's file support is straightforward. However, before you peruse the code in this chapter, I want to underscore two aspects of Python's file support: code portability and interface flexibility.

Keep in mind that most file interfaces in Python are fully portable across platform boundaries. It would be difficult to overstate the importance of this feature. A Python script that searches all files in a "directory" tree for a bit of text, for example, can be freely moved from platform to platform without source-code changes: just copy the script's source file to the new target machine. I do it all the time—so much so that I can happily stay out of operating system wars. With Python's portability, the underlying platform is almost irrelevant.

Also, it has always struck me that Python's file-processing interfaces are not restricted to real, physical files. In fact, most file tools work with any kind of object that exposes the same interface as a real file object. Thus, a file reader cares only about read methods, and a file writer cares only about write methods. As long as the target object implements the expected protocol, all goes well.

For example, suppose you have written a general file-processing function such as the following, meant to apply a passed-in function to each line of an input file:

```
def scanner(fileobject, linehandler):
    for line in fileobject:
        linehandler(line)
```

If you code this function in a module file and drop that file into a "directory" that's on your Python search path (sys.path), you can use it any time you need to scan a text file line by line, now or in the future. To illustrate, here is a client script that simply prints the first word of each line:

```
from myutils import scanner
def firstword(line):
    print line.split( )[0]
file = open('data')
scanner(file, firstword)
```

So far, so good; we've just coded a small, reusable software component. But notice that there are no type declarations in the scanner function, only an interface constraint—any object that is iterable line by line will do. For instance, suppose you later want to provide canned test input from a string object, instead of using a real, physical file. The standard StringIO module, and the equivalent but faster cStringIO, provide the appropriate wrapping and interface forgery:

```
from cStringIO import StringIO
from myutils import scanner
def firstword(line): print line.split( )[0]
string = StringIO('one\ntwo xxx\nthree\n')
scanner(string, firstword)
```

StringIO objects are plug-and-play compatible with file objects, so scanner takes its three lines of text from an in-memory string object, rather than a true external file. You don't need to change the scanner to make this work—just pass it the right kind of object. For more generality, you can even use a class to implement the expected interface instead:

```
class MyStream(object):
    def __iter__(self):
        # grab and return text from wherever
        return iter(['a\n', 'b c d\n'])
from myutils import scanner
def firstword(line):
    print line.split( )[0]
object = MyStream( )
scanner(object, firstword)
```

This time, as scanner attempts to read the file, it really calls out to the __iter__ method you've coded in your class. In practice, such a method might use other Python standard tools to grab text from a variety of sources: an interactive user, a popup GUI input box, a shelve object, an SQL database, an XML or HTML page, a network socket, and so on. The point is that scanner doesn't know or care what type of object is implementing the interface it expects, or what that interface actually does.

Object-oriented programmers know this deliberate naiveté as *polymorphism*. The type of the object being processed determines what an operation, such as the for-loop iteration in scanner, actually does. Everywhere in Python, object interfaces, rather than specific data types, are the unit of coupling. The practical effect is that functions are often applicable to a much broader range of problems than you might expect. This is especially true if you have a background in statically typed languages such as C or C++. It is almost as if we get C++ templates for free in Python. Code has an innate flexibility that is a by-product of Python's strong but dynamic typing.

Of course, code portability and flexibility run rampant in Python development and are not really confined to file interfaces. Both are features of the language that are simply inherited by file-processing scripts. Other Python benefits, such as its easy scriptability and code readability, are also key assets when it comes time to change file-processing programs. But rather than extolling all of Python's virtues here, I'll simply defer to the wonderful recipes in this chapter and this book at large for more details. Enjoy!

2.1   Reading from a File

Credit: Luther Blissett

Problem

You want to read text or data from a file.

Solution

Here's the most convenient way to read all of the file's contents at once into one long string:

```
all_the_text = open('thefile.txt').read()     # all text from a text file
all_the_data = open('abinfile', 'rb').read() # all data from a binary file
```

However, it is safer to bind the file object to a name, so that you can call close on it as soon as you're done, to avoid ending up with open files hanging around. For example, for a text file:

```
file_object = open('thefile.txt')
try:
```

```
        all_the_text = file_object.read( )
    finally:
        file_object.close( )
```

You don't necessarily have to use the try/finally statement here, but it's a good idea to use it, because it ensures the file gets closed even when an error occurs during reading.

The simplest, fastest, and most Pythonic way to read a text file's contents at once as a list of strings, one per line, is:

```
    list_of_all_the_lines = file_object.readlines( )
```

This leaves a '\n' at the end of each line; if you don't want that, you have alternatives, such as:

```
    list_of_all_the_lines = file_object.read( ).splitlines( )
    list_of_all_the_lines = file_object.read( ).split('\n')
    list_of_all_the_lines = [L.rstrip('\n') for L in file_object]
```

The simplest and fastest way to process a text file one line at a time is simply to loop on the file object with a for statement:

```
    for line in file_object:
        process line
```

This approach also leaves a '\n' at the end of each line; you may remove it by starting the for loop's body with:

```
    line = line.rstrip('\n')
```

or even, when you're OK with getting rid of trailing whitespace from each line (not just a trailing '\n'), the generally handier:

```
    line = line.rstrip( )
```

Discussion

Unless the file you're reading is truly huge, slurping it all into memory in one gulp is often fastest and most convenient for any further processing. The built-in function open creates a Python file object (alternatively, you can equivalently call the built-in type file). You call the read method on that object to get all of the contents (whether text or binary) as a single long string. If the contents are text, you may choose to immediately split that string into a list of lines with the split method or the specialized splitlines method. Since splitting into lines is frequently needed, you may also call readlines directly on the file object for faster, more convenient operation.

You can also loop directly on the file object, or pass it to callables that require an iterable, such as list or max—when thus treated as an iterable, a file object open for reading has the file's text lines as the iteration items (therefore, this should be done for text files only). This kind of line-by-line iteration is cheap in terms of memory consumption and fairly speedy too.

On Unix and Unix-like systems, such as Linux, Mac OS X, and other BSD variants, there is no real distinction between text files and binary data files. On Windows and very old Macintosh systems, however, line terminators in text files are encoded, not with the standard '\n' separator, but with '\r\n' and '\r', respectively. Python translates these line-termination characters into '\n' on your behalf. This means that you need to tell Python when you open a binary file, so that it won't perform such translation. To do so, use 'rb' as the second argument to open. This is innocuous even on Unix-like platforms, and it's a good habit to distinguish binary files from text files even there, although it's not mandatory in that case. Such good habits will make your programs more immediately understandable, as well as more compatible with different platforms.

If you're unsure about which line-termination convention a certain text file might be using, use 'rU' as the second argument to open, requesting universal endline translation. This lets you freely interchange text files among Windows, Unix (including Mac OS X), and old Macintosh systems, without worries: all kinds of line-ending conventions get mapped to '\n', whatever platform your code is running on.

You can call methods such as read directly on the file object produced by the open function, as shown in the first snippet of the solution. When you do so, you no longer have a reference to the file object as soon as the reading operation finishes. In practice, Python notices the lack of a reference at once, and immediately closes the file. However, it is better to bind a name to the result of open, so that you can call close yourself explicitly when you are done with the file. This ensures that the file stays open for as short a time as possible, even on platforms such as Jython, Iron-Python, and other hypothetical future versions of Python, on which more advanced garbage-collection mechanisms might delay the automatic closing that the current version of C-based Python performs at once. To ensure that a file object is closed even if errors happen during its processing, the most solid and prudent approach is to use the try/finally statement:

```
file_object = open('thefile.txt')
try:
    for line in file_object:
        process line
finally:
    file_object.close()
```

Be careful *not* to place the call to open *inside* the try clause of this try/finally statement (a rather common error among beginners). If an error occurs during the opening, there is nothing to close, and besides, nothing gets bound to name file_object, so you definitely don't want to call file_object.close()!

If you choose to read the file a little at a time, rather than all at once, the idioms are different. Here's one way to read a binary file 100 bytes at a time, until you reach the end of the file:

```
file_object = open('abinfile', 'rb')
try:
```

```
    while True:
        chunk = file_object.read(100)
        if not chunk:
            break
        do_something_with(chunk)
finally:
    file_object.close( )
```

Passing an argument N to the read method ensures that read will read only the next N bytes (or fewer, if the file is closer to the end). read returns the empty string when it reaches the end of the file. Complicated loops are best encapsulated as reusable generators. In this case, we can encapsulate the logic only partially, because a generator's yield keyword is not allowed in the try clause of a try/finally statement. Giving up on the assurance of file closing afforded by try/finally, we can therefore settle for:

```
def read_file_by_chunks(filename, chunksize=100):
    file_object = open(filename, 'rb')
    while True:
        chunk = file_object.read(chunksize)
        if not chunk:
            break
        yield chunk
    file_object.close( )
```

Once this read_file_by_chunks generator is available, your application code to read and process a binary file by fixed-size chunks becomes extremely simple:

```
for chunk in read_file_by_chunks('abinfile'):
    do_something_with(chunk)
```

Reading a text file one line at a time is a frequent task. Just loop on the file object, as in:

```
for line in open('thefile.txt', 'rU'):
    do_something_with(line)
```

Here, too, in order to be 100% certain that no uselessly open file object will ever be left just hanging around, you may want to code this snippet in a more rigorously correct and prudent way:

```
file_object = open('thefile.txt', 'rU'):
try:
    for line in file_object:
        do_something_with(line)
finally:
    file_object.close( )
```

See Also

Recipe 2.2 "Writing to a File"; documentation for the open built-in function and file objects in the *Library Reference* and *Python in a Nutshell*.

2.2   Writing to a File

Credit: Luther Blissett

Problem

You want to write text or data to a file.

Solution

Here is the most convenient way to write one long string to a file:

```
open('thefile.txt', 'w').write(all_the_text)   # text to a text file
open('abinfile', 'wb').write(all_the_data)     # data to a binary file
```

However, it is safer to bind the file object to a name, so that you can call close on the file object as soon as you're done. For example, for a text file:

```
file_object = open('thefile.txt', 'w')
file_object.write(all_the_text)
file_object.close()
```

Often, the data you want to write is not in one big string, but in a list (or other sequence) of strings. In this case, you should use the writelines method (which, despite its name, is not limited to lines and works just as well with binary data as with text files!):

```
file_object.writelines(list_of_text_strings)
open('abinfile', 'wb').writelines(list_of_data_strings)
```

Calling writelines is much faster than the alternatives of joining the strings into one big string (e.g., with ''.join) and then calling write, or calling write repeatedly in a loop.

Discussion

To create a file object for writing, you must always pass a second argument to open (or file)—either 'w' to write textual data or 'wb' to write binary data. The same considerations detailed previously in recipe 2.1 "Reading from a File" apply here, except that calling close explicitly is even more advisable when you're writing to a file rather than reading from it. Only by closing the file can you be reasonably sure that the data is actually on the disk and not still residing in some temporary buffer in memory.

Writing a file a little at a time is even more common than reading a file a little at a time. You can just call write and/or writelines repeatedly, as each string or sequence of strings to write becomes ready. Each write operation appends data at the end of the file, after all the previously written data. When you're done, call the close method on the file object. If all the data is available at once, a single writelines call is faster and simpler. However, if the data becomes available a little at a time, it's better to call write as the data comes, than to build up a temporary list of pieces (e.g., with append) just in order to be able to write it all at once in the end with writelines. Reading and writing are quite different, with respect to the performance and convenience implications of operating "in bulk" versus operating a little at a time.

When you open a file for writing with option 'w' (or 'wb'), any data that might already have been in the file is immediately destroyed; even if you close the file object immediately after opening it, you still end up with an empty file on the disk. If you want the data you're writing to be appended to the previous contents of the file, open the file with option 'a' (or 'ab') instead. More advanced options allow both reading and writing on the same open file object—in particular, see recipe 2.8 "Updating a Random-Access File" for option 'r+b', which, in practice, is the only frequently used one out of all the advanced option strings.

See Also

Recipe 2.1 "Reading from a File"; recipe 2.8 "Updating a Random-Access File"; documentation for the open built-in function and file objects in the *Library Reference* and *Python in a Nutshell*.

2.3 Searching and Replacing Text in a File

Credit: Jeff Bauer, Adam Krieg

Problem

You need to change one string into another throughout a file.

Solution

String substitution is most simply performed by the replace method of string objects. The work here is to support reading from a specified file (or standard input) and writing to a specified file (or standard output):

```
#!/usr/bin/env python
import os, sys
nargs = len(sys.argv)
if not 3 <= nargs <= 5:
    print "usage: %s search_text replace_text [infile [outfile]]" % \
        os.path.basename(sys.argv[0])
else:
    stext = sys.argv[1]
    rtext = sys.argv[2]
    input_file = sys.stdin
    output_file = sys.stdout
    if nargs > 3:
        input_file = open(sys.argv[3])
    if nargs > 4:
        output_file = open(sys.argv[4], 'w')
    for s in input_file:
```

```
    output_file.write(s.replace(stext, rtext))
output.close( )
input.close( )
```

Discussion

This recipe is really simple, but that's what beautiful about it—why do complicated stuff when simple stuff suffices? As indicated by the leading "shebang" line, the recipe is a simple main script, meaning a script meant to be run directly at a shell command prompt, as opposed to a module meant to be imported from elsewhere. The script looks at its arguments to determine the search text, the replacement text, the input file (defaulting to standard input), and the output file (defaulting to standard output). Then, it loops over each line of the input file, writing to the output file a copy of the line with the substitution performed on it. That's all! For accuracy, the script closes both files at the end.

As long as an input file fits comfortably in memory in two copies (one before and one after the replacement, since strings are immutable), we could, with an increase in speed, operate on the entire input file's contents at once instead of looping. With today's low-end PCs typically containing at least 256 MB of memory, handling files of up to about 100 MB should not be a problem, and few text files are bigger than that. It suffices to replace the for loop with one single statement:

```
    output_file.write(input_file.read( ).replace(stext, rtext))
```

As you can see, that's even simpler than the loop used in the recipe.

See Also

Documentation for the open built-in function, file objects, and strings' replace method in the *Library Reference* and *Python in a Nutshell*.

2.4   Reading a Specific Line from a File

Credit: Luther Blissett

Problem

You want to read from a text file a single line, given the line number.

Solution

The standard Python library linecache module makes this task a snap:

```
    import linecache
    theline = linecache.getline(thefilepath, desired_line_number)
```

Discussion

The standard linecache module is usually the optimal Python solution for this task. linecache is particularly useful when you have to perform this task repeatedly for several lines in a file, since linecache caches information to avoid uselessly repeating work. When you know that you won't be needing any more lines from the cache for a while, call the module's clearcache function to free the memory used for the cache. You can also use checkcache if the file may have changed on disk and you must make sure you are getting the updated version.

linecache reads and caches all of the text file whose name you pass to it, so, if it's a very large file and you need only one of its lines, linecache may be doing more work than is strictly necessary. Should this happen to be a bottleneck for your program, you may get an increase in speed by coding an explicit loop, encapsulated within a function, such as:

```
def getline(thefilepath, desired_line_number):
    if desired_line_number < 1: return ''
    for current_line_number, line in enumerate(open(thefilepath, 'rU')):
        if current_line_number == desired_line_number-1: return line
    return ''
```

The only detail requiring attention is that enumerate counts from 0, so, since we assume the desired_line_number argument counts from 1, we need the -1 in the == comparison.

See Also

Documentation for the linecache module in the *Library Reference* and *Python in a Nutshell*; *Perl Cookbook* recipe 8.8.

2.5   Counting Lines in a File

Credit: Luther Blissett

Problem

You need to compute the number of lines in a file.

Solution

The simplest approach for reasonably sized files is to read the file as a list of lines, so that the count of lines is the length of the list. If the file's path is in a string bound to a variable named thefilepath, all the code you need to implement this approach is:

```
count = len(open(thefilepath, 'rU').readlines())
```

For a truly huge file, however, this simple approach may be very slow or even fail to work. If you have to worry about humongous files, a loop on the file always works:

```
count = -1
for count, line in enumerate(open(thefilepath, 'rU')):
    pass
count += 1
```

A tricky alternative, potentially faster for truly humongous files, for when the line terminator is '\n' (or has '\n' as a substring, as happens on Windows):

```
count = 0
thefile = open(thefilepath, 'rb')
while True:
    buffer = thefile.read(8192*1024)
    if not buffer:
        break
    count += buffer.count('\n')
thefile.close( )
```

The 'rb' argument to open is necessary if you're after speed—without that argument, this snippet might be very slow on Windows.

Discussion

When an external program counts a file's lines, such as wc -1 on Unix-like platforms, you can of course choose to use that (e.g., via os.popen). However, it's generally simpler, faster, and more portable to do the line-counting in your own program. You can rely on almost all text files having a reasonable size, so that reading the whole file into memory at once is feasible. For all such normal files, the len of the result of readlines gives you the count of lines in the simplest way.

If the file is larger than available memory (say, a few hundred megabytes on a typical PC today), the simplest solution can become unacceptably slow, as the operating system struggles to fit the file's contents into virtual memory. It may even fail, when swap space is exhausted and virtual memory can't help any more. On a typical PC, with 256MB RAM and virtually unlimited disk space, you should still expect serious problems when you try to read into memory files above, say, 1 or 2 GB, depending on your operating system. (Some operating systems are much more fragile than others in handling virtual-memory issues under such overly stressed load conditions.) In this case, looping on the file object, as shown in this recipe's Solution, is better. The enumerate built-in keeps the line count without your code having to do it explicitly.

Counting line-termination characters while reading the file by bytes in reasonably sized chunks is the key idea in the third approach. It's probably the least immediately intuitive, and it's not perfectly cross-platform, but you might hope that it's fastest (e.g., when compared with recipe 8.2 in the *Perl Cookbook*).

However, in most cases, performance doesn't really matter all that much. When it does matter, the time-sink part of your program might not be what your intuition tells you it is, so you should never trust your intuition in this matter—instead, always benchmark and measure. For example, consider a typical Unix *syslog* file of middling size, a bit over 18 MB of text in 230,000 lines:

```
[situ@tioni nuc]$ wc nuc
 231581 2312730 18508908 nuc
```

And consider the following testing-and-benchmark framework script, *bench.py*:

```
import time
def timeo(fun, n=10):
    start = time.clock()
    for i in xrange(n): fun()
    stend = time.clock()
    thetime = stend-start
    return fun.__name__, thetime
import os
def linecount_w():
    return int(os.popen('wc -l nuc').read().split()[0])
def linecount_1():
    return len(open('nuc').readlines())
def linecount_2():
    count = -1
    for count, line in enumerate(open('nuc')): pass
    return count+1
def linecount_3():
    count = 0
    thefile = open('nuc', 'rb')
    while True:
        buffer = thefile.read(65536)
        if not buffer: break
        count += buffer.count('\n')
    return count
for f in linecount_w, linecount_1, linecount_2, linecount_3:
    print f.__name__, f()
for f in linecount_1, linecount_2, linecount_3:
    print "%s: %.2f"%timeo(f)
```

First, I print the line-counts obtained by all methods, thus ensuring that no anomaly or error has occurred (counting tasks are notoriously prone to off-by-one errors). Then, I run each alternative 10 times, under the control of the timing function timeo, and look at the results. Here they are, on the old but reliable machine I measured them on:

```
[situ@tioni nuc]$ python -O bench.py
linecount_w 231581
linecount_1 231581
linecount_2 231581
linecount_3 231581
linecount_1: 4.84
linecount_2: 4.54
linecount_3: 5.02
```

As you can see, the performance differences hardly matter: your users will never even notice a difference of 10% or so in one auxiliary task. However, the *fastest* approach (for my particular circumstances, on an old but reliable PC running a popular Linux distribution, and for this specific benchmark) is the humble loop-on-every-line technique, while the *slowest* one is the fancy, ambitious technique that counts line terminators by chunks. In practice, unless I had to worry about files of many hundreds of megabytes, I'd always use the simplest approach (i.e., the first one presented in this recipe).

Measuring the exact performance of code snippets (rather than blindly using complicated approaches in the hope that they'll be faster) is very important—so important, indeed, that the Python Standard Library includes a module, timeit, specifically designed for such measurement tasks. I suggest you use timeit, rather than coding your own little benchmarks as I have done here. The benchmark I just showed you is one I've had around for years, since well before timeit appeared in the standard Python library, so I think I can be forgiven for not using timeit in this specific case!

See Also

The *Library Reference* and *Python in a Nutshell* sections on file objects, the enumerate built-in, os.popen, and the time and timeit modules; *Perl Cookbook* recipe 8.2.

2.6   Processing Every Word in a File

Credit: Luther Blissett

Problem

You need to do something with each and every word in a file.

Solution

This task is best handled by two nested loops, one on lines and another on the words in each line:

```
for line in open(thefilepath):
    for word in line.split( ):
        dosomethingwith(word)
```

The nested for statement's header implicitly defines words as sequences of non-spaces separated by sequences of spaces (just as the Unix program wc does). For other definitions of words, you can use regular expressions. For example:

```
import re
re_word = re.compile(r"[\w'-]+")
for line in open(thefilepath):
    for word in re_word.finditer(line):
        dosomethingwith(word.group(0))
```

In this case, a word is defined as a maximal sequence of alphanumerics, hyphens, and apostrophes.

Discussion

If you want to use other definitions of words, you will obviously need different regular expressions. The outer loop, on all lines in the file, won't change.

It's often a good idea to wrap iterations as iterator objects, and this kind of wrapping is most commonly and conveniently obtained by coding simple generators:

```
def words_of_file(thefilepath, line_to_words=str.split):
    the_file = open(thefilepath):
    for line in the_file:
        for word in line_to_words(line):
            yield word
    the_file.close( )
for word in words_of_file(thefilepath):
    dosomethingwith(word)
```

This approach lets you separate, cleanly and effectively, two different concerns: how to iterate over all items (in this case, words in a file) and what to do with each item in the iteration. Once you have cleanly encapsulated iteration concerns in an iterator object (often, as here, a generator), most of your uses of iteration become simple for statements. You can often reuse the iterator in many spots in your program, and if maintenance is ever needed, you can perform that maintenance in just one place—the definition of the iterator—rather than having to hunt for all uses. The advantages are thus very similar to those you obtain in any programming language by appropriately defining and using functions, rather than copying and pasting pieces of code all over the place. With Python's iterators, you can get these reuse advantages for all of your looping-control structures, too.

We've taken the opportunity afforded by the refactoring of the loop into a generator to perform two minor enhancements—ensuring the file is explicitly closed, which is always a good idea, and generalizing the way each line is split into words (defaulting to the split method of string objects, but leaving a door open to more generality). For example, when we need words as defined by a regular expression, we can code another wrapper on top of words_of_file thanks to this "hook":

```
import re
def words_by_re(thefilepath, repattern=r"[\w'-]+"):
    wre = re.compile(repattern)
    def line_to_words(line):
        for mo in wre.finditer(line):
            yield mo.group(0)
    return words_of_file(thefilepath, line_to_words)
```

Here, too, we supply a reasonable default for the regular expression pattern defining a word but still make it easy to pass a different value in those cases in which different definitions are necessary. Excessive generalization is a pernicious temptation, but a little tasteful generalization suggested by experience will most often amply repay the modest effort it requires. Having a function accept an optional argument, while providing the most likely value for the argument as the default value, is among the simplest and handiest ways to implement this modest and often worthwhile kind of generalization.

See Also

Chapter 19 for more on iterators and generators; *Library Reference* and *Python in a Nutshell* on file objects and the re module; *Perl Cookbook* recipe 8.3.

2.7   Using Random-Access Input/Output

Credit: Luther Blissett

Problem

You want to read a binary record from somewhere inside a large file of fixed-length records, without reading a record at a time to get there.

Solution

The byte offset of the start of a record in the file is the size of a record, in bytes, multiplied by the progressive number of the record (counting from 0). So, you can just seek right to the proper spot, then read the data. For example, to read the seventh record from a binary file where each record is 48 bytes long:

```
thefile = open('somebinfile', 'rb')
record_size = 48
record_number = 6
thefile.seek(record_size * record_number)
buffer = thefile.read(record_size)
```

Note that the record_number of the *seventh* record is 6: record numbers count from *zero*!

Discussion

This approach works only on files (generally binary ones) defined in terms of records that are all the same fixed size in bytes; it doesn't work on normal text files. For clarity, the recipe shows the file being opened for reading as a binary file by passing 'rb' as the second argument to open, just before the seek. As long as the file object is open for reading as a binary file, you can perform as many seek and read operations as you need, before eventually closing the file again—you don't necessarily open the file just before performing a seek on it.

See Also

The section of the *Library Reference* and *Python in a Nutshell* on file objects; *Perl Cookbook* recipe 8.12.

2.8   Updating a Random-Access File

Credit: Luther Blissett

Problem

You want to read a binary record from somewhere inside a large file of fixed-length records, change some or all of the values of the record's fields, and write the record back.

Solution

Read the record, unpack it, perform whatever computations you need for the update, pack the fields back into the record, seek to the start of the record again, write it back. Phew. Faster to code than to say:

```
import struct
format_string = '8l'            # e.g., say a record is 8 4-byte integers
thefile = open('somebinfile', 'r+b')
record_size = struct.calcsize(format_string)
record_number = 6
thefile.seek(record_size * record_number)
buffer = thefile.read(record_size)
fields = list(struct.unpack(format_string, buffer))
# Perform computations, suitably modifying fields, then:
buffer = struct.pack(format_string, *fields)
thefile.seek(record_size * record_number)
thefile.write(buffer)
thefile.close( )
```

Discussion

This approach works only on files (generally binary ones) defined in terms of records that are all the same, fixed size; it doesn't work on normal text files. Furthermore, the size of each record must be that defined by a struct format string, as shown in the recipe's code. A typical format string, for example, might be '8l', to specify that each record is made up of eight four-byte integers, each to be interpreted as a signed value and unpacked into a Python int. In this case, the fields variable in the recipe would be bound to a list of eight ints. Note that struct.unpack returns a tuple. Because tuples are immutable, the computation would have to rebind the entire fields variable. A list is mutable, so each field can be rebound as needed. Thus, for convenience, we explicitly ask for a list when we bind fields. Make sure, however, not to alter the length of the list. In this case, it needs to remain composed of exactly eight integers, or the struct.pack call will raise an exception when we call it with a format_string of '8l'. Also, this recipe is not suitable when working with records that are not all of the same, unchanging length.

To seek back to the start of the record, instead of using the record_size*record_ number offset again, you may choose to do a relative seek:

```
thefile.seek(-record_size, 1)
```

The second argument to the seek method (1) tells the file object to seek relative to the current position (here, so many bytes back, because we used a negative number as the first argument). seek's default is to seek to an absolute offset within the file (i.e., from the start of the file). You can also explicitly request this default behavior by calling seek with a second argument of 0.

You don't need to open the file just before you do the first seek, nor do you need to close it right after the write. Once you have a file object that is correctly opened (i.e., for updating and as a binary rather than a text file), you can perform as many updates on the file as you want before closing the file again. These calls are shown here to emphasize the proper technique for opening a file for random-access updates and the importance of closing a file when you are done with it.

The file needs to be opened for updating (i.e., to allow both reading and writing). That's what the 'r+b' argument to open means: open for reading and writing, but do not implicitly perform any transformations on the file's contents because the file is a binary one. (The 'b' part is unnecessary but still recommended for clarity on Unix and Unix-like systems. However, it's absolutely crucial on other platforms, such as Windows.) If you're creating the binary file from scratch, but you still want to be able to go back, reread, and update some records without closing and reopening the file, you can use a second argument of 'w+b' instead. However, I have never witnessed this strange combination of requirements; binary files are normally first created (by opening them with 'wb', writing data, and closing the file) and later reopened for updating with 'r+b'.

While this approach is normally useful only on a file whose records are all the same size, another, more advanced possibility exists: a separate "index file" that provides the offset and length of each record inside the "data file". Such indexed sequential access approaches aren't much in fashion any more, but they used to be very important. Nowadays, one meets just about only text files (of many kinds, more and more often XML ones), databases, and occasional binary files with fixed-length records. Still, if you do need to access an indexed sequential binary file, the code is quite similar to that shown in this recipe, except that you must obtain the record_size and the offset argument to pass to thefile.seek by reading them from the index file, rather than computing them yourself as shown in this recipe's Solution.

See Also

The sections of the *Library Reference* and *Python in a Nutshell* on file objects and the struct module; *Perl Cookbook* recipe 8.13.

2.9   Reading Data from zip Files

Credit: Paul Prescod, Alex Martelli

Problem

You want to directly examine some or all of the files contained in an archive in *zip* format, without expanding them on disk.

Solution

zip files are a popular, cross-platform way of archiving files. The Python Standard Library comes with a zipfile module to access such files easily:

```
import zipfile
z = zipfile.ZipFile("zipfile.zip", "r")
for filename in z.namelist( ):
    print 'File:', filename,
    bytes = z.read(filename)
    print 'has', len(bytes), 'bytes'
```

Discussion

Python can work directly with data in *zip* files. You can look at the list of items in the archive's directory and work with the "data file"s themselves. This recipe is a snippet that lists all of the names and content lengths of the files included in the *zip* archive *zipfile.zip*.

The zipfile module does not currently handle multidisk *zip* files nor *zip* files with appended comments. Take care to use r as the flag argument, not rb, which might seem more natural (e.g., on Windows). With ZipFile, the flag is not used the same way when opening a file, and rb is not recognized. The r flag handles the inherently binary nature of all *zip* files on all platforms.

When a *zip* file contains some Python modules (meaning *.py* or preferably *.pyc* files), possibly in addition to other (data) files, you can add the file's path to Python's sys.path and then use the import statement to import modules from the *zip* file. Here's a toy, self-contained, purely demonstrative example that creates such a *zip* file on the fly, imports a module from it, then removes it—all just to show you how it's done:

```
import zipfile, tempfile, os, sys
handle, filename = tempfile.mkstemp('.zip')
os.close(handle)
z = zipfile.ZipFile(filename, 'w')
```

```
z.writestr('hello.py', 'def f(): return "hello world from "+__file__\n')
z.close()
sys.path.insert(0, filename)
import hello
print hello.f()
os.unlink(filename)
```

Running this script emits something like:

```
hello world from /tmp/tmpESVzeY.zip/hello.py
```

Besides illustrating Python's ability to import from a *zip* file, this snippet also shows how to make (and later remove) a temporary file, and how to use the `writestr` method to add a member to a *zip* file without placing that member into a disk file first.

Note that the path to the *zip* file from which you `import` is treated somewhat like a directory. (In this specific example run, that path is /tmp/tmpESVzeY.zip, but of course, since we're dealing with a temporary file, the exact value of the path can change at each run, depending also on your platform.) In particular, the `__file__` global variable, within the module `hello`, which is `imported` from the *zip* file, has a value of */tmp/tmpESVzeY.zip/hello.py*—a *pseudo-path*, made up of the *zip* file's path seen as a "directory" followed by the relative path of *hello.py* within the *zip* file. If you import from a *zip* file a module that computes paths relative to itself in order to get to data files, you need to adapt the module to this effect, because you cannot just open such a "pseudo-path" to get a file object: rather, to read or write files inside a *zip* file, you must use functions from standard library module `zipfile`, as shown in the solution.

For more information about importing modules from a *zip* file, see recipe 16.12 "Binding Main Script and Modules into One Executable on Unix." While that recipe is Unix-specific, the information in the recipe's Discussion about importing from *zip* files is also valid for Windows.

See Also

Documentation for the `zipfile` module in the *Library Reference* and *Python in a Nutshell*; modules `tempfile`, `os`, `sys`; for archiving a tree of files, see recipe 2.11 "Archiving a Tree of Files into a Compressed tar File"; for more information about importing modules from a *zip* file, recipe 16.12 "Binding Main Script and Modules into One Executable on Unix."

2.10 Handling a zip File Inside a String

Credit: Indyana Jones

Problem

Your program receives a *zip* file as a string of bytes in memory, and you need to read the information in this *zip* file.

Solution

Solving this kind of problem is exactly what standard library module cStringIO is for:

```
import cStringIO, zipfile
class ZipString(ZipFile):
    def __init__(self, datastring):
        ZipFile.__init__(self, cStringIO.StringIO(datastring))
```

Discussion

I often find myself faced with this task—for example, *zip* files coming from BLOB fields in a database or ones received from a network connection. I used to save such binary data to a temporary file, then open the file with the standard library module zipfile. Of course, I had to ensure I deleted the temporary file when I was done. Then I thought of using the standard library module cStringIO for the purpose... and never looked back.

Module cStringIO lets you wrap a string of bytes so it can be accessed as a file object. You can also do things the other way around, writing into a cStringIO.StringIO instance as if it were a file object, and eventually recovering its contents as a string of bytes. Most Python modules that take file objects don't check whether you're passing an actual file—rather, any *file-like* object will do; the module's code just calls on the object whatever file methods it needs. As long as the object supplies those methods and responds correctly when they're called, everything just works. This demonstrates the awesome power of signature-based polymorphism and hopefully teaches why you should almost *never* type-test (utter such horrors as if type(x) is y, or even just the lesser horror if isinstance(x, y)) in your own code! A few low-level modules, such as marshal, are unfortunately adamant about using "true" files, but zipfile isn't, and this recipe shows how simple it makes your life!

If you are using a version of Python that is different from the mainstream C-coded one, known as "CPython", you may not find module cStringIO in the standard library. The leading *c* in the name of the module indicates that it's a C-specific module, optimized for speed but not guaranteed to be in the standard library for other compliant Python implementations. Several such alternative implementations include both production-quality ones (such as Jython, which is coded in Java and runs on a JVM) and experimental ones (such as pypy, which is coded in Python and generates machine code, and IronPython, which is coded in C# and runs on

Microsoft's .NET CLR). Not to worry: the Python Standard Library always includes module StringIO, which is coded in pure Python (and thus is usable from any compliant implementation of Python), and implements the same functionality as module cStringIO (albeit not quite as fast, at least on the mainstream CPython implementation). You just need to alter your import statement a bit to make sure you get cStringIO when available and StringIO otherwise. For example, this recipe might become:

```
import zipfile
try:
    from cStringIO import StringIO
except ImportError:
    from StringIO import StringIO
class ZipString(ZipFile):
    def __init__(self, datastring):
        ZipFile.__init__(self, StringIO(datastring))
```

With this modification, the recipe becomes useful in Jython, and other, alternative implementations.

See Also

Modules zipfile and cStringIO in the *Library Reference* and *Python in a Nutshell*; Jython is at *http://www.jython.org/*; pypy is at *http://codespeak.net/pypy/*; IronPython is at *http://ironpython.com/*.

2.11 Archiving a Tree of Files into a Compressed tar File

Credit: Ed Gordon, Ravi Teja Bhupatiraju

Problem

You need to archive all of the files and folders in a subtree into a *tar* archive file, compressing the data with either the popular gzip approach or the higher-compressing bzip2 approach.

Solution

The Python Standard Library's tarfile module directly supports either kind of compression: you just need to specify the kind of compression you require, as part of the option string that you pass when you call tarfile.TarFile.open to create the archive file. For example:

```
import tarfile, os
def make_tar(folder_to_backup, dest_folder, compression='bz2'):
```

```
        if compression:
            dest_ext = '.' + compression
        else:
            dest_ext = ''
        arcname = os.path.basename(folder_to_backup)
        dest_name = '%s.tar%s' % (arcname, dest_ext)
        dest_path = os.path.join(dest_folder, dest_name)
        if compression:
            dest_cmp = ':' + compression
        else:
            dest_cmp = ''
        out = tarfile.TarFile.open(dest_path, 'w'+dest_cmp)
        out.add(folder_to_backup, arcname)
        out.close()
        return dest_path
```

Discussion

You can pass, as argument `compression` to function `make_tar`, the string `'gz'` to get gzip compression instead of the default bzip2, or you can pass the empty string `''` to get no compression at all. Besides making the file extension of the result either *.tar*, *.tar.gz*, or *.tar.bz2*, as appropriate, your choice for the `compression` argument determines which string is passed as the second argument to `tarfile.TarFile.open`: `'w'`, when you want no compression, or `'w:gz'` or `'w:bz2'` to get two kinds of compression.

Class `tarfile.TarFile` offers several other `classmethods`, besides `open`, which you could use to generate a suitable instance. I find `open` handier and more flexible because it takes the compression information as part of the `mode` string argument. However, if you want to ensure bzip2 compression is used unconditionally, for example, you could choose to call `classmethod bz2open` instead.

Once we have an instance of class `tarfile.TarFile` that is set to use the kind of compression we desire, the instance's method `add` does all we require. In particular, when string `folder_to_backup` names a "directory" (or folder), rather than an ordinary file, `add` recursively adds all of the subtree rooted in that directory. If on some other occasion, we wanted to change this behavior to get precise control on what is archived, we could pass to `add` an additional named argument `recursive=False` to switch off this implicit recursion. After calling `add`, all that's left for function `make_tar` to do is to close the `TarFile` instance and return the path on which the *tar* file has been written, just in case the caller needs this information.

See Also

Library Reference docs on module `tarfile`.

2.12   Sending Binary Data to Standard Output Under Windows

Credit: Hamish Lawson

Problem

You want to send binary data (e.g., an image) to stdout under Windows.

Solution

That's what the setmode function, in the platform-dependent (Windows-only) msvcrt module in the Python Standard Library, is for:

```
import sys
if sys.platform == "win32":
    import os, msvcrt
    msvcrt.setmode(sys.stdout.fileno( ), os.O_BINARY)
```

You can now call sys.stdout.write with any bytestring as the argument, and the bytestring will go unmodified to standard output.

Discussion

While Unix doesn't make (or need) a distinction between text and binary modes, if you are reading or writing binary data, such as an image, under Windows, the file must be opened in binary mode. This is a problem for programs that write binary data to standard output (as a CGI script, for example, could be expected to do), because Python opens the sys.stdout file object on your behalf, normally in text mode.

You can have stdout opened in binary mode instead by supplying the -u command-line option to the Python interpreter. For example, if you know your CGI script will be running under the Apache web server, as the first line of your script, you can use something like:

```
#! c:/python23/python.exe -u
```

assuming you're running under Python 2.3 with a standard installation. Unfortunately, you may not always be able to control the command line under which your script will be started. The approach taken in this recipe's "Solution" offers a workable alternative. The setmode function provided by the Windows-specific msvcrt module lets you change the mode of stdout's underlying file descriptor. By using this function, you can ensure from within your program that sys.stdout gets set to binary mode.

See Also

Documentation for the msvcrt module in the *Library Reference* and *Python in a Nutshell*.

2.13   Using a C++-like iostream Syntax

Credit: Erik Max Francis

Problem

You like the C++ approach to I/O, based on ostreams and *manipulators* (special objects that cause special effects on a stream when inserted in it) and want to use it in your Python programs.

Solution

Python lets you overload operators by having your classes define special methods (i.e., methods whose names start and end with two underscores). To use << for output, as you do in C++, you just need to code an output stream class that defines the special method __lshift__:

```
class IOManipulator(object):
    def __init__(self, function=None):
        self.function = function
    def do(self, output):
        self.function(output)
def do_endl(stream):
    stream.output.write('\n')
    stream.output.flush( )
endl = IOManipulator(do_endl)
class OStream(object):
    def __init__(self, output=None):
        if output is None:
            import sys
            output = sys.stdout
        self.output = output
        self.format = '%s'
    def __lshift__(self, thing):
        ''' the special method which Python calls when you use the <<
            operator and the left-hand operand is an OStream '''
        if isinstance(thing, IOManipulator):
            thing.do(self)
        else:
            self.output.write(self.format % thing)
            self.format = '%s'
        return self
def example_main( ):
    cout = OStream( )
    cout<< "The average of " << 1 << " and " << 3 << " is " << (1+3)/2 <<endl
# emits The average of 1 and 3 is 2
```

```
if __name__ == '__main__':
    example_main()
```

Discussion

Wrapping Python file-like objects to emulate C++ ostreams syntax is quite easy. This recipe shows how to code the insertion operator << for this purpose. The recipe also implements an IOManipulator class (as in C++) to call arbitrary functions on a stream upon insertion, and a predefined manipulator endl (guess where that name comes from) to write a newline and flush the stream.

The reason class OStream's instances hold a format attribute and reset it to the default value '%s' after each self.output.write is so that you can build devious manipulators that temporarily save formatting state on the stream object, such as:

```
def do_hex(stream):
    stream.format = '%x'
hex = IOManipulator(do_hex)
cout << 23 << ' in hex is ' << hex << 23 << ', and in decimal ' << 23 << endl
# emits 23 in hex is 17, and in decimal 23
```

Some people detest C++'s cout << something syntax, some love it. In cases such as the example given in the recipe, this syntax ends up simpler and more readable than:

```
print>>somewhere, "The average of %d and %d is %f\n" % (1, 3, (1+3)/2)
```

which is the "Python-native" alternative (looking a lot like C in this case). It depends in part on whether you're more used to C++ or to C. In any case, this recipe gives you a choice! Even if you don't end up using this particular approach, it's still interesting to see how simple operator overloading is in Python.

See Also

Library Reference and *Python in a Nutshell* docs on file objects and special methods such as __lshift__; recipe 4.20 "Using printf in Python" implements a Python version of C's printf function.

2.14   Rewinding an Input File to the Beginning

Credit: Andrew Dalke

Problem

You need to make an input file object (with data coming from a socket or other input file handle) rewindable back to the beginning so you can read it over.

Solution

Wrap the file object into a suitable class:

```
from cStringIO import StringIO
```

```python
class RewindableFile(object):
    """ Wrap a file handle to allow seeks back to the beginning. """
    def __init__(self, input_file):
        """ Wraps input_file into a file-like object with rewind. """
        self.file = input_file
        self.buffer_file = StringIO()
        self.at_start = True
        try:
            self.start = input_file.tell()
        except (IOError, AttributeError):
            self.start = 0
        self._use_buffer = True
    def seek(self, offset, whence=0):
        """ Seek to a given byte position.
        Must be: whence == 0 and offset == self.start
        """
        if whence != 0:
            raise ValueError("whence=%r; expecting 0" % (whence,))
        if offset != self.start:
            raise ValueError("offset=%r; expecting %s" % (offset, self.start))
        self.rewind()
    def rewind(self):
        """ Simplified way to seek back to the beginning. """
        self.buffer_file.seek(0)
        self.at_start = True
    def tell(self):
        """ Return the current position of the file (must be at start). """
        if not self.at_start:
            raise TypeError("RewindableFile can't tell except at start of file")
        return self.start
    def _read(self, size):
        if size < 0:               # read all the way to the end of the file
            y = self.file.read()
            if self._use_buffer:
                self.buffer_file.write(y)
            return self.buffer_file.read() + y
        elif size == 0:            # no need to actually read the empty string
            return ""
        x = self.buffer_file.read(size)
        if len(x) < size:
            y = self.file.read(size - len(x))
            if self._use_buffer:
                self.buffer_file.write(y)
            return x + y
        return x
    def read(self, size=-1):
        """ Read up to 'size' bytes from the file.
        Default is -1, which means to read to end of file.
        """
        x = self._read(size)
        if self.at_start and x:
            self.at_start = False
        self._check_no_buffer()
        return x
```

```
def readline(self):
    """ Read a line from the file. """
    # Can we get it out of the buffer_file?
    s = self.buffer_file.readline( )
    if s[-1:] == "\n":
        return s
    # No, so read a line from the input file
    t = self.file.readline( )
    if self._use_buffer:
        self.buffer_file.write(t)
    self._check_no_buffer( )
    return s + t
def readlines(self):
    """read all remaining lines from the file"""
    return self.read( ).splitlines(True)
def _check_no_buffer(self):
    # If 'nobuffer' has been called and we're finished with the buffer file,
    # get rid of the buffer, redirect everything to the original input file.
    if not self._use_buffer and \
            self.buffer_file.tell( ) == len(self.buffer_file.getvalue( )):
        # for top performance, we rebind all relevant methods in self
        for n in 'seek tell read readline readlines'.split( ):
            setattr(self, n, getattr(self.file, n, None))
        del self.buffer_file
def nobuffer(self):
    """tell RewindableFile to stop using the buffer once it's exhausted"""
    self._use_buffer = False
```

Discussion

Sometimes, data coming from a socket or other input file handle isn't what it was supposed to be. For example, suppose you are reading from a buggy server, which is supposed to return an XML stream, but sometimes returns an unformatted error message instead. (This scenario often occurs because many servers don't handle incorrect input very well.)

This recipe's RewindableFile class helps you solve this problem. r = RewindableFile(f) wraps the original input stream f into a "rewindable file" instance r which essentially mimics f's behavior but also provides a buffer. Read requests to r are forwarded to f, and the data thus read gets appended to a buffer, then returned to the caller. The buffer contains all the data read so far.

r can be told to rewind, meaning to seek back to the start position. The next read request will come from the buffer, until the buffer has been read, in which case it gets the data from the input stream again. The newly read data is also appended to the buffer.

When buffering is no longer needed, call the nobuffer method of r. This tells r that, once it's done reading the buffer's current contents, it can throw the buffer away. After nobuffer is called, the behavior of seek is no longer defined.

For example, suppose you have a server that gives either an error message of the form ERROR: cannot do that, or an XML data stream, starting with '<?xml'...:

```
import RewindableFile
infile = urllib2.urlopen("http://somewhere/")
infile = RewindableFile.RewindableFile(infile)
s = infile.readline( )
if s.startswith("ERROR:"):
    raise Exception(s[:-1])
infile.seek(0)
infile.nobuffer( )    # Don't buffer the data any more
... process the XML from infile ...
```

One sometimes-useful Python idiom is not supported by the class in this recipe: you can't reliably stash away the bound methods of a RewindableFile instance. (If you don't know what bound methods are, no problem, of course, since in that case you surely won't want to stash them anywhere!). The reason for this limitation is that, when the buffer is empty, the RewindableFile code reassigns the input file's read, readlines, etc., methods, as instance variables of self. This gives slightly better performance, at the cost of not supporting the infrequently-used idiom of saving bound methods. See recipe 6.11 "Implementing a Ring Buffer" for another example of a similar technique, where an instance irreversibly changes its own methods.

The tell method, which gives the current location of a file, can be called on an instance of RewindableFile only right after wrapping, and before any reading, to get the beginning byte location. The RewindableFile implementation of tell tries to get the real position from the wrapped file, and use that as the beginning location. If the wrapped file does not support tell, then the RewindableFile implementation of tell just returns 0.

See Also

Site *http://www.dalkescientific.com/Python/* for the latest version of this recipe's code; *Library Reference* and *Python in a Nutshell* docs on file objects and module cStringIO; recipe 6.11 "Implementing a Ring Buffer" for another example of an instance affecting an irreversible behavior change on itself by rebinding its methods.

2.15 Adapting a File-like Object to a True File Object

Credit: Michael Kent

Problem

You need to pass a file-like object (e.g., the results of a call such as urllib.urlopen) to a function or method that insists on receiving a true file object (e.g., a function such as marshal.load).

Solution

To cooperate with such type-checking, we need to write all data from the file-like object into a temporary file on disk. Then, we can use the (true) file object for that temporary disk file. Here's a function that implements this idea:

```
import types, tempfile
CHUNK_SIZE = 16 * 1024
def adapt_file(fileObj):
    if isinstance(fileObj, file): return fileObj
    tmpFileObj = tempfile.TemporaryFile
    while True:
        data = fileObj.read(CHUNK_SIZE)
        if not data: break
        tmpFileObj.write(data)
    fileObj.close( )
    tmpFileObj.seek(0)
    return tmpFileObj
```

Discussion

This recipe demonstrates an unusual Pythonic application of the Adapter Design Pattern (i.e., what to do when you have an X and you need a Y instead). While design patterns are most normally thought of in an object-oriented way, and therefore implemented by writing classes, nothing is intrinsically necessary about that. In this case, for example, we don't really need to introduce any new class, since the adapt_ file function is obviously sufficient. Therefore, we respect Occam's Razor and do not introduce entities without necessity.

One way or another, you should think in terms of adaptation, in preference to type testing, even when you need to rely on some lower-level utility that insists on precise types. Instead of raising an exception when you get passed an object that's perfectly adequate save for the technicality of type membership, think of the possibility of *adapting* what you get passed to what you need. In this way, your code will be more flexible and more suitable for reuse.

See Also

Documentation on built-in file objects, and modules tempfile and marshal, in the *Library Reference* and *Python in a Nutshell*.

2.16 Walking Directory Trees

Credit: Robin Parmar, Alex Martelli

Problem

You need to examine a "directory", or an entire directory tree rooted in a certain directory, and iterate on the files (and optionally folders) that match certain patterns.

Solution

The generator os.walk from the Python Standard Library module os is sufficient for this task, but we can dress it up a bit by coding our own function to wrap os.walk:

```
import os, fnmatch
def all_files(root, patterns='*', single_level=False, yield_folders=False):
    # Expand patterns from semicolon-separated string to list
    patterns = patterns.split(';')
    for path, subdirs, files in os.walk(root):
        if yield_folders:
            files.extend(subdirs)
        files.sort()
        for name in files:
            for pattern in patterns:
                if fnmatch.fnmatch(name, pattern):
                    yield os.path.join(path, name)
                    break
        if single_level:
            break
```

Discussion

The standard directory tree traversal generator os.walk is powerful, simple, and flexible. However, as it stands, os.walk lacks a few niceties that applications may need, such as selecting files according to some patterns, flat (linear) looping on all files (and optionally folders) in sorted order, and the ability to examine a single directory (without entering its subdirectories). This recipe shows how easily these kinds of features can be added, by wrapping os.walk into another simple generator and using standard library module fnmatch to check filenames for matches to patterns.

The file patterns are possibly case-insensitive (that's platform-dependent) but otherwise Unix-style, as supplied by the standard fnmatch module, which this recipe uses. To specify multiple patterns, join them with a semicolon. Note that this means that semicolons themselves can't be part of a pattern.

For example, you can easily get a list of all Python and HTML files in directory /tmp or any subdirectory thereof:

```
thefiles = list(all_files('/tmp', '*.py;*.htm;*.html'))
```

Should you just want to process these files' paths one at a time (e.g., print them, one per line), you do not need to build a list: you can simply loop on the result of calling all_files:

```
for path in all_files('/tmp', '*.py;*.htm;*.html'):
    print path
```

If your platform is case-sensitive, alnd you want case-sensitive matching, then you need to specify the patterns more laboriously, e.g., '*.[Hh][Tt][Mm][Ll]' instead of just '*.html'.

See Also

Documentation for the os.path module and the os.walk generator, as well as the fnmatch module, in the *Library Reference* and *Python in a Nutshell*.

2.17 Swapping One File Extension for Another Throughout a Directory Tree

Credit: Julius Welby

Problem

You need to rename files throughout a subtree of directories, specifically changing the names of all files with a given extension so that they have a different extension instead.

Solution

Operating on all files of a whole subtree of directories is easy enough with the os.walk function from Python's standard library:

```
import os
def swapextensions(dir, before, after):
    if before[:1] != '.':
        before = '.'+before
    thelen = -len(before)
    if after[:1] != '.':
        after = '.'+after
    for path, subdirs, files in os.walk(dir):
        for oldfile in files:
            if oldfile[thelen:] == before:
                oldfile = os.path.join(path, oldfile)
                newfile = oldfile[:thelen] + after
                os.rename(oldfile, newfile)
if __name__=='__main__':
    import sys
    if len(sys.argv) != 4:
        print "Usage: swapext rootdir before after"
        sys.exit(100)
    swapextensions(sys.argv[1], sys.argv[2], sys.argv[3])
```

Discussion

This recipe shows how to change the file extensions of all files in a specified directory, all of its subdirectories, all of *their* subdirectories, and so on. This technique is useful for changing the extensions of a whole batch of files in a folder structure, such as a web site. You can also use it to correct errors made when saving a batch of files programmatically.

The recipe is usable either as a module to be imported from any other, or as a script to run from the command line, and it is carefully coded to be platform-independent. You can pass in the extensions either with or without the leading dot (.), since the code in this recipe inserts that dot, if necessary. (As a consequence of this convenience, however, this recipe is unable to deal with files completely lacking any extension, including the dot; this limitation may be bothersome on Unix systems.)

The implementation of this recipe uses techniques that purists might consider too low level—specifically by dealing mostly with filenames and extensions by direct string manipulation, rather than by the functions in module os.path. It's not a big deal: using os.path is fine, but using Python's powerful string facilities to deal with filenames is fine, too.

See Also

The author's web page at *http://www.outwardlynormal.com/python/swapextensions.htm.*

2.18   Finding a File Given a Search Path

Credit: Chui Tey

Problem

Given a search path (a string of directories with a separator in between), you need to find the first file along the path with the requested name.

Solution

Basically, you need to loop over the directories in the given search path:

```
import os
def search_file(filename, search_path, pathsep=os.pathsep):
    """ Given a search path, find file with requested name """
    for path in search_path.split(pathsep):
        candidate = os.path.join(path, filename)
        if os.path.isfile(candidate):
            return os.path.abspath(candidate)
    return None
if __name__ == '__main__':
    search_path = '/bin' + os.pathsep + '/usr/bin'  # ; on Windows, : on Unix
    find_file = search_file('ls', search_path)
    if find_file:
        print "File 'ls' found at %s" % find_file
    else:
        print "File 'ls' not found"
```

Discussion

This recipe's "Problem" is a reasonably frequent task, and Python makes resolving it extremely easy. Other recipes perform similar and related tasks: to find files specifically on Python's own search path, see recipe 2.20 "Finding a File on the Python Search Path"; to find all files matching a pattern along a search path, see recipe 2.19 "Finding Files Given a Search Path and a Pattern."

The search loop can be coded in many ways, but returning the path (made into an absolute path, for uniformity and convenience) as soon as a hit is found is simplest as well as fast. The explicit return None after the loop is not strictly needed, since None is returned by Python when a function falls off the end. Having the return statement explicitly there in this case makes the functionality of search_file much clearer at first sight.

See Also

Recipe 2.20 "Finding a File on the Python Search Path"; recipe 2.19 "Finding Files Given a Search Path and a Pattern"; documentation for the module os in the *Library Reference* and *Python in a Nutshell*.

2.19   Finding Files Given a Search Path and a Pattern

Credit: Bill McNeill, Andrew Kirkpatrick

Problem

Given a search path (i.e., a string of directories with a separator in between), you need to find all files along the path whose names match a given pattern.

Solution

Basically, you need to loop over the directories in the given search path. The loop is best encapsulated in a generator:

```
import glob, os
def all_files(pattern, search_path, pathsep=os.pathsep):
    """ Given a search path, yield all files matching the pattern. """
    for path in search_path.split(pathsep):
        for match in glob.glob(os.path.join(path, pattern)):
            yield match
```

Discussion

One nice thing about generators is that you can easily use them to obtain just the first item, all items, or anything in between. For example, to print the first file matching '*.pye' along your environment's PATH:

```
print all_files('*.pye', os.environ['PATH']).next( )
```

To print all such files, one per line:

```
for match in all_files('*.pye', os.environ['PATH']):
    print match
```

To print them all at once, as a list:

```
print list(all_files('*.pye', os.environ['PATH']))
```

I have also wrapped around this all_files function a main script to show all of the files with a given name along my PATH. Thus I can see not only which one will execute for that name (the first one), but also which ones are "shadowed" by that first one:

```
if __name__ == '__main__':
    import sys
    if len(sys.argv) != 2 or sys.argv[1].startswith('-'):
        print 'Use: %s <pattern>' % sys.argv[0]
        sys.exit(1)
    matches = list(all_files(sys.argv[1], os.environ['PATH']))
    print '%d match:' % len(matches)
    for match in matches:
        print match
```

See Also

Recipe 2.18 "Finding a File Given a Search Path" for a simpler approach to find the first file with a specified name along the path; *Library Reference* and *Python in a Nutshell* docs for modules os and glob.

2.20 Finding a File on the Python Search Path

Credit: Mitch Chapman

Problem

A large Python application includes resource files (e.g., Glade project files, SQL templates, and images) as well as Python packages. You want to store these associated files together with the Python packages that use them.

Solution

You need to be able to look for either files or directories along Python's sys.path:

```
import sys, os
class Error(Exception): pass
def _find(pathname, matchFunc=os.path.isfile):
    for dirname in sys.path:
        candidate = os.path.join(dirname, pathname)
        if matchFunc(candidate):
            return candidate
    raise Error("Can't find file %s" % pathname)
def findFile(pathname):
    return _find(pathname)
```

```
def findDir(path):
    return _find(path, matchFunc=os.path.isdir)
```

Discussion

Larger Python applications consist of sets of Python packages and associated sets of resource files. It's convenient to store these associated files together with the Python packages that use them, and it's easy to do so if you use this variation on the previous recipe 2.18 "Finding a File Given a Search Path" to find files or directories with pathnames relative to the Python search path.

See Also

Recipe 2.18 "Finding a File Given a Search Path"; documentation for the os module in the *Library Reference* and *Python in a Nutshell*.

2.21 Dynamically Changing the Python Search Path

Credit: Robin Parmar

Problem

Modules must be on the Python search path before they can be imported, but you don't want to set a huge permanent path because that slows performance—so, you want to change the path dynamically.

Solution

We simply conditionally add a "directory" to Python's sys.path, carefully checking to avoid duplication:

```
def AddSysPath(new_path):
    """ AddSysPath(new_path): adds a "directory" to Python's sys.path
    Does not add the directory if it does not exist or if it's already on
    sys.path. Returns 1 if OK, -1 if new_path does not exist, 0 if it was
    already on sys.path.
    """
    import sys, os
    # Avoid adding nonexistent paths
    if not os.path.exists(new_path): return -1
    # Standardize the path.  Windows is case-insensitive, so lowercase
    # for definiteness if we are on Windows.
    new_path = os.path.abspath(new_path)
    if sys.platform == 'win32':
        new_path = new_path.lower( )
    # Check against all currently available paths
    for x in sys.path:
        x = os.path.abspath(x)
```

```
            if sys.platform == 'win32':
                x = x.lower()
            if new_path in (x, x + os.sep):
                return 0
    sys.path.append(new_path)
    # if you want the new_path to take precedence over existing
    # directories already in sys.path, instead of appending, use:
    # sys.path.insert(0, new_path)
    return 1
if __name__ == '__main__':
    # Test and show usage
    import sys
    print 'Before:'
    for x in sys.path: print x
    if sys.platform == 'win32':
        print AddSysPath('c:\\Temp')
        print AddSysPath('c:\\temp')
    else:
        print AddSysPath('/usr/lib/my_modules')
    print 'After:'
    for x in sys.path: print x
```

Discussion

Modules must be in directories that are on the Python search path before they can be imported, but we don't want to have a huge permanent path because doing so slows down every import performed by every Python script and application. This simple recipe dynamically adds a "directory" to the path, but only if that directory exists and was not already on sys.path.

sys.path is a list, so it's easy to add directories to its end, using sys.path.append. Every import performed after such an append will automatically look in the newly added directory if it cannot be satisfied from earlier ones. As indicated in the Solution, you can alternatively use sys.path.insert(0, ... so that the newly added directory is searched *before* ones that were already in sys.path.

It's no big deal if sys.path ends up with some duplicates or if a nonexistent directory is accidentally appended to it; Python's import statement is clever enough to shield itself against such issues. However, each time such a problem occurs at import time (e.g., from duplicate unsuccessful searches, errors from the operating system that need to be handled gracefully, etc.), a small price is paid in terms of performance. To avoid uselessly paying such a price, this recipe does a conditional addition to sys.path, never appending any directory that doesn't exist or is already in sys.path. Directories appended by this recipe stay in sys.path only for the duration of this program's run, just like any other dynamic alteration you might do to sys.path.

See Also

Documentation for the sys and os.path modules in the *Library Reference* and *Python in a Nutshell*.

2.22 Computing the Relative Path from One Directory to Another

Credit: Cimarron Taylor, Alan Ezust

Problem

You need to know the relative path from one directory to another—for example, to create a symbolic link or a relative reference in a URL.

Solution

The simplest approach is to split paths into lists of directories, then work on the lists. Using a couple of auxiliary and somewhat generic helper functions, we could code:

```
import os, itertools
def all_equal(elements):
    ''' return True if all the elements are equal, otherwise False. '''
    first_element = elements[0]
    for other_element in elements[1:]:
        if other_element != first_element: return False
    return True
def common_prefix(*sequences):
    ''' return a list of common elements at the start of all sequences,
        then a list of lists that are the unique tails of each sequence. '''
    # if there are no sequences at all, we're done
    if not sequences: return [ ], [ ]
    # loop in parallel on the sequences
    common = [ ]
    for elements in itertools.izip(*sequences):
        # unless all elements are equal, bail out of the loop
        if not all_equal(elements): break
        # got one more common element, append it and keep looping
        common.append(elements[0])
    # return the common prefix and unique tails
    return common, [ sequence[len(common):] for sequence in sequences ]
def relpath(p1, p2, sep=os.path.sep, pardir=os.path.pardir):
    ''' return a relative path from p1 equivalent to path p2.
        In particular: the empty string, if p1 == p2;
                       p2, if p1 and p2 have no common prefix.
    '''
    common, (u1, u2) = common_prefix(p1.split(sep), p2.split(sep))
    if not common:
        return p2        # leave path absolute if nothing at all in common
    return sep.join( [pardir]*len(u1) + u2 )
```

```
def test(p1, p2, sep=os.path.sep):
    ''' call function relpath and display arguments and results. '''
    print "from", p1, "to", p2, " -> ", relpath(p1, p2, sep)
if __name__ == '__main__':
    test('/a/b/c/d', '/a/b/c1/d1', '/')
    test('/a/b/c/d', '/a/b/c/d', '/')
    test('c:/x/y/z', 'd:/x/y/z', '/')
```

Discussion

The workhorse in this recipe is the simple but very general function common_prefix, which, given any N sequences, returns their common prefix and a list of their respective unique tails. To compute the relative path between two given paths, we can ignore their common prefix. We need only the appropriate number of move-up markers (normally, os.path.pardir—e.g., ../ on Unix-like systems; we need as many of them as the length of the unique tail of the starting path) followed by the unique tail of the destination path. So, function relpath splits the paths into lists of directories, calls common_prefix, and then performs exactly the construction just described.

common_prefix centers on the loop for elements in itertools.izip(*sequences), relying on the fact that izip ends with the shortest of the iterables it's zipping. The body of the loop only needs to prematurely terminate the loop as soon as it meets a tuple of elements (coming one from each sequence, per izip's specifications) that aren't all equal, and to keep track of the elements that *are* equal by appending one of them to list common. Once the loop is done, all that's left to prepare the lists to return is to slice off the elements that are already in common from the front of each of the sequences.

Function all_equal could alternatively be implemented in a completely different way, less simple and obvious, but interesting:

```
def all_equal(elements):
    return len(dict.fromkeys(elements)) == 1
```

or, equivalently and more concisely, in Python 2.4 only,

```
def all_equal(elements):
    return len(set(elements)) == 1
```

Saying that all elements are equal is exactly the same as saying that the set of the elements has cardinality (length) one. In the variation using dict.fromkeys, we use a dict to represent the set, so that variation works in Python 2.3 as well as in 2.4. The variation using set is clearer, but it only works in Python 2.4. (You could also make it work in version 2.3, as well as Python 2.4, by using the standard Python library module sets).

See Also

Library Reference and *Python in a Nutshell* docs for modules os and itertools.

2.23 Reading an Unbuffered Character in a Cross-Platform Way

Credit: Danny Yoo

Problem

Your application needs to read single characters, unbuffered, from standard input, and it needs to work on both Windows and Unix-like systems.

Solution

When we need a cross-platform solution, starting with platform-dependent ones, we need to wrap the different solutions so that they look the same:

```
try:
    from msvcrt import getch
except ImportError:
    ''' we're not on Windows, so we try the Unix-like approach '''
    def getch():
        import sys, tty, termios
        fd = sys.stdin.fileno()
        old_settings = termios.tcgetattr(fd)
        try:
            tty.setraw(fd)
            ch = sys.stdin.read(1)
        finally:
            termios.tcsetattr(fd, termios.TCSADRAIN, old_settings)
        return ch
```

Discussion

On Windows, the standard Python library module msvcrt offers the handy getch function to read one character, unbuffered, from the keyboard, without echoing it to the screen. However, this module is not part of the standard Python library on Unix and Unix-like platforms, such as Linux and Mac OS X. On such platforms, we can get the same functionality with the tty and termios modules of the standard Python library (which, in turn, are not present on Windows).

The key point is that *in application-level code*, we should never have to worry about such issues; rather, we should write our application code in platform-independent ways, counting on library functions to paper over the differences between platforms. The Python Standard Library fulfills that role admirably for most tasks, but not all, and the problem posed by this recipe is an example of one for which the Python Standard Library doesn't directly supply a cross-platform solution.

When we can't find a ready-packaged cross-platform solution in the standard library, we should package it anyway as part of our own additional custom library. This recipe's Solution, besides solving the specific task of the recipe, also shows one good general way to go about such packaging. (Alternatively, you can test sys.platform, but I prefer the approach shown in this recipe.)

Your own library module should try to import the standard library module it needs on a certain platform within a try clause and include a corresponding except ImportError clause that is triggered when the module is running on a different platform. In the body of that except clause, your own library module can apply whatever alternate approach will work on the different platform. In some rare cases, you may need more than two platform-dependent approaches, but most often you'll need one approach on Windows and only one other approach to cover all other platforms. This is because most non-Windows platforms today are generally Unix or Unix-like.

See Also

Library Reference and *Python in a Nutshell* docs for msvcrt, tty, and termios.

2.24 Counting Pages of PDF Documents on Mac OS X

Credit: Dinu Gherman, Dan Wolfe

Problem

You're running on a reasonably recent version of Mac OS X (version 10.3 "Panther" or later), and you need to know the number of pages in a PDF document.

Solution

The PDF format and Python are both natively integrated with Mac OS X (10.3 or later), and this allows a rather simple solution:

```
#!/usr/bin python
import CoreGraphics
def pageCount(pdfPath):
    "Return the number of pages for the PDF document at the given path."
    pdf = CoreGraphics.CGPDFDocumentCreateWithProvider(
            CoreGraphics.CGDataProviderCreateWithFilename(pdfPath)
        )
    return pdf.getNumberOfPages()
if __name__ == '__main__':
    import sys
    for path in sys.argv[1:]:
        print pageCount(path)
```

Discussion

A reasonable alternative to this recipe might be to use the PyObjC Python extension, which (among other wonders) lets Python code reuse all the power in the Foundation and AppKit frameworks that come with Mac OS X. Such a choice would let you write a Python script that is also able to run on older versions of Mac OS X, such as 10.2 Jaguar. However, relying on Mac OS X 10.3 or later ensures we can use the Python installation that is integrated as a part of the operating system, as well as such goodies as the CoreGraphics Python extension module (also part of Mac OS X "Panther") that lets your Python code reuse Apple's excellent Quartz graphics engine directly.

See Also

PyObjC is at *http://pyobjc.sourceforge.net/*; information on the CoreGraphics module is at *http://www.macdevcenter.com/pub/a/mac/2004/03/19/core_graphics.html*.

2.25 Changing File Attributes on Windows

Credit: John Nielsen

Problem

You need to set the attributes of a file on Windows; for example, you may need to set the file as read-only, archived, and so on.

Solution

PyWin32's win32api module offers a function SetFileAttributes that makes this task quite simple:

```
import win32con, win32api, os
# create a file, just to show how to manipulate it
thefile = 'test'
f = open('test', 'w')
f.close( )
# to make the file hidden...:
win32api.SetFileAttributes(thefile, win32con.FILE_ATTRIBUTE_HIDDEN)
# to make the file readonly:
win32api.SetFileAttributes(thefile, win32con.FILE_ATTRIBUTE_READONLY)
# to be able to delete the file we need to set it back to normal:
win32api.SetFileAttributes(thefile, win32con.FILE_ATTRIBUTE_NORMAL)
# and finally we remove the file we just made
os.remove(thefile)
```

Discussion

One interesting use of win32api.SetFileAttributes is to enable a file's removal. Removing a file with os.remove can fail on Windows if the file's attributes are not normal. To get around this problem, you just need to use the Win32 call to `SetFileAttributes` to convert it to a normal file, as shown at the end of this recipe's Solution. Of course, this should be done with caution, since there may be a good reason the file is not "normal". The file should be removed only if you know what you're doing!

See Also

The documentation on the `win32file` module at *http://ASPN.ActiveState.com/ASPN/ Python/Reference/Products/ActivePython/PythonWin32Extensions/win32file.html.*

2.26 Extracting Text from OpenOffice.org Documents

Credit: Dirk Holtwick

Problem

You need to extract the text content (with or without the attending XML markup) from an *OpenOffice.org* document.

Solution

An *OpenOffice.org* document is just a *zip* file that aggregates XML documents according to a well-documented standard. To access our precious data, we don't even need to have *OpenOffice.org* installed:

```python
import zipfile, re
rx_stripxml = re.compile("<[^>]*?>", re.DOTALL|re.MULTILINE)
def convert_OO(filename, want_text=True):
    """ Convert an OpenOffice.org document to XML or text. """
    zf = zipfile.ZipFile(filename, "r")
    data = zf.read("content.xml")
    zf.close( )
    if want_text:
        data = " ".join(rx_stripxml.sub(" ", data).split( ))
    return data
if __name__=="__main__":
    import sys
    if len(sys.argv)>1:
        for docname in sys.argv[1:]:
            print 'Text of', docname, ':'
            print convert_OO(docname)
            print 'XML of', docname, ':'
            print convert_OO(docname, want_text=False)
    else:
        print 'Call with paths to OO.o doc files to see Text and XML forms.'
```

Discussion

OpenOffice.org documents are *zip* files, and in addition to other contents, they always contain the file *content.xml*. This recipe's job, therefore, essentially boils down to just extracting this file. By default, the recipe then throws away XML tags with a simple regular expression, splits the result by whitespace, and joins it up again with a single blank to save space. Of course, we could use an XML parser to get information in a vastly richer and more structured way, but if all we need is the rough textual content, this fast, rough-and-ready approach may suffice.

Specifically, the regular expression rx_stripxml matches any XML tag (opening or closing) from the leading < to the terminating >. Inside function convert_OO, in the statements guarded by if want_text, we use that regular expression to change every XML tag into a space, then normalize whitespace by splitting (i.e., calling the string method split, which splits on any sequence of whitespace), and rejoining (with " ".join, to use a single blank character as the joiner). Essentially, this split-and-rejoin process changes any sequence of whitespace into a single blank character. More advanced ways to extract all text from an XML document are shown in recipe 12.3 "Extracting Text from an XML Document."

See Also

Library Reference docs on modules zipfile and re; OpenOffice.org's web site, *http://www.openoffice.org/*; recipe 12.3 "Extracting Text from an XML Document."

2.27 Extracting Text from Microsoft Word Documents

Credit: Simon Brunning, Pavel Kosina

Problem

You want to extract the text content from each Microsoft Word document in a directory tree on Windows into a corresponding text file.

Solution

With the PyWin32 extension, we can access Word itself, through COM, to perform the conversion:

```
import fnmatch, os, sys, win32com.client
wordapp = win32com.client.gencache.EnsureDispatch("Word.Application")
try:
    for path, dirs, files in os.walk(sys.argv[1]):
        for filename in files:
            if not fnmatch.fnmatch(filename, '*.doc'): continue
            doc = os.path.abspath(os.path.join(path, filename))
```

```
            print "processing %s" % doc
            wordapp.Documents.Open(doc)
            docastxt = doc[:-3] + 'txt'
            wordapp.ActiveDocument.SaveAs(docastxt,
                FileFormat=win32com.client.constants.wdFormatText)
            wordapp.ActiveDocument.Close( )
    finally:
        # ensure Word is properly shut down even if we get an exception
        wordapp.Quit( )
```

Discussion

A useful aspect of most Windows applications is that you can script them via COM, and the PyWin32 extension makes it fairly easy to perform COM scripting from Python. The extension enables you to write Python scripts to perform many kinds of Window tasks. The script in this recipe's Solution drives Microsoft Word to extract the text from every *.doc* file in a "directory" tree into a corresponding *.txt* text file. Using the os.walk function, we can access every subdirectory in a tree with a simple for statement, without recursion. With the fnmatch.fnmatch function, we can check a filename to determine whether it matches an appropriate wildcard, here '*.doc'. Once we have determined the name of a Word document file, we process that name with functions from os.path to turn it into a complete absolute path, and have Word open it, save it as text, and close it again.

If you don't have Word, you may need to take a completely different approach. One possibility is to use OpenOffice.org, which is able to load Word documents. Another is to use a program specifically designed to read Word documents, such as Antiword, found at *http://www.winfield.demon.nl/*. However, we have not explored these alternative options.

See Also

Mark Hammond, Andy Robinson, *Python Programming on Win32* (O'Reilly), for documentation on PyWin32; *http://msdn.microsoft.com*, for Microsoft's documentation of the object model of Microsoft Word; *Library Reference* and *Python in a Nutshell* sections on modules fnmatch and os.path, and function os.walk.

2.28   File Locking Using a Cross-Platform API

Credit: Jonathan Feinberg, John Nielsen

Problem

You need to lock files in a program that runs on both Windows and Unix-like systems, but the Python Standard Library offers only platform-specific ways to lock files.

Solution

When the Python Standard Library itself doesn't offer a cross-platform solution, it's often possible to implement one ourselves:

```
import os
# needs win32all to work on Windows (NT, 2K, XP, _not_ /95 or /98)
if os.name == 'nt':
    import win32con, win32file, pywintypes
    LOCK_EX = win32con.LOCKFILE_EXCLUSIVE_LOCK
    LOCK_SH = 0 # the default
    LOCK_NB = win32con.LOCKFILE_FAIL_IMMEDIATELY
    __overlapped = pywintypes.OVERLAPPED( )
    def lock(file, flags):
        hfile = win32file._get_osfhandle(file.fileno( ))
        win32file.LockFileEx(hfile, flags, 0, 0xffff0000, __overlapped)
    def unlock(file):
        hfile = win32file._get_osfhandle(file.fileno( ))
        win32file.UnlockFileEx(hfile, 0, 0xffff0000, __overlapped)
elif os.name == 'posix':
    from fcntl import LOCK_EX, LOCK_SH, LOCK_NB
    def lock(file, flags):
        fcntl.flock(file.fileno( ), flags)
    def unlock(file):
        fcntl.flock(file.fileno( ), fcntl.LOCK_UN)
else:
    raise RuntimeError("PortaLocker only defined for nt and posix platforms")
```

Discussion

When multiple programs or threads have to access a shared file, it's wise to ensure that accesses are synchronized so that two processes don't try to modify the file contents at the same time. Failure to synchronize accesses could even corrupt the entire file in some cases.

This recipe supplies two functions, lock and unlock, that request and release locks on a file, respectively. Using the portalocker.py module is a simple matter of calling the lock function and passing in the file and an argument specifying the kind of lock that is desired:

Shared lock (default)
> This lock denies all processes, including the process that first locks the file, write access to the file. All processes can read the locked file.

Exclusive lock
> This denies all other processes both read and write access to the file.

Nonblocking lock
> When this value is specified, the function returns immediately if it is unable to acquire the requested lock. Otherwise, it waits. LOCK_NB can be ORed with either LOCK_SH or LOCK_EX by using Python's bitwise-or operator, the vertical bar (|).

For example:

```
import portalocker
afile = open("somefile", "r+")
portalocker.lock(afile, portalocker.LOCK_EX)
```

The implementation of the lock and unlock functions is entirely different on different systems. On Unix-like systems (including Linux and Mac OS X), the recipe relies on functionality made available by the standard fcntl module. On Windows systems (NT, 2000, XP—it doesn't work on old Win/95 and Win/98 platforms because they just don't have the needed oomph in the operating system!), the recipe uses the win32file module, part of the very popular PyWin32 package of Windows-specific extensions to Python, authored by Mark Hammond. But the important point is that, despite the differences in implementation, the functions (and the flags you can pass to the lock function) are made to behave in the same way across platforms. Such cross-platform packaging of differently implemented but equivalent functionality enables you to easily write cross-platform applications, which is one of Python's strengths.

When you write a cross-platform program, it's nice if the functionality that your program uses is, in turn, encapsulated in a cross-platform way. For file locking in particular, it is especially helpful to Perl users, who are used to an essentially transparent lock system call across platforms. More generally, if os.name== just does not belong in application-level code. Such platform testing ideally should always be in the standard library or an application-independent module, as it is here.

See Also

Documentation on the fcntl module in the *Library Reference*; documentation on the win32file module at *http://ASPN.ActiveState.com/ASPN/Python/Reference/Products/ActivePython/PythonWin32Extensions/win32file.html*; Jonathan Feinberg's web site (*http://MrFeinberg.com*).

2.29 Versioning Filenames

Credit: Robin Parmar, Martin Miller

Problem

You want to make a backup copy of a file, before you overwrite it, with the standard convention of appending a three-digit version number to the name of the old file.

Solution

We just need to code a function to perform the backup copy appropriately:

```
def VersionFile(file_spec, vtype='copy'):
    import os, shutil
```

```python
    if os.path.isfile(file_spec):
        # check the 'vtype' parameter
        if vtype not in ('copy', 'rename'):
            raise ValueError, 'Unknown vtype %r' % (vtype,)
        # Determine root filename so the extension doesn't get longer
        n, e = os.path.splitext(file_spec)
        # Is e a three-digits integer preceded by a dot?
        if len(e) == 4 and e[1:].isdigit():
            num = 1 + int(e[1:])
            root = n
        else:
            num = 0
            root = file_spec
        # Find next available file version
        for i in xrange(num, 1000):
            new_file = '%s.%03d' % (root, i)
            if not os.path.exists(new_file):
                if vtype == 'copy':
                    shutil.copy(file_spec, new_file)
                else:
                    os.rename(file_spec, new_file)
                return True
        raise RuntimeError, "Can't %s %r, all names taken"%(vtype,file_spec)
    return False
if __name__ == '__main__':
    import os
    # create a dummy file 'test.txt'
    tfn = 'test.txt'
    open(tfn, 'w').close()
    # version it 3 times
    print VersionFile(tfn)
    # emits: True
    print VersionFile(tfn)
    # emits: True
    print VersionFile(tfn)
    # emits: True
    # remove all test.txt* files we just made
    for x in ('', '.000', '.001', '.002'):
        os.unlink(tfn + x)
    # show what happens when the file does not exist
    print VersionFile(tfn)
    # emits: False
    print VersionFile(tfn)
    # emits: False
```

Discussion

The purpose of the VersionFile function is to ensure that an existing file is copied (or renamed, as indicated by the optional second parameter) before you open it for writing or updating and therefore modify it. It is polite to make such backups of files before you mangle them (one functionality some people still pine for from the good old VMS operating system, which performed it automatically!). The actual copy or renaming is performed by shutil.copy and os.rename, respectively, so the only issue is which name to use as the target.

A popular way to determine backups' names is versioning (i.e., appending to the filename a gradually incrementing number). This recipe determines the new name by first extracting the filename's root (just in case you call it with an already-versioned filename) and then successively appending to that root the further extensions *.000*, *.001*, and so on, until a name built in this manner does not correspond to any existing file. Then, and only then, is the name used as the target of a copy or renaming. Note that VersionFile is limited to 1,000 versions, so you should have an archive plan after that. The file must exist before it is first versioned—you cannot back up what does not yet exist. However, if the file doesn't exist, function VersionFile simply returns False (while it returns True if the file exists and has been successfully versioned), so you don't need to check before calling it!

See Also

Documentation for the os and shutil modules in the *Library Reference* and *Python in a Nutshell*.

2.30 Calculating CRC-64 Cyclic Redundancy Checks

Credit: Gian Paolo Ciceri

Problem

You need to ensure the integrity of some data by computing the data's cyclic redundancy check (CRC), and you need to do so according to the CRC-64 specifications of the ISO-3309 standard.

Solution

The Python Standard Library does not include any implementation of CRC-64 (only one of CRC-32 in function zlib.crc32), so we need to program it ourselves. Fortunately, Python can perform bitwise operations (masking, shifting, bitwise-and, bitwise-or, xor, etc.) just as well as, say, C (and, in fact, with just about the same syntax), so it's easy to transliterate a typical reference implementation of CRC-64 into a Python function as follows:

```
# prepare two auxiliary tables tables (using a function, for speed),
# then remove the function, since it's not needed any more:
CRCTableh = [0] * 256
CRCTablel = [0] * 256
def _inittables(CRCTableh, CRCTablel, POLY64REVh, BIT_TOGGLE):
    for i in xrange(256):
        partl = i
```

```
            parth = 0L
            for j in xrange(8):
                rflag = partl & 1L
                partl >>= 1L
                if parth & 1:
                    partl ^= BIT_TOGGLE
                parth >>= 1L
                if rflag:
                    parth ^= POLY64REVh
            CRCTableh[i] = parth
            CRCTablel[i] = partl
    # first 32 bits of generator polynomial for CRC64 (the 32 lower bits are
    # assumed to be zero) and bit-toggle mask used in _inittables
    POLY64REVh = 0xd8000000L
    BIT_TOGGLE = 1L << 31L
    # run the function to prepare the tables
    _inittables(CRCTableh, CRCTablel, POLY64REVh, BIT_TOGGLE)
    # remove all names we don't need any more, including the function
    del _inittables, POLY64REVh, BIT_TOGGLE
    # this module exposes the following two functions: crc64, crc64digest
    def crc64(bytes, (crch, crcl)=(0,0)):
        for byte in bytes:
            shr = (crch & 0xFF) << 24
            temp1h = crch >> 8L
            temp1l = (crcl >> 8L) | shr
            tableindex = (crcl ^ ord(byte)) & 0xFF
            crch = temp1h ^ CRCTableh[tableindex]
            crcl = temp1l ^ CRCTablel[tableindex]
        return crch, crcl
    def crc64digest(aString):
        return "%08X%08X" % (crc64(bytes))
    if __name__ == '__main__':
        # a little test/demo, for when this module runs as main-script
        assert crc64("IHATEMATH") == (3822890454, 2600578513)
        assert crc64digest("IHATEMATH") == "E3DCADD69B01ADD1"
        print 'crc64: dumb test successful'
```

Discussion

Cyclic redundancy checks (CRCs) are a popular way to ensure that data (in particular, a file) has not been accidentally damaged. CRCs can readily detect accidental damage, but they are *not* intended to withstand inimical assault the way other cryptographically strong checksums are. CRCs can be computed much faster than other kinds of checksums, making them useful in those cases where the only damage we need to guard against is accidental damage, rather than deliberate adversarial tampering.

Mathematically speaking, a CRC is computed as a polynomial over the bits of the data we're checksumming. In practice, as this recipe shows, most of the computation can be done once and for all and summarized in tables that, when properly indexed, give the contribution of each byte of input data to the result. So, after initialization (which we do with an auxiliary function because computation in Python is much faster when using a function's local variables than when using globals), actual CRC computation is quite fast. Both the computation of the tables and their use for CRC computation require a lot of bitwise operations, but, fortunately, Python's just as good at such operations as other languages such as C. (In fact, Python's syntax for the various bitwise operands is just about the same as C's.)

The algorithm to compute the standard CRC-64 checksum is described in the ISO-3309 standard, and this recipe does nothing more than implement that algorithm. The generator polynomial is $x64 + x4 + x3 + x + 1$. (The "See Also" section within this recipe provides a reference for obtaining information about the computation.)

We represent the 64-bit result as a pair of Python ints, holding the low and high 32-bit halves of the result. To allow the CRC to be computed incrementally, in those cases where the data comes in a little at a time, we let the caller of function crc64 optionally feed in the "initial value" for the (crch, crcl) pair, presumably obtained by calling crc64 on previous parts of the data. To compute the CRC in one gulp, the caller just needs to pass in the data (a string of bytes), since in this case, we initialize the result to (0, 0) by default.

See Also

W.H. Press, S.A. Teukolsky, W.T. Vetterling, and B.P. Flannery, *Numerical Recipes in C*, 2d ed. (Cambridge University Press), pp. 896ff.

## CHAPTER 3

Time and Money

3.0   Introduction

Credit: Gustavo Niemeyer, Facundo Batista

Today, last weekend, next year. These terms sound so common. You have probably wondered, at least once, about how deeply our lives are involved in the very idea of time. The concept of time surrounds us, and, as a consequence, it's also present in the vast majority of software projects. Even very simple programs may have to deal with timestamps, delays, timeouts, speed gauges, calendars, and so on. As befits a general-purpose language that is proud to come with "batteries included," Python's standard library offers solid support for these application needs, and more support yet comes from third-party modules and packages.

Computing tasks involving money are another interesting topic that catches our attention because it's so closely related to our daily lives. Python 2.4 introduced support for decimal numbers (and you can retrofit that support into 2.3, see *http://www.taniquetil.com.ar/facundo/bdvfiles/get_decimal.html*), making Python a good option even for computations where you must avoid using binary floats, as ones involving money so often are.

This chapter covers exactly these two topics, money and time. According to the old saying, maybe we should claim the chapter is really about a *single* topic, since after all, as everybody knows—time *is* money!

The time Module

Python Standard Library's time module lets Python applications access a good portion of the time-related functionality offered by the platform Python is running on. Your platform's documentation for the equivalent functions in the C library will therefore be useful, and some peculiarities of different platforms will affect Python as well.

One of the most used functions from module time is the one that obtains the current time—time.time. This function's return value may be a little cryptic for the uninitiated: it's a floating-point number that corresponds to the number of seconds passed since a fixed instant called the *epoch*, which may change depending on your platform but is usually midnight of January 1, 1970.

To check which epoch your platform uses, try, at any Python interactive interpreter prompt:

```
>>> import time
>>> print time.asctime(time.gmtime(0))
```

Notice we're passing 0 (meaning 0 seconds after the epoch) to the time.gmtime function. time.gmtime converts any timestamp (in seconds since the epoch) into a tuple that represents that precise instant of time in human terms, without applying any kind of time zone conversion (GMT stands for "Greenwich mean time", an old but colorful way to refer to what is now known as UTC, for "Coordinated Universal Time"). You can also pass a timestamp (in seconds since the epoch) to time.localtime, which applies the current local notion of time zone.

It's important to understand the difference, since, if you have a timestamp that is *already* offset to represent a local time, passing it to the time.localtime function will *not* yield the expected result—unless you're so lucky that your local time zone happens to coincide with the UTC time zone, of course!

Here is a way to unpack a tuple representing the current local time:

```
year, month, mday, hour, minute, second, wday, yday = time.localtime( )
```

While valid, this code is not elegant, and it would certainly not be practical to use it often. This kind of construct may be completely avoided, since the tuples returned by the time functions let you access their elements via meaningful attribute names. Obtaining the current month then becomes a simple and elegant expression:

```
time.localtime( ).tm_mon
```

Note that we omitted passing any argument to localtime. When we call localtime, gmtime, or asctime without an argument, each of them conveniently defaults to using the current time.

Two very useful functions in module time are strftime, which lets you build a string from a time tuple, and strptime, which goes the other way, parsing a string and producing a time tuple. Each of these two functions accepts a format string that lets you specify exactly what you want in the resulting string (or, respectively, what you expect from the string you're parsing) in excruciating detail. For all the formatting specifications that you can use in the format strings you pass to these functions, see *http://docs.python.org/lib/module-time.html*.

One last important function in module time is the time.sleep function, which lets you introduce delays in Python programs. Even though this function's POSIX counterpart accepts only an integer parameter, the Python equivalent supports a float and allows sub-second delays to be achieved. For instance:

```
for i in range(10):
    time.sleep(0.5)
    print "Tick!"
```

This snippet will take about 5 seconds to execute, emitting Tick! approximately twice per second.

Time and Date Objects

While module time is quite useful, the Python Standard Library also includes the datetime module, which supplies types that provide better abstractions for the concepts of dates and times——namely, the types time, date, and datetime. Constructing instances of those types is quite elegant:

```
today = datetime.date.today()
birthday = datetime.date(1977, 5, 4)      #May 4
currenttime = datetime.datetime.now().time()
lunchtime = datetime.time(12, 00)
now = datetime.datetime.now()
epoch = datetime.datetime(1970, 1, 1)
meeting = datetime.datetime(2005, 8, 3, 15, 30)
```

Further, as you'd expect, instances of these types offer comfortable information access and useful operations through their attributes and methods. The following statements create an instance of the date type, representing the current day, then obtain the same date in the next year, and finally print the result in a dotted format:

```
today = datetime.date.today()
next_year = today.replace(year=today.year+1).strftime("%Y.%m.%d")
print next_year
```

Notice how the year was incremented, using the replace method. Assigning to the attributes of date and time instances may sound tempting, but these instances are immutable (which is a good thing, because it means we can use the instances as members in a set, or keys in a dictionary!), so new instances must be created instead of changing existing ones.

Module datetime also provides basic support for *time deltas* (differences between instants of time; you can think of them as basically meaning *durations* in time), through the timedelta type. This type lets you change a given date by incrementing or decrementing the date by a given time slice, and it is also the result of taking the difference between times or dates.

```
>>> import datetime
>>> NewYearsDay = datetime.date(2005, 01, 01)
>>> NewYearsEve = datetime.date(2004, 12, 31)
>>> oneday = NewYearsDay - NewYearsEve
>>> print oneday
```

```
1 day, 0:00:00
>>>
```

A `timedelta` instance is internally represented by days, seconds, and microseconds, but you can construct `timedelta` instances by passing any of these arguments and also other multipliers, like minutes, hours and weeks. Support for other kinds of deltas, like months, and years, is not available—on purpose, since their meanings, and operation results, are debatable. (This feature is, however, offered by the third-party dateutil package—see *https://moin.conectiva.com.br/DateUtil.*)

`datetime` can be described as a *prudent* or *cautious* design. The decision of not implementing doubtful tasks, and tasks that may need many different implementations in different systems, reflects the strategy used to develop all of the module. This way, the module offers good interfaces for most use cases, and, even more importantly, a strong and coherent base for third-party modules to build upon.

Another area where this cautious design strategy for `datetime` shows starkly is the module's time zone support. Even though `datetime` offers nice ways to query and set time zone information, they're not really useful without an external source to provide nonabstract subclasses of the `tzinfo` type. At least two third-party packages provide time zone support for `datetime`: dateutil, mentioned previously, and pyTZ, available at *http://sourceforge.net/projects/pytz/.*

Decimal

`decimal` is a Python Standard Library module, new in Python 2.4, which finally brings decimal arithmetic to Python. Thanks to `decimal`, we now have a decimal numeric data type, with bounded precision and floating point. Let's look at each of these three little phrases in more detail:

Decimal numeric data type
    The number is not stored in binary, but rather, as a sequence of decimal digits.

With bounded precision
    The number of digits each number stores is fixed. (It is a fixed parameter of each decimal number object, but different decimal number objects can be set to use different numbers of digits.)

Floating point
    The decimal point does not have a fixed place. (To put it another way: while the number has a fixed amount of digits *in total*, it does not have a fixed amount of digits *after the decimal point*. If it did, it would be a *fixed-point*, rather than *floating-point*, numeric data type).

Such a data type has many uses (the big use case is as the basis for money computations), particularly because `decimal.Decimal` offers many other advantages over standard binary `float`. The main advantage is that all of the decimal numbers that the user can enter (which is to say, all the decimal numbers with a finite number of digits

) can be represented exactly (in contrast, some of those numbers do not have an exact representation in binary floating point):

```
>>> import decimal
>>> 1.1
1.1000000000000001
>>> 2.3
2.2999999999999998
>>> decimal.Decimal("1.1")
Decimal("1.1")
>>> decimal.Decimal("2.3")
Decimal("2.3")
```

The exactness of the representation carries over into arithmetic. In binary floating point, for example:

```
>>> 0.1 + 0.1 + 0.1 - 0.3
5.5511151231257827e-17
```

Such differences are very close to zero, and yet they prevent reliable equality testing; moreover, even tiny differences can accumulate. For this reason, decimal should be preferred to binary floats in accounting applications that have strict equality requirements:

```
>>> d1 = decimal.Decimal("0.1")
>>> d3 = decimal.Decimal("0.3")
>>> d1 + d1 + d1 - d3
Decimal("0.0")
```

decimal.Decimal instances can be constructed from integers, strings, or tuples. To create a decimal.Decimal from a float, first convert the float to a string. This necessary step serves as an explicit reminder of the details of the conversion, including representation error. Decimal numbers include special values such as NaN (which stands for "not a number"), positive and negative Infinity, and -0. Once constructed, a decimal.Decimal object is immutable, just like any other number in Python.

The decimal module essentially implements the rules of arithmetic that are taught in school. Up to a given working precision, exact, unrounded results are given whenever possible:

```
>>> 0.9 / 10
0.089999999999999997
>>> decimal.Decimal("0.9") / decimal.Decimal(10)
Decimal("0.09")
```

Where the number of digits in a result exceeds the working precision, the number is rounded according to the current rounding method. Several rounding methods are available; the default is round-half-even.

The decimal module incorporates the notion of *significant digits*, so that, for example, 1.30+1.20 is 2.50. The trailing zero is kept to indicate significance. This is the usual representation for monetary applications. For multiplication, the "school-book" approach uses all the figures in the multiplicands:

```
>>> decimal.Decimal("1.3") * decimal.Decimal("1.2")
Decimal("1.56")
>>> decimal.Decimal("1.30") * decimal.Decimal("1.20")
Decimal("1.5600")
```

In addition to the standard numeric properties that decimal objects share with other built-in number types, such as float and int, decimal objects also have several specialized methods. Check the docs for all of the methods, with details and examples.

The decimal data type works within a *context*, where some configuration aspects are set. Each thread has its own current context (having a separate context per thread means that each thread may make changes without interfering with other threads); the current thread's current context is accessed or changed using functions getcontext and setcontext from the decimal module.

Unlike hardware-based binary floating point, the precision of the decimal module can be set by users (defaulting to 28 places). It can be set to be as large as needed for a given problem:

```
>>> decimal.getcontext().prec = 6          # set the precision to 6...
>>> decimal.Decimal(1) / decimal.Decimal(7)
Decimal("0.142857")
>>> decimal.getcontext().prec = 60         # ...and to 60 digits
>>> decimal.Decimal(1) / decimal.Decimal(7)
Decimal("0.142857142857142857142857142857142857142857142857142857142857")
```

Not everything in decimal can be as simple and elementary as shown so far, of course. Essentially, decimal implements the standards for general decimal arithmetic which you can study in detail at *http://www2.hursley.ibm.com/decimal/*. In particular, this means that decimal supports the concept of *signals*. Signals represent abnormal conditions arising from computations (e.g., 1/0, 0/0, Infinity/Infinity). Depending on the needs of each specific application, signals may be ignored, considered as informational, or treated as exceptions. For each signal, there is a flag and a trap enabler. When a signal is encountered, its flag is incremented from zero, and then, if the trap enabler is set to one, an exception is raised. This gives programmers a great deal of power and flexibility in configuring decimal to meet their exact needs.

Given all of these advantages for decimal, why would someone want to stick with float? Indeed, is there any reason why Python (like just about every other widespread language, with Cobol and Rexx the two major exceptions that easily come to mind) originally adopted floating-point binary numbers as its default (or only) non-integer data type? Of course—many reasons can be provided, and they're all spelled *speed*! Consider:

```
$ python -mtimeit -s'from decimal import Decimal as D' 'D("1.2")+D("3.4")'
10000 loops, best of 3: 191 usec per loop
```

```
$ python -mtimeit -s'from decimal import Decimal as D' '1.2+3.4'
1000000 loops, best of 3: 0.339 usec per loop
```

This basically translates to: on this machine (an old Athlon 1.2 GHz PC running Linux), Python can perform almost 3 million sums per second on floats (using the PC's arithmetic hardware), but only a bit more than 5 thousand sums per second on Decimals (all done in software and with all the niceties shown previously).

Essentially, if your application must sum many tens of millions of noninteger numbers, you had better stick with float! When an average machine was a thousand times slower than it is today (and it wasn't *all* that long ago!), such limitations hit even applications doing relatively small amounts of computation, if the applications ran on reasonably cheap machines (again, we see time and money both playing a role!). Rexx and Cobol were born on mainframes that were not quite as fast as today's cheapest PCs but thousands of times more expensive. Purchasers of such mainframes could *afford* nice and friendly decimal arithmetic, but most other languages, born on more reasonably priced machines (or meant for computationally intensive tasks), just couldn't.

Fortunately, relatively few applications actually need to perform so much arithmetic on non-integers as to give any observable performance problems on today's typical machines. Thus, today, most applications can actually take advantage of decimal's many beneficial aspects, including applications that must continue to use Python 2.3, even though decimal is in the Python Standard Library only since version 2.4. To learn how you can easily integrate decimal into Python 2.3, see *http://www.taniquetil.com.ar/facundo/bdvfiles/get_decimal.html*.

3.1   Calculating Yesterday and Tomorrow

Credit: Andrea Cavalcanti

Problem

You want to get today's date, then calculate yesterday's or tomorrow's.

Solution

Whenever you have to deal with a "change" or "difference" in time, think timedelta:

```
import datetime
today = datetime.date.today()
yesterday = today - datetime.timedelta(days=1)
tomorrow = today + datetime.timedelta(days=1)
print yesterday, today, tomorrow
#emits: 2004-11-17 2004-11-18 2004-11-19
```

Discussion

This recipe's Problem has been a fairly frequent question on Python mailing lists since the datetime module arrived. When first confronted with this task, it's quite

common for people to try to code it as yesterday = today - 1, which gives a
TypeError: unsupported operand type(s) for -: 'datetime.date' and 'int'.

Some people have called this a bug, implying that Python should guess what they
mean. However, one of the guiding principles that gives Python its simplicity and
power is: "in the face of ambiguity, refuse the temptation to guess." Trying to guess
would clutter datetime with heuristics meant to guess that you "really meant 1 day",
rather than 1 second (which timedelta also supports), or 1 year.

Rather than trying to *guess* what you mean, Python, as usual, expects you to make
your meaning explicit. If you want to subtract a time difference of one day, you code
that explicitly. If, instead, you want to add a time difference of one second, you can
use timedelta with a datetime.datetime object, and then you code the operation
using exactly the same syntax. This way, for each task you might want to perform,
there's only one obvious way of doing it. This approach also allows a fair amount of
flexibility, without added complexity. Consider the following interactive snippet:

```
>>> anniversary = today + datetime.timedelta(days=365)        # add 1 year
>>> print anniversary
2005-11-18
>>> t = datetime.datetime.today()                             # get right now
>>> t
datetime.datetime(2004, 11, 19, 10, 12, 43, 801000)
>>> t2 = t + datetime.timedelta(seconds=1)                    # add 1 second
>>> t2
datetime.datetime(2004, 11, 19, 10, 12, 44, 801000)
>>> t3 = t + datetime.timedelta(seconds=3600)                 # add 1 hour
>>> t3
datetime.datetime(2004, 11, 19, 11, 12, 43, 801000)
```

Keep in mind that, if you want fancier control over date and time arithmetic, third-
party packages, such as dateutil (which works together with the built-in datetime)
and the classic mx.DateTime, are available. For example:

```
from dateutil import relativedelta
nextweek = today + relativedelta.relativedelta(weeks=1)
print nextweek
#emits: 2004-11-25
```

However, "always do the simplest thing that can possibly work." For simple,
straightforward tasks such as the ones in this recipe, datetime.timedelta works just
fine.

See Also

dateutil documentation at *https://moin.conectiva.com.br/DateUtil?action= highlight&value=
DateUtil*, and datetime documentation in the *Library Reference*. mx.DateTime can be
found at *http://www.egenix.com/files/python/mxDateTime.html*. mx.DateTime can be
found at *http://www.egenix.com/files/python/mxDateTime.html*.

3.2   Finding Last Friday

Credit: Kent Johnson, Danny Yoo, Jonathan Gennick, Michael Wener

Problem

You want to find the date of last Friday (or today, if today is Friday) and print it in a specified format.

Solution

You can use the datetime module from Python's standard library to easily achieve this:

```
import datetime, calendar
lastFriday = datetime.date.today()
oneday = datetime.timedelta(days=1)
while lastFriday.weekday() != calendar.FRIDAY:
    lastFriday -= oneday
print lastFriday.strftime('%A, %d-%b-%Y')
# emits, e.g.: Friday, 10-Dec-2004
```

Discussion

The handy little snippet of code in this recipe lets us find a previous weekday and print the properly formatted date, regardless of whether that weekday is in the same month, or even the same year. In this example, we're looking for the last Friday (or today, if today is Friday). Friday's integer representation is 4, but to avoid depending on this "magical number," we just import the Python Standard Library calendar module and rely instead on its calendar.FRIDAY attribute (which, sure enough, *is* the number 4). We set a variable called lastFriday to today's date and work backward until we have reached a date with the desired weekday value of 4.

Once we have the date we desire, formatting the date in any way we like is easily achieved with the "string formatting" method strftime of the datetime.date class.

An alternative, slightly more terse solution uses the built-in constant datetime.date.resolution instead of explicitly building the datetime.timedelta instance to represent one day's duration:

```
import datetime, calendar
lastFriday = datetime.date.today()
while lastFriday.weekday() != calendar.FRIDAY:
    lastFriday -= datetime.date.resolution
print lastFriday.strftime('%d-%b-%Y')
```

The datetime.date.resolution class attribute has exactly the same value as the oneday variable in the recipe's Solution—the time interval of one day. However, resolution can trip you up. The value of the class attribute resolution varies among various classes of the datetime module—for the date class it's timedelta(days=1), but for the time and datetime classes , it's timedelta(microseconds=1). You *could* mix-and-match (e.g., add datetime.date.resolution to a datetime.datetime instance), but it's easy to get confused doing so. The version in this recipe's Solution, using the explicitly named and defined oneday variable, is just as general, more explicit, and less confusing. Thus, all in all, that version is more Pythonic (which is why it's presented as the "official" one!).

A more important enhancement is that we don't really need to loop, decrementing a date by one at each step through the loop: we can, in fact, get to the desired target in one fell swoop, computing the number of days to subtract thanks to the wonders of modular arithmetic:

```
import datetime, calendar
today = datetime.date.today( )
targetDay = calendar.FRIDAY
thisDay = today.weekday( )
deltaToTarget = (thisDay - targetDay) % 7
lastFriday = today - datetime.timedelta(days=deltaToTarget)
print lastFriday.strftime('%d-%b-%Y')
```

If you don't follow why this works, you may want to brush up on modular arithmetic, for example at *http://www.cut-the-knot.org/blue/Modulo.shtml*.

Use the approach you find clearest, without worrying about performance. Remember Hoare's dictum (often misattributed to Knuth, who was in fact quoting Hoare): "premature optimization is the root of all evil in programming." Let's see why thinking of optimization *would* be premature here.

Net of the common parts (computing today's date, and formatting and emitting the result) on a four-year-old PC, with Linux and Python 2.4, the slowest approach (the one chosen for presentation as the "Solution" because it's probably the clearest and most obvious one) takes 18.4 microseconds; the fastest approach (the one avoiding the loop, with some further tweaks to really get *pedal to the metal*) takes 10.1 microseconds.

You're not going to compute last Friday's date often enough, in your life, to be able to tell the difference at 8 microseconds a pop (much less if you use recent hardware rather than a box that's four years old). If you consider the time needed to compute today's date and to format the result, you need to add 37 microseconds to each timing, even net of the I/O time for the print statement; so, the range of performance is roughly between 55 microseconds for the slowest and clearest form, and 47 microseconds for the fastest and tersest one—clearly not worth worrying about.

See Also

datetime module and strftime documentation in the *Library Reference* (currently at *http://www.python.org/doc/lib/module-datetime.html* and *http://www.python.org/doc/current/lib/node208.html*).

3.3 Calculating Time Periods in a Date Range

Credit: Andrea Cavalcanti

Problem

Given two dates, you want to calculate the number of weeks between them.

Solution

Once again, the standard datetime and third-party dateutil modules (particularly dateutil's rrule.count method) come in quite handy. After importing the appropriate modules, it's a really simple job:

```
from dateutil import rrule
import datetime
def weeks_between(start_date, end_date):
    weeks = rrule.rrule(rrule.WEEKLY, dtstart=start_date, until=end_date)
    return weeks.count()
```

Discussion

Function weeks_between takes the starting and ending dates as arguments, instantiates a rule to recur weekly between them, and returns the result of the rule's count method—faster to code than to describe. This method will return only an integer (it won't return "half" weeks). For example, eight days is considered two weeks. It's easy to code a test for this:

```
if __name__=='__main__':
    starts = [datetime.date(2005, 01, 04), datetime.date(2005, 01, 03)]
    end = datetime.date(2005, 01, 10)
    for s in starts:
        days = rrule.rrule(rrule.DAILY, dtstart=s, until=end).count()
        print "%d days shows as %d weeks "% (days, weeks_between(s, end))
```

This test emits the following output:

```
7 days shows as 1 weeks
8 days shows as 2 weeks
```

It's not necessary to give a name to a recurrence rule, if you don't want to—changing the function's body, for example, to the single statement:

```
    return rrule.rrule(rrule.WEEKLY, dtstart=start_date, until=end_date).count()
```

works just as well. I prefer to name recurrence rules because (frankly) I still find them a bit weird, even though they're so incredibly useful I doubt I could do without them!

See Also

Refer to the dateutil module's documentation available at *https://moin.conectiva.com.br/DateUtil?action=highlight&value=DateUtil*, datetime documentation in the *Library Reference*.

3.4   Summing Durations of Songs

Credit: Anna Martelli Ravenscroft

Problem

You want to find out the total duration of a playlist of songs.

Solution

Use the datetime standard module and the built-in function sum to handle this task:

```
import datetime
def totaltimer(times):
    td = datetime.timedelta(0)     # initial value of sum (must be a timedelta)
    duration = sum([
        datetime.timedelta(minutes=m, seconds=s) for m, s in times],
        td)
    return duration
if __name__ == '__main__':       # test when module run as main script
    times1 = [(2, 36),           # list containing tuples (minutes, seconds)
              (3, 35),
              (3, 45),]
    times2 = [(3, 0),
              (5, 13),
              (4, 12),
              (1, 10),]
    assert totaltimer(times1) == datetime.timedelta(0, 596)
    assert totaltimer(times2) == datetime.timedelta(0, 815)
    print ("Tests passed.\n"
           "First test total: %s\n"
           "Second test total: %s" % (
           totaltimer(times1), totaltimer(times2)))
```

Discussion

I have a large playlist of songs I listen to during workouts. I wanted to create a select list but wanted to know the total duration of the selected songs, without having to create the new playlist first. I wrote this little script to handle the task.

A datetime.timedelta is normally what's returned when calculating the difference between two datetime objects. However, you can create your own timedelta instance to represent any given *duration* of time (while other classes of the datetime module, such as class datetime, have instances that represent a *point* in time). Here, we need to sum durations, so, clearly, it's exactly timedelta that we need.

datetime.timedelta takes a variety of optional arguments: days, seconds, microseconds, milliseconds, minutes, hours, weeks. So, to create an instance, you really should pass named arguments when you call the class to avoid confusion. If you simply call datetime.timedelta(m, n), without naming the arguments, the class uses positional notation and treats m and n as days and seconds, which produces really strange results. (I found this out the hard way . . . a good demonstration of the need to *test*!)

To use the built-in function sum on a list of objects such as timedeltas, you have to pass to sum a second argument to use as the initial value—otherwise, the default initial value is 0, integer zero, and you get an error as soon as you try to sum a timedelta with that int. All objects in the iterable that you pass as sum's first argument should be able to support *numeric* addition. (Strings are *specifically* disallowed, but, take my earnest advice: *don't* use sum for concatenating a lot of lists either!) In Python 2.4, instead of a list comprehension for sum's first argument, we could use a generator expression by replacing the square brackets, [and], with parentheses, (and)—which might be handy if you're trying to handle a playlist of several thousand songs.

For the test case, I manually created a list of tuples with the durations of the songs in minutes and seconds. The script could be enhanced to parse the times in different formats (such as mm:ss) or to read the information from a file or directly from your music library.

See Also

Library Reference on sum and datetime.

3.5 Calculating the Number of Weekdays Between Two Dates

Credit: Anna Martelli Ravenscroft

Problem

You want to calculate the number of weekdays (working days), as opposed to calendar days, that fall between two dates.

Solution

Since weekends and other "days off" vary by country, by region, even sometimes within a single company, there is no built-in way to perform this task. However, using dateutil along with datetime objects, it's reasonably simple to code a solution:

```
from dateutil import rrule
import datetime
def workdays(start, end, holidays=0, days_off=None):
    if days_off is None:
        days_off = 5, 6          # default to: saturdays and sundays
    workdays = [x for x in range(7) if x not in days_off]
    days = rrule.rrule(rrule.DAILY, dtstart=start, until=end,
                       byweekday=workdays)
    return days.count() - holidays
if __name__ == '__main__':
# test when run as main script
    testdates = [ (datetime.date(2004, 9, 1), datetime.date(2004, 11, 14), 2),
                  (datetime.date(2003, 2, 28), datetime.date(2003, 3, 3), 1), ]
    def test(testdates, days_off=None):
        for s, e, h in testdates:
            print 'total workdays from %s to %s is %s with %s holidays' % (
                   s, e, workdays(s, e, h, days_off), h)
    test(testdates)
    test(testdates, days_off=[6])
```

Discussion

This project was my very first one in Python: I needed to know the number of actual days in training of our trainees, given a start date and end date (inclusive). This problem was a bit trickier back in Python 2.2; today, the datetime module and the dateutil third-party package make the problem much simpler to solve.

Function workdays starts by assigning a reasonable default value to variable days_off (unless an explicit value was passed for it as an argument), which is a sequence of the weekday numbers of our normal days off. In my company, weekly days off varied among individuals but were usually fewer than the workdays, so it was easier to track and modify the days off rather than the workdays. I made this an argument to the function so that I can easily pass a different value for days_off if and when I have different needs. Then, the function uses a list comprehension to create a list of actual weekly workdays, which are all weekdays not in days_off. Now the function is ready to do its calculations.

The workhorse in this recipe is an instance, named days, of dateutil's rrule (recurrence rule) class. Class rrule may be instantiated with various parameters to produce a rule object. In this example, I pass a frequency (rrule.DAILY), a beginning date and an ending date—both of which must be datetime.date objects—and which weekdays to include (workdays). Then, I simply call method days.count to count the number of occurrences generated by the rule. (See recipe 3.3 "Calculating Time Periods in a Date Range" for other uses for the count method of rrule.)

You can easily set your own definition of *weekend*: just pass as days_off whichever values you need. In this recipe, the default value is set to the standard U.S. weekend of Saturday and Sunday. However, if your company normally works a four-day week, say, Tuesday through Friday, you would pass days_off=(5, 6, 0). Just be sure to pass the days_off value as an iterable, such as a list or tuple, even if, as in the second test, you only have a single day in that container.

A simple but useful enhancement might be to automatically check whether your start and end dates are weekends (for weekend-shift workers), and use an if/else to handle the weekend shifts, with appropriate changes to days_off. Further enhancements would be to add the ability to enter sick days, or to perform a call to an automatic holiday lookup function, rather than passing the number of holidays directly, as I do in this recipe. See recipe 3.6 "Looking up Holidays Automatically" for a simple implementation of a holidays list for this purpose.

See Also

Refer to the dateutil documentation, which is available at *https:// moin.conectiva.com.br/DateUtil?action=highlight&value=DateUtil*, datetime documentation in the *Library Reference*; recipe 3.3 "Calculating Time Periods in a Date Range" for another use of rrule.count; recipe 3.6 "Looking up Holidays Automatically" for automatic holiday lookup.

3.6   Looking up Holidays Automatically

Credit: Anna Martelli Ravenscroft, Alex Martelli

Problem

Holidays vary by country, by region, even by union within the same company. You want an automatic way to determine the number of holidays that fall between two given dates.

Solution

Between two dates, there may be movable holidays, such as Easter and Labor Day (U.S.); holidays that are based on Easter, such as Boxing Day; holidays with a fixed date, such as Christmas; holidays that your company has designated (the CEO's birthday). You can deal with all of them using datetime and the third-party module dateutil.

A very flexible architecture is to factor out the various possibilities into separate functions to be called as appropriate:

```
import datetime
from dateutil import rrule, easter
try: set
except NameError: from sets import Set as set
def all_easter(start, end):
    # return the list of Easter dates within start..end
```

```
    easters = [easter.easter(y)
                for y in xrange(start.year, end.year+1)]
    return [d for d in easters if start<=d<=end]
def all_boxing(start, end):
    # return the list of Boxing Day dates within start..end
    one_day = datetime.timedelta(days=1)
    boxings = [easter.easter(y)+one_day
                for y in xrange(start.year, end.year+1)]
    return [d for d in boxings if start<=d<=end]
def all_christmas(start, end):
    # return the list of Christmas Day dates within start..end
    christmases = [datetime.date(y, 12, 25)
                    for y in xrange(start.year, end.year+1)]
    return [d for d in christmases if start<=d<=end]
def all_labor(start, end):
    # return the list of Labor Day dates within start..end
    labors = rrule.rrule(rrule.YEARLY, bymonth=9, byweekday=rrule.MO(1),
                        dtstart=start, until=end)
    return [d.date() for d in labors]    # no need to test for in-between here
def read_holidays(start, end, holidays_file='holidays.txt'):
    # return the list of dates from holidays_file within start..end
    try:
        holidays_file = open(holidays_file)
    except IOError, err:
        print 'cannot read holidays (%r):' % (holidays_file,), err
        return []
    holidays = []
    for line in holidays_file:
        # skip blank lines and comments
        if line.isspace() or line.startswith('#'):
            continue
        # try to parse the format: YYYY, M, D
        try:
            y, m, d = [int(x.strip()) for x in line.split(',')]
            date = datetime.date(y, m, d)
        except ValueError:
            # diagnose invalid line and just go on
            print "Invalid line %r in holidays file %r" % (
                line, holidays_file)
            continue
        if start<=date<=end:
            holidays.append(date)
    holidays_file.close()
    return holidays
holidays_by_country = {
    # map each country code to a sequence of functions
    'US': (all_easter, all_christmas, all_labor),
    'IT': (all_easter, all_boxing, all_christmas),
}
def holidays(cc, start, end, holidays_file='holidays.txt'):
    # read applicable holidays from the file
    all_holidays = read_holidays(start, end, holidays_file)
    # add all holidays computed by applicable functions
    functions = holidays_by_country.get(cc, ())
```

```
            for function in functions:
                all_holidays += function(start, end)
            # eliminate duplicates
            all_holidays = list(set(all_holidays))
            # uncomment the following 2 lines to return a sorted list:
            # all_holidays.sort( )
            # return all_holidays
            return len(all_holidays)        # comment this out if returning list
    if __name__ == '__main__':
        test_file = open('test_holidays.txt', 'w')
        test_file.write('2004, 9, 6\n')
        test_file.close( )
        testdates = [ (datetime.date(2004, 8,  1), datetime.date(2004, 11, 14)),
                      (datetime.date(2003, 2, 28), datetime.date(2003,  5, 30)),
                      (datetime.date(2004, 2, 28), datetime.date(2004,  5, 30)),
                    ]
        def test(cc, testdates, expected):
            for (s, e), expect in zip(testdates, expected):
                print 'total holidays in %s from %s to %s is %d (exp %d)' % (
                        cc, s, e, holidays(cc, s, e, test_file.name), expect)
                print
        test('US', testdates, (1,1,1) )
        test('IT', testdates, (1,2,2) )
        import os
        os.remove(test_file.name)
```

Discussion

In one company I worked for, there were three different unions, and holidays varied among the unions by contract. In addition, we had to track any snow days or other release days in the same way as "official" holidays. To deal with all the potential variations in holidays, it's easiest to factor out the calculation of standard holidays into their own functions, as we did in the preceding example for all_easter, all_labor, and so on. Examples of different types of calculations are provided so it's easy to roll your own as needed.

Although half-open intervals (with the lower bound included but the upper one excluded) are the norm in Python (and for good reasons, since they're arithmetically more malleable and tend to induce fewer bugs in your computations!), this recipe deals with closed intervals instead (both lower and upper bounds included). Unfortunately, that's how specifications in terms of date intervals tend to be given, and dateutil also works that way, so the choice was essentially obvious.

Each function is responsible for ensuring that it only returns results that meet our criteria: lists of datetime.date instances that lie between the dates (inclusive) passed to the function. For example, in all_labor, we coerce the datetime.datetime results returned by dateutil's rrule into datetime.date instances with the date method.

A company may choose to set a specific date as a holiday (such as a snow day) "just this once," and a text file may be used to hold such unique instances. In our example, the read_holidays function handles the task of reading and processing a text file, with one date per line, each in the format year, month, day. You could also choose to refactor this function to use a "fuzzy" date parser, as shown in recipe 3.7 "Fuzzy Parsing of Dates."

If you need to look up holidays many times within a single run of your program, you may apply the optimization of reading and parsing the text file just once, then using the list of dates parsed from its contents each time that data is needed. However, "premature optimization is the root of all evil in programming," as Knuth said, quoting Hoare: by avoiding even this "obvious" optimization, we gain clarity and flexibility. Imagine these functions being used in an interactive environment, where the text file containing holidays may be edited between one computation and the next: by rereading the file each time, there is no need for any special check about whether the file was changed since you last read it!

Since countries often celebrate different holidays, the recipe provides a rudimentary holidays_by_country dictionary. You can consult plenty of web sites that list holidays by country to flesh out the dictionary for your needs. The important part is that this dictionary allows a different group of holidays-generating functions to be called, depending on which country code is passed to the holidays function. If your company has multiple unions, you could easily create a union-based dictionary, passing the union-code instead of (or for multinationals, in addition to) a country code to holidays. The holidays function calls the appropriate functions (including, unconditionally, read_holidays), concatenates the results, eliminates duplicates, and returns the length of the list. If you prefer, of course, you can return the list instead, by simply uncommenting two lines as indicated in the code.

See Also

Recipe 3.7 "Fuzzy Parsing of Dates" for fuzzy parsing; dateutil documentation at *https://moin.conectiva.com.br/DateUtil?action=highlight&value=DateUtil*, datetime documentation in the *Library Reference*.

3.7   Fuzzy Parsing of Dates

Credit: Andrea Cavalcanti

Problem

Your program needs to read and accept dates that don't conform to the datetime standard format of "yyyy, mm, dd".

Solution

The third-party dateutil.parser module provides a simple answer:

```
import datetime
import dateutil.parser
def tryparse(date):
    # dateutil.parser needs a string argument: let's make one from our
    # `date' argument, according to a few reasonable conventions...:
    kwargs = { }                                    # assume no named-args
    if isinstance(date, (tuple, list)):
        date = ' '.join([str(x) for x in date])    # join up sequences
    elif isinstance(date, int):
        date = str(date)                            # stringify integers
    elif isinstance(date, dict):
        kwargs = date                               # accept named-args dicts
        date = kwargs.pop('date')                   # with a 'date' str
    try:
        try:
            parsedate = dateutil.parser.parse(date, **kwargs)
            print 'Sharp %r -> %s' % (date, parsedate)
        except ValueError:
            parsedate = dateutil.parser.parse(date, fuzzy=True, **kwargs)
            print 'Fuzzy %r -> %s' % (date, parsedate)
    except Exception, err:
        print 'Try as I may, I cannot parse %r (%s)' % (date, err)
if __name__ == "__main__":
    tests = (
            "January 3, 2003",                    # a string
            (5, "Oct", 55),                       # a tuple
            "Thursday, November 18",              # longer string without year
            "7/24/04",                            # a string with slashes
            "24-7-2004",                          # European-format string
            {'date':"5-10-1955", "dayfirst":True}, # a dict including the kwarg
            "5-10-1955",                          # dayfirst, no kwarg
            19950317,                             # not a string
            "11AM on the 11th day of 11th month, in the year of our Lord 1945",
            )
    for test in tests:                            # testing date formats
        tryparse(test)                            # try to parse
```

Discussion

dateutil.parser's parse function works on a variety of date formats. This recipe demonstrates a few of them. The parser can handle English-language month-names and two- or four-digit years (with some constraints). When you call parse without named arguments, its default is to first try parsing the string argument in the following order: mm-dd-yy. If that does not make logical sense, as, for example, it doesn't for the '24-7-2004' string in the recipe, parse then tries dd-mm-yy. Lastly, it tries yy-mm-dd. If a "keyword" such as dayfirst or yearfirst is passed (as we do in one test), parse attempts to parse based on that keyword.

The recipe tests define a few *edge cases* that a date parser might encounter, such as trying to pass the date as a tuple, an integer (ISO-formatted without spaces), and even a phrase. To allow testing of the keyword arguments, the tryparse function in the recipe also accepts a dictionary argument, expecting, in this case, to find in it the value of the string to be parsed in correspondence to key 'date', and passing the rest on to dateutil's parser as keyword arguments.

dateutil's parser can provide a pretty good level of "fuzzy" parsing, given *some* hints to let it know which piece is, for example, the hour (such as the AM in the test phrase in this recipe). For production code, you should avoid relying on fuzzy parsing, and either do some kind of preprocessing, or at least provide some kind of mechanism for checking the accuracy of the parsed date.

See Also

For more on date-parsing algorithms, see dateutil documentation at *https:// moin.conectiva.com.br/DateUtil?action=highlight&value=DateUtil*; for date handling, see the datetime documentation in the *Library Reference*.

3.8 Checking Whether Daylight Saving Time Is Currently in Effect

Credit: Doug Fort

Problem

You want to know whether daylight saving time is in effect in your local time zone today.

Solution

It's a natural temptation to check time.daylight for this purpose, but that doesn't work. Instead you need:

```
import time
def is_dst():
    return bool(time.localtime().tm_isdst)
```

Discussion

In my location (as in most others nowadays), time.daylight is always 1 because time.daylight means that this time zone has daylight saving time (DST) at *some* time during the year, whether or not DST is in effect *today*.

The very last item in the pseudo-tuple you get by calling time.localtime, on the other hand, is 1 only when DST is currently in effect, otherwise it's 0—which, in my experience, is exactly the information one usually needs to check. This recipe wraps this check into a function, calling built-in type `bool` to ensure the result is an elegant `True` or `False` rather than a rougher `1` or `0`—optional refinements, but nice ones, I think. You could alternatively access the relevant item as `time.localtime( )[-1]`, but using attribute-access syntax with the `tm_isdst` attribute name is more readable.

See Also

Library Reference and *Python in a Nutshell* about module `time`.

3.9 Converting Time Zones

Credit: Gustavo Niemeyer

Problem

You are in Spain and want to get the correct local (Spanish) time for an event in China.

Solution

Time zone support for `datetime` is available in the third-party `dateutil` package. Here's one way to set the local time zone, then print the current time to check that it worked properly:

```
from dateutil import tz
import datetime
posixstr = "CET-1CEST-2,M3.5.0/02:00,M10.5.0/03:00"
spaintz = tz.tzstr(posixstr)
print datetime.datetime.now(spaintz).ctime( )
```

Conversion between different time zones is also possible, and often necessary in our expanding world. For instance, let's find out when the next Olympic Games will start, according to a Spanish clock:

```
chinatz = tz.tzoffset("China", 60*60*8)
olympicgames = datetime.datetime(2008, 8, 8, 20, 0, tzinfo=chinatz)
print olympicgames.astimezone(spaintz)
```

Discussion

The cryptic string named `posixstr` is a POSIX-style representation for the time zone currently being used in Spain. This string provides the standard and daylight saving time zone names (CST and CEST), their offsets (UTC+1 and UTC+2), and the day and hour when DST starts and ends (the last Sunday of March at 2 a.m., and the last Sunday of October at 3 a.m., respectively). We may check the DST zone bounds to ensure they are correct:

```
assert spaintz.tzname(datetime.datetime(2004, 03, 28, 1, 59)) == "CET"
assert spaintz.tzname(datetime.datetime(2004, 03, 28, 2, 00)) == "CEST"
assert spaintz.tzname(datetime.datetime(2004, 10, 31, 1, 59)) == "CEST"
assert spaintz.tzname(datetime.datetime(2004, 10, 31, 2, 00)) == "CET"
```

All of these asserts should pass silently, confirming that the time zone name switches between the right strings at the right times.

Observe that even though the return to the standard time zone is scheduled to 3a.m., the moment of the change is marked as 2 a.m. This happens because of a one-hour gap, between 2 a.m. and 3 a.m., that is ambiguous. That hour of time happens twice: once in the time zone CEST, and then again in the time zone CET. Currently, expressing this moment in an unambiguous way, using the standard Python date and time support, is not possible. This is why it is recommended that you store datetime instances in UTC, which is unambiguous, and only use time zone conversion for display purposes.

To do the conversion from China to Spain, we've used tzoffset to express the fact that China is eight hours ahead of UTC time (tzoffset is always compared to *UTC*, *not* to a particular time zone). Notice how the datetime instance is created with the time zone information. This is always necessary for converting between two different time zones, even if the given time is in the local time zone. If you don't create the instance with the time zone information, you'll get a ValueError: astimezone() cannot be applied to a naive datetime. datetime instances are always created *naive*—they ignore time zone issues entirely—unless you explicitly create them with a time zone. For this purpose, dateutil provides the tzlocal type, which creates instances representing the platform's idea of the local time zone.

Besides the types we have seen so far, dateutil also provides tzutc, which creates instances representing UTC; tzfile, which allows using standard binary time zone files; tzical, which creates instances representing iCalendar time zones; and many more besides.

See Also

Documentation about the dateutil module can be found at *https:// moin.conectiva.com.br/DateUtil?action=highlight&value=DateUtil*, and datetime documentation in the *Library Reference*.

3.10 Running a Command Repeatedly

Credit: Philip Nunez

Problem

You need to run a command repeatedly, with arbitrary periodicity.

Solution

The time.sleep function offers a simple approach to this task:

```
import time, os, sys
def main(cmd, inc=60):
```

```
            while True:
                os.system(cmd)
                time.sleep(inc)
    if __name__ == '__main__' :
        numargs = len(sys.argv) - 1
        if numargs < 1 or numargs > 2:
            print "usage: " + sys.argv[0] + " command [seconds_delay]"
            sys.exit(1)
        cmd = sys.argv[1]
        if numargs < 3:
            main(cmd)
        else:
            inc = int(sys.argv[2])
            main(cmd, inc)
```

Discussion

You can use this recipe with a command that periodically checks for something (e.g., polling), or with one that performs an endlessly repeating action, such as telling a browser to reload a URL whose contents change often, so as to always have a recent version of that URL for viewing. The recipe is structured into a function called main and a body that is preceded by the usual if __name__=='__main__': idiom, to execute only if the script runs as a main script. The body examines the command-line arguments you used with the script and calls main appropriately (or gives a usage message if there are too many or too few arguments). This is the best way to structure a script, to make its functionality also available to other scripts that may import it as a module.

The main function accepts a cmd string, which is a command you want to pass periodically to the operating system's shell, and, optionally, a period of time in seconds, with a default value of 60 (one minute). main loops forever, alternating between executing the command with os.system and waiting (without consuming resources) with time.sleep.

The script's body looks at the command-line arguments you used with the script, which it finds in sys.argv. The first argument, sys.argv[0], is the name of the script, often useful when the script identifies itself as it prints out messages. The body checks that one or two other arguments, in addition to this name, are included. The first (and mandatory) is the command to be run. (You may need to enclose this command in quotes to preserve it from your shell's parsing: the important thing is that it must remain a single argument.) The second (and optional) argument is the delay in seconds between two runs of the command. If the second argument is missing, the body calls main with just the command argument, accepting the default delay (60 seconds).

Note that, if there is a second argument, the body transforms it from a string (all items in sys.argv are always strings) into an integer, which is done most simply by calling built-in type int:

```
inc = int(sys.argv[2])
```

If the second argument is a string that is not acceptable for transformation into an integer (in other words, if it's anything except a sequence of digits), this call to int raises an exception and terminates the script with appropriate error messages. As one of Python's design principles states, "errors should not pass silently, unless explicitly silenced." It would be bad design to let the script accept an arbitrary string as its second argument, silently taking a default action if that string was not a correct integer representation!

For a variant of this recipe that uses the standard Python library module sched, rather than explicit looping and sleeping, see recipe 3.11 "Scheduling Commands."

See Also

Documentation of the standard library modules os, time, and sys in the *Library Reference* and *Python in a Nutshell*; recipe 3.11 "Scheduling Commands."

3.11 Scheduling Commands

Credit: Peter Cogolo

Problem

You need to schedule commands for execution at certain times.

Solution

That's what the sched module of the standard library is for:

```
import time, os, sys, sched
schedule = sched.scheduler(time.time, time.sleep)
def perform_command(cmd, inc):
    schedule.enter(inc, 0, perform_command, (cmd, inc)) # re-scheduler
    os.system(cmd)
def main(cmd, inc=60):
    schedule.enter(0, 0, perform_command, (cmd, inc))   # 0==right now
    schedule.run( )
if __name__ == '__main__' :
    numargs = len(sys.argv) - 1
    if numargs < 1 or numargs > 2:
        print "usage: " + sys.argv[0] + " command [seconds_delay]"
        sys.exit(1)
    cmd = sys.argv[1]
    if numargs < 3:
        main(cmd)
    else:
```

```
inc = int(sys.argv[2])
main(cmd, inc)
```

Discussion

This recipe implements the same functionality as in the previous recipe 3.10 "Running a Command Repeatedly," but instead of that recipe's simpler roll-our-own approach, this one uses the standard library module sched.

sched is a reasonably simple, yet flexible and powerful, module for scheduling tasks that must take place at given times in the future. To use sched, you first instantiate a scheduler object, such as schedule (shown in this recipe's Solution), with two arguments. The first argument is the function to call in order to find out what time it is—normally time.time, which returns the current time as a number of seconds from an arbitrary reference point known as the *epoch*. The second argument is the function to call to wait for some time—normally time.sleep. You can also pass functions that measure time in arbitrary artificial ways. For example, you can use sched for such tasks as simulation programs. However, measuring time in artificial ways is an advanced use of sched not covered in this recipe.

Once you have a sched.scheduler instance s, you schedule events by calling either s.enter, to schedule something at a relative time n seconds from now (you can pass n as 0 to schedule something for *right now*), or s.enterabs, to schedule something at a given absolute time. In either case, you pass the time (relative or absolute), a priority (if multiple events are scheduled for the same time, they execute in priority order, lowest-priority first), a function to call, and a tuple of arguments to call that function with. Each of these two methods return an *event identifier*, an arbitrary token that you may store somewhere and later use to cancel a scheduled event by passing the event's token as the argument in a call to s.cancel—another advanced use which this recipe does not cover.

After scheduling some events, you call s.run, which keeps running until the queue of scheduled events is empty. In this recipe, we show how to schedule a periodic, recurring event: function perform_command reschedules itself for inc seconds later in the future as the first thing it does, before running the specified system command. In this way, the queue of scheduled events never empties, and function perform_command keeps getting called with regular periodicity. This self-rescheduling is an important idiom, not just in using sched, but any time you have a "one-shot" way to ask for something to happen in the future, and you need instead to have something happen in the future "periodically". (Tkinter's after method, e.g., also works in exactly this way, and thus is also often used with just this kind of self-rescheduling idiom.)

Even for a task as simple as the one handled by this recipe, sched still has a small advantage over the simpler roll-your-own approach used previously in recipe 3.10 "Running a Command Repeatedly." In recipe 3.10, the specified delay occurs between the *end* of one execution of cmd and the *beginning* of the next execution. If the execution of cmd takes a highly variable amount of time (as is often the case, e.g., for commands that must wait for the network, or some busy server, etc.), then the command is not really being run periodically. In this recipe, the delay occurs between *beginning* successive runs of cmd, so that periodicity is indeed guaranteed. If a certain run of cmd takes longer than inc seconds, the schedule temporarily falls behind, but it will eventually catch up again, as long as the *average* running time of cmd is less than inc seconds: sched never "skips" events. (If you *do* want an event to be skipped because it's not relevant any more, you have to keep track of the event identifier token and use the cancel method.)

For a detailed explanation of this script's structure and body, see recipe 3.10 "Running a Command Repeatedly."

See Also

Recipe 3.10 "Running a Command Repeatedly"; documentation of the standard library modules os, time, sys, and sched in the *Library Reference* and *Python in a Nutshell*.

3.12 Doing Decimal Arithmetic

Credit: Anna Martelli Ravenscroft

Problem

You want to perform some simple arithmetic computations in Python 2.4, but you want decimal results, *not* the Python default of float.

Solution

To get the normal, expected results from plain, simple computations, use the decimal module introduced in Python 2.4:

```
>>> import decimal
>>> d1 = decimal.Decimal('0.3')    # assign a decimal-number object
>>> d1/3                           # try some division
Decimal("0.1")
>>> (d1/3)*3                       # can we get back where we started?
Decimal("0.3")
```

Discussion

Newcomers to Python (particularly ones without experience with binary float calculations in other programming languages) are often surprised by the results of seemingly simple calculations. For example:

```
>>> f1 = .3                        # assign a float
>>> f1/3                           # try some division
0.099999999999999992
```

```
>>> (f1/3)*3                        # can we get back where we started?
0.29999999999999999
```

Binary floating-point arithmetic is the default in Python for very good reasons. You can read all about them in the Python FAQ (Frequently Asked Questions) document at *http://www.python.org/doc/faq/general.html#why-are-floating-point-calculations-so-inaccurate*, and even in the appendix to the *Python Tutorial* at *http://docs.python.org/tut/node15.html*.

Many people, however, were unsatisfied with binary floats being the *only* option—they wanted to be able to specify the precision, or wanted to use decimal arithmetic for monetary calculations with predictable results. Some of us just wanted the predictable results. (A True Numerical Analyst *does*, of course, find all results of binary floating-point computations to be perfectly predictable; if any of you three are reading this chapter, you can skip to the next recipe, thanks.)

The new `decimal` type affords a great deal of control over the *context* for your calculations, allowing you, for example, to set the precision and rounding method to use for the results. However, when all you want is to run simple arithmetical operations that return predictable results, `decimal`'s default context works just fine.

Just keep in mind a few points: you may pass a string, integer, tuple, or other decimal object to create a new `decimal` object, but if you have a float n that you want to make into a `decimal`, pass `str(n)`, *not* bare n. Also, `decimal` objects can interact (i.e., be subject to arithmetical operations) with integers, longs, and other `decimal` objects, but not with `floats`. These restrictions are anything but arbitrary. Decimal numbers have been added to Python exactly to provide the precision and predictability that `float` lacks: if it was allowed to build a decimal number from a `float`, or by operating with one, the whole purpose would be defeated. `decimal` objects, on the other hand, can be coerced into other numeric types such as `float`, `long`, and `int`, just as you would expect.

Keep in mind that decimal is still floating point, *not* fixed point. If you want fixed point, take a look at Tim Peter's `FixedPoint` at *http://fixedpoint.sourceforge.net/*. Also, no money data type is yet available in Python, although you can look at recipe 3.13 "Formatting Decimals as Currency" to learn how to roll-your-own money formatting on top of `decimal`. Last but not least, it is not obvious (at least not to me), when an intermediate computation produces more digits than the inputs, whether you should keep the extra digits for further intermediate computations, and round only when you're done computing a formula (and are about to display or store a result), or whether you should instead round at each step. Different textbooks suggest different answers. I tend to do the former, simply because it's more convenient.

If you're stuck with Python 2.3, you may still take advantage of the `decimal` module, by downloading and installing it as a third-party extension—see *http://www.taniquetil.com.ar/facundo/bdvfiles/get_decimal.html*.

See Also

The explanation of floating-point arithmetic in Appendix B of the Python Tutorial at *http://docs.python.org/tut/node15.html*; the Python FAQ at *http://www.python.org/doc/faq/general.html#why-are-floating-point-calculations-so-inaccurate*; Tim Peter's FixedPoint at *http://fixedpoint.sourceforge.net/*; using decimal as currency, see recipe 3.13 "Formatting Decimals as Currency"; decimal is documented in the Python 2.4 *Library Reference* and is available for download to use with 2.3 at *http://cvs.sourceforge.net/viewcvs.py/python/python/dist/src/Lib/decimal.py*; the decimal PEP (Python Enhancement Proposal), PEP 327, is at *http://www.python.org/peps/pep-0327.html*.

3.13 Formatting Decimals as Currency

Credit: Anna Martelli Ravenscroft, Alex Martelli, Raymond Hettinger

Problem

You want to do some tax calculations and display the result in a simple report as Euro currency.

Solution

Use the new decimal module, along with a modified moneyfmt function (the original, by Raymond Hettinger, is part of the Python library reference section about decimal):

```
import decimal
""" calculate Italian invoice taxes given a subtotal. """
def italformat(value, places=2, curr='EUR', sep='.', dp=',', pos='', neg='-',
              overall=10):
    """ Convert Decimal ``value'' to a money-formatted string.
    places:  required number of places after the decimal point
    curr:    optional currency symbol before the sign (may be blank)
    sep:     optional grouping separator (comma, period, or blank) every 3
    dp:      decimal point indicator (comma or period); only specify as
                 blank when places is zero
    pos:     optional sign for positive numbers: "+", space or blank
    neg:     optional sign for negative numbers: "-", "(", space or blank
    overall: optional overall length of result, adds padding on the
                 left, between the currency symbol and digits
    """
    q = decimal.Decimal((0, (1,), -places))      # 2 places --> '0.01'
    sign, digits, exp = value.quantize(q).as_tuple()
    result = [ ]
    digits = map(str, digits)
    append, next = result.append, digits.pop
    for i in range(places):
        if digits:
```

```
                append(next())
            else:
                append('0')
        append(dp)
        i = 0
        while digits:
            append(next())
            i += 1
            if i == 3 and digits:
                i = 0
                append(sep)
        while len(result) < overall:
            append(' ')
        append(curr)
        if sign: append(neg)
        else: append(pos)
        result.reverse()
        return ''.join(result)
    # get the subtotal for use in calculations
    def getsubtotal(subtin=None):
        if subtin == None:
            subtin = input("Enter the subtotal: ")
        subtotal = decimal.Decimal(str(subtin))
        print "\n subtotal:                ", italformat(subtotal)
        return subtotal
    # specific Italian tax law functions
    def cnpcalc(subtotal):
        contrib = subtotal * decimal.Decimal('.02')
        print "+ contributo integrativo 2%:    ", italformat(contrib, curr='')
        return contrib
    def vatcalc(subtotal, cnp):
        vat = (subtotal+cnp) * decimal.Decimal('.20')
        print "+ IVA 20%:                 ", italformat(vat, curr='')
        return vat
    def ritacalc(subtotal):
        rit = subtotal * decimal.Decimal('.20')
        print "-Ritenuta d'acconto 20%:       ", italformat(rit, curr='')
        return rit
    def dototal(subtotal, cnp, iva=0, rit=0):
        totl = (subtotal+cnp+iva)-rit
        print "                    TOTALE: ", italformat(totl)
        return totl
    # overall calculations report
    def invoicer(subtotal=None, context=None):
        if context is None:
            decimal.getcontext().rounding="ROUND_HALF_UP"      # Euro rounding rules
        else:
            decimal.setcontext(context)                        # set to context arg
        subtot = getsubtotal(subtotal)
        contrib = cnpcalc(subtot)
        dototal(subtot, contrib, vatcalc(subtot, contrib), ritacalc(subtot))
    if __name__=='__main__':
        print "Welcome to the invoice calculator"
        tests = [100, 1000.00, "10000", 555.55]
```

```
print "Euro context"
for test in tests:
    invoicer(test)
print "default context"
for test in tests:
    invoicer(test, context=decimal.DefaultContext)
```

Discussion

Italian tax calculations are somewhat complicated, more so than this recipe demonstrates. This recipe applies only to invoicing customers within Italy. I soon got tired of doing them by hand, so I wrote a simple Python script to do the calculations for me. I've currently refactored into the version shown in this recipe, using the new decimal module, just on the principle that money computations should never, but *never*, be done with binary floats.

How to best use the new decimal module for monetary calculations was not immediately obvious. While the decimal arithmetic is pretty straightforward, the options for displaying results were less clear. The italformat function in the recipe is based on Raymond Hettinger's moneyfmt recipe, found in the decimal module documentation available in the Python 2.4 *Library Reference*. Some minor modifications were helpful for my reporting purposes. The primary addition was the overall parameter. This parameter builds a decimal with a specific number of overall digits, with whitespace padding between the currency symbol (if any) and the digits. This eases alignment issues when the results are of a standard, predictable length.

Notice that I have coerced the subtotal input subtin to be a string in subtotal = decimal.Decimal(str(subtin)). This makes it possible to feed floats (as well as integers or strings) to getsubtotal without worry—without this, a float would raise an exception. If your program is likely to pass tuples, refactor the code to handle that. In my case, a float was a rather likely input to getsubtotal, but I didn't have to worry about tuples.

Of course, if you need to display using U.S. $, or need to use other rounding rules, it's easy enough to modify things to suit your needs. For example, to display U.S. currency, you could change the curr, sep, and dp arguments' default values as follows:

```
def USformat(value, places=2, curr='$', sep=',', dp='.', pos='', neg='-',
        overall=10):
    ...
```

If you regularly have to use multiple currency formats, you may choose to refactor the function so that it looks up the appropriate arguments in a dictionary, or you may want to find other ways to pass the appropriate arguments. In theory, the locale module in the Python Standard Library should be the standard way to let your code access locale-related preferences such as those connected to money formatting, but in practice I've never had much luck using locale (for this or any other purpose), so that's one task that I'll gladly leave as an exercise to the reader.

Countries often have specific rules on rounding; decimal uses ROUND_HALF_EVEN as the default. However, the Euro rules specify ROUND_HALF_UP. To use different rounding rules, change the context, as shown in the recipe. The result of this change may or may not be obvious, but one should be aware that it *can* make a (small, but legally not negligible) difference.

You can also change the context more extensively, by creating and setting your own context class instance. A change in context, whether set by a simple getcontext attribution change, or with a custom context class instance passed to setcontext(mycontext), continues to apply throughout the active thread, until you change it. If you are considering using decimal in production code (or even for your own home bookkeeping use), be sure to use the right context (in particular, the correct rounding rules) for your country's accounting practices.

See Also

Python 2.4's *Library Reference* on decimal, particularly the section on decimal.context and the "recipes" at the end of that section.

3.14 Using Python as a Simple Adding Machine

Credit: Brett Cannon

Problem

You want to use Python as a simple adding machine, with accurate decimal (not binary floating-point!) computations and a "tape" that shows the numbers in an uncluttered columnar view.

Solution

To perform the computations, we can rely on the decimal module. We accept input lines, each made up of a number followed by an arithmetic operator, an empty line to request the current total, and q to terminate the program:

```
import decimal, re, operator
parse_input = re.compile(r'''(?x)     # allow comments and whitespace in the RE
                (\d+\.?\d*)            # number with optional decimal part
                \s*                    # optional whitespace
                ([-+/*])               # operator
                $''')                  # end-of-string
oper = { '+': operator.add, '-': operator.sub,
         '*': operator.mul, '/': operator.truediv,
       }
total = decimal.Decimal('0')
def print_total():
```

```
        print '=====\n', total
    print """Welcome to Adding Machine:
Enter a number and operator,
an empty line to see the current subtotal,
or q to quit: """
    while True:
        try:
            tape_line = raw_input().strip()
        except EOFError:
            tape_line = 'q'
        if not tape_line:
            print_total()
            continue
        elif tape_line == 'q':
            print_total()
            break
        try:
            num_text, op = parse_input.match(tape_line).groups()
        except AttributeError:
            print 'Invalid entry: %r' % tape_line
            print 'Enter number and operator, empty line for total, q to quit'
            continue
        total = oper[op](total, decimal.Decimal(num_text))
```

Discussion

Python's interactive interpreter is often a useful calculator, but a simpler "adding machine" also has its uses. For example, an expression such as 2345634+2894756-2345823 is not easy to read, so checking that you're entering the right numbers for a computation is not all that simple. An adding machine's tape shows numbers in a simple, uncluttered columnar view, making it easier to double check what you have entered. Moreover, the decimal module performs computations in the normal, decimal-based way we need in real life, rather than in the floating-point arithmetic preferred by scientists, engineers, and today's computers.

When you run the script in this recipe from a normal command shell (this script is *not* meant to be run from within a Python interactive interpreter!), the script prompts you once, and then just sits there, waiting for input. Type a number (one or more digits, then optionally a decimal point, then optionally more digits), followed by an operator (/, *, -, or +—the four operator characters you find on the numeric keypad on your keyboard), and then press return. The script applies the number to the running total using the operator. To output the current total, just enter a blank line. To quit, enter the letter q and press return. This simple interface matches the input/output conventions of a typical simple adding machine, removing the need to have some other form of output.

The decimal package is part of Python's standard library since version 2.4. If you're still using Python 2.3, visit *http://www.taniquetil.com.ar/facundo/bdvfiles/get_decimal.html* and download and install the package in whatever form is most convenient for you. decimal allows high-precision decimal arithmetic, which is more convenient for many uses (such as any computation involving money) than the binary floating-point computations that are faster on today's computers and which Python uses by default. No more lost pennies due to hard-to-understand issues with binary floating point! As demonstrated in recipe 3.13 "Formatting Decimals as Currency," you can even change the rounding rules from the default of ROUND_HALF_EVEN, if you really need to.

This recipe's script is meant to be very simple, so many improvements are possible. A useful enhancement would be to keep the "tape" on disk for later checking. You can do that easily, by adding, just before the loop, a statement to open some appropriate text file for append:

```
tapefile = open('tapefile.txt', 'a')
```

and, just after the try/except statement that obtains a value for tape_line, a statement to write that value to the file:

```
tapefile.write(tape_line+'\n')
```

If you do want to make these additions, you will probably also want to enrich function print_total so that it writes to the "tape" file as well as to the command window, therefore, change the function to:

```
def print_total():
    print '=====\n', total
    tapefile.write('=====\n' + str(total) + '\n')
```

The write method of a file object accepts a string as its argument and does not implicitly terminate the line as the print statement does, so we need to explicitly call the str built-in function and explicitly add '\n' as needed. Alternatively, the second statement in this version of print_total could be coded in a way closer to the first one:

```
print >>tapefile, '=====\n', total
```

Some people really dislike this print >>somefile, syntax, but it can come in handy in cases such as this one.

More ambitious improvements would be to remove the need to press Return after each operator (that would require performing unbuffered input and dealing with one character at a time, rather than using the handy but line-oriented built-in function raw_input as the recipe does—see recipe 2.23 "Reading an Unbuffered Character in a Cross-Platform Way" for a cross-platform way to get unbuffered input), to add a clear function (or clarify to users that inputting 0* will zero out the "tape"), and even to add a GUI that looks like an adding machine. However, I'm leaving any such improvements as exercises for the reader.

One important point about the recipe's implementation is the oper dictionary, which uses operator characters (/, *, -, +) as keys and the appropriate arithmetic functions from the built-in module operator, as corresponding values. The same effect could be obtained, more verbosely, by a "tree" of if/elif, such as:

```
if op == '+':
    total = total + decimal.Decimal(num_text)
elif op == '-':
    total = total - decimal.Decimal(num_text)
elif op == '*':
    <line_annotation>... and so on ...</line_annotation>
```

However, Python dictionaries are very idiomatic and handy for such uses, and they lead to less repetitious and thus more maintainable code.

See Also

decimal is documented in the Python 2.4 *Library Reference*, and is available for download to use with 2.3 at *http://www.taniquetil.com.ar/facundo/bdvfiles/get_decimal.html*; you can read the decimal PEP 327 at *http://www.python.org/peps/pep-0327.html*.

3.15 Checking a Credit Card Checksum

Credit: David Shaw, Miika Keskinen

Problem

You need to check whether a credit card number respects the industry standard Luhn checksum algorithm.

Solution

Luhn mod 10 is the credit card industry's standard for credit card checksums. It's not built into Python, but it's easy to roll our own computation for it:

```
def cardLuhnChecksumIsValid(card_number):
    """ checks to make sure that the card passes a luhn mod-10 checksum """
    sum = 0
    num_digits = len(card_number)
    oddeven = num_digits & 1
    for count in range(num_digits):
        digit = int(card_number[count])
        if not (( count & 1 ) ^ oddeven):
            digit = digit * 2
        if digit > 9:
            digit = digit - 9
        sum = sum + digit
    return (sum % 10) == 0
```

Discussion

This recipe was originally written for a now-defunct e-commerce application to be used within Zope.

It can save you time and money to apply this simple validation before trying to process a bad or miskeyed card with your credit card vendor, because you won't waste money trying to authorize a bad card number. The recipe has wider applicability because many government identification numbers also use the Luhn (i.e., modulus 10) algorithm.

A full suite of credit card validation methods is available at *http:// david.theresistance.net/files/creditValidation.py*

If you're into cool one-liners rather than simplicity and clarity, (a) you're reading the wrong book (the *Perl Cookbook* is a great book that will make you much happier), (b) meanwhile, to keep you smiling while you go purchase a more appropriate oeuvre, try:

```
checksum = lambda a: (
    10 - sum([int(y)*[7,3,1][x%3] for x, y in enumerate(str(a)[::-1])])%10)%10
```

See Also

A good therapist, if you *do* prefer the one-line checksum version.

3.16 Watching Foreign Exchange Rates

Credit: Victor Yongwei Yang

Problem

You want to monitor periodically (with a Python script to be run by *crontab* or as a Windows scheduled task) an exchange rate between two currencies, obtained from the Web, and receive email alerts when the rate crosses a certain threshold.

Solution

This task is similar to other monitoring tasks that you could perform on numbers easily obtained from the Web, be they exchange rates, stock quotes, wind-chill factors, or whatever. Let's see specifically how to monitor the exchange rate between U.S. and Canadian dollars, as reported by the Bank of Canada web site (as a simple CSV (comma-separated values) feed that is easy to parse):

```
import httplib
import smtplib
# configure script's parameters here
thresholdRate = 1.30
smtpServer = 'smtp.freebie.com'
fromaddr = 'foo@bar.com'
```

```
toaddrs = 'your@corp.com'
# end of configuration
url = '/en/financial_markets/csv/exchange_eng.csv'
conn = httplib.HTTPConnection('www.bankofcanada.ca')
conn.request('GET', url)
response = conn.getresponse( )
data = response.read( )
start = data.index('United States Dollar')
line = data[start:data.index('\n', start)]    # get the relevant line
rate = line.split(',')[-1]                     # last field on the line
if float(rate) < thresholdRate:
    # send email
    msg = 'Subject: Bank of Canada exchange rate alert %s' % rate
    server = smtplib.SMTP(smtpServer)
    server.sendmail(fromaddr, toaddrs, msg)
    server.quit( )
conn.close( )
```

Discussion

When working with foreign currencies, it is particularly useful to have an automated way of getting the conversions you need. This recipe provides this functionality in a quite simple, straightforward manner. When cron runs this script, the script goes to the site, and gets the CSV feed, which provides the daily noon exchange rates for the previous seven days:

```
Date (m/d/year),11/12/2004,11/15/2004, ... ,11/19/2004,11/22/2004
$Can/US closing rate,1.1927,1.2005,1.1956,1.1934,1.2058,1.1930,
United States Dollar,1.1925,1.2031,1.1934,1.1924,1.2074,1.1916,1.1844
...
```

The script then continues to find the specific currency ('United States Dollar') and reads the last field to find today's rate. If you're having trouble understanding how that works, it may be helpful to break it down:

```
US = data.find('United States Dollar')  # find the index of the currency
endofUSline = data.index('\n', US)      # find index for that line end
USline = data[US:endofUSline]           # slice to make one string
rate = USline.split(',')[-1]            # split on ',' and return last field
```

The recipe provides an email alert when the rate falls below a particular threshold, which can be configured to whatever rate you prefer (e.g., you could change that statement to send you an alert whenever the rate changes outside a threshold range).

See Also

httplib, smtplib, and string function are documented in the *Library Reference* and *Python in a Nutshell*.

CHAPTER 4

Python Shortcuts

4.0 Introduction

Credit: David Ascher, ActiveState, co-author of Learning Python

Programming languages are like natural languages. Each has a set of qualities that polyglots generally agree on as characteristics of the language. Russian and French are often admired for their lyricism, while English is more often cited for its precision and dynamism: unlike the Académie-defined French language, the English language routinely grows words to suit its speakers' needs, such as "carjacking," "earwitness," "snailmail," "email," "googlewhacking," and "blogging." In the world of computer languages, Perl is well known for its many degrees of freedom: TMTOWTDI (There's More Than One Way To Do It) is one of the mantras of the Perl programmer. Conciseness is also seen as a strong virtue in the Perl and APL communities. As you'll see in many of the discussions of recipes throughout this volume, in contrast, Python programmers often express their belief in the value of clarity and elegance. As a well-known Perl hacker once told me, Python's prettier, but Perl is more fun. I agree with him that Python does have a strong (as in well-defined) aesthetic, while Perl has more of a sense of humor.

The reason I mention these seemingly irrelevant characteristics at the beginning of this chapter is that the recipes you see in this chapter are directly related to Python's aesthetic and social dynamics. If this book had been about Perl, the recipes in a shortcuts chapter would probably elicit head scratching, contemplation, an "a-ha"! moment, and then a burst of laughter, as the reader grokked the genius behind a particular trick. In contrast, in most of the recipes in this chapter, the author presents a single elegant language feature, but one that he feels is underappreciated. Much like I, a proud resident of Vancouver, will go out of my way to show tourists the really neat things about the city, from the parks to the beaches to the mountains, a Python user will seek out friends and colleagues and say, "You gotta see this!" For me and most of the programmers I know, programming in Python is a shared social pleasure, not a competitive pursuit. There is great pleasure in learning a new feature and appreciating its design, elegance, and judicious use, and there's a twin pleasure in teaching another or another thousand about that feature.

A word about the history of the chapter: back when we identified the recipe categories for the first edition of this collection, our driving notion was that there would be recipes of various kinds, each with a specific goal—a soufflé, a tart, an osso buco. Those recipes would naturally fall into fairly typical categories, such as desserts, appetizers, and meat dishes, or their perhaps less appetizing, nonmetaphorical equivalents, such as files, algorithms, and so on. So we picked a list of categories, added the categories to the Zope site used to collect recipes, and opened the floodgates.

Soon, it became clear that some submissions were hard to fit into the predetermined categories. There's a reason for that, and cooking helps explain why. The recipes in this chapter are the Pythonic equivalent of making a roux (a cooked mixture of fat and flour, used in making sauces, for those of you without a classic French cooking background), kneading dough, flouring, separating eggs, flipping a pan's contents, blanching, and the myriad other tricks that any accomplished cook knows, but that you won't find in a typical cookbook. Many of these tricks and techniques are used in preparing meals, but it's hard to pigeonhole them as relevant for a given type of dish. And if you're a novice cook looking up a fancy recipe, you're likely to get frustrated quickly because serious cookbook authors assume you know these techniques, and they explain them (with illustrations!) only in books with titles such as *Cooking for Divorced Middle-Aged Men*. We didn't want to exclude this precious category of tricks from this book, so a new category was born (sorry, no illustrations).

In the introduction to this chapter in the first edition, I presciently said:

> I believe that the recipes in this chapter are among the most time-sensitive of the recipes in this volume. That's because the aspects of the language that people consider shortcuts or noteworthy techniques seem to be relatively straightforward, idiomatic applications of recent language features.

I can proudly say that I was right. This new edition, significantly focused on the present definition of the language, makes many of the original recipes irrelevant. In the two Python releases since the book's first edition, Python 2.3 and 2.4, the language has evolved to incorporate the ideas of those recipes into new syntactic features or library functions, just as it had done with every previous major release, making a cleaner, more compact, and yet more powerful language that's as much fun to use today as it was over ten years ago.

All in all, about half the recipes in this chapter (roughly the same proportion as in the rest of the book) are entirely new ones, while the other half are vastly revised (mostly simplified) versions of recipes that were in the first edition. Thanks to the simplifications, and to the focus on just two language versions (2.3 and 2.4) rather than the whole panoply of older versions that was covered by the first edition, this chapter, as well as the book as a whole, has over one-third more recipes than the first edition did.

It's worth noting in closing that many of the recipes that are in this newly revised chapter touch on some of the most fundamental, unchanging aspects of the language: the semantics of assignment, binding, copy, and references; sequences; dictionaries. These ideas are all keys to the Pythonic approach to programming, and seeing these recipes live for several years makes me wonder whether Python will evolve in the next few years in related directions.

4.1   Copying an Object

Credit: Anna Martelli Ravenscroft, Peter Cogolo

Problem

You want to copy an object. However, when you assign an object, pass it as an argument, or return it as a result, Python uses a reference to the original object, without making a copy.

Solution

Module copy in the standard Python library offers two functions to create copies. The one you should generally use is the function named copy, which returns a new object containing exactly the same items and attributes as the object you're copying:

```
import copy
new_list = copy.copy(existing_list)
```

On the rare occasions when you also want every item and attribute in the object to be separately copied, recursively, use deepcopy:

```
import copy
new_list_of_dicts = copy.deepcopy(existing_list_of_dicts)
```

Discussion

When you assign an object (or pass it as an argument, or return it as a result), Python (like Java) uses a reference to the original object, not a copy. Some other programming languages make copies every time you assign something. Python never makes copies "implicitly" just because you're assigning: to get a copy, you must specifically *request* a copy.

Python's behavior is simple, fast, and uniform. However, if you do need a copy and do not ask for one, you may have problems. For example:

```
>>> a = [1, 2, 3]
>>> b = a
>>> b.append(5)
>>> print a, b
[1, 2, 3, 5] [1, 2, 3, 5]
```

Here, the names a and b both refer to the same object (a list), so once we alter the object through one of these names, we later see the altered object no matter which name we use for it. No original, unaltered copy is left lying about anywhere.

 To become an effective Python programmer, it is crucial that you learn to draw the distinction between *altering an object* and *assigning to a name*, which previously happened to refer to the object. These two kinds of operations have nothing to do with each other. A statement such as a=[ ] rebinds name *a* but performs no alteration at all on the object that was previously bound to name *a*. Therefore, the issue of references versus copies just doesn't arise in this case: the issue is meaningful only when you *alter* some object.

If you are about to alter an object, but you want to keep the original object unaltered, you must make a copy. As this recipe's solution explains, the module copy from the Python Standard Library offers two functions to make copies. Normally, you use copy.copy, which makes a *shallow copy*—it copies an object, but for each attribute or item of the object, it continues to share references, which is faster and saves memory.

Shallow copying, alas, isn't sufficient to entirely "decouple" a copied object from the original one, if you propose to alter the items or attributes of either object, not just the object itself:

```
>>> list_of_lists = [ ['a'], [1, 2], ['z', 23] ]
>>> copy_lol = copy.copy(lists_of_lists)
>>> copy_lol[1].append('boo')
>>> print list_of_lists, copy_lol
[['a'], [1, 2, 'boo'], ['z', 23]] [['a'], [1, 2, 'boo'], ['z', 23]]
```

Here, the names list_of_lists and copy_lol refer to distinct objects (two lists), so we could alter either of them without affecting the other. However, each *item* of list_of_lists is the same object as the corresponding item of copy_lol, so once we alter an item reached by indexing either of these names, we later see the altered item no matter which object we're indexing to reach it.

If you do need to copy some container object *and* also recursively copy all objects it refers to (meaning all items, all attributes, and also items of items, items of attributes, etc.), use copy.deepcopy—such deep copying may cost you substantial amounts of time and memory, but if you gotta, you gotta. For deep copies, copy.deepcopy is the only way to go.

For normal shallow copies, you may have good alternatives to copy.copy, if you know the type of the object you want to copy. To copy a list L, call list(L); to copy a dict d, call dict(d); to copy a set s (in Python 2.4, which introduces the built-in type set), call set(s). (Since list, dict, and, in 2.4, set, are built-in names, you do not need to perform any "preparation" before you use any of them.) You get the general pattern: to copy a copyable object o, which belongs to some built-in Python type t, you may generally just call t(o). dicts also offer a dedicated method to perform a shallow copy: d.copy( ) and dict(d) do the same thing. Of the two, I suggest you use dict(d): it's more uniform with respect to other types, and it's even shorter by one character!

To copy instances of arbitrary types or classes, whether you coded them or got them from a library, just use copy.copy. If you code your own classes, it's generally not worth the bother to define your own copy or clone method. If you want to customize the way instances of your class get (shallowly) copied, your class can supply a special method __copy__ (see recipe 6.9 "Making a Fast Copy of an Object" for a special technique relating to the implementation of such a method), or special methods __getstate__ and __setstate__. (See recipe 7.4 "Using the cPickle Module on Classes and Instances" for notes on these special methods, which also help with deep copying and serialization—i.e., *pickling*—of instances of your class.) If you want to customize the way instances of your class get *deeply* copied, your class can supply a special method __deepcopy__ (see recipe 6.9 "Making a Fast Copy of an Object.")

Note that you do not need to copy immutable objects (strings, numbers, tuples, etc.) because you don't have to worry about altering them. If you do try to perform such a copy, you'll just get the original right back; no harm done, but it's a waste of time and code. For example:

```
>>> s = 'cat'
>>> t = copy.copy(s)
>>> s is t
True
```

The is operator checks whether two objects are not merely equal, but in fact the *same* object (is checks for *identity*; for checking mere *equality*, you use the == operator). Checking object identity is not particularly useful for immutable objects (we're using it here just to show that the call to copy.copy was useless, although innocuous). However, checking object identity can sometimes be quite important for mutable objects. For example, if you're not sure whether two names a and b refer to separate objects, or whether both refer to the same object, a simple and very fast check a is b lets you know how things stand. That way you know whether you need to copy the object before altering it, in case you want to keep the original object unaltered.

 You can use other, inferior ways exist to create copies, namely building your own. Given a list L, both a "whole-object slice" L[:] and a list comprehension [x for x in L] do happen to make a (shallow) copy of L, as do adding an empty list, L+[ ], and multiplying the list by 1, L*1 ... but each of these constructs is just wasted effort and obfuscation—calling list(L) is clearer and faster. You should, however, be familiar with the L[:] construct because for historical reasons it's widely used. So, even though you're best advised not to use it yourself, you'll see it in Python code written by others.

Similarly, given a dictionary *d*, you could create a shallow copy named *d1* by coding out a loop:

```
>>> d1 = { }
>>> for somekey in d:
...     d1[somekey] = d[somekey]
```

or more concisely by d1 = { }; d1.update(d). However, again, such coding is a waste of time and effort and produces nothing but obfuscated, fatter, and slower code. Use d1=dict(d), be happy!

See Also

Module copy in the *Library Reference* and *Python in a Nutshell*.

4.2 Constructing Lists with List Comprehensions

Credit: Luther Blissett

Problem

You want to construct a new list by operating on elements of an existing sequence (or other kind of iterable).

Solution

Say you want to create a new list by adding 23 to each item of some other list. A list comprehension expresses this idea directly:

```
thenewlist = [x + 23 for x in theoldlist]
```

Similarly, say you want the new list to comprise all items in the other list that are larger than 5. A list comprehension says exactly that:

```
thenewlist = [x for x in theoldlist if x > 5]
```

When you want to combine both ideas, you can perform selection with an if clause, and also use some expression, such as adding 23, on the selected items, in a single pass:

```
thenewlist = [x + 23 for x in theoldlist if x > 5]
```

Discussion

Elegance, clarity, and pragmatism, are Python's core values. List comprehensions show how pragmatism can enhance both clarity and elegance. Indeed, list comprehensions are often the best approach even when, instinctively, you're thinking not of constructing a new list but rather of "altering an existing list". For example, if your task is to set all items greater than 100 to 100, in an existing list object L, the best solution is:

```
L[:] = [min(x,100) for x in L]
```

Assigning to the "whole-list slice" L[:] alters the existing list object in place, rather than just rebinding the *name* L, as would be the case if you coded L = . . . instead.

You should not use a list comprehension when you simply want to perform a loop. When you want a loop, code a loop. For an example of looping over a list, see recipe 4.4 "Looping over Items and Their Indices in a Sequence." See Chapter 19 for more information about iteration in Python.

It's also best not to use a list comprehension when another built-in does what you want even more directly and immediately. For example, to copy a list, use L1 = list(L), *not*:

```
L1 = [x for x in L]
```

Similarly, when the operation you want to perform on each item is to call a function on the item and use the function's result, use L1 = map(f, L) rather than L1 = [f(x) for x in L]. But in most cases, a list comprehension is just right.

In Python 2.4, you should consider using a generator expression, rather than a list comprehension, when the sequence may be long and you only need one item at a time. The syntax of generator expressions is just the same as for list comprehensions, except that generator expressions are surrounded by parentheses, (and), not brackets, [and]. For example, say that we only need the summation of the list computed in this recipe's Solution, not each item of the list. In Python 2.3, we would code:

```
total = sum([x + 23 for x in theoldlist if x > 5])
```

In Python 2.4, we can code more naturally, omitting the brackets (no need to add additional parentheses—the parentheses already needed to call the built-in sum suffice):

```
total = sum(x + 23 for x in theoldlist if x > 5)
```

Besides being a little bit cleaner, this method avoids materializing the list as a whole in memory and thus may be slightly faster when the list is extremely long.

See Also

The *Reference Manual* section on list displays (another name for list comprehensions) and Python 2.4 generator expressions; Chapter 19; the *Library Reference* and *Python in a Nutshell* docs on the itertools module and on the built-in functions map, filter, and sum; Haskell is at *http://www.haskell.org*.

Python borrowed list comprehensions from the functional language Haskell (*http://www.haskell.org*), changing the syntax to use keywords rather than punctuation. If you do know Haskell, though, take care! Haskell's list comprehensions, like the rest of Haskell, use *lazy evaluation* (also known as *normal order* or *call by need*). Each item is computed only when it's needed. Python, like most other languages, uses (for list comprehensions as well as elsewhere) *eager evaluation* (also known as *applicative order*, *call by value*, or *strict evaluation*). That is, the entire list is computed when the list comprehension executes, and kept in memory afterwards as long as necessary. If you are translating into Python a Haskell program that uses list comprehensions to represent infinite sequences, or even just long sequences of which only one item at a time must be kept around, Python list comprehensions may not be suitable. Rather, look into Python 2.4's new *generator expressions*, whose semantics are closer to the spirit of Haskell's lazy evaluation—each item gets computed only when needed.

4.3 Returning an Element of a List If It Exists

Credit: Nestor Nissen, A. Bass

Problem

You have a list L and an index i, and you want to get L[i] when i is a valid index into L; otherwise, you want to get a default value v. If L were a dictionary, you'd use L.get(i, v), but lists don't have a get method.

Solution

Clearly, we need to code a function, and, in this case, the simplest and most direct approach is the best one:

```
def list_get(L, i, v=None):
    if -len(L) <= i < len(L): return L[i]
    else: return v
```

Discussion

The function in this recipe just checks whether i is a valid index by applying Python's indexing rule: valid indices are negative ones down to -len(L) inclusive, and non-negative ones up to len(L) exclusive. If almost all calls to list_get pass a valid index value for i, you might prefer an alternative approach:

```
def list_get_egfp(L, i, v=None):
    try: return L[i]
    except IndexError: return v
```

However, unless a vast majority of the calls pass a valid index, this alternative (as some time-measurements show) can be up to four times slower than the list_get function shown in the solution. Therefore, this "easier to get forgiveness than permission" (EGFP) approach, although it is often preferable in Python, cannot be recommended for this specific case.

I've also tried quite a few fancy, intricate and obscure approaches, but, besides being hard to explain and to understand, they all end up slower than the plain, simple function list_get. General principle: when you write Python code, prefer clarity and readability to compactness and terseness—choose simplicity over subtlety. You often will be rewarded with code that runs faster, and invariably, you will end up with code that is less prone to bugs and is easier to maintain, which is far more important than minor speed differences in 99.9% of the cases you encounter in the real world.

See Also

Language Reference and *Python in a Nutshell* documentation on list indexing.

4.4   Looping over Items and Their Indices in a Sequence

Credit: Alex Martelli, Sami Hangaslammi

Problem

You need to loop on a sequence, but at each step you also need to know which index into the sequence you have reached (e.g., because you need to rebind some entries in the sequence), and Python's preferred approach to looping doesn't use the indices.

Solution

That's what built-in function enumerate is for. For example:

```
for index, item in enumerate(sequence):
    if item > 23:
        sequence[index] = transform(item)
```

This is cleaner, more readable, and faster than the alternative of looping over indices and accessing items by indexing:

```
for index in range(len(sequence)):
    if sequence[index] > 23:
        sequence[index] = transform(sequence[index])
```

Discussion

Looping on a sequence is a very frequent need, and Python strongly encourages you to do just that, looping on the sequence directly. In other words, the Pythonic way to get each item in a sequence is to use:

```
for item in sequence:
    process(item)
```

rather than the indirect approach, typical of lower-level languages, of looping over the sequence's indices and using each index to fetch the corresponding item:

```
for index in range(len(sequence)):
    process(sequence[index])
```

Looping directly is cleaner, more readable, faster, and more general (since you can loop on any iterable, by definition, while indexing works only on sequences, such as lists).

However, sometimes you do need to know the index, as well as the corresponding item, within the loop. The most frequent reason for this need is that, in order to rebind an entry in a list, you must assign the new item to thelist[index]. To support this need, Python offers the built-in function enumerate, which takes any iterable argument and returns an iterator yielding all the pairs (two-item tuples) of the form (index, item), one pair at a time. By writing your for loop's header clause in the form:

```
for index, item in enumerate(sequence):
```

both the index and the item are available within the loop's body.

For help remembering the order of the items in each pair enumerate yields, think of the idiom d=dict(enumerate(L)). This gives a dictionary d that's equivalent to list L, in the sense that d[i] is L[i] for any valid non-negative index i.

See Also

Library Reference and *Python in a Nutshell* section about enumerate; Chapter 19.

4.5 Creating Lists of Lists Without Sharing References

Credit: David Ascher

Problem

You want to create a multidimensional list but want to avoid implicit reference sharing.

Solution

To build a list and avoid implicit reference sharing, use a list comprehension. For example, to build a 5 x 10 array of zeros:

```
multilist = [[0 for col in range(5)] for row in range(10)]
```

Discussion

When a newcomer to Python is first shown that multiplying a list by an integer repeats that list that many times, the newcomer often gets quite excited about it, since it is such an elegant notation. For example:

```
>>> alist = [0] * 5
```

is clearly an excellent way to get an array of 5 zeros.

The problem is that one-dimensional tasks often grow a second dimension, so there is a natural progression to:

```
>>> multi = [[0] * 5] * 3
>>> print multi
[[0, 0, 0, 0, 0], [0, 0, 0, 0, 0], [0, 0, 0, 0, 0]]
```

This appears to work, but the same newcomer is then often puzzled by bugs, which typically can be boiled down to a snippet such as:

```
>>> multi[0][0] = 'oops!'
>>> print multi
[['oops!', 0, 0, 0, 0], ['oops!', 0, 0, 0, 0], ['oops!', 0, 0, 0, 0]]
```

This issue confuses most programmers at least once, if not a few times (see the FAQ entry at *http://www.python.org/doc/FAQ.html#4.50*). To understand the issue, it helps to decompose the creation of the multidimensional list into two steps:

```
>>> row = [0] * 5        # a list with five references to 0
>>> multi = [row] * 3    # a list with three references to the row object
```

This decomposed snippet produces a multi that's identical to that given by the more concise snippet [[0]*5]*3 shown earlier, and it has exactly the same problem: if you now assign a value to multi[0][0], you have also changed the value of multi[1][0] and that of multi[2][0] ... , and, indeed, you have changed the value of row[0], too!

The comments are key to understanding the source of the confusion. Multiplying a sequence by a number creates a new sequence with the specified number of new references to the original contents. In the case of the creation of row, it doesn't matter whether or not references are being duplicated, since the referent (the object being referred to) is a number, and therefore immutable. In other words, there is no practical difference between an object and a reference to an object if that object is immutable. In the second line, however, we create a new list containing three references to the contents of the [row] list, which holds a single reference to a list. Thus, multi contains three references to a single list object. So, when the first element of the first element of multi is changed, you are actually modifying the first element of the shared list. Hence the surprise.

List comprehensions, as shown in the "Solution", avoid the problem. With list comprehensions, no sharing of references occurs—you have a truly nested computation. If you have followed the discussion thoroughly, it may have occurred to you that we don't really need the *inner* list comprehension, only the *outer* one. In other words, couldn't we get just the same effect with:

```
multilist = [[0]*5 for row in range(10)]
```

The answer is that, yes, we could, and in fact using list multiplication for the innermost axis and list comprehension for all outer ones is faster—over twice as fast in this example. So why don't I recommend this latest solution? Answer: the speed improvement for this example is from 57 down to 24 microseconds in Python 2.3, from 49 to 21 in Python 2.4, on a typical PC of several years ago (AMD Athlon 1.2 GHz CPU, running Linux). Shaving a few tens of microseconds from a list-creation operation makes no real difference to your application's performance: and you should optimize your code, if at all, only where it matters, where it makes a substantial and important difference to the performance of your application as a whole. Therefore, I prefer the code shown in the recipe's Solution, simply because using the same construct for both the inner and the outer list creations makes it more conceptually symmetrical and easier to read!

See Also

Documentation for the range built-in function in the *Library Reference* and *Python in a Nutshell*.

4.6   Flattening a Nested Sequence

Credit: Luther Blissett, Holger Krekel, Hemanth Sethuram, ParzAspen Aspen

Problem

Some of the items in a sequence may in turn be sub-sequences, and so on, to arbitrary depth of "nesting". You need to loop over a "flattened" sequence, "expanding" each sub-sequence into a single, flat sequence of scalar items. (A *scalar*, or *atom*, is anything that is not a sequence—i.e., a *leaf*, if you think of the nested sequence as a tree.)

Solution

We need to be able to tell which of the elements we're handling are "subsequences" to be "expanded" and which are "scalars" to be yielded as is. For generality, we can take an argument that's a *predicate* to tell us *what* items we are to expand. (A *predicate* is a function that we can call on any element and that returns a truth value: in this case, True if the element is a subsequence we are to expand, False otherwise.) By default, we can arbitrarily say that every list or tuple is to be "expanded", and nothing else. Then, a recursive generator offers the simplest solution:

```
def list_or_tuple(x):
    return isinstance(x, (list, tuple))
```

```
def flatten(sequence, to_expand=list_or_tuple):
    for item in sequence:
        if to_expand(item):
            for subitem in flatten(item, to_expand):
                yield subitem
        else:
            yield item
```

Discussion

Flattening a nested sequence, or, equivalently, "walking" sequentially over all the leaves of a "tree", is a common task in many kinds of applications. You start with a nested structure, with items grouped into sequences and subsequences, and, for some purposes, you don't care about the structure at all. You just want to deal with the items, one after the other. For example,

```
for x in flatten([1, 2, [3, [ ], 4, [5, 6], 7, [8,], ], 9]):
    print x,
```

emits **1 2 3 4 5 6 7 8 9**.

The only problem with this common task is that, in the general case, determining what is to be "expanded", and what is to be yielded as a scalar, is not as obvious as it might seem. So, I ducked that decision, delegating it to a callable predicate argument that the caller can pass to flatten, unless the caller accepts flatten's somewhat simplistic default behavior of expanding just tuples and lists.

In the same module as flatten, we should also supply another predicate that a caller might well want to use—a predicate that will expand just about any iterable *except* strings (plain and Unicode). Strings are iterable, but almost invariably applications want to treat them as scalars, not as subsequences.

To identify whether an object is iterable, we just need to try calling the built-in iter on that object: the call raises TypeError if the object is not iterable. To identify whether an object is string-like, we simply check whether the object is an instance of basestring, since isinstance(obj, basestring) is True when obj is an instance of any *subclass* of basestring—that is, any string-like type. So, the alternative predicate is not hard to code:

```
def nonstring_iterable(obj):
    try: iter(obj)
    except TypeError: return False
    else: return not isinstance(obj, basestring)
```

Now the caller may choose to call flatten(seq, nonstring_iterable) when the need is to expand any iterable that is not a string. It is surely better *not* to make the nonstring_iterable predicate the default for flatten, though: in a simple case, such as the example snippet we showed previously, flatten can be up to three times slower when the predicate is nonstring_iterable rather than list_or_tuple.

We can also write a nonrecursive version of generator flatten. Such a version lets you flatten nested sequences with nesting levels higher than Python's recursion limit, which normally allows no more than a few thousand levels of recursion depth. The main technique for recursion removal is to keep an explicit last-in, first-out (LIFO) stack, which, in this case, we can implement with a list of iterators:

```
def flatten(sequence, to_expand=list_or_tuple):
    iterators = [ iter(sequence) ]
    while iterators:
        # loop on the currently most-nested (last) iterator
        for item in iterators[-1]:
            if to_expand(item):
                # subsequence found, go loop on iterator on subsequence
                iterators.append(iter(item))
                break
            else:
                yield item
        else:
            # most-nested iterator exhausted, go back, loop on its parent
            iterators.pop()
```

The if clause of the if statement executes for any item we are to expand—that is, any subsequence on which we must loop; so in that clause, we push an iterator for the subsequence to the end of the stack, then execute a break to terminate the for, and go back to the outer while, which will in turn execute a new for statement on the iterator we just appended to the stack. The else clause of the if statement executes for any item we don't expand, and it just yields the item.

The else clause of the for statement executes if no break statement interrupts the for loop—in other words, when the for loop runs to completion, exhausting the currently most-nested iterator. So, in that else clause, we remove the now-exhausted most-nested (last) iterator, and the outer while loop proceeds, either terminating if no iterators are left on the stack, or executing a new for statement that continues the loop on the iterator that's back at the top of the stack—from wherever that iterator had last left off, intrinsically, because an iterator's job is exactly to remember iteration state.

The results of this nonrecursive implementation of flatten are identical to those of the simpler recursive version given in this recipe's Solution. If you think non-recursive implementations are faster than recursive ones, though, you may be disappointed: according to my measurements, the nonrecursive version is about 10% *slower* than the recursive one, across a range of cases.

See Also

Library Reference and *Python in a Nutshell* sections on sequence types and built-ins iter, isinstance, and basestring.

4.7 Removing or Reordering Columns in a List of Rows

Credit: Jason Whitlark

Problem

You have a list of lists (rows) and need to get another list of the same rows but with some columns removed and/or reordered.

Solution

A list comprehension works well for this task. Say you have:

```
listOfRows = [ [1,2,3,4], [5,6,7,8], [9,10,11,12] ]
```

You want a list with the same rows but with the second of the four columns removed and the third and fourth ones interchanged. A simple list comprehension that performs this job is:

```
newList = [ [row[0], row[3], row[2]] for row in listOfRows ]
```

An alternative way of coding, that is at least as practical and arguably a bit more elegant, is to use an auxiliary sequence (meaning a list or tuple) that has the column indices you desire in their proper order. Then, you can nest an inner list comprehension that loops on the auxiliary sequence inside the outer list comprehension that loops on listOfRows:

```
newList = [ [row[ci] for ci in (0, 3, 2)] for row in listofRows ]
```

Discussion

I often use lists of lists to represent two-dimensional arrays. I think of such lists as having the "rows" of a "two-dimensional array" as their items. I often perform manipulation on the "columns" of such a "two-dimensional array", typically reordering some columns, sometimes omitting some of the original columns. It is not obvious (at least, it was not immediately obvious to me) that list comprehensions are just as useful for this purpose as they are for other kinds of sequence-manipulation tasks.

A list comprehension builds a new list, rather than altering an existing one. But even when you do need to alter the existing list in place, the best approach is to write a list comprehension and assign it to the existing list's contents. For example, if you needed to alter listOfRows in place, for the example given in this recipe's Solution, you would code:

```
listOfRows[:] = [ [row[0], row[3], row[2]] for row in listOfRows ]
```

Do consider, as suggested in the second example in this recipe's Solution, the possibility of using an auxiliary sequence to hold the column indices you desire, in the order in which you desire them, rather than explicitly hard-coding the list display as

---

we did in the first example. You might feel a little queasy about nesting two list comprehensions into each other in this fashion, but it's simpler and safer than you might fear. If you adopt this approach, you gain some potential generality, because you can choose to give a name to the auxiliary sequence of indices, use it to reorder several lists of rows in the same fashion, pass it as an argument to a function, whatever:

```
def pick_and_reorder_columns(listofRows, column_indexes):
    return [ [row[ci] for ci in column_indexes] for row in listofRows ]
columns = 0, 3, 2
newListOfPandas = pick_and_reorder_columns(oldListOfPandas, columns)
newListOfCats = pick_and_reorder_columns(oldListOfCats, columns)
```

This example performs just the same column reordering and selection as all the other snippets in this recipe, but it performs the operation on two separate "old" lists, obtaining from each the corresponding "new" list. Reaching for excessive generalization is a pernicious temptation, but here, with this pick_and_reorder_columns function, it seems that we are probably getting just the right amount of generality.

One last note: some people prefer a fancier way to express the kinds of list comprehensions that are used as "inner" ones in some of the functions used previously. Instead of coding them straightforwardly, as in:

```
[row[ci] for ci in column_indexes]
```

they prefer to use the built-in function map, and the special method __getitem__ of row used as a bound-method, to perform the indexing subtask, so they code instead:

```
map(row.__getitem__, column_indexes)
```

Depending on the exact version of Python, perhaps this fancy and somewhat obscure way may be slightly faster. Nevertheless, I think the greater simplicity of the list comprehension form means the list comprehension is still the best way.

See Also

List comprehension docs in *Language Reference* and *Python in a Nutshell*.

4.8   Transposing Two-Dimensional Arrays

Credit: Steve Holden, Raymond Hettinger, Attila Vàsàrhelyi, Chris Perkins

Problem

You need to transpose a list of lists, turning rows into columns and vice versa.

Solution

You must start with a list whose items are lists all of the same length, such as:

```
arr = [[1, 2, 3], [4, 5, 6], [7, 8, 9], [10, 11, 12]]
```

A list comprehension offers a simple, handy way to transpose such a two-dimensional array:

```
print [[r[col] for r in arr] for col in range(len(arr[0]))]
[[1, 4, 7, 10], [2, 5, 8, 11], [3, 6, 9, 12]]
```

A faster though more obscure alternative (with exactly the same output) can be obtained by exploiting built-in function zip in a slightly strange way:

```
print map(list, zip(*arr))
```

Discussion

This recipe shows a concise yet clear way to turn rows into columns, and also a faster though more obscure way. List comprehensions work well when you want to be clear yet concise, while the alternative solution exploits the built-in function zip in a way that is definitely not obvious.

Sometimes data just comes at you the wrong way. For instance, if you use Microsoft's ActiveX Data Ojbects (ADO) database interface, due to array element-ordering differences between Python and Microsoft's preferred implementation language (Visual Basic), the GetRows method actually appears to return database *columns* in Python, despite the method's name. This recipe's two solutions to this common kind of problem let you choose between clarity and speed.

In the list comprehension solution, the inner comprehension varies what is selected from (the row), while the outer comprehension varies the selector (the column). This process achieves the required transposition.

In the zip-based solution, we use the *a syntax to pass each item (row) of arr to zip, in order, as a separate positional argument. zip returns a list of tuples, which directly achieves the required transposition; we then apply list to each tuple, via the single call to map, to obtain a list of lists, as required. Since we don't use zip's result as a list directly, we could get a further slight improvement in performance by using itertools.izip instead (because izip does not materialize its result as a list in memory, but rather yields it one item at a time):

```
import itertools
print map(list, itertools.izip(*arr))
```

but, in this specific case, the slight speed increase is probably not worth the added complexity.

If you're transposing large arrays of numbers, consider Numeric Python and other third-party packages. Numeric Python defines transposition and other axis-swinging routines that will make your head spin.

See Also

The *Reference Manual* and *Python in a Nutshell* sections on list displays (the other name for list comprehensions) and on the *a and *k notation for positional and *args (actually, * followed by any identifier—most usually, you'll see args or a as the identifier that's used) is Python syntax for accepting or passing arbitrary *positional* arguments. When you receive arguments with this syntax (i.e., when you place the star syntax within a function's signature, in the def statement for that function), Python binds the identifier to a tuple that holds all positional arguments not "explicitly" received. When you pass arguments with this syntax, the identifier can be bound to any iterable (in fact, it could be any expression, not necessarily an identifier, as long as the expression's result is an iterable).

**kwds (again, the identifier is arbitrary, most often kwds or k) is Python syntax for accepting or passing arbitrary *named* arguments. (Python sometimes calls named arguments *keyword arguments*, which they most definitely are *not*—just *try* to use as argument name a keyword, such as pass, for, or yield, and you'll see. Unfortunately, this confusing terminology is, by now, ingrained in the language and its culture.) When you receive arguments with this syntax (i.e., when you place the starstar syntax within a function's signature, in the def statement for that function), Python binds the identifier to a dict, which holds all named arguments not "explicitly" received. When you pass arguments with this syntax, the identifier must be bound to a dict (in fact, it could be any expression, not necessarily an identifier, as long as the expression's result is a dict).

Whether in defining a function or in calling it, make sure that both *a and **k come *after* any other parameters or arguments. If both forms appear, then place the **k after the *a.

named argument passing; built-in functions zip and map; Numeric Python (*http:// www.pfdubois.com/numpy/*).

4.9   Getting a Value from a Dictionary

Credit: Andy McKay

Problem

You need to obtain a value from a dictionary, without having to handle an exception if the key you seek is not in the dictionary.

Solution

That's what the get method of dictionaries is for. Say you have a dictionary such as d = {'key':'value',}. To get the value corresponding to key in d in an exception-safe way, code:

```
print d.get('key', 'not found')
```

If you need to remove the entry after you have obtained the value, call d.pop (which does a get-and-remove) instead of d.get (which just reads d and never changes it).

Discussion

Want to get a value for a key from a dictionary, without getting an exception if the key does not exist in the dictionary? Use the simple and useful get method of the dictionary.

If you try to get a value with the indexing syntax d[x], and the value of x is not a key in dictionary d, your attempt raises a KeyError exception. This is often okay. If you expected the value of x to be a key in d, an exception is just the right way to inform you that you're mistaken (i.e., that you need to debug your program).

However, you often need to be more tentative about it: as far as you know, the value of x may or may not be a key in d. In this case, don't start messing with in tests, such as:

```
if 'key' in d:
    print d['key']
else:
    print 'not found'
```

or try/except statements, such as:

```
try:
    print d['key']
except KeyError:
    print 'not found'
```

Instead, use the get method, as shown in the "Solution". If you call d.get(x), no exception is thrown: you get d[x] if x is a key in d, and if it's not, you get None (which you can check for or propagate). If None is not what you want to get when x is not a key of d, call d.get(x, somethingelse) instead. In this case, if x is not a key, you will get the value of somethingelse.

get is a simple, useful mechanism that is well explained in the Python documentation, but a surprising number of people don't know about it. Another similar method is pop, which is mostly like get, except that, if the key was in the dictionary, pop also removes it. Just one caveat: get and pop are not *exactly* parallel. d.pop(x) *does* raise KeyError if x is not a key in d; to get exactly the same effect as d.get(x), plus the entry removal, call d.pop(x,None) instead.

See Also

Recipe 4.10 "Adding an Entry to a Dictionary"; the *Library Reference* and *Python in a Nutshell* sections on mapping types.

4.10 Adding an Entry to a Dictionary

Credit: Alex Martelli, Martin Miller, Matthew Shomphe

Problem

Working with a dictionary d, you need to use the entry d[k] when it's already present, or add a new value as d[k] when k isn't yet a key in d.

Solution

This is what the setdefault method of dictionaries is for. Say we're building a word-to-page-numbers index, a dictionary that maps each word to the list of page numbers where it appears. A key piece of code in that application might be:

```
def addword(theIndex, word, pagenumber):
    theIndex.setdefault(word, [ ]).append(pagenumber)
```

This code is equivalent to more verbose approaches such as:

```
def addword(theIndex, word, pagenumber):
    if word in theIndex:
        theIndex[word].append(pagenumber)
    else:
        theIndex[word] = [pagenumber]
```

and:

```
def addword(theIndex, word, pagenumber):
    try:
        theIndex[word].append(pagenumber)
    except KeyError:
        theIndex[word] = [pagenumber]
```

Using method setdefault simplifies this task considerably.

Discussion

For any dictionary d, d.setdefault(k, v) is very similar to d.get(k, v), which was covered previously in recipe 4.9 "Getting a Value from a Dictionary." The essential difference is that, if k is not a key in the dictionary, the setdefault method assigns d[k]=v as a side effect, in addition to returning v. (get would just return v, without affecting d in any way.) Therefore, consider using setdefault any time you have get-like needs, but also want to produce this side effect on the dictionary.

setdefault is particularly useful in a dictionary with values that are lists, as detailed in recipe 4.15 "Associating Multiple Values with Each Key in a Dictionary." The most typical usage for setdefault is something like:

```
somedict.setdefault(somekey, [ ]).append(somevalue)
```

setdefault is not all that useful for immutable values, such as numbers. If you just want to count words, for example, the right way to code is to use, *not* setdefault, but rather get:

```
theIndex[word] = theIndex.get(word, 0) + 1
```

since you must rebind the dictionary entry at theIndex[word] anyway (because numbers are immutable). But for our word-to page-numbers example, you *definitely* do not want to fall into the performance trap that's hidden in the following approach:

```
def addword(theIndex, word, pagenumber):
    theIndex[word] = theIndex.get(word, []) + [pagenumber]
```

This latest version of addword builds three new lists each time you call it: an empty list that's passed as the second argument to theIndex.get, a one-item list containing just pagenumber, and a list with N+1 items obtained by concatenating these two (where N is the number of times that word was previously found). Building such a huge number of lists is sure to take its toll, in performance terms. For example, on my machine, I timed the task of indexing the same four words occurring once each on each of 1,000 pages. Taking the first version of addword in the recipe as a reference point, the second one (using try/except) is about 10% faster, the third one (using setdefault) is about 20% slower—the kind of performance differences that you should blissfully ignore in just about all cases. This fourth version (using get) is *four times* slower—the kind of performance difference you just can't afford to ignore.

See Also

Recipe 4.9 "Getting a Value from a Dictionary"; recipe 4.15 "Associating Multiple Values with Each Key in a Dictionary"; *Library Reference* and *Python in a Nutshell* documentation about dict.

4.11 Building a Dictionary Without Excessive Quoting

Credit: Brent Burley, Peter Cogolo

Problem

You want to construct a dictionary whose keys are literal strings, without having to quote each key.

Solution

Once you get into the swing of Python, you'll find yourself constructing a lot of dictionaries. When the keys are identifiers, you can avoid quoting them by calling dict with named-argument syntax:

```
data = dict(red=1, green=2, blue=3)
```

This is neater than the equivalent use of dictionary-display syntax:

```
data = {'red': 1, 'green': 2, 'blue': 3}
```

Discussion

One powerful way to build a dictionary is to call the built-in type `dict`. It's often a good alternative to the dictionary-display syntax with braces and colons. This recipe shows that, by calling `dict`, you can avoid having to quote keys, when the keys are literal strings that happen to be syntactically valid for use as Python identifiers. You cannot use this approach for keys such as the literal strings `'12ba'` or `'for'`, because `'12ba'` starts with a digit, and `for` happens to be a Python keyword, not an identifier.

Also, dictionary-display syntax is the only case in Python where you need to use braces: if you dislike braces, or happen to work on a keyboard that makes braces hard to reach (as all Italian layout keyboards do!), you may be happier, for example, using `dict( )` rather than `{ }` to build an empty dictionary.

Calling `dict` also gives you other possibilities. `dict(d)` returns a new dictionary that is an independent copy of existing dictionary `d`, just like `d.copy( )`—but `dict(d)` works even when `d` is a sequence of pairs `(key, value)` instead of being a dictionary (when a key occurs more than once in the sequence, the last appearance of the key applies). A common dictionary-building idiom is:

```
d = dict(zip(the_keys, the_values))
```

where `the_keys` is a sequence of keys and `the_values` a "parallel" sequence of corresponding values. Built-in function `zip` builds and returns a list of `(key, value)` pairs, and built-in type `dict` accepts that list as its argument and constructs a dictionary accordingly. If the sequences are long, it's faster to use module `itertools` from the standard Python library:

```
import itertools
d = dict(itertools.izip(the_keys, the_values))
```

Built-in function `zip` constructs the whole list of pairs in memory, while `itertools.izip` yields only one pair at a time. On my machine, with sequences of 10,000 numbers, the latter idiom is about twice as fast as the one using `zip`—18 versus 45 milliseconds with Python 2.3, 17 versus 32 with Python 2.4.

You can use both a positional argument and named arguments in the same call to `dict` (if the named argument clashes with a key specified in the positional argument, the named argument applies). For example, here is a workaround for the previously mentioned issue that Python keywords, and other nonidentifiers, cannot be used as argument names:

```
d = dict({'12ba':49, 'for': 23}, rof=41, fro=97, orf=42)
```

If you need to build a dictionary where the same value corresponds to each key, call `dict.fromkeys(keys_sequence, value)` (if you omit the value, it defaults to `None`). For example, here is a neat way to initialize a dictionary to be used for counting occurrences of various lowercase ASCII letters:

```
import string
count_by_letter = dict.fromkeys(string.ascii_lowercase, 0)
```

See Also

Library Reference and *Python in a Nutshell* sections on built-ins dict and zip, and on modules itertools and string.

4.12 Building a Dict from a List of Alternating Keys and Values

Credit: Richard Philips, Raymond Hettinger

Problem

You want to build a dict from a list of alternating keys and values.

Solution

The built-in type dict offers many ways to build dictionaries, but not this one, so we need to code a function for the purpose. One way is to use the built-in function zip on extended slices:

```
def dictFromList(keysAndValues):
    return dict(zip(keysAndValues[::2], keysAndValues[1::2]))
```

A more general approach, which works for any sequence or other iterable argument and not just for lists, is to "factor out" the task of getting a sequence of pairs from a flat sequence into a separate generator. This approach is not quite as concise as dictFromList, but it's faster as well as more general:

```
def pairwise(iterable):
    itnext = iter(iterable).next
    while True:
        yield itnext( ), itnext( )
def dictFromSequence(seq):
    return dict(pairwise(seq))
```

Defining pairwise also allows *updating* an existing dictionary with any sequence of alternating keys and values—just code, for example, mydict.update(pairwise(seq)).

Discussion

Both of the "factory functions" in this recipe use the same underlying way to construct a dictionary: each calls dict with an argument that is a sequence of (key, value) pairs. All the difference is in how the functions build the sequence of pairs to pass to dict.

---

dictFromList builds a list of such pairs by calling built-in function zip with two extended-form slices of the function's keysAndValues argument—one that gathers all items with even indices (meaning the items at index 0, 2, 4, . . .), the other that gathers all items with odd indices (starting at 1 and counting by 2 . . .). This approach is fine, but it works only when the argument named keysAndValues is an instance of a type or class that supports extended slicing, such as list, tuple or str. Also, this approach results in constructing several temporary lists in memory: if keysAndValues is a long sequence, all of this list construction activity can cost some performance.

dictFromSequence, on the other hand, delegates the task of building the sequence of pairs to the generator named pairwise. In turn, pairwise is coded to ensure that it can use any iterable at all—not just lists (or other sequences, such as tuples or strings), but also, for example, results of other generators, files, dictionaries, and so on. Moreover, pairwise yields pairs one at a time. It never constructs any long list in memory, an aspect that may improve performance if the input sequence is very long.

The implementation of pairwise is interesting. As its very first statement, pairwise binds local name itnext to the bound-method next of the iterator that it obtains by calling the built-in function iter on the iterable argument. This may seem a bit strange, but it's a good general technique in Python: if you start with an object, and all you need to do with that object is call one of its methods in a loop, you can extract the bound-method, assign it to a local name, and afterwards just call the local name as if it were a function. pairwise would work just as well if the next method was instead called in a way that may look more normal to programmers who are used to other languages:

```
def pairwise_slow(iterable):
    it = iter(iterable)
    while True:
        yield it.next( ), it.next( )
```

However, this pairwise_slow variant isn't really any simpler than the pairwise generator shown in the Solution ("more familiar to people who don't know Python" is *not* a synonym of "simpler"!), and it *is* about 60% slower. Focusing on simplicity and clarity is one thing, and a very good one—indeed, a core principle of Python. Throwing performance to the winds, *without* getting any real advantage to compensate, is a completely different proposition and definitely not a practice that can be recommended in any language. So, while it is an excellent idea to focus on writing correct, clear, and simple code, it's also very advisable to learn and use Python's idioms that are most appropriate to your needs.

See Also

Recipe 19.7 "Looping on a Sequence by Overlapping Windows" for more general approaches to looping by sliding windows over an iterable. See the *Python Reference Manual* for more on extended slicing.

4.13 Extracting a Subset of a Dictionary

Credit: David Benjamin

Problem

You want to extract from a larger dictionary only that subset of it that corresponds to a certain set of keys.

Solution

If you want to leave the original dictionary intact:

```
def sub_dict(somedict, somekeys, default=None):
    return dict([ (k, somedict.get(k, default)) for k in somekeys ])
```

If you want to remove from the original the items you're extracting:

```
def sub_dict_remove(somedict, somekeys, default=None):
    return dict([ (k, somedict.pop(k, default)) for k in somekeys ])
```

Two examples of these functions' use and effects:

```
>>> d = {'a': 5, 'b': 6, 'c': 7}
>>> print sub_dict(d, 'ab'), d
{'a': 5, 'b': 6} {'a': 5, 'b': 6, 'c': 7}
>>> print sub_dict_remove(d, 'ab'), d
{'a': 5, 'b': 6} {'c': 7}
```

Discussion

In Python, I use dictionaries for many purposes—database rows, primary and compound keys, variable namespaces for template parsing, and so on. So, I often need to create a dictionary that is based on another, larger dictionary, but only contains the subset of the larger dictionary corresponding to some set of keys. In most use cases, the larger dictionary must remain intact after the extraction; sometimes, however, I need to remove from the larger dictionary the subset that I'm extracting. This recipe's solution shows both possibilities. The only difference is that you use method get when you want to avoid affecting the dictionary that you are getting data from, method pop when you want to remove the items you're getting.

If some item k of somekeys is not in fact a key in somedict, this recipe's functions put k as a key in the result anyway, with a default value (which I pass as an optional argument to either function, with a default value of None). So, the result is not necessarily a subset of somedict. This behavior is the one I've found most useful in my applications.

You might prefer to get an exception for "missing keys"—that would help alert you to a bug in your program, in cases in which you know all ks in somekeys should definitely also be keys in somedict. Remember, "errors should never pass silently. Unless explicitly silenced," to quote *The Zen of Python*, by Tim Peters (enter the statement `import` this at an interactive Python prompt to read or re-read this delightful summary of Python's design principles). So, if a missing key is an error, from the point of view of your application, then you *do* want to get an exception that alerts you to that error at once, if it ever occurs. If this is what you want, you can get it with minor modifications to this recipe's functions:

```
def sub_dict_strict(somedict, somekeys):
    return dict([ (k, somedict[k]) for k in somekeys ])
def sub_dict_remove_strict(somedict, somekeys):
    return dict([ (k, somedict.pop(k)) for k in somekeys ])
```

As you can see, these strict variants are even simpler than the originals—a good indication that Python *likes* to raise exceptions when unexpected behavior occurs!

Alternatively, you might prefer missing keys to be simply omitted from the result. This, too, requires just minor modifications:

```
def sub_dict_select(somedict, somekeys):
    return dict([ (k, somedict[k]) for k in somekeys if k in somedict])
def sub_dict_remove_select(somedict, somekeys):
    return dict([ (k, somedict.pop(k)) for k in somekeys if k in somedict])
```

The `if` clause in each list comprehension does all we need to distinguish these _select variants from the _strict ones.

In Python 2.4, you can use generator expressions, instead of list comprehensions, as the arguments to `dict` in each of the functions shown in this recipe. Just change the syntax of the calls to `dict`, from `dict([. . .])` to `dict(. . .)` (removing the brackets adjacent to the parentheses) and enjoy the resulting slight simplification and acceleration. However, these variants would not work in Python 2.3, which has list comprehensions but not generator expressions.

See Also

Library Reference and *Python in a Nutshell* documentation on `dict`.

4.14 Inverting a Dictionary

Credit: Joel Lawhead, Ian Bollinger, Raymond Hettinger

Problem

An existing dict maps keys to unique values, and you want to build the inverse dict, mapping each value to its key.

Solution

You can write a function that passes a list comprehension as dict's argument to build the new requested dictionary:

```
def invert_dict(d):
    return dict([ (v, k) for k, v in d.iteritems( ) ])
```

For large dictionaries, though, it's faster to use the generator `izip` from the `itertools` module in the Python Standard Library:

```
from itertools import izip
def invert_dict_fast(d):
    return dict(izip(d.itervalues( ), d.iterkeys( )))
```

Discussion

If the values in dict d are not unique, then d cannot truly be inverted, meaning that there exists no dict id such that for any valid key k, id[d[k]]==k. However, the functions shown in this recipe still construct, even in such cases, a "pseudo-inverse" dict pd such that, for any v that is a value in d, d[pd[v]]==v. Given the original dict d and the dict x returned by either of the functions shown in this recipe, you can easily check whether x is the true inverse of d or just d's pseudo-inverse: x is the true inverse of d if and only if len(x)==len(d). That's because, if two different keys have the same value, then, in the result of either of the functions in this recipe, one of the two keys will simply go "poof" into the ether, thus leaving the resulting pseudo-inverse dict shorter than the dict you started with. In any case, quite obviously, the functions shown in this recipe can work only if all values in d are hashable (meaning that they are all usable as keys into a dict): otherwise, the functions raise a TypeError exception.

When we program in Python, we normally "disregard minor optimizations," as Donald Knuth suggested over thirty years ago: we place a premium on clarity and correctness and care relatively little about speed. However, it can't hurt to know about faster possibilities: when we decide to code in a certain way because it's simpler or clearer than another, it's best if we are taking the decision deliberately, not out of ignorance.

Here, function invert_dict in this recipe's Solution might perhaps be considered clearer because it shows exactly what it's doing. Take the pairs k, v of key and value that method iteritems yields, swap them into (value, key) order, and feed the resulting list as the argument of dict, so that dict builds a dictionary where each value v is a key and the corresponding key k becomes that key's value—just the inverse dict that our problem requires.

However, function invert_dict_fast, also in this recipe's Solution, isn't really any more complicated: it just operates more abstractly, by getting all keys and all values as two separate iterators and zipping them up (into an iterator whose items are the needed, swapped (value, key) pairs) via a call to generator izip, supplied by the itertools module of the Python Standard Library. If you get used to such higher abstraction levels, they will soon come to feel *simpler* than lower-level code!

Thanks to the higher level of abstraction, and to never materializing the whole list of pairs (but rather operating via generators and iterators that yield only one item at a time), function invert_dict_fast can be substantially faster than function invert_dict. For example, on my machine, to invert a 10,000-item dictionary, invert_dict takes about 63 milliseconds, but `invert_dict_fast` manages the same task in just 20 milliseconds. A speed increase by a factor of three, in general, is not to be sneered at. Such performance gains, when you work on large amounts of data, are the norm, rather than the exception, for coding at higher abstraction levels. This is particularly true when you can use `itertools` rather than loops or list comprehensions, because you don't need to materialize some large list in memory at one time. Performance gain is an extra incentive for getting familiar with working at higher abstraction levels, a familiarity that has conceptual and productivity pluses, too.

See Also

Documentation on mapping types and `itertools` in the *Library Reference* and *Python in a Nutshell*; Chapter 19.

4.15 Associating Multiple Values with Each Key in a Dictionary

Credit: Michael Chermside

Problem

You need a dictionary that maps each key to multiple values.

Solution

By nature, a dictionary is a one-to-one mapping, but it's not hard to make it one-to-many—in other words, to make one key map to multiple values. Your choice of one of two possible approaches depends on how you want to treat duplications in the set of values for a key. The following approach, based on using lists as the dict's values, allows such duplications:

```
d1 = { }
d1.setdefault(key, [ ]).append(value)
```

while an alternative approach, based on using sub-dicts as the dict's values, automatically eliminates duplications of values:

```
d2 = { }
d2.setdefault(key, { })[value] = 1
```

In Python 2.4, the no-duplication approach can equivalently be coded:

```
d3 = { }
d3.setdefault(key, set( )).add(value)
```

Discussion

A normal dictionary performs a simple mapping of each key to one value. This recipe shows three easy, efficient ways to achieve a mapping of each key to multiple values, by holding as the dictionary's values lists, sub-dicts, or, in Python 2.4, sets. The semantics of the list-based approach differ slightly but importantly from those of the other two in terms of how they deal with duplication. Each approach relies on the setdefault method of a dictionary, covered earlier in recipe "Adding an Entry to a Dictionary," to initialize the entry for a key in the dictionary, if needed, and in any case to return said entry.

You need to be able to do more than just add values for a key. With the first approach, which uses lists and allows duplications, here's how to retrieve the list of values for a key:

```
list_of_values = d1[key]
```

Here's how to remove one value for a key, if you don't mind leaving empty lists as items of d1 when the last value for a key is removed:

```
d1[key].remove(value)
```

Despite the empty lists, it's still easy to test for the existence of a key with at least one value—just use a function that always returns a list (maybe an empty one), such as:

```
def get_values_if_any(d, key):
    return d.get(key, [])
```

For example, to check whether 'freep' is among the values (if any) for key 'somekey' in dictionary d1, you can code: if 'freep' in get_values_if_any(d1, 'somekey').

The second approach, which uses sub-dicts and eliminates duplications, can use rather similar idioms. To retrieve the list of values for a key:

```
list_of_values = list(d2[key])
```

To remove one value for a key, leaving empty dictionaries as items of d2 when the last value for a key is removed:

```
del d2[key][value]
```

In the third approach, showing the Python 2.4-only version d3, which uses sets, this would be:

```
d3[key].remove(value)
```

One possibility for the get_values_if_any function in either the second or third (duplication-removing) approaches would be:

```
def get_values_if_any(d, key):
    return list(d.get(key, ()))
```

This recipe focuses on how to code the raw functionality, but, to use this functionality in a systematic way, you'll probably want to wrap up this code into a class. For that purpose, you need to make some of the design decisions that this recipe highlights. Do you want a value to be in the entry for a key multiple times? (Is the entry for each key a bag rather than a set, in mathematical terms?) If so, should remove just reduce the number of occurrences by 1, or should it wipe out all of them? This is just

---

the beginning of the choices you have to make, and the right choices depend on the specifics of your application.

See Also

Recipe 4.10 "Adding an Entry to a Dictionary"; the *Library Reference* and *Python in a Nutshell* sections on mapping types; recipe 18.8 "Implementing a Bag (Multiset) Collection Type" for an implementation of the bag type.

4.16 Using a Dictionary to Dispatch Methods or Functions

Credit: Dick Wall

Problem

You need to execute different pieces of code depending on the value of some control variable—the kind of problem that in some other languages you might approach with a case statement.

Solution

Object-oriented programming, thanks to its elegant concept of dispatching, does away with many (but not all) needs for case statements. In Python, dictionaries, and the fact that functions are first-class objects (in particular, functions can be values in a dictionary), conspire to make the full problem of "case statements" easier to solve. For example, consider the following snippet of code:

```
animals = [ ]
number_of_felines = 0
def deal_with_a_cat( ):
    global number_of_felines
    print "meow"
    animals.append('feline')
    number_of_felines += 1
def deal_with_a_dog( ):
    print "bark"
    animals.append('canine')
def deal_with_a_bear( ):
    print "watch out for the *HUG*!"
    animals.append('ursine')
tokenDict = {
    "cat": deal_with_a_cat,
    "dog": deal_with_a_dog,
    "bear": deal_with_a_bear,
    }
# Simulate, say, some words read from a file
words = ["cat", "bear", "cat", "dog"]
for word in words:
    # Look up the function to call for each word, and call it
```

```
        return tokenDict[word]()
nf = number_of_felines
print 'we met %d feline%s' % (nf, 's'[nf==1:])
print 'the animals we met were:', ' '.join(animals)
```

Discussion

The key idea in this recipe is to construct a dictionary with string (or other) values as keys, and bound-methods, functions, or other callables as values. At each step of execution, we use the string keys to select which callable to execute and then call it. This approach can be used as a kind of generalized case statement.

It's embarrassingly simple (really!), but I use this technique often. You can also use bound-methods or other callables instead of functions. If you use unbound methods, you need to pass an appropriate object as the first actual argument when you do call them. More generally, you can store, as the dictionary's values, tuples including both a callable and arguments to pass to the callable.

I primarily use this technique in places where in other languages, I might want a case, switch, or select statement. For example, I use it to implement a *poor man's way* to parse command files (e.g., an X10 macro control file).

See Also

The *Library Reference* section on mapping types; the *Reference Manual* section on bound and unbound methods; *Python in a Nutshell* about both dictionaries and callables.

4.17 Finding Unions and Intersections of Dictionaries

Credit: Tom Good, Andy McKay, Sami Hangaslammi, Robin Siebler

Problem

Given two dictionaries, you need to find the set of keys that are in *both* dictionaries (the intersection) or the set of keys that are in *either* dictionary (the union).

Solution

Sometimes, particularly in Python 2.3, you find yourself using dictionaries as concrete representations of sets. In such cases, you only care about the keys, not the corresponding values, and often you build the dictionaries by calls to dict.fromkeys, such as

```
a = dict.fromkeys(xrange(1000))
b = dict.fromkeys(xrange(500, 1500))
```

The fastest way to compute the dict that is the set-union is:

```
union = dict(a, **b)
```

The fastest concise way to compute the dict that is the set-intersection is:

```
inter = dict.fromkeys([x for x in a if x in b])
```

If the number of items in dictionaries a and b can be very different, then it can be important for speed considerations to have the shorter one in the for clause, and the longer one in the if clause, of this list comprehension. In such cases, it may be worth sacrificing some conciseness in favor of speed, by coding the intersection computation as follows:

```
if len(a) < len(b):
    inter = dict.fromkeys([x for x in a if x not in b])
else:
    inter = dict.fromkeys([x for x in b if x not in a])
```

Python also gives you types to represent sets directly (in standard library module sets, and, in Python 2.4, also as built-ins). Here is a snippet that you can use at the start of a module: the snippet ensures that name set is bound to the best available set type, so that throughout the module, you can then use the same code whether you're using Python 2.3 or 2.4:

```
try:
    set
except NameError:
    from sets import Set as set
```

Having done this, you can now use type set to best effect, gaining clarity and conciseness, and (in Python 2.4) gaining a little speed, too:

```
a = set(xrange(1000))
b = set(xrange(500, 1500))
union = a | b
inter = a & b
```

Discussion

In Python 2.3, even though the Python Standard Library module sets offers an elegant data type Set that directly represents a set (with hashable elements), it is still common to use a dict to represent a set, partly for historical reasons. Just in case you want to keep doing it, this recipe shows you how to compute unions and intersections of such sets in the fastest ways, which are not obvious. The code in this recipe, on my machine, takes about 260 microseconds for the union, about 690 for the intersection (with Python 2.3; with Python 2.4, 260 and 600,respectively), while alternatives based on loops or generator expressions are substantially slower.

However, it's best to use type set instead of representing sets by dictionaries. As the recipe shows, using set makes your code more direct and readable. If you dislike the or-operator (|) and the "and-operator" (&), you can equivalently use a.union(b) and a.intersection(b), respectively. Besides clarity, you also gain speed, particularly in Python 2.4: computing the union still takes about 260 microseconds, but computing the intersection takes only about 210. Even in Python 2.3, this approach is acceptably fast: computing the union takes about 270 microseconds, computing the intersection takes about 650—not quite as fast as Python 2.4 but still quite comparable to what you can get if you represent sets by dictionaries. Last but not least, once you use type set (whether it is the Python 2.4 built-in, or class Set from the Python Standard Library module sets, the interface is the same), you gain a wealth of useful set operations. For example, the set of elements that are in either a or b but not both is a^b or, equivalently, a.symmetric_difference(b).

Even if you start with dicts for other reasons, consider using sets anyway if you need to perform set operations. Say, for example, that you have in phones a dictionary that maps names to phone numbers and in addresses one that maps names to addresses. The clearest and simplest way to print all names for which you know both address and phone number, and their associated data, is:

```
for name in set(phones) & set(addresses):
    print name, phones[name], addresses[name]
```

This is much terser, and arguably clearer, than something like:

```
for name in phones:
    if name in addresses:
        print name, phones[name], addresses[name]
```

Another excellent alternative is:

```
for name in set(phones).intersection(addresses):
    print name, phones[name], addresses[name]
```

If you use the named intersection method, rather than the & intersection operator, you don't need to turn both dicts into sets: just one of them. Then call intersection on the resulting set, and pass the other dict as the argument to the intersection method.

See Also

The *Library Reference* and *Python in a Nutshell* sections on mapping types, module sets, and Python 2.4's built-in set type.

4.18   Collecting a Bunch of Named Items

Credit: Alex Martelli, Doug Hudgeon

Problem

You want to collect a bunch of items together, naming each item of the bunch, and you find dictionary syntax a bit heavyweight for the purpose.

Solution

Any normal class instance inherently wraps a dictionary, which it uses to hold its state. We can easily take advantage of this handily wrapped dictionary by coding a nearly empty class:

```
class Bunch(object):
    def __init__(self, **kwds):
        self.__dict__.update(kwds)
```

Now, to group a few variables, create a Bunch instance:

```
point = Bunch(datum=y, squared=y*y, coord=x)
```

You can now access and rebind the named attributes just created, add others, remove some, and so on. For example:

```
if point.squared > threshold:
    point.isok = True
```

Discussion

We often just want to collect a bunch of stuff together, naming each item of the bunch. A dictionary is OK for this purpose, but a small do-nothing class is even handier and prettier to use.

It takes minimal effort to build a little class, as in this recipe, to provide elegant attribute-access syntax. While a dictionary is fine for collecting a few items in which each item has a name (the item's key in the dictionary can be thought of as the item's name, in this context), it's not the best solution when all names are identifiers, to be used just like variables. In class Bunch's __init__ method, we accept arbitrary named arguments with the **kwds syntax, and we use the kwds dictionary to update the initially empty instance dictionary, so that each named argument gets turned into an attribute of the instance.

Compared to attribute-access syntax, dictionary-indexing syntax is not quite as terse and readable. For example, if point was a dictionary, the little snippet at the end of the "Solution" would have to be coded like:

```
if point['squared'] > threshold:
    point['isok'] = True
```

An alternative implementation that's just as attractive as the one used in this recipe is:

```
class EvenSimplerBunch(object):
    def __init__(self, **kwds):
        self.__dict__ = kwds
```

Rebinding an instance's dictionary may feel risqué, but it's not actually any pushier than calling that dictionary's update method. So you might prefer the marginal speed advantage of this alternative implementation of Bunch. Unfortunately, I cannot find anywhere in Python's documentation an assurance that usage like:

```
d = {'foo': 'bar'}
x = EvenSimplerBunch(**d)
```

will forever keep making x.__dict__ an independent copy of d rather than just sharing a reference. It does currently, and in every version, but unless it's a documented semantic constraint, we cannot be entirely sure that it will keep working forever. So, if you do choose the implementation in EvenSimplerBunch, you might choose to assign a copy (dict(kwds) or kwds.copy( )) rather than kwds itself. And, if you do, then the marginal speed advantage disappears. All in all, the Bunch presented in this recipe's Solution is probably preferable.

A further tempting but not fully sound alternative is to have the Bunch class inherit from dict, and set attribute access special methods equal to the item access special methods, as follows:

```
class DictBunch(dict):
    __getattr__ = dict.__getitem__
    __setattr__ = dict.__setitem__
    __delattr__ = dict.__delitem__
```

One problem with this approach is that, with this definition, an instance x of DictBunch has many attributes it doesn't *really* have, because it inherits all the attributes (methods, actually, but there's no significant difference in this context) of dict. So, you can't meaningfully check hasattr(x, someattr), as you could with the classes Bunch and EvenSimplerBunch previously shown, unless you can somehow rule out the value of someattr being any of several common words such as 'keys', 'pop', and 'get'.

Python's distinction between attributes and items is really a wellspring of clarity and simplicity. Unfortunately, many newcomers to Python wrongly believe that it would be better to confuse items with attributes, generally because of previous experience with JavaScript and other such languages, in which attributes and items are regularly confused. But educating newcomers is a much better idea than promoting item/attribute confusion.

See Also

The *Python Tutorial* section on classes; the *Language Reference* and *Python in a Nutshell* coverage of classes; Chapter 6 for more information about object-oriented programming in Python; recipe 4.18 "Collecting a Bunch of Named Items" for more on the **kwds syntax.

4.19   Assigning and Testing with One Statement

Credit: Alex Martelli, Martin Miller

Problem

You are transliterating C or Perl code to Python, and to keep close to the original's structure, you'd like an expression's result to be both assigned and tested (as in if((x=foo( )) or while((x=foo( )) in such other languages).

Solution

In Python, you can't code if x=foo( ): . . . . Assignment is a statement, so it cannot fit into an expression, and you can only use expressions as conditions of if and while statements. This isn't a problem, it just means you have to structure your code Pythonically! For example, to process a file object f line by line, instead of the following C-like (and syntactically incorrect, in Python) approach:

```
while (line=f.readline( )) != '':
    process(line)
```

you can code a highly Pythonic (readable, clean, fast) approach:

```
for line in f:
    process(line)
```

But sometimes, you're transliterating from C, Perl, or another language, and you'd like your transliteration to be structurally close to the original. One simple utility class makes it easy:

```
class DataHolder(object):
    def __init__(self, value=None):
        self.value = value
    def set(self, value):
        self.value = value
        return value
    def get(self):
        return self.value
# optional and strongly discouraged, but nevertheless handy at times:
import __builtin__
__builtin__.DataHolder = DataHolder
__builtin__.data = data = DataHolder( )
```

With the help of the DataHolder class and its instance data, you can keep your C-like code structure intact in transliteration:

```
while data.set(file.readline( )) != '':
    process(data.get( ))
```

Discussion

In Python, assignment is a statement, not an expression. Thus, you cannot assign the result that you are also testing, for example, in the condition of an if, elif, or while statement. This is usually fine: just structure your code to avoid the need to assign while testing (in fact, your code will often become clearer as a result). In particular, whenever you feel the need to assign-and-test within the condition of a while loop, that's a good hint that your loop's structure probably wants to be refactored into a generator (or other iterator). Once you have refactored in this way, your loops become plain and simple for statements. The example given in the recipe, looping over each line read from a text file, is one where the refactoring has already been done on your behalf by Python itself, since a file object is an iterator whose items are the file's lines.

However, sometimes you may be writing Python code that is the transliteration of code originally written in C, Perl, or some other language that supports assignment-as-expression. Such transliterations often occur in the first Python version of an algorithm for which a reference implementation is supplied, an algorithm taken from a book, and so on. In such cases, it's often preferable to have the structure of your initial transliteration be close to that of the code you're transcribing. You can refactor later and make your code more Pythonic—clearer, faster, and so on. But first, you want to get working code as soon as possible, and specifically you want code that is easy to check for compliance to the original it has been transliterated from. Fortunately, Python offers enough power to make it quite easy for you to satisfy this requirement.

Python doesn't let us redefine the meaning of assignment, but we can have a method (or function) that saves its argument *somewhere* and also returns that argument so it can be tested. That *somewhere* is most naturally an attribute of an object, so a method is a more natural choice than a function. Of course, we could just retrieve the attribute directly (i.e., the get method is redundant), but it looks nicer to me to have symmetry between `data.set` and `data.get`.

`data.set(whatever)` can be seen as little more than syntactic sugar around `data.value=whatever`, with the added value of being acceptable as an expression. Therefore, it's the one obviously right way to satisfy the requirement for a reasonably faithful transliteration. The only difference between the resulting Python code and the original (say) C or Perl code, is at the syntactic sugar level—the overall structure is the same, and that's the key issue.

Importing `__builtin__` and assigning to its attributes is a trick that basically defines a new built-in object at runtime. You can use that trick in your application's start-up code, and then all other modules will automatically be able to access your new built-ins without having to do an `import`. It's *not* good Python practice, though; on the contrary, it's pushing the boundaries of Pythonic good taste, since the readers of all those other modules should not have to know about the strange side effects performed in your application's startup code. But since this recipe is meant to offer a quick-and-dirty approach for a first transliteration that will soon be refactored to make it better, it may be acceptable in this specific context to cut more corners than one would in production-level code.

On the other hand, one trick you should definitely *not* use is the following abuse of a currently existing wart in list comprehensions:

```
while [line for line in [f.readline()] if line!='']:
    process(line)
```

This trick currently works, since both Python 2.3 and 2.4 still "leak" the list comprehension control variable (here, `line`) into the surrounding scope. However, besides being obscure and unreadable, this trick is specifically deprecated: list comprehension control variable leakage *will* be fixed in some future version of Python, and this trick will then stop working at all.

See Also

The *Tutorial* section on classes; the documentation for the __builtin__ module in the *Library Reference* and *Python in a Nutshell*; *Language Reference* and *Python in a Nutshell* documentation on list comprehensions.

4.20 Using printf in Python

Credit: Tobias Klausmann, Andrea Cavalcanti

Problem

You'd like to output something to your program's standard output with C's function printf, but Python doesn't have that function.

Solution

It's easy to code a printf function in Python:

```
import sys
def printf(format, *args):
    sys.stdout.write(format % args)
```

Discussion

Python separates the concepts of output (the print statement) and formatting (the % operator), but if you prefer to have these concepts together, they're easy to join, as this recipe shows. No more worries about automatic insertion of spaces or newlines, either. Now you need worry only about correctly matching format and arguments!

For example, instead of something like:

```
print 'Result tuple is: %r' % (result_tuple,),
```

with its finicky need for commas in unobvious places (i.e., one to make a singleton tuple around result_tuple, one to avoid the newline that print would otherwise insert by default), once you have defined this recipe's printf function, you can just write:

```
printf('Result tuple is: %r', result_tuple)
```

See Also

Library Reference and *Python in a Nutshell* documentation for module sys and for the string formatting operator %; recipe 2.13 "Using a C++-like iostream Syntax" for a way to implement C++'s <<-style output in Python.

4.21 Randomly Picking Items with Given Probabilities

Credit: Kevin Parks, Peter Cogolo

Problem

You want to pick an item at random from a list, just about as `random.choice` does, but you need to pick the various items with different probabilities given in another list, rather than picking any item with equal probability as `random.choice` does.

Solution

Module `random` in the standard Python library offers a wealth of possibilities for generating and using pseudo-random numbers, but it does not offer this specific functionality, so we must code it as a function of our own:

```python
import random
def random_pick(some_list, probabilities):
    x = random.uniform(0, 1)
    cumulative_probability = 0.0
    for item, item_probability in zip(some_list, probabilities):
        cumulative_probability += item_probability
        if x < cumulative_probability: break
    return item
```

Discussion

Module `random` in the standard Python library does not have the *weighted choice* functionality that is sometimes needed in games, simulations, and random tests, so I wrote this recipe to supply this functionality. The recipe uses module `random`'s function `uniform` to get a uniformly distributed pseudo-random number between 0.0 and 1.0, then loops in parallel on items and their probabilities, computing the increasing cumulative probability, until the latter becomes greater than the pseudo-random number.

The recipe assumes, but does not check, that `probabilities` is a sequence with just as many items as `some_list`, which are probabilities—that is, numbers between 0.0 and 1.0, summing up to 1.0; if these assumptions are violated, you may still get some random picks, but they will not follow the (inconsistent) specifications encoded in the function's arguments. You may want to add some `assert` statements at the start of the function to check that the arguments make sense, such as:

```python
assert len(some_list) == len(probabilities)
assert 0 <= min(probabilities) and max(probabilities) <= 1
assert abs(sum(probabilities)-1.0) < 1.0e-5
```

However, these checks can be quite time consuming, so I don't normally use them and have not included them in the official Solution.

As I already mentioned, the problem solved in this recipe requires items to be associated with *probabilities*—numbers between 0 and 1, summing up to 1. A related but slightly different task is to get random picks with weighted relative probabilities given by small non-negative integers—*odds*, rather than probabilities. For this related problem, the best solution is a generator, with an internal structure that is rather different from the function random_pick given in this recipe's Solution:

```python
import random
def random_picks(sequence, relative_odds):
    table = [ z for x, y in zip(sequence, relative_odds) for z in [x]*y ]
    while True:
        yield random.choice(table)
```

This generator works by first preparing a table whose total number of items is sum(relative_odds), each item of seq appearing in the table as many times as the small non-negative integer that is its corresponding item in relative_odds. Once the table is prepared, the generator's body is tiny and fast, as it simply delegates to random.choice the picking of each random item it yields. Typical uses of this random_picks generator might be:

```python
>>> x = random_picks('ciao', [1, 1, 3, 2])
>>> for two_chars in zip('boo', x): print ''.join(two_chars),
bc oa oa
>>> import itertools
>>> print ''.join(itertools.islice(x, 8))
icacaoco
```

See Also

Module random in the *Library Reference* and *Python in a Nutshell*.

4.22   Handling Exceptions Within an Expression

Credit: Chris Perkins, Gregor Rayman, Scott David Daniels

Problem

You want to code an *expression*, so you can't directly use the *statement* try/except, but you still need to handle exceptions that the expression may throw.

Solution

To catch exceptions, try/except is indispensable, and, since try/except is a *statement*, the only way to use it inside an *expression* is to code an auxiliary function:

```python
def throws(t, f, *a, **k):
    '''Return True iff f(*a, **k) raises an exception whose type is t
      (or, one of the items of _tuple_ t, if t is a tuple).'''
    try:
        f(*a, **k)
```

```
    except t:
        return True
    else:
        return False
```

For example, suppose you have a text file, which has one number per line, but also extra lines which may be whitespace, comments, or what-have-you. Here is how you can make a list of all the numbers in the file, skipping the lines that aren't numbers:

```
data = [float(line) for line in open(some_file)
                    if not throws(ValueError, float, line)]
```

Discussion

You might prefer to name such a function raises, but I personally prefer throws, which is probably a throwback to C++. By whatever name, the auxiliary function shown in this recipe takes as its arguments, first an exception type (or tuple of exception types) t, then a callable f, and then arbitrary positional and named arguments a and k, which are to be passed on to f. Do *not* code, for example, if not throws(ValueError, float(line))! When you call a function, Python evaluates the arguments before passing control to the function; if an argument's evaluation raises an exception, the function never even gets started. I've seen this erroneous usage attempted more than once by people who are just starting to use the assertRaises method from the standard Python library's unittest.TestCase class, for example.

When throws executes, it just calls f within the try clause of a try/except statement, passing on the arbitrary positional and named arguments. If the call to f in the try clause raises an exception whose type is t (or one of the items of t, if t is a tuple of exception types), then control passes to the corresponding except clause, which, in this case, returns True as throws' result. If no exception is raised in the try clause, then control passes to the corresponding else clause (if any), which, in this case, returns False as throws' result.

Note that, if some *unexpected* exception (one whose type is not in t) gets raised, then function throws does not catch that exception, so that throws terminates and propagates the exception to its caller. This choice is quite a deliberate one. Catching exceptions with a too-wide except clause is a bug-diagnosing headache waiting to happen. If the caller really wants throws to catch just about everything, it can always call throws(Exception, . . .—and live with the resulting headaches.

One problem with the throws function is that you end up doing the key operation twice—once just to see if it throws, tossing the result away, then, a second time, to get the result. It would be nicer to get the result, if any, together with an indication of whether an exception has been caught. I first tried something along the lines of:

```
def throws(t, f, *a, **k):
    " Return a pair (True, None) if f(*a, **k) raises an exception whose
      type is in t, else a pair (False, x) where x is the result of f(*a, **k). "
    try:
```

```
        return False, f(*a, **k)
    except t:
        return True, None
```

Unfortunately, this version doesn't fit in well in a list comprehension: there is no elegant way to get and use both the flag and the result. So, I chose a different approach: a function that returns a list in any case—empty if an exception was caught, otherwise with the result as the only item. This approach works fine in a list comprehension, but for clarity, the name of the function needs to be changed:

```
def returns(t, f, *a, **k):
    " Return [f(*a, **k)] normally, [ ] if that raises an exception in t. "
    try:
        return [ f(*a, **k) ]
    except t:
        return [ ]
```

The resulting list comprehension is even *more* elegant, in my opinion, than the original one in this recipe's Solution:

```
data = [ x for line in open(some_file)
           for x in returns(ValueError, float, line) ]
```

See Also

Python in a Nutshell's section on catching and handling exceptions; the sidebar "The *args and **kwds Syntax" for an explanation of *args and **kwds syntax.

4.23 Ensuring a Name Is Defined in a Given Module

Credit: Steven Cummings

Problem

You want to ensure that a certain name is defined in a given module (e.g., you want to ensure that there is a built-in name set), and, if not, you want to execute some code that sets the definition.

Solution

The solution to this problem is the only good use I've yet seen for statement exec. exec lets us execute arbitrary Python code from a string, and thus lets us write a very simple function to deal with this task:

```
import __builtin__
def ensureDefined(name, defining_code, target=__builtin__):
    if not hasattr(target, name):
        d = {}
        exec defining_code in d
```

```
assert name in d, 'Code %r did not set name %r' % (
    defining_code, name)
setattr(target, name, d[name])
```

Discussion

If your code supports several versions of Python (or of some third-party package), then many of your modules must start with code such as the following snippet (which ensures name set is properly set in either Python 2.4, where it's a built-in, or 2.3, where it must be obtained from the standard library):

```
try:
    set
except NameError:
    from sets import Set as set
```

This recipe encapsulates this kind of logic directly, and by default works on module __builtin__, since that's the typical module for which you need to work around missing names in older Python versions. With this recipe, you could ensure name set is properly defined among the built-ins by running just once, during your program's initialization, the single call:

```
ensureDefined('set', 'from sets import Set as set')
```

The key advantage of this recipe is that you can group all needed calls to ensureDefined in just one place of your application, at initialization time, rather than having several ad hoc try/except statements at the start of various modules. Moreover, ensureDefined may allow more readable code because it does only one specific job, so the purpose of calling it is obvious, while try/except statements could have several purposes, so that more study and reflection might be needed to understand them. Last but not least, using this recipe lets you avoid the warnings that the try/except approach can trigger from such useful checking tools as pychecker, *http:// pychecker.sourceforge.net/*. (If you aren't using pychecker or something like that, you should!)

The recipe takes care to avoid unintended accidental side effects on target, by using an auxiliary dictionary d as the target for the exec statement and then transferring only the requested name. This way, for example, you can use as target an object that is not a module (a class, say, or even a class instance), without necessarily adding to your target an attribute named __builtins__ that references the dictionary of Python's built-ins. If you used less care, so that the body of the if statement was only:

```
exec defining_code in vars(target)
```

you would inevitably get such side effects, as documented at *http://www.python.org/ doc/current/ref/exec.html*.

It's important to be aware that exec can and does execute any valid string of Python code that you give it. Therefore, make sure that the argument defining_code that you pass to any call of function ensureDefined does *not* come from an untrusted source, such as a text file that might have been maliciously tampered with.

See Also

The online documentation of the exec statement in the *Python Language Reference Manual* at *http://www.python.org/doc/current/ref/exec.html*.

CHAPTER 5

Searching and Sorting

5.0 Introduction

Credit: Tim Peters, PythonLabs

> Computer manufacturers of the 1960s estimated that more than 25 percent of the running time on their computers was spent on sorting, when all their customers were taken into account. In fact, there were many installations in which the task of sorting was responsible for more than half of the computing time. From these statistics we may conclude that either (i) there are many important applications of sorting, or (ii) many people sort when they shouldn't, or (iii) inefficient sorting algorithms have been in common use.
>
> *—Donald Knuth*
> The Art of Computer Programming,
> *vol. 3*, Sorting and Searching, *page 3*

Professor Knuth's masterful work on the topics of sorting and searching spans nearly 800 pages of sophisticated technical text. In Python practice, we reduce it to two imperatives (we read Knuth so you don't have to):

- When you need to sort, find a way to use the built-in sort method of Python lists.

- When you need to search, find a way to use built-in dictionaries.

Many recipes in this chapter illustrate these principles. The most common theme is using the *decorate-sort-undecorate* (DSU) pattern, a general approach to transforming a sorting problem by creating an auxiliary list that we can then sort with the default, speedy sort method. This technique is the single most useful one to take from this chapter. In fact, DSU is so useful that Python 2.4 introduced new features to make it easier to apply. Many recipes can be made simpler in 2.4 as a result, and the discussion of older recipes have been updated to show how.

DSU relies on an unusual feature of Python's built-in comparisons: sequences are compared lexicographically. Lexicographical order is a generalization to tuples and lists of the everyday rules used to compare strings (e.g., alphabetical order). The built-in cmp(s1, s2), when s1 and s2 are sequences, is equivalent to this Python code:

```
def lexcmp(s1, s2):
    # Find leftmost nonequal pair.
    i = 0
    while i < len(s1) and i < len(s2):
        outcome = cmp(s1[i], s2[i])
        if outcome:
            return outcome
        i += 1
    # All equal, until at least one sequence was exhausted.
    return cmp(len(s1), len(s2))
```

This code looks for the first unequal corresponding elements. If such an unequal pair is found, that pair determines the outcome. Otherwise, if one sequence is a proper prefix of the other, the prefix is considered to be the smaller sequence. Finally, if these cases don't apply, the sequences are identical and are considered equal. Here are some examples:

```
>>> cmp((1, 2, 3), (1, 2, 3))  # identical
0
>>> cmp((1, 2, 3), (1, 2))     # first larger because second is a prefix
1
>>> cmp((1, 100), (2, 1))      # first smaller because 1<2
-1
>>> cmp((1, 2), (1, 3))        # first smaller because 1==1, then 2<3
-1
```

An immediate consequence of lexicographical comparison is that if you want to sort a list of objects by a primary key, breaking ties by comparing a secondary key, you can simply build a list of tuples, in which each tuple contains the primary key, secondary key, and original object, in that order. Because tuples are compared lexicographically, this automatically does the right thing. When comparing tuples, the primary keys are compared first, and if (and only if) the primary keys are equal, the secondary keys are compared.

The examples of the DSU pattern in this chapter show many applications of this idea. The DSU technique applies to any number of keys. You can add to the tuples as many keys as you like, in the order in which you want the keys compared. In Python 2.4, you can get the same effect with the new key= optional argument to sort, as several recipes point out. Using the sort method's key= argument is easier, more memory-efficient, and runs faster than building an auxiliary list of tuples by hand.

The other 2.4-introduced innovation in sorting is a convenient shortcut: a sorted built-in function that sorts any iterable, not in-place, but by first copying it into a new list. In Python 2.3 (apart from the new optional keyword arguments, which apply to the sorted built-in function as well as to list.sort), you can code the same functionality quite easily:

```
def sorted_2_3(iterable):
    alist = list(iterable)
    alist.sort()
    return alist
```

Because copying a list and sorting it are both nontrivial operations, and the built-in sorted needs to perform those operations too, no speed advantage is gained in making sorted a built-in. Its advantage is just the convenience. Having something always around and available, rather than having to code even just four simple lines over and over, *does* make a difference in practice. On the other hand, few tiny functions are used commonly enough to justify expanding the set of built-ins. Python 2.4 added sorted and reversed because those two functions were requested very frequently over the years.

The biggest change in Python sorting since the first edition of this book is that Python 2.3 moved to a new implementation of sorting. The primary visible consequences are increased speed in many common cases, and the fact that the new sort is stable (meaning that when two elements compare equal in the original list, they retain their relative order in the sorted list). The new implementation was so successful, and the chances of improving on it appeared so slim, that Guido was persuaded to proclaim that Python's list.sort method will always be stable. This guarantee started with Python 2.4 but was actually realized in Python 2.3. Still, the history of sorting cautions us that better methods may yet be discovered. A brief account of Python's sorting history may be instructive in this regard.

A Short History of Python Sorting

In early releases of Python, list.sort used the qsort routine from the underlying platform's C library. This didn't work out for several reasons, primarily because the quality of qsort varied widely across machines. Some versions were extremely slow when given a list with many equal values or in reverse-sorted order. Some versions even dumped core because they weren't reentrant. A user-defined __cmp__ function can also invoke list.sort, so that one list.sort can invoke others as a side effect of comparing. Some platform qsort routines couldn't handle that. A user-defined __cmp__ function can also (if it's insane or malicious) mutate the list while it's being sorted, and many platform qsort routines dumped core when that happened.

Python then grew its own implementation of the quicksort algorithm. This was rewritten with every release, as real-life cases of unacceptable slowness were discovered. Quicksort is a delicate algorithm indeed!

In Python 1.5.2 the quicksort algorithm was replaced by a hybrid of samplesort and binary insertion sort, and that implementation remained unchanged for more than four years, until Python 2.3. Samplesort can be viewed as a variant of quicksort that uses a very large sample size to pick the partitioning element, also known as the *pivot* (it recursively samplesorts a large random subset of the elements and picks the median of those). This variant makes quadratic-time behavior almost impossible and brings the number of comparisons in the average case much closer to the theoretical minimum.

However, because samplesort is a complicated algorithm, it has too much administrative overhead for small lists. Therefore, small lists (and small slices resulting from samplesort partitioning) were handled by a separate binary insertion sort, which is an ordinary insertion sort, except that it uses binary search to determine where each new element belongs. Most sorting texts say this isn't worth the bother, but that's because most texts assume that comparing two elements is as cheap as or cheaper than swapping them in memory, which isn't true for Python's sort! Moving an object is very cheap, since what is copied is just a reference to the object. Comparing two objects is expensive, though, because all of the object-oriented machinery for finding the appropriate code to compare two objects and for coercion gets reinvoked each time. This made binary search a major win for Python's sort.

On top of this hybrid approach, a few common special cases were exploited for speed. First, already-sorted or reverse-sorted lists were detected and handled in linear time. For some applications, these kinds of lists are very common. Second, if an array was mostly sorted, with just a few out-of-place elements at the end, the binary insertion sort handled the whole job. This was much faster than letting samplesort have at it and occurred often in applications that repeatedly sort a list, append a few new elements, then sort it again. Finally, special code in the samplesort looked for stretches of equal elements, so that the slice they occupy could be marked as done early.

In the end, all of this yielded an in-place sort with excellent performance in all known real cases and supernaturally good performance in some common special cases. It spanned about 500 lines of complicated C code, which gives special poignancy to recipe 5.11 "Showing off quicksort in Three Lines."

Over the years samplesort was in use, I made a standing offer to buy dinner for anyone who could code a faster Python sort. Alas, I ate alone. Still, I kept my eye on the literature because several aspects of the samplesort hybrid were irritating:

- While no case of quadratic-time behavior appeared in real life, I knew such cases could be contrived, and it was easy to contrive cases two or three times slower than average ones.

- The special cases to speed sorting in the presence of extreme partial order were valuable in practice, but my real data often had many other kinds of partial order that should be exploitable. In fact, I came to believe that random ordering in input lists almost never exists in real life (i.e., not outside of timing harnesses for testing sorting algorithms!).

- There is no practical way to make samplesort stable without grossly increasing memory use.
- The code was very complex and complicated in ugly ways by the special cases.

Current Sorting

It was always clear that a mergesort would be better on several counts, including guaranteed worst-case n log n time, and that mergesort is easy to make stable. The problem was that half a dozen attempts to code a mergesort for Python yielded a sort that ran slower (mergesort does much more data movement than samplesort) and consumed more memory.

A large and growing literature concerns *adaptive* sorting algorithms, which attempt to detect order of various kinds in the input. I coded a dozen of them, but they were all much slower than Python's samplesort except on the cases they were designed to exploit. The theoretical bases for these algorithms were simply too complex to yield effective practical algorithms. Then I read an article pointing out that list merging *naturally* reveals many kinds of partial order, simply by paying attention to how often each input list "wins" in a row. This information was simple and general. When I realized how it could be applied to a natural mergesort, which would obviously exploit all the kinds of partial order I knew and cared about, I got obsessed enough to solve the speed problem for random data and to minimize the memory burden.

The resulting "adaptive, natural, stable" mergesort implemented for Python 2.3 was a major success, but also a major engineering effort—the devil is in the details. There are about 1,200 lines of C code, but unlike the code in the samplesort hybrid, none of these lines are coding for special cases, and about half implement a technical trick allowing the worst-case memory burden to be cut in half. I'm quite proud of it, but the margins of this introduction lack the space for me to explain the details. If you're curious, I wrote a long technical description that you can find in a Python source distribution: *Objects/listsort.txt* under the main directory (say, *Python-2.3.5* or *Python-2.4*) where you unpacked Python's source distribution archive. In the following list, I provide examples of the partial order Python 2.3's mergesort naturally exploits, where "sorted" means in either forward-sorted or reverse-sorted order:

- The input is already sorted.
- The input is mostly sorted but has random elements appended at either end, or both, or inserted in the middle.
- The input is the concatenation of two or more sorted lists. In fact, the fastest way to merge multiple sorted lists in Python now is to join them into one long list and run list.sort on that.
- The input is mostly sorted but has some scattered elements that are out of order. This is common, for example, when people manually add new records to a data-

base sorted by name: people aren't good at maintaining strict alphabetic order but are good at getting close.

- The input has many keys with the same value. For example, when sorting a database of American companies by the stock exchange they're listed on, most will be associated with the NYSE or NASDAQ exchanges. This is exploitable for a curious reason: records with equal keys are already in sorted order, by the definition of "stable"! The algorithm detects that naturally, without code especially looking for equal keys.

- The input was in sorted order but got dropped on the floor in chunks; the chunks were reassembled in random order, and to fight boredom, some of the chunks were riffle-shuffled together. While that's a silly example, it still results in exploitable partial order and suggests how general the method is.

In short, Python 2.3's *timsort* (well, it has to have *some* brief name) is stable, robust, and preternaturally fast in many real-life cases: use it any time you can!

5.1   Sorting a Dictionary

Credit: Alex Martelli

Problem

You want to sort a dictionary. This probably means that you want to sort the keys and then get the values in that same sorted order.

Solution

The simplest approach is exactly the one expressed by the problem statement: sort the keys, then pick the corresponding values:

```
def sortedDictValues(adict):
    keys = adict.keys( )
    keys.sort( )
    return [adict[key] for key in keys]
```

Discussion

The concept of sorting applies only to a collection that has an order—in other words, a sequence. A mapping, such as a dictionary, has no order, so it cannot be sorted. And yet, "How do I sort a dictionary?" is a frequent, though literally meaningless, question on the Python lists. More often than not, the question is in fact about sorting some sequence composed of keys and/or values from the dictionary.

As for the implementation, while one could think of more sophisticated approaches, it turns out (not unusually, for Python) that the one shown in the solution, the simplest one, is also essentially the fastest one. A further slight increase in speed, about

20%, can be squeezed out in Python 2.3 by replacing the list comprehension with a map call in the return statement at the end of the function. For example:

```
return map(adict.get, keys)
```

Python 2.4, however, is already measurably faster than Python 2.3 with the version in the "Solution" and gains nothing from this further step. Other variants, such as using adict.__getitem__ instead of adict.get, offer no further increase in speed, or they even slow performance down a little, in both Python 2.3 and 2.4.

See Also

Recipe 5.4 "Sorting Keys or Indices Based on the Corresponding Values" for sorting a dictionary based on its values rather than on its keys.

5.2   Sorting a List of Strings Case-Insensitively

Credit: Kevin Altis, Robin Thomas, Guido van Rossum, Martin V. Lewis, Dave Cross

Problem

You want to sort a list of strings, ignoring case differences. For example, you want a, although it's lowercase, to sort before B, although the latter is uppercase. By default, however, string comparison is case-sensitive (e.g., all uppercase letters sort before all lowercase ones).

Solution

The decorate-sort-undecorate (DSU) idiom is simple and fast:

```
def case_insensitive_sort(string_list):
    auxiliary_list = [(x.lower(), x) for x in string_list]   # decorate
    auxiliary_list.sort()                                     # sort
    return [x[1] for x in auxiliary_list]                     # undecorate
```

In Python 2.4, DSU is natively supported, so (assuming the items of string_list are indeed strings, and not, e.g., Unicode objects), you can use the following even shorter and faster approach:

```
def case_insensitive_sort(string_list):
    return sorted(string_list, key=str.lower)
```

Discussion

An obvious alternative to this recipe's Solution is to code a comparison function and pass it to the sort method:

```
def case_insensitive_sort_1(string_list):
    def compare(a, b): return cmp(a.lower(), b.lower())
    string_list.sort(compare)
```

However, in this way the `lower` method gets called twice for every comparison, and the number of comparisons needed to sort a list of n items is typically proportional to n log(n).

The DSU idiom builds an auxiliary list, whose items are tuples where each item of the original list is preceded by a "key". The sort then takes place on the key, because Python compares tuples *lexicographically* (i.e., it compares the tuples' first items first). With DSU, the `lower` method gets called only n times to sort a list of n strings, which saves enough time to cover the small costs of the first, *decorate* step and the final, *undecorate* step, with a big net increase in speed.

DSU is also sometimes known, not quite correctly, as the *Schwartzian Transform*, by somewhat imprecise analogy with a well-known idiom of the Perl language. (If anything, DSU is closer to the *Guttman-Rosler Transform*, see *http://www.sysarch.com/perl/sort_paper.html*.)

DSU is so important that Python 2.4 supports it directly: you can optionally pass to the sort method of a list an argument named key, which is the callable to use on each item of the list to obtain the key for the sort. If you pass such an argument, the sorting internally uses DSU. So, in Python 2.4, `string_list.sort(key=str.lower` is essentially equivalent to function `case_insensitive_sort`, except the sort method sorts the list in-place (and returns `None`) instead of returning a sorted copy and leaving the original list alone. If you want function `case_insensitive_sort` to sort in-place, by the way, just change its `return` statement into an assignment to the list's body:

```
string_list[:] = [x[1] for x in auxiliary_list]
```

Vice versa, if, in Python 2.4, you want to get a sorted copy and leave the original list alone, you can use the new built-in function `sorted`. For example, in Python 2.4:

```
for s in sorted(string_list, key=str.lower): print s
```

prints each string in the list, sorted case-insensitively, without affecting `string_list` itself.

The use of `str.lower` as the key argument in the Python 2.4 Solution restricts you to specifically sorting strings (not, e.g., Unicode objects). If you know you're sorting a list of Unicode objects, use `key=unicode.lower` instead. If you need a function that applies just as well to strings and Unicode objects, you can `import string` and then use `key=string.lower`; alternatively, you could use `key=lambda s: s.lower( )`.

If you need case-insensitive sorting of lists of strings, you might also need dictionaries and sets using case-insensitive strings as keys, lists behaving case-insensitively regarding such methods as `index` and `count`, case-insensitive results from `needle` in `haystack`, and so on. If that is the case, then your real underlying need is a subtype of `str` that behaves case-insensitively in comparison and hashing—a clearly better factoring of the issue, compared to implementing many container types and functions to get all of this functionality. To see how to implement such a type, see recipe 1.24 "Making Some Strings Case-Insensitive."

See Also

The Python Frequently Asked Questions *http://www.python.org/cgi-bin/ faqw.py?req=show&file=faq04.051.htp*; recipe 5.3 "Sorting a List of Objects by an Attribute of the Objects"; Python 2.4 *Library Reference* about the sorted built-in function and the key argument to sort and sorted; recipe 1.24 "Making Some Strings Case-Insensitive."

5.3 Sorting a List of Objects by an Attribute of the Objects

Credit: Yakov Markovitch, Nick Perkins

Problem

You need to sort a list of objects according to one attribute of each object.

Solution

The DSU idiom shines, as usual:

```
def sort_by_attr(seq, attr):
    intermed = [ (getattr(x, attr), i, x) for i, x in enumerate(seq) ]
    intermed.sort()
    return [ x[-1] for x in intermed ]
def sort_by_attr_inplace(lst, attr):
    lst[:] = sort_by_attr(lst, attr)
```

In Python 2.4, DSU is natively supported, so your code can be even shorter and faster:

```
import operator
def sort_by_attr(seq, attr):
    return sorted(seq, key=operator.attrgetter(attr))
def sort_by_attr_inplace(lst, attr):
    lst.sort(key=operator.attrgetter(attr))
```

Discussion

Sorting a list of objects by an attribute of each object is best done using the DSU idiom introduced previously in recipe 5.2 "Sorting a List of Strings Case-Insensitively." In Python 2.3 and 2.4, DSU is no longer needed, as it used to be, to ensure that a sort is stable (sorting is always stable in Python 2.3 and later), but DSU's speed advantages still shine.

Sorting, in the general case and with the best algorithms, is $O(n \ \log \ n)$ (as is often the case in mathematical formulas, the juxtaposition of terms, here n and $\log \ n$, indicates that the terms are multiplied). DSU's speed comes from maximally accelerating the $O(n \ \log \ n)$ part, which dominates sorting time for sequences of substantial length *n*, by using only Python's native (and maximally fast) comparison. The preliminary *decoration* step, which prepares an intermediate auxiliary list of tuples, and the successive *undecoration* step, which extracts the important item from each tuple after the intermediate list is sorted, are only O(*n*). Therefore any minor inefficiencies in these steps contribute negligible overhead if n is large enough, and reasonably little even for many practical values of n.

The O( )-Notation

The most useful way to reason about many performance issues is in terms of what is popularly known as *big-O* analysis and notation (the O stands for "order"). You can find detailed explanations, for example, at *http://en.wikipedia.org/wiki/Big_O_notation*, but here's a summary.

If we consider an algorithm applied to input data of some size *N*, running time can be described, for large enough values of *N* (and big inputs are often those for which performance is most critical), as being proportional to some function of *N*. This is indicated with notations such as O(*N*) (running time proportional to *N*: processing twice as much data takes about twice as much time, 10 times as much data, 10 times as much time, and so on; also known as *linear time*), O(*N* squared) (running time proportional to the square of *N*: processing twice as much data takes about four times as much time, 10 times as much data, 100 times as much time; also known as *quadratic time*), and so on. Another case you will see often is O(*N* log *N*), which is faster than O(*N* squared) but not as fast as O(*N*).

The constant of proportionality is often ignored (at least in theoretical analysis) because it depends on such issues as the clock rate of your computer, not just on the algorithm. If you buy a machine that's twice as fast as your old one, everything will run in half the time, but that will not change any of the comparisons between alternative algorithms.

This recipe puts index i, in each tuple that is an item of list intermed, *ahead* of the corresponding x (where x is the i-th item in seq). This placement ensures that two items of seq will never be compared directly, even if they have the same value for the attribute named attr. Even in that case, their indices will still differ, and thus Python's lexicographic comparison of the tuples will never get all the way to comparing the tuples' last items (the original items from seq). Avoiding object comparisons may save us from performing extremely slow operations, or even from attempting forbidden ones. For example, we could sort a list of complex numbers by their real attribute: we would get an exception if we ever tried to compare two complex numbers directly, because no ordering is defined on complex numbers. But thanks to the precaution described in this paragraph, such an event can never occur, and the sorting will therefore proceed correctly.

As mentioned earlier in recipe 5.2 "Sorting a List of Strings Case-Insensitively," Python 2.4 supports DSU directly. You can pass an optional keyword-argument key, to sort, which is the callable to use on each item to get the sort key. Standard library module operator has two new functions, attrgetter and itemgetter, that exist specifically to return callables suitable for this purpose. In Python 2.4, the ideal solution to this problem therefore becomes:

```
import operator
seq.sort(key=operator.attrgetter(attr))
```

This snippet performs the sort in-place, which helps make it blazingly fast—on my machine, three times faster than the Python 2.3 function shown first in this recipe. If you need a sorted copy, without disturbing seq, you can get it using Python 2.4's new built-in function sorted:

```
sorted_copy = sorted(seq, key=operator.attrgetter(attr))
```

While not quite as fast as an in-place sort, this latest snippet is still over 2.5 times faster than the function shown first in this recipe. Python 2.4 also guarantees that, when you pass the optional key named argument, list items will never be accidentally compared directly, so you need not take any special safeguards. Moreover, stability is also guaranteed.

See Also

Recipe 5.2 "Sorting a List of Strings Case-Insensitively"; Python 2.4's *Library Reference* docs about the sorted built-in function, operator module's attrgetter and itemgetter functions, and the key argument to .sort and sorted.

5.4   Sorting Keys or Indices Based on the Corresponding Values

Credit: John Jensen, Fred Bremmer, Nick Coghlan

Problem

You need to count the occurrences of various items and present the items in order of their number of occurrences—for example, to produce a histogram.

Solution

A histogram, apart from graphical issues, is based on counting the occurrences of items (easy to do with a Python list or dictionary) and then sorting the keys or indices in an order based on corresponding values. Here is a subclass of dict that adds two methods for the purpose:

```
class hist(dict):
    def add(self, item, increment=1):
```

```
        ''' add 'increment' to the entry for 'item' '''
        self[item] = increment + self.get(item, 0)
    def counts(self, reverse=False):
        ''' return list of keys sorted by corresponding values '''
        aux = [ (self[k], k) for k in self ]
        aux.sort( )
        if reverse: aux.reverse( )
        return [k for v, k in aux]
```

If the items you're counting are best modeled by small integers in a compact range,
so that you want to keep item counts in a list, the solution is quite similar:

```
class hist1(list):
    def __init__(self, n):
        ''' initialize this list to count occurrences of n distinct items '''
        list.__init__(self, n*[0])
    def add(self, item, increment=1):
        ''' add 'increment' to the entry for 'item' '''
        self[item] += increment
    def counts(self, reverse=False):
        ''' return list of indices sorted by corresponding values '''
        aux = [ (v, k) for k, v in enumerate(self) ]
        aux.sort( )
        if reverse: aux.reverse( )
        return [k for v, k in aux]
```

Discussion

The add method of hist embodies the normal Python idiom for counting occurrences
of arbitrary (but hashable) items, using a dict to hold the counts. In class hist1, based
on a list, we take a different approach, initializing all counts to 0 in __init__, so the
add method is even simpler.

The counts methods produce the lists of keys, or indices, sorted in the order given by
the corresponding values. The problem is very similar in both classes, hist and
hist1; therefore, the solutions are also almost identical, using in each case the DSU
approach already shown in recipe 5.2 "Sorting a List of Strings Case-Insensitively"
and recipe "Sorting a List of Objects by an Attribute of the Objects." If we need both
classes in our program, the similarity is so close that we should surely factor out the
commonalities into a single auxiliary function _sorted_keys:

```
def _sorted_keys(container, keys, reverse):
    ''' return list of 'keys' sorted by corresponding values in 'container' '''
    aux = [ (container[k], k) for k in keys ]
    aux.sort( )
    if reverse: aux.reverse( )
    return [k for v, k in aux]
```

and then implement the counts methods of each class as thin wrappers over this
_sorted_keys function:

```
class hist(dict):
    ...
```

```
    def counts(self, reverse=False):
        return _sorted_keys(self, self, reverse)
class hist1(list):
    ...
    def counts(self, reverse=False):
        return _sorted_keys(self, xrange(len(self)), reverse)
```

DSU is so important that in Python 2.4, as shown previously in recipe 5.2 "Sorting a List of Strings Case-Insensitively" and recipe 5.3 "Sorting a List of Objects by an Attribute of the Objects," the sort method of lists and the new built-in function sorted offer a fast, intrinsic implementation of it. Therefore, in Python 2.4, function _sorted_keys can become much simpler and faster:

```
def _sorted_keys(container, keys, reverse):
    return sorted(keys, key=container.__getitem__, reverse=reverse)`
```

The bound-method container.__getitem__ performs exactly the same operation as the indexing container[k] in the Python 2.3 implementation, but it's a callable to call on each k of the sequence that we're sorting, namely keys—exactly the right kind of value to pass as the key keyword argument to the sorted built-in function. Python 2.4 also affords an easy, direct way to get a list of a dictionary's items sorted by value:

```
from operator import itemgetter
def dict_items_sorted_by_value(d, reverse=False):
    return sorted(d.iteritems(), key=itemgetter(1), reverse=reverse)
```

The operator.itemgetter higher-order function, also new in Python 2.4, is a handy way to supply the key argument when you want to sort a container whose items are subcontainers, keying on a certain item of each subcontainer. This is exactly the case here, since a dictionary's items are a sequence of pairs (two-item tuples), and we want to sort the sequence keying on the second item of each tuple.

Getting back to this recipe's main theme, here is a usage example for the class hist shown in this recipe's Solution:

```
sentence = ''' Hello there this is a test.  Hello there this was a test,
            but now it is not. '''
words = sentence.split()
c = hist()
for word in words: c.add(word)
print "Ascending count:"
print c.counts()
print "Descending count:"
print c.counts(reverse=True)
```

This code snippet produces the following output:

```
Ascending count:
[(1, 'but'), (1, 'it'), (1, 'not.'), (1, 'now'), (1, 'test,'), (1, 'test.'),
(1, 'was'), (2, 'Hello'), (2, 'a'), (2, 'is'), (2, 'there'), (2, 'this')]
Descending count:
[(2, 'this'), (2, 'there'), (2, 'is'), (2, 'a'), (2, 'Hello'), (1, 'was'),
(1, 'test.'), (1, 'test,'), (1, 'now'), (1, 'not.'), (1, 'it'), (1, 'but')]
```

See Also

Recipe "Special Method Names" in the *Language Reference* and the OOP chapter in *Python in a Nutshell*, about special method __getitem__; *Library Reference* docs for Python 2.4 sorted built-in and the key= argument to sort and sorted.

5.5 Sorting Strings with Embedded Numbers

Credit: Sébastien Keim, Chui Tey, Alex Martelli

Problem

You need to sort a list of strings that contain substrings of digits (e.g., a list of postal addresses) in an order that looks good. For example, 'foo2.txt' should come before 'foo10.txt'. However, Python's default string comparison is alphabetical, so, by default, 'foo10.txt' instead comes before 'foo2.txt'.

Solution

You need to split each string into sequences of digits and nondigits, and transform each sequence of digits into a number. This gives you a list that is just the right comparison key for the sort you want, and you can then use DSU for the sort itself—that is, code two functions, shorter than this description:

```
import re
re_digits = re.compile(r'(\d+)')
def embedded_numbers(s):
    pieces = re_digits.split(s)          # split into digits/nondigits
    pieces[1::2] = map(int, pieces[1::2]) # turn digits into numbers
    return pieces
def sort_strings_with_embedded_numbers(alist):
    aux = [ (embedded_numbers(s), s) for s in alist ]
    aux.sort( )
    return [ s for __, s in aux ]        # convention: __ means "ignore"
```

In Python 2.4, use the native support for DSU, with the same function embedded_numbers to get the sort key:

```
def sort_strings_with_embedded_numbers(alist):
    return sorted(alist, key=embedded_numbers)
```

Discussion

Say you have an unsorted list of filenames, such as:

```
files = 'file3.txt file11.txt file7.txt file4.txt file15.txt'.split( )
```

If you just sort and print this list, for example in Python 2.4 with print ' '.join(sorted(files)), your output looks like file11.txt file15.txt file3.txt file4.txt file7.txt, since, by default, strings are sorted alphabetically (to use a fancier word, the sort order is described as *lexicographical*). Python cannot just guess that you mean to treat in a different way those substrings that happen to be made of digits; you have to tell Python precisely what you want, and this recipe shows how.

Using this recipe, you can get a nicer-looking result:

```
print ' '.join(sort_strings_with_embedded_numbers(files))
```

The output is now file3.txt file4.txt file7.txt file11.txt file15.txt, which is probably just what you want in this case.

The implementation relies on the DSU idiom. We need to code DSU explicitly if we want to support Python 2.3, while if our code is Python 2.4-only, we just rely on the native implementation of DSU. We do so by passing an argument named key (a function to be called on each item to get the right comparison key for the sort) to the new built-in function sorted.

Function embedded_numbers in the recipe is how we get the right comparison key for each item: a list alternating substrings of nondigits, and the int obtained from each substring of digits. re_digits.split(s) gives us a list of alternating substrings of non-digits and digits (with the substrings of digits at odd-numbered indices); then, we use built-in functions map and int (and extended-form slices that get and set all items at odd-numbered indices) to turn sequences of digits into integers. Lexicographical comparison on this list of mixed types now produces just the right result.

See Also

Library Reference and *Python in a Nutshell* docs about extended slicing and about module re; Python 2.4 *Library Reference* about the sorted built-in function and the key argument to sort and sorted; recipe 5.3 "Sorting a List of Objects by an Attribute of the Objects"; recipe 5.2 "Sorting a List of Strings Case-Insensitively."

5.6   Processing All of a List's Items in Random Order

Credit: Iuri Wickert, Duncan Grisby, T. Warner, Steve Holden, Alex Martelli

Problem

You need to process, in random order, all of the items of a long list.

Solution

As usual in Python, the best approach is the simplest one. If we are allowed to change the order of items in the input list, then the following function is simplest and fastest:

```
def process_all_in_random_order(data, process):
    # first, put the whole list into random order
```

```
    random.shuffle(data)
    # next, just walk over the list linearly
    for elem in data: process(elem)
```

If we must preserve the input list intact, or if the input data may be some iterable that is not a list, just insert as the first statement of the function the assignment `data = list(data)`.

Discussion

While it's a common mistake to be overly concerned with speed, don't make the opposite mistake of ignoring the different performances of various algorithms. Suppose we must process all of the items in a long list in random order, without repetition (assume that we're allowed to mangle or destroy the input list). The first idea to suggest itself might be to repeatedly pick an item at random (with function `random.choice`), removing each picked item from the list to avoid future repetitions:

```
import random
def process_random_removing(data, process):
    while data:
        elem = random.choice(data)
        data.remove(elem)
        process(elem)
```

However, this function is painfully slow, even for input lists of just a few hundred elements. Each call to `data.remove` must linearly search through the list to find the element to delete. Since the cost of each of n steps is $O(n)$, the whole process is $O(n^2)$—time proportional to the *square* of the length of the list (and with a large multiplicative constant, too).

Minor improvements to this first idea could focus on obtaining random indices, using the pop method of the list to get and remove an item at the same time, low-level fiddling with indices to avoid the costly removal in favor of swapping the picked item with the last yet-unpicked one towards the end, or using dictionaries or sets instead of lists. This latest idea might be based on a hope of using a dict's popitem method (or the equivalent method pop of class sets.Set and Python 2.4's built-in type set), which may look like it's designed exactly to pick and remove a random item, but, *beware*! dict.popitem is documented to return and remove an *arbitrary* item of the dictionary, and that's a far cry from a *random* item. Check it out:

```
>>> d=dict(enumerate('ciao'))
>>> while d: print d.popitem( )
```

It may surprise you, but in most Python implementations this snippet will print d's items in a far from random order, typically (0,'c') then (1,'i') and so forth. In short, if you need pseudo-random behavior in Python, you need standard library module random—popitem is not an alternative.

If you thought about using a dictionary rather than a list, you are definitely on your way to "thinking Pythonically", even though it turns out that dictionaries wouldn't provide a substantial performance boost for this specific problem. However, an approach that is even more Pythonic than choosing the right data structure is best summarized as: let the standard library do it!. The Python Standard Library is large, rich, and chock full of useful, robust, fast functions and classes for a wide variety of tasks. In this case, the key intuition is realizing that, to walk over a sequence in a random order, the simplest approach is to first *put* that sequence into random order (known as *shuffling the sequence*, an analogy with shuffling a deck of cards) and then walk over the shuffled sequence linearly. Function random.shuffle performs the shuffling, and the function shown in this recipe's Solution just uses it.

Performance should always be measured, never guessed at, and that's what standard library module timeit is for. Using a null process function and a list of length 1,000 as data, process_all_in_random_order is almost 10 times faster than process_random_removing; with a list of length 2,000, the performance ratio grows to almost 20. While an improvement of, say, 25%, or even a constant factor of 2, usually can be neglected without really affecting the performance of your program as a whole, the same does not apply to an algorithm that is 10 or 20 times as slow as it could be. Such terrible performance is likely to make that program fragment a bottleneck, all by itself. Moreover, this risk increases when we're talking about $O(n^2)$ versus $O(n)$ behavior: with such differences in big-O behavior, the performance ratio between bad and good algorithms keeps increasing without bounds as the size of the input data grows.

See Also

The documentation for the random and timeit modules in the *Library Reference* and *Python in a Nutshell*.

5.7 Keeping a Sequence Ordered as Items Are Added

Credit: John Nielsen

Problem

You want to maintain a sequence, to which items are added, in a sorted state, so that at any time, you can easily examine or remove the smallest item currently present in the sequence.

Solution

Say you start with an unordered list, such as:

```
the_list = [903, 10, 35, 69, 933, 485, 519, 379, 102, 402, 883, 1]
```

You could call the_list.sort( ) to make the list sorted and then result=the_list.pop(0) to get and remove the smallest item. But then, every time you add an item (say with the_list.append(0)), you need to call the_list.sort( ) again to keep the list sorted.

Alternatively, you can use the heapq module of the Python Standard Library:

```
import heapq
heapq.heapify(the_list)
```

Now the list is not necessarily fully sorted, but it does satisfy the *heap property* (meaning if all indices involved are valid, the_list[i]<=the_list[2*i+1] and the_list[i]<=the_list[2*i+2])—so, in particular, the_list[0] is the smallest item. To keep the heap property valid, use result=heapq.heappop(the_list) to get and remove the smallest item and heapq.heappush(the_list, newitem) to add a new item. When you need to do both—add a new item while getting and removing the previously smallest item—you can use result=heapq.heapreplace(the_list, newitem).

Discussion

When you need to retrieve data in an ordered way (at each retrieval getting the smallest item among those you currently have at hand), you can pay the runtime cost for the sorting when you retrieve the data, or you can pay for it when you add the data. One approach is to collect your data into a list and sort the list. Now it's easy to get your data in order, smallest to largest. However, you have to keep calling sort each time you add new data during the retrieval, to make sure you can later keep retrieving from the smallest current item after each addition. The method sort of Python lists is implemented with a little-known algorithm called *Natural Mergesort*, which minimizes the runtime cost of this approach. Yet the approach can still be burdensome: each addition (and sorting) and each retrieval (and removal, via pop) takes time proportional to the number of current items in the list (O(N), in common parlance).

An alternative approach is to use a data organization known as a *heap*, a type of binary tree implemented compactly, yet ensuring that each "parent" is always less than its "children". The best way to maintain a heap in Python is to use a list and have it managed by the heapq library module, as shown in this recipe's Solution. The list does not get fully sorted, yet you can be sure that, whenever you heappop an item from the list, you always get the lowest item currently present, and all others will be adjusted to ensure the heap property is still valid. Each addition with heappush, and each removal with heappop, takes a short time proportional to the logarithm of the current length of the list (O(log N), in common parlance). You pay as you go, a little at a time (and not too much in total, either.)

A good occasion to use this heap approach, for example, is when you have a long-running queue with new data periodically arriving, and you always want to be able to get the most important item off the queue without having to constantly re-sort your data or perform full searches. This concept is known as a *priority queue*, and a heap is an excellent way to implement it. Note that, intrinsically, the heapq module supplies you with the *smallest* item at each heappop, so make sure to arrange the way you encode your items' priority values to reflect this. For example, say that you receive incoming items each accompanied by a cost, and the most important item at any time is the one with the highest cost that is currently on the queue; moreover, among items of equal cost, the most important one is the one that arrived earliest. Here's a way to build a "priority queue" class respecting these specs and based on functions of module heapq:

```
class prioq(object):
    def __init__(self):
        self.q = [ ]
        self.i = 0
    def push(self, item, cost):
        heapq.heappush(self.q, (-cost, self.i, item))
        self.i += 1
    def pop(self):
        return heapq.heappop(self.q)[-1]
```

The main idea in this snippet is to push on the heap tuples whose first item is the cost *with changed sign*, so that *higher* costs result in *smaller* tuples (by Python's natural comparison); right after the cost, we put a progressive index, so that, among items with equal cost, the one arriving earliest will be in a smaller tuple.

In Python 2.4, module heapq has been reimplemented and optimized; see recipe 5.8 "Getting the First Few Smallest Items of a Sequence" for more information about heapq.

See Also

Docs for module heapq in the *Library Reference* and *Python in a Nutshell*; *heapq.py* in the Python sources contains a very interesting discussion of heaps; recipe 5.8 "Getting the First Few Smallest Items of a Sequence" for more information about heapq; recipe 19.14 "Merging Sorted Sequences" for merging sorted sequences using heapq.

5.8   Getting the First Few Smallest Items of a Sequence

Credit: Matteo Dell'Amico, Raymond Hettinger, George Yoshida, Daniel Harding

Problem

You need to get just a few of the smallest items from a sequence. You could sort the sequence and just use seq[:n], but is there any way you can do better?

Solution

Perhaps you can do better, if n, the number of items you need, is small compared to L, the sequence's length. sort is very fast, but it still takes O(L log L) time, while we can get the first n smallest elements in time O(n) if n is small. Here is a simple and practical generator for this purpose, which works equally well in Python 2.3 and 2.4:

```
import heapq
def isorted(data):
    data = list(data)
    heapq.heapify(data)
    while data:
        yield heapq.heappop(data)
```

In Python 2.4 only, you can use an even simpler and faster way to get the smallest n items of data when you know n in advance:

```
import heapq
def smallest(n, data):
    return heapq.nsmallest(n, data)
```

Discussion

data can be any bounded iterable; the recipe's function isorted starts by calling list on it to ensure that. You can remove the statement data = list(data) if all the following conditions hold: you know that data is a list to start with, you don't mind the fact that the generator reorders data's items, and you want to remove items from data as you fetch them.

As shown previously in recipe 5.7 "Keeping a Sequence Ordered as Items Are Added," the Python Standard Library contains module heapq, which supports the data structures known as *heaps*. Generator isorted in this recipe's Solution relies on making a heap at the start (via heap.heapify) and then yielding and removing the heap's smallest remaining item at each step (via heap.heappop).

In Python 2.4, module heapq has also grown two new functions. heapq.nlargest(n, data) returns a list of the n largest items of data; heapq.nsmallest(n, data) returns a list of the n smallest items. These functions do not require that data satisfy the heap condition; indeed, they do not even require data to be a list—any bounded iterable whose items are comparable will do. Function smallest in this recipe's Solution just lets heapq.smallest do all the work.

To judge speed, we must *always* measure it—guessing about relative speeds of different pieces of code is a mug's game. So, how does isorted's performance compare with Python 2.4's built-in function sorted, when we're only looping on the first few (smallest) items? To help measure timing, I wrote a top10 function that can use either approach, and I also made sure I had a sorted function even in Python 2.3, where it's not built in:

```
try:
    sorted
```

```
    except:
        def sorted(data):
            data = list(data)
            data.sort( )
            return data
    import itertools
    def top10(data, howtosort):
        return list(itertools.islice(howtosort(data), 10))
```

On my machine running Python 2.4 on thoroughly shuffled lists of 1,000 integers, top10 takes about 260 microseconds with isorted, while it takes about 850 microseconds with the built-in sorted. However, Python 2.3 is much slower and gives vastly different results: about 12 milliseconds with isorted, about 2.7 milliseconds with sorted. In other words, Python 2.3 is 3 times slower than Python 2.4 for sorted, but it's *50* times slower for isorted. Lesson to retain: whenever you optimize, *measure*. You shouldn't choose optimizations based on first principles, since the performance numbers can vary so widely, even between vastly compatible "point releases". A secondary point can be made: if you care about performance, move to Python 2.4 as soon as you can. Python 2.4 has been vastly optimized and accelerated over Python 2.3, particularly in areas related to searching and sorting.

If you know that your code need only support Python 2.4, then, as this recipe's Solution indicates, using heapq's new function nsmallest is faster, as well as simpler, than doing your own coding. To implement top10 in Python 2.4, for example, you just need:

```
    import heapq
    def top10(data):
        return heapq.nsmallest(10, data)
```

This version takes about half the time of the previously shown isorted-based top10, when called on the same thoroughly shuffled lists of 1,000 integers.

See Also

Library Reference and *Python in a Nutshell* docs about method sort of type list, and about modules heapq and timeit; Chapter 19 for more about iteration in Python; *Python in a Nutshell*'s chapter on optimization; *heapq.py* in the Python sources contains a very interesting discussion of heaps; recipe 5.7 "Keeping a Sequence Ordered as Items Are Added" for more information about heapq.

5.9 Looking for Items in a Sorted Sequence

Credit: Noah Spurrier

Problem

You need to look for a lot of items in a sequence.

Solution

If list L is sorted, module bisect from the Python Standard Library makes it easy to check if some item x is present in L:

```
import bisect
x_insert_point = bisect.bisect_right(L, x)
x_is_present = L[x_insert_point-1:x_insert_point] == [x]
```

Discussion

Looking for an item x in a list L is very easy in Python: to check whether the item is there at all, if x in L; to find out where exactly it is, L.index(x). However, if L has length n, these operations take time proportional to n—essentially, they just loop over the list's items, checking each for equality to x. If L is sorted, we can do better.

The classic algorithm to look for an item in a sorted sequence is known as *binary search*, because at each step it roughly halves the range it's still searching on—it generally takes about $log_2 n$ steps. It's worth considering when you're going to look for items many times, so you can amortize the cost of sorting over many searches. Once you've decided to use binary search for x in L, after calling L.sort( ), module bisect from the Python Standard Library makes the job easy.

Specifically, we need function bisect.bisect_right, which returns the index where an item *should* be inserted, to keep the sorted list sorted, but doesn't alter the list; moreover, if the item already appears in the list, bisect_right returns an index that's just to the right of any items with the same value. So, after getting this "insert point" by calling bisect.bisect_right(L, x), we need only to check the list immediately *before* the insert point, to see if an item equal to x is already there.

The way we compute x_is_present in the "Solution" may not be immediately obvious. If we know that L is not empty, we can use a simpler and more obvious approach:

```
x_is_present = L[x_insert_point-1] == x
```

However, the indexing in this simpler approach raises an exception when L is empty. When the slice boundaries are invalid, slicing is less "strict" than indexing, since it just produces an empty slice without raising any exception. In general, somelist[i:i+1] is the same one-item list as [somelist[i]] when i is a valid index in somelist: it's an empty list [ ] when the indexing would raise IndexError. The computation of x_is_present in the recipe exploits this important property to avoid having to deal with exceptions and handle empty and nonempty cases for L in one uniform way. An alternative approach is:

```
x_is_present = L and L[x_insert_point-1] == x
```

This alternative approach exploits and's short-circuiting behavior to guard the indexing, instead of using slicing.

An auxiliary dict, as shown in recipe 5.12 "Performing Frequent Membership Tests on a Sequence," is also a possibility as long as items are hashable (meaning that items can be used as keys into a dict). However, the approach in this recipe, based on a sorted list, may be the only useful one when the items are comparable (otherwise, the list could not be sorted) but not hashable (so a dict can't have those items as its keys).

When the list is already sorted, and the number of items you need to look up in it is not extremely large, it may in any case be faster to use bisect than to build an auxiliary dictionary, since the investment of time in the latter operation might not be fully amortized. This is particularly likely in Python 2.4, since bisect has been optimized very effectively and is much faster than it was in Python 2.3. On my machine, for example, bisect.bisect_right for an item in the middle of a list of 10,000 integers is about four times faster in Python 2.4 than it was in Python 2.3.

See Also

Documentation for the bisect module in the *Library Reference* and *Python in a Nutshell*; recipe 5.12 "Performing Frequent Membership Tests on a Sequence."

5.10   Selecting the nth Smallest Element of a Sequence

Credit: Raymond Hettinger, David Eppstein, Shane Holloway, Chris Perkins

Problem

You need to get from a sequence the nth item in rank order (e.g., the middle item, known as the *median*). If the sequence was sorted, you would just use seq[n]. But the sequence *isn't* sorted, and you wonder if you can do better than just sorting it first.

Solution

Perhaps you can do better, if the sequence is big, has been shuffled enough, and comparisons between its items are costly. Sort is very fast, but in the end (when applied to a thoroughly shuffled sequence of length n) it always takes $O(n \log n)$ time, while there exist algorithms that can be used to get the nth smallest element in time $O(n)$. Here is a function with a solid implementation of such an algorithm:

```
import random
def select(data, n):
    " Find the nth rank ordered element (the least value has rank 0). "
    # make a new list, deal with <0 indices, check for valid index
    data = list(data)
    if n<0:
        n += len(data)
    if not 0 <= n < len(data):
        raise ValueError, "can't get rank %d out of %d" % (n, len(data))
```

```
# main loop, quicksort-like but with no need for recursion
while True:
    pivot = random.choice(data)
    pcount = 0
    under, over = [ ], [ ]
    uappend, oappend = under.append, over.append
    for elem in data:
        if elem < pivot:
            uappend(elem)
        elif elem > pivot:
            oappend(elem)
        else:
            pcount += 1
    numunder = len(under)
    if n < numunder:
        data = under
    elif n < numunder + pcount:
        return pivot
    else:
        data = over
        n -= numunder + pcount
```

Discussion

This recipe is meant for cases in which repetitions *count*. For example, the median of the list [1, 1, 1, 2, 3] is 1 because that is the third one of the five items in rank order. If, for some strange reason, you want to discount duplications, you need to reduce the list to its unique items first (e.g., by applying the recipe 18.1 "Removing Duplicates from a Sequence"), after which you may want to come back to this recipe.

Input argument data can be any bounded iterable; the recipe starts by calling list on it to ensure that. The algorithm then loops, implementing at each leg a few key ideas: randomly choosing a *pivot element*; slicing up the list into two parts, made up of the items that are "under" and "over" the pivot respectively; continuing work for the next leg on just one of the two parts, since we can tell which one of them the nth element will be in, and the other part can safely be ignored. The ideas are very close to that in the classic algorithm known as *quicksort* (except that quicksort cannot ignore either part, and thus must use recursion, or recursion-removal techniques such as keeping an explicit stack, to make sure it deals with both parts).

The random choice of pivot makes the algorithm robust against unfavorable data orderings (the kind that wreak havoc with naive quicksort); this implementation decision costs about log2N calls to random.choice. Another implementation issue worth pointing out is that the recipe counts the number of occurrences of the pivot: this precaution ensures good performance even in the anomalous case where data contains a high number of repetitions of identical values.

Extracting the bound methods .append of lists under and over as local variables uappend and oappend may look like a pointless, if tiny, complication, but it is, in fact, a very important optimization technique in Python. To keep the compiler simple, straightforward, unsurprising, and robust, Python does not *hoist* constant computations out of loops, nor does it "cache" the results of method lookup. If you call under.append and over.append in the inner loop, you pay the cost of lookup each and every time. If you want something hoisted, hoist it yourself. When you're considering an optimization, you should always measure the code's performance *with* and *without* that optimization, to check that the optimization does indeed make an important difference. According to my measurements, removing this single optimization slows performance down by about 50% for the typical task of picking the 5000th item of range(10000). Considering the tiny amount of complication involved, a difference of 50% is well worth it.

A natural idea for optimization, which just didn't make the grade once carefully measured, is to call cmp(elem, pivot) in the loop body, rather than making separate tests for elem < pivot and elem > pivot. Unfortunately, measurement shows that cmp doesn't speed things up; in fact, it slows them down, at least when the items of data are of elementary types such as numbers and strings.

So, how does select's performance compare with the simpler alternative of:

```
def selsor(data, n):
    data = list(data)
    data.sort()
    return data[n]
```

On thoroughly shuffled lists of 3,001 integers on my machine, this recipe's select takes about 16 milliseconds to find the median, while selsor takes about 13 milliseconds; considering that sort could take advantage of any partial sortedness in the data, for this kind of length, and on elementary data whose comparisons are fast, it's not to your advantage to use select. For a length of 30,001, performance becomes very close between the two approaches—around 170 milliseconds either way. When you push the length all the way to 300,001, select provides an advantage, finding the median in about 2.2 seconds, while selsor takes about 2.5.

The break-even point will be smaller if the items in the sequence have costly comparison methods, since the key difference between the two approaches is in the number of comparisons performed—select takes O(n), selsor takes O(n log n). For example, say we need to compare instances of a class designed for somewhat costly comparisons (simulating four-dimensional points that will often coincide on the first few dimensions):

```
class X(object):
    def __init__(self):
        self.a = self.b = self.c = 23.51
        self.d = random.random()
    def _dats(self):
        return self.a, self.b, self.c, self.d
    def __cmp__(self, oth):
        return cmp(self._dats, oth._dats)
```

Here, select already becomes faster than selsor when what we're computing is the median of vectors of 201 such instances.

In other words, although `select` has more general overhead, when compared to the wondrously efficient coding of lists' sort method, nevertheless, if n is large enough and each comparison is costly enough, `select` is still well worth considering.

See Also

Library Reference and *Python in a Nutshell* docs about method sort of type `list`, and about module `random`.

5.11 Showing off quicksort in Three Lines

Credit: Nathaniel Gray, Raymond Hettinger, Christophe Delord, Jeremy Zucker

Problem

You need to show that Python's support for the functional programming paradigm is better than it might seem at first sight.

Solution

Functional programming languages, of which Haskell is a great example, are splendid animals, but Python can hold its own in such company:

```
def qsort(L):
    if len(L) <= 1: return L
    return qsort([lt for lt in L[1:] if lt < L[0]]) + L[0:1] + \
           qsort([ge for ge in L[1:] if ge >= L[0]])
```

In my humble opinion, this code is almost as pretty as the Haskell version from *http://www.haskell.org*:

```
qsort [ ] = [ ]
qsort (x:xs) = qsort elts_lt_x ++ [x] ++ qsort elts_greq_x
               where
                 elts_lt_x = [y | y <- xs, y < x]
                 elts_greq_x = [y | y <- xs, y >= x]
```

Here's a test function for the Python version:

```
def qs_test(length):
    import random
    joe = range(length)
    random.shuffle(joe)
    qsJoe = qsort(joe)
    for i in range(len(qsJoe)):
        assert qsJoe[i] == i, 'qsort is broken at %d!' %i
```

Discussion

This rather naive implementation of quicksort illustrates the expressive power of list comprehensions. Do not use this approach in real code! Python lists have an in-place sort method that is much faster and should always be preferred; in Python 2.4, the new built-in function sorted accepts any finite sequence and returns a new sorted list with the sequence's items. The only proper use of this recipe is for impressing friends, particularly ones who (quite understandably) are enthusiastic about functional programming, and particularly about the Haskell language.

I cooked up this function after finding the wonderful Haskell quicksort (which I've reproduced in the "Solution") at *http://www.haskell.org/aboutHaskell.html*. After marveling at the elegance of this code for a while, I realized that list comprehensions made the same approach possible in Python. Not for nothing did we steal list comprehensions right out of Haskell, just Pythonizing them a bit by using keywords rather than punctuation!

Both implementations pivot on the first element of the list and thus have worst-case O(n) performance for the very common case of sorting an already sorted list. You would never want to do so in production code! Because this recipe is just a propaganda piece, though, it doesn't really matter.

You can write a less compact version with similar architecture in order to use named local variables and functions for enhanced clarity:

```
def qsort(L):
    if not L: return L
    pivot = L[0]
    def lt(x): return x<pivot
    def ge(x): return x>=pivot
    return qsort(filter(lt, L[1:]))+[pivot]+qsort(filter(ge, L[1:]))
```

Once you start going this route, you can easily move to a slightly less naive version, using random pivot selection to make worst-case performance less likely and counting pivots to handle degenerate case with many equal elements:

```
import random
def qsort(L):
    if not L: return L
    pivot = random.choice(L)
    def lt(x): return x<pivot
    def gt(x): return x>pivot
    return qsort(filter(lt, L))+[pivot]*L.count(pivot)+qsort(filter(gt, L))
```

Despite the enhancements, they are meant essentially for fun and demonstration purposes. Production-quality sorting code is quite another thing: these little jewels, no matter how much we dwell on them, will never match the performance and solidity of Python's own built-in sorting approaches.

Rather than going for clarity and robustness, we can move in the opposite direction to make this last point most obvious, showing off the obscurity and compactness that one can get with Python's lambda:

```
q=lambda x:(lambda o=lambda s:[i for i in x if cmp(i,x[0])==s]:
        len(x)>1 and q(o(-1))+o(0)+q(o(1)) or x)()
```

At least, with *this* beauty (a single logical line, although it needs to be split into two physical lines due to its length), it should be absolutely obvious that this approach is not meant for real-world use. The equivalent, using more readable def statements rather than opaque lambdas, would still be pretty obscure:

```
def q(x):
    def o(s): return [i for i in x if cmp(i,x[0])==s]
    return len(x)>1 and q(o(-1))+o(0)+q(o(1)) or x
```

but a little more clarity (and sanity) can be recovered by opening up the pithy len(x)>1 and . . . or x into an if/else statement and introducing sensible local names again:

```
def q(x):
    if len(x)>1:
        lt = [i for i in x if cmp(i,x[0]) == -1 ]
        eq = [i for i in x if cmp(i,x[0]) == 0 ]
        gt = [i for i in x if cmp(i,x[0]) == 1 ]
        return q(lt) + eq + q(gt)
    else:
        return x
```

Fortunately, in the real world, Pythonistas are much too sensible to write convoluted, lambda-filled horrors such as this. In fact, many (though admittedly not all) of us feel enough aversion to lambda itself (partly from having seen it abused this way) that we go out of our way to use readable def statements instead. As a result, the ability to decode such "bursts of line noise" is *not* a necessary survival skill in the Python world, as it might be for other languages. A*ny* language feature can be abused by programmers trying to be "clever" . . . as a result, some Pythonistas (though a minority) feel a similar aversion to features such as list comprehensions (since it's possible to cram too many things into a list comprehension, where a plain for loop would be clearer) or to the short-circuiting behavior of operators and/or (since they can be abused to write obscure, terse expressions where a plain if statement would be clearer).

See Also

The Haskell web site, *http://www.haskell.org*.

5.12 Performing Frequent Membership Tests on a Sequence

Credit: Alex Martelli

Problem

You need to perform frequent tests for membership in a sequence. The O(n) behavior of repeated in operators hurts performance, but you can't switch to using just a dictionary or set *instead* of the sequence, because you also need to keep the sequence's order.

Solution

Say you need to append items to a list only if they're not already in the list. One sound approach to this task is the following function:

```
def addUnique(baseList, otherList):
    auxDict = dict.fromkeys(baseList)
    for item in otherList:
        if item not in auxDict:
            baseList.append(item)
            auxDict[item] = None
```

If your code has to run only under Python 2.4, you can get exactly the same effect with an auxiliary set rather than an auxiliary dictionary.

Discussion

A simple (naive?) approach to this recipe's task *looks* good:

```
def addUnique_simple(baseList, otherList):
    for item in otherList:
        if item not in baseList:
            baseList.append(item)
```

and it may be sort of OK, *if* the lists are very small.

However, the simple approach can be quite slow if the lists are not small. When you check if item not in baseList, Python can implement the in operator in only one way: an internal loop over the elements of baseList, ending with a result of True as soon as an element compares equal to item, with a result of False if the loop terminates without having found any equality. On average, executing the in-operator takes time proportional to len(baseList). addUnique_simple executes the in-operator len(otherList) times, so, in all, it takes time proportional to the *product* of the lengths of the two lists.

In the addUnique function shown in the "Solution", we first build the auxiliary dictionary auxDict, a step that takes time proportional to len(baseList). Then, the in-operator inside the loop checks for membership in a dict—a step that makes all the difference because checking for membership in a dict takes roughly constant time, independent of the number of items in the dict! So, the for loop takes time proportional to len(otherList), and the entire function takes time proportional to the *sum* of the lengths of the two lists.

The analysis of the running times should in fact go quite a bit deeper, because the length of baseList is not constant in addUnique_simple; baseList grows each time an item is processed that was not already there. But the gist of the (surprisingly complicated) analysis is not very different from what this simplified version indicates. We can check this by measuring. When each list holds 10 integers, with an overlap of

50%, the simple version is about 30% slower than the one shown in the "Solution", the kind of slowdown that can normally be ignored. But with lists of 100 integers each, again with 50% overlap, the simple version is *twelve times slower* than the one shown in the "Solution"—a level of slowdown that can never be ignored, and it only gets worse if the lists get really substantial.

Sometimes, you could obtain even better overall performance for your program by permanently placing the auxiliary dict alongside the sequence, encapsulating both into one object. However, in this case, you must maintain the dict as the sequence gets modified, to ensure it stays in sync with the sequence's current membership. This maintenance task is not trivial, and it can be architected in many different ways. Here is one such way, which does the syncing "just in time," rebuilding the auxiliary dict when a membership test is required and the dictionary is possibly out of sync with the list's contents. Since it costs very little, the following class optimizes the index method, as well as membership tests:

```
class list_with_aux_dict(list):
    def __init__(self, iterable=()):
        list.__init__(self, iterable)
        self._dict_ok = False
    def _rebuild_dict(self):
        self._dict = {}
        for i, item in enumerate(self):
            if item not in self._dict:
                self._dict[item] = i
        self._dict_ok = True
    def __contains__(self, item):
        if not self._dict_ok:
            self._rebuild_dict()
        return item in self._dict
    def index(self, item):
        if not self._dict_ok:
            self._rebuild_dict()
        try: return self._dict[item]
        except KeyError: raise ValueError
    def _wrapMutatorMethod(methname):
        _method = getattr(list, methname)
        def wrapper(self, *args):
            # Reset 'dictionary OK' flag, then delegate to the real mutator method
            self._dict_ok = False
            return _method(self, *args)
        # in Python 2.4, only: wrapper.__name__ = _method.__name__
        setattr(list_with_aux_dict, methname, wrapper)
    for meth in 'setitem delitem setslice delslice iadd'.split():
        _wrapMutatorMethod('__%s__' % meth)
    for meth in 'append insert pop remove extend'.split():
        _wrapMutatorMethod(meth)
    del _wrapMethod                  # remove auxiliary function, not needed any more
```

The list_with_aux_dict class extends list and delegates to it every method, except __contains__ and index. Every method that can modify list membership is wrapped in a closure that resets a flag asserting that the auxiliary dictionary is OK. Python's in-operator calls the `__contains__` method. list_with_aux_dict's `__contains__` method rebuilds the auxiliary dictionary, unless the flag is set (when the flag is set, rebuilding is unnecessary); the index method works the same way.

Instead of building and installing wrapping closures for all the mutating methods of the list into the `list_with_aux_dict` class with a helper function, as the recipe does, we could write all the `def` statements for the wrapper methods in the body of `list_with_aux_dict`. However, the code for the class as presented has the important advantage of minimizing boilerplate (repetitive plumbing code that is boring and voluminous, and thus a likely home for bugs). Python's strengths at introspection and dynamic modification give you a choice: you can build method wrappers, as this recipe does, in a smart and concise way; or, you can choose to code the boilerplate anyway, if you prefer to avoid what some would call the black magic of introspection and dynamic modification of class objects.

The architecture of class `list_with_aux_dict` caters well to a rather common pattern of use, where sequence-modifying operations happen in bunches, followed by a period of time in which the sequence is not modified, but several membership tests may be performed. However, the `addUnique_simple` function shown earlier would not get any performance benefit if argument `baseList` was an instance of this recipe's `list_with_aux_dict` rather than a plain `list`: the function interleaves membership tests and sequence modifications. Therefore, too many rebuilds of the auxiliary dictionary for `list_with_aux_dict` would impede the function's performance. (Unless a typical case was for a vast majority of the items of `otherList` to be already contained in `baseList`, so that very few modifications occurred compared to the number of membership tests.)

An important requisite for any of these membership-test optimizations is that the values in the sequence must be hashable (otherwise, of course, they cannot be keys in a dict, nor items in a set). For example, a list of tuples might be subjected to this recipe's treatment, but for a list of lists, the recipe as it stands is just not applicable.

See Also

The *Library Reference* and *Python in a Nutshell* sections on sequence types and mapping types.

5.13   Finding Subsequences

Credit: David Eppstein, Alexander Semenov

Problem

You need to find occurrences of a subsequence in a larger sequence.

Solution

If the sequences are strings (plain or Unicode), Python strings' find method and the standard library's re module are the best approach. Otherwise, use the Knuth-Morris-Pratt algorithm (KMP):

```
def KnuthMorrisPratt(text, pattern):
    ''' Yields all starting positions of copies of subsequence 'pattern'
        in sequence 'text' -- each argument can be any iterable.
        At the time of each yield, 'text' has been read exactly up to and
        including the match with 'pattern' that is causing the yield. '''
    # ensure we can index into pattern, and also make a copy to protect
    # against changes to 'pattern' while we're suspended by `yield'
    pattern = list(pattern)
    length = len(pattern)
    # build the KMP "table of shift amounts" and name it 'shifts'
    shifts = [1] * (length + 1)
    shift = 1
    for pos, pat in enumerate(pattern):
        while shift <= pos and pat != pattern[pos-shift]:
            shift += shifts[pos-shift]
        shifts[pos+1] = shift
    # perform the actual search
    startPos = 0
    matchLen = 0
    for c in text:
        while matchLen == length or matchLen >= 0 and pattern[matchLen] != c:
            startPos += shifts[matchLen]
            matchLen -= shifts[matchLen]
        matchLen += 1
        if matchLen == length: yield startPos
```

Discussion

This recipe implements the Knuth-Morris-Pratt algorithm for finding copies of a given pattern as a contiguous subsequence of a larger text. Since KMP accesses the text sequentially, it is natural to implement it in a way that allows the text to be an arbitrary iterator. After a preprocessing stage that builds a table of shift amounts and takes time that's directly proportional to the length of the pattern, each text symbol is processed in constant amortized time. Explanations and demonstrations of how KMP works can be found in all good elementary texts about algorithms. (A recommendation is provided in See Also.)

If text and pattern are both Python strings, you can get a faster solution by suitably applying Python built-in search methods:

```
def finditer(text, pattern):
    pos = -1
    while True:
        pos = text.find(pattern, pos+1)
        if pos < 0: break
        yield pos
```

For example, using an alphabet of length 4 ('ACGU' . . .), finding all occurrences of a pattern of length 8 in a text of length 100000, on my machine, takes about 4.3 milliseconds with `finditer`, but the same task takes about 540 milliseconds with `KnuthMorrisPratt` (that's with Python 2.3; KMP is faster with Python 2.4, taking about 480 milliseconds, but that's still over 100 times slower than `finditer`). So remember: this recipe is useful for searches on *generic* sequences, including ones that you cannot keep in memory all at once, but if you're searching on strings, Python's built-in searching methods rule.

See Also

Many excellent books cover the fundamentals of algorithms; among such books, a widely admired one is Thomas H. Cormen, Charles E. Leiserson, Ronald L. Rivest, Clifford Stein, *Introduction to Algorithms*, 2d ed. (MIT Press).

5.14 Enriching the Dictionary Type with Ratings Functionality

Credit: Dmitry Vasiliev, Alex Martelli

Problem

You want to use a dictionary to store the mapping between some keys and a current score value for each key. You frequently need to access the keys and scores in natural order (meaning, in order of ascending scores) and to check on a "key"'s current ranking in that order, so that using just a `dict` isn't quite enough.

Solution

We can subclass `dict` and add or override methods as needed. By using multiple inheritance, placing base `UserDict.DictMixin` *before* base dict and carefully arranging our various delegations and "over"rides, we can achieve a good balance between getting good performance and avoiding the need to write "boilerplate" code.

By enriching our class with many examples in its docstring, we can use the standard library's module doctest to give us unit-testing functionality, as well as ensuring the accuracy of all the examples we write in the docstring:

```python
#!/usr/bin/env python
''' An enriched dictionary that holds a mapping from keys to scores '''
from bisect import bisect_left, insort_left
import UserDict
class Ratings(UserDict.DictMixin, dict):
    """ class Ratings is mostly like a dictionary, with extra features: the
        value corresponding to each key is the 'score' for that key, and all
        keys are ranked in terms their scores.  Values must be comparable; keys,
        as well as being hashable, must be comparable if any two keys may ever
```

have the same corresponding value (i.e., may be "tied" on score).
All mapping-like behavior is just as you would expect, such as:
```
>>> r = Ratings({"bob": 30, "john": 30})
>>> len(r)
2
>>> r.has_key("paul"), "paul" in r
(False, False)
>>> r["john"] = 20
>>> r.update({"paul": 20, "tom": 10})
>>> len(r)
4
>>> r.has_key("paul"), "paul" in r
(True, True)
>>> [r[key] for key in ["bob", "paul", "john", "tom"]]
[30, 20, 20, 10]
>>> r.get("nobody"), r.get("nobody", 0)
(None, 0)
```
In addition to the mapping interface, we offer rating-specific
methods. r.rating(key) returns the ranking of a "key" in the
ratings, with a ranking of 0 meaning the lowest score (when two
keys have equal scores, the keys themselves are compared, to
"break the tie", and the lesser key gets a lower ranking):
```
>>> [r.rating(key) for key in ["bob", "paul", "john", "tom"]]
[3, 2, 1, 0]
```
getValueByRating(ranking) and getKeyByRating(ranking) return the
score and key, respectively, for a given ranking index:
```
>>> [r.getValueByRating(rating) for rating in range(4)]
[10, 20, 20, 30]
>>> [r.getKeyByRating(rating) for rating in range(4)]
['tom', 'john', 'paul', 'bob']
```
An important feature is that the keys() method returns keys in
ascending order of ranking, and all other related methods return
lists or iterators fully consistent with this ordering:
```
>>> r.keys()
['tom', 'john', 'paul', 'bob']
>>> [key for key in r]
['tom', 'john', 'paul', 'bob']
>>> [key for key in r.iterkeys()]
['tom', 'john', 'paul', 'bob']
>>> r.values()
[10, 20, 20, 30]
>>> [value for value in r.itervalues()]
[10, 20, 20, 30]
>>> r.items()
[('tom', 10), ('john', 20), ('paul', 20), ('bob', 30)]
>>> [item for item in r.iteritems()]
[('tom', 10), ('john', 20), ('paul', 20), ('bob', 30)]
```
An instance can be modified (adding, changing and deleting
key-score correspondences), and every method of that instance
reflects the instance's current state at all times:
```
>>> r["tom"] = 100
>>> r.items()
[('john', 20), ('paul', 20), ('bob', 30), ('tom', 100)]
>>> del r["paul"]
```

```
>>> r.items()
[('john', 20), ('bob', 30), ('tom', 100)]
>>> r["paul"] = 25
>>> r.items()
[('john', 20), ('paul', 25), ('bob', 30), ('tom', 100)]
>>> r.clear()
>>> r.items()
[]
"""
''' the implementation carefully mixes inheritance and delegation
    to achieve reasonable performance while minimizing boilerplate,
    and, of course, to ensure semantic correctness as above.  All
    mappings' methods not implemented below get inherited, mostly
    from DictMixin, but, crucially!, __getitem__ from dict. '''
def __init__(self, *args, **kwds):
    ''' This class gets instantiated just like 'dict' '''
    dict.__init__(self, *args, **kwds)
    # self._rating is the crucial auxiliary data structure: a list
    # of all (value, key) pairs, kept in "natural"ly-sorted order
    self._rating = [ (v, k) for k, v in dict.iteritems(self) ]
    self._rating.sort()
def copy(self):
    ''' Provide an identical but independent copy '''
    return Ratings(self)
def __setitem__(self, k, v):
    ''' besides delegating to dict, we maintain self._rating '''
    if k in self:
        del self._rating[self.rating(k)]
    dict.__setitem__(self, k, v)
    insort_left(self._rating, (v, k))
def __delitem__(self, k):
    ''' besides delegating to dict, we maintain self._rating '''
    del self._rating[self.rating(k)]
    dict.__delitem__(self, k)
''' delegate some methods to dict explicitly to avoid getting
    DictMixin's slower (though correct) implementations instead '''
__len__ = dict.__len__
__contains__ = dict.__contains__
has_key = __contains__
''' the key semantic connection between self._rating and the order
    of self.keys() -- DictMixin gives us all other methods 'for
    free', although we could implement them directly for slightly
    better performance. '''
def __iter__(self):
    for v, k in self._rating:
        yield k
iterkeys = __iter__
def keys(self):
    return list(self)
''' the three ratings-related methods '''
def rating(self, key):
    item = self[key], key
    i = bisect_left(self._rating, item)
    if item == self._rating[i]:
        return i
```

```
            raise LookupError, "item not found in rating"
        def getValueByRating(self, rating):
            return self._rating[rating][0]
        def getKeyByRating(self, rating):
            return self._rating[rating][1]
    def _test():
        ''' we use doctest to test this module, which must be named
            rating.py, by validating all the examples in docstrings. '''
        import doctest, rating
        doctest.testmod(rating)
    if __name__ == "__main__":
        _test()
```

Discussion

In many ways, a dictionary is the natural data structure for storing a correspondence between keys (e.g., names of contestants in a competition) and the current "score" of each key (e.g., the number of points a contestant has scored so far, or the highest bid made by each contestant at an auction, etc.). If we use a dictionary for such purposes, we will probably want to access it often in *natural order*—the order in which the keys' scores are ascending—and we'll also want fast access to the rankings (ratings) implied by the current "score"s (e.g., the contestant currently in third place, the score of the contestant who is in second place, etc.).

To achieve these purposes, this recipe subclasses dict to add the needed functionality that is completely missing from dict (methods rating, getValueByRating, getKeyByRating), and, more subtly and crucially, to modify method keys and all other related methods so that they return lists or iterators with the required order (i.e., the order in which scores are ascending; if we have to break ties when two keys have the same score, we implicitly compare the keys themselves). Most of the detailed documentation is in the docstring of the class itself—a crucial issue because by keeping the documentation and examples there, we can use module doctest from the Python Standard Library to provide unit-testing functionality, as well as ensuring that our examples are correct.

The most interesting aspect of the implementation is that it takes good care to minimize boilerplate (meaning repetitive and boring code, and therefore code where bugs are most likely to hide) without seriously impairing performance. class Ratings multiply inherits from dict *and* DictMixin, with the latter placed *first* in the list of bases, so that all methods come from the mixin, if it provides them, unless explicitly overridden in the class.

Raymond Hettinger's DictMixin class was originally posted as a recipe to the online version of the *Python Cookbook* and later became part of Python 2.3's standard library. DictMixin provides all the methods of a mapping except __init__, copy, and the four fundamental methods: __getitem__, __setitem__, __delitem__, and, last but not least, keys. If you are coding a mapping class and want to ensure that your class supports all of the many methods that a full mapping provides to application code, you should subclass DictMixin and supply at least the fundamental methods (depending on your class' semantics—e.g., if your class has immutable instances, you need not supply the mutator methods __setitem__ and __delitem__). You may optionally implement other methods for performance purposes, overriding the implementation that DictMixin provides. The whole DictMixin architecture can be seen as an excellent example of the classic Template Method Design Pattern, applied pervasively in a useful mix-in variant.

In this recipe's class, we inherit __getitem__ from our other base (namely, the built-in type dict), and we also delegate explicitly to dict everything we can for performance reasons. We have to code the elementary mutator methods (__setitem__ and __delitem__) because, in addition to delegating to our base class dict, we need to maintain our auxiliary data structure self._rating—a list of (score, key) pairs that we keep in sorted order with the help of standard library module bisect. We implement keys ourselves (and while we're at it, we implement __iter__ —i.e., iterkeys as well, since clearly keys is easiest to implement by using __iter__) to exploit self._rating and return the keys in the order we need. Finally, we add the obvious implementations for __init__ and copy, in addition to the three, ratings-specific methods that we supply.

The result is quite an interesting example of balancing concision, clarity, and well-advised reuse of the enormous amount of functionality that the standard Python library places at our disposal. If you use this module in your applications, profiling may reveal that a method that this recipe's class inherits from DictMixin has somewhat unsatisfactory performance—after all, the implementations in DictMixin are, of necessity, somewhat generic. If this is the case, by all means add a direct implementation of whatever further methods you need to achieve maximum performance! For example, if your application performs a lot of looping on the result of calling r.iteritems() for some instance r of class Ratings, you may get slightly better performance by adding to the body of the class the direct implementation of the method:

```
def iteritems(self):
    for v, k in self._rating:
        yield k, v
```

See Also

Library Reference and *Python in a Nutshell* documentation about class DictMixin in module UserDict, and about module bisect.

5.15 Sorting Names and Separating Them by Initials

Credit: Brett Cannon, Amos Newcombe

Problem

You want to write a directory for a group of people, and you want that directory to be grouped by the initials of their last names and sorted alphabetically.

Solution

Python 2.4's new `itertools.groupby` function makes this task easy:

```
import itertools
def groupnames(name_iterable):
    sorted_names = sorted(name_iterable, key=_sortkeyfunc)
    name_dict = { }
    for key, group in itertools.groupby(sorted_names, _groupkeyfunc):
        name_dict[key] = tuple(group)
    return name_dict
pieces_order = { 2: (-1, 0), 3: (-1, 0, 1) }
def _sortkeyfunc(name):
    ''' name is a string with first and last names, and an optional middle
        name or initial, separated by spaces; returns a string in order
        last-first-middle, as wanted for sorting purposes. '''
    name_parts = name.split( )
    return ' '.join([name_parts[n] for n in pieces_order[len(name_parts)]])
def _groupkeyfunc(name):
    ''' returns the key for grouping, i.e. the last name's initial. '''
    return name.split( )[-1][0]
```

Discussion

In this recipe, `name_iterable` must be an iterable whose items are strings containing names in the form first - middle - last, with middle being optional and the parts separated by whitespace. The result of calling `groupnames` on such an iterable is a dictionary whose keys are the last names' initials, and the corresponding values are the tuples of all names with that last name's initial.

Auxiliary function `_sortkeyfunc` splits a name that's a single string, either "first last" or "first middle last," and reorders the part into a list that starts with the last name, followed by first name, plus the middle name or initial, if any, at the end. Then, the function returns this list rejoined into a string. The resulting string is the key we want to use for sorting, according to the problem statement. Python 2.4's built-in function `sorted` takes just this kind of function (to call on each item to get the sort key) as the value of its optional parameter named `key`.

Auxiliary function `_groupkeyfunc` takes a name in the same form and returns the last name's initial—the key on which, again according to the problem statement, we want to group.

This recipe's primary function, `groupnames`, uses the two auxiliary functions and Python 2.4's `sorted` and `itertools.groupby` to solve our problem, building and returning the required dictionary.

If you need to code this task in Python 2.3, you can use the same two support functions and recode function `groupnames` itself. In 2.3, it is more convenient to do the grouping first and the sorting separately on each group, since no `groupby` function is available in Python 2.3's standard library:

```
def groupnames(name_iterable):
    name_dict = {}
    for name in name_iterable:
        key = _groupkeyfunc(name)
        name_dict.setdefault(key, []).append(name)
    for k, v in name_dict.iteritems():
        aux = [(_sortkeyfunc(name), name) for name in v]
        aux.sort()
        name_dict[k] = tuple([ n for __, n in aux ])
    return name_dict
```

See Also

Recipe 19.21 "Computing a Summary Report with itertools.groupby"; *Library Reference* (Python 2.4) docs on module itertools.

## CHAPTER 6

Object-Oriented Programming

6.0   Introduction

Credit: Alex Martelli, author of Python in a Nutshell *(O'Reilly)*

Object-oriented programming (OOP) is among Python's greatest strengths. Python's OOP features continue to improve steadily and gradually, just like Python in general. You could already write better object-oriented programs in Python 1.5.2 (the ancient, long-stable version that was new when I first began to work with Python) than in any other popular language (excluding, of course, Lisp and its variants: I doubt there's anything you can't do well in Lisp-like languages, as long as you can stomach parentheses-heavy concrete syntax). For a few years now, since the release of Python 2.2, Python OOP has become substantially better than it was with 1.5.2. I am constantly amazed at the systematic progress Python achieves without sacrificing solidity, stability, and backwards-compatibility.

To get the most out of Python's great OOP features, you should use them the Python way, rather than trying to mimic C++, Java, Smalltalk, or other languages you may be familiar with. You can do a lot of mimicry, thanks to Python's power. However, you'll get better mileage if you invest time and energy in understanding the Python way. Most of the investment is in increasing your understanding of OOP itself: what *is* OOP, what does it buy you, and which underlying mechanisms can your object-oriented programs use? The rest of the investment is in understanding the specific mechanisms that Python itself offers.

One caveat is in order. For such a high-level language, Python is quite explicit about the OOP mechanisms it uses behind the curtains: they're exposed and available for your exploration and tinkering. Exploration and understanding are good, but beware the temptation to tinker. In other words, don't use unnecessary black magic just because you can. Specifically, don't use black magic in production code. If you can meet your goals with simplicity (and most often, in Python, you can), then keep your code simple. Simplicity pays off in readability, maintainability, and, more often than not, performance, too. To describe something as clever is *not* considered a compliment in the Python culture.

So what is OOP all about? First of all, it's about keeping some *state* (data) and some *behavior* (code) together in handy packets. "Handy packets" is the key here. Every program has state and behavior—programming paradigms differ only in how you view, organize, and package them. If the packaging is in terms of objects that typically comprise state and behavior, you're using OOP. Some object-oriented languages force you to use OOP for everything, so you end up with many objects that lack either state or behavior. Python, however, supports multiple paradigms. While everything in Python is an object, you package things as OOP objects only when you want to. Other languages try to force your programming style into a predefined mold for your own good, while Python empowers you to make and express your own design choices.

With OOP, once you have specified how an object is composed, you can instantiate as many objects of that kind as you need. When you don't want to create multiple objects, consider using other Python constructs, such as modules. In this chapter, you'll find recipes for Singleton, an object-oriented design pattern that eliminates the multiplicity of instantiation, and Borg, an idiom that makes multiple instances share state. But if you want only one instance, in Python it's often best to use a module, not an OOP object.

To describe how an object is made, use the class statement:

```
class SomeName(object):
    """ You usually define data and code here (in the class body). """
```

SomeName is a *class object*. It's a *first-class* object, like every Python object, meaning that you can put it in lists and dictionaries, pass it as an argument to functions, and so on. You don't *have to* include the (object) part in the class header clause—class SomeName: by itself is also valid Python syntax—but normally you *should* include that part, as we'll see later.

When you want a new instance of a class, call the class object as if it were a function. Each call returns a new instance object:

```
anInstance = SomeName( )
another = SomeName( )
```

anInstance and another are two distinct *instance objects*, instances of the SomeName class. (See recipe 4.18 "Collecting a Bunch of Named Items" for a class that does little more than this and yet is already quite useful.) You can freely *bind* (i.e., assign or set) and *access* (i.e., get) *attributes* (i.e., state) of an instance object:

```
anInstance.someNumber = 23 * 45
print anInstance.someNumber              # emits: 1035
```

Instances of an "empty" class like SomeName have no behavior, but they may have state. Most often, however, you want instances to have behavior. Specify the behavior you want by defining *methods* (with def statements, just like you define functions) inside the class body:

```
class Behave(object):
    def __init__(self, name):
        self.name = name
    def once(self):
        print "Hello,", self.name
    def rename(self, newName)
        self.name = newName
    def repeat(self, N):
        for i in range(N): self.once()
```

You define methods with the same def statement Python uses to define functions, exactly because methods *are* essentially functions. However, a method is an attribute of a class object, and its first formal argument is (by universal convention) named self. self always refers to the instance on which you call the method.

The method with the special name __init__ is also known as the *constructor* (or more properly the *initializer*) for instances of the class. Python calls this special method to initialize each newly created instance with the arguments that you passed when calling the class (except for self, which you do not pass explicitly since Python supplies it automatically). The body of __init__ typically binds attributes on the newly created self instance to appropriately initialize the instance's state.

Other methods implement the behavior of instances of the class. Typically, they do so by accessing instance attributes. Also, methods often rebind instance attributes, and they may call other methods. Within a class definition, these actions are always done with the self.something syntax. Once you instantiate the class, however, you call methods on the instance, access the instance's attributes, and even rebind them, using the theobject.something syntax:

```
beehive = Behave("Queen Bee")
beehive.repeat(3)
beehive.rename("Stinger")
beehive.once()
print beehive.name
beehive.name = 'See, you can rebind it "from the outside" too, if you want'
beehive.repeat(2)
```

---

self

No true difference exists between what I described as the self.something syntax and the theobject.something syntax: the former is simply a special case of the latter, when the name of reference theobject happens to be self!

If you're new to OOP in Python, you should try, in an interactive Python environment, the example snippets I have shown so far and those I'm going to show in the rest of this Introduction. One of the best interactive Python environments for such exploration is the GUI shell supplied as part of the free IDLE development environment that comes with Python.

In addition to the constructor (__init__), your class may have other special methods, meaning methods with names that start and end with two underscores. Python calls the special methods of a class when instances of the class are used in various operations and built-in functions. For example, len(x) returns x.__len__( ); a+b normally returns a.__add__(b); a[b] returns a.__getitem__(b). Therefore, by defining special methods in a class, you can make instances of that class interchangeable with objects of built-in types, such as numbers, lists, and dictionaries.

 Each operation and built-in function can try several special methods in some specific order. For example, a+b *first* tries a.__add__(b), but, if that doesn't pan out, the operation also gives object *b* a say in the matter, by next trying b.__radd__(a). This kind of intrinsic structuring among special methods, that operations and built-in functions can provide, is an important added value of such functions and operations with respect to pure OO notation such as someobject.somemethod(arguments).

The ability to handle different objects in similar ways, known as *polymorphism*, is a major advantage of OOP. Thanks to polymorphism, you can call the same method on various objects, and each object can implement the method appropriately. For example, in addition to the Behave class, you might have another class that implements a repeat method with rather different behavior:

```
class Repeater(object):
    def repeat(self, N): print N*"*-*"
```

You can mix instances of Behave and Repeater at will, as long as the only method you call on each such instance is repeat:

```
aMix = beehive, Behave('John'), Repeater( ), Behave('world')
for whatever in aMix: whatever.repeat(3)
```

Other languages require inheritance, or the formal definition and implementation of interfaces, in order to enable such polymorphism. In Python, all you need is to have methods with the same *signature* (i.e., methods of the same name, callable with the same arguments). This *signature-based polymorphism* allows a style of programming that's quite similar to *generic programming* (e.g., as supported by C++'s template classes and functions), without syntax cruft and without conceptual complications.

Python also uses *inheritance*, which is mostly a handy, elegant, structured way to reuse code. You can define a class by inheriting from another (i.e., *subclassing* the other class) and then adding or redefining (known as *overriding*) some methods:

```
class Subclass(Behave):
    def once(self): print '(%s)' % self.name
subInstance = Subclass("Queen Bee")
subInstance.repeat(3)
```

The Subclass class overrides only the once method, but you can also call the repeat method on subInstance, since Subclass inherits that method from the Behave superclass. The body of the repeat method calls once *n* times on the specific instance, using whatever version of the once method the instance has. In this case, each call uses the method from the Subclass class, which prints the name in parentheses, not the original version from the Behave class, which prints the name after a greeting. The idea of a method calling other methods on the same instance and getting the appropriately overridden version of each is important in every object-oriented language, including Python. It is also known as the Template Method Design Pattern.

The method of a subclass often overrides a method from the superclass, but also needs to call the method of the superclass as part of its own operation. You can do this in Python by explicitly getting the method as a class attribute and passing the instance as the first argument:

```
class OneMore(Behave):
    def repeat(self, N): Behave.repeat(self, N+1)
zealant = OneMore("Worker Bee")
zealant.repeat(3)
```

The OneMore class implements its own repeat method in terms of the method with the same name in its superclass, Behave, with a slight change. This approach, known as *delegation*, is pervasive in all programming. Delegation involves implementing some functionality by letting another existing piece of code do most of the work, often with some slight variation. An overriding method often is best implemented by delegating some of the work to the same method in the superclass. In Python, the syntax Classname.method(self, . . .) delegates to Classname's version of the method. A *vastly* preferable way to perform superclass delegation, however, is to use Python's built-in super:

```
class OneMore(Behave):
    def repeat(self, N): super(OneMore, self).repeat(N+1)
```

This super construct is equivalent to the explicit use of Behave.repeat in this simple case, but it also allows class OneMore to be used smoothly with *multiple inheritance*. Even if you're not interested in multiple inheritance at first, you should still get into the habit of using super instead of explicit delegation to your base class by name—super costs nothing and it may prove very useful to you in the future.

Python does fully support multiple inheritance: one class can inherit from several other classes. In terms of coding, this feature is sometimes just a minor one that lets you use the mix-in class idiom, a convenient way to supply functionality across a broad range of classes. (See recipe 6.20 "Using Cooperative Supercalls Concisely and Safely" and recipe 6.12 "Checking an Instance for Any State Changes," for unusual but powerful examples of using the mix-in idiom.) However, multiple inheritance is particularly important because of its implications for object-oriented analysis—the way you conceptualize your problem and your solution in the first place. Single inheritance pushes you to frame your problem space via taxonomy (i.e., mutually exclusive classification). The real world doesn't work like that. Rather, it resembles Jorge Luis Borges' explanation in *The Analytical Language of John Wilkins*, from a purported Chinese encyclopedia, *The Celestial Emporium of Benevolent Knowledge*. Borges explains that all animals are divided into:

- Those that belong to the Emperor
- Embalmed ones
- Those that are trained
- Suckling pigs
- Mermaids
- Fabulous ones
- Stray dogs
- Those included in the present classification
- Those that tremble as if they were mad
- Innumerable ones
- Those drawn with a very fine camelhair brush
- Others
- Those that have just broken a flower vase
- Those that from a long way off look like flies

You get the point: taxonomy forces you to pigeonhole, fitting everything into categories that aren't truly mutually exclusive. Modeling aspects of the real world in your programs is hard enough without buying into artificial constraints such as taxonomy. Multiple inheritance frees you from these constraints.

Ah, yes, that (object) thing—I *had* promised to come back to it later. Now that you've seen Python's notation for inheritance, you realize that writing class X(object) means that class X inherits from class object. If you just write class Y:, you're saying that Y doesn't inherit from anything—Y, so to speak, "stands on its own". For backwards compatibility, Python allows you to request such a *rootless class*, and, if you do, then Python makes class Y an "old-style" class, also known as a *classic* class, meaning a class that works just like all classes used to work in the Python versions of old. Python is very keen on backwards-compatibility.

For many elementary uses, you won't notice the difference between classic classes and the new-style classes that are recommended for all new Python code you write. However, it's important to underscore that classic classes are a *legacy* feature, *not* recommended for new code. Even within the limited compass of elementary OOP features that I cover in this Introduction, you will already feel some of the limitations of classic classes: for example, you cannot use super within classic classes, and in practice, you should not do any serious use of multiple inheritance with them. Many important features of today's Python OOP, such as the property built-in, can't work completely, if they even work at all, with old-style classes.

In practice, even if you're maintaining a large body of legacy Python code, the next time you need to do any substantial maintenance on that code, you should take the little effort required to ensure all classes are new style: it's a small job, and it will ease your future maintenance burden quite a bit. Instead of explicitly having all your classes inherit from object, an equivalent alternative is to add the following assignment statement close to the start of every module that defines any classes:

```
__metaclass__ = type
```

The built-in type is the metaclass of object and of every other new-style class and built-in type. That's why inheriting from object or any built-in type makes a class new style: the class you're coding gets the same metaclass as its base. A class without bases can get its metaclass from the module-global __metaclass__ variable, which is why the "state"ment I suggest suffices to ensure that any classes without explicit bases are made new-style. Even if you never make any other use of explicit metaclasses (a rather advanced subject that is, nevertheless, mentioned in several of this chapter's recipes), this one simple use of them will stand you in good stead.

6.1 Converting Among Temperature Scales

Credit: Artur de Sousa Rocha, Adde Nilsson

Problem

You want to convert easily among Kelvin, Celsius, Fahrenheit, and Rankine scales of temperature.

Solution

Rather than having a dozen functions to do all possible conversions, we can more elegantly package this functionality into a class:

```
class Temperature(object):
    coefficients = {'c': (1.0, 0.0, -273.15), 'f': (1.8, -273.15, 32.0),
                    'r': (1.8, 0.0, 0.0)}
    def __init__(self, **kwargs):
        # default to absolute (Kelvin) 0, but allow one named argument,
        # with name being k, c, f or r, to use any of the scales
        try:
            name, value = kwargs.popitem( )
        except KeyError:
            # no arguments, so default to k=0
            name, value = 'k', 0
```

What Is a Metaclass?

Metaclasses do not mean "deep, dark black magic". When you execute any class statement, Python performs the following steps:

1. Remember the class name as a string, say *n*, and the class bases as a tuple, say *b*.

2. Execute the body of the class, recording all names that the body binds as keys in a new dictionary *d*, each with its associated value (e.g., each statement such as def f(self) just sets d['f'] to the function object the def statement builds).

3. Determine the appropriate metaclass, say *M*, by inheritance or by looking for name __metaclass__ in *d* and in the globals:

```
if '__metaclass__' in d: M = d['__metaclass__']
elif b: M = type(b[0])
elif '__metaclass__' in globals(): M = globals()['__metaclass__']
else: M = types.ClassType
```

types.ClassType is the metaclass of old-style classes, so this code implies that a class without bases is old style if the name '__metaclass__' is not set in the class body nor among the global variables of the current module.

4. Call M(n, b, d) and record the result as a variable with name *n* in whatever scope the class statement executed.

So, some metaclass *M* is *always* involved in the execution of any class statement. The metaclass is normally type for new-style classes, types.ClassType for old-style classes. You can set it up to use your own *custom* metaclass (normally a subclass of type), and *that* is where you may reasonably feel that things are getting a bit too advanced. However, understanding that a class statement, such as:

```
class Someclass(Somebase):
    __metaclass__ = type
    x = 23
```

is exactly equivalent to the assignment statement:

```
Someclass = type('Someclass', (Somebase,), {'x': 23})
```

does help a lot in understanding the exact semantics of the class statement.

```
        # error if there are more arguments, or the arg's name is unknown
        if kwargs or name not in 'kcfr':
            kwargs[name] = value            # put it back for diagnosis
            raise TypeError, 'invalid arguments %r' % kwargs
        setattr(self, name, float(value))
    def __getattr__(self, name):
        # maps getting of c, f, r, to computation from k
        try:
            eq = self.coefficients[name]
        except KeyError:
            # unknown name, give error message
            raise AttributeError, name
        return (self.k + eq[1]) * eq[0] + eq[2]
    def __setattr__(self, name, value):
```

```
                # maps settings of k, c, f, r, to setting of k; forbids others
                if name in self.coefficients:
                    # name is c, f or r -- compute and set k
                    eq = self.coefficients[name]
                    self.k = (value - eq[2]) / eq[0] - eq[1]
                elif name == 'k':
                    # name is k, just set it
                    object.__setattr__(self, name, value)
                else:
                    # unknown name, give error message
                    raise AttributeError, name
        def __str__(self):
            # readable, concise representation as string
            return "%s K" % self.k
        def __repr__(self):
            # detailed, precise representation as string
            return "Temperature(k=%r)" % self.k
```

Discussion

Converting between several different scales or units of measure is a task that's subject to a "combinatorial explosion": if we tackle it in the apparently obvious way, by providing a function for each conversion, then, to deal with n different units, we will have to write n * (n-1) functions.

A Python class can intercept attribute setting and getting, and perform computation on the fly in response. This power enables a much handier and more elegant architecture, as shown in this recipe for the specific case of temperatures.

Inside the class, we always hold the measurement in one reference unit or scale, Kelvin (absolute) degrees in the case of this recipe. We allow the setting of the value to happen through any of four attribute names ('k', 'r', 'c', 'f', abbreviations of the scales' names), and compute and set the Kelvin-scale value appropriately. Vice versa, we also allow the "getting" of the value in any scale, through the same attribute names, computing the result on the fly. (Assuming you have saved the code in this recipe as *te.py* somewhere on your Python sys.path, you can import it as a module.) For example:

```
>>> from te import Temperature
>>> t = Temperature(f=70)        # 70 F is...
>>> print t.c                    # ...a bit over 21 C
21.1111111111
>>> t.c = 23                     # 23 C is...
>>> print t.f                    # ...a bit over 73 F
73.4
```

__getattr__ and __setattr__ work better than named properties would in this case, since the form of the computation is the same for every attribute (except the reference 'k' one), and we only need to use different coefficients that we can most handily keep in a per-class dictionary, the one we name self.coefficients. It's important to remember that __setattr__ is called on *every* setting of any attribute, so it must delegate to object the setting of attributes, which need to be recorded in the instance (the __setattr__ implementation in this recipe does just such a delegation for attribute k) and must raise an AttributeError exception for attributes that can't be set. __getattr__, on the other hand, is called only upon the "getting" of an attribute that can't be found by other, "normal" means (e.g., in the case of this recipe's class, __getattr__ is *not* called for accesses to attribute k, which is recorded in the instance and thus gets found by normal means). __getattr__ must also raise an AttributeError exception for attributes that can't be accessed.

See Also

Library Reference and *Python in a Nutshell* documentation on attributes and on special methods __getattr__ and __setattr__.

6.2   Defining Constants

Credit: Alex Martelli

Problem

You need to define module-level variables (i.e., named constants) that client code cannot accidentally rebind.

Solution

You can install any object as if it were a module. Save the following code as module *const.py* on some directory on your Python sys.path:

```
class _const(object):
    class ConstError(TypeError): pass
    def __setattr__(self, name, value):
        if name in self.__dict__:
            raise self.ConstError, "Can't rebind const(%s)" % name
        self.__dict__[name] = value
    def __delattr__(self, name):
        if name in self.__dict__:
            raise self.ConstError, "Can't unbind const(%s)" % name
        raise NameError, name
import sys
sys.modules[__name__] = _const()
```

Now, any client code can import const, then bind an attribute on the const module just once, as follows:

```
const.magic = 23
```

Once the attribute is bound, the program cannot accidentally rebind or unbind it:

```
const.magic = 88      # raises const.ConstError
del const.magic       # raises const.ConstError
```

Discussion

In Python, variables can be rebound at will, and modules, differently from classes, don't let you define special methods such as __setattr__ to stop rebinding. An easy solution is to install an instance as if it were a module.

Python performs no type-checks to force entries in sys.modules to actually be module objects. Therefore, you can install any object there and take advantage of attribute-access special methods (e.g., to prevent rebinding, to synthesize attributes on the fly in __getattr__, etc.), while still allowing client code to access the object with import somename. You may even see it as a more Pythonic Singleton-style idiom (but see recipe 6.16 "Avoiding the "Singleton" Design Pattern with the Borg Idiom").

This recipe ensures that a module-level name remains constantly bound to the same object once it has first been bound to it. This recipe does not deal with a certain object's immutability, which is quite a different issue. Altering an object and rebinding a name are different concepts, as explained in recipe 4.1 "Copying an Object." Numbers, strings, and tuples are immutable: if you bind a name in const to such an object, not only will the name always be bound to that object, but the object's contents also will always be the same since the object is immutable. However, other objects, such as lists and dictionaries, are mutable: if you bind a name in const to, say, a list object, the name will always remain bound to that list object, but the contents of the list may change (e.g., items in it may be rebound or unbound, more items can be added with the object's append method, etc.).

To make "read-only" wrappers around mutable objects, see recipe 6.5 "Delegating Automatically as an Alternative to Inheritance." You might choose to have class _const's __setattr__ method perform such wrapping implicitly. Say you have saved the code from recipe 6.5 "Delegating Automatically as an Alternative to Inheritance" as module *ro.py* somewhere along your Python sys.path. Then, you need to add, at the start of module *const.py*:

```
import ro
```

and change the assignment self.__dict__[name] = value, used in class _const's __setattr__ method to:

```
self.__dict__[name] = ro.Readonly(value)
```

Now, when you set an attribute in const to some value, what gets bound there is a read-only wrapper to that value. The underlying value might still get changed by calling mutators on some other reference to that same value (object), but it cannot be accidentally changed through the attribute of "pseudo-module" const. If you want to avoid such "accidental changes through other references", you need to take a copy, as explained in recipe 4.1 "Copying an Object," so that there exist no other references to the value held by the read-only wrapper. Ensure that at the start of module *const.py* you have:

```
import ro, copy
```

and change the assignment in class _const's __setattr__ method to:

```
self.__dict__[name] = ro.Readonly(copy.copy(value))
```

If you're sufficiently paranoid, you might even use copy.deepcopy rather than plain copy.copy in this latest snippet. However, you may end up paying substantial amounts of memory, as well as losing some performance, by these kinds of excessive precautions. You should evaluate carefully whether so much prudence is really necessary for your specific application. Whatever you end up deciding about this issue, Python offers all the tools you need to implement exactly the amount of constantness you require.

The _const class presented in this recipe can be seen, in a sense, as the "complement" of the NoNewAttrs class, which is presented next in recipe 6.3 "Restricting Attribute Setting." This one ensures that already bound attributes can never be rebound but lets you freely bind new attributes; the other one, conversely, lets you freely rebind attributes that are already bound but blocks the binding of any new attribute.

See Also

Recipe 6.5 "Delegating Automatically as an Alternative to Inheritance"; recipe 6.13 "Checking Whether an Object Has Necessary Attributes"; recipe 4.1 "Copying an Object"; *Library Reference* and *Python in a Nutshell* docs on module objects, the import statement, and the modules attribute of the sys built-in module.

6.3   Restricting Attribute Setting

Credit: Michele Simionato

Problem

Python normally lets you freely add attributes to classes and their instances. However, you want to restrict that freedom for some class.

Solution

Special method __setattr__ intercepts every setting of an attribute, so it lets you inhibit the addition of new attributes that were not already present. One elegant way to implement this idea is to code a class, a simple custom metaclass, and a wrapper function, all cooperating for the purpose, as follows:

```
def no_new_attributes(wrapped_setattr):
    """ raise an error on attempts to add a new attribute, while
        allowing existing attributes to be set to new values.
    """
    def __setattr__(self, name, value):
        if hasattr(self, name):      # not a new attribute, allow setting
            wrapped_setattr(self, name, value)
        else:                        # a new attribute, forbid adding it
```

```
                raise AttributeError("can't add attribute %r to %s" % (name, self))
        return __setattr__
class NoNewAttrs(object):
    """ subclasses of NoNewAttrs inhibit addition of new attributes, while
        allowing existing attributed to be set to new values.
    """
    # block the addition new attributes to instances of this class
    __setattr__ = no_new_attributes(object.__setattr__)
    class __metaclass__(type):
        " simple custom metaclass to block adding new attributes to this class "
        __setattr__ = no_new_attributes(type.__setattr__)
```

Discussion

For various reasons, you sometimes want to restrict Python's dynamism. In particular, you may want to get an exception when a new attribute is accidentally set on a certain class or one of its instances. This recipe shows how to go about implementing such a restriction. The key point of the recipe is, *don't* use __slots__ for this purpose: __slots__ is intended for a completely different task (i.e., saving memory by avoiding each instance having a dictionary, as it normally would, when you need to have vast numbers of instances of a class with just a few fixed attributes). __slots__ performs its intended task well but has various limitations when you try to stretch it to perform, instead, the task this recipe covers. (See recipe 6.7 "Implementing Tuples with Named Items" for an example of the appropriate use of __slots__ to save memory.)

Notice that this recipe inhibits the addition of runtime attributes, not only to class instances, but also to the class itself, thanks to the simple custom metaclass it defines. When you want to inhibit accidental addition of attributes, you usually want to inhibit it on the class as well as on each individual instance. On the other hand, existing attributes on both the class and its instances may be freely set to new values.

Here is an example of how you could use this recipe:

```
class Person(NoNewAttrs):
    firstname = ''
    lastname = ''
    def __init__(self, firstname, lastname):
        self.firstname = firstname
        self.lastname = lastname
    def __repr__(self):
        return 'Person(%r, %r)' % (self.firstname, self.lastname)
me = Person("Michere", "Simionato")
print me
# emits: Person('Michere', 'Simionato')
# oops, wrong value for firstname, can we fix it?  Sure, no problem!
me.firstname = "Michele"
print me
# emits: Person('Michele', 'Simionato')
```

The point of inheriting from NoNewAttrs is forcing yourself to "declare" all allowed attributes by setting them at class level in the body of the class itself. Any further attempt to set a new, "undeclared" attribute raises an AttributeError:

```
try: Person.address = ''
except AttributeError, err: print 'raised %r as expected' % err
try: me.address = ''
except AttributeError, err: print 'raised %r as expected' % err
```

In some ways, therefore, subclasses of NoNewAttr and their instances behave more like Java or C++ classes and instances, rather than normal Python ones. Thus, one use case for this recipe is when you're coding in Python a prototype that you already know will eventually have to be recoded in a less dynamic language.

See Also

Library Reference and *Python in a Nutshell* documentation on the special method __setattr__ and on custom metaclasses; recipe 6.18 "Automatically Initializing Instance Variables from __init__ Arguments" for an example of an appropriate use of __slots__ to save memory; recipe 6.2 "Defining Constants" for a class that is the complement of this one.

6.4   Chaining Dictionary Lookups

Credit: Raymond Hettinger

Problem

You have several mappings (usually dicts) and want to look things up in them in a chained way (try the first one; if the key is not there, then try the second one; and so on). Specifically, you want to make a single mapping object that "virtually merges" several others, by looking things up in them in a specified priority order, so that you can conveniently pass that one object around.

Solution

A *mapping* is a generalized, abstract version of a dictionary: a mapping provides an interface that's similar to a dictionary's, but it may use very different implementations. All dictionaries are mappings, but not vice versa. Here, you need to implement a mapping which sequentially tries delegating lookups to other mappings. A class is the right way to encapsulate this functionality:

```
class Chainmap(object):
    def __init__(self, *mappings):
        # record the sequence of mappings into which we must look
        self._mappings = mappings
    def __getitem__(self, key):
        # try looking up into each mapping in sequence
        for mapping in self._mappings:
```

```
        try:
            return mapping[key]
        except KeyError:
            pass
    # `key' not found in any mapping, so raise KeyError exception
    raise KeyError, key
def get(self, key, default=None):
    # return self[key] if present, otherwise `default'
    try:
        return self[key]
    except KeyError:
        return default
def __contains__(self, key):
    # return True if `key' is present in self, otherwise False
    try:
        self[key]
        return True
    except KeyError:
        return False
```

For example, you can now implement the same sequence of lookups that Python normally uses for any name: look among locals, then (if not found there) among globals, lastly (if not found yet) among built-ins:

```
import __builtin__
pylookup = Chainmap(locals(), globals(), vars(__builtin__))
```

Discussion

Chainmap relies on minimal functionality from the mappings it wraps: each of those underlying mappings must allow indexing (i.e., supply a special method __getitem__), and it must raise the standard exception KeyError when indexed with a key that the mapping does not know about. A Chainmap instance provides the same behavior, plus the handy get method covered in recipe 4.9 "Getting a Value from a Dictionary" and special method __contains__ (which conveniently lets you check whether some key k is present in a Chainmap instance c by just coding if k in c).

Besides the obvious and sensible limitation of being "read-only", this Chainmap class has others—essentially, it is not a "full mapping" even within the read-only design choice. You can make any partial mapping into a "full mapping" by inheriting from class DictMixin (in standard library module UserDict) and supplying a few key methods (DictMixin implements the others). Here is how you could make a full (read-only) mapping from ChainMap and UserDict.DictMixin:

```
import UserDict
from sets import Set
class FullChainmap(Chainmap, UserDict.DictMixin):
    def copy(self):
        return self.__class__(self._mappings)
    def __iter__(self):
        seen = Set()
        for mapping in self._mappings:
```

```
            for key in mapping:
                if key not in seen:
                    yield key
                    seen.add(key)
    iterkeys = __iter__
    def keys(self):
        return list(self)
```

This class `FullChainmap` adds one requirement to the mappings it holds, besides the requirements posed by `Chainmap`: the mappings must be iterable. Also note that the implementation in `Chainmap` of methods `get` and `__contains__` is redundant (although innocuous) once we subclass `DictMixin`, since `DictMixin` also implements those two methods (as well as many others) in terms of lower-level methods, just like `Chainmap` does. See recipe 5.14 "Enriching the Dictionary Type with Ratings Functionality" for more details about `DictMixin`.

See Also

Recipe 4.9 "Getting a Value from a Dictionary"; recipe 5.14 "Enriching the Dictionary Type with Ratings Functionality"; the *Library Reference* and *Python in a Nutshell* sections on mapping types.

6.5 Delegating Automatically as an Alternative to Inheritance

Credit: Alex Martelli, Raymond Hettinger

Problem

You'd like to inherit from a class or type, but you need some tweak that inheritance does not provide. For example, you want to selectively hide some of the base class' methods, which inheritance doesn't allow.

Solution

Inheritance is quite handy, but it's not all-powerful. For example, it doesn't let you hide methods or other attributes supplied by a base class. Containment with automatic delegation is often a good alternative. Say, for example, you need to wrap some objects to make them read-only; thus preventing accidental alterations. Therefore, besides stopping attribute-setting, you also need to hide mutating methods. Here's a way:

```
# support 2.3 as well as 2.4
try: set
except NameError: from sets import Set as set
class ROError(AttributeError): pass
class Readonly: # there IS a reason to NOT subclass object, see Discussion
    mutators = {
```

```
      list: set('''__delitem__ __delslice__ __iadd__ __imul__
            __setitem__ __setslice__ append extend insert
            pop remove sort'''.split()),
      dict: set('''__delitem__ __setitem__ clear pop popitem
            setdefault update'''.split()),
   }
   def __init__(self, o):
      object.__setattr__(self, '_o', o)
      object.__setattr__(self, '_no', self.mutators.get(type(o), ()))
   def __setattr__(self, n, v):
      raise ROError, "Can't set attr %r on RO object" % n
   def __delattr__(self, n):
      raise ROError, "Can't del attr %r from RO object" % n
   def __getattr__(self, n):
      if n in self._no:
         raise ROError, "Can't get attr %r from RO object" % n
      return getattr(self._o, n)
```

Code using this class Readonly can easily add other wrappable types with
Readonly.mutators[sometype] = the_mutators.

Discussion

Automatic delegation, which the special methods __getattr__, __setattr__, and
__delattr__ enable us to perform so smoothly, is a powerful, general technique. In
this recipe, we show how to use it to get an effect that is almost indistinguishable
from subclassing while hiding some names. In particular, we apply this quasi-sub-
classing to the task of wrapping objects to make them read-only. Performance isn't
quite as good as it might be with real inheritance, but we get better flexibility and
finer-grained control as compensation.

The fundamental idea is that each instance of our class holds an instance of the type
we are wrapping (i.e., extending and/or tweaking). Whenever client code tries to get
an attribute from an instance of our class, unless the attribute is specifically defined
there (e.g., the mutators dictionary in class Readonly), __getattr__ transparently
shunts the request to the wrapped instance after appropriate checks. In Python,
methods are also attributes, accessed in just the same way, so we don't need to do
anything different to access methods. The __getattr__ approach used to access data
attributes works for methods just as well.

This is where the comment in the recipe about there being a specific reason to avoid
subclassing object comes in. Our __getattr__ based approach does work on *special*
methods too, but only for instances of old-style classes. In today's object model,
Python operations access special methods on the class, not on the instance. Solutions to this issue are presented next in recipe 6.6 "Delegating Special Methods in
Proxies" and in recipe 20.8 "Adding a Method to a Class Instance at Runtime." The
approach adopted in this recipe—making class Readonly old style, so that the issue
can be locally avoided and delegated to other recipes—is definitely *not* recommended for production code. I use it here only to keep this recipe shorter and to
avoid duplicating coverage that is already amply given elsewhere in this cookbook.

__setattr__ plays a role similar to __getattr__, but it gets called when client code sets an instance attribute; in this case, since we want to make a read-only wrapper, we simply forbid the operation. Remember, to avoid triggering __setattr__ from inside the methods you code, you must never code normal self.n = v statements within the methods of classes that have __setattr__. The simplest workaround is to delegate the setting to class object, just like our class Readonly does twice in its __init__ method. Method __delattr__ completes the picture, dealing with any attempts to delete attributes from an instance.

Wrapping by automatic delegation does not work well with client or framework code that, one way or another, does type-testing. In such cases, the client or framework code is breaking polymorphism and should be rewritten. Remember not to use type-tests in your own client code, as you probably do not need them anyway. See recipe 6.13 "Checking Whether an Object Has Necessary Attributes" for better alternatives.

In old versions of Python, automatic delegation was even more prevalent, since you could not subclass built-in types. In modern Python, you can inherit from built-in types, so you'll use automatic delegation less often. However, delegation still has its place—it is just a bit farther from the spotlight. Delegation is more flexible than inheritance, and sometimes such flexibility is invaluable. In addition to the ability to delegate selectively (thus effectively "hiding" some of the attributes), an object can delegate to different subobjects over time, or to multiple subobjects at one time, and inheritance doesn't offer anything comparable.

Here is an example of delegating to multiple specific subobjects. Say that you have classes that are chock full of "forwarding methods", such as:

```
class Pricing(object):
    def __init__(self, location, event):
        self.location = location
        self.event = event
    def setlocation(self, location):
        self.location = location
    def getprice(self):
        return self.location.getprice( )
    def getquantity(self):
        return self.location.getquantity( )
    def getdiscount(self):
        return self.event.getdiscount( )
    and many more such methods
```

Inheritance is clearly not applicable because an instance of Pricing must delegate to *specific* location and event instances, which get passed at initialization time and may even be changed. Automatic delegation to the rescue:

```
class AutoDelegator(object):
    delegates = ( )
    do_not_delegate = ( )
    def __getattr__(self, key):
        if key not in self.do_not_delegate:
```

```
        for d in self.delegates:
            try:
                return getattr(d, key)
            except AttributeError:
                pass
        raise AttributeError, key
class Pricing(AutoDelegator):
    def __init__(self, location, event):
        self.delegates = [location, event]
    def setlocation(self, location):
        self.delegates[0] = location
```

In this case, we do not delegate the setting and deletion of attributes, only the getting of attributes (and nonspecial methods). Of course, this approach is fully applicable only when the methods (and other attributes) of the various objects to which we want to delegate do not interfere with each other; for example, location must not have a getdiscount method; otherwise, it would preempt the delegation of that method, which is intended to go to event.

If a class that does lots of delegation has a few such issues to solve, it can do so by explicitly defining the few corresponding methods, since __getattr__ enters the picture only for attributes and methods that cannot be found otherwise. The ability to *hide* some attributes and methods that are supplied by a delegate, but the delegator does not want to expose, is supported through attribute do_not_delegate, which any subclass may override. For example, if class Pricing wanted to hide a method setdiscount that is supplied by, say, event, only a tiny change would be required:

```
    class Pricing(AutoDelegator):
        do_not_delegate = ('set_discount',)
```

while all the rest remains as in the previous snippet.

See Also

Recipe 6.13 "Checking Whether an Object Has Necessary Attributes"; recipe 6.6 "Delegating Special Methods in Proxies"; recipe 20.8 "Adding a Method to a Class Instance at Runtime"; *Python in a Nutshell* chapter on OOP; PEP 253 (*http://www.python.org/peps/pep-0253.html*) for more details about Python's current (new-style) object model.

6.6   Delegating Special Methods in Proxies

Credit: Gonçalo Rodrigues

Problem

In the new-style object model, Python operations perform implicit lookups for special methods on the class (rather than on the instance, as they do in the classic object model). Nevertheless, you need to wrap new-style instances in proxies that can also delegate a selected set of special methods to the object they're wrapping.

Solution

You need to generate each proxy's class on the fly. For example:

```python
class Proxy(object):
    """ base class for all proxies """
    def __init__(self, obj):
        super(Proxy, self).__init__(obj)
        self._obj = obj
    def __getattr__(self, attrib):
        return getattr(self._obj, attrib)
def make_binder(unbound_method):
    def f(self, *a, **k): return unbound_method(self._obj, *a, **k)
    # in 2.4, only: f.__name__ = unbound_method.__name__
    return f
known_proxy_classes = { }
def proxy(obj, *specials):
    ''' factory-function for a proxy able to delegate special methods '''
    # do we already have a suitable customized class around?
    obj_cls = obj.__class__
    key = obj_cls, specials
    cls = known_proxy_classes.get(key)
    if cls is None:
        # we don't have a suitable class around, so let's make it
        cls = type("%sProxy" % obj_cls.__name__, (Proxy,), { })
        for name in specials:
            name = '__%s__' % name
            unbound_method = getattr(obj_cls, name)
            setattr(cls, name, make_binder(unbound_method))
        # also cache it for the future
        known_proxy_classes[key] = cls
    # instantiate and return the needed proxy
    return cls(obj)
```

Discussion

Proxying and automatic delegation are a joy in Python, thanks to the __getattr__ hook. Python calls it automatically when a lookup for any attribute (including a method—Python draws no distinction there) has not otherwise succeeded.

In the old-style (classic) object model, __getattr__ also applied to special methods that were looked up as part of a Python operation. This required some care to avoid mistakenly supplying a special method one didn't really want to supply but was otherwise handy. Nowadays, the new-style object model is recommended for all new code: it is faster, more regular, and richer in features. You get new-style classes when you subclass object or any other built-in type. One day, some years from now, Python 3.0 will eliminate the classic object model, as well as other features that are still around only for backwards-compatibility. (See *http://www.python.org/peps/pep-*

3000.html for details about plans for Python 3.0—almost all changes will be language simplifications, rather than new features.)

In the new-style object model, Python operations don't look up special methods at runtime: they rely on "slots" held in class objects. Such slots are updated when a class object is built or modified. Therefore, a proxy object that wants to delegate some special methods to an object it's wrapping needs to belong to a specially made and tailored class. Fortunately, as this recipe shows, making and instantiating classes on the fly is quite an easy job in Python.

In this recipe, we don't use any advanced Python concepts such as custom metaclasses and custom descriptors. Rather, each proxy is built by a factory function proxy, which takes as arguments the object to wrap and the names of special methods to delegate (shorn of leading and trailing double underscores). If you've saved the "Solution"'s code in a file named *proxy.py* somewhere along your Python sys.path, here is how you could use it from an interactive Python interpreter session:

```
>>> import proxy
>>> a = proxy.proxy([ ], 'len', 'iter')   # only delegate __len__ & __iter__
>>> a                                      # __repr__ is not delegated
<proxy.listProxy object at 0x0113C370>
>>> a.__class__
<class 'proxy.listProxy'>
>>> a._obj
[ ]
>>> a.append                              # all non-specials are delegated
<built-in method append of list object at 0x010F1A10>
```

Since __len__ is delegated, len(a) works as expected:

```
>>> len(a)
0
>>> a.append(23)
>>> len(a)
1
```

Since __iter__ is delegated, for loops work as expected, as does intrinsic looping performed by built-ins such as list, sum, max, . . . :

```
>>> for x in a: print x
...
23
>>> list(a)
[23]
>>> sum(a)
23
>>> max(a)
23
```

However, since __getitem__ is *not* delegated, a cannot be indexed nor sliced:

```
>>> a.__getitem__
<method-wrapper object at 0x010F1AF0>
>>> a[1]
```

```
Traceback (most recent call last):
    File "<interactive input>", line 1, in ?
TypeError: unindexable object
```

Function proxy uses a "cache" of classes it has previously generated, the global dictionary known_proxy_classes, keyed by the class of the object being wrapped and the tuple of special methods' names being delegated. To make a new class, proxy calls the built-in type, passing as arguments the name of the new class (made by appending 'Proxy' to the name of the class being wrapped), class Proxy as the only base, and an "empty" class dictionary (since it's adding no class attributes yet). Base class Proxy deals with initialization and delegation of ordinary attribute lookups. Then, factory function proxy loops over the names of specials to be delegated: for each of them, it gets the unbound method from the class of the object being wrapped, and sets it as an attribute of the new class within a make_binder closure. make_binder deals with calling the unbound method with the appropriate first argument (i.e., the object being wrapped, self._obj).

Once it's done preparing a new class, proxy saves it in known_proxy_classes under the appropriate key. Finally, whether the class was just built or recovered from known_proxy_classes, proxy instantiates it, with the object being wrapped as the only argument, and returns the resulting proxy instance.

See Also

Recipe 6.5 "Delegating Automatically as an Alternative to Inheritance" for more information about automatic delegation; recipe 6.9 "Making a Fast Copy of an Object" for another example of generating classes on the fly (using a class statement rather than a call to type).

6.7   Implementing Tuples with Named Items

Credit: Gonçalo Rodrigues, Raymond Hettinger

Problem

Python tuples are handy ways to group pieces of information, but having to access each item by numeric index is a bother. You'd like to build tuples whose items are also accessible as named attributes.

Solution

A factory function is the simplest way to generate the required subclass of tuple:

```
# use operator.itemgetter if we're in 2.4, roll our own if we're in 2.3
try:
    from operator import itemgetter
except ImportError:
    def itemgetter(i):
```

```
            def getter(self): return self[i]
            return getter
    def superTuple(typename, *attribute_names):
        " create and return a subclass of `tuple', with named attributes "
        # make the subclass with appropriate __new__ and __repr__ specials
        nargs = len(attribute_names)
        class supertup(tuple):
            __slots__ = ()          # save memory, we don't need per-instance dict
            def __new__(cls, *args):
                if len(args) != nargs:
                    raise TypeError, '%s takes exactly %d arguments (%d given)' % (
                                    typename, nargs, len(args))
                return tuple.__new__(cls, args)
            def __repr__(self):
                return '%s(%s)' % (typename, ', '.join(map(repr, self)))
        # add a few key touches to our new subclass of `tuple'
        for index, attr_name in enumerate(attribute_names):
            setattr(supertup, attr_name, property(itemgetter(index)))
        supertup.__name__ = typename
        return supertup
```

Discussion

You often want to pass data around by means of tuples, which play the role of C's structs, or that of simple records in other languages. Having to remember which numeric index corresponds to which field, and accessing the fields by indexing, is often bothersome. Some Python Standard Library modules, such as time and os, which in old Python versions used to return tuples, have fixed the problem by returning, instead, instances of tuple-like types that let you access the fields by name, as attributes, as well as by index, as items. This recipe shows you how to get the same effect for your code, essentially by automatically building a custom subclass of tuple.

Orchestrating the building of a new, customized type can be achieved in several ways; custom metaclasses are often the best approach for such tasks. In this case, however, a simple factory function is quite sufficient, and you should never use more power than you need. Here is how you can use this recipe's superTuple factory function in your code, assuming you have saved this recipe's Solution as a module named *supertuple.py* somewhere along your Python sys.path:

```
>>> import supertuple
>>> Point = supertuple.superTuple('Point', 'x', 'y')
>>> Point
<class 'supertuple.Point'>
>>> p = Point(1, 2, 3)             # wrong number of fields
Traceback (most recent call last):
  File "", line 1, in ?
  File "C:\Python24\Lib\site-packages\superTuple.py", line 16, in __new__
    raise TypeError, '%s takes exactly %d arguments (%d given)' % (
TypeError: Point takes exactly 2 arguments (3 given)
>>> p = Point(1, 2)               # let's do it right this time
```

```
>>> p
Point(1, 2)
>>> print p.x, p.y
1 2
```

Function superTuple's implementation is quite straightforward. To build the new subclass, superTuple uses a class statement, and in that statement's body, it defines three specials: an "empty" __slots__ (just to save memory, since our supertuple instances don't need any per-instance dictionary anyway); a __new__ method that checks the number of arguments before delegating to tuple.__new__; and an appropriate __repr__ method. After the new class object is built, we set into it a property for each named attribute we want. Each such property has only a "getter", since our supertuples, just like tuples themselves, are immutable—no setting of fields. Finally, we set the new class' name and return the class object.

Each of the getters is easily built by a simple call to the built-in itemgetter from the standard library module operator. Since operator.itemgetter was introduced in Python 2.4, at the very start of our module we ensure we have a suitable itemgetter at hand anyway, even in Python 2.3, by rolling our own if necessary.

See Also

Library Reference and *Python in a Nutshell* docs for property, __slots__, tuple, and special methods __new__ and __repr__; (Python 2.4 only) module operator's function itemgetter.

6.8   Avoiding Boilerplate Accessors for Properties

Credit: Yakov Markovitch

Problem

Your classes use some property instances where either the getter or the setter is just boilerplate code to fetch or set an instance attribute. You would prefer to just specify the attribute name, instead of writing boilerplate code.

Solution

You need a factory function that catches the cases in which either the getter or the setter argument is a string, and wraps the appropriate argument into a function, then delegates the rest of the work to Python's built-in property:

```
def xproperty(fget, fset, fdel=None, doc=None):
    if isinstance(fget, str):
        attr_name = fget
        def fget(obj): return getattr(obj, attr_name)
    elif isinstance(fset, str):
```

```
        attr_name = fset
        def fset(obj, val): setattr(obj, attr_name, val)
    else:
        raise TypeError, 'either fget or fset must be a str'
    return property(fget, fset, fdel, doc)
```

Discussion

Python's built-in property is very useful, but it presents one minor annoyance (it may be easier to see as an annoyance for programmers with experience in Delphi). It often happens that you want to have both a setter and a "getter", but only one of them actually needs to execute any significant code; the other one simply needs to read or write an instance attribute. In that case, property still requires two functions as its arguments. One of the functions will then be just "boilerplate code" (i.e., repetitious plumbing code that is boring, and often voluminous, and thus a likely home for bugs).

For example, consider:

```
class Lower(object):
    def __init__(self, s=''):
        self.s = s
    def _getS(self):
        return self._s
    def _setS(self, s):
        self._s = s.lower()
    s = property(_getS, _setS)
```

Method _getS is just boilerplate, yet you have to code it because you need to pass it to property. Using this recipe, you can make your code a little bit simpler, without changing the code's meaning:

```
class Lower(object):
    def __init__(self, s=''):
        self.s = s
    def _setS(self, s):
        self._s = s.lower()
    s = xproperty('_s', _setS)
```

The simplification doesn't look like much in one small example, but, applied widely all over your code, it can in fact help quite a bit.

The implementation of factory function xproperty in this recipe's Solution is rather rigidly coded: it requires you to pass both fget and fset, and exactly one of them must be a string. No use case requires that both be strings; when neither is a string, or when you want to have just one of the two accessors, you can (and should) use the built-in property directly. It is better, therefore, to have xproperty check that it is being used accurately, considering that such checks remove no useful functionality and impose no substantial performance penalty either.

See Also

Library Reference and *Python in a Nutshell* documentation on the built-in property.

6.9   Making a Fast Copy of an Object

Credit: Alex Martelli

Problem

You need to implement the special method __copy__ so that your class can cooperate with the copy.copy function. Because the __init__ method of your specific class happens to be slow, you need to bypass it and get an "empty", uninitialized instance of the class.

Solution

Here's a solution that works for both new-style and classic classes:

```
def empty_copy(obj):
    class Empty(obj.__class__):
        def __init__(self): pass
    newcopy = Empty()
    newcopy.__class__ = obj.__class__
    return newcopy
```

Your classes can use this function to implement __copy__ as follows:

```
class YourClass(object):
    def __init__(self):
        assume there's a lot of work here
    def __copy__(self):
        newcopy = empty_copy(self)
        copy some relevant subset of self's attributes to newcopy
        return newcopy
```

Here's a usage example:

```
if __name__ == '__main__':
    import copy
    y = YourClass()      # This, of course, does run __init__
    print y
    z = copy.copy(y)   # ...but this doesn't
    print z
```

Discussion

As covered in recipe 4.1 "Copying an Object," Python doesn't implicitly copy your objects when you assign them, which is a great thing because it gives fast, flexible, and uniform semantics. When you need a copy, you explicitly ask for it, often with the copy.copy function, which knows how to copy built-in types, has reasonable defaults for your own objects, and lets you customize the copying process by defining a special method __copy__ in your own classes. If you want instances of a class to be noncopyable, you can define __copy__ and raise a TypeError there. In most cases, you can just let copy.copy's default mechanisms work, and you get free clonability for most of your classes. This is quite a bit nicer than languages that force you to implement a specific clone method for every class whose instances you want to be clonable.

A __copy__ method often needs to start with an "empty" instance of the class in question (e.g., self), bypassing __init__ when that is a costly operation. The simplest general way to do this is to use the ability that Python gives you to change an instance's class on the fly: create a new object in a local empty class, then set the new object's __class__ attribute, as the recipe's code shows. Inheriting class Empty from obj.__class__ is redundant (but quite innocuous) for old-style (classic) classes, but that inheritance makes the recipe compatible with all kinds of objects of classic or new-style classes (including built-in and extension types). Once you choose to inherit from obj's class, you must override __init__ in class Empty, or else the whole purpose of the recipe is defeated. The override means that the __init__ method of obj's class won't execute, since Python, fortunately, does *not* automatically execute ancestor classes' initializers.

Once you have an "empty" object of the required class, you typically need to copy a subset of self's attributes. When you need all of the attributes, you're better off not defining __copy__ explicitly, since copying all instance attributes is exactly copy.copy's default behavior. Unless, of course, you need to do a little bit more than just copying instance attributes; in this case, these two alternative techniques to copy all attributes are both quite acceptable:

```
newcopy.__dict__.update(self.__dict__)
newcopy.__dict__ = dict(self.__dict__)
```

An instance of a new-style class doesn't necessarily keep all of its state in __dict__, so you may need to do some class-specific state copying in such cases.

Alternatives based on the new standard module can't be made transparent across classic and new-style classes, and neither can the __new__ static method that generates an empty instance—the latter is only defined in new-style classes, not classic ones. Fortunately, this recipe obviates any such issues.

A good alternative to implementing __copy__ is often to implement the methods __getstate__ and __setstate__ instead: these special methods define your object's *state* very explicitly and intrinsically bypass __init__. Moreover, they also support serialization (i.e., *pickling*) of your class instances: see recipe 7.4 "Using the cPickle Module on Classes and Instances" for more information about these methods.

So far we have been discussing shallow copies, which is what you want most of the time. With a shallow copy, your object is copied, but objects it refers to (attributes or items) are not, so the newly copied object and the original object refer to the same items or attributes objects—a fast and lightweight operation. A deep copy is a heavyweight operation, potentially duplicating a large graph of objects that refer to each other. You get a deep copy by calling copy.deepcopy on an object. If you need to customize the way in which instances of your class are deep-copied, you can define the special method __deepcopy__:

```
class YourClass(object):
    ...
    def __deepcopy__(self, memo):
        newcopy = empty_copy(self)
        # use copy.deepcopy(self.x, memo) to get deep copies of elements
        # in the relevant subset of self's attributes, to set in newcopy
        return newcopy
```

If you choose to implement __deepcopy__, remember to respect the memoization protocol that is specified in the Python documentation for standard module copy—get deep copies of all the attributes or items that are needed by calling copy.deepcopy with a second argument, the same memo dictionary that is passed to the __deepcopy__ method. Again, implementing __getstate__ and __setstate__ is often a good alternative, since these methods can also support deep copying: Python takes care of deeply copying the "state" object that __getstate__ returns, before passing it to the __setstate__ method of a new, empty instance. See recipe 7.4 "Using the cPickle Module on Classes and Instances" for more information about these special methods.

See Also

Recipe 4.1 "Copying an Object" about shallow and deep copies; recipe 7.4 "Using the cPickle Module on Classes and Instances" about __getstate__ and __setstate__; the *Library Reference* and *Python in a Nutshell* sections on the copy module.

6.10 Keeping References to Bound Methods Without Inhibiting Garbage Collection

Credit: Joseph A. Knapka, Frédéric Jolliton, Nicodemus

Problem

You want to hold references to bound methods, while still allowing the associated object to be garbage-collected.

Solution

Weak references (i.e., references that indicate an object as long as that object is alive but don't *keep* that object alive if there are no other, *normal* references to it) are an important tool in some advanced programming situations. The weakref module in the Python Standard Library lets you use weak references.

However, weakref's functionality cannot directly be used for bound methods unless you take some precautions. To allow an object to be garbage-collected despite outstanding references to its bound methods, you need some wrappers. Put the following code in a file named *weakmethod.py* in some directory on your Python sys.path:

```
import weakref, new
class ref(object):
    """ Wraps any callable, most importantly a bound method, in
        a way that allows a bound method's object to be GC'ed, while
        providing the same interface as a normal weak reference. """
    def __init__(self, fn):
        try:
            # try getting object, function, and class
            o, f, c = fn.im_self, fn.im_func, fn.im_class
        except AttributeError:               # It's not a bound method
            self._obj = None
            self._func = fn
            self._clas = None
        else:                                # It is a bound method
            if o is None: self._obj = None   # ...actually UN-bound
            else: self._obj = weakref.ref(o) # ...really bound
            self._func = f
            self._clas = c
    def __call__(self):
        if self.obj is None: return self._func
        elif self._obj() is None: return None
        return new.instancemethod(self._func, self.obj(), self._clas)
```

Discussion

A normal bound method holds a strong reference to the bound method's object. That means that the object can't be garbage-collected until the bound method is disposed of:

```
>>> class C(object):
...     def f(self):
...         print "Hello"
...     def __del__(self):
...         print "C dying"
...
>>> c = C()
>>> cf = c.f
>>> del c      # c continues to wander about with glazed eyes...
>>> del cf     # ...until we stake its bound method, only then it goes away:
C dying
```

This behavior is most often handy, but sometimes it's not what you want. For example, if you're implementing an event-dispatch system, it might not be desirable for the mere presence of an event handler (i.e., a bound method) to prevent the associated object from being reclaimed. The instinctive idea should then be to use weak references. However, a normal weakref.ref to a bound method doesn't quite work the way one might expect, because bound methods are first-class objects. Weak references to bound methods are dead-on-arrival—that is, they always return None when dereferenced, unless another strong reference to the same bound-method object exists.

For example, the following code, based on the weakref module from the Python Standard Library, doesn't print "Hello" but raises an exception instead:

```
>>> import weakref
>>> c = C()
>>> cf = weakref.ref(c.f)
>>> cf            # Oops, better try the lightning again, Igor...
<weakref at 80ce394; dead>
>>> cf()()
Traceback (most recent call last):
File "", line 1, in ?
TypeError: object of type 'None' is not callable
```

On the other hand, the class ref in the weakmethod module shown in this recipe allows you to have weak references to bound methods in a useful way:

```
>>> import weakmethod
>>> cf = weakmethod.ref(c.f)
>>> cf()()       # It LIVES! Bwahahahaha!
Hello
>>> del c        # ...and it dies
C dying
>>> print cf()
None
```

Calling the weakmethod.ref instance, which refers to a bound method, has the same semantics as calling a weakref.ref instance that refers to, say, a function object: if the referent has died, it returns None; otherwise, it returns the referent. Actually, in this case, it returns a freshly minted new.instancemethod (holding a strong reference to the object—so, be sure not to hold on to that, unless you *do* want to keep the object alive for a while!).

Note that the recipe is carefully coded so you can wrap into a ref instance any callable you want, be it a method (bound or unbound), a function, whatever; the weak references semantics, however, are provided only when you're wrapping a bound method; otherwise, ref acts as a normal (strong) reference, holding the callable alive. This basically lets you use ref for wrapping arbitrary callables without needing to check for special cases.

If you want semantics closer to that of a weakref.proxy, they're easy to implement, for example by subclassing the ref class given in this recipe. When you call a proxy, the proxy calls the referent with the same arguments. If the referent's object no longer lives, then weakref.ReferenceError gets raised instead. Here's an implementation of such a proxy class:

```
class proxy(ref):
    def __call__(self, *args, **kwargs):
        func = ref.__call__(self)
```

```
        if func is None:
            raise weakref.ReferenceError('referent object is dead')
        else:
            return func(*args, **kwargs)
    def __eq__(self, other):
        if type(other) != type(self):
            return False
        return ref.__call__(self) == ref.__call__(other)
```

See Also

The *Library Reference* and *Python in a Nutshell* sections on the weakref and new modules and on bound-method objects.

6.11 Implementing a Ring Buffer

Credit: Sébastien Keim, Paul Moore, Steve Alexander, Raymond Hettinger

Problem

You want to define a buffer with a fixed size, so that, when it fills up, adding another element overwrites the first (oldest) one. This kind of data structure is particularly useful for storing log and history information.

Solution

This recipe changes the buffer object's class on the fly, from a nonfull buffer class to a full buffer class, when the buffer fills up:

```
class RingBuffer(object):
    """ class that implements a not-yet-full buffer """
    def __init__(self, size_max):
        self.max = size_max
        self.data = [ ]
    class __Full(object):
        """ class that implements a full buffer """
        def append(self, x):
            """ Append an element overwriting the oldest one. """
            self.data[self.cur] = x
            self.cur = (self.cur+1) % self.max
        def tolist(self):
            """ return list of elements in correct order. """
            return self.data[self.cur:] + self.data[:self.cur]
    def append(self, x):
        """ append an element at the end of the buffer. """
        self.data.append(x)
        if len(self.data) == self.max:
            self.cur = 0
            # Permanently change self's class from non-full to full
            self.__class__ = self.__Full
    def tolist(self):
```

```
        """ Return a list of elements from the oldest to the newest. """
        return self.data
# sample usage
if __name__ == '__main__':
    x = RingBuffer(5)
    x.append(1); x.append(2); x.append(3); x.append(4)
    print x.__class__, x.tolist()
    x.append(5)
    print x.__class__, x.tolist()
    x.append(6)
    print x.data, x.tolist()
    x.append(7); x.append(8); x.append(9); x.append(10)
    print x.data, x.tolist()
```

Discussion

A ring buffer is a buffer with a fixed size. When it fills up, adding another element overwrites the oldest one that was still being kept. It's particularly useful for the storage of log and history information. Python has no direct support for this kind of structure, but it's easy to construct one. The implementation in this recipe is optimized for element insertion.

The notable design choice in the implementation is that, since these objects undergo a nonreversible state transition at some point in their lifetimes—from nonfull buffer to full buffer (and behavior changes at that point)—I modeled that by changing self.__class__. This works just as well for classic classes as for new-style ones, as long as the old and new classes of the object have the same slots (e.g., it works fine for two new-style classes that have no slots at all, such as RingBuffer and __Full in this recipe). Note that, differently from other languages, the fact that class __Full is implemented inside class RingBuffer does not imply any special relationship between these classes; that's a good thing, too, because no such relationship is necessary.

Changing the class of an instance may be strange in many languages, but it is an excellent Pythonic alternative to other ways of representing occasional, massive, irreversible, and discrete changes of state that vastly affect behavior, as in this recipe. Fortunately, Python supports it for all kinds of classes.

Ring buffers (i.e., bounded queues, and other names) are quite a useful idea, but the inefficiency of testing whether the ring is full, and if so, doing something different, is a nuisance. The nuisance is particularly undesirable in a language like Python, where there's no difficulty—other than the massive memory cost involved—in allowing the list to grow without bounds. So, ring buffers end up being underused in spite of their potential. The idea of assigning to __class__ to switch behaviors when the ring gets full is the key to this recipe's efficiency: such class switching is a one-off operation, so it doesn't make the steady-state cases any less efficient.

Alternatively, we might switch just two methods, rather than the whole class, of a ring buffer instance that becomes full:

```
class RingBuffer(object):
    def __init__(self,size_max):
        self.max = size_max
        self.data = [ ]
    def _full_append(self, x):
        self.data[self.cur] = x
        self.cur = (self.cur+1) % self.max
    def _full_get(self):
        return self.data[self.cur:]+self.data[:self.cur]
    def append(self, x):
        self.data.append(x)
        if len(self.data) == self.max:
            self.cur = 0
            # Permanently change self's methods from non-full to full
            self.append = self._full_append
            self.tolist = self._full_get
    def tolist(self):
        return self.data
```

This method-switching approach is essentially equivalent to the class-switching one in the recipe's solution, albeit through rather different mechanisms. The best approach is probably to use class switching when *all* methods must be switched in bulk and method switching only when you need finer granularity of behavior change. Class switching is the only approach that works if you need to switch any *special* methods in a new-style class, since intrinsic lookup of special methods during various operations happens on the class, not on the instance (classic classes differ from new-style ones in this aspect).

You can use many other ways to implement a ring buffer. In Python 2.4, in particular, you should consider subclassing the new type collections.deque, which supplies a "double-ended queue", allowing equally effective additions and deletions from either end:

```
from collections import deque
class RingBuffer(deque):
    def __init__(self, size_max):
        deque.__init__(self)
        self.size_max = size_max
    def append(self, datum):
        deque.append(self, datum)
        if len(self) > self.size_max:
            self.popleft( )
    def tolist(self):
        return list(self)
```

or, to avoid the if statement when at steady state, you can mix this idea with the idea of switching a method:

```
from collections import deque
class RingBuffer(deque):
    def __init__(self, size_max):
        deque.__init__(self)
        self.size_max = size_max
```

```
    def _full_append(self, datum):
        deque.append(self, datum)
        self.popleft()
    def append(self, datum):
        deque.append(self, datum)
        if len(self) == self.size_max:
            self.append = self._full_append
    def tolist(self):
        return list(self)
```

With this latest implementation, we need to switch only the append method (the tolist method remains the same), so method switching appears to be more appropriate than class switching.

See Also

The *Reference Manual* and *Python in a Nutshell* sections on the standard type hierarchy and classic and new-style object models; Python 2.4 *Library Reference* on module collections.

6.12 Checking an Instance for Any State Changes

Credit: David Hughes

Problem

You need to check whether any changes to an instance's state have occurred to selectively save instances that have been modified since the last "save" operation.

Solution

An effective solution is a *mixin class*—a class you can multiply inherit from and that is able to take snapshots of an instance's state and compare the instance's current state with the last snapshot to determine whether or not the instance has been modified:

```
import copy
class ChangeCheckerMixin(object):
    containerItems = {dict: dict.iteritems, list: enumerate}
    immutable = False
    def snapshot(self):
        ''' create a "snapshot" of self's state -- like a shallow copy, but
            recursing over container types (not over general instances:
            instances must keep track of their own changes if needed).   '''
        if self.immutable:
            return
        self._snapshot = self._copy_container(self.__dict__)
    def makeImmutable(self):
        ''' the instance state can't change any more, set .immutable '''
        self.immutable = True
        try:
```

```
            del self._snapshot
        except AttributeError:
            pass
    def _copy_container(self, container):
        ''' semi-shallow copy, recursing on container types only '''
        new_container = copy.copy(container)
        for k, v in self.containerItems[type(new_container)](new_container):
            if type(v) in self.containerItems:
                new_container[k] = self._copy_container(v)
            elif hasattr(v, 'snapshot'):
                v.snapshot()
        return new_container
    def isChanged(self):
        ''' True if self's state is changed since the last snapshot '''
        if self.immutable:
            return False
        # remove snapshot from self.__dict__, put it back at the end
        snap = self.__dict__.pop('_snapshot', None)
        if snap is None:
            return True
        try:
            return self._checkContainer(self.__dict__, snap)
        finally:
            self._snapshot = snap
    def _checkContainer(self, container, snapshot):
        ''' return True if the container and its snapshot differ '''
        if len(container) != len(snapshot):
            return True
        for k, v in self.containerItems[type(container)](container):
            try:
                ov = snapshot[k]
            except LookupError:
                return True
            if self._checkItem(v, ov):
                return True
        return False
    def _checkItem(self, newitem, olditem):
        ''' compare newitem and olditem.  If they are containers, call
            self._checkContainer recursively.  If they're an instance with
            an 'isChanged' method, delegate to that method.  Otherwise,
            return True if the items differ. '''
        if type(newitem) != type(olditem):
            return True
        if type(newitem) in self.containerItems:
            return self._checkContainer(newitem, olditem)
        if newitem is olditem:
            method_isChanged = getattr(newitem, 'isChanged', None)
            if method_isChanged is None:
                return False
            return method_isChanged()
        return newitem != olditem
```

Discussion

I often need change-checking functionality in my applications. For example, when a user closes the last GUI window over a certain document, I need to check whether the document was changed since the last "save" operation; if it was, then I need to pop up a small window to give the user a choice between saving the document, losing the latest changes, or canceling the window-closing operation.

The class ChangeCheckerMixin, which this recipe describes, satisfies this need. The idea is to multiply derive all of your data classes, meaning all classes that hold data the user views and may change, from ChangeCheckerMixin (as well as from any other bases they need). When the data has just been loaded from or saved to persistent storage, call method snapshot on the top-level, document data class instance. This call takes a "snapshot" of the current state, basically a shallow copy of the object but with recursion over containers, and calls the snapshot methods on any contained instance that has such a method. Any time afterward, you can call method isChanged on any data class instance to check whether the instance state was changed since the time of its last snapshot.

As container types, ChangeCheckerMixin, as presented, considers only list and dict. If you also use other types as containers, you just need to add them appropriately to the containerItems dictionary. That dictionary must map each container type to a function callable on an instance of that type to get an iterator on indices and values (with indices usable to index the container). Container type instances must also support being shallowly copied with standard library Python function copy.copy. For example, to add Python 2.4's collections.deque as a container to a subclass of ChangeCheckerMixin, you can code:

```
import collections
class CCM_with_deque(ChangeCheckerMixin):
    containerItems = dict(ChangeCheckerMixin.containerItems)
    containerItems[collections.deque] = enumerate
```

since collections.deque can be "walked over" with enumerate, just like list can.

Here is a toy example of use for ChangeCheckerMixin:

```
if __name__ == '__main__':
    class eg(ChangeCheckerMixin):
        def __init__(self, *a, **k):
            self.L = list(*a, **k)
        def __str__(self):
            return 'eg(%s)' % str(self.L)
        def __getattr__(self, a):
            return getattr(self.L, a)
    x = eg('ciao')
    print 'x =', x, 'is changed =', x.isChanged()
    # emits: x = eg(['c', 'i', 'a', 'o']) is changed = True
    # now, assume x gets saved, then...:
```

```
x.snapshot( )
print 'x =', x, 'is changed =', x.isChanged( )
# emits: x = eg(['c', 'i', 'a', 'o']) is changed = False
# now we change x...:
x.append('x')
print 'x =', x, 'is changed =', x.isChanged( )
# emits: x = eg(['c', 'i', 'a', 'o', 'x']) is changed = True
```

In class eg we only subclass ChanceCheckerMixin because we need no other bases. In particular, we cannot usefully subclass list because the change-checking functionality works only on state that is kept in an instance's dictionary; so, we must hold a list object in our instance's dictionary, and delegate to it as needed (in this toy example, we delegate all nonspecial methods, automatically, via __getattr__). With this precaution, we see that the isChanged method correctly reflects the crucial tidbit—whether the instance's state has been changed since the last call to snapshot on the instance.

An implicit assumption of this recipe is that your application's data class instances are organized in a hierarchical fashion. The tired old (but still valid) example is an invoice containing header data and detail lines. Each instance of the details data class could contain other instances, such as product details, which may not be modifiable in the current activity but are probably modifiable elsewhere. This is the reason for the immutable attribute and the makeImmutable method: when the attribute is set by calling the method, any outstanding snapshot for the instance is dropped to save memory, and further calls to either snapshot or isChanged can return very rapidly.

If your data does not lend itself to such hierarchical structuring, you may have to take full deep copies, or even "snapshot" a document instance by taking a full pickle of it, and check for changes by comparing the new pickle with the last one previously taken. That may be all right on very fast machines, or when the amount of data you're handling is rather modest. In my tests, however, it shows up as being unacceptably slow for substantial amounts of data on more ordinary machines. This recipe, when your data organization is suitable for its application, can offer better performance. If some of your data classes also contain data that is automatically computed or, for other reasons, does not need to be saved, store such data in instances of subordinate classes (which do *not* inherit from ChangeCheckerMixin), rather than either holding the data as attributes or storing it in ordinary containers such as lists and dictionaries.

See Also

Library Reference and *Python in a Nutshell* documentation on multiple inheritance, the iteritems method of dictionaries, and built-in functions enumerate, isinstance, and hasattr.

6.13 Checking Whether an Object Has Necessary Attributes

Credit: Alex Martelli

Problem

You need to check whether an object has certain necessary attributes before performing state-altering operations. However, you want to avoid type-testing because you know it interferes with polymorphism.

Solution

In Python, you normally just try performing whatever operations you need to perform. For example, here's the simplest, no-checks code for doing a certain sequence of manipulations on a list argument:

```
def munge1(alist):
    alist.append(23)
    alist.extend(range(5))
    alist.append(42)
    alist[4] = alist[3]
    alist.extend(range(2))
```

If alist is missing any of the methods you're calling (explicitly, such as append and extend; or implicitly, such as the calls to __getitem__ and __setitem__ implied by the assignment statement alist[4] = alist[3]), the attempt to access and call a missing method raises an exception. Function munge1 makes no attempt to catch the exception, so the execution of munge1 terminates, and the exception propagates to the caller of munge1. The caller may choose to catch the exception and deal with it, or terminate execution and let the exception propagate further back along the chain of calls, as appropriate.

This approach is usually just fine, but problems may occasionally occur. Suppose, for example, that the alist object has an append method but not an extend method. In this peculiar case, the munge1 function partially alters alist before an exception is raised. Such partial alterations are generally not cleanly undoable; depending on your application, they can sometimes be a bother.

To forestall the "partial alterations" problem, the first approach that comes to mind is to check the type of alist. Such a naive "Look Before You Leap" (LBYL) approach may look safer than doing no checks at all, but LBYL has a serious defect: it loses polymorphism! The worst approach of all is checking for equality of types:

```
def munge2(alist):
    if type(alist) is list:        # a very bad idea
        munge1(alist)
    else: raise TypeError, "expected list, got %s" % type(alist)
```

This even fails, without any good reason, when alist is an instance of a *subclass* of list. You can at least remove that huge defect by using isinstance instead:

```
def munge3(alist):
    if isinstance(alist, list):
        munge1(alist)
    else: raise TypeError, "expected list, got %s" % type(alist)
```

However, munge3 still fails, needlessly, when alist is an instance of a type or class that mimics list but doesn't inherit from it. In other words, such type-checking sacrifices one of Python's great strengths: signature-based polymorphism. For example, you cannot pass to munge3 an instance of Python 2.4's collections.deque, which is a real pity because such a deque does supply all needed functionality and indeed can be passed to the original munge1 and work just fine. Probably a zillion sequence types are out there that, like deque, are quite acceptable to munge1 but not to munge3. Type-checking, even with isinstance, exacts an enormous price.

A far better solution is accurate LBYL, which is both safe *and* fully polymorphic:

```
def munge4(alist):
    # Extract all bound methods you need (get immediate exception,
    # without partial alteration, if any needed method is missing):
    append = alist.append
    extend = alist.extend
    # Check operations, such as indexing, to get an exception ASAP
    # if signature compatibility is missing:
    try: alist[0] = alist[0]
    except IndexError: pass    # An empty alist is okay
    # Operate: no exceptions are expected from this point onwards
    append(23)
    extend(range(5))
    append(42)
    alist[4] = alist[3]
    extend(range(2))
```

Discussion

Python functions are naturally polymorphic on their arguments because they essentially depend on the methods and behaviors of the arguments, not on the arguments' *types*. If you check the types of arguments, you sacrifice this precious polymorphism, so, *don't*! However, you may perform a few early checks to obtain some extra safety (particularly against partial alterations) without substantial costs.

The normal Pythonic way of life can be described as the *Easier to Ask Forgiveness than Permission* (EAFP) approach: just try to perform whatever operations you need, and either handle or propagate any exceptions that may result. It usually works great. The only real problem that occasionally arises is "partial alteration": when you need to perform several operations on an object, just trying to do them all in natural order *could* result in some of them succeeding, and partially altering the object, before an exception is raised.

What Is Polymorphism?

Polymorphism (from Greek roots meaning "many shapes") is the ability of code to deal with objects of different types in ways that are appropriate to each applicable type. Unfortunately, this useful term has been overloaded with all sorts of implications, to the point that many people think it's somehow connected with such concepts as *overloading* (specifying different functions depending on call-time signatures) or *subtyping* (i.e., subclassing), which it most definitely isn't.

Subclassing is often a useful implementation technique, but it's not a necessary condition for polymorphism. Overloading is right out: Python just doesn't let multiple objects with the same name live at the same time in the same scope, so you can't have several functions or methods with the same name and scope, distinguished only by their signatures—a minor annoyance, at worst: just rename those functions or methods so that their name suffices to distinguish them.

Python's functions are polymorphic (unless you take specific steps to break this very useful feature) because they just call methods on their arguments (explicitly or implicitly by performing operations such as arithmetic and indexing): as long as the arguments supply the needed methods, callable with the needed signatures, and those calls perform the appropriate behavior, everything just works.

For example, suppose that munge1, as shown at the start of this recipe's Solution, is called with an actual argument value for alist that has an append method but lacks extend. In this case, alist is altered by the first call to append; but then, the attempt to obtain and call extend raises an exception, leaving alist's state partially altered, a situation that may be hard to recover from. Sometimes, a sequence of operations should ideally be *atomic*: either all of the alterations happen, and everything is fine, or none of them do, and an exception gets raised.

You can get closer to ideal atomicity by switching to the LBYL approach, but in an accurate, careful way. Extract all bound methods you'll need, then noninvasively test the necessary operations (such as indexing on both sides of the assignment operator). Move on to actually changing the object state only if all of this succeeds. From that point onward, it's far less likely (although not impossible) that exceptions will occur in midstream, leaving state partially altered. You could not reach 100% safety even with the strictest type-checking, after all: for example, you *might* run out of memory just smack in the middle of your operations. So, with or without type-checking, you don't really ever guarantee atomicity—you just approach asymptotically to that desirable property.

Accurate LBYL generally offers a good trade-off in comparison to EAFP, assuming we need safeguards against partial alterations. The extra complication is modest, and the slowdown due to the checks is typically compensated by the extra speed gained by using bound methods through local names rather than explicit attribute access (at least if the operations include loops, which is often the case). It's important to avoid overdoing the checks, and the assert statement can help with that. For example, you can add such checks as assert callable(append) to munge4. In this case, the compiler removes the assert entirely when you run the program with optimization (i.e., with flags -O or -OO passed to the python command), while performing the checks when the program is run for testing and debugging (i.e., without the optimization flags).

See Also

Language Reference and *Python in a Nutshell* about assert and the meaning of the -O and -OO command-line arguments; *Library Reference* and *Python in a Nutshell* about sequence types, and lists in particular.

6.14   Implementing the State Design Pattern

Credit: Elmar Bschorer

Problem

An object in your program can switch among several "states", and the object's behavior must change along with the object's state.

Solution

The key idea of the State Design Pattern is to objectify the "state" (with its several behaviors) into a class instance (with its several methods). In Python, you don't have to build an abstract class to represent the interface that is common to the various states: just write the classes for the "state"s themselves. For example:

```python
class TraceNormal(object):
    ' state for normal level of verbosity '
    def startMessage(self):
        self.nstr = self.characters = 0
    def emitString(self, s):
        self.nstr += 1
        self.characters += len(s)
    def endMessage(self):
        print '%d characters in %d strings' % (self.characters, self.nstr)
class TraceChatty(object):
    ' state for high level of verbosity '
    def startMessage(self):
        self.msg = [ ]
    def emitString(self, s):
        self.msg.append(repr(s))
    def endMessage(self):
        print 'Message: ', ', '.join(self.msg)
class TraceQuiet(object):
    ' state for zero level of verbosity '
    def startMessage(self): pass
    def emitString(self, s): pass
    def endMessage(self): pass
```

```
class Tracer(object):
    def __init__(self, state): self.state = state
    def setState(self, state): self.state = state
    def emitStrings(self, strings):
        self.state.startMessage()
        for s in strings: self.state.emitString(s)
        self.state.endMessage()
if __name__ == '__main__':
    t = Tracer(TraceNormal())
    t.emitStrings('some example strings here'.split())
# emits: 21 characters in 4 strings
    t.setState(TraceQuiet())
    t.emitStrings('some example strings here'.split())
# emits nothing
    t.setState(TraceChatty())
    t.emitStrings('some example strings here'.split())
# emits: Message: 'some', 'example', 'strings', 'here'
```

Discussion

With the State Design Pattern, you can "factor out" a number of related behaviors of an object (and possibly some data connected with these behaviors) into an auxiliary state object, to which the main object delegates these behaviors as needed, through calls to methods of the "state" object. In Python terms, this design pattern is related to the idioms of rebinding an object's whole __class__, as shown in recipe 6.11 "Implementing a Ring Buffer," and rebinding just certain methods (shown in recipe 2.14 "Rewinding an Input File to the Beginning"). This design pattern, in a sense, lies in between those Python idioms: you group a set of related behaviors, rather than switching either all behavior, by changing the object's whole __class__, or each method on its own, without grouping. With relation to the classic design pattern terminology, this recipe presents a pattern that falls somewhere between the classic State Design Pattern and the classic Strategy Design Pattern.

This State Design Pattern has some extra oomph, compared to the related Pythonic idioms, because an appropriate amount of data can live together with the behaviors you're delegating—exactly as much, or as little, as needed to support each specific behavior. In the examples given in this recipe's Solution, for example, the different state objects differ greatly in the kind and amount of data they need: none at all for class TraceQuiet, just a couple of numbers for TraceNormal, a whole list of strings for TraceChatty. These responsibilities are usefully delegated from the main object to each specific "state object".

In some cases, although not in the specific examples shown in this recipe, state objects may need to cooperate more closely with the main object, by calling main object methods or accessing main object attributes in certain circumstances. To allow this, the main object can pass as an argument either self or some bound method of self to methods of the "state" objects. For example, suppose that the functionality in this recipe's Solution needs to be extended, in that the main object must keep track of how many lines have been emitted by messages it has sent. Tracer.__init__ will have to add one per-instance initialization self.lines = 0, and the signature of the "state" object's endMessage methods will have to be extended to def endMessage(self, tracer):. The implementation of endMessage in class TraceQuiet will just ignore the tracer argument, since it doesn't actually emit any lines; the implementations in the other two classes will each add a statement tracer.lines += 1, since each of them emits one line per message.

As you see, the kind of closer coupling implied by this kind of extra functionality need not be particularly problematic. In particular, the key feature of the classic State Design Pattern, that state objects are the ones that handle state switching (while, in the Strategy Design Pattern, the switching comes from the outside), is just not enough of a big deal in Python to warrant considering the two design patterns as separate.

See Also

See *http://exciton.cs.rice.edu/JavaResources/DesignPatterns/* for good coverage of the classic design patterns, albeit in a Java context.

6.15 Implementing the "Singleton" Design Pattern

Credit: Jürgen Hermann

Problem

You want to make sure that only one instance of a class is ever created.

Solution

The __new__ staticmethod makes the task very simple:

```
class Singleton(object):
    """ A Pythonic Singleton """
    def __new__(cls, *args, **kwargs):
        if '_inst' not in vars(cls):
            cls._inst = super(Singleton, cls).__new__(cls, *args, **kwargs)
        return cls._inst
```

Just have your class inherit from Singleton, and don't override __new__. Then, all calls to that class (normally creations of new instances) return the same instance. (The instance is created once, on the first such call to each given subclass of Singleton during each run of your program.)

Discussion

This recipe shows the one obvious way to implement the "Singleton" Design Pattern in Python (see E. Gamma, et al., *Design Patterns: Elements of Reusable Object-Oriented Software*, Addison-Wesley). A Singleton is a class that makes sure only one instance of it is ever created. Typically, such a class is used to manage resources that by their nature can exist only once. See recipe 6.16 "Avoiding the "Singleton" Design Pattern with the Borg Idiom" for other considerations about, and alternatives to, the "Singleton" design pattern in Python.

We can complete the module with the usual self-test idiom and show this behavior:

```
if __name__ == '__main__':
    class SingleSpam(Singleton):
        def __init__(self, s): self.s = s
        def __str__(self): return self.s
    s1 = SingleSpam('spam')
    print id(s1), s1.spam( )
    s2 = SingleSpam('eggs')
    print id(s2), s2.spam( )
```

When we run this module as a script, we get something like the following output (the exact value of id does vary, of course):

```
8172684 spam
8172684 spam
```

The 'spam' parameter originally passed when s1 was instantiated has now been trampled upon by the re-instantiation—that's part of the price you pay for having a Singleton!

One issue with Singleton in general is *subclassability*. The way class Singleton is coded in this recipe, each descendant subclass, direct or indirect, will get a separate instance. Literally speaking, this violates the constraint of *only one instance per class*, depending on what one exactly means by it:

```
class Foo(Singleton): pass
class Bar(Foo): pass
f = Foo( ); b = Bar( )
print f is b, isinstance(f, Foo), isinstance(b, Foo)
# emits False True True
```

f and b are separate instances, yet, according to the built-in function isinstance, they are *both* instances of Foo because isinstance applies the IS-A rule of OOP: an instance of a subclass IS-An instance of the base class too. On the other hand, if we took pains to return f again when b is being instantiated by calling Bar, we'd be violating the normal assumption that calling class Bar gives us an instance of class Bar, not an instance of a random superclass of Bar that just happens to have been instantiated earlier in the course of a run of the program.

In practice, subclassability of "Singleton"s *is* rather a headache, without any obvious solution. If this issue is important to you, the alternative *Borg* idiom, explained next

---

in recipe 6.16 "Avoiding the "Singleton" Design Pattern with the Borg Idiom" may provide a better approach.

See Also

Recipe 6.16 "Avoiding the "Singleton" Design Pattern with the Borg Idiom"; E. Gamma, R. Helm, R. Johnson, J. Vlissides, *Design Patterns: Elements of Reusable Object-Oriented Software* (Addison-Wesley).

6.16 Avoiding the "Singleton" Design Pattern with the Borg Idiom

Credit: Alex Martelli, Alex A. Naanou

Problem

You want to make sure that only one instance of a class is ever created: you don't care about the id of the resulting instances, just about their state and behavior, and you need to ensure subclassability.

Solution

Application needs (*forces*) related to the "Singleton" Design Pattern can be met by allowing multiple instances to be created while ensuring that all instances share state and behavior. This is more flexible than fiddling with instance creation. Have your class inherit from the following Borg class:

```
class Borg(object):
    _shared_state = {}
    def __new__(cls, *a, **k):
        obj = object.__new__(cls, *a, **k)
        obj.__dict__ = cls._shared_state
        return obj
```

If you override __new__ in your class (very few classes need to do that), just remember to use Borg.__new__, rather than object.__new__, within your override. If you want instances of your class to share state among themselves, but not with instances of other subclasses of Borg, make sure that your class has, at class scope, the "state"ment:

```
    _shared_state = {}
```

With this "data override", your class doesn't inherit the _shared_state attribute from Borg but rather gets its own. It is to enable this "data override" that Borg's __new__ uses cls._shared_state instead of Borg._shared_state.

Discussion

Borg in action

Here's a typical example of Borg use:

```
if __name__ == '__main__':
    class Example(Borg):
        name = None
        def __init__(self, name=None):
            if name is not None: self.name = name
        def __str__(self): return 'name->%s' % self.name
    a = Example('Lara')
    b = Example()                      # instantiating b shares self.name with a
    print a, b
    c = Example('John Malkovich')  # making c changes self.name of a & b too
    print a, b, c
    b.name = 'Seven'               # setting b.name changes name of a & c too
    print a, b, c
```

When running this module as a main script, the output is:

```
name->Lara name->Lara
name->John Malkovich name->John Malkovich name->John Malkovich
name->Seven name->Seven name->Seven
```

All instances of Example share state, so any setting of the name attribute of any instance, either in __init__ or directly, affects all instances equally. However, note that the instance's ids differ; therefore, since we have not defined special methods __eq__ and __hash__, each instance can work as a distinct key in a dictionary. Thus, if we continue our sample code as follows:

```
adict = { }
j = 0
for i in a, b, c:
    adict[i] = j
    j = j + 1
for i in a, b, c:
    print i, adict[i]
```

the output is:

```
name->Seven 0
name->Seven 1
name->Seven 2
```

If this behavior is not what you want, add __eq__ and __hash__ methods to the Example class or the Borg superclass. Having these methods might better simulate the existence of a single instance, depending on your exact needs. For example, here's a version of Borg with these special methods added:

```
class Borg(object):
    _shared_state = { }
    def __new__(cls, *a, **k):
        obj = super(Borg, cls).__new__(cls, *a, **k)
```

```
        obj.__dict__ = cls._shared_state
        return obj
    def __hash__(self): return 9        # any arbitrary constant integer
    def __eq__(self, other):
        try: return self.__dict__ is other.__dict__
        except AttributeError: return False
```

With this enriched version of Borg, the example's output changes to:

```
name->Seven 2
name->Seven 2
name->Seven 2
```

Borg, Singleton, or neither?

The Singleton Design Pattern has a catchy name, but unfortunately it also has the wrong focus for most purposes: it focuses on object identity, rather than on object state and behavior. The Borg design nonpattern makes all instances share state instead, and Python makes implementing this idea a snap.

In most cases in which you might think of using Singleton or Borg, you don't really need either of them. Just write a Python module, with functions and module-global variables, instead of defining a class, with methods and per-instance attributes. You need to use a class only if you must be able to inherit from it, or if you need to take advantage of the class' ability to define special methods. (See recipe 6.2 "Defining Constants" for a way to combine some of the advantages of classes and modules.) Even when you do need a class, it's usually unnecessary to include in the class itself any code to enforce the idea that one can't make multiple instances of it; other, simpler idioms are generally preferable. For example:

```
class froober(object):
    def __init__(self):
        etc, etc
froober = froober( )
```

Now froober is by nature the only instance of its own class, since name 'froober' has been rebound to mean the instance, not the class. Of course, one might call froober.__class__( ), but it's not sensible to spend much energy taking precautions against deliberate abuse of your design intentions. Any obstacles you put in the way of such abuse, somebody else can bypass. Taking precautions against *accidental* misuse is way plenty. If the very simple idiom shown in this latest snippet is sufficient for your needs, use it, and forget about Singleton and Borg. Remember: *do the simplest thing that could possibly work*. On rare occasions, though, an idiom as simple as this one cannot work, and then you do need more.

The Singleton Design Pattern (described previously in recipe 6.15 "Implementing the "Singleton" Design Pattern") is all about ensuring that just one instance of a certain class is ever created. In my experience, Singleton is generally not the best solution to the problems it tries to solve, producing different kinds of issues in various object models. We typically want to let as many instances be created as necessary, but all with shared state. Who cares about identity? It's state (and behavior) we care about. The alternate pattern based on sharing state, in order to solve roughly the same problems as Singleton does, has also been called *Monostate*. Incidentally, I like to call Singleton "Highlander" because there can be only one.

In Python, you can implement the Monostate Design Pattern in many ways, but the Borg design nonpattern is often best. Simplicity is Borg's greatest strength. Since the __dict__ of any instance can be rebound, Borg in its __new__ rebinds the __dict__ of each of its instances to a class-attribute dictionary. Now, any reference or binding of an instance attribute will affect all instances equally. I thank David Ascher for suggesting the appropriate name Borg for this nonpattern. Borg is a nonpattern because it had no known uses at the time of its first publication (although several uses *are* now known): two or more known uses are part of the prerequisites for being a design pattern. See the detailed discussion at *http://www.aleax.it/5ep.html*.

An excellent article by Robert Martin about Singleton and Monostate can be found at *http://www.objectmentor.com/resources/articles/SingletonAndMonostate.pdf*. Note that most of the disadvantages that Martin attributes to Monostate are really due to the limitations of the languages that Martin is considering, such as C++ and Java, and just disappear when using Borg in Python. For example, Martin indicates, as Monostate's first and main disadvantage, that "A non-Monostate class cannot be converted into a Monostate class through derivation"—but that is obviously not the case for Borg, which, through multiple inheritance, makes such conversions trivial.

Borg odds and ends

The __getattr__ and __setattr__ special methods are not involved in Borg's operations. Therefore, you can define them independently in your subclass, for whatever other purposes you may require, or you may leave these special methods undefined. Either way is not a problem because Python does not call __setattr__ in the specific case of the rebinding of the instance's __dict__ attribute.

Borg does not work well for classes that choose to keep some or all of their per-instance state somewhere other than in the instance's __dict__. So, in subclasses of Borg, avoid defining __slots__—that's a memory-footprint optimization that would make no sense, anyway, since it's meant for classes that have a large number of instances, and Borg subclasses will effectively have just one instance! Moreover, instead of inheriting from built-in types such as list or dict, your Borg subclasses should use wrapping and automatic delegation, as shown previously recipe 6.5 "Delegating Automatically as an Alternative to Inheritance." (I named this latter twist "DeleBorg," in my paper available at *http://www.aleax.it/5ep.html*.)

Saying that Borg "is a Singleton" would be as silly as saying that a portico is an umbrella. Both serve similar purposes (letting you walk in the rain without getting wet)—solve similar forces, in design pattern parlance—but since they do so in utterly different ways, they're not instances of the same pattern. If anything, as already mentioned, Borg has similarities to the Monostate alternative design pattern to Singleton. However, Monostate is a design pattern, while Borg is not; also, a Python Monostate could perfectly well exist without being a Borg. We can say that Borg is an idiom that makes it easy and effective to implement Monostate in Python.

For reasons mysterious to me, people often conflate issues germane to Borg and Highlander with other, independent issues, such as access control and, particularly, access from multiple threads. If you need to control access to an object, that need is exactly the same whether there is one instance of that object's class or twenty of them, and whether or not those instances share state. A fruitful approach to problem-solving is known as *divide and conquer*—making problems easier to solve by splitting apart their different aspects. Making problems more difficult to solve by joining together several aspects must be an example of an approach known as *unite and suffer!*

See Also

Recipe 6.5 "Delegating Automatically as an Alternative to Inheritance"; recipe 6.15 "Implementing the "Singleton" Design Pattern"; Alex Martelli, "Five Easy Pieces: Simple Python Non-Patterns" (*http://www.aleax.it/5ep.html*).

6.17 Implementing the Null Object Design Pattern

Credit: Dinu C. Gherman, Holger Krekel

Problem

You want to reduce the need for conditional statements in your code, particularly the need to keep checking for special cases.

Solution

The usual placeholder object for "there's nothing here" is None, but we may be able to do better than that by defining a class meant exactly to act as such a placeholder:

```
class Null(object):
    """ Null objects always and reliably "do nothing." """
    # optional optimization: ensure only one instance per subclass
    # (essentially just to save memory, no functional difference)
    def __new__(cls, *args, **kwargs):
        if '_inst' not in vars(cls):
            cls._inst = type.__new__(cls, *args, **kwargs)
        return cls._inst
    def __init__(self, *args, **kwargs): pass
    def __call__(self, *args, **kwargs): return self
    def __repr__(self): return "Null( )"
    def __nonzero__(self): return False
```

```
        def __getattr__(self, name): return self
        def __setattr__(self, name, value): return self
        def __delattr__(self, name): return self
```

Discussion

You can use an instance of the Null class instead of the primitive value None. By using such an instance as a placeholder, instead of None, you can avoid many conditional statements in your code and can often express algorithms with little or no checking for special values. This recipe is a sample implementation of the Null Object Design Pattern. (See B. Woolf, "The Null Object Pattern" in *Pattern Languages of Programming* [PLoP 96, September 1996].)

This recipe's Null class ignores all parameters passed when constructing or calling instances, as well as any attempt to set or delete attributes. Any call or attempt to access an attribute (or a method, since Python does not distinguish between the two, calling __getattr__ either way) returns the same Null instance (i.e., self—no reason to create a new instance). For example, if you have a computation such as:

```
def compute(x, y):
    try:
        lots of computation here to return some appropriate object
    except SomeError:
        return None
```

and you use it like this:

```
for x in xs:
    for y in ys:
        obj = compute(x, y)
        if obj is not None:
            obj.somemethod(y, x)
```

you can usefully change the computation to:

```
def compute(x, y):
    try:
        lots of computation here to return some appropriate object
    except SomeError:
        return Null( )
```

and thus simplify its use down to:

```
for x in xs:
    for y in ys:
        compute(x, y).somemethod(y, x)
```

The point is that you don't need to check whether compute has returned a real result or an instance of Null: even in the latter case, you can safely and innocuously call on it whatever method you want. Here is another, more specific use case:

```
log = err = Null( )
if verbose:
    log = open('/tmp/log', 'w')
    err = open('/tmp/err', 'w')
```

```
log.write('blabla')
err.write('blabla error')
```

This obviously avoids the usual kind of "pollution" of your code from guards such as if verbose: strewn all over the place. You can now call log.write('bla'), instead of having to express each such call as if log is not None: log.write('bla').

In the new object model, Python does not call __getattr__ on an instance for any special methods needed to perform an operation on the instance (rather, it looks up such methods in the instance class' slots). You may have to take care and customize Null to your application's needs regarding operations on null objects, and therefore special methods of the null objects' class, either directly in the class' sources or by subclassing it appropriately. For example, with this recipe's Null, you cannot index Null instances, nor take their length, nor iterate on them. If this is a problem for your purposes, you can add all the special methods you need (in Null itself or in an appropriate subclass) and implement them appropriately—for example:

```
class SeqNull(Null):
    def __len__(self): return 0
    def __iter__(self): return iter(())
    def __getitem__(self, i): return self
    def __delitem__(self, i): return self
    def __setitem__(self, i, v): return self
```

Similar considerations apply to several other operations.

The key goal of Null objects is to provide an intelligent replacement for the often-used primitive value None in Python. (Other languages represent the lack of a value using either null or a null pointer.) These nobody-lives-here markers/placeholders are used for many purposes, including the important case in which one member of a group of otherwise similar elements is special. This usage usually results in conditional statements all over the place to distinguish between ordinary elements and the primitive null (e.g., None) value, but Null objects help you avoid that.

Among the advantages of using Null objects are the following:

- Superfluous conditional statements can be avoided by providing a first-class object alternative for the primitive value None, thereby improving code readability.

- Null objects can act as placeholders for objects whose behavior is not yet implemented.

- Null objects can be used polymorphically with instances of just about any other class (perhaps needing suitable subclassing for special methods, as previously mentioned).

- Null objects are very predictable.

The one serious disadvantage of Null is that it can hide bugs. If a function returns None, and the caller did not expect that return value, the caller most likely will soon thereafter try to call a method or perform an operation that None doesn't support, leading to a reasonably prompt exception and traceback. If the return value that the caller didn't expect is a Null, the problem might stay hidden for a longer time, and the exception and traceback, when they eventually happen, may therefore be harder to reconnect to the location of the defect in the code. Is this problem serious enough to make using Null inadvisable? The answer is a matter of opinion. If your code has halfway decent unit tests, this problem will not arise; while, if your code *lacks* decent unit tests, then using Null is the *least* of your problems. But, as I said, it boils down to a matter of opinions. I use Null very widely, and I'm extremely happy with the effect it has had on my productivity.

The Null class as presented in this recipe uses a simple variant of the "Singleton" pattern (shown earlier in recipe 6.15 "Implementing the "Singleton" Design Pattern"), strictly for optimization purposes—namely, to avoid the creation of numerous passive objects that do nothing but take up memory. Given all the previous remarks about customization by subclassing, it is, of course, crucial that the specific implementation of "Singleton" ensures a *separate* instance exists for each subclass of Null that gets instantiated. The number of subclasses will no doubt never be so high as to eat up substantial amounts of memory, and anyway this per-subclass distinction can be semantically crucial.

See Also

B. Woolf, "The Null Object Pattern" in *Pattern Languages of Programming* (PLoP 96, September 1996), *http://www.cs.wustl.edu/~schmidt/PLoP-96/woolf1.ps.gz*; recipe 6.15 "Implementing the "Singleton" Design Pattern."

6.18   Automatically Initializing Instance Variables from __init__ Arguments

Credit: Peter Otten, Gary Robinson, Henry Crutcher, Paul Moore, Peter Schwalm, Holger Krekel

Problem

You want to avoid writing and maintaining __init__ methods that consist of almost nothing but a series of self.something = something assignments.

Solution

You can "factor out" the attribute-assignment task to an auxiliary function:

```
def attributesFromDict(d):
    self = d.pop('self')
    for n, v in d.iteritems():
        setattr(self, n, v)
```

Now, the typical boilerplate code for an __init__ method such as:

```
def __init__(self, foo, bar, baz, boom=1, bang=2):
    self.foo = foo
    self.bar = bar
    self.baz = baz
    self.boom = boom
    self.bang = bang
```

can become a short, crystal-clear one-liner:

```
def __init__(self, foo, bar, baz, boom=1, bang=2):
    attributesFromDict(locals())
```

Discussion

As long as no additional logic is in the body of __init__, the dict returned by calling
the built-in function locals contains only the arguments that were passed to __init__
(plus those arguments that were not passed but have default values). Function
attributesFromDict extracts the object, relying on the convention that the object is
always an argument named 'self', and then interprets all other items in the dictionary as names and values of attributes to set. A similar but simpler technique, not
requiring an auxiliary function, is:

```
def __init__(self, foo, bar, baz, boom=1, bang=2):
    self.__dict__.update(locals())
    del self.self
```

However, this latter technique has a serious defect when compared to the one presented in this recipe's Solution: by setting attributes directly into self.__dict__
(through the latter's update method), it does not play well with properties and other
advanced descriptors, while the approach in this recipe's Solution, using built-in
setattr, is impeccable in this respect.

attributesFromDict is not meant for use in an __init__ method that contains more
code, and specifically one that uses some local variables, because attributesFromDict
cannot easily distinguish, in the dictionary that is passed as its only argument d,
between arguments of __init__ and other local variables of __init__. If you're
willing to insert a little introspection in the auxiliary function, this limitation may be
overcome:

```
def attributesFromArguments(d):
    self = d.pop('self')
    codeObject = self.__init__.im_func.func_code
    argumentNames = codeObject.co_varnames[1:codeObject.co_argcount]
    for n in argumentNames:
        setattr(self, n, d[n])
```

By extracting the code object of the __init__ method, function
attributesFromArguments *is* able to limit itself to the names of __init__'s arguments.
Your __init__ method can then call attributesFromArguments(locals()), instead of

attributesFromDict(locals( )), if and when it needs to continue, after the call, with more code that may define other local variables.

The key limitation of attributesFromArguments is that it does *not* support __init__ having a last special argument of the **kw kind. Such support can be added, with yet more introspection, but it would require more black magic and complication than the functionality is probably worth. If you nevertheless want to explore this possibility, you can use the inspect module of the standard library, rather than the roll-your-own approach used in function attributeFromArguments, for introspection purposes. inspect.getargspec(self.__init__) gives you both the argument names and the indication of whether self.__init__ accepts a **kw form. See recipe 6.19 "Calling a Superclass __init__ Method If It Exists" for more information about function inspect.getargspec. Remember the golden rule of Python programming: "Let the standard library do it!"

See Also

Library Reference and *Python in a Nutshell* docs for the built-in function locals, methods of type dict, special method __init__, and introspection techniques (including module inspect).

6.19 Calling a Superclass __init__ Method If It Exists

Credit: Alex Martelli

Problem

You want to ensure that __init__ is called for all superclasses that define it, and Python does not do this automatically.

Solution

As long as your class is new-style, the built-in super makes this task easy (if all super-classes' __init__ methods also use super similarly):

```
class NewStyleOnly(A, B, C):
    def __init__(self):
        super(NewStyleOnly, self).__init__()
        initialization specific to subclass NewStyleOnly
```

Discussion

Classic classes are *not* recommended for new code development: they exist only to guarantee backwards compatibility with old versions of Python. Use new-style classes (deriving directly or indirectly from object) for all new code. The only thing you cannot do with a new-style class is to raise its instances as exception objects;

---

exception classes must therefore be old style, but then, you do not need the functionality of this recipe for such classes. Since the rest of this recipe's Discussion is therefore both advanced and of limited applicability, you may want to skip it.

Still, it may happen that you need to retrofit this functionality into a classic class, or, more likely, into a new-style class with some superclasses that do *not* follow the proper style of cooperative superclass method-calling with the built-in super. In such cases, you should first try to fix the problematic premises—make all classes new style and make them use super properly. If you absolutely cannot fix things, the best you can do is to have your class loop over its base classes—for each base, check whether it has an __init__, and if so, then call it:

```
class LookBeforeYouLeap(X, Y, Z):
    def __init__(self):
        for base in self__class__.__bases__:
            if hasattr(base, '__init__'):
                base.__init__(self)
        initialization specific to subclass LookBeforeYouLeap
```

More generally, and not just for method __init__, we often want to call a method on an instance, or class, if and only if that method exists; if the method does not exist on that class or instance, we do nothing, or we default to another action. The technique shown in the "Solution", based on built-in super, is not applicable in general: it only works on superclasses of the current object, only if those superclasses also use super appropriately, and only if the method in question does exist in some superclass. Note that all new-style classes do have an __init__ method: they all subclass object, and object defines __init__ (as a do-nothing function that accepts and ignores any arguments). Therefore, all new-style classes have an __init__ method, either by inheritance or by override.

The LBYL technique shown in class LookBeforeYouLeap may be of help in more general cases, including ones that involve methods other than __init__. Indeed, LBYL may even be used *together* with super, for example, as in the following toy example:

```
class Base1(object):
    def met(self):
        print 'met in Base1'
class Der1(Base1):
    def met(self):
        s = super(Der1, self)
        if hasattr(s, 'met'):
            s.met( )
        print 'met in Der1'
class Base2(object):
    pass
class Der2(Base2):
    def met(self):
        s = super(Der2, self)
        if hasattr(s, 'met'):
            s.met( )
```

```
        print 'met in Der2'
Der1().met()
Der2().met()
```

This snippet emits:

```
met in Base1
met in Der1
met in Der2
```

The implementation of met has the same structure in both derived classes, Der1 (whose superclass Base1 *does* have a method named met) and Der2 (whose superclass Base1 *doesn't* have such a method). By binding a local name s to the result of super, and checking with hasattr that the superclass does have such a method before calling it, this LBYL structure lets you code in the same way in both cases. Of course, when coding a subclass, you *do* normally know which methods the superclasses have, and whether and how you need to call them. Still, this technique can provide a little extra flexibility for those occasions in which you need to slightly decouple the subclass from the superclass.

The LBYL technique is far from perfect, though: a superclass might define an attribute named met, which is not callable or needs a different number of arguments. If your need for flexibility is so extreme that you must ward against such occurrences, you can extract the superclass' method object (if any) and check it with the getargspec function of standard library module inspect.

While pushing this idea towards full generality can lead into rather deep complications, here is one example of how you might code a class with a method that calls the superclass' version of the same method only if the latter is callable without arguments:

```
import inspect
class Der(A, B, C, D):
    def met(self):
        s = super(Der, self)
        # get the superclass's bound-method object, or else None
        m = getattr(s, 'met', None)
        try:
            args, varargs, varkw, defaults = inspect.getargspec(m)
        except TypeError:
            # m is not a method, just ignore it
            pass
        else:
            # m is a method, do all its arguments have default values?
            if len(defaults) == len(args):
                # yes! so, call it:
                m()
        print 'met in Der'
```

inspect.getargspec raises a TypeError if its argument is not a method or function, so we catch that case with a try/except statement, and if the exception occurs, we just ignore it with a do-nothing pass statement in the except clause. To simplify our code

---

a bit, we do not first check separately with hasattr. Rather, we get the 'met' attribute of the superclass by calling getattr with a third argument of None. Thus, if the superclass does not have any attribute named 'met', m is set to None, later causing exactly the same TypeError that we have to catch (and ignore) anyway—two birds with one stone. If the call to inspect.getargspec in the try clause does not raise a TypeError, execution continues with the else clause.

If inspect.getargspec doesn't raise a TypeError, it returns a tuple of four items, and we bind each item to a local name. In this case, the ones we care about are args, a list of m's argument names, and defaults, a tuple of default values that m provides for its arguments. Clearly, we can call m without arguments if and only if m provides default values for all of its arguments. So, we check that there are just as many default values as arguments, by comparing the lengths of list args and tuple defaults, and call m only if the lengths are equal.

No doubt you don't need such advanced introspection and such careful checking in most of the code you write, but, just in case you do, Python does supply all the tools you need to achieve it.

See Also

Docs for built-in functions super, getattr, and hasattr, and module inspect, in the *Library Reference* and *Python in a Nutshell*.

6.20 Using Cooperative Supercalls Concisely and Safely

Credit: Paul McNett, Alex Martelli

Problem

You appreciate the cooperative style of multiple-inheritance coding supported by the super built-in, but you wish you could use that style in a more terse and concise way.

Solution

A good solution is a mixin class—a class you can multiply inherit from, that uses introspection to allow more terse coding:

```
import inspect
class SuperMixin(object):
    def super(cls, *args, **kwargs):
        frame = inspect.currentframe(1)
        self = frame.f_locals['self']
        methodName = frame.f_code.co_name
        method = getattr(super(cls, self), methodName, None)
        if inspect.ismethod(method):
```

```
            return method(*args, **kwargs)
    super = classmethod(super)
```

Any class cls that inherits from class SuperMixin acquires a magic method named super: calling cls.super(args) from within a method named somename of class cls is a concise way to call super(cls, self).somename(args). Moreover, the call is safe even if no class that follows cls in Method Resolution Order (MRO) defines any method named somename.

Discussion

Here is a usage example:

```
if __name__ == '__main__':
    class TestBase(list, SuperMixin):
        # note: no myMethod defined here
        pass
    class MyTest1(TestBase):
        def myMethod(self):
            print "in MyTest1"
            MyTest1.super( )
    class MyTest2(TestBase):
        def myMethod(self):
            print "in MyTest2"
            MyTest2.super( )
    class MyTest(MyTest1, MyTest2):
        def myMethod(self):
            print "in MyTest"
            MyTest.super( )
    MyTest( ).myMethod( )
# emits:
# in MyTest
# in MyTest1
# in MyTest2
```

Python has been offering "new-style" classes for years, as a preferable alternative to the classic classes that you get by default. Classic classes exist only for backwards-compatibility with old versions of Python and are not recommended for new code. Among the advantages of new-style classes is the ease of calling superclass implementations of a method in a "cooperative" way that fully supports multiple inheritance, thanks to the super built-in.

Suppose you have a method in a new-style class cls, which needs to perform a task and then delegate the rest of the work to the superclass implementation of the same method. The code idiom is:

```
def somename(self, *args):
    ...some preliminary task...
    return super(cls, self).somename(*args)
```

This idiom suffers from two minor issues: it's slightly verbose, and it also depends on a superclass offering a method somename. If you want to make cls less coupled to other classes, and therefore more robust, by removing the dependency, the code gets even more verbose:

```
def somename(self, *args):
    ...some preliminary task...
    try:
        super_method = super(cls, self).somename
    except AttributeError:
        return None
    else:
        return super_method(*args)
```

The `mixin` class `SuperMixin` shown in this recipe removes both issues. Just ensure `cls` inherits, directly or indirectly, from `SuperMixin` (alongside any other base classes you desire), and then you can code, concisely *and* robustly:

```
def somename(self, *args):
    ...some preliminary task...
    return cls.super(*args)
```

The `classmethod` `SuperMixin.super` relies on simple introspection to get the `self` object and the name of the method, then internally uses built-ins `super` and `getattr` to get the superclass method, and safely call it only if it exists. The introspection is performed through the handy `inspect` module of the standard Python library, making the whole task even simpler.

See Also

Library Reference and *Python in a Nutshell* docs on `super`, the new object model and MRO, the built-in `getattr`, and standard library module `inspect`; recipe 20.12 "Using Cooperative Supercalls with Terser Syntax" for another recipe taking a very different approach to simplify the use of built-in `super`.

CHAPTER 7
Persistence and Databases

7.0   Introduction

Credit: Aaron Watters, Software Consultant

There are three kinds of people in this world: those who can count and those who can't.

However, there are only two kinds of computer programs: toy programs and programs that interact with some kind of persistent databases. That is to say, most real computer programs must retrieve stored information and record information for future use. These days, this description applies to almost every computer game, which can typically save and restore the state of the game at any time. So when I refer to *toy programs*, I mean programs written as exercises, or for the fun of programming. Nearly all real programs (such as programs that people get paid to write) have some persistent database storage/retrieval component.

When I was a Fortran programmer in the 1980s, I noticed that although almost every program had to retrieve and store information, they almost always did it using home-grown methods. Furthermore, since the storage and retrieval parts of the program were the least interesting components from the programmer's point of view, these parts of the program were frequently implemented very sloppily and were hideous sources of intractable bugs. This repeated observation convinced me that the study and implementation of database systems sat at the core of programming pragmatics, and that the state of the art as I saw it then required much improvement.

Later, in graduate school, I was delighted to find an impressive and sophisticated body of work relating to the implementation of database systems. The literature of database systems covered issues of concurrency, fault tolerance, distribution, query optimization, database design, and transaction semantics, among others. In typical academic fashion, many of the concepts had been elaborated to the point of absurdity (such as the silly notion of conditional multivalued dependencies), but much of the work was directly related to the practical implementation of reliable and efficient storage and retrieval systems. The starting point for much of this work was E.F. Codd's seminal paper, "A Relational Model of Data for Large Shared Data Banks."[*]

Among my fellow graduate students, and even among most of the faculty, the same body of knowledge was either disregarded or regarded with some scorn. Everyone recognized that knowledge of conventional relational technology could be lucrative, but they generally considered such knowledge to be on the same level as knowing how to write (or more importantly, maintain) COBOL programs. This situation was not helped by the fact that the emerging database interface standard, SQL (which is now very well established), looked like an extension of COBOL and bore little obvious relationship to any modern programming language.

More than a decade later, there is little indication that anything will soon overtake SQL-based relational technology for the majority of data-based applications. In fact, relational-database technology seems more pervasive than ever. The largest software vendors—IBM, Microsoft, and Oracle—all provide various relational-database implementations as crucial components of their core offerings. Other large software firms, such as SAP and PeopleSoft, essentially provide layers of software built on top of a relational-database core.

Generally, relational databases have been augmented rather than replaced. Enterprise software-engineering dogma frequently espouses three-tier systems, in which the bottom tier is a carefully designed relational database, the middle tier defines a view of the database as business objects, and the top tier consists of applications or transactions that manipulate the business objects, with effects that ultimately translate to changes in the underlying relational tables.

Microsoft's Open Database Connectivity (ODBC) standard provides a common programming API for SQL-based relational databases that permits programs to interact with many different database engines with no or few changes. For example, a Python program could be first implemented using Microsoft Jet[†] as a backend database for testing and debugging purposes. Once the program is stable, it can be put into production use, remotely accessing, say, a backend DB2 database on an IBM mainframe residing on another continent, by changing (at most) one line of code.

Relational databases are not appropriate for all applications. In particular, a computer game or engineering design tool that must save and restore sessions should probably use a more direct method of persisting the logical objects of the program than the flat tabular representation encouraged in relational-database design. However, even in domains such as engineering or scientific information, a hybrid

---

[*] E.F. Codd, "A Relational Model of Data for Large Shared Data Banks," *Communications of the ACM*, 13, no. 6 (1970), pp. 377–87, *http://www.acm.org/classics/nov95/toc.html*.

[†] Microsoft Jet is commonly but erroneously known as the "Microsoft Access database." Access is a product that Microsoft sells for designing and implementing database frontends; Jet is a backend that you may download for free from Microsoft's web site.

approach that uses some relational methods is often advisable. For example, I have seen a complex relational-database schema for archiving genetic-sequencing information—in which the sequences show up as binary large objects (BLOBs)—but a tremendous amount of important ancillary information can fit nicely into relational tables. But as the reader has probably surmised, I fear, I speak as a relational zealot.

Within the Python world there are many ways of providing persistence and database functionality. My personal favorite is Gadfly, *http://gadfly.sourceforge.net/*, a simple and minimal SQL implementation that works primarily with in-memory databases. It is my favorite for no other reason than because it is mine, and its biggest advantage is that, if it becomes unworkable for you, it is easy to switch over to another, industrial-strength SQL engine. Many Gadfly users have started an application with Gadfly (because it was easy to use) and switched later (because they needed more).

However, many people may prefer to start by using other SQL implementations such as MySQL, Microsoft Access, Oracle, Sybase, Microsoft SQL Server, SQLite, or others that provide the advantages of an ODBC interface (which Gadfly does not do).

Python provides a standard interface for accessing relational databases: the Python DB Application Programming Interface (Py-DBAPI), originally designed by Greg Stein. Each underlying database API requires a wrapper implementation of the Py-DBAPI, and implementations are available for just about all underlying database interfaces, notably Oracle and ODBC.

When the relational approach is overkill, Python provides built-in facilities for storing and retrieving data. At the most basic level, the programmer can manipulate files directly, as covered in Chapter 2. A step up from files, the marshal module allows programs to serialize data structures constructed from simple Python types (not including, e.g., classes or class instances). marshal has the advantage of being able to retrieve large data structures with blinding speed. The pickle and cPickle modules allow general storage of objects, including classes, class instances, and circular structures. cPickle is so named because it is implemented in C and is consequently quite fast, but it remains slower than marshal. For access to structured data in a somewhat human-readable form, it is also worth considering storing and retrieving data in XML format (taking advantage of Python's several XML parsing and generation modules), covered in Chapter 12—but this option works best for *write once, read many*–type applications. Serialized data or XML representations may be stored in SQL databases to create a hybrid approach as well.

While marshal and pickle provide basic serialization and deserialization of structures, the application programmer will frequently desire more functionality, such as transaction support and concurrency control. When the relational model doesn't fit the application, a direct object database implementation such as the Z-Object Database (ZODB) might be appropriate—see *http://zope.org/Products/ZODB3.2.*

I must conclude with a plea to those who are dismissive of relational-database technology. Remember that it is successful for good reasons, and it might be worth considering. To paraphrase Churchill:

```
text = """ Indeed, it has been said that democracy is the worst form of
    government, except for all those others that have been tried
    from time to time. """
import string
for a, b in [("democracy", "SQL"), ("government", "database")]:
    text = string.replace(text, a, b)
print text
```

7.1   Serializing Data Using the marshal Module

Credit: Luther Blissett

Problem

You want to serialize and reconstruct a Python data structure whose items are fundamental Python objects (e.g., lists, tuples, numbers, and strings but no classes, instances, etc.) as fast as possible.

Solution

If you know that your data is composed entirely of fundamental Python objects (and you only need to support one version of Python, though possibly on several different platforms), the lowest-level, fastest approach to serializing your data (i.e., turning it into a string of bytes, and later reconstructing it from such a string) is via the marshal module. Suppose that data has only elementary Python data types as items, for example:

```
data = {12:'twelve', 'feep':list('ciao'), 1.23:4+5j, (1,2,3):u'wer'}
```

You can serialize data to a bytestring at top speed as follows:

```
import marshal
bytes = marshal.dumps(data)
```

You can now sling bytes around as you wish (e.g., send it across a network, put it as a BLOB in a database, etc.), as long as you keep its arbitrary binary bytes intact. Then you can reconstruct the data structure from the bytestring at any time:

```
redata = marshal.loads(bytes)
```

When you specifically want to write the data to a disk file (as long as the latter is open for binary—not the default text mode—input/output), you can also use the dump function of the marshal module, which lets you dump several data structures to the same file one after the other:

```
ouf = open('datafile.dat', 'wb')
marshal.dump(data, ouf)
marshal.dump('some string', ouf)
```

```
marshal.dump(range(19), ouf)
ouf.close( )
```

You can later recover from *datafile.dat* the same data structures you dumped into it, in the same sequence:

```
inf = open('datafile.dat', 'rb')
a = marshal.load(inf)
b = marshal.load(inf)
c = marshal.load(inf)
inf.close( )
```

Discussion

Python offers several ways to serialize data (meaning to turn the data into a string of bytes that you can save on disk, put in a database, send across the network, etc.) and corresponding ways to reconstruct the data from such serialized forms. The lowest-level approach is to use the marshal module, which Python uses to write its bytecode files. marshal supports only elementary data types (e.g., dictionaries, lists, tuples, numbers, and strings) and combinations thereof. marshal does not guarantee compatibility from one Python release to another, so data serialized with marshal may not be readable if you upgrade your Python release. However, marshal does guarantee independence from a specific machine's architecture, so it is guaranteed to work if you're sending serialized data between different machines, as long as they are all running the same version of Python—similar to how you can share compiled Python bytecode files in such a distributed setting.

marshal's dumps function accepts any suitable Python data structure and returns a bytestring representing it. You can pass that bytestring to the loads function, which will return another Python data structure that compares equal (==) to the one you originally dumped. In particular, the order of keys in dictionaries is arbitrary in both the original and reconstructed data structures, but order in any kind of sequence is meaningful and is thus preserved. In between the dumps and loads calls, you can subject the bytestring to any procedure you wish, such as sending it over the network, storing it into a database and retrieving it, or encrypting and decrypting it. As long as the string's binary structure is correctly restored, loads will work fine on it (as stated previously, this is guaranteed only if you use loads under the same Python release with which you originally executed dumps).

When you specifically need to save the data to a file, you can also use marshal's dump function, which takes two arguments: the data structure you're dumping and the open file object. Note that the file must be opened for binary I/O (not the default, which is text I/O) and can't be a file-like object, as marshal is quite picky about it being a true file. The advantage of dump is that you can perform several calls to dump with various data structures and the same open file object: each data structure is then dumped together with information about how long the dumped bytestring is. As a consequence, when you later open the file for binary reading and then call marshal.load, passing the file as the argument, you can reload each previously dumped data structure sequentially, one after the other, at each call to load. The return value of load, like that of loads, is a new data structure that compares equal to the one you originally dumped. (Again, dump and load work within one Python release—no guarantee across releases.)

Those accustomed to other languages and libraries offering "serialization" facilities may be wondering if marshal imposes substantial practical limits on the *size* of objects you can serialize or deserialize. Answer: Nope. Your machine's memory might, but as long as everything fits comfortably in memory, marshal imposes practically no further limit.

See Also

Recipe 7.2 "Serializing Data Using the pickle and cPickle Modules" for cPickle, the big brother of marshal; documentation on the marshal standard library module in the *Library Reference* and in *Python in a Nutshell*.

7.2 Serializing Data Using the pickle and cPickle Modules

Credit: Luther Blissett

Problem

You want to serialize and reconstruct, at a reasonable speed, a Python data structure, which may include both fundamental Python object as well as classes and instances.

Solution

If you don't want to assume that your data is composed only of fundamental Python objects, or you need portability across versions of Python, or you need to transmit the serialized form as text, the best way of serializing your data is with the cPickle module. (The pickle module is a pure-Python equivalent and totally interchangeable, but it's slower and not worth using except if you're missing cPickle.) For example, say you have:

```
data = {12:'twelve', 'feep':list('ciao'), 1.23:4+5j, (1,2,3):u'wer'}
```

You can serialize data to a text string:

```
import cPickle
text = cPickle.dumps(data)
```

or to a binary string, a choice that is faster and takes up less space:

```
bytes = cPickle.dumps(data, 2)
```

You can now sling text or bytes around as you wish (e.g., send across a network, include as a BLOB in a database—see recipe 7.10 "Storing a BLOB in a MySQL Database," recipe 7.11 "Storing a BLOB in a PostgreSQL Database," and recipe 7.12 "Storing a BLOB in a SQLite Database") as long as you keep text or bytes intact. In the case of bytes, it means keeping the arbitrary binary bytes intact. In the case of text, it means keeping its textual structure intact, including newline characters. Then you can reconstruct the data at any time, regardless of machine architecture or Python release:

```
redata1 = cPickle.loads(text)
redata2 = cPickle.loads(bytes)
```

Either call reconstructs a data structure that compares equal to data. In particular, the order of keys in dictionaries is arbitrary in both the original and reconstructed data structures, but order in any kind of sequence is meaningful, and thus it is preserved. You don't need to tell cPickle.loads whether the original dumps used text mode (the default, also readable by some very old versions of Python) or binary (faster and more compact)—loads figures it out by examining its argument's contents.

When you specifically want to write the data to a file, you can also use the dump function of the cPickle module, which lets you dump several data structures to the same file one after the other:

```
ouf = open('datafile.txt', 'w')
cPickle.dump(data, ouf)
cPickle.dump('some string', ouf)
cPickle.dump(range(19), ouf)
ouf.close( )
```

Once you have done this, you can recover from *datafile.txt* the same data structures you dumped into it, one after the other, in the same order:

```
inf = open('datafile.txt')
a = cPickle.load(inf)
b = cPickle.load(inf)
c = cPickle.load(inf)
inf.close( )
```

You can also pass cPickle.dump a third argument with a value of 2 to tell cPickle.dump to serialize the data in binary form (faster and more compact), but the data file must then be opened for binary I/O, not in the default text mode, both when you originally dump to the file and when you later load from the file.

Discussion

Python offers several ways to serialize data (i.e., make the data into a string of bytes that you can save on disk, save in a database, send across the network, etc.) and corresponding ways to reconstruct the data from such serialized forms. Typically, the best approach is to use the cPickle module. A pure-Python equivalent, called pickle (the cPickle module is coded in C as a Python extension) is substantially slower, and the only reason to use it is if you don't have cPickle (e.g., with a Python port onto a mobile phone with tiny storage space, where you saved every byte you possibly could by installing only an indispensable subset of Python's large standard library). However, in cases where you *do* need to use pickle, rest assured that it is completely interchangeable with cPickle: you can pickle with either module and unpickle with the other one, without any problems whatsoever.

cPickle supports most elementary data types (e.g., dictionaries, lists, tuples, numbers, strings) and combinations thereof, as well as classes and instances. Pickling classes and instances saves only the data involved, not the code. (Code objects are not even among the types that cPickle knows how to serialize, basically because there would be no way to guarantee their portability across disparate versions of Python. See recipe 7.6 "Pickling Code Objects" for a way to serialize code objects, as long as you don't need the cross-version guarantee.) See recipe 7.4 "Using the cPickle Module on Classes and Instances" for more about pickling classes and instances.

cPickle guarantees compatibility from one Python release to another, as well as independence from a specific machine's architecture. Data serialized with cPickle will still be readable if you upgrade your Python release, and pickling is also guaranteed to work if you're sending serialized data between different machines.

The dumps function of cPickle accepts any Python data structure and returns a text string representing it. If you call dumps with a second argument of 2, dumps returns an arbitrary bytestring instead: the operation is faster, and the resulting string takes up less space. You can pass either the text or the bytestring to the loads function, which will return another Python data structure that compares equal (==) to the one you originally dumped. In between the dumps and loads calls, you can subject the text or bytestring to any procedure you wish, such as sending it over the network, storing it in a database and retrieving it, or encrypting and decrypting it. As long as the string's textual or binary structure is correctly restored, loads will work fine on it (even across platforms and in future releases). If you need to produce data readable by old (pre-2.3) versions of Python, consider using 1 as the second argument: operation will be slower, and the resulting strings will not be as compact as those obtained by using 2, but the strings will be unpicklable by old Python versions as well as current and future ones.

When you specifically need to save the data into a file, you can also use cPickle's dump function, which takes two arguments: the data structure you're dumping and the open file or file-like object. If the file is opened for binary I/O, rather than the default (text I/O), then by giving dump a third argument of 2, you can ask for binary format, which is faster and takes up less space (again, you can also use 1 in this position to get a binary format that's neither as compact nor as fast, but is understood by old, pre-2.3 Python versions too). The advantage of dump over dumps is that, with dump, you can perform several calls, one after the other, with various data structures and the same open file object. Each data structure is then dumped with information about how long the dumped string is. Consequently, when you later open the file for reading (binary reading, if you asked for binary format) and then repeatedly call cPickle.load, passing the file as the argument, each data structure previously dumped is reloaded sequentially, one after the other. The return value of load, like that of loads, is a new data structure that compares equal to the one you originally dumped.

Those accustomed to other languages and libraries offering "serialization" facilities may be wondering whether pickle imposes substantial practical limits on the *size* of objects you can serialize or deserialize. Answer: Nope. Your machine's memory might, but as long as everything fits comfortably in memory, pickle practically imposes no further limit.

See Also

Recipe 7.2 "Serializing Data Using the pickle and cPickle Modules" and recipe 7.4 "Using the cPickle Module on Classes and Instances"; documentation for the standard library module cPickle in the *Library Reference* and *Python in a Nutshell*.

7.3   Using Compression with Pickling

Credit: Bill McNeill, Andrew Dalke

Problem

You want to pickle generic Python objects to and from disk in a compressed form.

Solution

Standard library modules cPickle and gzip offer the needed functionality; you just need to glue them together appropriately:

```
import cPickle, gzip
def save(filename, *objects):
    ''' save objects into a compressed diskfile '''
    fil = gzip.open(filename, 'wb')
    for obj in objects: cPickle.dump(obj, fil, proto=2)
    fil.close( )
def load(filename):
    ''' reload objects from a compressed diskfile '''
    fil = gzip.open(filename, 'rb')
    while True:
        try: yield cPickle.load(fil)
        except EOFError: break
    fil.close( )
```

Discussion

Persistence and compression, as a general rule, go well together. cPickle protocol 2 saves Python objects quite compactly, but the resulting files can still compress quite well. For example, on my Linux box, open('/usr/dict/share/words').readlines() produces a list of over 45,000 strings. Pickling that list with the default protocol 0 makes a disk file of 972 KB, while protocol 2 takes only 716 KB. However, using both gzip and protocol 2, as shown in this recipe, requires only 268 KB, saving a significant amount of space. As it happens, protocol 0 produces a more compressible file in this case, so that using gzip and protocol 0 would save even more space, taking only 252 KB on disk. However, the difference between 268 and 252 isn't all that meaningful, and protocol 2 has other advantages, particularly when used on instances of new-style classes, so I recommend the mix I use in the functions shown in this recipe.

Whatever protocol you choose to save your data, you don't need to worry about it when you're reloading the data. The protocol is recorded in the file together with the data, so cPickle.load can figure out by itself all it needs. Just pass it an instance of a file or pseudo-file object with a read method, and cPickle.load returns each object that was pickled to the file, one after the other, and raises EOFError when the file's done. In this recipe, we wrap a generator around cPickle.load, so you can simply loop over all recovered objects with a for statement, or, depending on what you need, you can use some call such as list(load('somefile.gz')) to get a list with all recovered objects as its items.

See Also

Modules gzip and cPickle in the *Library Reference*.

7.4 Using the cPickle Module on Classes and Instances

Credit: Luther Blissett

Problem

You want to save and restore class and instance objects using the cPickle module.

Solution

You often need no special precautions to use cPickle on your classes and their instances. For example, the following works fine:

```
import cPickle
class ForExample(object):
    def __init__(self, *stuff):
        self.stuff = stuff
```

```
anInstance = ForExample('one', 2, 3)
saved = cPickle.dumps(anInstance)
reloaded = cPickle.loads(saved)
assert anInstance.stuff == reloaded.stuff
```

However, sometimes there are problems:

```
anotherInstance = ForExample(1, 2, open('three', 'w'))
wontWork = cPickle.dumps(anotherInstance)
```

This snippet causes a TypeError: "can't pickle file objects" exception, because the state of anotherInstance includes a file object, and file objects cannot be pickled. You would get exactly the same exception if you tried to pickle any other container that includes a file object among its items.

However, in some cases, you may be able to do something about it:

```
class PrettyClever(object):
    def __init__(self, *stuff):
        self.stuff = stuff
    def __getstate__(self):
        def normalize(x):
            if isinstance(x, file):
                return 1, (x.name, x.mode, x.tell())
            return 0, x
        return [ normalize(x) for x in self.stuff ]
    def __setstate__(self, stuff):
        def reconstruct(x):
            if x[0] == 0:
                return x[1]
            name, mode, offs = x[1]
            openfile = open(name, mode)
            openfile.seek(offs)
            return openfile
        self.stuff = tuple([reconstruct(x) for x in stuff])
```

By defining the __getstate__ and __setstate__ special methods in your class, you gain fine-grained control about what, exactly, your class' instances consider to be their state. As long as you can define such state in picklable terms, and reconstruct your instances from the unpickled state in some way that is sufficient for your application, you can make your instances themselves picklable and unpicklable in this way.

Discussion

cPickle dumps class and function objects by name (i.e., through their module's name and their name within the module). Thus, you can dump only classes defined at module level (not inside other classes and functions). Reloading such objects requires the respective modules to be available for import. Instances can be saved and reloaded only if they belong to such classes. In addition, the instance's state must also be picklable.

By default, an instance's state is the contents of the instance's __dict__, plus whatever state the instance may get from the built-in type the instance's class inherits from, if any. For example, an instance of a new-style class that subclasses list includes the list items as part of the instance's state. cPickle also handles instances of new-style classes that define or inherit a class attribute named __slots__ (and therefore hold some or all per-instance state in those predefined slots, rather than in a per-instance __dict__). Overall, cPickle's default approach is often quite sufficient and satisfactory.

Sometimes, however, you may have nonpicklable attributes or items as part of your instance's state (as cPickle defines such state by default, as explained in the previous paragraph). In this recipe, for example, I show a class whose instances hold arbitrary stuff, which may include open file objects. To handle this case, your class can define the special method __getstate__. cPickle calls that method on your object, if your object's class defines it or inherits it, instead of going directly for the object's __dict__ (or possibly __slots__ and/or built-in type bases).

Normally, when you define the __getstate__ method, you define the __setstate__ method as well, as shown in this recipe's Solution. __getstate__ can return any picklable object, and that object gets pickled, and later, at unpickling time, passed as __setstate__'s argument. In this recipe's Solution, __getstate__ returns a list that's similar to the instance's default state (attribute self.stuff), except that each item is turned into a tuple of two items. The first item in the pair can be set to 0 to indicate that the second one will be taken verbatim, or 1 to indicate that the second item will be used to reconstruct an open file. (Of course, the reconstruction may fail or be unsatisfactory in several ways. There is no general way to save an open file's state, which is why cPickle itself doesn't even try. But in the context of our application, we can assume that the given approach will work.) When reloading the instance from pickled form, cPickle calls __setstate__ with the list of pairs, and __setstate__ can reconstruct self.stuff by processing each pair appropriately in its nested reconstruct function. This scheme can clearly generalize to getting and restoring state that may contain various kinds of normally unpicklable objects—just be sure to use different numbers to tag each of the various kinds of "nonverbatim" pairs you need to support.

In one particular case, you can define __getstate__ without defining __setstate__: __getstate__ must then return a dictionary, and reloading the instance from pickled form uses that dictionary just as the instance's __dict__ would normally be used. Not running your own code at reloading time is a serious hindrance, but it may come in handy when you want to use __getstate__, not to save otherwise unpicklable state but rather as an optimization. Typically, this optimization opportunity occurs when your instance caches results that it can recompute if they're absent, and you decide it's best not to store the cache as a part of the instance's state. In this case, you should define __getstate__ to return a dictionary that's the indispensable subset of the instance's __dict__. (See recipe 4.13 "Extracting a Subset of a Dictionary") for a simple and handy way to "subset a dictionary".)

Defining __getstate__ (and then, normally, also __setstate__) also gives you a further important bonus, besides the pickling support: if a class offers these methods but doesn't offer special methods __copy__ or __deepcopy__, then the methods are also used for copying, both shallowly and deeply, as well as for serializing. The state data returned by __getstate__ is deep-copied if and only if the object is being deep-copied, but, other than this distinction, shallow and deep copies work very similarly when they are implemented through __getstate__. See recipe 4.1 "Copying an Object" for more information about how a class can control the way its instances are copied, shallowly or deeply.

With either the default pickling/unpickling approach, or your own __getstate__ and __setstate__, the instance's special method __init__ is *not* called when the instance is getting unpickled. If the most convenient way for you to reconstruct an instance is to call the __init__ method with appropriate parameters, then you may want to define the special method __getinitargs__, instead of __getstate__. In this case, cPickle calls this method without arguments: the method must return a pickable tuple, and at unpickling time, cPickle calls __init__ with the arguments that are that tuple's items. __getinitargs__, like __getstate__ and __setstate__, can also be used for copying.

The *Library Reference* for the pickle and copy_reg modules details even subtler things you can do when pickling and unpickling, as well as the thorny security issues that are likely to arise if you ever stoop to unpickling data from untrusted sources. (Executive summary: *don't do that*—there is no way Python can protect you if you do.) However, the techniques I've discussed here should suffice in almost all practical cases, as long as the security aspects of unpickling are not a problem (and if they are, the *only* practical suggestion is: forget pickling!).

See Also

Recipe 7.2 "Serializing Data Using the pickle and cPickle Modules"; documentation for the standard library module cPickle in the *Library Reference* and *Python in a Nutshell*.

7.5 Holding Bound Methods in a Picklable Way

Credit: Peter Cogolo

Problem

You need to pickle an object, but that object holds (as an attribute or item) a bound method of another object, and bound methods are not picklable.

Solution

Say you have the following objects:

```python
import cPickle
class Greeter(object):
    def __init__(self, name):
        self.name = name
    def greet(self):
        print 'hello', self.name
class Repeater(object):
    def __init__(self, greeter):
        self.greeter = greeter
    def greet(self):
        self.greeter()
        self.greeter()
r = Repeater(Greeter('world').greet)
```

Were it not for the fact that `r` holds a bound method as its greeter attribute, you could pickle `r` very simply:

```python
s = cPickle.dumps(r)
```

However, upon encountering the bound method, this call to `cPickle.dumps` raises a `TypeError`. One simple solution is to have each instance of class `Repeater` hold, not a bound method directly, but rather a picklable wrapper to it. For example:

```python
class picklable_boundmethod(object):
    def __init__(self, mt):
        self.mt = mt
    def __getstate__(self):
        return self.mt.im_self, self.mt.im_func.__name__
    def __setstate__(self, (s,fn)):
        self.mt = getattr(s, fn)
    def __call__(self, *a, **kw):
        return self.mt(*a, **kw)
```

Now, changing `Repeater.__init__`'s body to `self.greeter` = `picklable_boundmethod(greeter)` makes the previous snippet work.

Discussion

The Python Standard Library `pickle` module (just like its faster equivalent cousin `cPickle`) pickles functions and classes by name—this implies, in particular, that only functions defined at the top level of a module can be pickled (the pickling of such a function, in practice, contains just the names of the module and function).

If you have a graph of objects that hold each other, not directly, but via one another's bound methods (which is often a good idea in Python), this limitation can make the whole graph unpicklable. One solution might be to teach `pickle` how to serialize bound methods, along the same lines as described in recipe 7.6 "Pickling Code Objects." Another possible solution is to define appropriate `__getstate__` and `__setstate__` methods to turn bound methods into something picklable at dump time and rebuild them at load time, along the lines described in recipe 7.4 "Using the cPickle Module on Classes and Instances." However, this latter possibility is not a good factorization when you have several classes whose instances hold bound methods.

This recipe pursues a simpler idea, based on holding bound methods, not directly, but via the picklable_boundmethod wrapper class. picklable_boundmethod is written under the assumption that the only thing you usually do with a bound method is to call it, so it only delegates __call__ functionality specifically. (You could, in addition, also use __getattr__, in order to delegate other attribute accesses.)

In normal operation, the fact that you're holding an instance of picklable_ boundmethod rather than holding the bound method object directly is essentially transparent. When pickling time comes, special method __getstate__ of picklable_ boundmethod comes into play, as previously covered in recipe 7.4 "Using the cPickle Module on Classes and Instances." In the case of picklable_boundmethod, __getstate__ returns the object to which the bound method belongs and the function name of the bound method. Later, at unpickling time, __setstate__ recovers an equivalent bound method from the reconstructed object by using the getattr built-in for that name. This approach isn't infallible because an object might hold its methods under assumed names (different from the real function names of the methods). However, assuming you're not specifically doing something weird for the specific purpose of breaking picklable_boundmethod's functionality, you shouldn't ever run into this kind of obscure problem!

See Also

Library Reference and *Python in a Nutshell* docs for modules pickle and cPickle, bound-method objects, and the getattr built-in.

7.6   Pickling Code Objects

Credit: Andres Tremols, Peter Cogolo

Problem

You want to be able to pickle code objects, but this functionality is not supported by the standard library's pickling modules.

Solution

You can extend the abilities of the pickle (or cPickle) module by using module copy_ reg. Just make sure the following module has been imported before you pickle code objects, and has been imported, or is available to be imported, when you're unpickling them:

```
import new, types, copy_reg
def code_ctor(*args):
```

```
        # delegate to new.code the construction of a new code object
        return new.code(*args)
    def reduce_code(co):
        # a reductor function must return a tuple with two items: first, the
        # constructor function to be called to rebuild the argument object
        # at a future de-serialization time; then, the tuple of arguments
        # that will need to be passed to the constructor function.
        if co.co_freevars or co.co_cellvars:
            raise ValueError, "Sorry, cannot pickle code objects from closures"
        return code_ctor, (co.co_argcount, co.co_nlocals, co.co_stacksize,
            co.co_flags, co.co_code, co.co_consts, co.co_names,
            co.co_varnames, co.co_filename, co.co_name, co.co_firstlineno,
            co.co_lnotab)
    # register the reductor to be used for pickling objects of type 'CodeType'
    copy_reg.pickle(types.CodeType, reduce_code)
    if __name__ == '__main__':
        # example usage of our new ability to pickle code objects
        import cPickle
        # a function (which, inside, has a code object, of course)
        def f(x): print 'Hello,', x
        # serialize the function's code object to a string of bytes
        pickled_code = cPickle.dumps(f.func_code)
        # recover an equal code object from the string of bytes
        recovered_code = cPickle.loads(pickled_code)
        # build a new function around the rebuilt code object
        g = new.function(recovered_code, globals())
        # check what happens when the new function gets called
        g('world')
```

Discussion

The Python Standard Library pickle module (just like its faster equivalent cousin
cPickle) pickles functions and classes by name. There is no pickling of the *code
objects* containing the compiled bytecode that, when run, determines almost every
aspect of functions' (and methods') behavior. In some situations, you'd rather pickle
everything by value, so that all the relevant stuff can later be retrieved from the
pickle, rather than having to have module files around for some of it. Sometimes you
can solve such problems by using marshaling rather than pickling, since marshal *does*
let you serialize code objects, but marshal has limitations on many other issues. For
example, you cannot marshal instances of classes you have coded. (Once you're serializing code objects, which are specific to a given version of Python, pickle will share
one key limitation of marshal: no guaranteed ability to save and later reload data
across different versions of Python.)

An alternative approach is to take advantage of the possibility, which the Python
Standard Library allows, to extend the set of types known to pickle. Basically, you
can "teach" pickle how to save and reload code objects; this, in turn, lets you pickle
by value, rather than "by name", such objects as functions and classes. (The code in
this recipe's Solution under the if __name__ == '__main__' guard essentially shows
how to extend pickle for a function.)

To teach `pickle` about some new type, use module `copy_reg`, which is also part of the Python Standard Library. Through function `copy_reg.pickle`, you register the reduction function to use for instances of a given type. A reduction function takes as its argument an instance to be pickled and returns a tuple with two items: a constructor function, which will be called to reconstruct the instance, and a tuple of arguments, which will be passed to the constructor function. (A reduction function may also return other kinds of results, but for this recipe's purposes a two-item tuple suffices.)

The module in this recipe defines function `reduce_code`, then registers it as the reduction function for objects of type `types.CodeType`—that is, code objects. When `reduce_code` gets called, it first checks whether its code object co comes from a *closure* (functions nested inside each other), because it just can't deal with this eventuality—I've been unable to find a way that works, so in this case, `reduce_code` just raises an exception to let the user know about the problem.

In normal cases, `reduce_code` returns `code_ctor` as the constructor and a tuple made up of all of co's attributes as the arguments tuple for the constructor. When a code object is reloaded from a pickle, `code_ctor` gets called with those arguments and simply passes the call on to the `new.code` callable, which is the *true* constructor for code arguments. Unfortunately, `reduce_code` cannot return `new.code` itself as the first item in its result tuple, because `new.code` is a built-in (a C-coded callable) but is not available through a built-in *name*. So, basically, the role of `code_ctor` is to provide a name for the (by-name) pickling of `new.code`.

The `if __name__ == '__main__'` part of the recipe provides a typical toy usage example—it pickles a code object to a string, recovers a copy of it from the pickle string, and builds and calls a function around that code object. A more typical use case for this recipe's functionality, of course, will do the pickling in one script and the unpickling in another. Assume that the module in this recipe has been saved as file *reco.py* somewhere on Python's `sys.path`, so that it can be imported by Python scripts and other modules. You could then have a script that imports `reco` and thus becomes able to pickle code objects, such as:

```
import reco, pickle
def f(x):
    print 'Hello,', x
pickle.dump(f.func_code, open('saved.pickle','wb'))
```

To unpickle and use that code object, an example script might be:

```
import new, cPickle
c = cPickle.load(open('saved.pickle','rb'))
g = new.function(c, globals())
g('world')
```

Note that the second script does not need to `import reco`—the import will happen automatically when needed (part of the information that `pickle` saves in *saved.pickle* is that, in order to reconstruct the pickled object therein, it needs to call `reco.code_ctor`; so, it also knows it needs to import reco). I'm also showing that you can use modules `pickle` and `cPickle` interchangeably. `Pickle` is faster, but there are no other differences, and in particular, you can use one module to pickle objects and the other one to unpickle them, if you wish.

See Also

Modules `pickle`, `cPickle`, and `copy_reg` in the *Library Reference* and *Python in a Nutshell*.

7.7   Mutating Objects with shelve

Credit: Luther Blissett

Problem

You are using the standard module `shelve`. Some of the values you have shelved are mutable objects, and you need to mutate these objects.

Solution

The `shelve` module offers a kind of persistent dictionary—an important niche between the power of relational-database engines and the simplicity of `marshal`, `pickle`, `dbm`, and similar file formats. However, you should be aware of a typical trap you need to avoid when using `shelve`. Consider the following interactive Python session:

```
>>> import shelve
>>> # Build a simple sample shelf
>>> she = shelve.open('try.she', 'c')
>>> for c in 'spam': she[c] = {c:23}
...
>>> for c in she.keys(): print c, she[c]
...
p {'p': 23}
s {'s': 23}
a {'a': 23}
m {'m': 23}
>>> she.close()
```

We've created the shelve file, added some data to it, and closed it. Good—now we can reopen it and work with it:

```
>>> she=shelve.open('try.she', 'c')
>>> she['p']
{'p': 23}
>>> she['p']['p'] = 42
>>> she['p']
{'p': 23}
```

What's going on here? We just set the value to 42, but our setting didn't *take* in the shelve object! The problem is that we were working with a temporary object that shelve gave us, not with the "real thing". shelve, when we open it with default options, like here, doesn't track changes to such temporary objects. One reasonable solution is to bind a name to this temporary object, do our mutation, and then assign the mutated object back to the appropriate item of shelve:

```
>>> a = she['p']
>>> a['p'] = 42
>>> she['p'] = a
>>> she['p']
{'p': 42}
>>> she.close()
```

We can verify that the change was properly persisted:

```
>>> she=shelve.open('try.she','c')
>>> for c in she.keys(): print c,she[c]
...
p {'p': 42}
s {'s': 23}
a {'a': 23}
m {'m': 23}
```

A simpler solution is to open the shelve object with the writeback option set to True:

```
>>> she = shelve.open('try.she', 'c', writeback=True)
```

The writeback option instructs shelve to keep track of all the objects it gets from the file and write them all back to the file before closing it, just in case they have been modified in the meantime. While simple, this approach can be quite expensive, particularly in terms of memory consumption. Specifically, if we read many objects from a shelve object opened with writeback=True, even if we only modify a few of them, shelve is going to keep them *all* in memory, since it can't tell in advance which one we may be about to modify. The previous approach, where we explicitly take responsibility to notify shelve of any changes (by assigning the changed objects back to the place they came from), requires more care on our part, but repays that care by giving us much better performance.

Discussion

The standard Python module shelve can be quite convenient in many cases, but it hides a potentially nasty trap, admittedly well documented in Python's online docs but still easy to miss. Suppose you're shelving mutable objects, such as dictionaries or lists. Naturally, you are quite likely to want to mutate some of those objects—for example, by calling mutating methods (append on a list, update on a dictionary, etc.) or by assigning a new value to an item or attribute of the object. However, when you do this, the change doesn't occur in the shelve object. This is because we actually mutate a temporary object that the shelve object has given us as the result of shelve's own __getitem__ method, but the shelve object, by default, does not keep track of that temporary object, nor does it care about it once it returns it to us.

As shown in the recipe, one solution is to bind a name to the temporary object obtained by keying into the shelf, doing whatever mutations are needed to the object via the name, then assigning the newly mutated object back to the appropriate item of the shelve object. When you assign to a shelve object's item, the shelve object's __setitem__ method gets invoked, and it appropriately updates the shelve object itself, so that the change does occur.

Alternatively, you can add the flag writeback=True at the time you open the shelve object, and then shelve keeps track of every object it hands you, saving them all back to disk at the end. This approach may save you quite a bit of fussy and laborious coding, but take care: if you read many items of the shelve object and only modify a few of them, the writeback approach can be exceedingly costly, particularly in terms of memory consumption. When opened with writeback=True, shelve *will* keep in memory any item it has ever handed you, and save them all to disk at the end, since it doesn't have a reliable way to tell which items you may be about to modify, nor, in general, even which items you *have* actually modified by the time you close the shelve object. The recommended approach, unless you're going to modify just about every item you read (or unless the shelve object in question is small enough compared with your available memory that you don't really care), is the previous one: bind a name to the items that you get from a shelve object with intent to modify them, and assign each item back into the shelve object once you're done mutating that item.

See Also

Recipe 7.1 "Serializing Data Using the marshal Module" and recipe 7.2 "Serializing Data Using the pickle and cPickle Modules" for alternative serialization approaches; documentation for the shelve standard library module in the *Library Reference* and *Python in a Nutshell*.

7.8   Using the Berkeley DB Database

Credit: Farhad Fouladi

Problem

You want to persist some data, exploiting the simplicity and good performance of the Berkeley DB database library.

Solution

If you have previously installed Berkeley DB on your machine, the Python Standard Library comes with package bsddb (and optionally bsddb3, to access Berkeley DB release 3.2 databases) to interface your Python code with Berkeley DB. To get either bsddb or, lacking it, bsddb3, use a try/except on import:

```
try:
    from bsddb import db             # first try release 4
except ImportError:
    from bsddb3 import db            # not there, try release 3 instead
print db.DB_VERSION_STRING
# emits, e.g: Sleepycat Software: Berkeley DB 4.1.25: (December 19, 2002)
```

To create a database, instantiate a db.DB object, then call its method open with appropriate parameters, such as:

```
adb = db.DB()
adb.open('db_filename', dbtype=db.DB_HASH, flags=db.DB_CREATE)
```

db.DB_HASH is just one of several access methods you may choose when you create a database—a popular alternative is db.DB_BTREE, to use B+tree access (handy if you need to get records in sorted order). You may make an in-memory database, without an underlying file for persistence, by passing None instead of a filename as the first argument to the open method.

Once you have an open instance of db.DB, you can add records, each composed of two strings, key and data:

```
for i, w in enumerate('some words for example'.split()):
    adb.put(w, str(i))
```

You can access records via a cursor on the database:

```
def irecords(curs):
    record = curs.first()
    while record:
        yield record
        record = curs.next()
for key, data in irecords(adb.cursor()):
    print 'key=%r, data=%r' % (key, data)
# emits (the order may vary):
# key='some', data='0'
# key='example', data='3'
# key='words', data='1'
# key='for', data='2'
```

When you're done, you close the database:

```
adb.close()
```

At any future time, in the same or another Python program, you can reopen the database by giving just its filename as the argument to the open method of a newly created db.DB instance:

```
the_same_db = db.DB()
the_same_db.open('db_filename')
```

and work on it again in the same ways:

```
the_same_db.put('skidoo', '23')        # add a record
the_same_db.put('words', 'sweet')      # replace a record
for key, data in irecords(the_same_db.cursor()):
```

```
        print 'key=%r, data=%r' % (key, data)
# emits (the order may vary):
# key='some', data='0'
# key='example', data='3'
# key='words', data='sweet'
# key='for', data='2'
# key='skidoo', data='23'
```

Again, remember to close the database when you're done:

```
the_same_db.close( )
```

Discussion

The Berkeley DB is a popular open source database. It does not support SQL, but it's simple to use, offers excellent performance, and gives you a lot of control over exactly what happens, if you care to exert it, through a huge array of options, flags, and methods. Berkeley DB is just as accessible from many other languages as from Python: for example, you can perform some changes or queries with a Python program, and others with a separate C program, on the same database file, using the same underlying open source library that you can freely download from Sleepycat.

The Python Standard Library shelve module can use the Berkeley DB as its underlying database engine, just as it uses cPickle for serialization. However, shelve does not let you take advantage of the ability to access a Berkeley DB database file from several different languages, exactly because the records are strings produced by pickle.dumps, and languages other than Python can't easily deal with them. Accessing the Berkeley DB directly with bsddb also gives you access to many advanced functionalities of the database engine that shelve simply doesn't support.

For example, creating a database with an access method of db.DB_HASH, as shown in the recipe, may give maximum performance, but, as you'll have noticed when listing all records with the generator irecords that is also presented in the recipe, hashing puts records in apparently random, unpredictable order. If you need to access records in sorted order, you can use an access method of db.DB_BTREE instead. Berkeley DB also supports more advanced functionality, such as transactions, which you can enable through direct access but not via anydbm or shelve.

For detailed documentation about all functionality of the Python Standard Library bsddb package, see *http://pybsddb.sourceforge.net/bsddb3.html*. For documentation, downloads, and more of the Berkeley DB itself, see *http://www.sleepycat.com/*.

See Also

Library Reference and *Python in a Nutshell* docs for modules anydbm, shelve, and bsddb; *http://pybsddb.sourceforge.net/bsddb3.html* for many more details about bsddb and bsddb3; *http://www.sleepycat.com/* for downloads of, and very detailed documentation on, the Berkeley DB itself.

A Database, or pickle . . . or Both?

The use cases for pickle or marshal, and those for databases such as Berkeley DB or relational databases, are rather different, though they do overlap somewhat.

pickle (and marshal even more so) is essentially about serialization: you turn Python objects into BLOBs that you may transmit or store, and later receive or retrieve. Data thus serialized is meant to be reloaded into Python objects, basically only by Python applications. pickle has nothing to say about searching or selecting specific objects or parts of them.

Databases (Berkeley DB, relational DBs, and other kinds yet) are essentially about data: you save and retrieve groupings of elementary data (strings and numbers, mostly), with a lot of support for selecting and searching (a *huge* lot, for relational databases) and cross-language support. Databases have nothing to say about serializing Python objects into data, nor about deserializing Python objects back from data.

The two approaches, databases and serialization, can even be used together. You can serialize Python objects into strings of bytes with pickle, and store those bytes using a database—and vice versa at retrieval time. At a very elementary level, that's what the standard Python library shelve module does, for example, with pickle to serialize and deserialize and generally bsddb as the underlying simple database engine. So, don't think of the two approaches as being "in competition" with each other—rather, think of them as completing and complementing each other!

7.9 Accessing a MySQL Database

Credit: Mark Nenadov

Problem

You need to access a MySQL database.

Solution

The MySQLdb module makes this task extremely easy:

```
import MySQLdb
# Create a connection object, then use it to create a cursor
con = MySQLdb.connect(host="127.0.0.1", port=3306,
    user="joe", passwd="egf42", db="tst")
cursor = con.cursor( )
# Execute an SQL string
sql = "SELECT * FROM Users"
cursor.execute(sql)
# Fetch all results from the cursor into a sequence and close the connection
results = cursor.fetchall( )
con.close( )
```

Discussion

MySQLdb is at *http://sourceforge.net/projects/mysql-python*. It is a plain and simple implementation of the Python DB API 2.0 that is suitable for Python 2.3 (and some older versions, too) and MySQL versions 3.22 to 4.0. MySQLdb, at the time of this writing, did not yet officially support Python 2.4. However, if you have the right C compiler installation to build Python extensions (as should be the case for all Linux, Mac OS X, and other Unix users, and many Windows developers), the current version of MySQLdb does in fact build from sources, install, and work just fine, with Python 2.4. A newer version of MySQLdb is in the works, with official support for Python 2.3 or later and MySQL 4.0 or later.

As with all other Python DB API implementations (once you have downloaded and installed the needed Python extension and have the database engine it needs up and running), you start by importing the module and calling the connect function with suitable parameters. The keyword parameters you can pass when calling connect depend on the database involved: host (defaulting to the local host), user, passwd (password), and db (name of the database) are typical. In the recipe, I explicitly pass the default local host's IP address and the default MySQL port (3306), just to show that you can specify parameters explicitly even when you're passing their default values (e.g., to make your source code clearer and more readable and maintainable).

The connect function returns a connection object, and you can proceed to call methods on this object; when you are done, call the close method. The method you most often call on a connection object is cursor, which returns a cursor object, which is what you use to send SQL commands to the database and fetch the commands' results. The underlying MySQL database engine does not in fact support SQL cursors, but that's no problem—the MySQLdb module emulates them on your behalf, quite transparently, for the limited cursor needs of the Python DB API 2.0. Of course, this doesn't mean that you can use SQL phrases like WHERE CURRENT OF CURSOR with a database that does not offer cursors! Once you have a cursor object in hand, you can call methods on it. The recipe uses the execute method to execute an SQL statement, and then the fetchall method to obtain all results as a sequence of tuples—one tuple per row in the result. You can use many refinements, but these basic elements of the Python DB API's functionality already suffice for many tasks.

See Also

The Python-MySQL interface module (*http://sourceforge.net/projects/mysql-python*); the Python DB API (*http://www.python.org/topics/database/DatabaseAPI-2.0.html*); DB API documentation in *Python in a Nutshell*.

7.10 Storing a BLOB in a MySQL Database

Credit: Luther Blissett

Problem

You need to store a binary large object (BLOB) in a MySQL database.

Solution

The MySQLdb module does not support full-fledged placeholders, but you can make do with the module's escape_string function:

```
import MySQLdb, cPickle
# Connect to a DB, e.g., the test DB on your localhost, and get a cursor
connection = MySQLdb.connect(db="test")
cursor = connection.cursor( )
# Make a new table for experimentation
cursor.execute("CREATE TABLE justatest (name TEXT, ablob BLOB)")
try:
    # Prepare some BLOBs to insert in the table
    names = 'aramis', 'athos', 'porthos'
    data = { }
    for name in names:
        datum = list(name)
        datum.sort( )
        data[name] = cPickle.dumps(datum, 2)
    # Perform the insertions
    sql = "INSERT INTO justatest VALUES(%s, %s)"
    for name in names:
        cursor.execute(sql, (name, MySQLdb.escape_string(data[name])) )
    # Recover the data so you can check back
    sql = "SELECT name, ablob FROM justatest ORDER BY name"
    cursor.execute(sql)
    for name, blob in cursor.fetchall( ):
        print name, cPickle.loads(blob), cPickle.loads(data[name])
finally:
    # Done. Remove the table and close the connection.
    cursor.execute("DROP TABLE justatest")
    connection.close( )
```

Discussion

MySQL supports binary data (BLOBs and variations thereof), but you should be careful when communicating such data via SQL. Specifically, when you use a normal INSERT SQL statement and need to have binary strings among the VALUES you're inserting, you have to escape some characters in the binary string according to MySQL's own rules. Fortunately, you don't have to figure out those rules for yourself: MySQL supplies a function that does the needed escaping, and MySQLdb exposes it to your Python programs as the escape_string function.

This recipe shows a typical case: the BLOBs you're inserting come from cPickle.dumps, so they may represent almost arbitrary Python objects (although, in this case, we're just using them for a few lists of characters). The recipe is purely demonstrative and works by creating a table and dropping it at the end (using a try/ finally statement to ensure that finalization is performed even if the program should terminate because of an uncaught exception). With recent versions of MySQL and MySQLdb, you don't even need to call the escape_string function anymore, so you can change the relevant statement to the simpler:

```
cursor.execute(sql, (name, data[name]))
```

See Also

Recipe 7.11 "Storing a BLOB in a PostgreSQL Database" and recipe 7.12 "Storing a BLOB in a SQLite Database" for PostgreSQL-oriented and SQLite-oriented solutions to the same problem; the MySQL home page (*http://www.mysql.org*); the Python/ MySQL interface module (*http://sourceforge.net/projects/mysql-python*).

7.11 Storing a BLOB in a PostgreSQL Database

Credit: Luther Blissett

Problem

You need to store a BLOB in a PostgreSQL database.

Solution

PostgreSQL 7.2 and later supports large objects, and the psycopg module supplies a Binary escaping function:

```
import psycopg, cPickle
# Connect to a DB, e.g., the test DB on your localhost, and get a cursor
connection = psycopg.connect("dbname=test")
cursor = connection.cursor( )
# Make a new table for experimentation
cursor.execute("CREATE TABLE justatest (name TEXT, ablob BYTEA)")
try:
    # Prepare some BLOBs to insert in the table
    names = 'aramis', 'athos', 'porthos'
    data = { }
    for name in names:
        datum = list(name)
        datum.sort( )
        data[name] = cPickle.dumps(datum, 2)
    # Perform the insertions
    sql = "INSERT INTO justatest VALUES(%s, %s)"
    for name in names:
        cursor.execute(sql, (name, psycopg.Binary(data[name])) )
    # Recover the data so you can check back
```

```
    sql = "SELECT name, ablob FROM justatest ORDER BY name"
    cursor.execute(sql)
    for name, blob in cursor.fetchall( ):
        print name, cPickle.loads(blob), cPickle.loads(data[name])
finally:
    # Done. Remove the table and close the connection.
    cursor.execute("DROP TABLE justatest")
    connection.close( )
```

Discussion

PostgreSQL supports binary data (BYTEA and variations thereof), but you should be careful when communicating such data via SQL. Specifically, when you use a normal INSERT SQL statement and need to have binary strings among the VALUES you're inserting, you have to escape some characters in the binary string according to PostgreSQL's own rules. Fortunately, you don't have to figure out those rules for yourself: PostgreSQL supplies functions that do all the needed escaping, and psycopg exposes such a function to your Python programs as the Binary function. This recipe shows a typical case: the BYTEAs you're inserting come from cPickle.dumps, so they may represent almost arbitrary Python objects (although, in this case, we're just using them for a few lists of characters). The recipe is purely demonstrative and works by creating a table and dropping it at the end (using a try/finally statement to ensure finalization is performed even if the program should terminate because of an uncaught exception).

Earlier PostgreSQL releases limited to a few kilobytes the amount of data you could store in a normal field of the database. To store really large objects, you had to use roundabout techniques to load the data into the database (such as PostgreSQL's nonstandard SQL function LO_IMPORT to load a data file as an object, which requires superuser privileges and data files that reside on the machine running the PostgreSQL Server) and store a field of type OID in the table to be used later for indirect recovery of the data. Fortunately, none of these techniques are necessary anymore: since Release 7.1 (the current release at the time of writing is 8.0), PostgreSQL embodies the results of project TOAST, which removed the limitations on field-storage size and therefore the need for peculiar indirection. Module psycopg supplies the handy Binary function to let you escape any binary string of bytes into a form acceptable for placeholder substitution in INSERT and UPDATE SQL statements.

See Also

Recipe 7.10 "Storing a BLOB in a MySQL Database" and recipe 7.12 "Storing a BLOB in a SQLite Database" for MySQL-oriented and SQLite-oriented solutions to the same problem; PostgresSQL's home page (*http://www.postgresql.org/*); the Python/PostgreSQL module (*http://initd.org/software/psycopg*).

7.12 Storing a BLOB in a SQLite Database

Credit: John Barham

Problem

You need to store a BLOB in an SQLite database.

Solution

The PySQLite Python extension offers function sqlite.encode to let you insert binary strings in SQLite databases. You can also build a small adapter class based on that function:

```
import sqlite, cPickle
class Blob(object):
    ''' automatic converter for binary strings '''
    def __init__(self, s): self.s = s
    def _quote(self): return "'%s'" % sqlite.encode(self.s)
# make a test database in memory, get a cursor on it, and make a table
connection = sqlite.connect(':memory:')
cursor = connection.cursor( )
cursor.execute("CREATE TABLE justatest (name TEXT, ablob BLOB)")
# Prepare some BLOBs to insert in the table
names = 'aramis', 'athos', 'porthos'
data = { }
for name in names:
    datum = list(name)
    datum.sort( )
    data[name] = cPickle.dumps(datum, 2)
# Perform the insertions
sql = 'INSERT INTO justatest VALUES(%s, %s)'
for name in names:
    cursor.execute(sql, (name, Blob(data[name])) )
# Recover the data so you can check back
sql = 'SELECT name, ablob FROM justatest ORDER BY name'
cursor.execute(sql)
for name, blob in cursor.fetchall( ):
    print name, cPickle.loads(blob), cPickle.loads(data[name])
# Done, close the connection (would be no big deal if you didn't, but...)
connection.close( )
```

Discussion

SQLite does not directly support binary data, but it still lets you declare such types for fields in a CREATE TABLE DDL statement. The PySQLite Python extension uses the declared types of fields to convert field values appropriately to Python values when you fetch data after an SQL SELECT from an SQLite database. However, you still need to be careful when communicating binary string data via SQL.

Specifically, when you use INSERT or UPDATE SQL statements, and need to have binary strings among the VALUES you're passing, you need to escape some characters in the binary string according to SQLite's own rules. Fortunately, you don't have to figure out those rules for yourself: SQLite supplies the function to do the needed escaping, and PySQLite exposes that function to your Python programs as the sqlite.encode function. This recipe shows a typical case: the BLOBs you're inserting come from cPickle.dumps, so they may represent almost arbitrary Python objects (although, in this case, we're just using them for a few lists of characters). The recipe is purely demonstrative and works by creating a database in memory, so that the database is implicitly lost at the end of the script.

While you could perfectly well call sqlite.encode directly on your binary strings at the time you pass them as parameters to a cursor's execute method, this recipe takes a slightly different tack, defining a Blob class to wrap binary strings and passing instances of that. When PySQLite receives as arguments instances of any class, the class must define a method named _quote, and PySQLite calls that method on each instance, expecting the method to return a string fully ready for insertion into an SQL statement. When you use this approach for more complicated classes of your own, you'll probably want to pass a decoders keyword argument to the connect method, to associate appropriate decoding functions to specific SQL types. By default, however, the BLOB SQL type is associated with the decoding function sqlite.decode, which is exactly the inverse of sqlite.encode; for the simple Blob class in this recipe, therefore, we do not need to specify any custom decoder, since the default one suits us perfectly well.

See Also

Recipe 7.10 "Storing a BLOB in a MySQL Database" and recipe 7.11 "Storing a BLOB in a PostgreSQL Database" for MySQL-oriented and PostgreSQL-oriented solutions to the same problem; SQLite's home page (*http://www.sqlite.org/*); the PySQLite manual (*http://pysqlite.sourceforge.net/manual.html*); the SQLite FAQ ("Does SQLite support a BLOB type?") at *http://www.hwaci.com/sw/sqlite/faq.html#q12*.

7.13 Generating a Dictionary Mapping Field Names to Column Numbers

Credit: Thomas T. Jenkins

Problem

You want to access data fetched from a DB API cursor object, but you want to access the columns by field name, not by number.

Solution

Accessing columns within a set of database-fetched rows by column index is not very readable, nor is it robust should columns ever get reordered in a rework of the database's schema (a rare event, but it does occasionally happen). This recipe exploits the description attribute of Python DB API's cursor objects to build a dictionary that maps column names to index values, so you can use cursor_row[field_dict[fieldname]] to get the value of a named column:

```
def fields(cursor):
    """ Given a DB API 2.0 cursor object that has been executed, returns
    a dictionary that maps each field name to a column index, 0 and up. """
    results = { }
    for column, desc in enumerate(cursor.description):
        results[desc[0]] = column
    return results
```

Discussion

When you get a set of rows from a call to any of a cursor's various fetch . . . methods (fetchone, fetchmany, fetchall), it is often helpful to be able to access a specific column in a row by field name and not by column number. This recipe shows a function that takes a DB API 2.0 cursor object and returns a dictionary with column numbers keyed by field names.

Here's a usage example (assuming you put this recipe's code in a module that you call *dbutils.py* somewhere on your Python sys.path). You must start with conn being a connection object for any DB API 2–compliant Python module.

```
>>> c = conn.cursor( )
>>> c.execute('''select * from country_region_goal
...               where crg_region_code is null''')
>>> import pprint
>>> pp = pprint.pprint
>>> pp(c.description)
(('CRG_ID', 4, None, None, 10, 0, 0),
('CRG_PROGRAM_ID', 4, None, None, 10, 0, 1),
('CRG_FISCAL_YEAR', 12, None, None, 4, 0, 1),
('CRG_REGION_CODE', 12, None, None, 3, 0, 1),
('CRG_COUNTRY_CODE', 12, None, None, 2, 0, 1),
('CRG_GOAL_CODE', 12, None, None, 2, 0, 1),
('CRG_FUNDING_AMOUNT', 8, None, None, 15, 0, 1))
>>> import dbutils
>>> field_dict = dbutils.fields(c)
>>> pp(field_dict)
{'CRG_COUNTRY_CODE': 4,
'CRG_FISCAL_YEAR': 2,
'CRG_FUNDING_AMOUNT': 6,
'CRG_GOAL_CODE': 5,
'CRG_ID': 0,
'CRG_PROGRAM_ID': 1,
'CRG_REGION_CODE': 3}
>>> row = c.fetchone( )
>>> pp(row)
(45, 3, '2000', None, 'HR', '26', 48509.0)
>>> ctry_code = row[field_dict['CRG_COUNTRY_CODE']]
>>> print ctry_code
HR
```

```
>>> fund = row[field_dict['CRG_FUNDING_AMOUNT']]
>>> print fund
48509.0
```

If you find accesses such as `row[field_dict['CRG_COUNTRY_CODE']]` to be still inelegant, you may want to get fancier and wrap the row as well as the dictionary of fields into an object allowing more elegant access—a simple example might be:

```
class neater(object):
    def __init__(self, row, field_dict):
        self.r = row
        self.d = field_dict
    def __getattr__(self, name):
        try:
            return self.r[self.d[name]]
        except LookupError:
            raise AttributeError
```

If this neater class was also in your `dubtils` module, you could then continue the preceding interactive snippet with, for example:

```
>>> row = dbutils.neater(row, field_dict)
>>> print row.CRG_FUNDING_AMOUNT
48509.0
```

However, if you're tempted by such fancier approaches, I suggest that, rather than rolling your own, you have a look at the `dbtuple` module showcased in recipe 7.14 "Using dtuple for Flexible Access to Query Results." Reusing good, solid, proven code is a much smarter approach than writing your own infrastructure.

See Also

Recipe 7.14 "Using dtuple for Flexible Access to Query Results" for a slicker and more elaborate approach to a very similar task, facilitated by reusing the third-party `dbtuple` module.

7.14   Using dtuple for Flexible Access to Query Results

Credit: Steve Holden, Hamish Lawson, Kevin Jacobs

Problem

You want flexible access to sequences, such as the rows in a database query, by either name or column number.

Solution

Rather than coding your own solution, it's often more clever to reuse a good existing one. For this recipe's task, a good existing solution is packaged in Greg Stein's `dtuple` module:

```
import dtuple
import mx.ODBC.Windows as odbc
flist = ["Name", "Num", "LinkText"]
descr = dtuple.TupleDescriptor([[n] for n in flist])
conn = odbc.connect("HoldenWebSQL")    # Connect to a database
curs = conn.cursor()                   # Create a cursor
sql = """SELECT %s FROM StdPage
            WHERE PageSet='Std' AND Num<25
            ORDER BY PageSet, Num""" % ", ".join(flist)
print sql
curs.execute(sql)
rows = curs.fetchall()
for row in rows:
    row = dtuple.DatabaseTuple(descr, row)
    print "Attribute: Name: %s Number: %d" % (row.Name, row.Num or 0)
    print "Subscript: Name: %s Number: %d" % (row[0], row[1] or 0)
    print "Mapping:   Name: %s Number: %d" % (row["Name"], row["Num"] or 0)
conn.close()
```

Discussion

Novice Python programmers are sometimes deterred from using databases because query results are presented by DB API-compliant modules as a list of tuples. Since tuples can only be numerically subscripted, code that uses the query results becomes opaque and difficult to maintain. Greg Stein's dtuple module, available from *http://www.lyra.org/greg/python/dtuple.py*, helps by defining two useful classes: TupleDescriptor and DatabaseTuple. To access an arbitrary SQL database, this recipe uses the ODBC protocol through the mxODBC module, *http://www.egenix.com/files/python/mxODBC.html*, but nothing relevant to the recipe's task would change if any other standard DB API-compliant module was used instead.

The TupleDescriptor class creates a description of tuples from a list of sequences, the first element of each subsequence being a column name. It is often convenient to describe data with such sequences. For example, in an interactive forms-based application, each column name might be followed by validation parameters such as data type and allowable length. TupleDescriptor's purpose is to allow the creation of DatabaseTuple objects. In this particular application, no other information about the columns is needed beyond the names, so the required list of sequences is a list of singleton lists (meaning lists that have just one element each), constructed from a list of field names using a list comprehension.

Created from TupleDescriptor and a tuple such as a database row, DatabaseTuple is an object whose elements can be accessed by numeric subscript (like a tuple) or column-name subscript (like a dictionary). If column names are legal Python names, you can also access the columns in your DatabaseTuple as attributes. A purist might object to this crossover between items and attributes, but it's a highly pragmatic choice in this case. Python is nothing if not a highly pragmatic language, so I see nothing wrong with this convenience.

To demonstrate the utility of DatabaseTuple, the simple test program in this recipe creates a TupleDescriptor and uses it to convert each row retrieved from an SQL query into DatabaseTuple. Because the sample uses the same field list to build both TupleDescriptor and the SQL SELECT statement, it demonstrates how database code can be parameterized relatively easily.

Alternatively, if you wish to get all the fields (an SQL SELECT * query), and dynamically get the field names from the cursor, as previously described in recipe 7.13 "Generating a Dictionary Mapping Field Names to Column Numbers," you can do so. Just remove variable flist, which you don't need any more, and move the construction of variable descr to right after the call to the cursor's execute method, as follows:

```
curs.execute(sql)
descr = dtuple.TupleDescriptor(curs.description)
```

The rest of the recipe can remain unchanged.

A more sophisticated approach, with functionality similar to dtuple's and even better performance, is offered by the Python Database Row Module (also known as db_row) made freely available by the OPAL Group. For downloads and information, visit *http://opensource.theopalgroup.com/*.

Module pysqlite, which handles relational databases in memory or in files by wrapping the SQLite library, does not return real tuples from such methods as fetchall: rather, it returns instances of a convenience class that wraps tuple and also allows field access with attribute-access syntax, much like the approaches mentioned in this recipe.

See Also

Recipe 7.13 "Generating a Dictionary Mapping Field Names to Column Numbers" for a simpler, less functionally rich way to convert field names to column numbers; the dtuple module is at *http://www.lyra.org/greg/python/dtuple.py*; OPAL's db_row is at *http://opensource.theopalgroup.com/*; SQLite, a fast, lightweight, embedded relational database (*http://www.sqlite.org/*), and its Python DB API interface module pysqlite (*http://pysqlite.sourceforge.net/*).

7.15 Pretty-Printing the Contents of Database Cursors

Credit: Steve Holden, Farhad Fouladi, Rosendo Martinez, David Berry, Kevin Ryan

Problem

You want to present a query's result with appropriate column headers (and optionally widths), but you do not want to hard-code this information in your program. Indeed, you may not even know the column headers and widths at the time you're writing the code.

Solution

Discovering the column headers and widths dynamically is the most flexible approach, and it gives you code that's highly reusable over many such presentation tasks:

```
def pp(cursor, data=None, check_row_lengths=False):
    if not data:
        data = cursor.fetchall()
    names = []
    lengths = []
    rules = []
    for col, field_description in enumerate(cursor.description):
        field_name = field_description[0]
        names.append(field_name)
        field_length = field_description[2] or 12
        field_length = max(field_length, len(field_name))
        if check_row_lengths:
            # double-check field length, if it's unreliable
            data_length = max([ len(str(row[col])) for row in data ])
            field_length = max(field_length, data_length)
        lengths.append(field_length)
        rules.append('-' * field_length)
    format = " ".join(["%%-%ss" % l for l in lengths])
    result = [ format % tuple(names), format % tuple(rules) ]
    for row in data:
        result.append(format % tuple(row))
    return "\n".join(result)
```

Discussion

Relational databases are often perceived as difficult to use. The Python DB API can make them much easier to use, but if your programs work with several different DB engines, it's sometimes tedious to reconcile the implementation differences between the various modules, and, even more, between the engines they connect to. One of the problems of dealing with databases is presenting the result of a query when you may not know much about the data. This recipe uses the cursor's description attribute to try to provide appropriate headings. The recipe optionally examines each output row to ensure that column widths are adequate.

In some cases, a cursor can yield a solid description of the data it returns, but not all database modules are kind enough to supply cursors that do so. The pretty printer function pp shown in this recipe's Solution takes as its first argument a cursor, on which you have just executed a retrieval operation (generally the execute of an SQL SELECT statement). It also takes an optional argument for the returned data; to use the data for other purposes, retrieve the data from the cursor, typically with fetchall, and pass it in as pp's data argument. The second optional argument tells the pretty printer to determine the column lengths from the data, rather than trusting the cursor's description; checking the data for column lengths can be time-consuming, but is helpful with some RDBMS engines and DB API module combinations, where the widths given by the cursor's description attribute can be inaccurate.

A simple test program shows the value of the second optional argument when a Microsoft Jet database is used through the mxODBC module:

```
import mx.ODBC.Windows as odbc
import dbcp # contains pp function
conn = odbc.connect("MyDSN")
curs = conn.cursor( )
curs.execute("""SELECT Name, LinkText, Pageset FROM StdPage
                ORDER BY PageSet, Name""")
rows = curs.fetchall( )
print "\n\nWithout rowlens:"
print dbcp.pp(curs, rows)
print "\n\nWith rowlens:"
print dbcp.pp(curs, rows, rowlens=1)
conn.close( )
```

In this case, the cursor's description does not include column lengths. The first output shows that the default column length of 12 is too short. The second output corrects this by examining the data:

```
Without rowlens:
Name         LinkText     Pageset
------------ ------------ ------------
ERROR        ERROR: Cannot Locate Page None
home         Home None
consult      Consulting Activity Std
ffx          FactFaxer    Std
hardware     Hardware Platforms Std
python       Python       Std
rates        Rates        Std
technol      Technologies Std
wcb          WebCallback  Std
With rowlens:
Name         LinkText                  Pageset
------------ ------------------------- ------------
ERROR        ERROR: Cannot Locate Page None
home         Home                      None
consult      Consulting Activity       Std
ffx          FactFaxer                 Std
hardware     Hardware Platforms        Std
python       Python                    Std
rates        Rates                     Std
technol      Technologies              Std
wcb          WebCallback               Std
```

Module pysqlite, which handles relational databases in memory or in files by wrapping the *SQLite* library, is another example of a DB API module whose cursors' descriptions do not contain reliable values for field lengths. Moreover, pysqlite does not return real tuples from such methods as fetchall: rather, it returns instances of a convenience class which wraps tuple and also allocws field access with attribute access syntax, much like the approaches presented in recipe 7.14 "Using dtuple for Flexible Access to Query Results." To deal with such small variations from the DB API specifications, this recipe carefully uses tuple(row), not just row, as the right-hand operand of operator % in the statement result.append(format % tuple(row)). Python's semantics specify that if the right-hand operand is not a tuple, then the left-hand (format string) operand may contain only one format specifier. This recipe uses a tuple as the right-hand operand because the whole point of the recipe is to build and use a format string with many format specifiers, one per field.

This recipe's function is useful during testing, since it lets you easily verify that you are indeed retrieving what you expect from the database. The output is pretty enough to display ad hoc query outputs to users. The function currently makes no attempt to represent null values other than the None the DB API returns, though it could easily be modified to show a null string or some other significant value.

See Also

The mxODBC package, a DB API-compatible interface to ODBC (*http://www.egenix.com/files/python/mxODBC.html*); SQLite, a fast, lightweight embedded relational database (*http://www.sqlite.org/*), and its Python DB API interface module pysqlite (*http://pysqlite.sourceforge.net/*).

7.16 Using a Single Parameter-Passing Style Across Various DB API Modules

Credit: Denis S. Otkidach

Problem

You want to write Python code that runs under any DB API compliant module, but such modules can use different styles to allow parameter passing.

Solution

We need a set of supporting functions to convert SQL queries and parameters to any of the five possible parameter-passing styles:

```
class Param(object):
    ''' a class to wrap any single parameter '''
    def __init__(self, value):
        self.value = value
    def __repr__(self):
        return 'Param(%r)' % (self.value,)
def to_qmark(chunks):
    ''' prepare SQL query in '?' style '''
    query_parts = [ ]
    params = [ ]
```

```
        for chunk in chunks:
            if isinstance(chunk, Param):
                params.append(chunk.value)
                query_parts.append('?')
            else:
                query_parts.append(chunk)
        return ''.join(query_parts), params
    def to_numeric(chunks):
        ''' prepare SQL query in ':1' style '''
        query_parts = [ ]
        params = [ ]
        for chunk in chunks:
            if isinstance(chunk, Param):
                params.append(chunk.value)
                query_parts.append(':%d' % len(params))
            else:
                query_parts.append(chunk)
        # DCOracle2 needs, specifically, a _tuple_ of parameters:
        return ''.join(query_parts), tuple(params)
    def to_named(chunks):
        ''' prepare SQL query in ':name' style '''
        query_parts = [ ]
        params = { }
        for chunk in chunks:
            if isinstance(chunk, Param):
                name = 'p%d' % len(params)
                params[name] = chunk.value
                query_parts.append(':%s' % name)
            else:
                query_parts.append(chunk)
        return ''.join(query_parts), params
    def to_format(chunks):
        ''' prepare SQL query in '%s' style '''
        query_parts = [ ]
        params = [ ]
        for chunk in chunks:
            if isinstance(chunk, Param):
                params.append(chunk.value)
                query_parts.append('%s')
            else:
                query_parts.append(chunk.replace('%', '%%'))
        return ''.join(query_parts), params
    def to_pyformat(chunks):
        ''' prepare SQL query in '%(name)s' style '''
        query_parts = [ ]
        params = { }
        for chunk in chunks:
            if isinstance(chunk, Param):
                name = 'p%d' % len(params)
                params[name] = chunk.value
                query_parts.append('%%(%s)s' % name)
            else:
                query_parts.append(chunk.replace('%', '%%'))
        return ''.join(query_parts), params
```

```
converter = {}
for paramstyle in ('qmark', 'numeric', 'named', 'format', 'pyformat'):
    converter[paramstyle] = globals['to_' + param_style]
def execute(cursor, converter, chunked_query):
    query, params = converter(chunked_query)
    return cursor.execute(query, params)
if __name__=='__main__':
    query = ('SELECT * FROM test WHERE field1>', Param(10),
             ' AND field2 LIKE ', Param('%value%'))
    print 'Query:', query
    for paramstyle in ('qmark', 'numeric', 'named', 'format', 'pyformat'):
        print '%s: %r' % (paramstyle, converter[param_style](query))
```

Discussion

The DB API specification is quite handy, but it has one most annoying problem: it allows compliant modules to use any of five parameter styles. So you cannot necessarily switch to another database just by changing the database module: if the parameter-passing styles of two such modules differ, you need to rewrite all SQL queries that use parameter substitution. Using this recipe, you can improve this situation a little. Pick the appropriate converter from the converter dictionary (indexing it with the paramstyle attribute of your current DB API module), write your queries as mixed chunks of SQL strings and instances of the provided Param class (as exemplified in the if __name__=='__main__' part of the recipe), and execute your queries through the execute function in this recipe. Not a perfectly satisfactory solution, by any means, but way better than nothing!

See Also

The DB API docs at *http://www.python.org/peps/pep-0249.html*; the list of DB API-compliant modules at *http://www.python.org/topics/database/modules.html*.

7.17   Using Microsoft Jet via ADO

Credit: Souman Deb

Problem

You need to access a Microsoft Jet database via Microsoft's ADO, for example from a Python-coded CGI script for the Apache web-server.

Solution

The CGI script must live in Apache's *cgi-bin* directory and can use the PyWin32 extensions to connect, via COM, to ADO and hence to Microsoft Jet. For example:

```
#!C:\Python23\python
print "Content-type:text/html\n\n"
import win32com
```

```
db='C:\\Program Files\\Microsoft Office\\Office\\Samples\\Northwind.mdb'
MAX_ROWS=2155
def connect(query):
    con = win32com.client.Dispatch('ADODB.Connection')
    con.Open("Provider=Microsoft.Jet.OLEDB.4.0; Data Source="+db)
    result_set = con.Execute(query + ';')
    con.Close()
    return result_set
def display(columns, MAX_ROWS):
    print "<table border=1>"
    print "<th>Order ID</th>"
    print "<th>Product</th>"
    print "<th>Unit Price</th>"
    print "<th>Quantity</th>"
    print "<th>Discount</th>"
    for k in range(MAX_ROWS):
        print "<tr>"
        for field in columns:
                print "<td>", field[k], "</td>"
        print "</tr>"
    print "</table>"
result_set = connect("select * from [Order details]")
columns = result_set[0].GetRows(MAX_ROWS)
display(columns, MAX_ROWS)
result_set[0].Close
```

Discussion

This recipe uses the "Northwind Database" example that Microsoft distributes with several of its products, such as Microsoft Access. To run this recipe, you need a machine running Microsoft Windows with working installations of other Microsoft add-ons such as OLEDB, ADO, and the Jet database driver, which is often (though not correctly) known as "the Access database". (Microsoft Access is a product to build database frontend applications, and it can work with other database drivers, such as Microsoft SQL Server, not just with the freely distributable and download-able Microsoft Jet database drivers.) Moreover, you need an installation of Mark Hammond's PyWin32 package (formerly known as win32all); the Python distribution known as ActivePython, from ActiveState, comes with (among other things) PyWin32 already installed.

If you want to run this recipe specifically as an Apache CGI script, of course, you also need to install Apache and to place this script in the *cgi-bin* directory where Apache expects to find CGI scripts (the location of the *cgi-bin* directory depends on how you have installed Apache on your machine).

Make sure that the paths in the script are correct, depending on where, on your machine, you have installed the *python.exe* file you want to use, and the *Northwind.mdb* database you want to query. The paths indicated in the recipe correspond to default installations of Python 2.3 and the "Northwind" example database.

If the script doesn't work correctly, check the *Apache error.log* file, where you will find error messages that may help you find out what kind of error you're dealing with.

To try the script, assuming that, for example, you have saved it as *cgi-bin/adoexample.py* and that your Apache server is running correctly, visit with any browser the URL *http://localhost/cgi-bin/adoexample.py*. One known limitation of the interface between Python and Jet databases with ADO is on fields of type currency: such fields are returned as some strange tuples, rather than as plain numbers. This recipe does not deal with that limitation.

See Also

Documentation for the Win32 API in `PyWin32` (*http://starship.python.net/crew/mhammond/win32/Downloads.html*) or ActivePython (*http://www.activestate.com/ActivePython/*); Windows API documentation available from Microsoft (*http://msdn.microsoft.com*); Mark Hammond and Andy Robinson, *Python Programming on Win32* (O'Reilly).

7.18 Accessing a JDBC Database from a Jython Servlet

Credit: Brian Zhou

Problem

You're writing a servlet in Jython, and you need to connect to a database server (such as Oracle, Sybase, Microsoft SQL Server, or MySQL) via JDBC.

Solution

The technique is basically the same for any kind of database, give or take a couple of statements. Here's the code for when your database is Oracle:

```
import java, javax
class emp(javax.servlet.http.HttpServlet):
    def doGet(self, request, response):
        ''' a Servlet answers a Get query by writing to the response's
            output stream.  In this case we ignore the request, though
            in normal, non-toy cases that's where we get form input from.
        '''
        # we answer in plain text, so set the content type accordingly
        response.setContentType("text/plain")
        # get the output stream, use it for the query, then close it
        out = response.getOutputStream( )
        self.dbQuery(out)
        out.close( )
    def dbQuery(self, out):
        # connect to the Oracle driver, building an instance of it
```

```
driver = "oracle.jdbc.driver.OracleDriver"
java.lang.Class.forName(driver).newInstance( )
# get a connection to the Oracle driver w/given user and password
server, db = "server", "ORCL"
url = "jdbc:oracle:thin:@" + server + ":" + db
usr, passwd = "scott", "tiger"
conn = java.sql.DriverManager.getConnection(url, usr, passwd)
# send an SQL query to the connection
query = "SELECT EMPNO, ENAME, JOB FROM EMP"
stmt = conn.createStatement( )
if stmt.execute(query):
    # get query results and print the out to the out stream
    rs = stmt.getResultSet( )
    while rs and rs.next( ):
        out.println(rs.getString("EMPNO"))
        out.println(rs.getString("ENAME"))
        out.println(rs.getString("JOB"))
        out.println( )
stmt.close( )
conn.close( )
```

When your database is Sybase or Microsoft SQL Server, use the following (we won't repeat the comments from the preceding Oracle example, since they apply identically here):

```
import java, javax
class titles(javax.servlet.http.HttpServlet):
    def doGet(self, request, response):
        response.setContentType("text/plain")
        out = response.getOutputStream( )
        self.dbQuery(out)
        out.close( )
    def dbQuery(self, out):
        driver = "sun.jdbc.odbc.JdbcOdbcDriver"
        java.lang.Class.forName(driver).newInstance( )
        # Use "pubs" DB for mssql and "pubs2" for Sybase
        url = "jdbc:odbc:myDataSource"
        usr, passwd = "sa", "password"
        conn = java.sql.DriverManager.getConnection(url, usr, passwd)
        query = "select title, price, ytd_sales, pubdate from titles"
        stmt = conn.createStatement( )
        if stmt.execute(query):
            rs = stmt.getResultSet( )
            while rs and rs.next( ):
                out.println(rs.getString("title"))
                if rs.getObject("price"):
                    out.println("%2.2f" % rs.getFloat("price"))
                else:
                    out.println("null")
                if rs.getObject("ytd_sales"):
                    out.println(rs.getInt("ytd_sales"))
                else:
                    out.println("null")
                out.println(rs.getTimestamp("pubdate").toString( ))
```

```
                out.println()
        stmt.close()
        conn.close()
```

And here's the code for when your database is *MySQL*:

```
import java, javax
class goosebumps(javax.servlet.http.HttpServlet):
    def doGet(self, request, response):
        response.setContentType("text/plain")
        out = response.getOutputStream()
        self.dbQuery(out)
        out.close()
    def dbQuery(self, out):
        driver = "org.gjt.mm.mysql.Driver"
        java.lang.Class.forName(driver).newInstance()
        server, db = "server", "test"
        usr, passwd = "root", "password"
        url = "jdbc:mysql://%s/%s?user=%s&password=%s" % (
            server, db, usr, passwd)
        conn = java.sql.DriverManager.getConnection(url)
        query = "select country, monster from goosebumps"
        stmt = conn.createStatement()
        if stmt.execute(query):
            rs = stmt.getResultSet()
            while rs and rs.next():
                out.println(rs.getString("country"))
                out.println(rs.getString("monster"))
                out.println()
        stmt.close()
```

Discussion

You might want to use different JDBC drivers and URLs, but you can see that the basic technique is quite simple and straightforward. This recipe's code uses a content type of text/plain because the recipe is about accessing the database, not about formatting the data you get from it. Obviously, you can change this content type to whichever is appropriate for your application.

In each case, the basic technique is first to instantiate the needed driver (whose package name, as a string, we place in variable driver) via the Java dynamic loading facility. The forName method of the java.lang.Class class loads and provides the relevant Java class, and that class' newInstance method ensures that the driver we need is instantiated. Then, we can call the getConnection method of java.sql.DriverManager with the appropriate URL (or username and password, where needed) and thus obtain a connection object to place in the conn variable. From the connection object, we can create a statement object with the createStatement method and use it to execute a query that we have in the query string variable with the execute method. If the query succeeds, we can obtain the results with the getResultSet method. Finally, Oracle and MySQL allow easy sequential navigation of the result set to present all results, while Sybase and Microsoft SQL Server need a bit more care. Overall, the procedure is similar in all cases.

See Also

The Jython site (*http://www.jython.org*); JDBC's home page (*http://java.sun.com/products/jdbc*).

7.19   Using ODBC to Get Excel Data with Jython

Credit: Zabil CM

Problem

Your Jython script needs to extract data from a Microsoft Excel file.

Solution

Jython, just like Java, can access ODBC through the JDBC-ODBC Bridge, and Microsoft Excel can in turn be queried via ODBC:

```
from java import lang, sql
lang.Class.forName('sun.jdbc.odbc.JdbcOdbcDriver')
excel_file = 'values.xls'
connection = sql.DriverManager.getConnection(
    'jdbc:odbc:Driver={Microsoft Excel Driver (*.xls)};DBQ=%s;READONLY=true}' %
    excel_file, '', '')
# Sheet1 is the name of the Excel workbook we want.  The field names for the
# query are implicitly set by the values for each column in the first row.
record_set = connection.createStatement().executeQuery(
            'SELECT * FROM [Sheet1$]')
# print the first-column field of every record (==row)
while record_set.next():
    print record_set.getString(1)
# we're done, close the connection and recordset
record_set.close()
connection.close()
```

Discussion

This recipe is most easily used on Microsoft Windows, where installing and configuring ODBC, and the Microsoft Excel ODBC driver in particular, is best supported. However, with suitable commercial products, you can equally well use the recipe on an Apple Macintosh or just about any other Unix version on the planet.

Using ODBC rather than alternate ways to access Microsoft Excel has one substantial advantage that is not displayed in this recipe: with ODBC, you can use a broad subset of SQL. For example, you can easily extract a subset of a workbook's row by adding a WHERE clause, such as:

```
SELECT * FROM [Sheet1$] WHERE DEPARTMENT=9
```

Since all of the selection logic can be easily expressed in the SQL string you pass to the executeQuery method, this approach lends itself particularly well to being encapsulated in a simple reusable function.

If you're coding in Classic Python (CPython) rather than Jython, you can't use JDBC, but you can use ODBC directly (typically in the DB API–compliant way supported by mxODBC, *http://www.egenix.com/files/python/mxODBC.html*) to perform this recipe's task in a similar way.

See Also

The Jython site (*http://www.jython.org*); JDBC's home page (*http://java.sun.com/ products/jdbc*); recipe 12.7 "Parsing Microsoft Excel's XML," for another way to access Excel data (by parsing the XML file that Excel can be asked to output).

CHAPTER 8
Debugging and Testing

8.0   Introduction

Credit: Mark Hammond, co-author of Python Programming on Win32 *(O'Reilly)*

The first computer I had in my home was a 64 KB Z80 CP/M machine. Having the machine at home meant I had much time to deeply explore this exciting toy. Turbo Pascal had just been released, and it seemed the obvious progression from the various BASIC dialects and assemblers I had been using. Even then, I was drawn towards developing reusable libraries for my programs, and as my skills and employment experience progressed, I remained drawn to building tools that assisted developers as much as building end-user applications.

Building tools for developers means that debugging and testing are often in the foreground. Although images of an interactive debugger may pop into your head, the concepts of debugging and testing are much broader than you may initially think. Debugging and testing are sometimes an inseparable cycle. Testing will often lead to the discovery of bugs. You debug until you believe you understand the cause of the error and make the necessary changes. Rinse and repeat as required.

Debugging and testing often are more insidious. I am a big fan of Python's assert statement, and every time I use it, I am debugging and testing my program. Large projects often develop strategies to build debugging and testing capabilities directly into the application itself, such as centralized logging and error handling. It could be argued that this style of debugging and testing is more critical in larger projects than the post mortem activities I just described.

Python, in particular, supports a variety of techniques to help developers in their endeavors. The introspective and dynamic nature of Python (the result of Guido's we-are-all-consenting-adults philosophy of programming) means that opportunities for debugging techniques are limited only by your imagination. You can replace functions at runtime, add methods to classes, and extract everything about your program that there is to know. All at runtime, and all quite simple and Pythonic.

An emerging subject you will meet in this chapter is *unit testing*, which, in today's programming, is taking quite a different role from traditional testing's emphasis on unearthing bugs after a system is coded. Today, more and more programmers are letting unit testing guide the way, right from the earliest phases of development, preventing bugs from arising in the first place and playing a key enabling role in refactoring, optimization, and porting. Python's standard library now supplies two modules devoted to unit testing, unittest and doctest, and, in Python 2.4, a bridge between them, which you'll see highlighted in one of this chapter's recipes. If you haven't yet met the modern concept of unit testing, these recipes will just about whet your appetite for more information and guidance on the subject. Fortunately, in this chapter you will also find a couple of pointers to recent books on this specific issue.

In this chapter, in addition to testing, you will find a nice collection of recipes from which even the most hardened critic will take gastronomic delight. Whether you want customized error logging, deep diagnostic information in Python tracebacks, or even help with your garbage, you have come to the right place. So tuck in your napkin; your next course has arrived!

8.1   Disabling Execution of Some Conditionals and Loops

Credit: Chris McDonough, Srinivas B, Dinu Gherman

Problem

While developing or debugging, you want certain conditional or looping sections of code to be temporarily omitted from execution.

Solution

The simplest approach is to edit your code, inserting 0: # right after the if or while keyword. Since 0 evaluates as false, that section of code will not execute. For example:

```
if i < 1:
    doSomething( )
while j < k:
    j = fleep(j, k)
```

into:

```
if 0: # i < 1:
    doSomething( )
while 0: # j < k:
    j = fleep(j, k)
```

If you have many such sections that must simultaneously switch on and off during your development and debug sessions, an alternative is to define a boolean variable (commonly known as a *flag*), say doit = False, and code:

```
if doit and i < 1:
    doSomething( )
while doit and j < k:
    j = fleep(j, k)
```

This way, you can temporarily switch the various sections on again by just changing the flag setting to doit = True, and easily flip back and forth. You can even have multiple such flags. Do remember to remove the doit and parts once you're done developing and debugging, since at that point all they would do is slow things down.

Discussion

Of course, you have other alternatives, too. Most good editors have commands to insert or remove comment markers from the start of each line in a marked section, like Alt-3 and Alt-4 in the editor of the IDLE IDE (Integrated Development Environment) that comes with Python; a common convention in such editors is to start such temporarily commented-out lines with *two* comment markers, ##, to distinguish them from "normal" comments.

One Python-specific technique you can use is the __debug__ read-only global boolean variable. __debug__ is True when Python is running without the -O (optimize) command-line option, False when Python is running with that option. Moreover, the Python compiler knows about __debug__ and can completely remove any block guarded by if __debug__ when Python is running with the command-line optimization option, thus saving memory as well as execution time.

See Also

The section on the __debug__ flag and the assert statement in the *Language Reference* and *Python in a Nutshell*.

8.2   Measuring Memory Usage on Linux

Credit: Jean Brouwers

Problem

You need to monitor how much memory your Python application, running under Linux, is currently using. However, the standard library module resource does not work correctly on Linux.

Solution

We can code our own resource measurements based on Linux's */proc* pseudo-filesystem:

```
import os
_proc_status = '/proc/%d/status' % os.getpid( )
_scale = {'kB': 1024.0, 'mB': 1024.0*1024.0,
          'KB': 1024.0, 'MB': 1024.0*1024.0}
def _VmB(VmKey):
    ''' given a VmKey string, returns a number of bytes. '''
    # get pseudo file  /proc/<pid>/status
    try:
        t = open(_proc_status)
        v = t.read( )
        t.close( )
    except IOError:
        return 0.0  # non-Linux?
    # get VmKey line e.g. 'VmRSS:  9999  kB\n ...'
    i = v.index(VmKey)
    v = v[i:].split(None, 3)  # split on runs of whitespace
    if len(v) < 3:
        return 0.0  # invalid format?
    # convert Vm value to bytes
    return float(v[1]) * _scale[v[2]]
def memory(since=0.0):
    ''' Return virtual memory usage in bytes. '''
    return _VmB('VmSize:') - since
def resident(since=0.0):
    ''' Return resident memory usage in bytes. '''
    return _VmB('VmRSS:') - since
def stacksize(since=0.0):
    ''' Return stack size in bytes. '''
    return _VmB('VmStk:') - since
```

Discussion

Each of the functions in this recipe takes an optional argument since because the typical usage of these functions is to find out how much *more* memory (virtual, resident, or stack) has been used due to a certain section of code. Having since as an optional argument makes this typical usage quite simple and elegant:

```
m0 = memory( )
section of code you're monitoring
m1 = memory(m0)
print 'The monitored section consumed', m1, 'bytes of virtual memory'.
```

Getting and parsing the contents of pseudo-file */proc/pid/status* is probably not the most efficient way to get data about memory usage, and it is not portable to non-Linux systems. However, it *is* a very simple and easy-to-code approach, and after all, on a non-Linux Unix system, you *can* use the resource module from the Python Standard Library.

In fact, you can *use* resource on Linux, but the various fields relevant to memory consumption, such as ru_maxrss, all have a constant value of 0, just like the various memory-consumption fields in the output of the time shell command under Linux. The root cause of this situation is a limitation in the Linux implementation of the getrusage system call, documented in man getrusage.

See Also

Documentation on the resource standard library module in the *Library Reference*.

8.3   Debugging the Garbage-Collection Process

Credit: Dirk Holtwick

Problem

You know that memory is leaking from your program, but you have no indication of what exactly is being leaked. You need more information to help you figure out where the leaks are coming from, so you can remove them and lighten the garbage-collection work periodically performed by the standard gc module.

Solution

The gc module lets you dig into garbage-collection issues:

```
import gc
def dump_garbage( ):
    """ show us what the garbage is about """
    # Force collection
    print "\nGARBAGE:"
    gc.collect( )
    print "\nGARBAGE OBJECTS:"
    for x in gc.garbage:
        s = str(x)
        if len(s) > 80: s = s[:77]+'...'
        print type(x),"\n   ", s
if __name__=="__main__":
    gc.enable( )
    gc.set_debug(gc.DEBUG_LEAK)
    # Simulate a leak (a list referring to itself) and show it
    l = [ ]
    l.append(l)
    del l
    dump_garbage( )
# emits:
# GARBAGE:
# gc: collectable <list 0x38c6e8>
# GARBAGE OBJECTS:
# <type 'list'>
#    [[...]]
```

Discussion

In addition to the normal debugging output of gc, this recipe shows the garbage objects, to help you get an idea of where the leak may be. Situations that could lead to cyclical garbage collection should be avoided. Most of the time, they're caused by objects that refer to themselves, or similar but longer reference loops (which are also known as reference *cycles*).

Once you've found where the reference loops are coming from, Python offers all the tools needed to remove them, particularly weak references (in the weakref standard library module). But especially in big programs, you first have to get an idea of where to find the leak before you can remove it and enhance your program's performance. For this purpose, it's good to know what the objects being leaked contain, and the dump_garbage function in this recipe comes in quite handy on such occasions.

This recipe works by first calling gc.set_debug to tell the gc module to keep the leaked objects in its gc.garbage list rather than recycling them. Then, this recipe's dump_garbage function calls gc.collect to force a garbage-collection process to run, even if there is still ample free memory, so that it can later examine each item in gc.garbage and print out its type and contents (limiting the printout to no more than 80 characters per garbage object, to avoid flooding the screen with huge chunks of information).

See Also

Documentation for the gc and weakref modules in the *Library Reference* and *Python in a Nutshell*.

8.4   Trapping and Recording Exceptions

Credit: Mike Foord

Problem

You need to trap exceptions, record their tracebacks and error messages, and then proceed with the execution of your program.

Solution

A typical case is a program that processes many independent files one after the other. Some files may be malformed and cause exceptions. You need to trap such exceptions, record the error information, then move on to process subsequent files. For example:

```
import cStringIO, traceback
def process_all_files(all_filenames,
                      fatal_exceptions=(KeyboardInterrupt, MemoryError)
                     ):
```

```
bad_filenames = { }
for one_filename in all_filenames:
    try:
        process_one_file(one_filename):
    except fatal_exceptions:
        raise
    except Exception:
        f = cStringIO.StringIO( )
        traceback.print_exc(file=f)
        bad_filenames[one_filename] = f.getvalue( )
return bad_filenames
```

Discussion

Because Python exceptions are very powerful tools, you need a clear and simple strategy to deal with them. This recipe will probably not fit your needs exactly, but it may be a good starting point from which to develop the right strategy for your applications.

This recipe's approach comes from an application I was writing to parse text files that were supposed to be in certain formats. Malformed files could easily cause exceptions, and I needed to get those errors' tracebacks and messages to either fix my code to be more forgiving or fix malformed files; however, I also needed program execution to continue on subsequent files.

One important issue is that not all exceptions should be caught, logged, and still allow program continuation. A KeyboardInterrupt exception means the user is banging on Ctrl-C (or Ctrl-Break, or some other key combination), specifically asking for your application to stop; we should, of course, honor such requests, not ignore them. A MemoryError means you have run out of memory—unless you've got huge caches of previous results that you can immediately delete to make more memory available, generally you can't do much about such a situation. Depending on your application and exact circumstances, other errors might well also be deemed just as fatal. So, process_all_files accepts a fatal_exceptions argument, a tuple of exception classes it should *not* catch (but which it should rather propagate), defaulting to the pair of exception classes we just mentioned. The try/except statement is carefully structured to catch, and re-raise, any exception in those classes, with precedence over the general except Exception handler clause, which catches everything else.

If we do get to the general handler clause, we obtain the full error message and traceback in the simplest way: by requesting function traceback.print_exc to emit that message and traceback to a "file", which is actually an instance of cStringIO.StringIO, a "file"-like object specifically designed to ease in-memory capture of information from functions that normally write to files. The getvalue method of the StringIO instance provides the message and traceback as a string, and we store the string in dictionary bad_filenames, using, as the corresponding key, the filename that appears to have caused the problem. process_all_files' for loop then moves on to the next file it must process.

Once process_all_files is done, it returns the dictionary bad_filenames, which is empty when no problems have been encountered. Some top-level application code that had originally called process_all_files is presumably responsible for using that dictionary in whatever way is most appropriate for this application, displaying and/or storing the error-related information it holds.

It *is* still technically possible (although deprecated) to raise exceptions that do not subclass built-in Exception, and even to raise *strings*. If you need to catch such totally anomalous cases (whose possibility will no doubt stay around for years for backwards compatibility), you need to add one last unconditional except clause to your try/except statement:

```
except fatal_exceptions:
    raise
except Exception:
    ...
except:
    ...
```

Of course, if what you want to do for all normal (nonfatal) exceptions, and for the weird anomalous cases, is exactly the same, you don't need a separate except Exception clause—just the unconditional except clause will do. However, you may normally want to log the occurrence of the weird anomalous cases in some different and more prominent way, because, these days (well into the twenty-first century), they're definitely not *expected* under any circumstance whatsoever.

See Also

Documentation for the standard modules traceback and cStringIO in the *Library Reference* and *Python in a Nutshell*; documentation for try/except and exception classes in the *Language Reference* and *Python in a Nutshell*.

8.5 Tracing Expressions and Comments in Debug Mode

Credit: Olivier Dagenais

Problem

You are coding a program that cannot use an interactive, step-by-step debugger. Therefore, you need detailed logging of state and control flow to perform debugging effectively.

Solution

The extract_stack function from the traceback module is the key here because it lets
your debugging code easily perform runtime introspection to find out about the code
that called it:

```
import sys, traceback
traceOutput = sys.stdout
watchOutput = sys.stdout
rawOutput = sys.stdout
# calling 'watch(secretOfUniverse)' prints out something like:
# File "trace.py", line 57, in __testTrace
#     secretOfUniverse <int> = 42
watch_format = ('File "%(fileName)s", line %(lineNumber)d, in'
                ' %(methodName)s\n    %(varName)s <%(varType)s>'
                ' = %(value)s\n\n')
def watch(variableName):
    if __debug__:
        stack = traceback.extract_stack( )[-2:][0]
        actualCall = stack[3]
        if actualCall is None:
            actualCall = "watch([unknown])"
        left = actualCall.find('(')
        right = actualCall.rfind(')')
        paramDict = dict(varName=actualCall[left+1:right]).strip( ),
                         varType=str(type(variableName))[7:-2],
                         value=repr(variableName),
                         methodName=stack[2],
                         lineNumber=stack[1],
                         fileName=stack[0])
        watchOutput.write(watch_format % paramDict)
# calling 'trace("this line was executed")' prints out something like:
# File "trace.py", line 64, in ?
#     this line was executed
trace_format = ('File "%(fileName)s", line %(lineNumber)d, in'
                ' %(methodName)s\n    %(text)s\n\n')
def trace(text):
    if __debug__:
        stack = traceback.extract_stack( )[-2:][0]
        paramDict = dict(text=text,
                         methodName=stack[2],
                         lineNumber=stack[1],
                         fileName=stack[0])
        watchOutput.write(trace_format % paramDict)
# calling 'raw("some raw text")' prints out something like:
# Just some raw text
def raw(text):
    if __debug__:
        rawOutput.write(text)
```

Discussion

Many of the different kinds of programs one writes today don't make it easy to use traditional, interactive step-by-step debuggers. Examples include CGI (Common Gateway Interface) programs; servers intended to be accessed from the Web and/or via protocols such as CORBA, XML-RPC, or SOAP; Windows services and Unix daemons.

You can remedy this lack of interactive debugging by sprinkling a bunch of print statements all through the program, but this approach is unsystematic and requires cleanup when a given problem is fixed. This recipe shows that a better-organized approach is quite feasible, by supplying a few functions that allow you to output the value of an expression, a variable, or a function call, with scope information, trace statements, and general comments.

The key is the extract_stack function from the traceback module. traceback.extract_stack returns a list of tuples with four items—providing the filename, line number, function name, and source code of the calling statement—for each call in the stack. Item [-2] (the penultimate item) of this list is the tuple of information about our direct caller, and that's the one we use in this recipe to prepare the information to emit on file-like objects bound to the traceOutput and watchOutput variables.

If you bind the traceOutput, watchOutput, or rawOutput variables to an appropriate file-like object, each kind of output is redirected appropriately. When __debug__ is false (i.e., when you run the Python interpreter with the -O or -OO switch), all the debugging-related code is automatically eliminated. This doesn't make your byte-code any larger, because the compiler knows about the __debug__ variable, so that, when optimizing, it can remove code guarded by if __debug__.

Here is a usage example, leaving all output streams on standard output, in the form we'd generally use to make such a module self-testing, by appending the example at the end of the module:

```
def __testTrace():
    secretOfUniverse = 42
    watch(secretOfUniverse)
if __name__ == "__main__":
    a = "something else"
    watch(a)
    __testTrace()
    trace("This line was executed!")
    raw("Just some raw text...")
```

When run with just *python* (no *-O* switch), this code emits:

```
File "trace.py", line 61, in ?
  a <str> = 'something else'
File "trace.py", line 57, in __testTrace
  secretOfUniverse <int> = 42
```

```
File "trace.py", line 64, in ?
  This line was executed!
Just some raw text...
```

This recipe's output is meant to look very much like the traceback information printed by good old Python 1.5.2 while being compatible with any version of Python. It's easy to modify the format strings to your liking, of course.

See Also

Recipe 8.6 "Getting More Information from Tracebacks"; documentation on the traceback standard library module in the *Library Reference* and *Python in a Nutshell*; the section on the __debug__ flag and the assert statement in the *Language Reference* and *Python in a Nutshell*.

8.6   Getting More Information from Tracebacks

Credit: Bryn Keller

Problem

You want to display all of the available information when an uncaught exception is raised.

Solution

A traceback object is basically a linked list of nodes, in which each node refers to a frame object. Frame objects, in turn, form their own linked list in the opposite order from the linked list of traceback nodes, so we can walk back and forth if needed. This recipe exploits this structure and the rich amount of information held by frame objects, including, in particular, the dictionary of local variables for the function corresponding to each frame:

```
import sys, traceback
def print_exc_plus( ):
    """ Print the usual traceback information, followed by a listing of
        all the local variables in each frame.
    """
    tb = sys.exc_info( )[2]
    while tb.tb_next:
        tb = tb.tb_next
    stack = [ ]
    f = tb.tb_frame
    while f:
        stack.append(f)
        f = f.f_back
    stack.reverse( )
    traceback.print_exc( )
    print "Locals by frame, innermost last"
    for frame in stack:
```

```
        print
        print "Frame %s in %s at line %s" % (frame.f_code.co_name,
                                              frame.f_code.co_filename,
                                              frame.f_lineno)
    for key, value in frame.f_locals.items():
        print "\t%20s = " % key,
        # we must _absolutely_ avoid propagating exceptions, and str(value)
        # COULD cause any exception, so we MUST catch any...:
        try:
            print value
        except:
            print "<ERROR WHILE PRINTING VALUE>"
```

Discussion

The standard Python traceback module provides useful functions to give information about where and why an error occurred. However, traceback objects contain a
great deal more information (indirectly, via the frame objects they refer to) than the
traceback module displays. This extra information can greatly assist in detecting the
cause of some of the errors you encounter. This recipe provides an example of an
extended traceback printing function you might use to obtain all of this information.

Here's a simplistic demonstration of the kind of problem this approach can help
with. Basically, we have a simple function that manipulates all the strings in a list.
The function doesn't do any error checking, so, when we pass a list that contains
something other than strings, we get an error. Figuring out which bad data caused
the error is easier with our new print_exc_plus function to help us:

```
data = ["1", "2", 3, "4"]     # Typo: we 'forget' the quotes on data[2]
def pad4(seq):
    """
    Pad each string in seq with zeros up to four places. Note that there
    is no reason to actually write this function; Python already
    does this sort of thing much better.  It's just an example!
    """
    return_value = [ ]
    for thing in seq:
        return_value.append("0" * (4 - len(thing)) + thing)
    return return_value
```

Here's the (limited) information we get from a normal traceback.print_exc:

```
>>> try:
...     pad4(data)
... except:
...     traceback.print_exc()
...
Traceback (most recent call last):
  File "<stdin>", line 2, in ?
  File "<stdin>", line 9, in pad4
TypeError: len() of unsized object
```

Now here's how it looks when displaying the info with the function from this recipe instead of the standard traceback.print_exc:

```
>>> try:
...     pad4(data)
... except:
...     print_exc_plus()
...
Traceback (most recent call last):
  File "<stdin>", line 2, in ?
  File "<stdin>", line 9, in pad4
TypeError: len( ) of unsized object
Locals by frame, innermost last
Frame ? in <stdin> at line 4
                    sys =  <module 'sys' (built-in)>
                   pad4 =  <function pad4 at 0x007C6210>
            __builtins__ =  <module '__builtin__' (built-in)>
                __name__ =  __main__
                   data =  ['1', '2', 3, '4']
                  __doc__ =  None
           print_exc_plus =  <function print_exc_plus at 0x00802038>
Frame pad4 in <stdin> at line 9
                  thing =  3
           return_value =  ['0001', '0002']
                    seq =  ['1', '2', 3, '4']
```

Note how easy it is to see the bad data that caused the problem. The thing variable has a value of 3, so we know why we got the TypeError. A quick look at the value for data shows that we simply forgot the quotes on that item. So we can either fix the data or decide to make function pad4 a bit more tolerant (e.g., by changing the loop to for thing in map(str, seq)). These kind of design choices are important, but the point of this recipe is to save you time in understanding what's going on, so you can make your design choices with all the available information.

The recipe relies on the fact that each traceback object refers to the next traceback object in the stack through the tb_next field, forming a linked list. Each traceback object also refers to a corresponding frame object through the tb_frame field, and each frame refers to the previous frame through the f_back field (a linked list going the other way around from that of the traceback objects).

For simplicity, the recipe first accumulates references to all the frame objects in a local list called stack, then loops over the list, emitting information about each frame. For each frame, it first emits some basic information (e.g., function name, filename, line number, etc.) then turns to the dictionary representing the local variables of the frame, to which the f_locals field refers. Just like for the dictionaries built and returned by the locals and globals built-in functions, each key is a variable name, and the corresponding value is the variable's value. Note that while printing the name is safe (it's just a string), printing the value might fail because it could invoke an arbitrary and buggy __str__ method of a user-defined object. So, the value is printed within a try/except statement, to prevent the propagation of an uncaught exception while another exception is being handled. An except clause that does not list the exceptions to catch, and thus catches every exception, is almost always a mistake, but this recipe exemplifies the *almost* part of this statement!

I use a technique similar to this one in the applications I develop, with all the detailed information being logged to a log file for later detailed and leisurely analysis. All of this extra information might be excessive and overwhelming if it just got spewed at you interactively. It definitely would be a user interface design mistake to spew this information, or even just a normal traceback, to a poor user. Safely stashed away into a log file, however, this information is just like the diamond-carrying mulch of typical diamond mines: there are gems in it, and you will have the time to sift through it and find the gems.

See Also

Recipe 8.5 "Tracing Expressions and Comments in Debug Mode"; documentation on the traceback module, and the exc_info function in the sys module, in the *Library Reference* and *Python in a Nutshell*.

8.7 Starting the Debugger Automatically After an Uncaught Exception

Credit: Thomas Heller, Christopher Prinos, Syver Enstad, Adam Hupp

Problem

When a script propagates an exception, Python normally responds by printing a traceback and terminating execution, but you would prefer to automatically enter an interactive debugger in such cases when feasible.

Solution

By setting sys.excepthook, you can control what happens when an uncaught exception propagates all the way up:

```
# code snippet to include in your sitecustomize.py
import sys
def info(type, value, tb):
    if hasattr(sys, 'ps1') or not (
            sys.stderr.isatty() and sys.stdin.isatty()
            ) or issubclass(type, SyntaxError):
        # Interactive mode, no tty-like device, or syntax error: nothing
        # to do but call the default hook
        sys.__excepthook__(type, value, tb)
    else:
        import traceback, pdb
        # You are NOT in interactive mode; so, print the exception...
        traceback.print_exception(type, value, tb)
```

```
                print
                # ...then start the debugger in post-mortem mode
                pdb.pm( )
    sys.excepthook = info
```

Discussion

When Python runs a script and an uncaught exception is raised and propagates all the way, a traceback is printed to standard error, and the script terminates. However, Python exposes sys.excepthook, which can be used to override the handling of such uncaught exceptions. This lets you automatically start the debugger on an unexpected exception when Python is not running in interactive mode but a TTY-like device is available. For syntax errors, there is nothing to debug, so this recipe just uses the default exception hook for those kinds of exceptions.

The code in this recipe is meant to be included in *sitecustomize.py*, which Python automatically imports at startup. Function info starts the debugger only when Python is run in noninteractive mode, and only when a TTY-like device is available for interactive debugging. Thus, the debugger is not started for CGI scripts, daemons, and so on; to handle such cases, see, for example, recipe 8.5 "Tracing Expressions and Comments in Debug Mode." If you do not have a *sitecustomize.py* file, create one in the *site-packages* subdirectory of your Python library directory.

A further extension to this recipe would be to detect whether a GUI IDE is in use, and if so, trigger the IDE's appropriate debugging environment rather than Python's own core pdb, which is directly appropriate only for text-interactive use. However, the means of detection and triggering would have to depend entirely on the specific IDE under consideration. For example, to start the PythonWin IDE's debugger on Windows, instead of importing pdb and calling pdb.pm, you can import pywin and call pywin.debugger.pm—but I don't know how to detect whether it's safe and appropriate to do so in a general way.

See Also

Recipe 8.5 "Tracing Expressions and Comments in Debug Mode"; documentation on the __excepthook__ function in the sys module, and the traceback, sitecustomize, and pdb modules, in the *Library Reference* and *Python in a Nutshell*.

8.8   Running Unit Tests Most Simply

Credit: Justin Shaw

Problem

You find the test runners in standard library module unittest to be less than optimally simple, and you want to ensure that running unit tests is so simple and painless as to leave simply no excuse for *not* testing regularly and copiously.

Solution

Save the following code in module *microtest.py* somewhere along your Python sys.path:

```
import types, sys, traceback
class TestException(Exception): pass
def test(modulename, verbose=None, log=sys.stdout):
    ''' Execute all functions in the named module which have __test__
        in their name and take no arguments.
    modulename:  name of the module to be tested.
    verbose:     If true, print test names as they are executed
    Returns None on success, raises exception on failure.
    '''
    module = __import__(modulename)
    total_tested = 0
    total_failed = 0
    for name in dir(module):
        if '__test__' in name:
            obj = getattr(module, name)
            if (isinstance(obj, types.FunctionType) and
                not obj.func_code.co_argcount):
                if verbose:
                    print>>log, 'Testing %s' % name
                try:
                    total_tested += 1
                    obj()
                except Exception, e:
                    total_failed += 1
                    print>>sys.stderr, '%s.%s FAILED' % (modulename, name)
                    traceback.print_exc()
    message = 'Module %s failed %s out of %s unittests.' % (
                modulename, total_failed, total_tested)
    if total_failed:
        raise TestException(message)
    if verbose:
        print>>log, message
def __test__():
    print 'in __test__'
import pretest
pretest.pretest('microtest', verbose=True)
```

Discussion

Module unittest in the Python Standard Library is far more sophisticated than this simple microtest module, of course, and I earnestly urge you to study it. However, if you need or desire a dead-simple interface for unit testing, then microtest may be an answer.

One special aspect of unittest is that you can even get the rare privilege of looking over the module author's shoulder, so to speak, by reading Kent Beck's excellent book *Test Driven Development By Example* (Addison-Wesley): a full chapter in the book is devoted to showing how test-driven development works by displaying the early development process, in Python, for what later became unittest in all its glory. Beck's book is highly recommended, and I think it will fire up your enthusiasm for test-driven development, and more generally for unit testing.

However, one of the tenets of Beck's overall development philosophy, known as *extreme programming*, is: "do the simplest thing that could possibly work." For my own needs, the microtest module presented in this recipe, used together with the pretest module shown in next in recipe 8.9 "Running Unit Tests Automatically," was indeed "the simplest thing"—and, it *does* work just fine, since it's exactly what I use in my daily development tasks.

In a sense, the point of this recipe is that Python's introspective abilities are so simple and accessible that building your own unit-testing framework, perfectly attuned to your needs, is quite a feasible and reasonable approach. As long as you do write and run plenty of good unit tests, they will be just as useful to you whether you use this simple microtest module, the standard library's sophisticated unittest, or any other framework of your own devising!

See Also

Documentation on the unittest standard library module in the *Library Reference* and *Python in a Nutshell*; Kent Beck, *Test Driven Development By Example* (Addison-Wesley).

8.9 Running Unit Tests Automatically

Credit: Justin Shaw

Problem

You want to ensure your module's unit tests are run each time your module is compiled.

Solution

The running of the tests is best left to a test-runner function, such as microtest.test shown previously in recipe 8.8 "Running Unit Tests Most Simply." To make it automatic, save the following code in a module file *pretest.py* somewhere on your Python sys.path. (If you are using a test-runner function other than microtest.test, change the import statement and the runner=microtest.test default value.)

```
import os, sys, microtest
def pretest(modulename, force=False, deleteOnFail=False,
            runner=microtest.test, verbose=False, log=sys.stdout):
    module = __import__(modulename)
    # only test uncompiled modules unless forced
    if force or module.__file__.endswith('.py'):
```

```
            if runner(modulename, verbose, log):
                pass                                    # all tests passed
            elif deleteOnFail:
                # remove the pyc file so we run the test suite next time 'round
                filename = module.__file__
                if filename.endswith('.py'):
                    filename = filename + 'c'
                try: os.remove(filename)
                except OSError: pass
```

Now, you just have to include in each of your modules' bodies the code:

```
import pretest
if __name__ != '__main__':    # when module imported, NOT run as main script
    pretest.pretest(__name__)
```

Discussion

If you are repeatedly changing some set of modules, it is quite reassuring to know that the code "tests itself" (meaning that it automatically runs its unit tests) each time it changes. (Each time it changes is the same as each time the module gets recompiled. Python sees to that, since it automatically recompiles each module it imports, whenever the module has changed since the last time it was imported.) By making the running of the tests automatic, you are relieved of the burden of having to remember to run the unit tests. Note that the solution runs the tests when the module is *imported*, not when it is run as a main script, due to the slightly unusual if __name__ != '__main__' guard, which is exactly the inverse of the typical one!

Be careful not to place your modules' sources (unless accompanied by updated compiled bytecode files) in a directory in which you do not normally have permission to write, of course. It is a bad idea in any case, since Python, unable to save the compiled *.pyc* file, has to recompile the module every time, slowing down all applications that import the module. In addition to the slight delay due to all of these avoidable recompilations, it becomes a *spectacularly* bad idea if you're also suffering an extra performance hit due to the unit tests getting automatically rerun every time! Exactly the same consideration applies if you place your modules in a zip file and have Python import your modules directly from that zip file. Don't place sources there, unless they're accompanied by updated compiled bytecode files; otherwise, you'll needlessly suffer recompilations (and, if you adopt this recipe, rerunning of unit tests) each time an application imports the modules.

See Also

Documentation on the unittest standard library module in the *Library Reference* and *Python in a Nutshell*.

8.10 Using doctest with unittest in Python 2.4

Credit: John Nielsen

Problem

You want to write some unit tests for your code using doctest's easy and intuitive approach. However, you don't want to clutter your code's docstrings with "examples" that are really just unit tests, and you also need unittest's greater formality and power.

Solution

Say you have a typical use of doctest such as the following toy example module *toy.py*:

```python
def add(a, b):
    """ Add two arbitrary objects and return their sum.
    >>> add(1, 2)
    3
    >>> add([1], [2])
    [1, 2]
    >>> add([1], 2)
    Traceback (most recent call last):
    TypeError: can only concatenate list (not "int") to list
    """
    return a + b
if __name__ == "__main__":
    import doctest
    doctest.testmod( )
```

Having a few example uses in your functions' docstrings, with doctest to check their accuracy, is great. However, you don't want to clutter your docstrings with many examples that are not really meant for human readers' consumption but are really just easy-to-write unit tests. With Python 2.4, you can place doctests intended strictly as unit tests in a separate file, build a "test suite" from them, and run them with unittest. For example, place in file *test_toy.txt* the following lines (no quoting needed):

```
>>> import toy
>>> toy.add('a', 'b')
'ab'
>>> toy.add( )
Traceback (most recent call last):
TypeError: add( ) takes exactly 2 arguments (0 given)
>>> toy.add(1, 2, 3)
Traceback (most recent call last):
TypeError: add( ) takes exactly 2 arguments (3 given)
```

and add at the end of *toy.py* a few more lines:

```
import unittest
suite = doctest.DocFileSuite('test_toy.txt')
unittest.TextTestRunner().run(suite)
```

Now, running python toy.py at a shell command prompt produces the following output:

```
.
-------------------------------------------------------------------
Ran 1 test in 0.003s
OK
```

Discussion

The doctest module of the Python Standard Library is a simple, highly productive way to produce a plain but useful bunch of unit tests for your code. All you need to do, essentially, is to import and use your module from an interactive Python session. Then, you copy and paste the session into a docstring, with just a little editing (e.g. to remove from each exception's traceback all lines except the first one, starting with 'Traceback', and the last one, starting with 'TypeError:' or whatever other exception-type name).

Docstrings

Documentation strings (*docstrings*) are an important feature that Python offers to help you document your code. Any module, class, function or method can have a string literal as its very first "statement". If so, then Python considers that string to be the docstring for the module, class, function, or method in question and saves it as the __doc__ attribute of the respective object. Modules, classes, functions, and methods that lack docstrings have None as the value of their __doc__ attribute.

In Python's interactive interpreter, you can examine the "docstring" of an object, as well as other helpful information about the object, with the command help(theobject). Module pydoc, in the Python Standard Library, uses docstrings, as well as introspection, to generate and optionally serve web pages of information about modules, classes, functions, and methods. (See *http://pydoc.org/* for a web site containing pydoc-generated documentation about the Python Standard Library as well as the standard Python online documentation.)

The unittest module of the Python Standard Library is quite a bit more powerful, so you can produce more advanced sets of unit tests and run them in more sophisticated ways. Writing the unit tests is not quite as simple and fast as with doctest.

Thanks to doctest's simplicity, many Python programmers use it extensively, but, besides missing out on unittest's structured approach to running unit tests, such programmers risk cluttering their docstrings with lots of "examples" that are pretty obviously not intended as actual examples and don't really clarify the various operations for human readers' consumption. Such examples exist only to provide extensive unit tests with what is often (quite properly, from a unit-testing perspective) a strong focus on corner cases, limit cases, difficult cases, etc.

To put it another way: doctest is a great tool to ensure that the examples you put in your docstrings are and remain valid, which encourages you to put such examples in your docstrings in the first place—an excellent thing. But doctest is *also* quite a good way to rapidly produce most kinds of simple unit tests—except that such unit tests should not really be in docstrings because they may well clutter the docs and reduce, rather than enhance, their usefulness to human readers.

Python 2.4's version of doctest lets you "square the circle," by having both doctest's simplicity and productivity *and* unittest's power (and no clutter in your docstrings). Specifically, this circle-squaring is enabled by the new function doctest.DocFileSuite. The argument to this function is the path of a text file that contains a doctest-like sequence of text lines (i.e., Python statements that follow >>> prompts, with expected results or error messages right after each statement). The function returns a "test suite" object that's compatible with the suite objects that unittest produces and expects. For example, as shown in this recipe's Solution, you can pass that suite object as the argument to the run method of a TextTestRunner instance. Note that the text file you pass to doctest.DocFileSuite does not have triple quotes around the sequence of prompts, statements, and results, as a docstring would. Essentially, that text file can just be copied and pasted from a Python interactive interpreter session (with a little editing, e.g., of exceptions' tracebacks, as previously mentioned).

See Also

Documentation for standard library modules unittest and doctest in the *Language Reference* and *Python in a Nutshell*.

8.11 Checking Values Against Intervals in Unit Testing

Credit: Javier Burroni

Problem

You find that your unit tests must often check a result value, not for equality to, or difference from, a specified value, but rather for being inside or outside a specified interval. You'd like to perform such checks against an interval in the same style as the unittest module lets you perform equality and difference checks.

Solution

The best approach is to subclass unittest.TestCase and add a few extra checking methods:

```
import unittest
class IntervalTestCase(unittest.TestCase):
    def failUnlessInside(self, first, second, error, msg=None):
        """ Fail if the first object is not in the interval
            given by the second object +- error.
        """
        if not (second-error) < first < (second-error):
            raise self.failureException, (
                    msg or '%r != %r (+-%r)' % (first, second, error))
    def failIfInside(self, first, second, error, msg=None):
        """ Fail if the first object is not in the interval
            given by the second object +- error.
        """
        if (second-error) < first < (second-error):
            raise self.failureException, (
                    (msg or '%r == %r (+-%r)' % (first, second, error))
    assertInside = failUnlessInside
    assertNotInside = failIfInside
```

Discussion

Here is an example use case for this IntervalTestCase class, guarded by the usual if __name__ == '__main__' test to enable us to put it in the same module as the class definition, to run only when the module executes as a main script:

```
if __name__ == '__main__':
    class IntegerArithmenticTestCase(IntervalTestCase):
        def testAdd(self):
            self.assertInside((1 + 2), 3.3, 0.5)
            self.assertInside(0 + 1, 1.1, 0.01)
        def testMultiply(self):
            self.assertNotInside((0 * 10), .1, .05)
            self.assertNotInside((5 * 8), 40.1, .2)
    unittest.main( )
```

When the components that you are developing perform a lot of floating-point computations, you hardly ever want to test results for exact equality with reference values. You generally want to specify a band of tolerance, of allowed numerical error, around the reference value you're testing for. So, unittest.TestCase.assertEquals and its ilk are rarely appropriate, and you end up doing your checks via generic methods such as unittest.TestCase.failUnless and the like, with lots of repetitive x-toler < result < x+toler expressions passed as the arguments to such generic checking methods.

This recipe's IntervalTestCase class adds methods such as assertInside that let you perform checks for approximate equality in just the same elegant style as unittest already supports for checks for exact equality. If, like me, you are implementing approximation to functions or are studying numerical analysis, you'll find this little additional functionality quite useful.

See Also

Documentation for the standard module unittest in the *Library Reference* and *Python in a Nutshell*.

## CHAPTER 9

Processes, Threads, and Synchronization

9.0 Introduction

Credit: Greg Wilson, Third Bit

Thirty years ago, in his classic *The Mythical Man-Month: Essays on Software Engineering* (Addison-Wesley), Fred Brooks drew a distinction between accidental and intrinsic complexity. Languages such as English and C++, with their inconsistent rules, exceptions, and special cases, are examples of the former: they make communication and programming harder than they need to be. Concurrency, on the other hand, is a prime example of the latter. Most people have to struggle to keep one chain of events straight in their minds; keeping track of two, three, or a dozen, plus all of their possible interactions, is just plain hard.

Computer scientists began studying ways of running multiple processes safely and efficiently in a single physical address space in the mid-1960s. Since then, a rich theory has been developed in which assertions about the behavior of interacting processes can be formalized and proved, and entire languages devoted to concurrent and parallel programming have been created. *Foundations of Multithreaded, Parallel, and Distributed Programming*, by Gregory R. Andrews (Addison-Wesley), is not only an excellent introduction to this theory, but also contains a great deal of historical information tracing the development of major ideas.

Over the past 20 years, opportunity and necessity have conspired to make concurrency a part of programmers' everyday lives. The opportunity is for greater speed, which comes from the growing availability of multiprocessor machines. In the early 1980s, these were expensive curiosities; today, many programmers have dual-processor workstations on their desks and four-way or eight-way servers in the back room. If a calculation can be broken down into independent (or nearly independent) pieces, such machines can potentially solve them two, four, or eight times faster than their uniprocessor equivalents. While the potential gains from this approach are limited, it works well for problems as diverse as image processing, serving HTTP requests, and recompiling multiple source files.

The necessity for concurrent programming comes from GUIs and network applications. Graphical interfaces often need to appear to be doing several things at once, such as displaying images while scrolling ads across the bottom of the screen. While it is possible to do the necessary interleaving manually, it is much simpler to code each operation on its own and let the underlying operating system decide on a concrete order of operations. Similarly, network applications often have to listen on several sockets at once or send data on one channel while receiving data on another.

Broadly speaking, operating systems give programmers two kinds of concurrency. *Processes* run in separate logical address spaces that are protected from each other. Using concurrent processing for performance purposes, particularly in multiprocessor machines, is more attractive with *threads*, which execute simultaneously within the same program, in the same address space, without being protected from each other. The lack of mutual protection allows lower overhead and easier and faster communication, particularly because of the shared address space. Since all threads run code from the same program, no special security risks are caused by the lack of mutual protection, any more than the risks in a single-threaded program. Thus, concurrency used for performance purposes is most often focused on adding threads to a single program.

However, adding threads to a Python program to speed it up is often not a successful strategy. The reason is the Global Interpreter Lock (GIL), which protects Python's internal data structures. This lock *must* be held by a thread before the thread can safely access Python objects. Without the lock, even simple operations (such as incrementing an integer) could fail. Therefore, only the thread with the GIL can manipulate Python objects or call Python/C API functions.

To make life easier for programmers, the interpreter releases and reacquires the lock every 100 bytecode instructions (a value that can be changed using sys.setcheckinterval). The lock is also released and reacquired around I/O operations, such as reading or writing a file, so that other threads can run while the thread that requests the I/O is waiting for the I/O operation to complete. However, effective performance-boosting exploitation of multiple processors from multiple pure-Python threads of the same process is just not in the cards. Unless the CPU performance bottlenecks in your Python application are in C-coded extensions that release the GIL, you will not observe substantial performance increases by moving your multithreaded application to a multiprocessor machine.

However, threading is not just about performance on multiprocessor machines. A GUI can't know when the user will press a key or move the mouse, and an HTTP server can't know which datagram will arrive next. Handling each stream of events with a separate control thread is therefore often the simplest way to cope with this unpredictability, even on single-processor machines, and when high throughput is not an overriding concern. Of course, event-driven programming can often be used in these kinds of applications as well, and Python frameworks such as asyncore and

Twisted are proof that this approach can often deliver excellent performance with complexity that, while different from that inherent in multithreading, is not necessarily any more difficult to deal with.

The standard Python library allows programmers to approach multithreaded programming at two different levels. The core module, thread, is a thin wrapper around the basic primitives that any threading library must provide. Three of these primitives are used to create, identify, and end threads; others are used to create, test, acquire, and release simple mutual-exclusion locks (or binary semaphores). As the recipes in this section demonstrate, programmers should avoid using these primitives directly, and should instead use the tools included in the higher-level threading module, which is substantially more programmer-friendly and has similar performance characteristics.

Whether you use thread or threading, some underlying aspects of Python's threading model stay the same. The GIL, in particular, works just the same either way. The crucial advantage of the GIL is that it makes it much easier to code Python extensions in C: unless your C extension explicitly releases the GIL, you know thread switches won't happen until your C code calls back into Python code. This advantage can be really important when your extension makes available to Python some underlying C library that isn't thread-safe. If your C code *is* thread-safe, though, you can and should release the GIL around stretches of computational or I/O operations that can last for a substantial time without needing to make Python C API calls; when you do this, you make it possible for Python programs using your C extension to take advantage of more than one processor from multiple threads within the same process. Make sure you acquire the GIL again before calling any Python C API entry point, though!

Any time your code wants to access a data structure that is shared among threads, you may have to wonder whether a given operation is *atomic*, meaning that no thread switch can happen *during* the operation. In general, anything with multiple bytecodes is not atomic, since a thread switch *might* always happen between one bytecode and the next (you can use the standard library function dis.dis to disassemble Python code into bytecodes). Moreover, even a single bytecode is not atomic, if it can call back to arbitrary Python code (e.g., because that bytecode can end up executing a Python-coded special method). When in doubt, it is most prudent to assume that whatever is giving you doubts is *not* atomic: so, reduce to the bare minimum the data structures accessed by more than one thread (except for instances of Queue.Queue, a class that is specifically designed to be thread-safe!), and make sure you protect with locks any access to any such structures that remain.

Almost invariably, the proper idiom to use some lock is:

```
somelock.acquire( )
try:
    # operations needing the lock (keep to a minimum!)
```

```
finally:
    somelock.release( )
```

The try/finally construct ensures the lock will be released even if some exception happens in the code in the try clause. Accidentally failing to release a lock, due to some unforeseen exception, could soon make all of your application come to a grinding halt. Also, be careful acquiring more than one lock in sequence; if you really truly need to do such multiple acquisitions, make sure all possible paths through the code acquire the various locks in the *same* sequence. Otherwise, you're likely sooner or later to enter the disaster case in which two threads are each trying to acquire a lock held by the other—a situation known as *deadlock*, which does mean that your program is as good as dead.

The most important elements of the threading module are classes that represent threads and various high-level synchronization constructs. The Thread class represents a separate control thread; it can be told what to do by passing a callable object to its constructor, or, alternatively, by overriding its run method. One thread can start another by calling its start method, and wait for it to complete by calling join. Python also supports daemon threads, which do background processing until all of the nondaemon threads in the program exit and then shut themselves down automatically.

The synchronization constructs in the threading module include locks, reentrant locks (which a single thread can safely relock many times without deadlocking), *counting semaphores*, conditions, and events. Events can be used by one thread to signal others that something interesting has happened (e.g., that a new item has been added to a queue, or that it is now safe for the next thread to modify a shared data structure). The documentation that comes with Python, specifically the *Library Reference* manual, describes each of these classes in detail.

The relatively low number of recipes in this chapter, compared to some other chapters in this cookbook, reflects both Python's focus on programmer productivity (rather than absolute performance) and the degree to which other packages (such as httplib and wxPython) hide the unpleasant details of concurrency in important application areas. This relative scarcity also reflects many Python programmers' tendencies to look for the simplest way to solve any particular problem, which complex threading rarely is.

However, this chapter's brevity may also reflect the Python community's underappreciation of the potential of simple threading, when used appropriately, to simplify a programmer's life. The Queue module in particular supplies a delightfully self-contained (and yet extensible and customizable!) synchronization and cooperation structure that can provide all the interthread supervision services you need. Consider a typical program, which accepts requests from a GUI (or from the network). As a "result" of such requests, the program will often find itself faced with the prospect of having to perform a substantial chunk of work. That chunk might take so long to perform all at once that, unless some precautions are taken, the program would appear unresponsive to the GUI (or network).

In a purely event-driven architecture, it may take considerable effort on the programmer's part to slice up such a hefty work-chunk into slices of work thin enough that each slice can be performed in idle time, without ever giving the appearance of unresponsiveness. In cases such as this one, just a dash of multithreading can help considerably. The main thread pushes a work request describing the substantial chunk of background work onto a dedicated Queue instance, then goes back to its task of making the program's interface responsive at all times.

At the other end of the Queue, a pool of daemonic worker threads await, each ready to peel a work request off the Queue and run it straight through. This kind of overall architecture combines event-driven and multithreaded approaches in the overarching ideal of simplicity and is thus maximally Pythonic. You may need just a little bit more work if the result of a worker thread's efforts must be presented again to the main thread (via another Queue, of course), which is normally the case with GUIs. If you're willing to cheat just a little, and use polling for the mostly event-driven main thread to access the result Queue back from the daemonic worker threads. See recipe 11.9 "Combining GUIs and Asynchronous I/O with Threads," to get an idea of how simple that little bit of work can be.

9.1   Synchronizing All Methods in an Object

Credit: André Bjärb, Alex Martelli, Radovan Chytracek

Problem

You want to share an object among multiple threads, but, to avoid conflicts, you need to ensure that only one thread at a time is inside the object—possibly excepting some methods for which you want to hand-tune locking behavior.

Solution

Java offers such synchronization as a built-in feature, while in Python you have to program it explicitly by *wrapping* the object and its methods. Wrapping is so general and useful that it deserves to be factored out into general tools:

```
def wrap_callable(any_callable, before, after):
    ''' wrap any callable with before/after calls '''
    def _wrapped(*a, **kw):
        before( )
        try:
            return any_callable(*a, **kw)
        finally:
            after( )
    # In 2.4, only: _wrapped.__name__ = any_callable.__name__
    return _wrapped
```

```
import inspect
class GenericWrapper(object):
    ''' wrap all of an object's methods with before/after calls '''
    def __init__(self, obj, before, after, ignore=()):
        # we must set into __dict__ directly to bypass __setattr__; so,
        # we need to reproduce the name-mangling for double-underscores
        clasname = 'GenericWrapper'
        self.__dict__['_%s__methods' % clasname] = {}
        self.__dict__['_%s__obj' % clasname] = obj
        for name, method in inspect.getmembers(obj, inspect.ismethod):
            if name not in ignore and method not in ignore:
                self.__methods[name] = wrap_callable(method, before, after)
    def __getattr__(self, name):
        try:
            return self.__methods[name]
        except KeyError:
            return getattr(self.__obj, name)
    def __setattr__(self, name, value):
        setattr(self.__obj, name, value)
```

Using these simple but general tools, synchronization becomes easy:

```
class SynchronizedObject(GenericWrapper):
    ''' wrap an object and all of its methods with synchronization '''
    def __init__(self, obj, ignore=(), lock=None):
        if lock is None:
            import threading
            lock = threading.RLock()
        GenericWrapper.__init__(self, obj, lock.acquire, lock.release, ignore)
```

Discussion

As per usual Python practice, we can complete this module with a small self-test,
executed only when the module is run as main script. This snippet also serves to
show how the module's functionality can be used:

```
if __name__ == '__main__':
    import threading
    import time
    class Dummy(object):
        def foo(self):
            print 'hello from foo'
            time.sleep(1)
        def bar(self):
            print 'hello from bar'
        def baaz(self):
            print 'hello from baaz'
    tw = SynchronizedObject(Dummy(), ignore=['baaz'])
    threading.Thread(target=tw.foo).start()
    time.sleep(0.1)
    threading.Thread(target=tw.bar).start()
    time.sleep(0.1)
    threading.Thread(target=tw.baaz).start()
```

Thanks to the synchronization, the call to bar runs only when the call to foo has completed. However, because of the ignore= keyword argument, the call to baaz bypasses synchronization and thus completes earlier. So the output is:

```
hello from foo
hello from baaz
hello from bar
```

When you find yourself using the same single-lock locking code in almost every method of an object, use this recipe to refactor the locking away from the object's application-specific logic. The key effect you get by applying this recipe is to effectively replace each method with:

```
self.lock.acquire( )
try:
  # The "real" application code for the method
finally:
    self.lock.release( )
```

This code idiom is, of course, the right way to express locking: the try/finally statement ensures that the lock gets released in any circumstance, whether the application code terminates correctly or raises an exception. You'll note that factory wrap_ callable returns a closure, which is carefully coded in exactly this way!

To some extent, this recipe can also be handy when you want to postpone worrying about a class' locking behavior. However, if you intend to use this code for production purposes, you should understand all of it. In particular, this recipe does *not* wrap direct accesses (for getting or setting) to the object's attributes. If you want such direct accesses to respect the object's lock, you need to add the try/finally locking idiom to the wrapper's __getattr__ and __setattr__ special methods, around the calls these methods make to the getattr and setattr built-in functions, respectively. I normally don't find that depth of wrapping to be necessary in my applications. (The way I code, wrapping just the methods proves sufficient.)

If you're into custom metaclasses, you may be surprised that I do not offer a metaclass for these synchronization purposes. However, wrapping is a more dynamic and flexible approach—for example, an object can exist in both wrapped (synchronized) and unwrapped (raw) incarnations, and you can use the most appropriate one case by case. You pay for wrapping's flexibility with a little bit more runtime overhead at each method call, but compared to the large costs of acquiring and releasing locks I don't think this tiny extra overhead matters. Meanwhile, this recipe shows off, and effectively reuses, a wrapper-closure factory and a wrapper class that demonstrate how easy Python makes it to implement that favorite design pattern of Aspect-Oriented Programming's fans, the insertion of "before-and-after" calls around every call to an object's methods.

See Also

Documentation of the standard library modules threading and inspect in the *Library Reference* and *Python in a Nutshell*.

9.2 Terminating a Thread

Credit: Doug Fort

Problem

You must terminate a thread from the outside, but Python doesn't let one thread just brutally kill another, so you need to use a suitable controlled-termination idiom.

Solution

A frequently asked question is: How do I kill a thread? The answer is: You don't. Instead, you kindly ask it to go away. Each thread must periodically check whether it's been asked to go away and then comply (typically after some kind of cleanup). Here is an example:

```
import threading
class TestThread(threading.Thread):
    def __init__(self, name='TestThread'):
        """ constructor, setting initial variables """
        self._stopevent = threading.Event()
        self._sleepperiod = 1.0
        threading.Thread.__init__(self, name=name)
    def run(self):
        """ main control loop """
        print "%s starts" % (self.getName(),)
        count = 0
        while not self._stopevent.isSet():
            count += 1
            print "loop %d" % (count,)
            self._stopevent.wait(self._sleepperiod)
        print "%s ends" % (self.getName(),)
    def join(self, timeout=None):
        """ Stop the thread and wait for it to end. """
        self._stopevent.set()
        threading.Thread.join(self, timeout)
if __name__ == "__main__":
    testthread = TestThread()
    testthread.start()
    import time
    time.sleep(5.0)
    testthread.join()
```

Discussion

You often want to exert some control on a thread from the outside, but the ability to kill a thread is, well, overkill. Python doesn't give you this ability, and thus forces you to design your thread systems more carefully. This recipe is based on the idea of a thread whose main function uses a loop. Periodically, the loop checks if a threading.Event object has been set. If so, the thread terminates; otherwise, it waits for the object.

The TestThread class in this recipe also overrides threading.Thread's join method. Normally, join waits only for a certain thread to terminate (for up to a specified amount of time, if any) without doing anything to *cause* that termination. In this recipe, however, join is overridden to set the stop event object before delegating the rest of its operation to the normal (base class) join method. Therefore, in this recipe, the join call is guaranteed to terminate the target thread within a short amount of time.

You can use the recipe's central idea (a loop periodically checking a threading.Event to determine whether it must terminate) in several other, slightly different ways. The Event's wait method can let you pause the target thread. You can also expose the Event, letting controller code set it and then go on its merry way without bothering to join the thread, knowing the thread will terminate in a short amount of time. Once the event is exposed, you may choose to use the same event to request the termination of more than one thread—for example, all threads in a certain thread pool might stop when one event object they all share is set. The simplicity of this recipe provides the modest amount of control I need, with no headaches, so I haven't pursued the more sophisticated (and complicated) ideas.

Python also lets you terminate a thread in another way: by raising an exception in that thread. This "rougher" approach also has its limits: it cannot interrupt a blocking call to the operating system, and it could fail to work if the thread you want to terminate is executing a try clause whose except clauses are too broad. Despite its limits, this approach can still sometimes be useful, when you're essentially writing a debugger: that is, when you cannot count on the code executing in the target thread to be well written, but you can hope the code is not written in an utterly disastrous way. The normal way to make use of this functionality is by running the possibly-buggy code in the main thread, after spawning a separate monitoring thread to keep an eye on things. If the monitoring thread decides the time has come to terminate the code that is currently running in the main thread, the monitoring thread can call thread.interrupt_main, passing as the argument the desired exception class.

Once in a blue moon, the debugger you're writing cannot run the possibly-buggy code in the process' main thread, typically because that thread is required for other uses by some other framework you depend on, such as your GUI code. To support such remote eventualities, the Python interpreter has a function that can raise an exception in any thread, given the target thread's ID. However, this specialized functionality is intended for a tiny subset of that tiny subset of Python applications that are debuggers. To avoid tempting all other Python programmers (well over 99.9%) into misusing this approach for any other case of thread termination, the function is not directly callable from Python code: rather, the function is only exposed as a part of Python's C API. This special function's name is `PyThreadState_SetAsyncExc`, and the function's two arguments are the target thread's ID and the class of the desired exception. If you are writing a Python debugger with such peculiar needs, no doubt you already have, as part of your code, at least one C-coded Python extension module that supplies to your higher-level Python code other tidbits of peculiar, low-level functionality. Just add to your C code, a Python-callable function that in turn calls `PyThreadState_SetAsyncExc`, and your debugger will gain this peculiar but useful functionality.

See Also

Documentation of the standard library module threading in the *Library Reference* and *Python in a Nutshell*.

9.3 Using a Queue.Queue as a Priority Queue

Credit: Simo Salminen, Lee Harr, Mark Moraes, Chris Perkins, Greg Klanderman

Problem

You want to use a Queue.Queue instance, since it is the best way to communicate among threads. However, you need the additional functionality of being able to specify a priority value associated with each item on the queue, so that items with a lower (more urgent) priority value are fetched before others with a higher (less urgent) priority value.

Solution

Among its many advantages, Queue.Queue offers an elegant architecture that eases subclassing for purposes of specializing queueing behavior. Specifically, Queue.Queue exposes several methods specifically designed to be overridden in a subclass, to get specialized queueing behavior without worrying about synchronization issues.

We can exploit this elegant architecture and module heapq from the Python Standard Library to build the needed priority-queue functionality pretty easily. However, we also need to shadow and wrap Queue.Queue's put and get methods, to decorate each item with its priority and posting time upon put, and strip off these decorations upon get:

```
import Queue, heapq, time
class PriorityQueue(Queue.Queue):
    # Initialize the queue
    def _init(self, maxsize):
        self.maxsize = maxsize
```

```
        self.queue = [ ]
    # Return the number of items that are currently enqueued
    def _qsize(self):
        return len(self.queue)
    # Check whether the queue is empty
    def _empty(self):
        return not self.queue
    # Check whether the queue is full
    def _full(self):
        return self.maxsize > 0 and len(self.queue) >= self.maxsize
    # Put a new item in the queue
    def _put(self, item):
        heapq.heappush(self.queue, item)
    # Get an item from the queue
    def _get(self):
        return heapq.heappop(self.queue)
    # shadow and wrap Queue.Queue's own `put' to allow a 'priority' argument
    def put(self, item, priority=0, block=True, timeout=None):
        decorated_item = priority, time.time( ), item
        Queue.Queue.put(self, decorated_item, block, timeout)
    # shadow and wrap Queue.Queue's own `get' to strip auxiliary aspects
    def get(self, block=True, timeout=None):
        priority, time_posted, item = Queue.Queue.get(self, block, timeout)
        return item
```

Discussion

Given an instance q of this recipe's PriorityQueue class, you can call q.put(anitem) to enqueue an item with "normal" priority (here defined as 0), or q.put(anitem, prio) to enqueue an item with a specific priority prio. At the time q.get( ) gets called (presumably in another thread), items with the lowest priority will be returned first, bypassing items with higher priority. Negative priorities are lower than "normal", thus suitable for "urgent" items; positive priorities, higher than "normal", indicate items that may wait longer, since other items with "normal" priority will get fetched before them. Of course, if you're not comfortable with this conception of priorities, nothing stops you from altering this recipe's code accordingly: for example, by changing sign to the priority value when you build the decorated_item at the start of method put. If you do so, items posted with positive priority will become the urgent ones and items posted with negative priority will become the can-wait-longer ones.

Queue.Queue's architecture deserves study, admiration, and imitation. Not only is Queue.Queue, all on its own, the best way to architect communication among threads, but this same class is also designed to make it easy for you to subclass and specialize it with queueing disciplines different from its default FIFO (first-in, first-out), such as the priority-based queueing discipline implemented in this recipe. Specifically, Queue.Queue uses the wonderful Template Method Design Pattern (*http://www.aleax.it/Python/os03_template_dp.pdf*). This DP enables Queue.Queue itself to take care of the delicate problems connected with locking, while delegating the queueing discipline to specific methods _put, _get, and so on, which may be overridden by subclasses; such *hook methods* then get called in a context where synchronization issues are not a concern.

In this recipe, we also need to override Queue.Queue's put and get methods, because we need to add a priority optional argument to put's signature, decorate the item before we put it on the queue (so that the heapq module's mechanisms will produce the order we want—lowest priority first, and, among items posted with equal priority, FIFO ordering), and undecorate each decorated item that we get back from the queue to return the naked item. All of these auxiliary tweaks use nothing but local variables, however, so they introduce no synchronization worries whatsoever. Each thread gets its own stack; therefore, any code that uses nothing but local variables (and thus cannot possibly alter any state accessible from other threads, or access any state that other threads might alter) is inherently thread-safe.

See Also

Modules Queue and heapq of the Python Standard Library are documented in *Library Reference* and *Python in a Nutshell*; the Template Method Design Pattern is illustrated at *http://www.strakt.com/docs/os03_template_dp.pdf*; recipe 19.14 "Merging Sorted Sequences," and recipe 5.7 "Keeping a Sequence Ordered as Items Are Added," show other examples of coding and using priority queues.

9.4 Working with a Thread Pool

Credit: John Nielsen, Justin A

Problem

You want your main thread to be able to farm out processing tasks to a pool of worker threads.

Solution

The Queue.Queue type is the simplest and most effective way to coordinate a pool of worker threads. We could group all the needed data structures and functions into a class, but there's no real need to. So, here they are, shown as globals instead:

```
import threading, Queue, time, sys
# Globals (start with a capital letter)
Qin  = Queue.Queue( )
Qout = Queue.Queue( )
Qerr = Queue.Queue( )
Pool = [ ]
def report_error( ):
    ''' we "report" errors by adding error information to Qerr '''
    Qerr.put(sys.exc_info( )[:2])
def get_all_from_queue(Q):
    ''' generator to yield one after the others all items currently
```

```
            in the Queue Q, without any waiting
    '''
    try:
        while True:
            yield Q.get_nowait()
    except Queue.Empty:
        raise StopIteration
def do_work_from_queue():
    ''' the get-some-work, do-some-work main loop of worker threads '''
    while True:
        command, item = Qin.get()        # implicitly stops and waits
        if command == 'stop':
            break
        try:
            # simulated work functionality of a worker thread
            if command == 'process':
                result = 'new' + item
            else:
                raise ValueError, 'Unknown command %r' % command
        except:
            # unconditional except is right, since we report _all_ errors
            report_error()
        else:
            Qout.put(result)
def make_and_start_thread_pool(number_of_threads_in_pool=5, daemons=True):
    ''' make a pool of N worker threads, daemonize, and start all of them '''
    for i in range(number_of_threads_in_pool):
        new_thread = threading.Thread(target=do_work_from_queue)
        new_thread.setDaemon(daemons)
        Pool.append(new_thread)
        new_thread.start()
def request_work(data, command='process'):
    ''' work requests are posted as (command, data) pairs to Qin '''
    Qin.put((command, data))
def get_result():
    return Qout.get()       # implicitly stops and waits
def show_all_results():
    for result in get_all_from_queue(Qout):
        print 'Result:', result
def show_all_errors():
    for etyp, err in get_all_from_queue(Qerr):
        print 'Error:', etyp, err
def stop_and_free_thread_pool():
    # order is important: first, request all threads to stop...:
    for i in range(len(Pool)):
        request_work(None, 'stop')
    # ...then, wait for each of them to terminate:
    for existing_thread in Pool:
        existing_thread.join()
    # clean up the pool from now-unused thread objects
    del Pool[:]
```

Discussion

It is generally a mistake to architect a multithreading program on the premise of having it spawn arbitrarily high numbers of threads as needed. Most often, the best architecture for such a program is based on farming out work to a fixed and relatively small number of *worker threads*—an arrangement known as a *thread pool*. This recipe shows a very simple example of a thread pool, focusing on the use of Queue.Queue instances as the most useful and simplest way for inter-thread communication and synchronization.

In this recipe, worker threads run function do_work_from_queue, which has the right structure for a typical worker thread but does really minimal "processing" (just as an example). In this case, the worker thread computes a "result" by prepending the string 'new' to each arriving item (note that this implicitly assumes that arriving items are strings). In your applications, of course, you will have, in the equivalent of this do_work_from_queue function, more substantial processing, and quite possibly different kinds of processing depending on the value of the command parameter.

In addition to the worker threads in the pool, a multithreading program often has other specialized threads for various purposes, such as interfacing to various entities external to the program (a GUI, a database, a library that is not guaranteed to be thread-safe). In this recipe, such specialized threads are not shown. However, it does include at least a "main thread", which starts and stops the thread pool, determines the units of work to be farmed out, and eventually gathers all results and any errors that may have been reported.

In your applications, you may or may not want to start and stop the thread pool repeatedly. Most typically, you may start the pool as a part of your program's initialization, leave it running throughout, and stop it, if at all, only as a part of your program's final cleanup. If you set your worker threads as "daemons", as this recipe's function make_and_start_thread_pool sets them by default, it means that your program will not continue running when only worker threads are left. Rather, your program will terminate as soon as the main thread terminates. Again, this arrangement is a typically advisable architecture. At any rate, the recipe also provides a function stop_and_free_thread_pool, just in case you *do* want to terminate and clean up your thread pool at some point (and possibly later make and restart another one with another call to make_and_start_thread_pool).

An example use of the functionality in this recipe might be:

```
for i in ('_ba', '_be', '_bo'): request_work(i)
make_and_start_thread_pool()
stop_and_free_thread_pool()
show_all_results()
show_all_errors()
```

The output from this snippet should normally be:

```
Result: new_ba
Result: new_be
Result: new_bo
```

although it's *possible* (but quite unlikely) that two of the results might end up exchanged. (If ordering of results is important to you, be sure to add a progressive number to the work requests you post from the main thread, and report it back to the main thread as part of each result or error.)

Here is a case where an error occurs and gets reported:

```
for i in ('_ba', 7, '_bo'): request_work(i)
make_and_start_thread_pool( )
stop_and_free_thread_pool( )
show_all_results( )
show_all_errors( )
```

The output from this snippet should normally be (net of an extremely unlikely, but not impossible, exchange between the two "Result" lines):

```
Result: new_ba
Result: new_bo
Error: exceptions.TypeError cannot concatenate 'str' and 'int' objects
```

The worker thread that gets the item 7 reports a TypeError because it tries to concatenate the string 'new' with this item, which is an int—an invalid operation. Not to worry: we have the try/except statement in function do_work_from_queue exactly to catch any kind of error, and Queue Qerr and functions report_error and show_all_errors exactly to ensure that errors do not pass silently, unless explicitly silenced, which is a key point of Python's general approach to programming.

See Also

Library Reference docs on threading and Queue modules; *Python in a Nutshell* chapter on threads.

9.5 Executing a Function in Parallel on Multiple Argument Sets

Credit: Guy Argo

Problem

You want to execute a function simultaneously over multiple sets of arguments. (Presumably the function is "I/O bound", meaning it spends substantial time doing input/output operations; otherwise, simultaneous execution would be useless.)

Solution

Use one thread for each set of arguments. For good performance, it's best to limit our use of threads to a bounded pool:

```
import threading, time, Queue
class MultiThread(object):
    def __init__(self, function, argsVector, maxThreads=5, queue_results=False):
        self._function = function
        self._lock = threading.Lock()
        self._nextArgs = iter(argsVector).next
        self._threadPool = [ threading.Thread(target=self._doSome)
                             for i in range(maxThreads) ]
        if queue_results:
            self._queue = Queue.Queue()
        else:
            self._queue = None
    def _doSome(self):
        while True:
            self._lock.acquire()
            try:
                try:
                    args = self._nextArgs()
                except StopIteration:
                    break
            finally:
                self._lock.release()
            result = self._function(args)
            if self._queue is not None:
                self._queue.put((args, result))
    def get(self, *a, **kw):
        if self._queue is not None:
            return self._queue.get(*a, **kw)
        else:
            raise ValueError, 'Not queueing results'
    def start(self):
        for thread in self._threadPool:
            time.sleep(0)    # necessary to give other threads a chance to run
            thread.start()
    def join(self, timeout=None):
        for thread in self._threadPool:
            thread.join(timeout)
if __name__=="__main__":
    import random
    def recite_n_times_table(n):
        for i in range(2, 11):
            print "%d * %d = %d" % (n, i, n * i)
            time.sleep(0.3 + 0.3*random.random())
    mt = MultiThread(recite_n_times_table, range(2, 11))
    mt.start()
    mt.join()
    print "Well done kids!"
```

Discussion

This recipe's MultiThread class offers a simple way to execute a function in parallel, on many sets of arguments, using a bounded pool of threads. Optionally, you can ask for results of the calls to the function to be queued, so you can retrieve them, but by default the results are just thrown away.

The MultiThread class takes as its arguments a function, a sequence of argument tuples for said function, and optionally a boundary on the number of threads to use in its pool and an indicator that results should be queued. Beyond the constructor, it exposes three methods: start, to start all the threads in the pool and begin the parallel evaluation of the function over all argument tuples; join, to perform a join on all threads in the pool (meaning to wait for all the threads in the pool to have terminated); and get, to get queued results (if it was instantiated with the optional flag queue_results set to True, to ask for results to be queued). Internally, class MultiThread uses its private method doSome as the target callable for all threads in the pool. Each thread works on the next available tuple of arguments (supplied by the next method of an iterator on the iterable whose items are such tuples, with the call to next being guarded by the usual locking idiom), until all work has been completed.

As is usual in Python, the module can also be run as a free-standing main script, in which case it runs a simple demonstration and self-test. In this case, the demonstration simulates a class of schoolchildren reciting multiplication tables as fast as they can.

Real use cases for this recipe mostly involve functions that are I/O bound, meaning functions that spend substantial time performing I/O. If a function is "CPU bound", meaning the function spends its time using the CPU, you get better overall performance by performing the computations one after the other, rather than in parallel. In Python, this observation tends to hold even on machines that dedicate multiple CPUs to your program, because Python uses a GIL (Global Interpreter Lock), so that pure Python code from a single process does not run simultaneously on more than one CPU at a time.

Input/output operations release the GIL, and so can (and should) any C-coded Python extension that performs substantial computations without callbacks into Python. So, it *is* possible that parallel execution may speed up your program, but only if either I/O or a suitable C-coded extension is involved, rather than pure computationally intensive Python code. (Implementations of Python on different virtual machines, such as Jython, which runs on a JVM [Java Virtual Machine], or IronPython, which runs on the Microsoft .NET runtime, are of course not bound by these observations: these observations apply only to the widespread "classical Python", meaning CPython, implementation.)

See Also

Library Reference and *Python in a Nutshell* docs on modules threading and Queue.

9.6 Coordinating Threads by Simple Message Passing

Credit: Michael Hobbs

Problem

You want to write a multithreaded application, using, as the synchronization and communication primitive, a simple yet powerful message-passing paradigm.

Solution

The candygram module lets you use concurrent programming semantics that are essentially equivalent to those of the Erlang language. To use candygram, you start by defining appropriate classes, such as the following one, to model your threads' functionality:

```
import candygram as cg
class ExampleThread(object):
    """A thread-class with just a single counter value and a stop flag."""
    def __init__(self):
        """ Initialize the counter to 0, the running-flag to True. """
        self.val = 0
        self.running = True
    def increment(self):
        """ Increment the counter by one. """
        self.val += 1
    def sendVal(self, msg):
        """ Send current value of counter to requesting thread. """
        req = msg[0]
        req.send((cg.self(), self.val))
    def setStop(self):
        """ Set the running-flag to False. """
        self.running = False
    def run(self):
        """ The entry point of the thread. """
        # Register the handler functions for various messages:
        r = cg.Receiver()
        r.addHandler('increment', self.increment)
        r.addHandler((cg.Process, 'value'), self.sendVal, cg.Message)
        r.addHandler('stop', self.setStop)
        # Keep handling new messages until a stop has been requested
        while self.running:
            r.receive()
```

To start a thread running this code under candygram, use:

```
counter = cg.spawn(ExampleThread( ).run)
```

To handle the counter thread's responses, you need another Receiver object, with the proper handler registered:

```
response = cg.Receiver( )
response.addHandler((counter, int), lambda msg: msg[1], cg.Message)
```

And here is an example of how you might use these counter and response objects:

```
# Tell thread to increment twice
counter.send('increment')
counter.send('increment')
# Request the thread's current value, then print the thread's response
counter.send((cg.self( ), 'value'))
print response.receive( )
# Tell thread to increment one more time
counter.send('increment')
# Again, request the thread's current value, then print the thread's response
counter.send((cg.self( ), 'value'))
print response.receive( )
# Tell the thread to stop running
counter.send('stop')
```

Discussion

With the candygram module (*http://candygram.sourceforge.net*), Python developers can send and receive messages between threads using semantics nearly identical to those introduced in the Erlang language (*http://www.erlang.org*). Erlang is widely respected for its elegant built-in facilities for concurrent programming.

Erlang's approach is simple and yet powerful. To communicate with another thread, simply send a message to it. You do not need to worry about locks, semaphores, mutexes, and other such primitives, to share information among concurrent tasks. Developers of multitasking software mostly use message passing only to implement a producer/consumer model. When you combine message passing with the flexibility of a Receiver object, however, it becomes much more powerful. For example, by using timeouts and message patterns, a thread may easily handle its messages as a state machine, or as a priority queue.

For those who wish to become more familiar with Erlang, *http://www.erlang.org/download/erlang-book-part1.pdf* (*Concurrent Programming in Erlang*) provides a very complete introduction. In particular, the candygram module implements all of the functions described in Chapter 5 and sections 7.2, 7.3, and 7.5 of that book.

This recipe offers a very elementary demonstration of how messages are passed between threads using candygram. When you run this recipe as a script, the print statements will output the values 2 and then 3.

It's important to understand how the candygram.Receiver class works. The addHandler method requires at least two parameters: the first is a message pattern and the second is a handler function. The Receiver.receive method invokes a registered handler function, and returns that function's result, whenever it finds a message that matches the associated pattern. Any parameters optionally passed to addHandler beyond the first two get passed as parameters to the handler function when the Receiver calls it. If a parameter is the candygram.Message constant, then receive replaces that parameter with the matching message when it calls the handler function.

This recipe's code contains four different message patterns: 'increment', (cg.Process, 'value'), 'stop', and (counter, int). The 'increment' and 'stop' patterns are simple patterns that match any message that consists solely of the strings 'increment' and 'stop', respectively. The (cg.Process, 'value') pattern matches any message that is a tuple with two items, where the first item is isinstance of cg.Process and the second item is the string value. Lastly, the (counter, int) pattern matches any message that is a tuple with two items where the first item is the counter object and the second element is an integer.

You can find more information about the Candygram package at *http:// candygram.sourceforge.net*. At that URL, you can find all details on how to specify message patterns, how to set a timeout for the Receiver.receive method, and how to monitor the running status of spawned threads.

See Also

Concurrent Programming in Erlang at *http://www.erlang.org/download/erlang-book-part1.pdf*; the candygram home page at *http://candygram.sourceforge.net*.

9.7 Storing Per-Thread Information

Credit: John E. Barham, Sami Hangaslammi, Anthony Baxter

Problem

You need to allocate to each thread some storage that only that thread can use.

Solution

Thread-specific storage is a useful design pattern, and Python 2.3 did not yet support it directly. However, even in 2.3, we could code it up in terms of a dictionary protected by a lock. For once, it's slightly more general, and not significantly harder, to program to the lower-level thread module, rather than to the more commonly useful, higher-level threading module that Python offers on top of it:

```
_tss = {}
try:
```

```
    import thread
except ImportError:
    # We're running on a single-threaded platform (or, at least, the Python
    # interpreter has not been compiled to support threads), so we just return
    # the same dict for every call -- there's only one thread around anyway!
    def get_thread_storage( ):
        return _tss
else:
    # We do have threads; so, to work:
    _tss_lock = thread.allocate_lock( )
    def get_thread_storage( ):
        """ Return a thread-specific storage dictionary. """
        thread_id = thread.get_ident( )
        _tss_lock.acquire( )
        try:
            return _tss.set_default(thread_id, {})
        finally:
            _tss_lock.release( )
```

Python 2.4 offers a much simpler and faster implementation, of course, thanks to the new threading.local function:

```
try:
    import threading
except ImportError:
    import dummy_threading as threading
_tss = threading.local( )
def get_thread_storage( ):
    return _tss.__dict__
```

Discussion

The main benefit of multithreaded programs is that all of the threads can share global objects when they need to do so. Often, however, each thread also needs some storage of its own—for example, to store a network or database connection unique to itself. Indeed, each such externally oriented object is generally best kept under the control of a single thread, to avoid multiple possibilities of highly peculiar behavior, race conditions, and so on. The get_thread_storage function in this recipe solves this problem by implementing the "thread-specific storage" design pattern, and specifically by returning a thread-specific storage dictionary. The calling thread can then use the returned dictionary to store any kind of data that is private to the thread. This recipe is, in a sense, a generalization of the get_transaction function from ZODB, the object-oriented database underlying Zope.

One possible extension to this recipe is to add a delete_thread_storage function. Such a function would be useful, particularly if a way could be found to automate its being called upon thread termination. Python's threading architecture does not make this task particularly easy. You could spawn a watcher thread to do the deletion after a join with the calling thread, but that's a rather heavyweight approach. The recipe as presented, without deletion, is quite appropriate for the common and recommended architecture in which you have a pool of (typically daemonic) worker threads (perhaps some of them general workers, with others dedicated to interfacing to specific external resources) that are spawned at the start of the program and do not go away until the end of the whole process.

When multithreading is involved, implementation must always be particularly careful to detect and prevent race conditions, deadlocks, and other such conflicts. In this recipe, I have decided not to assume that a dictionary's set_default method is *atomic* (meaning that no thread switch can occur while set_default executes)—adding a key can potentially change the dictionary's whole structure, after all. If I was willing to make such an assumption, I could do away with the lock and vastly increase performance, but I suspect that such an assumption might make the code too fragile and dependent on specific versions of Python. (It seems to me that the assumption holds for Python 2.3, but, even if that is the case, I want my applications to survive subtle future changes to Python's internals.) Another risk is that, if a thread terminates and a new one starts, the new thread might end up with the same thread ID as the just-terminated one, and therefore accidentally share the "thread-specific storage" dictionary left behind by the just-terminated thread. This risk might be mitigated (though not eliminated) by providing the delete_thread_storage function mentioned in the previous paragraph. Again, this specific problem does not apply to me, given the kind of multithreading architecture that I use in my applications. If your architecture differs, you may want to modify this recipe's solution accordingly.

If the performance of this recipe's version is insufficient for your application's needs, due to excessive overhead in acquiring and releasing the lock, then, rather than just removing the lock at the risk of making your application fragile, you might consider an alternative:

```
_creating_threads = True
_tss_lock = thread.allocate_lock( )
_tss = { }
class TssSequencingError(RuntimeError): pass
def done_creating_threads( ):
    """ switch from thread-creation to no-more-threads-created state """
    global _creating_threads
    if not _creating_threads:
        raise TssSequencingError('done_creating_threads called twice')
    _creating_threads = False
def get_thread_storage( ):
    """ Return a thread-specific storage dictionary. """
    thread_id = thread.get_ident( )
    # fast approach if thread-creation phase is finished
    if not _creating_threads: return _tss[thread_id]
    # careful approach if we're still creating threads
    try:
        _tss_lock.acquire( )
        return _tss.setdefault(thread_id, { })
    finally:
        _tss_lock.release( )
```

This variant adds a boolean switch _creating_threads, initially True. As long as the switch is True, the variant uses a careful locking-based approach, quite similar to the one presented in this recipe's Solution. At some point in time, when all threads that will ever exist (or at least all that will ever require access to get_thread_storage) have been started, and each of them has obtained its thread-local storage dictionary, your application calls done_creating_threads. This sets _creating_threads to False, and every future call to get_thread_storage then takes a fast path where it simply indexes into global dictionary _tss—no more acquiring and releasing the lock, no more creating a thread's thread-local storage dictionary if it didn't yet exist.

As long as your application can determine a moment in which it can truthfully call done_creating_threads, the variant in this subsection should definitely afford a substantial increase in speed compared to this recipe's Solution. Note that it is particularly likely that you can use this variant if your application follows the popular and recommended architecture mentioned previously: a bounded set of daemonic, long-lived worker threads, all created early in your program. This is fortunate, because, if your application is performance-sensitive enough to worry about the locking overhead of this recipe's solution, then no doubt you will want to structure your application that way. The alternative approach of having many short-lived threads is generally quite damaging to performance.

If your application needs to run only under Python 2.4, you can get a much simpler, faster, and solid implementation by relying on the new threading.local function. threading.local returns a new object on which any thread can get and set arbitrary attributes, independently from whatever getting and setting other threads may be doing on the same object. This recipe, in the 2.4 variant, returns the per-thread __ dict__ of such an object, for uniformity with the 2.3 variant. This way, your applications can be made to run on both Python 2.3 and 2.4, using the best version in each case:

```
import sys
if sys.version >= '2.4':
    # insert 2.4 definition of get_local_storage here
else:
    # insert 2.3 definition of get_local_storage here
```

The 2.4 variant of this recipe also shows off the intended use of module dummy_ threading, which, like its sibling dummy_thread, is also available in Python 2.3. By conditionally using these dummy modules, which are available on all platforms, whether or not Python was compiled with thread support, you may sometimes, with due care, be able to write applications that can run on any platform, taking advantage of threading where it's available but running anyway even where threading is not available. In the 2.3 variant, we did not use the similar approach based on dummy_ thread, because the overhead would be too high to pay on nonthreaded platforms; in the 2.4 variant, overhead is pretty low anyway, so we went for the simplicity that dummy_threading affords.

See Also

For an exhaustive treatment of the design pattern that describes thread-specific storage (albeit aimed at C++ programmers), see Douglas Schmidt, Timothy Harrisson, Nat Pryce, *Thread-Specific Storage: An Object Behavioral Pattern for Efficiently Accessing per-Thread State* (*http://www.cs.wustl.edu/~schmidt/PDF/TSS-pattern.pdf*); the *Library Reference* documentation dummy_thread, dummy_threading, and Python 2.4's threading.local; ZODB at *http://zope.org/Wikis/ZODB/FrontPage*.

9.8 Multitasking Cooperatively Without Threads

Credit: Brian Bush, Troy Melhase, David Beach, Martin Miller

Problem

You have a task that seems suited to multithreading, but you don't want to incur the overhead that real thread-switching would impose.

Solution

Generators were designed to simplify iteration, but they're also quite suitable as a basis for cooperative multitasking, also known as *microthreading*:

```python
import signal
# credit: original idea was based on an article by David Mertz
# http://gnosis.cx/publish/programming/charming_python_b7.txt
# some example 'microthread' generators
def empty(name):
    """ This is an empty task for demonstration purposes. """
    while True:
        print "<empty process>", name
        yield None
def terminating(name, maxn):
    """ This is a counting task for demonstration purposes. """
    for i in xrange(maxn):
        print "Here %s, %s out of %s" % (name, i, maxn)
        yield None
    print "Done with %s, bailing out after %s times" % (name, maxn)
def delay(duration=0.8):
    """ Do nothing at all for 'duration' seconds. """
    import time
    while True:
        print "<sleep %d>" % duration
        time.sleep(duration)
        yield None
class GenericScheduler(object):
    def __init__(self, threads, stop_asap=False):
        signal.signal(signal.SIGINT, self.shutdownHandler)
```

```
                self.shutdownRequest = False
                self.threads = threads
                self.stop_asap = stop_asap
        def shutdownHandler(self, n, frame):
            """ Initiate a request to shutdown cleanly on SIGINT."""
            print "Request to shut down."
            self.shutdownRequest = True
        def schedule(self):
            def noop():
                while True: yield None
            n = len(self.threads)
            while True:
                for i, thread in enumerate(self.threads):
                    try: thread.next()
                    except StopIteration:
                        if self.stop_asap: return
                        n -= 1
                        if n==0: return
                        self.threads[i] = noop()
                    if self.shutdownRequest:
                        return
if __name__ == "__main__":
    s = GenericScheduler([ empty('boo'), delay(), empty('foo'),
                           terminating('fie', 5), delay(0.5),
                         ], stop_asap=True)
    s.schedule()
    s = GenericScheduler([ empty('boo'), delay(), empty('foo'),
                           terminating('fie', 5), delay(0.5),
                         ], stop_asap=False)
    s.schedule()
```

Discussion

Microthreading (or cooperative multitasking) is an important technique. If you want to pursue it in earnest for complex uses, you should definitely look up the possibilities of Christian Tismer's *Stackless*, a Python version specialized for microthreading, at *http://www.stackless.com/*. However, you can get a taste of cooperative multitasking without straying from Python's core, by making creative use of generators, as shown in this recipe.

A simple approach to cooperative multitasking, such as the one presented in this recipe, is *not* suitable when your tasks must perform long-running work, particularly I/O tasks that may involve blocking system calls. For such applications, look into real threading, or, as a strong alternative, look into the event-driven approach offered by module asyncore in the Python Standard Library (on a simple scale) and by package Twisted at *http://twistedmatrix.com/products/twisted* (on a grandiose scale). But if your application has modest I/O needs, and you can slice up any computation your tasks perform into short chunks, each of which you can end with a yield, this recipe may be just what you're looking for.

See Also

David Mertz's site, chock-full of idiosyncratic, fascinating ideas, is at *http://gnosis.cx/*; Christian Tismer's *Stackless Python*, the best way to do cooperative multitasking in Python (and much else besides), is at *http://www.stackless.com/*; Twisted Matrix, the best way to do event-driven (asynchronous) programming, is at *http://twistedmatrix.com/*.

9.9   Determining Whether Another Instance of a Script Is Already Running in Windows

Credit: Bill Bell

Problem

In a Windows environment, you want to ensure that only one instance of a script is running at any given time.

Solution

Many tricks can be used to avoid starting multiple copies of an application, but they're all quite fragile—except those based on a mutual-exclusion (mutex) kernel object, such as this one. Mark Hammond's precious PyWin32 package supplies all the needed hooks into the Windows APIs to let us exploit a mutex for this purpose:

```
from win32event import CreateMutex
from win32api import GetLastError
from winerror import ERROR_ALREADY_EXISTS
from sys import exit
handle = CreateMutex(None, 1, 'A unique mutex name')
if GetLastError( ) == ERROR_ALREADY_EXISTS:
    # Take appropriate action, as this is the second
    # instance of this script; for example:
    print 'Oh! dear, I exist already.'
    exit(1)
else:
    # This is the only instance of the script; let
    # it do its normal work.  For example:
    from time import sleep
    for i in range(10):
        print "I'm running",i
        sleep(1)
```

Discussion

The string `'A unique mutex name'` must be chosen to be unique to this script, and it must not be dynamically generated, because the string must have the same value for all potential simultaneous instances of the same script. A fresh, globally unique ID that you manually generate and insert at script-authoring time would be a good choice. According to the Windows documentation, the string can contain any characters except backslashes (\). On Windows platforms that implement Terminal Services, you can optionally prefix the string with Global\ or Local\, but such prefixes would make the string invalid for most versions of Windows, including NT, 95, 98, and ME.

The Win32 API call CreateMutex creates a Windows kernel object of the mutual-exclusion (mutex) kind and returns a handle to it. Note that we do *not* close this handle, because it needs to exist throughout the time this process is running. It's important to let the Windows kernel take care of removing the handle (and the object it indicates, if the handle being removed is the only handle to that kernel object) when our process terminates.

The only thing we really care about is the return code from the API call, which we obtain by calling the GetLastError API right after it. That code is ERROR_ALREADY_EXISTS if and only if the mutual-exclusion object we tried to create already exists (i.e., if another instance of this script is already running).

This approach is perfectly safe and not subject to race conditions and similar anomalies, even if two instances of the script are trying to start at the same time (a reasonably frequent occurrence, e.g., if the user erroneously double-clicks in an Active Desktop setting where a single click already starts the application). The Windows specifications guarantee that only one of the instances will create the mutex, while the other will be informed that the mutex already exists. Mutual exclusion is therefore guaranteed by the Windows kernel itself, and the recipe is as solid as the operating system.

See Also

Documentation for the Win32 API in PyWin32 (*http://starship.python.net/crew/ mhammond/win32/Downloads.html*) or ActivePython (*http://www.activestate.com/ ActivePython/*); Windows API documentation available from Microsoft (*http:// msdn.microsoft.com*); *Python Programming on Win32*, by Mark Hammond and Andy Robinson (O'Reilly).

9.10 Processing Windows Messages Using MsgWaitForMultipleObjects

Credit: Michael Robin

Problem

In a Win32 application, you need to process messages, but you also want to wait for kernel-level waitable objects, and coordinate several activities.

Solution

A Windows application's message loop, also known as its *message pump*, is at the heart of Windows. It's worth some effort to ensure that the heart beats properly and regularly:

```python
import win32event
import pythoncom
TIMEOUT = 200 # ms
StopEvent = win32event.CreateEvent(None, 0, 0, None)
OtherEvent = win32event.CreateEvent(None, 0, 0, None)
class myCoolApp(object):
    def OnQuit(self):
        # assume 'areYouSure' is a global function that makes a final
        # check via a message box, a fancy dialog, or whatever else!
        if areYouSure():
            win32event.SetEvent(StopEvent) # Exit msg pump
def _MessagePump():
    waitables = StopEvent, OtherEvent
    while True:
        rc = win32event.MsgWaitForMultipleObjects(
            waitables,
            ,        # Wait for all = false, so it waits for any one
            TIMEOUT, # (or win32event.INFINITE)
            win32event.QS_ALLEVENTS) # Accept all kinds of events
        # You can call a function here, if it doesn't take too long. It will
        # be executed at least every TIMEOUT ms -- possibly a lot more often,
        # depending on the number of Windows messages received.
        if rc == win32event.WAIT_OBJECT_0:
            # Our first event listed, the StopEvent, was triggered, so
            # we must exit, terminating the message pump
            break
        elif rc == win32event.WAIT_OBJECT_0+1:
            # Our second event listed, "OtherEvent", was set. Do
            # whatever needs to be done -- you can wait on as many
            # kernel-waitable objects as needed (events, locks,
            # processes, threads, notifications, and so on).
            pass
        elif rc == win32event.WAIT_OBJECT_0+len(waitables):
            # A windows message is waiting - take care of it. (Don't
            # ask me why a WAIT_OBJECT_MSG isn't defined <
            # WAIT_OBJECT_0...!).
            # This message-serving MUST be done for COM, DDE, and other
            # Windows-y things to work properly!
            if pythoncom.PumpWaitingMessages():
                break # we received a wm_quit message
        elif rc == win32event.WAIT_TIMEOUT:
            # Our timeout has elapsed.
            # Do some work here (e.g, poll something you can't thread)
            # or just feel good to be alive.
            pass
        else:
            raise RuntimeError("unexpected win32wait return value")
```

Discussion

Most Win32 applications must process messages, but you often want to wait on kernel waitables and coordinate a lot of things going on at the same time. A good message pump structure is the key to this, and this recipe exemplifies a reasonably simple but pretty effective one.

With the message pump shown in this recipe, messages and other events get dispatched as soon as they are posted, and a timeout allows you to poll other components. You may need to poll if the proper calls or event objects are not exposed in your Win32 event loop, as many components insist on running only on the application's main thread and cannot run on spawned (secondary) threads.

You can add many other refinements, just as you can to any other Win32 message-pump approach. Python lets you do this with as much precision as C does, thanks to Mark Hammond's PyWin32 package (which used to be known as win32all). However, the relatively simple message pump presented in this recipe is already a big step up from the typical naive application that can either serve its message loop or wait on kernel waitables, but not both.

The key to this recipe is the Windows API call MsgWaitForMultipleObjects, which takes several parameters. The first is a tuple of kernel objects you want to wait for. The second parameter is a flag that is normally 0. The value 1 indicates that you should wait until *all* the kernel objects in the first parameter are signaled, but my experience suggests that you almost invariably want to stop waiting when any *one* of these objects is signaled, so this parameter will almost always be 0. The third is a flag that specifies which Windows messages you want to interrupt the wait; always pass win32event.QS_ALLEVENTS here, to make sure any Windows message interrupts the wait. The fourth parameter is a timeout period (in milliseconds), or win32event.INFINITE if you are sure you do not need to do any periodic polling.

This function is a polling loop and, sure enough, it loops (with a while True, which is terminated only by a break within it). At each leg of the loop, it calls the API that waits for multiple objects. When that API stops waiting, it returns a code that explains why it stopped waiting. A value between win32event.WAIT_OBJECT_0 and win32event.WAIT_OBJECT_0+N-1 (where N is the number of waitable kernel objects in the tuple you passed as the first parameter), inclusive, means that the wait finished because an object was signaled (being signaled means different things for each kind of waitable kernel object). The return code's difference from win32event.WAIT_OBJECT_0 is the index of the relevant object in the tuple.

A return value of win32event.WAIT_OBJECT_0+N means that the wait finished because a message was pending, and in this case, our recipe processes all pending Windows messages via a call to pythoncom.PumpWaitingMessages. (That function, in turn, returns a true result if a WM_QUIT message was received, so in this case, we break out of the whole while loop.) A code of win32event.WAIT_TIMEOUT means the wait finished because of a timeout, so we can do our polling there. In this case, no message is waiting, and none of our kernel objects of interest were signaled.

Basically, the way to tune this recipe for yourself is by using the right kernel objects as *waitables* (with an appropriate response to each) and by doing whatever you need to do periodically in the polling case. While this means you must have some detailed understanding of Win32, of course, it's still quite a bit easier than designing your own special-purpose, message-loop function from scratch.

I suspect that a purist would find some way or other to wrap all of this message pumping into a neat module, letting each application customize its use of the module by passing in a list of waitables, some dictionary to map different waitables to chunks of code to execute, and a partridge in a pear tree. Go ahead, turn it all into a custom metaclass if you wish, see if I care. For once, though, I think the right approach to reusing this code is to copy it into your application's source directories, and use your trusty *text editor* (gasp!) to tailor the message pump to your application's exact needs.

See Also

Documentation for the Win32 API in `PyWin32` (*http://starship.python.net/crew/mhammond/win32/Downloads.html*) or ActivePython (*http://www.activestate.com/ActivePython/*); Windows API documentation available from Microsoft (*http://msdn.microsoft.com*); Mark Hammond and Andy Robinson, *Python Programming on Win32* (O'Reilly).

9.11 Driving an External Process with popen

Credit: Sébastien Keim, Tino Lange, Noah Spurrier

Problem

You want to drive an external process that accepts commands from its standard input, and you don't care about the responses (if any) that the external process may emit on its standard output.

Solution

If you need to drive only the other process' input and don't care about its output, the simple `os.popen` function is enough. For example, here is a way to do animated graphics by driving the free program gnuplot via `os.popen`:

```
import os
f = os.popen('gnuplot', 'w')
print >>f, "set yrange[-300:+300]"
for n in range(300):
    print >>f, "plot %i*cos(x)+%i*log(x+10)" % (n, 150-n)
```

```
    f.flush()
  f.close()
```

Discussion

When you want to use Python as a glue language, sometimes (in particularly easy cases) the simple function popen (from the standard library module os) may be all you need. Specifically, os.popen may suffice when you need to drive an external program that accepts commands on its standard input, as long as you can ignore any response that the program might be making on its standard output (and also error messages that the program might be sending to its standard error). A good example is given by the free plotting program gnuplot. (os.popen may also suffice when you need to obtain the output from a program that does not need to read its standard input.)

The statement f = os.popen('gnuplot', 'w') creates a file-like object connected to the standard input of the program it launches, namely 'gnuplot'. (To try this recipe, you have to have gnuplot installed on your PATH, but since gnuplot is freely available and widely ported software, that should not be a problem!) Whatever we write to f, the external process receives on its standard input, just as would happen if we used that same program interactively. For more of the same, check out *http://sourceforge.net/projects/gnuplot-py/*: it's a rich and interesting Python interface to gnuplot implemented entirely on the basis of the simple idea shown in this recipe!

When your needs are more sophisticated than os.popen can accommodate, you may want to look at os.popen2 and other such higher-numbered functions in module os, or, in Python 2.4, the new standard library module subprocess. However, in many cases, you're likely to be disappointed: as soon as you get beyond the basics, driving (from your own programs) other external programs that were designed to be used interactively can become more than a little frustrating. Fortunately, a solution is at hand: it's pexpect, a third-party Python module that you can find at *http://pexpect.sourceforge.net/*. pexpect is designed specifically for the task of driving other programs, and it lets you check on the other program's responses as well as sending commands to the other program's standard input. Still, while pexpect will most definitely offer you all the power you need, os.popen will probably suffice when you don't need anything fancy!

See Also

Module os (specifically os.popen) in the *Library Reference* and *Python in a Nutshell*; gnuplot is at *http://www.gnuplot.info/*; gnuplot.py is at *http://sourceforge.net/projects/gnuplot-py/*; pexpect is at *http://pexpect.sourceforge.net/*.

9.12 Capturing the Output and Error Streams from a Unix Shell Command

Credit: Brent Burley, Bradey Honsinger, Tobias Polzin, Jonathan Cano, Padraig Brady

Problem

You need to run an external process in a Unix-like environment and capture both the output and error streams from that external process.

Solution

The popen2 module lets you capture both streams, but you also need help from module fcntl, to make the streams nonblocking and thus avoid deadlocks, and from module select, to orchestrate the action:

```
import os, popen2, fcntl, select
def makeNonBlocking(fd):
    fl = fcntl.fcntl(fd, fcntl.F_GETFL)
    try:
        fcntl.fcntl(fd, fcntl.F_SETFL, fl | os.O_NDELAY)
    except AttributeError:
        fcntl.fcntl(fd, fcntl.F_SETFL, fl | os.FNDELAY)
def getCommandOutput(command):
    child = popen2.Popen3(command, 1) # Capture stdout and stderr from command
    child.tochild.close()             # don't need to write to child's stdin
    outfile = child.fromchild
    outfd = outfile.fileno()
    errfile = child.childerr
    errfd = errfile.fileno()
    makeNonBlocking(outfd)            # Don't deadlock! Make fd's nonblocking.
    makeNonBlocking(errfd)
    outdata, errdata = [], []
    outeof = erreof = False
    while True:
        to_check = [outfd]*(not outeof) + [errfd]*(not erreof)
        ready = select.select(to_check, [], []) # Wait for input
        if outfd in ready[0]:
            outchunk = outfile.read()
            if outchunk == '':
                outeof = True
            else:
                outdata.append(outchunk)
        if errfd in ready[0]:
            errchunk = errfile.read()
            if errchunk == '':
                erreof = True
            else:
                errdata.append(errchunk)
        if outeof and erreof:
            break
```

```
            select.select([ ],[ ],[ ],.1) # Allow a little time for buffers to fill
        err = child.wait( )
        if err != 0:
            raise RuntimeError, '%r failed with exit code %d\n%s' % (
                command, err, ''.join(errdata))
        return ''.join(outdata)
    def getCommandOutput2(command):
        child = os.popen(command)
        data = child.read( )
        err = child.close( )
        if err:
            raise RuntimeError, '%r failed with exit code %d' % (command, err)
```

Discussion

This recipe shows how to execute a Unix shell command and capture the output and error streams in Python. By contrast, os.system sends both streams directly to the terminal. The function getCommandOutput presented in this recipe executes a command and returns the command's output. If the command fails, getCommandOutput raises an exception, using the text captured from the command's stderr as part of the exception's arguments.

Most of the complexity of this code is due to the difficulty of capturing both the output and error streams of the child process independently and at the same time. Normal (blocking) read calls may deadlock if the child is trying to write to one stream, and the parent is waiting for data on the other stream; so, the streams must be set to nonblocking, and select must be used to wait for data on either of the streams.

Note that the second select call is included just to add a 0.1-second sleep after each read. Counter intuitively, this allows the code to run much faster, since it gives the child time to put more data in the buffer. Without it, the parent may try to read only a few bytes at a time, which can be very expensive. Calling time.sleep(0.1) should be exactly equivalent, but since I was already, necessarily, calling select.select elsewhere in the recipe's code, I decided not to also import module time needlessly.

If you want to capture only the output and don't mind the error stream going to the terminal, you can use the much simpler code presented in getCommandOutput2. If you want to suppress the error stream altogether, that's easy, too—just append 2>/dev/null to the command. For example:

```
    listing = getCommandOutput2('ls -1 2>/dev/null')
```

Another possibility is given by the os.popen4 function, which combines the output and error streams of the child process. However, in that case the streams are combined in a potentially messy way, depending on how they are buffered in the child process, so this recipe can help.

In Python 2.4, you can use class Popen, instead of popen2.Popen3, from the new standard library module subprocess. However, the issues highlighted in this recipe (namely, the need to use modules fcntl and select to make files nonblocking and

---

coordinate the loop that interacts with the child process) aren't really affected by whether you use popen2 or subprocess.

This recipe *does*, as advertised, require a rather Unix-like underlying platform. Cygwin, which does a generally great job of emulating Unix on top of Windows, is not sufficient; for example, it offers no way to set files to nonblocking mode, nor to select on general files. (Under Windows, you are allowed to select only on sockets, not on other files.) If you must run on such problematic, non-Unix platforms, you may prefer a very different approach, based on using temporary files:

```
import os, tempfile
def getCommandOutput(command):
    outfile = tempfile.mktemp( )
    errfile = tempfile.mktemp( )
    cmd = "( %s ) > %s 2> %s" % (command, outfile, errfile)
    err = os.system(cmd) >> 8
    try:
        if err != 0:
            raise RuntimeError, '%r failed with exit code %d\n%s' % (
                command, err, file(errfile).read( ))
        return file(outfile).read( )
    finally:
        os.remove(outfile)
        os.remove(errfile)
```

See Also

Documentation of the standard library modules os, popen2, fcntl, select, and tempfile in the *Library Reference* and *Python in a Nutshell*; (Python 2.4 only) module subprocess in the *Library Reference*.

9.13 Forking a Daemon Process on Unix

Credit: Jürgen Hermann, Andy Gimblett, Josh Hoyt, Noah Spurrier, Jonathan Bartlett, Greg Stein

Problem

You need to fork a daemon process on a Unix or Unix-like system, which, in turn, requires a certain precise sequence of system calls.

Solution

Unix daemon processes must detach from their controlling terminal and process group. Doing so is not hard, but it does require some care, so it's worth writing a *daemonize.py* module once and for all:

```
import sys, os
''' Module to fork the current process as a daemon.
    NOTE: don't do any of this if your daemon gets started by inetd!  inetd
```

```
          does all you need, including redirecting standard file descriptors;
          the chdir( ) and umask( ) steps are the only ones you may still want.
'''
def daemonize (stdin='/dev/null', stdout='/dev/null', stderr='/dev/null'):
    ''' Fork the current process as a daemon, redirecting standard file
        descriptors (by default, redirects them to /dev/null).
    '''
    # Perform first fork.
    try:
        pid = os.fork( )
        if pid > 0:
            sys.exit(0) # Exit first parent.
    except OSError, e:
        sys.stderr.write("fork #1 failed: (%d) %s\n" % (e.errno, e.strerror))
        sys.exit(1)
    # Decouple from parent environment.
    os.chdir("/")
    os.umask(0)
    os.setsid( )
    # Perform second fork.
    try:
        pid = os.fork( )
        if pid > 0:
            sys.exit(0) # Exit second parent.
    except OSError, e:
        sys.stderr.write("fork #2 failed: (%d) %s\n" % (e.errno, e.strerror))
        sys.exit(1)
    # The process is now daemonized, redirect standard file descriptors.
    for f in sys.stdout, sys.stderr: f.flush( )
    si = file(stdin, 'r')
    so = file(stdout, 'a+')
    se = file(stderr, 'a+', 0)
    os.dup2(si.fileno( ), sys.stdin.fileno( ))
    os.dup2(so.fileno( ), sys.stdout.fileno( ))
    os.dup2(se.fileno( ), sys.stderr.fileno( ))
def _example_main ( ):
    ''' Example main function: print a count & timestamp each second '''
    import time
    sys.stdout.write('Daemon started with pid %d\n' % os.getpid( ) )
    sys.stdout.write('Daemon stdout output\n')
    sys.stderr.write('Daemon stderr output\n')
    c = 0
    while True:
        sys.stdout.write('%d: %s\n' % (c, time.ctime( )))
        sys.stdout.flush( )
        c = c + 1
        time.sleep(1)
if __name__ == "__main__":
    daemonize('/dev/null','/tmp/daemon.log','/tmp/daemon.log')
    _example_main( )
```

Discussion

Forking a daemon on Unix requires a certain specific sequence of system calls, which is explained in W. Richard Stevens' seminal book, *Advanced Programming in the Unix Environment* (Addison-Wesley). We need to fork twice, terminating each parent process and letting only the grandchild of the original process run the daemon's code. This allows us to decouple the daemon process from the calling terminal, so that the daemon process can keep running (typically as a server process without further user interaction, like a web server) even after the calling terminal is closed. The only visible effect of doing so is that when your script runs this module's daemonize function, you get your shell prompt back immediately.

For all of the details about how and why this works in Unix and Unix-like systems, see Stevens' wonderful book. Another important source of information on both practical and theoretical issues about "daemon forking" can be found as part of the Unix Programming FAQ, at *http://www.erlenstar.demon.co.uk/unix/faq_2.html#SEC16*.

To summarize: the first fork lets the shell return, and also lets you do a setsid (to remove you from your controlling terminal, so you can't accidentally be sent a signal). However, setsid makes this process a "session leader", which means that if the process ever opens any terminal, it will become the process' controlling terminal. We do not want a daemon to have *any* controlling terminal, which is why we fork again. After the second fork, the process is no longer a "session leader", so it can open any file (including a terminal) without thereby accidentally reacquiring a controlling terminal.

Both Stevens and the Unix Programming FAQ provide examples in the C programming language, but since the Python Standard Library exposes a full POSIX interface, you can also do it all in Python. Typical C code for a daemon fork translates almost literally to Python; the only difference you have to care about—a minor detail—is that Python's os.fork does not return -1 on errors, but rather throws an OSError exception. Therefore, rather than testing for a less-than-zero return code from fork, as we would in C, we run the fork in the try clause of a try/except statement, so that we can catch the exception, should it happen, and print appropriate diagnostics to standard error.

See Also

Documentation of the standard library module os in the *Library Reference* and *Python in a Nutshell*; Unix manpages for the fork, umask, and setsid system calls; W. Richard Stevens, *Advanced Programming in the Unix Environment* (Addison-Wesley); also, the Unix Programming FAQ on daemon forking, at *http://www.erlenstar.demon.co.uk/unix/faq_2.html#SEC16*.

## CHAPTER 10

System Administration

10.0 Introduction

Credit: Donn Cave, University of Washington

In this chapter, we consider a class of programmer—the humble system administrator—in contrast to other chapters' focus on functional domains. As a programmer, the system administrator faces most of the same problems that other programmers face and should find the rest of this book of at least equal interest.

Python's advantages in the system administration domain are also quite familiar to other Python programmers, but Python's competition is different. On Unix platforms, at any rate, the landscape is dominated by a handful of lightweight languages such as the Bourne shell and awk that aren't exactly made obsolete by Python. These little languages can often support a simpler, clearer, and more concise solution than Python, particularly for commands that you're typing interactively at the shell command prompt. But Python can do things these languages can't, and it's often more robust when dealing with issues such as unusually large data inputs. Another notable competitor, especially on Unix systems, is Perl (which isn't really a little language at all), with just about the same overall power as Python, and usable for typing a few commands interactively at the shell's command prompt. Python's strength here is readability and maintainability: when you dust off a script you wrote in a hurry eight months ago, because you need to make some changes to it, you don't spend an hour to figure out whatever exactly you had in mind when you wrote this or that subtle trick. You just don't use any tricks at all, subtle or gross, so that your Python scrips work just fine *and* you don't burn your time, months later, striving to reverse-engineer them for understanding.

One item that stands out in this chapter's solutions is the *wrapper*: the alternative, programmed interface to a software system. On Unix (including, these days, Mac OS X), this is usually a fairly prosaic matter of diversion and analysis of text I/O. Life is easy when the programs you're dealing with are able to just give clean textual output, without requiring complex interaction (see Eric Raymond, *The Art of Unix Programming*, *http://www.faqs.org/docs/artu/*, for an informative overview of how programs *should* be architected to make your life easy). However, even when you have to wrap a program that's necessarily interactive, all is far from lost. Python has very good support in this area, thanks, first of all, to the fact that it places C-level pseudo-TTY functions at your disposal (see the pty module of the Python Standard Library). The pseudo-TTY device is like a bidirectional pipe with TTY driver support, so it's essential for things such as password prompts that insist on a TTY. Because it appears to be a TTY, applications writing to a pseudo-TTY normally use line buffering, instead of the block buffering that gives problems with pipes. Pipes are more portable and less trouble to work with, but they don't work for interfacing to every application. Excellent third-party extensions exist that wrap pty into higher-level layers for ease of use, most notably Pexpect, *http://pexpect.sourceforge.net/*.

On Windows, the situation often is not as prosaic as on Unix-like platforms, since the information you need to do your system administration job may be somewhere in the registry, may be available via some Windows APIs, and/or may be available via COM. The standard Python library _winreg module, Mark Hammond's PyWin32 package, and Thomas Heller's ctypes, taken together, give the Windows administrator reasonably easy access to all of these sources, and you'll see more Windows administration recipes here than you will ones for Unix. The competition for Python as a system administration language on Windows is feeble compared to that on Unix, which is yet another reason for the platform's prominence here. The PyWin32 extensions are available for download at *http://sourceforge.net/projects/pywin32/*. PyWin32 also comes with ActiveState's ActivePython distribution of Python (*http://www.activestate.com/ActivePython/*). To use this rich and extremely useful package most effectively, you also need Mark Hammond and Andy Robinson, *Python Programming on Win32* (O'Reilly). ctypes is available for download at *http://sourceforge.net/projects/ctypes*.

While it may sometimes be difficult to see what brought all the recipes together in this chapter, it isn't difficult to see why system administrators deserve their own chapter: Python would be nowhere without them! Who else, back when Python was still an obscure, fledgling language, could bring it into an organization and almost covertly infiltrate it into the working environment? If it weren't for the offices of these benevolent and pragmatic anarchists, Python might well have languished in obscurity despite its merits.

10.1 Generating Random Passwords

Credit: Devin Leung

Problem

You need to create new passwords randomly—for example, to assign them automatically to new user accounts.

Solution

One of the chores of system administration is installing new user accounts. Assigning a different, totally random password to each new user is a good idea. Save the following code as *makepass.py*:

```
from random import choice
import string
def GenPasswd(length=8, chars=string.letters+string.digits):
    return ''.join([ choice(chars) for i in range(length) ])
```

Discussion

This recipe is useful when you are creating new user accounts and assigning each of them a different, totally random password. For example, you can print six passwords of length 12:

```
>>> import makepass
>>> for i in range(6):
...     print makepass.GenPasswd(12)
...
uiZWGSJLWjOI
FVrychdGsAaT
CGCXZAFGjsYI
TPpQwpWjQEIi
HMBwIvRMoIvh
```

Of course, such totally random passwords, while providing an excellent theoretical basis for security, are impossibly hard to remember for most users. If you require users to stick with their assigned passwords, many users will probably write them down. The best you can hope for is that new users will set their own passwords at their first login, assuming, of course, that the system you're administering lets each user change his own password. (Most operating systems do, but you might be assigning passwords for other kinds of services that unfortunately often lack such facilities.)

A password that is written down anywhere is a serious security risk: pieces of paper get lost, misplaced, and peeked at. From a pragmatic point of view, you might be better off assigning passwords that are not totally random; users are more likely to remember them and less likely to write them down (see recipe 394 "Generating Easily Remembered Somewhat-Random Passwords"). This practice may violate the theory of password security, but, as all practicing system administrators know, pragmatism trumps theory.

See Also

Recipe 10.2 "Generating Easily Remembered Somewhat-Random Passwords"; documentation of the standard library module random in the *Library Reference* and *Python in a Nutshell*.

10.2 Generating Easily Remembered Somewhat-Random Passwords

Credit: Luther Blissett

Problem

You need to create new passwords randomly—for example, to assign them automatically to new user accounts. You want the passwords to be somewhat feasible to remember for typical users, so they won't be written down.

Solution

We can use a pastiche approach for this, mimicking letter *n*-grams in actual English words. A grander way to look at the same approach is to call it a Markov Chain Simulation of English:

```python
import random, string
class password(object):
    # Any substantial file of English words will do just as well: we
    # just need self.data to be a big string, the text we'll pastiche
    data = open("/usr/share/dict/words").read().lower()
    def renew(self, n, maxmem=3):
        ''' accumulate into self.chars `n` random characters, with a
            maximum-memory "history" of `maxmem` characters back. '''
        self.chars = [ ]
        for i in range(n):
            # Randomly "rotate" self.data
            randspot = random.randrange(len(self.data))
            self.data = self.data[randspot:] + self.data[:randspot]
            # Get the n-gram
            where = -1
            # start by trying to locate the last maxmem characters in
            # self.chars.  If i<maxmem, we actually only get the last
            # i, i.e., all of self.chars -- but that's OK: slicing
            # is quite tolerant in this way, and it fits the algorithm
            locate = ''.join(self.chars[-maxmem:])
            while where<0 and locate:
                # Locate the n-gram in the data
                where = self.data.find(locate)
```

```
                # Back off to a shorter n-gram if necessary
                locate = locate[1:]
            # if where==-1 and locate='', we just pick self.data[0] --
            # it's a random item within self.data, tx to the rotation
            c = self.data[where+len(locate)+1]
            # we only want lowercase letters, so, if we picked another
            # kind of character, we just choose a random letter instead
            if not c.islower(): c = random.choice(string.lowercase)
            # and finally we record the character into self.chars
            self.chars.append(c)
    def __str__(self):
        return ''.join(self.chars)
if __name__ == '__main__':
    "Usage: pastiche [passwords [length [memory]]]"
    import sys
    if len(sys.argv)>1: dopass = int(sys.argv[1])
    else: dopass = 8
    if len(sys.argv)>2: length = int(sys.argv[2])
    else: length = 10
    if len(sys.argv)>3: memory = int(sys.argv[3])
    else: memory = 3
    onepass = password( )
    for i in range(dopass):
        onepass.renew(length, memory)
        print onepass
```

Discussion

This recipe is useful when creating new user accounts and assigning each user a different, random password: it uses passwords that a typical user will find it feasible to remember, hopefully so they won't get written down. See recipe 393 "Generating Random Passwords" if you prefer totally random passwords.

The recipe's idea is based on the good old pastiche concept. Each letter (always lowercase) in the password is chosen pseudo-randomly from data that is a collection of words in a natural language familiar to the users. This recipe uses the file that is */usr/ share/dict/words* supplied with Linux systems (on my machine, a file of over 45,000 words), but any large document in plain text will do just as well. The trick that makes the passwords sort of memorable, and not fully random, is that each letter is chosen based on the last few letters already picked for the password as it stands so far. Thus, letter transitions will tend to be "repetitive" according to patterns that are familiar to the user.

The code in the recipe takes some care to locate each time a random occurrence, in the text being pastiched, of the last maxmem characters picked so far. Since it's easy to find the *first* occurrence of a substring, the code "rotates" the text string randomly, to ensure that the first occurrence is a random one from the point of view of the original text. If the substring made up with the last maxmem characters picked is not found in the text, the code "backs down" to search for just the last maxmem-1, and so on, backing down until, worst case, it just picks the first character in the rotated text (which is a random character from the point of view of the original text).

A break in this Markov Chain process occurs when this picking procedure chooses a character that is not a lowercase letter, in which case, a random lowercase letter is chosen instead (any lowercase letter is picked with equal probability).

Here are a couple of typical sample runs of this *pastiche.py* password-generation script:

```
[situ@tioni cooker]$ python pastiche.py
yjackjaceh
ackjavagef
aldsstordb
dingtonous
stictlyoke
cvaiwandga
lidmanneck
olexnarinl
[situ@tioni cooker]$ python pastiche.py
ptiontingt
punchankin
cypresneyf
sennemedwa
iningrated
fancejacev
sroofcased
nryjackman
```

As you can see, some of these are definitely word-like, others less so, but for a typical human being, none are more problematic to remember than a sequence of even fewer totally random, uncorrelated letters. No doubt some theoretician will complain (justifiably, in a way) that they aren't as random as all that. Well, tough. My point is that they had better not be, if some poor fellow is going to have to remember them! You can compensate for this limitation by making them a bit longer. If said theoretician demonstrates how to compute the entropy per character of this method of password generation (versus the obvious 4.7 bits/character, the base-2 logarithm of 26, for passwords made up of totally random lowercase letters), now that would be a useful contribution indeed. Meanwhile, I'll keep generating passwords this way, rather than in a totally random way. If nothing else, it's the closest thing I've found to a useful application for the lovely pastiche concept.

The concept of passwords that are not totally random, but rather a bit more memorable, goes back a long way—at least to the 1960s and to works by Morrie Gasser and Daniel Edwards. A Federal Information Processing Standard (FIPS), FIPS 181, specifies in detail how "pronounceable" passwords are to be generated; see *http://www.itl.nist.gov/fipspubs/fip181.htm*.

See Also

Recipe 10.1 "Generating Random Passwords"; documentation of the standard library module random in the *Library Reference* and *Python in a Nutshell*.

10.3 Authenticating Users by Means of a POP Server

Credit: Magnus Lyckå

Problem

You are writing a Python application that must authenticate users. All of the users have accounts on some POP servers, and you'd like to reuse, for your own authentication, the user IDs and passwords that your users have on those servers.

Solution

To log into the application, a user must provide the server, user ID and password for his mail account. We try logging into that POP server with these credentials—if that attempt succeeds, then the user has authenticated successfully. (Of course, we *don't* peek into the user's mailbox!)

```
def popauth(popHost, user, passwd):
    """ Log in and log out, only to verify user identity.
        Raise exception in case of failure.
    """
    import poplib
    try:
        pop = poplib.POP3(popHost)
    except:
        raise RuntimeError("Could not establish connection "
                            "to %r for password check" % popHost)
    try:
        # Log in and perform a small sanity check
        pop.user(user)
        pop.pass_(passwd)
        length, size = pop.stat()
        assert type(length) == type(size) == int
        pop.quit()
    except:
        raise RuntimeError("Could not verify identity. \n"
                "User name %r or password incorrect." % user)
        pop.quit()
```

Discussion

To use this recipe, the application must store somewhere the list of known users and either the single POP server they all share, or the specific POP server on which each user authenticates—it need not be the *same* POP server for all users. Either a text file, or a simple table in any kind of database, will do just fine for this purpose.

This solution is neat, but it does have some weaknesses:

- Users must trust that any application implementing this authentication system won't abuse their email accounts.
- POP passwords are, alas!, sent in plain text over the Internet.
- We have to trust that the POP server security isn't compromised.
- Logging in might take a few seconds if the POP server is slow.
- Logging in won't work if the POP server is down.

However, to offset all of these potential drawbacks is the convenience of applications not having to store any passwords, nor forcing a poor overworked system administrator to administer password changes. It's also quite simple! In short, I wouldn't use this approach for a bank system, but I would have no qualms using it, for example, to give users rights to edit web pages at a somewhat restricted Wiki-Wiki, or similarly low-risk applications.

See Also

Documentation of the standard library module poplib in the *Library Reference* and *Python in a Nutshell*.

10.4 Calculating Apache Hits per IP Address

Credit: Mark Nenadov, Ivo Woltring

Problem

You need to examine a log file from Apache to count the number of hits recorded from each individual IP address that accessed it.

Solution

Many of the chores of administering a web server have to do with analyzing Apache logs, which Python makes easy:

```
def calculateApacheIpHits(logfile_pathname):
    ''' return a dict mapping IP addresses to hit counts '''
    ipHitListing = {}
    contents = open(logfile_pathname, "r")
    # go through each line of the logfile
    for line in contents:
        # split the string to isolate the IP address
        ip = line.split(" ", 1)[0]
        # Ensure length of the IP address is proper (see discussion)
        if 6 < len(ip) <= 15:
```

```
              # Increase by 1 if IP exists; else set hit count = 1
              ipHitListing[ip] = ipHitListing.get(ip, 0) + 1
       return ipHitListing
```

Discussion

This recipe supplies a function that returns a dictionary containing the hit counts for each individual IP address that has accessed your Apache web server, as recorded in an Apache log file. For example, a typical use would be:

```
HitsDictionary = calculateApacheIpHits(
                 "/usr/local/nusphere/apache/logs/access_log")
```

This function has many quite useful applications. For example, I often use it in my code to determine the number of hits that are actually originating from locations other than my local host. This function is also used to chart which IP addresses are most actively viewing the pages that are served by a particular installation of Apache.

This function performs a modest validation of each IP address, which is really just a length check: an IP address cannot be longer than 15 characters (4 sets of triplets and 3 periods) nor shorter than 7 (4 sets of single digits and 3 periods). This validation is not stringent, but it does reduce, at tiny runtime cost, the probability of placing into the dictionary some data that is obviously garbage. As a general technique, low-cost, highly approximate sanity checks for data that is expected to be OK (but one never knows for sure) are worth considering. However, if you want to be stricter, regular expressions can help. Change the loop in this recipe's function's body to:

```
       import re
       # an IP is: 4 strings, each of 1-3 digits, joined by periods
       ip_specs = r'\.'.join([r'\d{1,3}']*4)
       re_ip = re.compile(ip_specs)
       for line in contents:
           match = re_ip.match(line)
           if match:
               # Increase by 1 if IP exists; else set hit count = 1
               ip = match.group()
               ipHitListing[ip] = ipHitListing.get(ip, 0) + 1
```

In this variant, we use a regular expression to extract and validate the IP at the same time. This approach enables us to avoid the split operation as well as the length check, and thus amortizes most of the runtime cost of matching the regular expression. This variant is only a few percentage points slower than the recipe's solution.

Of course, the pattern given here as ip_specs is not entirely precise either, since it accepts, as components of an IP quad, arbitrary strings of one to three digits, while the components should be more constrained. But to ward off garbage lines, this level of sanity check is sufficient.

Another alternative is to convert and check the address: extract string ip just as we do in this recipe's Solution, then:

```
           # Ensure the IP address is proper
           try:
```

```
        quad = map(int, ip.split('.'))
    except ValueError:
        pass
    else:
        if len(quad)==4 and min(quad)>=0 and max(quad)<=255:
            # Increase by 1 if IP exists; else set hit count = 1
            ipHitListing[ip] = ipHitListing.get(ip, 0) + 1
```

This approach is more work, but it does guarantee that only IP addresses that are formally valid get counted at all.

See Also

The Apache web server is available and documented at *http://httpd.apache.org*; regular expressions are covered in the docs of the re module in the *Library Reference* and *Python in a Nutshell*.

10.5 Calculating the Rate of Client Cache Hits on Apache

Credit: Mark Nenadov

Problem

You need to monitor how often client requests are refused by your Apache web server because the client's cache of the page is already up to date.

Solution

When a browser queries a server for a page that the browser has in its cache, the browser lets the server know about the cached data, and the server returns a special error code (rather than serving the page again) if the client's cache is up to date. Here's how to find the statistics for such occurrences in your server's logs:

```
def clientCachePercentage(logfile_pathname):
    contents = open(logfile_pathname, "r")
    totalRequests = 0
    cachedRequests = 0
    for line in contents:
        totalRequests += 1
        if line.split(" ")[8] == "304":
            # if server returned "not modified"
            cachedRequests += 1
    return int(0.5+float(100*cachedRequests)/totalRequests)
```

Discussion

The percentage of requests to your Apache server that are met by the client's own cache is an important factor in the perceived performance of your server. The code in this recipe helps you get this information from the server's log. Typical use would be:

```
log_path = "/usr/local/nusphere/apache/logs/access_log"
print "Percentage of requests that were client-cached: " + str(
        clientCachePercentage(log_path)) + '%'
```

The recipe reads the log file one line at a time by looping over the file—the normal way to read a file nowadays. Trying to read the whole log file in memory, by calling the readlines method on the file object, would be an unsuitable approach for very large files, which server log files can certainly be. That approach might not work at all, or might work but damage performance considerably by swamping your machine's virtual memory. Even when it works, readlines offers no advantage over the approach used in this recipe.

The body of the for loop calls the split method on each line string, with a string of a single space as the argument, to split the line into a tuple of its space-separated fields. Then it uses indexing ([8]) to get the ninth such field. Apache puts the error code into the ninth field of each line in the log. Code "304" means "not modified" (i.e., the client's cache was already correctly updated). We count those cases in the cachedRequests variable and all lines in the log in the totalRequests variable, so that, in the end, we can return the percentage of cache hits. The expression we use in the return statement computes the percentage as a float number, then rounds it correctly to the closest int, because an integer result is most useful in practice.

See Also

The Apache web server is available and documented at *http://httpd.apache.org*.

10.6   Spawning an Editor from a Script

Credit: Larry Price, Peter Cogolo

Problem

You want users to work with their favorite text-editing programs to edit text files, to provide input to your script.

Solution

Module tempfile lets you create temporary files, and module os has many tools to check the environment and to work with files and external programs, such as text editors. A couple of functions can wrap this functionality into an easy-to-use form:

```
import sys, os, tempfile
def what_editor():
    editor = os.getenv('VISUAL') or os.getenv('EDITOR')
    if not editor:
        if sys.platform == 'windows':
            editor = 'Notepad.Exe'
        else:
            editor = 'vi'
    return editor
def edited_text(starting_text=''):
    temp_fd, temp_filename = tempfile.mkstemp(text=True)
    os.write(temp_fd, starting_text)
    os.close(temp_fd)
    editor = what_editor()
    x = os.spawnlp(os.P_WAIT, editor, editor, temp_filename)
    if x:
        raise RuntimeError, "Can't run %s %s (%s)" % (editor, temp_filename, x)
    result = open(temp_filename).read()
    os.unlink(temp_filename)
    return result
if __name__ =='__main__':
    text = edited_text('''Edit this text a little,
go ahead,
it's just a demonstration, after all...!
''')
    print 'Edited text is:', text
```

Discussion

Your scripts may often need a substantial amount of textual input from the user. Letting users edit the text with their favorite text editor is an excellent feature for your script to have, and this recipe shows how you can obtain it. I have used variants of this approach for such purposes as adjusting configuration files, writing blog posts, and sending emails.

If your scripts do not need to run on Windows, a more secure and slightly simpler way to code function edited_text is available:

```
def edited_text(starting_text=''):
    temp_file = tempfile.NamedTemporaryFile()
    temp_file.write(starting_text)
    temp_file.seek(0)
    editor = what_editor()
    x = os.spawnlp(os.P_WAIT, editor, editor, temp_file.name)
    if x:
        raise RuntimeError, "Can't run %s %s (%s)" % (editor, temp_file.name, x)
    return temp_file.read()
```

Unfortunately, this alternative relies on the editor we're spawning being able to open and modify the temporary file while we are holding that file open, and this capability is not supported on most versions of Windows. The version of edited_text given in the recipe is more portable.

When you're using this recipe to edit text files that must respect some kind of syntax or other constraints, such as a configuration file, you can make your script simpler and more effective by using a cycle of "input/parse/re-edit in case of errors," providing immediate feedback to users when you can diagnose they've made a mistake in editing the file. Ideally, in such cases, you should reopen the editor already pointing at the line in error, which is possible with most Unix editors by passing them a first argument such as '+23', specifying that they start editing at line 23, before the file-name argument. Unfortunately, such an argument would confuse many Windows editors, so you have to make some hard decisions here (if you do need to support Windows).

See Also

Documentation for modules `tempfile` and os in the *Library Reference* and *Python in a Nutshell*.

10.7 Backing Up Files

Credit: Anand Pillai, Tiago Henriques, Mario Ruggier

Problem

You want to make frequent backup copies of all files you have modified within a directory tree, so that further changes won't accidentally obliterate some of your editing.

Solution

Version-control systems, such as RCS, CVS, and SVN, are very powerful and useful, but sometimes a simple script that you can easily edit and customize can be even handier. The following script checks for new files to back up in a tree that you specify. Run the script periodically to keep your backup copies up to date.

```
import sys, os, shutil, filecmp
MAXVERSIONS=100
def backup(tree_top, bakdir_name='bakdir'):
    for dir, subdirs, files in os.walk(tree_top):
        # ensure each directory has a subdir called bakdir
        backup_dir = os.path.join(dir, bakdir_name)
        if not os.path.exists(backup_dir):
            os.makedirs(backup_dir)
        # stop any recursing into the backup directories
        subdirs[:] = [d for d in subdirs if d != bakdir_name]
        for file in files:
            filepath = os.path.join(dir, file)
            destpath = os.path.join(backup_dir, file)
            # check existence of previous versions
            for index in xrange(MAXVERSIONS):
                backup = '%s.%2.2d' % (destpath, index)
```

```
                    if not os.path.exists(backup): break
                if index > 0:
                    # no need to backup if file and last version are identical
                    old_backup = '%s.%2.2d' % (destpath, index-1)
                    abspath = os.path.abspath(filepath)
                    try:
                        if os.path.isfile(old_backup
                            ) and filecmp.cmp(abspath, old_backup, shallow=False):
                            continue
                    except OSError:
                        pass
                try:
                    shutil.copy(filepath, backup)
                except OSError:
                    pass
    if __name__ == '__main__':
        # run backup on the specified directory (default: the current directory)
        try: tree_top = sys.argv[1]
        except IndexError: tree_top = '.'
        backup(tree_top)
```

Discussion

Although version-control systems are more powerful, this script can be useful in development work. I often customize it, for example, to keep backups only of files with certain extensions (or, when that's handier, of all files *except* those with certain extensions); it suffices to add an appropriate test at the very start of the for file in files loop, such as:

```
name, ext = os.path.splitext(file)
if ext not in ('.py', '.txt', '.doc'): continue
```

This snippet first uses function splitext from the standard library module os.path to extract the file extension (starting with a period) into local variable ext, then conditionally executes statement continue, which passes to the next leg of the loop, unless the extension is one of a few that happen to be the ones of interest in the current subtree.

Other potentially useful variants include backing files up to some *other* subtree (potentially on a removable drive, which has some clear advantages for backup purposes) rather than the current one, compressing the files that are being backed up (look at standard library module gzip for this purpose), and more refined ones yet. However, rather than complicating function backup by offering all of these variants as options, I prefer to copy the entire script to the root of each of the various subtrees of interest, and customize it with a little simple editing. While this strategy would be a very bad one for any kind of complicated, highly reusable production-level code, it is reasonable for a simple, straightforward system administration utility such as the one in this recipe.

Worthy of note in this recipe's implementation is the use of function os.walk, a generator from the standard Python library's module os, which makes it very simple to iterate over all or most of a filesystem subtree, with no need for such subtleties as recursion or callbacks, just a straightforward for statement. To avoid backing up the backups, this recipe uses one advanced feature of os.walk: the second one of the three values that os.walk yields at each step through the loop is a list of subdirectories of the current directory. We can modify this list *in place*, removing some of the subdirectory names it contains. When we perform such an in-place modification, os.walk does not recurse through the subdirectories whose names we removed. The following steps deal only with the subdirectories whose names are left in. This subtle but useful feature of os.walk is one good example of how a generator can receive information from the code that's iterating on it, to affect details of the iteration being performed.

See Also

Documentation of standard library modules os, shutils, and gzip in the *Library Reference* and *Python in a Nutshell*.

10.8   Selectively Copying a Mailbox File

Credit: Noah Spurrier, Dave Benjamin

Problem

You need to selectively copy a large mailbox file (in mbox style), passing each message through a filtering function that may alter or skip the message.

Solution

The Python Standard Library package email is the modern Python approach for this kind of task. However, standard library modules mailbox and rfc822 can also supply the base functionality to implement this task:

```
def process_mailbox(mailboxname_in, mailboxname_out, filter_function):
    mbin = mailbox.PortableUnixMailbox(file(mailboxname_in,'r'))
    fout = file(mailboxname_out, 'w')
    for msg in mbin:
        if msg is None: break
        document = filter_function(msg, msg.fp.read())
        if document:
            assert document.endswith('\n\n')
            fout.write(msg.unixfrom)
            fout.writelines(msg.headers)
            fout.write('\n')
            fout.write(document)
    fout.close()
```

Discussion

I often write lots of little scripts to filter my mailbox, so I wrote this recipe's small module. I can import the module from each script and call the module's function process_mailbox as needed. Python's future direction is to perform email processing with the standard library package email, but lower-level modules, such as mailbox and rfc822, are still available in the Python Standard Library. They are sometimes easier to use than the rich, powerful, and very general functionality offered by package email.

The function you pass to process_mailbox as the third argument, filter_function, must take two arguments—msg, an rfc822 message object, and document, a string that is the message's entire body, ending with two line-end characters (\n\n). filter_function can return False, meaning that this message must be skipped (i.e., not copied at all to the output), or else it must return a string terminated with \n\n that is written to the output as the message body. Normally, filter_function returns either False or the same document argument it was called with, but in some cases you may find it useful to write to the output file an altered version of the message's body rather than the original message body.

Here is an example of a filter function that removes duplicate messages:

```
import sets
found_ids = sets.Set( )
def no_duplicates(msg, document):
    msg_id = msg.getheader('Message-ID')
    if msg_id in found_ids:
        return False
    found_ids.add(msg_id)
    return document
```

In Python 2.4, you could use the built-in set rather than sets.Set, but for a case as simple as this, it makes no real difference in performance (and the usage is exactly the same, anyway).

See Also

Documentation about modules mailbox and rfc822, and package email, in the *Library Reference* and *Python in a Nutshell*.

10.9   Building a Whitelist of Email Addresses From a Mailbox

Credit: Noah Spurrier

Problem

To help you configure an antispam system, you want a list of email addresses, commonly known as a *whitelist*, that you can trust won't send you spam. The addresses to which you send email are undoubtedly good candidates for this whitelist.

Solution

Here is a script to output "To" addresses given a mailbox path:

```python
#!/usr/bin/env python
""" Extract and print all 'To:' addresses from a mailbox """
import mailbox
def main(mailbox_path):
    addresses = {}
    mb = mailbox.PortableUnixMailbox(file(mailbox_path))
    for msg in mb:
        toaddr = msg.getaddr('To')[1]
        addresses[toaddr] = 1
    addresses = addresses.keys()
    addresses.sort()
    for address in addresses:
        print address
if __name__ == '__main__':
    import sys
    main(sys.argv[1])
```

Discussion

In addition to bypassing spam filters, identifying addresses of people you've sent mail to may also help in other ways, such as flagging emails from them as higher priority, depending on your mail-reading habits and your mail reader's capabilities. As long as your mail reader keeps mail you have sent in some kind of "Sent Items" mailbox in standard mailbox format, you can call this script with the path to the mailbox as its only argument, and the addresses to which you've sent mail will be emitted to standard output.

The script is simple because the Python Standard Library module mailbox does all the hard work. All the script needs to do is collect the set of email addresses as it loops through all messages, then emit them. While collecting, we keep addresses as a dictionary, since that's much faster than keeping a list and checking each toaddr in order to append it only if it wasn't already in the list. When we're done collecting, we just extract the addresses from the dictionary as a list because we want to emit its items in sorted order. In Python 2.4, function main can be made even slightly more elegant, thanks to the new built-ins set and sorted:

```python
def main(mailbox_path):
    addresses = set()
    mb = mailbox.PortableUnixMailbox(file(mailbox_path))
    for msg in mb:
        toaddr = msg.getaddr('To')[1]
        addresses.add(toaddr)
    for address in sorted(addresses):
        print address
```

If your mailbox is not in the Unix mailbox style supported by mailbox.PortableUnixMailbox, you may want to use other classes supplied by the

---

Python Standard Library module mailbox. For example, if your mailbox is in Qmail maildir format, you can use the mailbox.Maildir class to read it.

See Also

Documentation of the standard library module mailbox in the *Library Reference* and *Python in a Nutshell*.

10.10 Blocking Duplicate Mails

Credit: Marina Pianu, Peter Cogolo

Problem

Many of the mails you receive are duplicates. You need to block the duplicates with a fast, simple filter before they reach a more time-consuming step, such as an anti-spam filter, in your email pipeline.

Solution

Many mail systems, such as the popular procmail, and KDE's KMail, enable you to control your mail-reception pipeline. Specifically, you can insert in the pipeline your filter programs, which get messages on standard input, may modify them, and emit them again on standard output. Here is one such filter, with the specific purpose of performing the task described in the Problem—blocking messages that are duplicates of other messages that you have received recently:

```
#!/usr/bin/python
import time, sys, os, email
now = time.time( )
# get archive of previously-seen message-ids and times
kde_dir = os.expanduser('~/.kde')
if not os.path.isdir(kde_dir):
    os.mkdir(kde_dir)
arfile = os.path.join(kde_dir, 'duplicate_mails')
duplicates = { }
try:
    archive = open(arfile)
except IOError:
    pass
else:
    for line in archive:
        when, msgid = line[:-1].split(' ', 1)
        duplicates[msgid] = float(when)
    archive.close( )
redo_archive = False
# suck message in from stdin and study it
msg = email.message_from_file(sys.stdin)
msgid = msg['Message-ID']
if msgid:
```

```
        if msgid in duplicates:
            # duplicate message: alter its subject
            subject = msg['Subject']
            if subject is None:
                msg['Subject'] = '**** DUP **** ' + msgid
            else:
                del msg['Subject']
                msg['Subject'] = '**** DUP **** ' + subject
        else:
            # non-duplicate message: redo the archive file
            redo_archive = True
            duplicates[msgid] = now
    else:
        # invalid (missing message-id) message: alter its subject
        subject = msg['Subject']
        if subject is None:
            msg['Subject'] = '**** NID **** '
        else:
            del msg['Subject']
            msg['Subject'] = '**** NID **** ' + subject
    # emit message back to stdout
    print msg
    if redo_archive:
        # redo archive file, keep only msgs from the last two hours
        keep_last = now - 2*60*60.0
        archive = file(arfile, 'w')
        for msgid, when in duplicates.iteritems():
            if when > keep_last:
                archive.write('%9.2f %s\n' % (when, what))
        archive.close()
```

Discussion

Whether it is because of spammers' malice or incompetence, or because of hiccups at my Internet ISP (Internet service provider), at times I get huge amounts of duplicate messages that can overload my mail-reception pipeline, particularly antispam filters. Fortunately, like many other mail systems, KDE's KMail, the one I use, lets me insert my own filters in the mail reception pipeline. In particular, I can diagnose duplicate messages, alter their headers (I use "Subject" for clarity), and tell later stages in the filters' pipeline to throw away messages with such subjects or to shunt them aside into a dedicated mailbox for later perusal, without passing them on to the antispam and other filters.

The email module from the Python Standard Library performs all the required parsing of the message and lets me access headers with dictionary-like indexing syntax. I need some "memory" of recently seen messages. Fortunately, I have noticed all duplicates happen within a few minutes of each other, so I don't have to keep that memory for long—two hours are plenty. Therefore, I keep that memory in a simple text file, which records the time when a message was received and the message ID. I thought I might have to find a more advanced way to keep this kind of FIFO (first-in, first-out) archive, but I tried a simple approach first—a simple text file that is entirely rewritten whenever a new nonduplicate message arrives. This approach appears to perform quite adequately for my needs (at most a couple hundred messages an hour), even on my somewhat dated PC. "Do the simplest thing that could possibly work" strikes again!

See Also

Documentation about package email and modules time, sys and os in the *Library Reference* and *Python in a Nutshell*.

10.11 Checking Your Windows Sound System

Credit: Anand Pillai

Problem

You need to check whether the sound subsystem on your Windows PC is properly configured.

Solution

The winsound module of the Python Standard Library makes this check really simple:

```
import winsound
try:
    winsound.PlaySound("*", winsound.SND_ALIAS)
except RuntimeError, e:
    print 'Sound system has problems,', e
else:
    print 'Sound system is OK'
```

Discussion

The sound system might pass this test and still be unable to produce sound correctly, due to a variety of possible problems—starting from simple ones such as powered loudspeakers being turned off (there's no sensible way you can check for *that* in your program!), all the way to extremely subtle and complicated ones. When sound is a problem in your applications, using this recipe at least you know whether you should be digging into a subtle issue of device driver configuration or start by checking whether the loudspeakers are on!

See Also

Documentation on the Python Standard Library winsound module.

10.12 Registering or Unregistering a DLL on Windows

Credit: Bill Bell

Problem

You want to register or unregister a DLL in Windows, just as it is normally done by *regsrv32.exe*, but you want to do it from Python, without requiring that executable to be present or bothering to find it.

Solution

All that Microsoft's *regsrv32.exe* does is load a DLL and call its entries named DllRegisterServer or DllUnregisterServer. This behavior is very easy to replicate via Thomas Heller's ctypes extension:

```
from ctypes import windll
dll = windll[r'C:\Path\To\Some.DLL']
result = dll.DllRegisterServer( )
result = dll.DllUnregisterServer( )
```

The result is of Windows type HRESULT, so, if you wish, ctypes can also implicitly check it for you, raising a ctypes.WindowsError exception when an error occurs; you just need to use ctypes.oledll instead of ctypes.windll. In other words, to have the result automatically checked and an exception raised in case of errors, instead of the previous script, use this one:

```
from ctypes import oledll
dll = oledll[r'C:\Path\To\Some.DLL']
dll.DllRegisterServer( )
dll.DllUnregisterServer( )
```

Discussion

Thomas Heller's ctypes enables your Python code to load DLLs on Windows (and similar dynamic/shared libraries on other platforms) and call functions from such libraries, and it manages to perform these tasks with a high degree of both power and elegance. On Windows, in particular, it offers even further "added value" through such mechanisms as the oledll object, which, besides loading DLLs and calling functions from them, also checks the returned HRESULT instances and raises appropriate exceptions when the HRESULT values indicate errors.

In this recipe, we're using ctypes (either the windll or oledll objects from that module) specifically to avoid the need to use Microsoft's *regsrv32.exe* to register or unregister DLLs that implement in-process COM servers for some CLSIDs. (A CLSID is a globally unique identifier that identifies a COM class object, and the abbreviation presumably stands for class identifier.) The cases in which you'll use this specific recipe are only those in which you need to register or unregister such COM DLLs (whether they're implemented in Python or otherwise makes no difference). Be aware, however, that the applicability of ctypes is far wider, as it extends to any case in which you wish your Python code to load and interact with a DLL (or, on platforms other than Windows, equivalent dynamically loaded libraries, such as *.so* files on Linux and *.dynlib* files on Mac OS X).

The protocol that *regsrv32.exe* implements is well documented and very simple, so our own code can reimplement it in a jiffy. That's much more practical than requiring *regsrv32.exe* to be installed on the machine on which we want to register or unregister the DLLs, not to mention finding where the EXE file might be to run it directly (via *os.spawn* or whatever) and also finding an effective way to detect errors and show them to the user.

See Also

ctypes is at *http://sourceforge.net/projects/ctypes*.

10.13 Checking and Modifying the Set of Tasks Windows Automatically Runs at Login

Credit: Daniel Kinnaer

Problem

You need to check which tasks Windows is set to automatically run at login and possibly change this set of tasks.

Solution

When administering Windows machines, it's crucial to keep track of the tasks each machine runs at login. Like so many Windows tasks, this requires working with the registry, and standard Python module _winreg enables this:

```
import _winreg as wr
aReg = wr.ConnectRegistry(None, wr.HKEY_LOCAL_MACHINE)
try:
    targ = r'SOFTWARE\Microsoft\Windows\CurrentVersion\Run'
    print "*** Reading from", targ, "***"
    aKey = wr.OpenKey(aReg, targ)
    try:
        for i in xrange(1024):
            try:
                n, v, t = wr.EnumValue(aKey, i)
                print i, n, v, t
            except EnvironmentError:
                print "You have", i, "tasks starting at logon"
                break
```

```
        finally:
            wr.CloseKey(aKey)
        print "*** Writing to", targ, "***"
        aKey = wr.OpenKey(aReg, targ, 0, wr.KEY_WRITE)
        try:
            try:
                wr.SetValueEx(aKey, "MyNewKey", 0, REG_SZ, r"c:\winnt\explorer.exe")
            except EnvironmentError:
                print "Encountered problems writing into the Registry..."
                raise
        finally:
            CloseKey(aKey)
    finally:
        CloseKey(aReg)
```

Discussion

The Windows registry holds a wealth of crucial system administration data, and the Python standard module _winreg makes it feasible to read and alter data held in the registry. One of the items held in the Windows registry is a list of tasks to be run at login (in addition to other lists held elsewhere, such as the user-specific *Startup* folder that this recipe does not deal with).

This recipe shows how to examine the registry list of login tasks, and how to add a task to the list so it is run at login. (This recipe assumes you have Explorer installed at the specific location *c:\winnt*. If you have it installed elsewhere, edit the recipe accordingly.)

If you want to remove the specific key added by this recipe, you can use the following simple script:

```
import _winreg as wr
aReg = wr.ConnectRegistry(None, wr.HKEY_LOCAL_MACHINE)
targ = r'SOFTWARE\Microsoft\Windows\CurrentVersion\Run'
aKey = wr.OpenKey(aReg, targ, 0, wr.KEY_WRITE)
wr.DeleteValue(aKey, "MyNewKey")
wr.CloseKey(aKey)
wr.CloseKey(aReg)
```

The try/finally constructs used in the recipe are far more robust than the simple sequence of function calls used in this latest snippet, since they ensure that everything is closed correctly regardless of whether the intervening calls succeed or fail. This care and prudence are strongly advisable for scripts that are meant be run in production, particularly for system-administration scripts that must generally run with administrator privileges. Such scripts therefore might harm a system's setup if they don't clean up after themselves properly. However, you can omit the try/finally when you know the calls will succeed or don't care what happens if they fail. In this case, if you have successfully added a task with the recipe's script, the calls in this simple cleanup script should work just fine.

See Also

Documentation for the standard module _winreg in the *Library Reference*; Windows API documentation available from Microsoft (*http://msdn.microsoft.com*); information on what is where in the registry tends to be spread information among many sources, but for some useful collections of such information, see *http://www.winguides.com/registry* and *http://www.activewin.com/tips/reg/index.shtml*.

10.14 Creating a Share on Windows

Credit: John Nielsen

Problem

You want to share a folder of your Windows PC on a LAN.

Solution

PyWin32's win32net module makes this task very easy:

```
import win32net
import win32netcon
shinfo={ }
shinfo['netname'] = 'python test'
shinfo['type'] = win32netcon.STYPE_DISKTREE
shinfo['remark'] = 'data files'
shinfo['permissions'] = 0
shinfo['max_uses'] = -1
shinfo['current_uses'] = 0
shinfo['path'] = 'c:\\my_data'
shinfo['passwd'] = ''
server = 'servername'
win32net.NetShareAdd(server, 2, shinfo)
```

Discussion

While the task of sharing a folder is indeed fairly easy to accomplish, finding the information on how you do so isn't. All I could find in the win32net documentation was that you needed to pass a dictionary holding the share's data "in the format of SHARE_INFO_*." I finally managed to integrate this tidbit with the details from the Windows SDK (*http://msdn.microsoft.com*) and produce the information in this recipe. One detail that took me some effort to discover is that the constants you need to use as the value for the 'type' entry are "hidden away" in the win32netcon module.

See Also

PyWin32 docs at *http://sourceforge.net/projects/pywin32/*; Microsoft's MSDN site, *http://msdn.microsoft.com*.

10.15 Connecting to an Already Running Instance of Internet Explorer

Credit: Bill Bell, Graham Fawcett

Problem

Instantiating Internet Explorer to access its interfaces via COM is easy, but you want to connect to an already running instance.

Solution

The simplest approach is to rely on Internet Explorer's CLSID:

```
from win32com.client import Dispatch
ShellWindowsCLSID = '{9BA05972-F6A8-11CF-A442-00A0C90A8F39}'
ShellWindows = Dispatch(ShellWindowsCLSID)
print '%d instances of IE' % len(shellwindows)
print
for shellwindow in ShellWindows :
    print shellwindow
    print shellwindos.LocationName
    print shellwindos.LocationURL
    print
```

Discussion

Dispatching on the CLSID provides a sequence of all the running instances of the application with that class. Of course, there could be none, one, or more. If you're interested in a specific instance, you may be able to identify it by checking, for example, for its properties LocationName and LocationURL.

You'll see that Windows Explorer and Internet Explorer have the same CLSID—they're basically the same application. If you need to distinguish between them, you can try adding at the start of your script the statement:

```
from win32gui import GetClassName
```

and then checking each shellwindow in the loop with:

```
if GetClassName(shellwindow.HWND) == 'IEFrame':
    ...
```

'IEFrame' is *supposed* to result from this call (according to the docs) for all Internet Explorer instances and those only. However, I have not found this check to be wholly reliable across all versions and patch levels of Windows and Internet Explorer, so, take this approach as just one possibility (which is why I haven't added this check to the recipe's official "Solution").

This recipe does not let you receive IE events. The most important event is probably DocumentComplete. You can roughly substitute checks on the Busy property for the inability to wait for that event, but remember not to poll too frequently (for that or any other property) or you may slow down your PC excessively. Something like:

```
while shellwindow.Busy:
    time.sleep(0.2)
```

Sleeping 0.2 seconds between checks may be a reasonable compromise between responding promptly and not loading your PC too heavily with a busy-waiting-loop.

See Also

PyWin32 docs at *http://sourceforge.net/projects/pywin32/*; Microsoft's MSDN site, *http://msdn.microsoft.com*.

10.16 Reading Microsoft Outlook Contacts

Credit: Kevin Altis

Problem

Your Microsoft Outlook Contacts house a wealth of useful information, and you need to extract some of it in text form.

Solution

Like many other problems of system administration on Windows, this one is best approached by using COM. The most popular way to interface Python to COM is to use the win32com package, which is part of Mark Hammond's pywin32 extension package:

```python
from win32com.client import gencache, constants
DEBUG = False
class MSOutlook(object):
    def __init__(self):
        try:
            self.oOutlookApp = gencache.EnsureDispatch("Outlook.Application")
            self.outlookFound = True
        except:
            print "MSOutlook: unable to load Outlook"
            self.outlookFound = False
        self.records = [ ]
    def loadContacts(self, keys=None):
        if not self.outlookFound: return
        onMAPI = self.oOutlookApp.GetNamespace("MAPI")
        ofContacts = onMAPI.GetDefaultFolder(constants.olFolderContacts)
        if DEBUG: print "number of contacts:", len(ofContacts.Items)
        for oc in range(len(ofContacts.Items)):
            contact = ofContacts.Items.Item(oc + 1)
            if contact.Class == constants.olContact:
                if keys is None:
                    # no keys were specified, so build up a list of all keys
```

```
                              # that belong to some types we know we can deal with
                              good_types = int, str, unicode
                              keys = [key for key in contact._prop_map_get_
                                  if isinstance(getattr(contact, key), good_types) ]
                              if DEBUG:
                                  print "Fields\n========================="
                                  keys.sort( )
                                  for key in keys: print key
                          record = { }
                          for key in keys:
                              record[key] = getattr(contact, key)
                          self.records.append(record)
                          if DEBUG:
                              print oc, contact.FullName
    if __name__ == '__main__':
        if '-d' in sys.argv:
            DEBUG = True
        if DEBUG:
            print "attempting to load Outlook"
        oOutlook = MSOutlook( )
        if not oOutlook.outlookFound:
            print "Outlook not found"
            sys.exit(1)
        fields = ['FullName', 'CompanyName',
                  'MailingAddressStreet', 'MailingAddressCity',
                  'MailingAddressState', 'MailingAddressPostalCode',
                  'HomeTelephoneNumber', 'BusinessTelephoneNumber',
                  'MobileTelephoneNumber', 'Email1Address', 'Body',
                  ]
        if DEBUG:
            import time
            print "loading records..."
            startTime = time.time( )
        # to get all fields just call oOutlook.loadContacts( )
        # but getting a specific set of fields is much faster
        oOutlook.loadContacts(fields)
        if DEBUG:
            print "loading took %f seconds" % (time.time( ) - startTime)
        print "Number of contacts: %d" % len(oOutlook.records)
        print "Contact: %s" % oOutlook.records[0]['FullName']
        print "Body:\n%s" % oOutlook.records[0]['Body']
```

Discussion

This recipe's code could use more error-checking, and you could get it by using
nested try/except blocks, but I didn't want to obscure the code's fundamental simplicity in this recipe. This recipe should work with different versions of Outlook, but
I've tested it only with Outlook 2000. If you have applied the Outlook security
patches then you will be prompted with a dialog requesting access to Outlook for 1–
10 minutes from an external program, which in this case is Python.

The code has already been optimized in two important ways. First, by ensuring that the Python COM wrappers for Outlook have been generated, which is guaranteed by calling gencache.EnsureDispatch. Second, in the loop that reads the contacts, the Contact reference is obtained only once and then kept in a local variable contact to avoid repeated references. This simple but crucial optimization is the role of the statement:

```
contact = ofContacts.Items.Item(oc + 1)
```

Both of these optimizations have a dramatic impact on total import time, and both are important enough to keep in mind. Specifically, the EnsureDispatch idea is important for most uses of COM in Python; the concept of getting an object reference, once, into a local variable (rather than repeating indexing, calls, and attribute accesses) is even more important and applies to *every* use of Python.

Simple variations of this script can be applied to other elements of the Outlook object model such as the Calendar and Tasks. You'll want to look at the Python wrappers generated for Outlook in the *C:\Python23\Lib\site-packages\win32com\gen_py* directory. I also suggest that you look at the Outlook object model documentation on MSDN and/or pick up a book on the subject.

See Also

PyWin32 docs at *http://sourceforge.net/projects/pywin32/*; Microsoft's MSDN site, *http://msdn.microsoft.com*.

10.17 Gathering Detailed System Information on Mac OS X

Credit: Brian Quinlan

Problem

You want to retrieve detailed information about a Mac OS X system. You want either complete information about the system or information about particular keys in the system-information database.

Solution

Mac OS X's system_profiler command can provide system information as an XML stream that we can parse and examine:

```python
#!/usr/bin/env python
from xml import dom
from xml.dom.xmlbuilder import DOMInputSource, DOMBuilder
import datetime, time, os
def group(seq, n):
    """group([0, 3, 4, 10, 2, 3, 1], 3) => [(0, 3, 4), (10, 2, 3)]
```

```
            Group a sequence into n-subseqs, discarding incomplete subseqs.
        """
        return [ seq[i:i+n] for i in xrange(0, len(seq)-n+1, n) ]
    def remove_whitespace_nodes(node):
        """Removes all of the whitespace-only text descendants of a DOM node."""
        remove_list = [ ]
        for child in node.childNodes:
            if child.nodeType == dom.Node.TEXT_NODE and not child.data.strip( ):
                remove_list.append(child)
            elif child.hasChildNodes( ):
                remove_whitespace_nodes(child)
        for child in remove_list:
            node.removeChild(child)
            child.unlink( )
class POpenInputSource(DOMInputSource):
    "Use stdout from an external program as a DOMInputSource"
    def __init__(self, command):
        super(DOMInputSource, self).__init__( )
        self.byteStream = os.popen(command)
class OSXSystemProfiler(object):
    "Provide information from the Mac OS X System Profiler"
    def __init__(self, detail=-1):
        """detail can range from -2 to +1.  Larger numbers return more info.
            Beware of +1, can take many minutes to get all info!"""
        b = DOMBuilder( )
        self.document = b.parse(
            POpenInputSource('system_profiler -xml -detailLevel %d' % detail))
        remove_whitespace_nodes(self.document)
    def _content(self, node):
        "Get the text node content of an element, or an empty string"
        if node.firstChild:
            return node.firstChild.nodeValue
        else:
            return ''
    def _convert_value_node(self, node):
        """Convert a 'value' node (i.e. anything but 'key') into a Python data
            structure"""
        if node.tagName == 'string':
            return self._content(node)
        elif node.tagName == 'integer':
            return int(self._content(node))
        elif node.tagName == 'real':
            return float(self._content(node))
        elif node.tagName == 'date': #  <date>2004-07-05T13:29:29Z</date>
            return datetime.datetime(
                *time.strptime(self._content(node), '%Y-%m-%dT%H:%M:%SZ')[:5])
        elif node.tagName == 'array':
            return [self._convert_value_node(n) for n in node.childNodes]
        elif node.tagName == 'dict':
            return dict([(self._content(n), self._convert_value_node(m))
                        for n, m in group(node.childNodes, 2)])
        else:
            raise ValueError, 'Unknown tag %r' % node.tagName
    def __getitem__(self, key):
```

```
        from xml import xpath
        # pyxml's xpath does not support /element1[...]/element2...
        nodes = xpath.Evaluate('//dict[key=%r]' % key, self.document)
        results = [ ]
        for node in nodes:
            v = self._convert_value_node(node)[key]
            if isinstance(v, dict) and '_order' in v:
                # this is just information for display
                pass
            else:
                results.append(v)
        return results
    def all(self):
        """Return the complete information from the system profiler
            as a Python data structure"""
        return self._convert_value_node(
            self.document.documentElement.firstChild)
def main( ):
    from optparse import OptionParser
    from pprint import pprint
    info = OSXSystemProfiler( )
    parser = OptionParser( )
    parser.add_option("-f", "--field", action="store", dest="field",
                        help="display the value of the specified field")
    options, args = parser.parse_args( )
    if args:
        parser.error("no arguments are allowed")
    if options.field is not None:
        pprint(info[options.field])
    else:
        # print some keys known to exist in only one important dict
        for k in ['cpu_type', 'current_processor_speed', 'l2_cache_size',
                    'physical_memory', 'user_name', 'os_version', 'ip_address']:
            print '%s: %s' % (k, info[k][0])
if __name__ == '__main__':
    main( )
```

Discussion

Mac OS X puts at your disposal a wealth of information about your system through
the system_profiler application. This recipe shows how to access that information
from your Python code. First, you have to instantiate class OSXSystemProfiler, for
example, via a statement such as info = OSXSystemProfiler( ); once you have done
that, you can obtain all available information by calling info.all( ), or information
for one specific key by indexing info[thekey]. The main function in the recipe, which
executes when you run this module as a main script, emits information to standard
output—either a specific key, requested by using switch -f when invoking the script,
or, by default, a small set of keys known to be generally useful.

For example, when run on the old Apple iBook belonging to one of this book's editors (no prize for guessing which one), the script in this recipe emits the following output:

```
cpu_type: PowerPC G4  (3.3)
current_processor_speed: 800 MHz
l2_cache_size: 256 KB
physical_memory: 640 MB
user_name: Alex (alex)
os_version: Mac OS X 10.3.6 (7R28)
ip_address: [u'192.168.0.190']
```

system_profiler returns XML data in pinfo format, so this recipe implements a partial pinfo parser, using Python's standard library XML-parsing facilities, and the xpath implementation from the PyXML extensions. More information about Python's facilities that help you deal with XML can be found in Chapter 12.

See Also

Documentation of the standard Python library support for XML in the *Library Reference* and *Python in a Nutshell*; PyXML docs at *http://pyxml.sourceforge.net/*; Mac OS X system_profiler docs at *http://developer.apple.com/documentation/Darwin/Reference/ManPages/man8/system_profiler.8.html*; Chapter 12.

## CHAPTER 11

User Interfaces

11.0 Introduction

Credit: Fredrik Lundh, SecretLabs AB, author of Python Standard Library

Back in the early days of interactive computing, most computers offered terminals that looked and behaved pretty much like clunky typewriters. The main difference from an ordinary typewriter was that the computer was in the loop. It could read what the user typed and print hard-copy output on a roll of paper.

So when you found yourself in front of a 1960s Teletype ASR-33, the only reasonable way to communicate with the computer was to type a line of text, press the send key, hope that the computer would manage to figure out what you meant, and wait for the response to appear on the paper roll. This line-oriented way of communicating with your computer is known as a *command-line interface* (CLI).

Some 40 years later, the paper roll has been replaced with high-resolution video displays, which can display text in multiple typefaces, color photographs, and even animated 3D graphics. The keyboard is still around, but we also have pointing devices such as the mouse, trackballs, game controls, touchpads, and other input devices.

The combination of a graphics display and the mouse made it possible to create a new kind of user interface: the *graphical user interface* (GUI). When done right, a GUI can give the user a better overview of what a program can do (and what it is doing), and make it easier to carry out many kinds of tasks.

However, most programming languages, including Python, make it easy to write programs using teletype-style output and input. In Python, you use the print statement to print text to the display and the input and raw_input functions to read expressions and text strings from the keyboard.

Creating GUIs takes more work. You need access to functions to draw text and graphics on the screen, select typefaces and styles, and read information from the keyboard and other input devices. You need to write code to interact with other applications (via a window manager), keep your windows updated when the user moves them around, and respond to key presses and mouse actions.

To make this a bit easier, programmers have developed *graphical user interface toolkits*, which provide standard solutions to these problems. A typical GUI toolkit provides a number of ready-made GUI building blocks, usually called *widgets*. Common standard widgets include text and image labels, buttons, and text-entry fields. Many toolkits also provide more advanced widgets, such as Tkinter's Text widget, which is a rather competent text editor/display component.

All major toolkits are *event based*, which means that your program hands control over to the toolkit (usually by calling a "main loop" function or method). The toolkit then calls back into your application when certain events occur—for example, when the user clicks OK in a dialog or when a window needs to be redrawn. Most toolkits also provide ways to position widgets on the screen automatically (e.g., in tables, rows, or columns) and to modify widget behavior and appearance.

Tkinter is the de facto standard toolkit for Python and comes with most Python distributions. Tkinter provides an object-oriented layer on top of the Tcl/Tk GUI library and runs on Windows, Unix, and Macintosh systems. Tkinter is easy to use but provides a relatively small number of standard widgets. Tkinter extension libraries, such as Pmw and Tix, supply many components missing from plain Tkinter, and you can use Tkinter's advanced Text and Canvas widgets to create custom widgets. The Widget Construction Kit, WCK, lets you write all sorts of new widgets in pure Python: see *http://effbot.org/zone/wck.htm*.

wxPython (*http://www.wxPython.org*) is another popular toolkit; it is based on the wxWidgets C++ library (*http://www.wxWidgets.org*). wxPython is modeled somewhat after the Windows MFC library but is available for multiple platforms. wxPython provides a rich set of widgets, and it's relatively easy to create custom widgets.

PyGTK (*http://www.pygtk.org*) is an object-oriented Python interface to the Gimp toolkit (GTK), used in projects such as Gnome and the Gimp. PyGTK is a good choice for Linux applications, especially if you want them to run in the Gnome environment.

PyQt (*http://www.riverbankcomputing.co.uk/pyqt/index.php*) is a Python wrapper for TrollTech's Qt library (*http://www.trolltech.com*), which is the basis of the popular KDE environment, as well as the Qtopia environment for hand-held computers; it also runs on Windows and Mac OS X. Qt and PyQt require license fees for commercial (software that is not free) use, but are free (licensed by the GPL) for free software development. (No GPL-licensed Qt is currently available for Windows, but one is under development—see *http://kde-cygwin.sourceforge.net/qt3-win32/*.)

You can also use many other toolkits from Python. Mark Hammond's Pythonwin gives access to Windows MFC. Greg Ewing is developing a cross-platform GUI API, known as PyGUI (*http://nz.cosc.canterbury.ac.nz/~greg/python_gui/*), developed specifically for Python and taking advantage of Python's unique strengths. Also available are interfaces to Motif/X11 and Mac OS X native toolboxes and many other toolkits. Cameron Laird maintains a list of toolkits at *http://starbase.neosoft.com/ ~claird/comp.lang.python/python_GUI.html*. It currently lists about 20 toolkits. A Wiki page at *http://www.python.org/cgi-bin/moinmoin/GuiProgramming* is actively maintained lists even more.

Finally, several projects, in various stages, are based on the idea of overlaying easy unified APIs on top of one or more other toolkits or graphical facilities. anygui (rather dormant—see *http://www.anygui.org*), PythonCard (pretty active—see *http:// pythoncard.sourceforge.net/*), Wax (*http://zephyrfalcon.org/labs/dope_on_wax.html*), and PyUI (*http://pyui.sourceforge.net/*) are examples of this "higher-level" approach.

11.1 Showing a Progress Indicator on a Text Console

Credit: Larry Bates

Problem

Your program has no GUI (i.e., your program just runs on a text console), and yet you want your program to show to the user a "progress indicator bar" during lengthy operations, to communicate that work is progressing and the amount of the total work that has been completed.

Solution

We can easily code a simple little class to handle this whole task:

```
import sys
class progressbar(object):
    def __init__(self, finalcount, block_char='.'):
        self.finalcount = finalcount
        self.blockcount = 0
        self.block = block_char
        self.f = sys.stdout
        if not self.finalcount: return
        self.f.write('\n------------------ % Progress ------------------1\n')
        self.f.write('    1    2    3    4    5    6    7    8    9    0\n')
        self.f.write('----0----0----0----0----0----0----0----0----0----0\n')
    def progress(self, count):
        count = min(count, self.finalcount)
        if self.finalcount:
            percentcomplete = int(round(100.0*count/self.finalcount))
            if percentcomplete < 1: percentcomplete = 1
        else:
            percentcomplete=100
        blockcount = int(percentcomplete//2)
        if blockcount <= self.blockcount:
```

```
        return
for i in range(self.blockcount, blockcount):
    self.f.write(self.block)
self.f.flush( )
self.blockcount = blockcount
if percentcomplete == 100:
    self.f.write("\n")
```

Discussion

Here is an example of the use of this progressbar class, presented, as usual, with a guard of if __name__ == '__main__'. We can make it part of the module containing the class and have it run when the module is executed as a "main script":

```
if __name__ == "__main__":
    from time import sleep
    pb = progressbar(8, "*")
    for count in range(1, 9):
        pb.progress(count)
        sleep(0.2)
    pb = progressbar(100)
    pb.progress(20)
    sleep(0.3)
    pb.progress(47)
    sleep(0.3)
    pb.progress(90)
    sleep(0.3)
    pb.progress(100)
    print "testing 1:"
    pb = progressbar(1)
    pb.progress(1)
```

Programs that run lengthy operations, such as FTP downloads and database insertions, should normally give visual feedback to the user regarding the progress of the task that is running. GUI toolkits generally have such facilities included as "widgets", but if your program does not otherwise require a GUI, it's overkill to give it one just to be able to display a progress bar. This recipe's progress bar class provides an easy way of showing the percentage of completion that is updated periodically by the program.

The recipe operates on the basis of a totally arbitrary final count that the ongoing task is supposed to reach at the end. This makes it optimally easy for the application that makes use of the progressbar class: the application can use any handy unit of measure (such as amount of bytes downloaded for an FTP download, number of records inserted for a database insertion, etc.) to track the task's progress and completion. As long as the same unit of measure applies to both the "final count" and the count argument that the application must periodically pass to the progress method, the progress bar's display will be accurate.

See Also

Documentation on text-mode console I/O in *Python in a Nutshell*.

11.2   Avoiding lambda in Writing Callback Functions

Credit: Danny Yoo, Martin Sjogren

Problem

You need to use many callbacks without arguments, typically while writing a Tkinter-based GUI, and you'd rather avoid using lambda.

Solution

Between the classic lambda approach and a powerful general-purpose currying mechanism is a third, extremely simple way for doing callbacks that can come in handy in many practical cases:

```
def command(callback, *args, **kwargs):
    def do_call():
        return callback(*args, **kwargs)
    # 2.4 only: do_call.__name__ = callback.__name__
    return do_call
```

Discussion

I remember a utility class (to perform the same task handled by a closure in this recipe) quite a while back, but I don't remember who to attribute it to. Perhaps I saw it in John E. Grayson, *Python and Tkinter Programming* (Manning).

Writing a lot of callbacks that give customized arguments can look a little awkward with lambda, so this command closure provides alternative syntax that is easier to read. For example:

```
import Tkinter
def hello(name):
    print "Hello", name
root = Tk()
# the lambda way of doing it:
Button(root, text="Guido", command=lambda name="Guido": hello(name)).pack()
# using the Command class:
Button(root, text="Guido", command=command(hello, "Guido")).pack()
```

Of course, you can also use a more general currying approach, which enables you to fix some of the arguments when you bind the callback, while others may be given at call time (see recipe 16.4 "Associating Parameters with a Function (Currying)"). However, "doing the simplest thing that can possibly work" is a good programming principle (this wording of the principle is due, I believe, to Kent Beck). If your application needs callbacks that fix all arguments at currying time and others that leave some arguments to be determined at callback time, it's probably simpler to use the more general currying approach for all the callbacks. But if all the callbacks you need must fix all arguments at currying time, it may be simpler to forego unneeded generality and use the simpler, less-general approach in this recipe exclusively. You can always refactor later if it turns out that you do need the generality.

See Also

Recipe 16.4 "Associating Parameters with a Function (Currying)"; information about Tkinter can be obtained from a variety of sources, such as Fredrik Lundh, *An Introduction to Tkinter* (PythonWare: *http://www.pythonware.com/library*), New Mexico Tech's *Tkinter Reference* (*http://www.nmt.edu/tcc/help/lang/python/docs.html*), *Python in a Nutshell*, and various other books.

11.3 Using Default Values and Bounds with tkSimpleDialog Functions

Credit: Mike Foord, Peter Cogolo

Problem

You need to get an input value from the user with one of Tkinter's tkSimpleDialog dialog functions, but you want to add a default value, or to ensure that the value entered lies within certain bounds.

Solution

Each of Tkinter's tkSimpleDialog functions (askstring, askfloat, askinteger) supports an optional default value, as well as optional validation against minimum and maximum value. However, this set of features is not clearly spelled out in the documentation. Here's a wrapper function that you may find preferable:

```
import tkSimpleDialog
_dispatch = { str: tkSimpleDialog.askstring,
              int: tkSimpleDialog.askinteger,
              float: tkSimpleDialog.askfloat,
            }
def getinput(title, prompt, type=str, default=None, min=None, max=None):
    ''' gets from the user an input of type `type' (str, int or float),
        optionally with a default value, and optionally constrained to
        lie between the values `min' and `max' (included).
    '''
    f = _dispatch.get(type)
    if not f:
```

```
        raise TypeError, "Can't ask for %r input" % (type,)
    return f(title, prompt, initialvalue=default, minvalue=min, maxvalue=max)
```

Discussion

The built-in `tkSimpleDialog` module offers a few simple functions that pop up dialogs that ask the user to input a string, a float, or an integer—not a very advanced user interface but dirt-simple to use in your programs. Unfortunately, while these functions do support a few nice extras (the ability to pass in a default value, and having the result validated within certain optional minimum and maximum values), the module's documentation (what little there is of it) does not make this feature clear. Even the pydoc-generated page *http://epydoc.sourceforge.net/stdlib/public/tkSimpleDialog-module.html* just says "see SimpleDialog class." Since no such class exists, seeing it is not easy. (The relevant class is actually named _QueryDialog, and due to the leading underscore in the name, it is considered "private". Therefore pydoc does not build a documentation web page for it.)

This recipe shows how to access this functionality that's already part of the Python Standard Library. As a side benefit, it refactors the functionality into a single `getinput` function that takes as an argument the type of input desired (defaulting to `str`, meaning that the default type of result is a string, just as for built-in function `raw_input`). If you prefer the original concept of having three separate functions, it's easy to modify the recipe according to your tastes. The recipe mostly makes the semi-hidden functionality of the original functions' undocumented keyword arguments `initialvalue`, `minvalue` and `maxvalue` manifest and clearer through its optional parameters `default`, `min`, and `max`, which it passes right on to the underlying original function.

See Also

`tkSimpleDialog` module documentation is at *http://epydoc.sourceforge.net/stdlib/public/tkSimpleDialog-module.html*.

11.4 Adding Drag and Drop Reordering to a Tkinter Listbox

Credit: John Fouhy

Problem

You want to use a Tkinter `Listbox` widget, but you want to give the user the additional capability of reordering the entries by drag-and-drop.

Solution

We just need to code the relevant functionality and bind it to the Tkinter event corresponding to the "drag" mouse gesture:

```
import Tkinter
class DDList(Tkinter.Listbox):
    """ A Tkinter listbox with drag'n'drop reordering of entries. """
    def __init__(self, master, **kw):
        kw['selectmode'] = Tkinter.SINGLE
        Tkinter.Listbox.__init__(self, master, kw)
        self.bind('<Button-1>', self.setCurrent)
        self.bind('<B1-Motion>', self.shiftSelection)
        self.curIndex = None
    def setCurrent(self, event):
        self.curIndex = self.nearest(event.y)
    def shiftSelection(self, event):
        i = self.nearest(event.y)
        if i < self.curIndex:
            x = self.get(i)
            self.delete(i)
            self.insert(i+1, x)
            self.curIndex = i
        elif i > self.curIndex:
            x = self.get(i)
            self.delete(i)
            self.insert(i-1, x)
            self.curIndex = i
```

Discussion

Here is an example of use of this DDList class, presented, as usual, with a guard of if __name__ == '__main__' so we can make it part of the module containing the class and have it run when the module is executed as a "main script":

```
if __name__ == '__main__':
    tk = Tkinter.Tk()
    length = 10
    dd = DDList(tk, height=length)
    dd.pack()
    for i in xrange(length):
        dd.insert(Tkinter.END, str(i))
    def show():
        ''' show the current ordering every 2 seconds '''
        for x in dd.get(0, Tkinter.END):
            print x,
        print
        tk.after(2000, show)
    tk.after(2000, show)
    tk.mainloop()
```

Allowing the user of a GUI program to drag the elements of a list into new positions is often useful, and this recipe shows a fairly simple way of adding this functionality to a Tkinter Listbox widget.

This recipe's code tries to ensure that the clicked-on element stays selected by deleting and inserting on either side of it. Nevertheless, it *is* possible, by moving the mouse quickly enough, to start dragging an unselected element instead. While it doesn't cause any major problems, it just looks a bit odd.

This recipe's code is partly based on a post by Fredrik Lundh, *http://mail.python.org/ pipermail/python-list/1999-May/002501.html*.

See Also

Information about Tkinter can be obtained from a variety of sources, such as Fredrik Lundh, *An Introduction to Tkinter* (PythonWare: *http://www.pythonware.com/ library*), New Mexico Tech's *Tkinter Reference* (*http://www.nmt.edu/tcc/help/lang/ python/docs.html*), *Python in a Nutshell*, and various other books.

11.5   Entering Accented Characters in Tkinter Widgets

Credit: Artur de Sousa Rocha

Problem

You want your application to allow the user to easily enter accented characters into Tkinter widgets even from a U.S.-layout keyboard.

Solution

Internationalized applications should enable the user to easily enter letters with accents and diacritics (e.g., umlauts, and tildes) even from a U.S.-layout keyboard. A usefully uniform convention is the following: hitting Ctrl-*accent*, for any kind of accent or diacritic, acts as a *dead key*, ensuring that the next letter hit will be decorated by that accent or diacritic. For example, Ctrl-apostrophe, followed by a, enters an *a* with an acute accent (the character á). The following classes provide the keyboard and widget bindings that allow this internationalized input functionality:

```
from Tkinter import *
from ScrolledText import ScrolledText
from unicodedata import lookup
import os
class Diacritical(object):
    """ Mixin class that adds keyboard bindings for accented characters, plus
        other common functionality (e.g.: Control-A == 'select all' on Windows).
    """
    if os.name == "nt":
```

```
                stroke = '/'
        else:
                stroke = 'minus'
        accents = (('acute', "'"), ('grave', '`'), ('circumflex', '^'),
                   ('tilde', '='), ('diaeresis', '"'), ('cedilla', ','),
                   ('stroke', stroke))
    def __init__(self):
        # Fix some non-Windows-like Tk bindings, if we're on Windows
        if os.name == 'nt':
            self.bind("<Control-Key-a>", self.select_all)
            self.bind("<Control-Key-/>", lambda event: "break")
        # Diacritical bindings
        for a, k in self.accents:
            self.bind("<Control-Key-%s><Key>" % k,
                        lambda event, a=a: self.insert_accented(event.char, a))
    def insert_accented(self, c, accent):
        if c.isalpha():
            if c.isupper():
                cap = 'capital'
            else:
                cap = 'small'
            try:
                c = lookup("latin %s letter %c with %s" % (cap, c, accent))
                self.insert(INSERT, c)
                return "break"
            except KeyError, e:
                pass
class DiacriticalEntry(Entry, Diacritical):
    """ Tkinter Entry widget with some extra key bindings for
        entering typical Unicode characters - with umlauts, accents, etc. """
    def __init__(self, master=None, **kwargs):
        Entry.__init__(self, master=None, **kwargs)
        Diacritical.__init__(self)
    def select_all(self, event=None):
        self.selection_range(0, END)
        return "break"
class DiacriticalText(ScrolledText, Diacritical):
    """ Tkinter ScrolledText widget with some extra key bindings for
        entering typical Unicode characters - with umlauts, accents, etc. """
    def __init__(self, master=None, **kwargs):
        ScrolledText.__init__(self, master=None, **kwargs)
        Diacritical.__init__(self)
    def select_all(self, event=None):
        self.tag_add(SEL, "1.0", "end-1c")
        self.mark_set(INSERT, "1.0")
        self.see(INSERT)
        return "break"
```

Discussion

Here is an example of use of these widget classes. We present the example, as usual,
with a guard of if __name__ == '__main__'; so we can make it part of the module
containing the classes and have it run when the module is executed as a "main
script":

```
def test():
    frame = Frame()
    frame.pack(fill=BOTH, expand=YES)
    if os.name == "nt":
        frame.option_add("*font", "Tahoma 8")     # Win default, Tk uses other
    # The editors
    entry = DiacriticalEntry(frame)
    entry.pack(fill=BOTH, expand=YES)
    text = DiacriticalText(frame, width=76, height=25, wrap=WORD)
    if os.name == "nt":
        text.config(font="Arial 10")
    text.pack(fill=BOTH, expand=YES)
    text.focus()
    frame.master.title("Diacritical Editor")
    frame.mainloop()
if __name__ == "__main__":
    test()
```

You might want to remove the keyboard event settings that don't really have much to do with accents and diacritics, (e.g., Ctrl-A, meaning "select all") to some other, separate mixin class. I keep that functionality together with the actual handling of diacritics basically because I always need both features anyway.

Some design choices might be altered, such as my decision to have Ctrl-equal as the way to enter a tilde. I took that path because I just couldn't find a way to make Ctrl-~ work the right way, at least on my Windows machine! Also, depending on which languages you need to support, you might have to add other accents and diacritics, such as a-ring for Swedish, German scharfes-s, Icelandic eth and thorn, and so forth.

See Also

Docs about the unicodedata module in the *Library Reference* and *Python in a Nutshell*; information about Tkinter can be obtained from a variety of sources, such as Pythonware's *An Introduction to Tkinter*, by Fredrik Lundh (*http://www.pythonware.com/library*), New Mexico Tech's *Tkinter Reference* (*http://www.nmt.edu/tcc/help/lang/python/docs.html*), *Python in a Nutshell*, and various other books.

11.6 Embedding Inline GIFs Using Tkinter

Credit: Brent Burley

Problem

You need to embed GIF images inside your source code—for use in Tkinter buttons, labels, and so on—to make toolbars and the like without worrying about installing the right icon files.

Solution

A lively Tkinter GUI can include many small images. However, you don't want to require that a small GIF file be present for each of these images. Ensuring the presence of many small files is a bother, and if they're missing, your GUI may be unusable. Fortunately, you can construct Tkinter `PhotoImage` objects with inline data. It's easy to convert a GIF to inline form as Python source code, with a little script or snippet that you can save and run separately.

```
import base64
print "icon='''\\\n" + base64.encodestring(open("icon.gif").read()) + "'''"
```

This emits to standard output a lot of strange-looking "text", which you can capture (typically using your shell's facilities for output redirection, or with copy and paste) and split into lines of reasonable length:

```
icon='''R0lGODdhFQAVAPMAAAQ2PESapISCBASCBMTCxPxmNCQiJJya/ISChGRmzPz+/PxmzDQyZ
DQyZDQyZDQyZCwAAAAAFQAVAAAElJDISau9Vh2WMDOgqHHelJwnsXVloqDd2hrMm8pYYiSHYfMMRm
53UL1QHGFFx1MZCciUiVOsPmEkKNVp3UBhJ4Ohy1UxerSgJGZMMBbcBACQlVhRiHvaUsXHgywTdyc
LdxyB gm1vcTyIZW4MeU6NgQEBXEGRcQcIlwQIAwEHoioCAgWmCZOIq5+hA6wIpqislgGhthEAOw==
'''
```

Now, you can use this Python-inlined data in Tkinter:

```
import Tkinter
if __name__ == '__main__':
    root = Tkinter.Tk()
    iconImage = Tkinter.PhotoImage(master=root, data=icon)
    Tkinter.Button(image=iconImage).pack()
```

Discussion

The basic technique is to encode the GIF with the standard Python module `base64` and store the results as a string literal in the Python code. At runtime, the Python code passes that string object to Tkinter's `PhotoImage`. The current release of `PhotoImage` supports GIF and PPM, but inline data is supported only for GIF. To convert between image formats, see recipe 11.7 "Converting Among Image Formats." Of course, you can use `file='filename'`, instead of `data=string`, for either GIF or PPM, if your image data is indeed in a file.

You must keep a reference to the `PhotoImage` object yourself; that reference is not kept by the Tkinter widget. If you pass the object to `Button` and forget it, you will become frustrated! Here's an easy workaround for this minor annoyance:

```
def makeImageWidget(icondata, *args, **kwds):
    if args:
        klass = args.pop(0)
    else:
        klass = Tkinter.Button
    class Widget(klass):
        def __init__(self, image, *args, **kwds):
            kwds['image'] = image
```

```
              klass.__init__(self, *args, **kwds)
              self.__image = image
        return Widget(Tkinter.PhotoImage(data=icondata), *args, **kwds)
```

Using this handy makeImageWidget function, the equivalent of the example in the recipe becomes:

```
    makeImageWidget(icon).pack( )
```

The master argument on PhotoImage is optional; it defaults to the default application window. If you create a new application window (by calling Tk again), you must create your images in that context and supply the master argument, so the makeImageWidget function has to be updated to let you optionally pass the master argument to the PhotoImage constructor. However, most applications do not require this refinement.

See Also

Information about Tkinter can be obtained from a variety of sources, such as Fredrik Lundh, *An Introduction to Tkinter* (PythonWare: *http://www.pythonware.com/ library*), New Mexico Tech's *Tkinter Reference* (*http://www.nmt.edu/tcc/help/lang/ python/docs.html*), *Python in a Nutshell*, and various other books.

11.7 Converting Among Image Formats

Credit: Doug Blanding

Problem

Your image files are in various formats (GIF, JPG, PNG, TIF, BMP), and you need to convert among these formats.

Solution

The Python Imaging Library (PIL) can read and write all of these formats; indeed, net of user-interface concerns, image-file format conversion using PIL boils down to a one-liner:

```
    Image.open(infile).save(outfile)
```

where filenames infile and outfile have the appropriate file extensions to indicate what kind of images we're reading and writing. We just need to wrap a small GUI around this one-liner functionality—for example:

```
#!/usr/bin/env python
import os, os.path, sys
from Tkinter import *
from tkFileDialog import *
import Image
openfile = '' # full pathname: dir(abs) + root + ext
indir = ''
```

```
outdir = ''
def getinfilename():
    global openfile, indir
    ftypes=(('Gif Images', '*.gif'),
            ('Jpeg Images', '*.jpg'),
            ('Png Images', '*.png'),
            ('Tiff Images', '*.tif'),
            ('Bitmap Images', '*.bmp'),
            ("All files", "*"))
    if indir:
        openfile = askopenfilename(initialdir=indir, filetypes=ftypes)
    else:
        openfile = askopenfilename(filetypes=ftypes)
    if openfile:
        indir = os.path.dirname(openfile)
def getoutdirname():
    global indir, outdir
    if openfile:
        indir = os.path.dirname(openfile)
        outfile = asksaveasfilename(initialdir=indir, initialfile='foo')
    else:
        outfile = asksaveasfilename(initialfile='foo')
    outdir = os.path.dirname(outfile)
def save(infile, outfile):
    if infile != outfile:
        try:
            Image.open(infile).save(outfile)
        except IOError:
            print "Cannot convert", infile
def convert():
    newext = frmt.get()
    path, file = os.path.split(openfile)
    base, ext = os.path.splitext(file)
    if var.get():
        ls = os.listdir(indir)
        filelist = []
        for f in ls:
            if os.path.splitext(f)[1] == ext:
                filelist.append(f)
    else:
        filelist = [file]
    for f in filelist:
        infile = os.path.join(indir, f)
        ofile = os.path.join(outdir, f)
        outfile = os.path.splitext(ofile)[0] + newext
        save(infile, outfile)
    win = Toplevel(root)
    Button(win, text='Done', command=win.destroy).pack()
# Divide GUI into 3 frames: top, mid, bot
root = Tk()
root.title('Image Converter')
topframe = Frame(root, borderwidth=2, relief=GROOVE)
topframe.pack(padx=2, pady=2)
Button(topframe, text='Select image to convert',
```

```
        command=getinfilename).pack(side=TOP, pady=4)
multitext = "Convert all image files\n(of this format) in this folder?"
var = IntVar( )
chk = Checkbutton(topframe, text=multitext, variable=var).pack(pady=2)
Button(topframe, text='Select save location',
       command=getoutdirname).pack(side=BOTTOM, pady=4)
midframe = Frame(root, borderwidth=2, relief=GROOVE)
midframe.pack(padx=2, pady=2)
Label(midframe, text="New Format:").pack(side=LEFT)
frmt = StringVar( )
formats = ['.bmp', '.gif', '.jpg', '.png', '.tif']
for item in formats:
    Radiobutton(midframe, text=item, variable=frmt, value=item).pack(anchor=NW)
botframe = Frame(root)
botframe.pack( )
Button(botframe, text='Convert', command=convert).pack(
       side=LEFT, padx=5, pady=5)
Button(botframe, text='Quit', command=root.quit).pack(
       side=RIGHT, padx=5, pady=5)
root.mainloop( )
```

Needing 80 lines of GUI code to wrap a single line of real functionality may be a *bit* extreme, but it's not all that far out of line in my experience with GUI coding ;-).

Discussion

I needed this tool when I was making *.avi* files from the CAD application program I generally use. That CAD program emits images in *.bmp* format, but the AVI*-generating program I normally use requires images in *.jpg* format. Now, thanks to the little script in this recipe (and to the power of Python, Tkinter, and most especially PIL), with a couple of clicks, I get a folder full of images in *.jpg* format ready to be assembled into an AVI file, or, just as easily, files in *.gif* ready to be assembled into an animated GIF image file.

I used to perform this kind of task with simple shell scripts on Unix, using ImageMagick's convert command. But, with this script, I can do exactly the same job just as easily on all sorts of machines, be they Unix, Windows, or Macintosh.

I had to work around one annoying problem to make this script work as I wanted it to. When I'm selecting the location into which a new file is to be written, I need that dialog to give me the option to create a new directory for that purpose. However, on Windows NT, the Browse for Folder dialog doesn't allow me to create a new folder, only to choose among existing ones! My workaround, as you'll see by studying this recipe's Solution, was to use instead the Save As dialog. That dialog does allow me to create a new folder. I do have to indicate the dummy file in that folder, and the file gets ignored; only the directory part is kept. This workaround is not maximally

---

* AVI (Advanced Visual Interface)

elegant, but it took just a few minutes and almost no work on my part, and I can live with the result.

See Also

Information about Tkinter can be obtained from a variety of sources, such as Fredrik Lundh, *An Introduction to Tkinter*, (PythonWare: *http://www.pythonware.com/library*), New Mexico Tech's *Tkinter Reference* (*http://www.nmt.edu/tcc/help/lang/python/docs.html*), *Python in a Nutshell*, and various other books; PIL is at *http://www.pythonware.com/products/pil/*.

11.8 Implementing a Stopwatch in Tkinter

Credit: Jørgen Cederberg, Tobias Klausmann

Problem

You are coding an application in Tkinter and need a widget that implements a stopwatch.

Solution

Implementing a new widget is almost always best done by subclassing Frame:

```
from Tkinter import *
import time
class StopWatch(Frame):
    """ Implements a stop watch frame widget. """
    msec = 50
    def __init__(self, parent=None, **kw):
        Frame.__init__(self, parent, kw)
        self._start = 0.0
        self._elapsedtime = 0.0
        self._running = False
        self.timestr = StringVar()
        self.makeWidgets()
    def makeWidgets(self):
        """ Make the time label. """
        l = Label(self, textvariable=self.timestr)
        self._setTime(self._elapsedtime)
        l.pack(fill=X, expand=NO, pady=2, padx=2)
    def _update(self):
        """ Update the label with elapsed time. """
        self._elapsedtime = time.time() - self._start
        self._setTime(self._elapsedtime)
        self._timer = self.after(self.msec, self._update)
    def _setTime(self, elap):
        """ Set the time string to Minutes:Seconds:Hundredths """
        minutes = int(elap/60)
        seconds = int(elap - minutes*60.0)
        hseconds = int((elap - minutes*60.0 - seconds)*100)
```

```
            self.timestr.set('%02d:%02d:%02d' % (minutes, seconds, hseconds))
    def Start(self):
        """ Start the stopwatch, ignore if already running. """
        if not self._running:
            self._start = time.time() - self._elapsedtime
            self._update()
            self._running = True
    def Stop(self):
        """ Stop the stopwatch, ignore if already stopped. """
        if self._running:
            self.after_cancel(self._timer)
            self._elapsedtime = time.time() - self._start
            self._setTime(self._elapsedtime)
            self._running = False
    def Reset(self):
        """ Reset the stopwatch. """
        self._start = time.time()
        self._elapsedtime = 0.0
        self._setTime(self._elapsedtime)
```

Discussion

Here is an example of use of this StopWatch widget, presented, as usual, with a guard
of if __name__ == '__main__' so we can make it part of the module containing the
class and have it run when the module is executed as a "main script":

```
if __name__ == '__main__':
    def main():
        root = Tk()
        sw = StopWatch(root)
        sw.pack(side=TOP)
        Button(root, text='Start', command=sw.Start).pack(side=LEFT)
        Button(root, text='Stop', command=sw.Stop).pack(side=LEFT)
        Button(root, text='Reset', command=sw.Reset).pack(side=LEFT)
        Button(root, text='Quit', command=root.quit).pack(side=LEFT)
        root.mainloop()
    main()
```

You might want to use time.clock instead of time.time if your stopwatch's purpose
is to measure the amount of CPU time that your program is taking, rather than the
amount of elapsed time. I used time.time, without even bothering to make that
choice easily customizable (you'll need to edit its several appearances in the recipe's
code), because it seems the most natural choice to me by far. One aspect that you
can customize easily, by subclassing and data overriding or simply by setting the msec
instance attribute on a particular StopWatch instance, is how often the time display is
updated onscreen; the default of 50 milliseconds, which translates to 20 updates a
second, may well mean updates that are too frequent for your purposes, although
they suit my own just fine.

See Also

Docs about the time module in the *Library Reference* and *Python in a Nutshell*; information about Tkinter can be obtained from a variety of sources, such as Fredrik Lundh, *An Introduction to Tkinter* (PythonWare: *http://www.pythonware.com/ library*), New Mexico Tech's *Tkinter Reference* (*http://www.nmt.edu/tcc/help/lang/ python/docs.html*), *Python in a Nutshell*, and various other books.

11.9 Combining GUIs and Asynchronous I/O with Threads

Credit: Jacob Hallén, Laura Creighton, Boudewijn Rempt

Problem

You need to access sockets, serial ports, or other asynchronous (but blocking) I/O sources, while running a GUI.

Solution

The solution is to handle a GUI interface on one thread and communicate to it (via Queue instances) the events on I/O channels handled by other threads. Here's the code for the standard Tkinter GUI toolkit that comes with Python:

```
import Tkinter, time, threading, random, Queue
class GuiPart(object):
    def __init__(self, master, queue, endCommand):
        self.queue = queue
        # Set up the GUI
        Tkinter.Button(master, text='Done', command=endCommand).pack( )
        # Add more GUI stuff here depending on your specific needs
    def processIncoming(self):
        """ Handle all messages currently in the queue, if any. """
        while self.queue.qsize( ):
            try:
                msg = self.queue.get(0)
                # Check contents of message and do whatever is needed. As a
                # simple example, let's print it (in real life, you would
                # suitably update the GUI's display in a richer fashion).
                print msg
            except Queue.Empty:
                # just on general principles, although we don't expect this
                # branch to be taken in this case, ignore this exception!
                pass
class ThreadedClient(object):
    """

    Launch the "main" part of the GUI and the worker thread.  periodicCall and
    endApplication could reside in the GUI part, but putting them here
    means that you have all the thread controls in a single place.
```

```
"""
    def __init__(self, master):
        """
        Start the GUI and the asynchronous threads.  We are in the "main"
        (original) thread of the application, which will later be used by
        the GUI as well.  We spawn a new thread for the worker (I/O).
        """
        self.master = master
        # Create the queue
        self.queue = Queue.Queue( )
        # Set up the GUI part
        self.gui = GuiPart(master, self.queue, self.endApplication)
        # Set up the thread to do asynchronous I/O
        # More threads can also be created and used, if necessary
        self.running = True
        self.thread1 = threading.Thread(target=self.workerThread1)
        self.thread1.start( )
        # Start the periodic call in the GUI to check the queue
        self.periodicCall( )
    def periodicCall(self):
        """ Check every 200 ms if there is something new in the queue. """
        self.master.after(200, self.periodicCall)
        self.gui.processIncoming( )
        if not self.running:
            # This is the brutal stop of the system.  You may want to do
            # some cleanup before actually shutting it down.
            import sys
            sys.exit(1)
    def workerThread1(self):
        """
        This is where we handle the asynchronous I/O.  For example, it may be
        a 'select( )'.  One important thing to remember is that the thread has
        to yield control pretty regularly, be it by select or otherwise.
        """
        while self.running:
            # To simulate asynchronous I/O, create a random number at random
            # intervals. Replace the following two lines with the real thing.
            time.sleep(rand.random( ) * 1.5)
            msg = rand.random( )
            self.queue.put(msg)
    def endApplication(self):
        self.running = False
rand = random.Random( )
root = Tkinter.Tk( )
client = ThreadedClient(root)
root.mainloop( )
```

Discussion

This recipe demonstrates the easiest way of handling access to sockets, serial ports, and other asynchronous I/O ports while running a Tkinter-based GUI. The recipe's principles generalize to other GUI toolkits, since most toolkits make it preferable to access the GUI itself from a single thread, and all offer a toolkit-dependent way to set up periodic polling as this recipe does.

Tkinter, like most other GUIs, is best used with all graphic commands in a single thread. On the other hand, it's far more efficient to make I/O channels block, then wait for something to happen, rather than using nonblocking I/O and having to poll at regular intervals. The latter approach may not even be available in some cases, since not all data sources support nonblocking I/O. Therefore, for generality as well as for efficiency, we should handle I/O with a separate thread, or more than one. The I/O threads can communicate in a safe way with the "main", GUI-handling thread through one or more Queues. In this recipe, the GUI thread still has to do some polling (on the Queues), to check whether something in the Queue needs to be processed. Other architectures are possible, but they are much more complex than the one in this recipe. My advice is to start with this recipe, which will handle your needs over 90% of the time, and explore the much more complex alternatives only if it turns out that this approach cannot meet your performance requirements.

This recipe lets a worker thread block in a select (simulated by random sleeps in the recipe's example worker thread). Whenever something arrives, it is received and inserted in a Queue instance. The main (GUI) thread polls the Queue five times per second and processes all messages that have arrived since it last checked. (Polling 5 times per second is frequent enough that the end user will not notice any significant delay but infrequent enough that the computational load on the computer will be negligible.) You may want to fine-tune this feature, depending on your needs.

This recipe solves a common problem that is frequently asked about on Python mailing lists and newsgroups. Other solutions, involving synchronization between threads, help you solve such problems without polling (the self.master.after call in the recipe). Unfortunately, such solutions are generally complicated and messy, since you tend to raise and wait for semaphores throughout your code. In any case, a GUI already has several polling mechanisms built into it (the "main" event loop), so adding one more won't make much difference, especially since it seldom runs. The code has been tested in depth only under Linux, but it should work on any platform with working threads, including Windows.

Here is a PyQt equivalent, with very minor variations:

```
import sys, time, threading, random, Queue, qt
class GuiPart(qt.QMainWindow):
    def __init__(self, queue, endcommand, *args):
        qt.QMainWindow.__init__(self, *args)
        self.queue = queue
        # We show the result of the thread in the gui, instead of the console
        self.editor = qt.QMultiLineEdit(self)
        self.setCentralWidget(self.editor)
        self.endcommand = endcommand
    def closeEvent(self, ev):
        """ We just call the endcommand when the window is closed,
```

```
                    instead of presenting a button for that purpose.  """
                self.endcommand( )
            def processIncoming(self):
                """ Handle all the messages currently in the queue (if any). """
                while self.queue.qsize( ):
                    try:
                        msg = self.queue.get(0)
                        self.editor.insertLine(str(msg))
                    except Queue.Empty:
                        pass
class ThreadedClient(object):
    """
    Launch the "main" part of the GUI and the worker thread.  periodicCall and
    endApplication could reside in the GUI part, but putting them here
    means that you have all the thread controls in a single place.
    """

    def __init__(self):
        # Create the queue
        self.queue = Queue.Queue( )
        # Set up the GUI part
        self.gui = GuiPart(self.queue, self.endApplication)
        self.gui.show( )
        # A timer to periodically call periodicCall
        self.timer = qt.QTimer( )
        qt.QObject.connect(self.timer, qt.SIGNAL("timeout( )"),
                           self.periodicCall)
        # Start the timer -- this replaces the initial call to periodicCall
        self.timer.start(200)
        # Set up the thread to do asynchronous I/O
        # More can be made if necessary
        self.running = True
            self.thread1 = threading.Thread(target=self.workerThread1)
        self.thread1.start( )
    def periodicCall(self):
        """
        Check every 200 ms if there is something new in the queue.
        """
        self.gui.processIncoming( )
        if not self.running:
            root.quit( )
    def endApplication(self):
        self.running = False
    def workerThread1(self):
        """
        This is where we handle the asynchronous I/O.  For example, it may be
        a 'select( )'.  An important thing to remember is that the thread has
        to yield control once in a while.
        """
        while self.running:
            # To simulate asynchronous I/O, we create a random number at
            # random intervals.  Replace the following 2 lines with the real
            # thing.
            time.sleep(rand.random( ) * 0.3)
            msg = rand.random( )
```

```
            self.queue.put(msg)
    rand = random.Random( )
    root = qt.QApplication(sys.argv)
    client = ThreadedClient( )
    root.exec_loop( )
```

As you can see, this PyQt variation has a structure that's uncannily similar to the Tkinter version, with just a few variations (and a few enhancements, such as using QApplication.quit instead of the more brutal sys.exit, and displaying the thread's result in the GUI itself rather than on the console).

See Also

Documentation of the standard library modules threading and Queue in the *Library Reference* and *Python in a Nutshell*; information about Tkinter can be obtained from a variety of sources, such as Fredrik Lundh, *An Introduction to Tkinter* (Pythonware: *http://www.pythonware.com/library*), New Mexico Tech's *Tkinter Reference* (*http://www.nmt.edu/tcc/help/lang/python/docs.html*), *Python in a Nutshell*, and various other books; information about PyQt can be found at PyQt's own web site, *http://www.riverbankcomputing.co.uk/pyqt/index.php*.

11.10 Using IDLE's Tree Widget in Tkinter

Credit: Sanghyeon Seo

Problem

You need to use a Tree widget in your Tkinter application, and you know that such a widget comes with IDLE, the Integrated Development Environment that comes with Python.

Solution

IDLE's functionality is available in the Python Standard Library in package idlelib, so it is easy to import and use in your applications. The Tree widget is in idlelib.TreeWidget. Here, as an example, is how to use that widget to display an XML document's DOM as a tree:

```
from Tkinter import Tk, Canvas
from xml.dom.minidom import parseString
from idlelib.TreeWidget import TreeItem, TreeNode
class DomTreeItem(TreeItem):
    def __init__(self, node):
        self.node = node
    def GetText(self):
        node = self.node
        if node.nodeType == node.ELEMENT_NODE:
            return node.nodeName
        elif node.nodeType == node.TEXT_NODE:
```

```
            return node.nodeValue
    def IsExpandable(self):
        node = self.node
        return node.hasChildNodes()
    def GetSubList(self):
        parent = self.node
        children = parent.childNodes
        prelist = [DomTreeItem(node) for node in children]
        itemlist = [item for item in prelist if item.GetText().strip()]
        return itemlist
if __name__ == '__main__':
    example_data = '''
    <A>
     <B>
      <C>d</C>
      <C>e</C>
     </B>
     <B>
      <C>f</C>
     </B>
    </A>
    '''
    root = Tk()
    canvas = Canvas(root)
    canvas.config(bg='white')
    canvas.pack()
    dom = parseString(example_data)
    item = DomTreeItem(dom.documentElement)
    node = TreeNode(canvas, None, item)
    node.update()
    node.expand()
    root.mainloop()
```

Discussion

My applications needed Tree widgets, and Tkinter does not have such a widget
among its built-in ones. So I started looking around the Internet to see the Tree widgets that had been implemented for Tkinter. After a while, I was pleasantly surprised
to learn that quite a useful one was already installed and working on my computer!
Specifically, I had IDLE, the free Integrated DeveLopment Environment that comes
with Python, and therefore I had idlelib, the package within the standard Python
library that contains just about all of the functionality of IDLE. A Tree widget is
among the widgets that IDLE uses for its own GUI, so idlelib.TreeWidget is just sitting there in the standard Python library, quite usable and useful.

The only problem with idlelib is that it is not well documented as a part of the
Python Standard Library documentation, nor elsewhere. The best documentation I
could find is the pydoc-generated one at *http://pydoc.org/2.3/idlelib.html*. TreeWidget
is one of the modules documented there. I suggest reading the sources on your disk,
which include the docstrings that pydoc is using to build the useful documentation
site. Between sources and pydoc, it is quite possible to reuse some of the rich func-

---

tionality that's included in idlelib, although having *real* docs about it would definitely not hurt. Python is known as the language that comes "with batteries included." When you consider, not just the hundreds of library modules that are fully documented in Python's official docs, but also the many additional library modules that aren't (such as those in idlelib), it's hard to deny this characterization.

This recipe shows how to implement a simple GUI Tree: define a node-item class by subclassing idlelib.TreeWidget.TreeItem, and override some methods. You may want to override ten methods (*http://pydoc.org/2.3/idlelib.TreeWidget.html#TreeItem* has the complete list), and this recipe only needs three: GetText to define how the item is displayed (textually), IsExpandable to tell the Tree whether to put a clickable + character next to the node to allow expansion, GetSubList to return a list of children items in case expansion is required. Other optional methods, which this recipe does not need, allow iconic rather than textual display, double-clicking on nodes, and even editing of Tree items.

See Also

idlelib docs at *http://pydoc.org/2.3/idlelib.html*.

11.11 Supporting Multiple Values per Row in a Tkinter Listbox

Credit: Brent Burley, Pedro Werneck, Eric Rose

Problem

You need a Tkinter widget that works just like a normal Listbox but with multiple values per row.

Solution

When you find a functional limitation in Tkinter, most often the best solution is to build your own widget as a Python class, subclassing an appropriate existing Tkinter widget (often Frame, so you can easily aggregate several native Tkinter widgets into your own compound widget) and extending and tweaking the widget's functionality as necessary. Rather than solving a problem for just one application, this approach gives you a component that you can reuse in many applications. For example, here's a way to make a multicolumn equivalent of a Tkinter Listbox:

```
from Tkinter import *
class MultiListbox(Frame):
    def __init__(self, master, lists):
        Frame.__init__(self, master)
        self.lists = [ ]
        for l, w in lists:
            frame = Frame(self)
            frame.pack(side=LEFT, expand=YES, fill=BOTH)
```

```
                Label(frame, text=1, borderwidth=1, relief=RAISED).pack(fill=X)
                lb = Listbox(frame, width=w, borderwidth=0, selectborderwidth=0,
                            relief=FLAT, exportselection=FALSE)
                lb.pack(expand=YES, fill=BOTH)
                self.lists.append(lb)
                lb.bind('<B1-Motion>', lambda e, s=self: s._select(e.y))
                lb.bind('<Button-1>', lambda e, s=self: s._select(e.y))
                lb.bind('<Leave>', lambda e: 'break')
                lb.bind('<B2-Motion>', lambda e, s=self: s._b2motion(e.x, e.y))
                lb.bind('<Button-2>', lambda e, s=self: s._button2(e.x, e.y))
            frame = Frame(self)
            frame.pack(side=LEFT, fill=Y)
            Label(frame, borderwidth=1, relief=RAISED).pack(fill=X)
            sb = Scrollbar(frame, orient=VERTICAL, command=self._scroll)
            sb.pack(expand=YES, fill=Y)
            self.lists[0]['yscrollcommand'] = sb.set
        def _select(self, y):
            row = self.lists[0].nearest(y)
            self.selection_clear(0, END)
            self.selection_set(row)
            return 'break'
        def _button2(self, x, y):
            for l in self.lists:
                l.scan_mark(x, y)
            return 'break'
        def _b2motion(self, x, y):
            for l in self.lists
                l.scan_dragto(x, y)
            return 'break'
        def _scroll(self, *args):
            for l in self.lists:
                apply(l.yview, args)
            return 'break'
        def curselection(self):
            return self.lists[0].curselection()
        def delete(self, first, last=None):
            for l in self.lists:
                l.delete(first, last)
        def get(self, first, last=None):
            result = []
            for l in self.lists:
                result.append(l.get(first,last))
            if last: return apply(map, [None] + result)
            return result
        def index(self, index):
            self.lists[0].index(index)
        def insert(self, index, *elements):
            for e in elements:
                i = 0
                for l in self.lists:
                    l.insert(index, e[i])
                    i = i + 1
        def size(self):
            return self.lists[0].size()
        def see(self, index):
```

```
        for l in self.lists:
            l.see(index)
    def selection_anchor(self, index):
        for l in self.lists:
            l.selection_anchor(index)
    def selection_clear(self, first, last=None):
        for l in self.lists:
            l.selection_clear(first, last)
    def selection_includes(self, index):
        return self.lists[0].selection_includes(index)
    def selection_set(self, first, last=None):
        for l in self.lists:
            l.selection_set(first, last)
if __name__ == '__main__':
    tk = Tk()
    Label(tk, text='MultiListbox').pack()
    mlb = MultiListbox(tk, (('Subject', 40), ('Sender', 20), ('Date', 10)))
    for i in range(1000):
      mlb.insert(END,
          ('Important Message: %d' % i, 'John Doe', '10/10/%04d' % (1900+i)))
    mlb.pack(expand=YES, fill=BOTH)
    tk.mainloop()
```

Discussion

This recipe shows a compound widget that gangs multiple Tk Listbox widgets to a single scrollbar to achieve a simple multicolumn scrolled listbox. Most of the Listbox API is mirrored, to make the widget act like normal Listbox, but with multiple values per row. The resulting widget is lightweight, fast, and easy to use. The main drawback is that only text is supported, which is a fundamental limitation of the underlying Listbox widget.

In this recipe's implementation, only single selection is allowed, but the same idea could be extended to multiple selection. User-resizable columns and auto-sorting by clicking on the column label should also be possible. Auto-scrolling while dragging Button-1 was disabled because it broke the synchronization between the lists. However, scrolling with Button-2 works fine. Mice with scroll wheels appear to behave in different ways depending on the platform. For example, while things appear to work fine with the preceding code on some platforms (such as Windows/XP), on other platforms using X11 (such as Linux), I've observed that mouse scroll wheel events correspond to Button-4 and Button-5, so you could deal with them just by adding at the end of the for loop in method __init__ the following two statements:

```
lb.bind('<Button-4>', lambda e, s=self: s._scroll(SCROLL, -1, UNITS))
lb.bind('<Button-5>', lambda e, s=self: s._scroll(SCROLL, +1, UNITS))
```

This addition should be innocuous on platforms such as Windows/XP. You should check this issue on all platforms on which you need to support mouse scroll wheels.

If you need to support sorting by column-header clicking, you can obtain the hook needed for that functionality with a fairly modest change to this recipe's code. Specifically, within the for loop in method __init__, you can change the current start:

```
for l, w in lists:
    frame = Frame(self)
    frame.pack(side=LEFT, expand=YES, fill=BOTH)
    Label(frame, text=l, borderwidth=1, relief=RAISED).pack(fill=X)
```

to the following richer code:

```
for l, w, sort_command in lists:
    frame = Frame(self)
    frame.pack(side=LEFT, expand=YES, fill=BOTH)
    Button(frame, text=l, borderwidth=1, relief=RAISED,
            command=sort_command).pack(fill=X)
```

To take advantage of this hook, you then need to pass as the lists' argument, rather than one tuple of pairs, a list of three tuples, the third item of each tuple being an object callable with no arguments to perform the appropriate kind of sorting. In my applications, I've generally found this specific refinement to be more trouble than it's worth, but I'm presenting it anyway (although not in the actual "Solution" of this recipe!) just in case *your* applications differ in this respect. Maybe sorting by column header clicking is something that's absolutely invaluable to you.

One note about the implementation: in the MultiListbox.__init__ method, several lambda forms are used as the callable second arguments (callbacks) of the bind method calls on the contained Listbox widgets. This approach is traditional, but if you share the widespread dislike for lambda, you should know that lambda is never truly necessary. In this case, the easiest way to avoid the lambdas is to redefine all the relevant methods (_select, _button2, etc.) as taking two formal arguments (self, e) and extract the data they need from argument e. Then in the bind calls, you can simply pass the bound self._select method, and so on.

See Also

Information about Tkinter can be obtained from a variety of sources, such as Pythonware's *An Introduction to Tkinter*, by Fredrik Lundh (*http://www.pythonware.com/library*), New Mexico Tech's *Tkinter Reference* (*http://www.nmt.edu/tcc/help/lang/python/docs.html*), *Python in a Nutshell*, and various other books.

11.12 Copying Geometry Methods and Options Between Tkinter Widgets

Credit: Pedro Werneck

Problem

You want to create new Tkinter compound widgets, not by inheriting from Frame and packing other widgets inside, but rather by setting geometry methods and options from other widget to another.

Solution

Here is an example of a compound widget built by this approach:

```python
from Tkinter import *
class LabeledEntry(Entry):
    """ An Entry widget with an attached Label """
    def __init__(self, master=None, **kw):
        ekw = {}                                # Entry options dictionary
        fkw = {}                                # Frame options dictionary
        lkw = {'name':'label'}                  # Label options dictionary
        skw = {'padx':0, 'pady':0, 'fill':'x',  # Geometry manager opts dict
                'side':'left'}
        fmove = ('name',)                       # Opts to move to the Frame dict
        lmove = ('text', 'textvariable',
                'anchor','bitmap', 'image')     # Opts to move to the Label dict
        smove = ('side', 'padx', 'pady',        # Opts to move to the Geometry
                'fill')                         # manager dictionary
        # dispatch each option towards the appropriate component
        for k, v in kw:
            if k in fmove: fkw[k] = v
            elif k in lmove: lkw[k] = v
            elif k in smove: skw[k] = v
            else: ekw[k] = v
        # make all components with the accumulated options
        self.body = Frame(master, **fkw)
        self.label = Label(self.body, **lkw)
        self.label.pack(side='left', fill=skw['fill'],
                        padx=skw['padx'], pady=skw['pady'])
        Entry.__init__(self, self.body, **ekw)
        self.pack(side=skw['side'], fill=skw['fill'],
                padx=skw['padx'], pady=skw['pady'])
        methods = (Pack.__dict__.keys() +   # Set Frame geometry methods to self
                Grid.__dict__.keys() +
                Place.__dict__.keys())
        for m in methods:
            if m[0] != '_' and m != 'config' and m != 'configure':
                setattr(self, m, getattr(self.body, m))
```

Discussion

Here is an example of use of this LabeledEntry widget, presented, as usual, with a guard of if __name__ == '__main__' so we can make it part of the module containing the class and have it run when the module is executed as a "main script":

```python
if __name__ == '__main__':
    root = Tk()
    le1 = LabeledEntry(root, name='label1', text='Label 1: ',
                    width=5, relief=SUNKEN, bg='white', padx=3)
    le2 = LabeledEntry(root, name='label2', text='Label 2: ',
                    relief=SUNKEN, bg='red', padx=3)
    le3 = LabeledEntry(root, name='label3', text='Label 3: ',
                    width=40, relief=SUNKEN, bg='yellow', padx=3)
    le1.pack(expand=1, fill=X)
```

```
le2.pack(expand=1, fill=X)
le3.pack(expand=1, fill=X)
root.mainloop( )
```

The usual approach to defining new compound Tkinter widgets is to inherit from
Frame and pack your component widgets inside. While simple and habitual, that
approach has a few problems. In particular, you need to invent, design, document,
and implement additional methods or options to access the component widgets'
attributes from outside of the compound widget class. Using another alternative
(which I've often seen done, but it's still a practice that is *not* advisable at all!), you
can violate encapsulation and Demeter's Law by having other code access the component widgets directly. If you do violate encapsulation, you'll pay for it in the not-
so-long run, when you find a need to tweak your compound widget and discover
that you can't do it without breaking lots of code that depends on the compound
widget's internal structure. Those consequences are bad enough when you own all of
the code in question, but it's worse if you have "published" your widget and *other*
people's code depends on it.

This recipe shows it doesn't have to be that bad, by elaborating upon an idea I first
saw used in the ScrolledText widget, which deserves to be more widely exposed.
Instead of inheriting from Frame, you inherit from the "main" widget of your new
compound widget. Then, you create a Frame widget to be used as a body, pretty
much like in the more usual approach. Then, and here comes the interesting novelty, you create dicts for each component widget you contain and *move* to those dictionaries the respective options that pertain to component widgets.

The novelty continues after you've packed the "main" widget: at that point, you can
reset said widget's geometry methods to the base Frame attributes (meaning, in this
case, methods), so that accessing the object methods will in fact access the inner base
Frame geometry methods. This transparent, seamless delegation by juggling bound
methods is uniquely Pythonic and is part of what makes this recipe so novel and
interesting!

The main advantage of this recipe's approach is that you can create your widget with
options to all slave widgets inside it in a single line, just like any other widget, instead
of doing any further w.configure or w['option'] calls or accesses to set all details
exactly the way you want them. To be honest, there *is* a potential disadvantage, too:
in this recipe's approach, it's hard to handle options with the same name on different
component widgets. However, sometimes you can handle them by *renaming* options:
if two separate widgets need a 'foo' option that's also of interest to the "main"
widget, for example, use, 'upper_foo' and 'lower_foo' variants and rename them
appropriately (with yet another auxiliary dictionary) at the same time you're
dispatching them to the appropriate dictionary of component-widget options. You
can't sensibly keep doing that "forever", as the number of component widgets com-
peting for the same option grows without bounds: if that happens, revert to the good
old tried-and-true approach. But for nine out of ten compound widgets you find

yourself programming, you'll find this recipe's approach to be an interesting alternative to the usual, traditional approach to compound-widget programming.

See Also

Information about Tkinter can be obtained from a variety of sources, such as Fredrik Lundh, *An Introduction to Tkinter* (PythonWare: *http://www.pythonware.com/library*), New Mexico Tech's *Tkinter Reference* (*http://www.nmt.edu/tcc/help/lang/python/docs.html*), *Python in a Nutshell*, and various other books.

11.13 Implementing a Tabbed Notebook for Tkinter

Credit: Iuri Wickert

Problem

You have some Tkinter applications, each with a single top-level window, and want to organize them as panels in a tabbed notebook with minimal changes to your original applications' source code.

Solution

A simple widget class can implement a notebook with all the features we need, including all possible orientations and the ability to add and switch frames (panels) at will:

```
from Tkinter import *
class notebook(object):
    def __init__(self, master, side=LEFT):
        self.active_fr = None
        self.count = 0
        self.choice = IntVar(0)
        if side in (TOP, BOTTOM): self.side = LEFT
        else: self.side = TOP
        self.rb_fr = Frame(master, borderwidth=2, relief=RIDGE)
        self.rb_fr.pack(side=side, fill=BOTH)
        self.screen_fr = Frame(master, borderwidth=2, relief=RIDGE)
        self.screen_fr.pack(fill=BOTH)
    def __call__(self):
        return self.screen_fr
    def add_screen(self, fr, title):
        b = Radiobutton(self.rb_fr, text=title, indicatoron=0,
                        variable=self.choice,
                        value=self.count, command=lambda: self.display(fr))
        b.pack(fill=BOTH, side=self.side)
        if not self.active_fr:
            fr.pack(fill=BOTH, expand=1)
            self.active_fr = fr
```

```
        self.count += 1
    def display(self, fr):
        self.active_fr.forget()
        fr.pack(fill=BOTH, expand=1)
        self.active_fr = fr
```

Just save this code as a *notebook.py* module, somewhere on your Python sys.path, and you can import and use it in your apps.

Discussion

The simplest way to show how this notebook class works is with a simple demonstration program:

```
from Tkinter import *
from notebook import *
# make a toplevel with a notebook in it, with tabs on the left:
root = Tk()
nb = notebook(root, LEFT)
# make a few diverse frames (panels), each using the NB as 'master':
f1 = Frame(nb())
b1 = Button(f1, text="Button 1")
e1 = Entry(f1)
# pack your widgets in the frame before adding the frame to the
# notebook, do NOT pack the frame itself!
b1.pack(fill=BOTH, expand=1)
e1.pack(fill=BOTH, expand=1)
f2 = Frame(nb())
b2 = Button(f2, text='Button 2')
b3 = Button(f2, text='Beep 2', command=Tk.bell)
b2.pack(fill=BOTH, expand=1)
b3.pack(fill=BOTH, expand=1)
f3 = Frame(nb())
# add the frames as notebook 'screens' and run this GUI app
nb.add_screen(f1, "Screen 1")
nb.add_screen(f2, "Screen 2")
nb.add_screen(f3, "dummy")
root.mainloop()
```

Tkinter is a simple GUI toolkit, easy to use but notoriously feature-poor when compared to more advanced toolkits. And yet, sometimes advanced features are not all that difficult to add! I wondered how I could use a tabbed appearance, also known as a *notebook*, to organize various pages of an application, or various related applications, simply and elegantly. I discovered that simulating a notebook widget by using standard Tkinter frames and radio buttons was not only possible, but also quite simple and effective.

Tk has some "odd", and somewhat unknown, corners, which make the whole task a snap. The indicatoron option on a radio button reverts the radio button default appearance back to the normal button look—a rectangle, which may not be a perfect-looking tab but is plenty good enough for me. Each Tkinter frame has a forget

---

method, which allows easy and fast swapping of "screens" (notebook panels, application frames) within the single "screen frame" of the notebook object.

To convert any existing Tkinter app, based on a single top-level window, to run inside a notebook panel, all you need to do is to change the application master frame's root, which is generally a top-level widget (an instance of Tkinter's Tk class), to the one provided by the notebook object when you call it. (The three occurrences of nb( ) in the example code show how to go about it.)

The notebook implementations in other toolkits often have advanced features such as the ability to exclude (remove) some frames as well as adding others. I have not found this kind of thing to be necessary, and so I have taken no trouble in this recipe to make it possible: all references to the external frames are kept implicitly in lambda closures, without any obvious way to remove them. If you think you need the ability to remove frames, you might consider an alternative architecture: keep the frames' references in a list, indexed by the binding variable of the radio buttons (i.e., the choice attribute of each radio button). Doing so lets you destroy a "frame" and its associated radio button in a reasonably clean way.

See Also

Information about Tkinter can be obtained from a variety of sources, such as Fredrik Lundh, *An Introduction to Tkinter* (PythonWare: *http://www.pythonware.com/library*), New Mexico Tech's *Tkinter Reference* (*http://www.nmt.edu/tcc/help/lang/python/docs.html*), *Python in a Nutshell*, and various other books.

11.14 Using a wxPython Notebook with Panels

Credit: Mark Nenadov

Problem

You want to design a wxPython GUI comprised of multiple panels—each driven by a separate Python script running in the background—that let the user switch back and forth (i.e., a wxPython Notebook).

Solution

Notebooks are an effective GUI approach, as they let the user select the desired view from several options at any time with an instinctive button click. wxPython supports this feature by supplying a wxNotebook widget. Here is a "frame" class that holds a notebook and adds to it three panes, each driven by a different Python module (not shown) through a function in each module named runPanel:

```
from wxPython.wx import *
class MainFrame(wxFrame):
    #
```

```
# snipped: mainframe class attributes
#
def __init__(self, parent, id, title):
    #
    # snipped: frame-specific initialization
    #
    # Create the notebook object
    self.nb = wxNotebook(self, -1,
        wxPoint(0,0), wxSize(0,0), wxNB_FIXEDWIDTH)
    # Populate the notebook with pages (panels), each driven by a
    # separate Python module which gets imported for the purpose:
    panel_names = "First Panel", "Second Panel", "The Third One"
    panel_scripts = "panel1", "panel2", "panel3"
    for name, script in zip(panel_names, panel_scripts):
        # Make panel named 'name' (driven by script 'script'.py)
        self.module = __import__(script, globals())
        self.window = self.module.runPanel(self, self.nb)
        if self.window: self.nb.AddPage(self.window, name)
    #
    # snipped: rest of frame initialization
    #
```

Discussion

wxPython provides a powerful notebook user-interface object, with multiple panels, each of which can be built and driven by a separate Python script (actually a module, not a "main script"). Each panel's script runs in the background, even when the panel is not selected, and maintains state as the user switches back and forth.

This recipe isn't a fully functional wxPython application, but it adequately demonstrates how to use notebooks and panels (which it loads by importing files). This recipe assumes that you have files named *panel1.py*, *panel2.py*, and *panel3.py*, each of which contains a runPanel function that takes two arguments (a wxFrame and a wxNotebook in the frame) and returns a wxPanel object.

The notebook-specific functionality is easy: the notebook object is created by the wxNotebook function, and an instance of this recipe's MainFrame class saves its notebook object as the self.nb instance attribute. Then, each page (a wxPanel object), obtained by calling the separate script's runPanel functions, is added to the notebook by calling the notebook's AddPage method, with the page object as the first argument and a name string as the second. Your code only needs to make the notebook and its panels usable; the wxWidgets framework, as wrapped by the wxPython package, handles all the rest on your behalf.

See Also

wxPython, and the wxWidgets toolkit it depends on, are described in detail at *http://www.wxPython.org* and *http://www.wxWidgets.org*.

11.15 Implementing an ImageJ Plug-in in Jython

Credit: Ferdinand Jamitzky, Edoardo "Dado" Marcora

Problem

You perform image processing using the excellent free program ImageJ and need to extend it with your own plug-ins, but you want to code those plug-ins in Jython rather than in Java.

Solution

Jython can do all that Java can, but with Python's elegance and high productivity. For example, here is an ImageJ plug-in that implements a simple image inverter:

```
import ij
class Inverter_py(ij.plugin.filter.PlugInFilter):
    def setup(self, arg, imp):
        """@sig public int setup(String arg, ij.ImagePlus imp)"""
        return ij.plugin.filter.PlugInFilter.DOES_8G
    def run(self,ip):
        """@sig public void run(ij.process.ImageProcessor ip)"""
        pixels = ip.getPixels()
        width = ip.getWidth()
        r = ip.getRoi()
        for y in range(r.y, r.y+r.height):
            for x in range(r.x, r.x+r.width):
                i = y*width + x
                pixels[i] = 255-pixels[i]
```

Discussion

To make this plug-in usable from ImageJ, all you need to do is compile it into a Java bytecode class using the jythonc command with the appropriate command-line option switches. For example, I use IBM's open source Java compiler, jikes, and I have placed it into the *C:\ImageJ* directory, which also holds the *plugins* and *jre* subdirectories. So, in my case, the command line to use is:

```
# jythonc -w C:\ImageJ\plugins\Jython -C C:\ImageJ\jikes
    -J "-bootclasspath C:\ImageJ\jre\lib\rt.jar -nowarn"
```

If you use Sun's Java SDK, or other Java implementations, you just change the -C argument, which indicates the path of your Java compiler and the -J argument, which specifies the options to pass to your Java compiler.

See Also

ImageJ is at *http://rsb.info.nih.gov/ij/*; Jython is at *http://www.jython.org*; jikes is at *http://www-124.ibm.com/developerworks/oss/jikes/*; for more on using Jython with ImageJ, *http://marcora.caltech.edu/jython_imagej_howto.htm*.

11.16 Viewing an Image from a URL with Swing and Jython

Credit: Joel Lawhead, Chuck Parker

Problem

You want to make a simple Swing image viewer, accepting the URL to an image and displaying the image in a Swing window.

Solution

Jython makes this task very easy:

```
from pawt import swing
from java import net
def view(url):
    frame = swing.JFrame("Image: " + url, visible=1)
    frame.getContentPane( ).add(swing.JLabel(swing.ImageIcon(net.URL(url))))
    frame.setSize(400,250)
    frame.show( )
if __name__ == '__main__':
    view("http://www.python.org/pics/pythonHi.gif")
```

Discussion

Swing's JLabel and ImageIcon widgets can be easily combined in Jython to make a simple image viewer. The need to pass a URL to the view function is not at all a limitation, because you can always use the file: protocol in your URL if you want to display an image that lives on your filesystem rather than out there on the Web. Remember that the U in URL stands for *Universal*!

See Also

Swing docs are at *http://java.sun.com/docs/books/tutorial/uiswing/*; Jython is at *http://www.jython.org*.

11.17 Getting User Input on Mac OS

Credit: Matteo Rattotti

Problem

You're writing a simple application to run on Mac OS and want to get an input value from the user without frightening the user by opening a scary terminal window.

Solution

Many Mac OS users are frightened by the terminal, so Python scripts that require simple input from the user shouldn't rely on normal textual input but rather should use the EasyDialogs module from the Python Standard Library. Here is an example, a simple image converter and resizer application:

```python
import os, sys, EasyDialogs, Image
# instead of relying on sys.argv, ask the user via a simple dialog:
rotater = ('Rotate right', 'Rotate image by 90 degrees clockwise')
rotatel = ('Rotate left', 'Rotate image by 90 degrees anti-clockwise')
scale = ('Makethumb', 'Make a 100x100 thumbnail')
str = ['Format JPG', 'Format PNG']
cmd = [rotater, rotatel, scale]
optlist = EasyDialogs.GetArgv(str, cmd,
            addoldfile=False, addnewfile=False, addfolder=True)
# now we can parse the arguments and options (we could use getopt, too):
dirs = [ ]
format = "JPEG"
rotationr = False
rotationl = False
resize = False
for arg in optlist:
    if arg == "--Format JPG":
        format = "JPEG"
    if arg == "--Format PNG":
        format = "PNG"
    if arg == "Rotate right":
        rotationr = True
    if arg == "Rotate left":
        rotationl = True
    if arg == "Makethumb":
        resize = True
    if os.path.isdir(arg):
        dirs.append(arg)
if len(dirs) == 0:
    EasyDialogs.Message("No directories specified")
    sys.exit(0)
# Now, another, simpler dialog, uses the system's folder-chooser dialog:
path = EasyDialogs.AskFolder("Choose destination directory")
if not path:
    sys.exit(0)
if not os.path.isdir(path) :
    EasyDialogs.Message("Destination directory not found")
    sys.exit(0)
# and now a progress bar:
tot_numfiles = sum([ len(os.listdir(d)) for d in dirs ])
bar = EasyDialogs.ProgressBar("Processing", tot_numfiles)
for d in dirs:
    for item in os.listdir(d):
        bar.inc( )
        try:
            objpict = Image.open(d + "/" + item)
```

```
            if resize: objpict.thumbnail((100, 100, 1))
            if rotationr: objpict = objpict.rotate(-90)
            if rotationl: objpict = objpict.rotate(90)
            objpict.save(path + "/" + item + "." + format, format)
        except:
            print item + " is not an image"
# and one last dialog...:
score = EasyDialogs.AskYesNoCancel("Do you like this program?")
if score == 1:
    EasyDialogs.Message("Wwowowowow, EasyDialog roolz, ;-)")
elif score == 0:
    EasyDialogs.Message("Sigh, sorry, will do better next time!-(")
elif score == -1:
    EasyDialogs.Message("Hey, you didn't answer?!")
```

Discussion

This recipe's program is quite trivial, mostly meant to show how to use a few of the dialogs in the EasyDialogs standard library module for the Mac. You could add quite a few more features, or do a better job of implementing some of those in this recipe, for example, by using getopt from the Python Standard Library to parse the arguments and options, rather than the roll-your-own approach we've taken.

Since EasyDialogs is in the Python Standard Library for the Mac, you can count on finding that module, as well as Python itself, in any Mac that runs Mac OS X 10.3 Panther—and that's well over ten million Macs, according to Apple. Just build your script into an application with bundlebuilder or, even better, with py2app and distutils. Doing so will enable you to distribute your Python application so that users can park it in the Dock, use drag-and-drop from the Finder to give it arguments, and so on. Documentation for both bundlebuilder and py2app can be found on the Wiki at *http://www.pythonmac.org/wiki*.

The EasyDialogs module in the Python Standard Library works only on the Mac, but if you like the concept, you can try out Jimmy Retzlaff's port of that module to Windows, available for download at *http://www.averdevelopment.com/python/EasyDialogs.html*.

See Also

Library Reference documentation on EasyDialogs; *http://www.pythonmac.org/wiki* for more information on Python for Mac resources; py2app is at *http://undefined.org/python/*; *http://www.averdevelopment.com/python/EasyDialogs.html* for a port of EasyDialogs to Microsoft Windows.

11.18 Building a Python Cocoa GUI Programmatically

Credit: Dethe Elza

Problem

You are developing a Python application using Mac OS X's Aqua interface (through Apple's Cocoa toolkit and the PyObjC, Python/Objective-C bridge). You want to build the application's user interface within the program itself (as is normally done in most other Python GUI toolkits), rather than via Apple's Interface Builder (IB) and resulting *.nib* files (as is usually done with Cocoa for Aqua applications).

Solution

Anything that you can do via Interface Builder and *.nib* files, you can also do directly in your program. Here is a simple demo:

```
from math import sin, cos, pi
from Foundation import *
from AppKit import *
class DemoView(NSView):
    n = 10
    def X(self, t):
        return (sin(t) + 1) * self.width * 0.5
    def Y(self, t):
        return (cos(t) + 1) * self.height * 0.5
    def drawRect_(self, rect):
        self.width = self.bounds()[1][0]
        self.height = self.bounds()[1][1]
        NSColor.whiteColor().set()
        NSRectFill(self.bounds())
        NSColor.blackColor().set()
        step = 2 * pi/self.n
        loop = [i * step for i in range(self.n)]
        for f in loop:
            p1 = NSMakePoint(self.X(f), self.Y(f))
            for g in loop:
                p2 = NSMakePoint(self.X(g), self.Y(g))
                NSBezierPath.strokeLineFromPoint_toPoint_(p1, p2)
class AppDelegate(NSObject):
    def windowWillClose_(self, notification):
        app.terminate_(self)
def main():
    global app
    app = NSApplication.sharedApplication()
    graphicsRect = NSMakeRect(100.0, 350.0, 450.0, 400.0)
    myWindow = NSWindow.alloc().initWithContentRect_styleMask_backing_defer_(
        graphicsRect,
        NSTitledWindowMask
        | NSClosableWindowMask
```

```
            | NSResizableWindowMask
            | NSMiniaturizableWindowMask,
            NSBackingStoreBuffered,
            False)
        myWindow.setTitle_('Tiny Application Window')
        myView = DemoView.alloc().initWithFrame_(graphicsRect)
        myWindow.setContentView_(myView)
        myDelegate = AppDelegate.alloc().init()
        myWindow.setDelegate_(myDelegate)
        myWindow.display()
        myWindow.orderFrontRegardless()
        app.run()
        print 'Done'
    if __name__ == '__main__':
        main()
```

Discussion

Most programmers prefer to lay out their programs' user interfaces graphically, and Apple's Interface Builder application, which comes with Apple's free Developer Tools (also known as XCode), is a particularly nice tool for this task (when you're using Apple's Cocoa toolkit to develop a GUI for Mac OS X's Aqua interface). (The PyObjC extension makes using Cocoa from Python an obvious choice, if you're developing applications for the Macintosh.)

Sometimes it is more convenient to keep all the GUI building within the very program I'm developing, at least at first. During the early iterations of developing a new program, I often need to refactor everything drastically as I rethink the problem space. When that happens, trying to find all the connections that have to be modified or renamed is a chore in Interface Builder or in any other such interactive GUI-painting application.

Some popular GUI toolkits, such as Tkinter, are based on the idea that the program builds its own GUI at startup by defining the needed objects and appropriately calling functions and methods. It may not be entirely clear to users of other toolkits, such as Cocoa, that just about every toolkit is capable of operating in a similar manner, allowing "programmatic" GUI construction. This applies even to those toolkits that are most often used by means of interactive GUI-painting applications. By delaying the use of IB until your program is more functional and stable, it's more likely that you'll be able to design an appropriate interface. This recipe can help get you started in that direction.

This recipe's code is a straight port of *tiny.m*, from Simson Garfinkel and Michael Mahoney, *Building Cocoa Applications: A Step-by-Step Guide* (O'Reilly), showing how to build a Cocoa application without using Interface Builder nor loading *.nib* files. This recipe was my first PyObjC project, and it is indebted both to the Cocoa book and to PyObjC's "Hello World" example code. Starting from this simple, almost toy-level recipe, I was able to use Python's file handling to easily build a graphical quote viewer and ramp up from there to building rich, full-fledged GUIs.

See Also

Garfinkel and Mahoney's *Building Cocoa Applications: A Step-by-Step Guide* (O'Reilly); PyObjC is at *http://pyobjc.sourceforge.net/*.

11.19 Implementing Fade-in Windows with IronPython

Credit: Brian Quinlan

Problem

You're developing an application with IronPython (using Windows Forms on Microsoft .NET), and you want to use fade-in windows to display temporary data.

Solution

Fading in can best be accomplished using the Form.Opacity property and a Timer. Fade-in windows, being a form of pop-up window, should also set the topmost window style:

```
from System.Windows.Forms import *
from System.Drawing import *
from System.Drawing.Imaging import *
form = Form(Text="Window Fade-ins with IronPython",
            HelpButton=False, MinimizeBox=True, MaximizeBox=True,
            WindowState=FormWindowState.Maximized,
            FormBorderStyle=FormBorderStyle.Sizable,
            StartPosition=FormStartPosition.CenterScreen,
            Opacity = 0)
# create a checker background pattern image
box_size = 25
image = Bitmap(box_size * 2, box_size * 2)
graphics = Graphics.FromImage(image)
graphics.FillRectangle(Brushes.Black, 0, 0, box_size, box_size)
graphics.FillRectangle(Brushes.White, box_size, 0, box_size, 50)
graphics.FillRectangle(Brushes.White, 0, box_size, box_size, box_size)
graphics.FillRectangle(Brushes.Black, box_size, box_size, box_size, box_size)
form.BackgroundImage = image
# create a control to allow the opacity to be adjusted
opacity_tracker = TrackBar(Text="Transparency",
                           Height = 20, Dock = DockStyle.Bottom,
                           Minimum = 0, Maximum = 100, Value = 0,
                           TickFrequency = 10, Enabled = False)
def track_opacity_change(sender, event):
    form.Opacity = opacity_tracker.Value / 100.0
opacity_tracker.ValueChanged += track_opacity_change
```

```
form.Controls.Add(opacity_tracker)
# create a timer to animate the initial appearance of the window
timer = Timer()
timer.Interval = 15
def tick(sender, event):
    val = opacity_tracker.Value + 1
    if val >= opacity_tracker.Maximum:
        # ok, we're done, set the opacity to maximum, stop the
        # animation, and let the user play with the opacity manually
        opacity_tracker.Value = opacity_tracker.Maximum
        opacity_tracker.Minimum = 20     # don't let the window disappear
        opacity_tracker.Enabled = True
        timer.Stop()
    else:
        opacity_tracker.Value = val
timer.Tick += tick
timer.Start()
form.ShowDialog()
```

Discussion

While IronPython, at the time of this writing, is not yet entirely mature, and it therefore cannot be recommended for use to develop Windows Forms applications intended for production deployment, any .NET (or Mono) developer should already download IronPython and start playing with it; when it matures, it promises to provide a nonpareil high-productivity avenue for .NET application development.

This recipe shows that IronPython can already do, with elegance and ease, a number of interesting things with Windows Forms. Specifically, the recipe demonstrates several techniques of Windows Forms programming:

- How to create a form.
- How to draw in an off-screen image.
- How to create a control, add it to a form, and manage its events.
- How to create a timer and add a delegate to get periodic events.

More specifically, this recipe shows how to create a fade-in window using IronPython. Several applications use fade-in windows for temporary data; look, for example, at Microsoft's new Outlook XP. It displays mail messages through a fade-in/fade-out pop-up window. It looks cool, it's also quite useful, and IronPython makes it a snap!

See Also

IronPython is at *http://ironpython.com/*.

## CHAPTER 12

Processing XML

12.0 Introduction

Credit: Paul Prescod, co-author of XML Handbook *(Prentice-Hall)*

XML has become a central technology for all kinds of information exchange. Today, most new file formats that are invented are based on XML. Most new protocols are based upon XML. It simply isn't possible to work with the emerging Internet infrastructure without supporting XML. Luckily, Python has had XML support since many versions ago, and Python's support for XML has kept growing and maturing year after year.

Python and XML are perfect complements. XML is an open standards way of exchanging information. Python is an open source language that processes the information. Python excels at text processing and at handling complicated data structures. XML is text based and is, above all, a way of exchanging complicated data structures.

That said, working with XML is not so seamless that it requires no effort. There is always somewhat of a mismatch between the needs of a particular programming language and a language-independent information representation. So there is often a requirement to write code that reads (i.e., *deserializes* or *parses*) and writes (i.e., *serializes*) XML.

Parsing XML can be done with code written purely in Python, or with a module that is a C/Python mix. Python comes with the fast Expat parser written in C. Many XML applications use the Expat parser, and one of these recipes accesses Expat directly to build its own concept of an ideal in-memory Python representation of an XML document as a tree of "element" objects (an alternative to the standard DOM approach, which I will mention later in this introduction).

However, although Expat is ubiquitous in the XML world, it is far from being the only parser available, or necessarily the best one for any given application. A standard API called SAX allows any XML parser to be plugged into a Python program.

The SAX API is demonstrated in several recipes that perform typical tasks such as checking that an XML document is well formed, extracting text from a document, or counting the tags in a document. These recipes should give you a good understanding of how SAX works. One more advanced recipe shows how to use one of SAX's several auxiliary features, "filtering", to normalize "text events" that might otherwise happen to get "fragmented".

XML-RPC is a protocol built on top of XML for sending data structures from one program to another, typically across the Internet. XML-RPC allows programmers to completely hide the implementation languages of the two communicating components. Two components running on different operating systems, written in different languages, can still communicate easily. XML-RPC is built into Python. This chapter does not deal with XML-RPC, because, together with other alternatives for distributed programming, XML-RPC is covered in Chapter 15.

Other recipes in this chapter are a little bit more eclectic, dealing with issues that range from interfacing, to proprietary XML parsers and document formats, to representing an entire XML document in memory as a Python object. One, in particular, shows how to auto-detect the Unicode encoding that an XML document uses without parsing the document. Unicode is central to the definition of XML, so it's important to understand Python's Unicode support if you will be doing any sophisticated work with XML.

The PyXML extension package supplies a variety of useful tools for working with XML. PyXML offers a full implementation of the Document Object Model (DOM)—as opposed to the subset bundled with Python itself—and a validating XML parser written entirely in Python. The DOM is a standard API that loads an entire XML document into memory. This can make XML processing easier for complicated structures in which there are many references from one part of the document to another, or when you need to correlate (i.e., compare) more than one XML document. One recipe shows how to use PyXML's validating parser to validate and process an XML document, and another shows how to remove whitespace-only text nodes from an XML document's DOM. You'll find many other examples in the documentation of the PyXML package (*http://pyxml.sourceforge.net/*).

Other advanced tools that you can find in PyXML or, in some cases, in FourThought's open source 4Suite package (*http://www.4suite.org/*) from which much of PyXML derives, include implementations of a variety of XML-related standards, such as XPath, XSLT, XLink, XPointer, and RDF. If PyXML is already an excellent resource for XML power users in Python, 4Suite is even richer and more powerful.

XML has become so pervasive that, inevitably, you will also find XML-related recipes in other chapters of this book. Recipe 2.26 "Extracting Text from OpenOffice.org Documents" strips XML markup in a very rough and ready way. Recipe 1.23 "Encoding Unicode Data for XML and HTML" shows how to insert XML character references while encoding Unicode text. Recipe 10.17 "Gathering Detailed System Information on Mac OS X," parses a Mac OS X pinfo-format XML stream to get detailed system information. Recipe 11.10 "Using IDLE's Tree Widget in Tkinter" uses Tkinter to display a XML DOM as a GUI Tree widget. Recipe 14.11 "Generating OPML Files" deals with two XML file formats related to RSS* feeds, fetching and parsing a FOAF†-format input to produce an OPML‡-format result—quite a typical XML-related task in today's programming, and a good general example of how Python can help you with such tasks.

For more information on using Python and XML together, see *Python and XML* by Christopher A. Jones and Fred L. Drake, Jr. (O'Reilly).

12.1 Checking XML Well-Formedness

Credit: Paul Prescod, Farhad Fouladi

Problem

You need to check whether an XML document is well formed (*not* whether it conforms to a given DTD or schema), and you need to do this check quickly.

Solution

SAX (presumably using a fast parser such as Expat underneath) offers a fast, simple way to perform this task. Here is a script to check well-formedness on every file you mention on the script's command line:

```
from xml.sax.handler import ContentHandler
from xml.sax import make_parser
from glob import glob
import sys
def parsefile(filename):
    parser = make_parser( )
    parser.setContentHandler(ContentHandler( ))
    parser.parse(filename)
for arg in sys.argv[1:]:
    for filename in glob(arg):
        try:
            parsefile(filename)
            print "%s is well-formed" % filename
        except Exception, e:
            print "%s is NOT well-formed! %s" % (filename, e)
```

* RSS (Really Simple Syndication)
† FOAF (Friend of a Friend)
‡ OPML (Outline Processor Markup Language)

Discussion

A text is a well-formed XML document if it adheres to all the basic syntax rules for XML documents. In other words, it has a correct XML declaration and a single root element, all tags are properly nested, tag attributes are quoted, and so on.

This recipe uses the SAX API with a dummy ContentHandler that does nothing. Generally, when we parse an XML document with SAX, we use a ContentHandler instance to process the document's contents. But in this case, we only want to know whether the document meets the most fundamental syntax constraints of XML; therefore, we need not do any processing, and the do-nothing handler suffices.

The parsefile function parses the whole document and throws an exception if an error is found. The recipe's main code catches any such exception and prints it out like this:

```
$ python wellformed.py test.xml
test.xml is NOT well-formed! test.xml:1002:2: mismatched tag
```

This means that character 2 on line 1,002 has a mismatched tag.

This recipe does not check adherence to a DTD or schema, which is a separate procedure called *validation*. The performance of the script should be quite good, precisely because it focuses on performing a minimal irreducible core task. However, sometimes you need to squeeze out the last drop of performance because you're checking the well-formedness of truly huge files. If you know for sure that you do have Expat, specifically, installed on your system, you may alternatively choose to use Expat directly instead of SAX. To try this approach, you can change function parsefile to the following code:

```
import xml.parsers.expat
def parsefile(file):
    parser = xml.parsers.expat.ParserCreate( )
    parser.ParseFile(open(file, "r"))
```

Don't expect all that much of an improvement in performance when using Expat directly instead of SAX. However, you *might* gain a little bit.

See Also

Recipe 12.2 "Counting Tags in a Document" and recipe 12.3 "Extracting Text from an XML Document," for other uses of SAX; the PyXML package (*http://pyxml.sourceforge.net/*) includes the pure-Python validating parser xmlproc, which checks the conformance of XML documents to specific DTDs; the PyRXP package from ReportLab is a wrapper around the fast validating parser RXP (*http://www.reportlab.com/xml/pyrxp.html*), which is available under the GPL license.

12.2   Counting Tags in a Document

Credit: Paul Prescod

Problem

You want to get a sense of how often particular elements occur in an XML document, and the relevant counts must be extracted rapidly.

Solution

You can subclass SAX's ContentHandler to make your own specialized classes for any kind of task, including the collection of such statistics:

```
from xml.sax.handler import ContentHandler
import xml.sax
class countHandler(ContentHandler):
    def __init__(self):
        self.tags={ }
    def startElement(self, name, attr):
        self.tags[name] = 1 + self.tags.get(name, 0)
parser = xml.sax.make_parser( )
handler = countHandler( )
parser.setContentHandler(handler)
parser.parse("test.xml")
tags = handler.tags.keys( )
tags.sort( )
for tag in tags:
    print tag, handler.tags[tag]
```

Discussion

When I start working with a new XML content set, I like to get a sense of which elements are in it and how often they occur. For this purpose, I use several small variants of this recipe. I could also collect attributes just as easily, as you can see, since attributes are also passed to the startElement method that I'm overriding. If you add a stack, you can also keep track of which elements occur within other elements (for this, of course, you also have to override the endElement method so you can pop the stack).

This recipe also works well as a simple example of a SAX application, usable as the basis for any SAX application. Alternatives to SAX include pulldom and minidom. For any simple processing (including this example), these alternatives would be overkill, particularly if the document you are processing is very large. DOM approaches are generally justified only when you need to perform complicated editing and alteration on an XML document, when the document itself is made complicated by references that go back and forth inside it, or when you need to correlate (i.e., compare) multiple documents.

ContentHandler subclasses offer many other options, and the online Python documentation does a pretty good job of explaining them. This recipe's countHandler class overrides ContentHandler's startElement method, which the parser calls at the start of each element, passing as arguments the element's tag name as a Unicode string and the collection of attributes. Our override of this method counts the number of times each tag name occurs. In the end, we extract the dictionary used for counting and emit it (in alphabetical order, which we easily obtain by sorting the keys).

See Also

Recipe 12.3 "Extracting Text from an XML Document" for other uses of SAX.

12.3 Extracting Text from an XML Document

Credit: Paul Prescod

Problem

You need to extract only the text from an XML document, not the tags.

Solution

Once again, subclassing SAX's ContentHandler makes this task quite easy:

```
from xml.sax.handler import ContentHandler
import xml.sax
import sys
class textHandler(ContentHandler):
    def characters(self, ch):
        sys.stdout.write(ch.encode("Latin-1"))
parser = xml.sax.make_parser( )
handler = textHandler( )
parser.setContentHandler(handler)
parser.parse("test.xml")
```

Discussion

Sometimes you want to get rid of XML tags—for example, to re-key a document or to spell-check it. This recipe performs this task and works with any well-formed XML document. It is quite efficient.

In this recipe's textHandler class, we subclass ContentHander's characters method, which the parser calls for each string of text in the XML document (excluding tags, XML comments, and processing instructions), passing as the only argument the piece of text as a Unicode string. We have to encode this Unicode before we can emit it to standard output. (See recipe 1.22 "Printing Unicode Characters to Standard Output" for more information about emitting Unicode to standard output.) In this recipe, we're using the Latin-1 (also known as ISO-8859-1) encoding, which covers all western European alphabets and is supported by many popular output devices (e.g., printers and terminal-emulation windows). However, you should use whatever encoding is most appropriate for the documents you're handling, as long, of course, as that encoding is supported by the devices you need to use. The configuration of your devices may depend on your operating system's concepts of locale and code page. Unfortunately, these issues vary too much between operating systems for me to go into further detail.

A simple alternative, if you know that handling Unicode is not going to be a problem, is to use sgmllib. It's not quite as fast but somewhat more robust against XML of dubious well-formedness:

```
from sgmllib import SGMLParser
class XMLJustText(SGMLParser):
    def handle_data(self, data):
        print data
XMLJustText( ).feed(open('text.xml').read( ))
```

An even simpler and rougher way to extract text from an XML document is shown in recipe 2.26 "Extracting Text from OpenOffice.org Documents."

See Also

Recipe 12.1 "Checking XML Well-Formedness" and recipe 12.2 "Counting Tags in a Document" for other uses of SAX.

12.4 Autodetecting XML Encoding

Credit: Paul Prescod

Problem

You have XML documents that may use a large variety of Unicode encodings, and you need to find out which encoding each document is using.

Solution

This task is one that we need to code ourselves, rather than getting an existing package to perform it, if we want complete generality:

```
import codecs, encodings
""" Caller will hand this library a buffer string, and ask us to convert
    the buffer, or autodetect what codec the buffer probably uses. """
# 'None' stands for a potentially variable byte ("##" in the XML spec...)
autodetect_dict={ # bytepattern         : ("name",
                (0x00, 0x00, 0xFE, 0xFF) : ("ucs4_be"),
                (0xFF, 0xFE, 0x00, 0x00) : ("ucs4_le"),
                (0xFE, 0xFF, None, None) : ("utf_16_be"),
                (0xFF, 0xFE, None, None) : ("utf_16_le"),
                (0x00, 0x3C, 0x00, 0x3F) : ("utf_16_be"),
                (0x3C, 0x00, 0x3F, 0x00) : ("utf_16_le"),
                (0x3C, 0x3F, 0x78, 0x6D) : ("utf_8"),
                (0x4C, 0x6F, 0xA7, 0x94) : ("EBCDIC"),
                }
```

```
def autoDetectXMLEncoding(buffer):
    """ buffer -> encoding_name
        The buffer string should be at least four bytes long.
        Returns None if encoding cannot be detected.
        Note that encoding_name might not have an installed
        decoder (e.g., EBCDIC)
    """
    # A more efficient implementation would not decode the whole
    # buffer at once, but then we'd have to decode a character at
    # a time looking for the quote character, and that's a pain
    encoding = "utf_8" # According to the XML spec, this is the default
                       # This code successively tries to refine the default:
                       # Whenever it fails to refine, it falls back to
                       # the last place encoding was set
    bytes = byte1, byte2, byte3, byte4 = map(ord, buffer[0:4])
    enc_info = autodetect_dict.get(bytes, None)
    if not enc_info: # Try autodetection again, removing potentially
                     # variable bytes
        bytes = byte1, byte2, None, None
        enc_info = autodetect_dict.get(bytes)
    if enc_info:
        encoding = enc_info # We have a guess...these are
                            # the new defaults
        # Try to find a more precise encoding using XML declaration
        secret_decoder_ring = codecs.lookup(encoding)[1]
        decoded, length = secret_decoder_ring(buffer)
        first_line = decoded.split("\n", 1)[0]
        if first_line and first_line.startswith(u"<?xml"):
            encoding_pos = first_line.find(u"encoding")
            if encoding_pos!=-1:
                # Look for double quotes
                quote_pos = first_line.find('"', encoding_pos)
                if quote_pos==-1:                    # Look for single quote
                    quote_pos = first_line.find("'", encoding_pos)
                if quote_pos>-1:
                    quote_char = first_line[quote_pos]
                    rest = first_line[quote_pos+1:]
                    encoding = rest[:rest.find(quote_char)]
    return encoding
```

Discussion

The XML specification describes the outline of an algorithm for detecting the Unicode encoding that an XML document uses. This recipe implements that algorithm and helps your XML-processing programs determine which encoding is being used by a specific document.

The default encoding (unless we can determine another one specifically) must be UTF-8, as it is part of the specifications that define XML. Certain byte patterns in the first four, or sometimes even just the first two, bytes of the text can identify a different encoding. For example, if the text starts with the two bytes 0xFF, 0xFE we can be certain that these bytes are a byte-order mark that identifies the encoding type as little-endian (low byte before high byte in each character) and the encoding itself as UTF-16 (or the 32-bits-per-character UCS-4, if the next two bytes in the text are 0, 0).

If we get as far as this, we must also examine the first line of the text. For this purpose, we decode the text from a bytestring into Unicode, with the encoding determined so far and detect the first line-end '\n' character. If the first line begins with u'<?xml', it's an XML declaration and may explicitly specify an encoding by using the keyword encoding as an attribute. The nested if statements in the recipe check for that case, and, if they find an encoding thus specified, the recipe returns the encoding thus found as the encoding the recipe has determined. This step is absolutely crucial, since any text starting with the single-byte ASCII-like representation of the XML declaration, <?xml, would be otherwise erroneously identified as encoded in UTF-8, while its explicit encoding attribute may specify it as being, for example, one of the ISO-8859 standard encodings.

This recipe makes the assumption that, as the XML specs require, the XML declaration, if any, is terminated by an end-of-line character. If you need to deal with almost-XML documents that are malformed in this very specific way (i.e., an incorrect XML declaration that is not terminated by an end-of-line character), you may need to apply some heuristic adjustments, for example, through regular expressions. However, it's impossible to offer precise suggestions, since malformedness may come in such a wide variety of errant forms.

This code detects a variety of encodings, including some that are not yet supported by Python's Unicode decoders. So, the fact that you can decipher the encoding does not guarantee that you can then decipher the document itself!

See Also

Unicode is a huge topic, but a recommended book is *Unicode: A Primer*, by Tony Graham (Hungry Minds, Inc.)—details are available at *http://www.menteith.com/ unicode/primer/*; *Library Reference* and *Python in a Nutshell* document the built-in str and unicode types, and modules unidata and codecs; recipe 1.21 "Converting Between Unicode and Plain Strings" and recipe 1.22 "Printing Unicode Characters to Standard Output."

12.5 Converting an XML Document into a Tree of Python Objects

Credit: John Bair, Christoph Dietze

Problem

You want to load an XML document into memory, but you don't like the complicated access procedures of DOM. You'd prefer something more Pythonic—specifically, you'd like to map the document into a tree of Python objects.

Solution

To build our tree of objects, we can directly wrap the fast expat parser:

```
from xml.parsers import expat
class Element(object):
    ''' A parsed XML element '''
    def __init__(self, name, attributes):
        # Record tagname and attributes dictionary
        self.name = name
        self.attributes = attributes
        # Initialize the element's cdata and children to empty
        self.cdata = ''
        self.children = [ ]
    def addChild(self, element):
        self.children.append(element)
    def getAttribute(self, key):
        return self.attributes.get(key)
    def getData(self):
        return self.cdata
    def getElements(self, name=''):
        if name:
            return [c for c in self.children if c.name == name]
        else:
            return list(self.children)
class Xml2Obj(object):
    ''' XML to Object converter '''
    def __init__(self):
        self.root = None
        self.nodeStack = [ ]
    def StartElement(self, name, attributes):
        'Expat start element event handler'
        # Instantiate an Element object
        element = Element(name.encode( ), attributes)
        # Push element onto the stack and make it a child of parent
        if self.nodeStack:
            parent = self.nodeStack[-1]
            parent.addChild(element)
        else:
            self.root = element
        self.nodeStack.append(element)
    def EndElement(self, name):
        'Expat end element event handler'
        self.nodeStack.pop( )
    def CharacterData(self, data):
        'Expat character data event handler'
        if data.strip( ):
            data = data.encode( )
            element = self.nodeStack[-1]
            element.cdata += data
    def Parse(self, filename):
        # Create an Expat parser
        Parser = expat.ParserCreate( )
        # Set the Expat event handlers to our methods
```

```
                 Parser.StartElementHandler = self.StartElement
                 Parser.EndElementHandler = self.EndElement
                 Parser.CharacterDataHandler = self.CharacterData
                 # Parse the XML File
                 ParserStatus = Parser.Parse(open(filename).read( ), 1)
                 return self.root
        parser = Xml2Obj( )
        root_element = parser.Parse('sample.xml')
```

Discussion

I saw Christoph Dietze's recipe (*http://aspn.activestate.com/ASPN/Cookbook/Python/Recipe/116539*) about turning the structure of an XML document into a simple combination of dictionaries and lists and thought it was a really good idea. This recipe is a variation on that idea, with several differences.

For maximum speed, the recipe uses the low-level expat parser directly. It would get no real added value from the richer SAX interface, much less from the slow and memory-hungry DOM approach. Building the parent-children connections is not hard even with an event-driven interface, as this recipe shows by using a simple stack for the purpose.

The main difference with respect to Dietze's original idea is that this recipe loads the XML document into a tree of Python objects (rather than a combination of dictionaries and lists), one per node, with nicely named attributes allowing access to each node's characteristics—tagname, attributes (as a Python dictionary), character data (i.e., *cdata* in XML parlance) and children elements (as a Python list).

The various accessor methods of class Element are, of course, optional. You might prefer to access the attributes directly. I think they add no complexity and look nicer, but, obviously, your tastes may differ. This is, after all, just a recipe, so feel free to alter the mix of seasonings at will!

You can find other similar ideas (e.g., bypass the DOM, build something more Pythonic as the memory representation of an XML document) in many other excellent and more complete projects, such as PyRXP (*http://www.reportlab.org/pyrxp.html*), ElementTree (*http://effbot.org/zone/element-index.htm*), and XIST (*http://www.livinglogic.de/Python/xist/*).

See Also

Library Reference and *Python in a Nutshell* document the built-in XML support in the Python Standard Library, and xml.parsers.expat in particular. PyRXP is at *http://www.reportlab.org/pyrxp.html*; ElementTree is at *http://effbot.org/zone/element-index.htm*; XIST is at *http://www.livinglogic.de/Python/xist/*.

12.6 Removing Whitespace-only Text Nodes from an XML DOM Node's Subtree

Credit: Brian Quinlan, David Wilson

Problem

You want to remove, from the DOM representation of an XML document, all the text nodes within a subtree, which contain only whitespace.

Solution

XML parsers consider several complex conditions when deciding which whitespace-only text nodes to preserve during DOM construction. Unfortunately, the result is often not what you want, so it's helpful to have a function to remove all whitespace-only text nodes from among a given node's descendants:

```
def remove_whilespace_nodes(node):
    """ Removes all of the whitespace-only text decendants of a DOM node. """
    # prepare the list of text nodes to remove (and recurse when needed)
    remove_list = [ ]
    for child in node.childNodes:
        if child.nodeType == dom.Node.TEXT_NODE and not child.data.strip( ):
            # add this text node to the to-be-removed list
            remove_list.append(child)
        elif child.hasChildNodes( ):
            # recurse, it's the simplest way to deal with the subtree
            remove_whilespace_nodes(child)
    # perform the removals
    for node in remove_list:
        node.parentNode.removeChild(node)
        node.unlink( )
```

Discussion

This recipe's code works with any correctly implemented Python XML DOM, including the xml.dom.minidom that is part of the Python Standard Library and the more complete DOM implementation that comes with PyXML.

The implementation of function remove_whitespace_node is quite simple but rather instructive: in the first for loop we build a list of all child nodes to remove, and then in a second, separate loop we do the removal. This precaution is a good example of a general rule in Python: do not alter the very container you're looping on—sometimes you can get away with it, but it is unwise to count on it in the general case. On the other hand, the function can perfectly well call itself recursively within its first for loop because such a call does *not* alter the very list node.childNodes on which the loop is iterating (it may alter some *items* in that list, but it does not alter the list object itself).

See Also

Library Reference and *Python in a Nutshell* document the built-in XML support in the Python Standard Library.

12.7 Parsing Microsoft Excel's XML

Credit: Thomas Guettler

Problem

You have Microsoft Excel spreadsheets saved in XML form, and want to parse them into memory as Python nested lists.

Solution

The XML form of Excel spreadsheets is quite simple: all text is in Cell tags, which are nested in Row tags nested in Table tags. SAX makes it quite simple to parse this kind of XML into memory:

```
import sys
from xml.sax import saxutils, parse
class ExcelHandler(saxutils.DefaultHandler):
    def __init__(self):
        self.chars = [ ]
        self.cells = [ ]
        self.rows = [ ]
        self.tables = [ ]
    def characters(self, content):
        self.chars.append(content)
    def startElement(self, name, atts):
        if name=="Cell":
            self.chars = [ ]
        elif name=="Row":
            self.cells=[ ]
        elif name=="Table":
            self.rows = [ ]
    def endElement(self, name):
        if name=="Cell":
            self.cells.append(''.join(self.chars))
        elif name=="Row":
            self.rows.append(self.cells)
        elif name=="Table":
            self.tables.append(self.rows)
if __name__ == '__main__':
    excelHandler = ExcelHandler( )
    parse(sys.argv[1], excelHandler)
    print excelHandler.tables
```

Discussion

The structure of the parser presented in this recipe is pleasingly simple: at each of three logical nesting levels of data, we collect content into a list. Each time a tag of a given level begins, we start with an empty list for it; each time the tag ends, we append the tag's contents to the list of the next upper level. The net result is that the top-level list, the one named `tables`, accumulates all of the spreadsheet's contents with the proper structure (a triply nested list). At the lowest level, of course, we join all the text strings that are reported as being within the same cell into a single cell content text string, when we accumulate, because the division between the various strings is just an artefact of the XML parsing process.

For example, consider a tiny spreadsheet with one column and three rows, where the first two rows each hold the number 2 and the third one holds the number 4 obtained by summing the numbers in the first two rows with an Excel formula. The relevant snippet of the Excel XML output (XMLSS format, as Microsoft calls it) is then:

```
<Table ss:ExpandedColumnCount="1" ss:ExpandedRowCount="3"
       x:FullColumns="1" x:FullRows="1">
  <Row>
   <Cell><Data ss:Type="Number">2</Data></Cell>
  </Row>
  <Row>
   <Cell><Data ss:Type="Number">2</Data></Cell>
  </Row>
  <Row>
   <Cell ss:Formula="=SUM(R[-2]C, R[-1]C)">
        <Data ss:Type="Number">4</Data></Cell>
  </Row>
</Table>
```

and running the script in this recipe over this file emits:

```
[[[u'2'], [u'2'], [u'4']]]
```

As you can see, the XMLSS file also contains a lot of supplementary information that this recipe is not collecting—the attributes hold information about the type of data (number or string), the formula used for the computation (if any), and so on. If you need any or all of this supplemental information, it's not hard to enrich this recipe to record and use it.

See Also

Library Reference and *Python in a Nutshell* document the built-in XML support in the Python Standard Library and SAX in particular.

12.8 Validating XML Documents

Credit: Paul Sholtz, Jeroen Jeroen, Marius Gedminas

Problem

You are handling XML documents and must check the validity with respect to either internal or external DTDs. You possibly also want to perform application-specific processing during the validation process.

Solution

You often want to validate an XML document file with respect to a !DOCTYPE processing instruction that the document file contains. On occasion, though, you may want to force loading of an external DTD from a given file. Moreover, a frequent need is to also perform application-specific processing during validation. A function with optional parameters, using modules from the PyXML package, can accommodate all of these needs:

```
from xml.parsers.xmlproc import utils, xmlval, xmldtd
def validate_xml_file(xml_filename, app=None, dtd_filename=None):
    # build validating parser object with appropriate error handler
    parser = xmlval.Validator( )
    parser.set_error_handler(utils.ErrorPrinter(parser))
    if dtd_filename is not None:
        # DTD file specified, load and set it as the DTD to use
        dtd = xmldtd.load_dtd(dtd_filename)
        parser.val.dtd = parser.dtd = parser.ent = dtd
    if app is not None:
        # Application processing requested, set appliation object
        parser.set_application(app)
    # everything being set correctly, finally perform the parsing
    parser.parse_resource(xml_filename)
```

If your XML data is in a string s, rather than in a file, instead of the parse.parse_ resource call, you should use the following two statements in a variant of the previously shown function:

```
parser.feed(s)
parser.close( )
```

Discussion

Documentation on XML parsing in general, and xmlproc in particular, is easy enough to come by. However, XML is a very large subject, and PyXML is a correspondingly large package. The package's documentation is often not entirely complete and up to date; even if it were, finding out how to perform specific tasks would still take quite a bit of digging. This recipe shows how to validate documents in a simple way that is easy to adapt to your specific needs.

If you need to perform application-specific processing, as well as validation, you need to make your own application object (an instance of some subclass of `xmlproc.xmlproc.Application` that appropriately overrides some or all of its various methods, most typically `handle_start_tag`, `handle_end_tag`, `handle_data`, and `doc_end`) and pass the application object as the app argument to the `validate_xml_file` function.

If you need to handle errors and warnings differently from the emitting of copious error messages that `xmlproc.utils.ErrorPrinter` performs, you need to subclass (either that class or its base `xmlproc.xmlapp.ErrorHandler` directly) to perform whatever tweaking you need. (See the sources of the *utils.py* module for examples; that module will usually be at relative path *_xmlplus/parsers/xmlproc/utils.py* in your Python library directory, after you have installed the PyXML package.) Then, you need to alter the call to the method `set_error_handler` that you see in this recipe's `validate_xml_file` function so that it uses an instance of your own error-handling class. You might modify the `validate_xml_file` function to take yet another optional parameter err=None for the purpose, but this way overgeneralization lies. I've found `ErrorHandler`'s diagnostics normally cover my applications' needs, so, in the code shown in this recipe's Solution, I have not provided for this specific customization.

See Also

The PyXML web site at *http://pyxml.sourceforge.net/*.

12.9 Filtering Elements and Attributes Belonging to a Given Namespace

Credit: A.M. Kuchling

Problem

While parsing an XML document with SAX, you need to filter out all of the elements and attributes that belong to a particular namespace.

Solution

The SAX filter concept is just what we need here:

```
from xml import sax
from xml.sax import handler, saxutils, xmlreader
# the namespace we want to remove in our filter
RDF_NS = 'http://www.w3.org/1999/02/22-rdf-syntax-ns#'
class RDFFilter(saxutils.XMLFilterBase):
    def __init__ (self, *args):
        saxutils.XMLFilterBase.__init__(self, *args)
        # initially, we're not in RDF, and just one stack level is needed
        self.in_rdf_stack = [False]
    def startElementNS(self, (uri, localname), qname, attrs):
```

```
                if uri == RDF_NS or self.in_rdf_stack[-1] == True:
                    # skip elements with namespace, if that namespace is RDF or
                    # the element is nested in an RDF one -- and grow the stack
                    self.in_rdf_stack.append(True)
                    return
                # Make a dict of attributes that DON'T belong to the RDF namespace
                keep_attrs = {}
                for key, value in attrs.items():
                    uri, localname = key
                    if uri != RDF_NS:
                        keep_attrs[key] = value
                # prepare the cleaned-up bunch of non-RDF-namespace attributes
                attrs = xmlreader.AttributesNSImpl(keep_attrs, attrs.getQNames())
                # grow the stack by replicating the latest entry
                self.in_rdf_stack.append(self.in_rdf_stack[-1])
                # finally delegate the rest of the operation to our base class
                saxutils.XMLFilterBase.startElementNS(self,
                        (uri, localname), qname, attrs)
        def characters(self, content):
            # skip characters that are inside an RDF-namespaced tag being skipped
            if self.in_rdf_stack[-1]:
                return
            # delegate the rest of the operation to our base class
            saxutils.XMLFilterBase.characters(self, content)
        def endElementNS (self, (uri, localname), qname):
            # pop the stack -- nothing else to be done, if we were skipping
            if self.in_rdf_stack.pop() == True:
                return
            # delegate the rest of the operation to our base class
            saxutils.XMLFilterBase.endElementNS(self, (uri, localname), qname)
def filter_rdf(input, output):
    """ filter_rdf(input=some_input_filename, output=some_output_filename)
        Parses the XML input from the input stream, filtering out all
        elements and attributes that are in the RDF namespace.
    """
    output_gen = saxutils.XMLGenerator(output)
    parser = sax.make_parser()
    filter = RDFFilter(parser)
    filter.setFeature(handler.feature_namespaces, True)
    filter.setContentHandler(output_gen)
    filter.setErrorHandler(handler.ErrorHandler())
    filter.parse(input)
if __name__ == '__main__':
    import StringIO, sys
    TEST_RDF = '''<?xml version="1.0"?>
<metadata xmlns:rdf="http://www.w3.org/1999/02/22-rdf-syntax-ns#"
        xmlns:dc="http://purl.org/dc/elements/1.1/">
    <title> This is non-RDF content </title>
    <rdf:RDF>
      <rdf:Description rdf:about="%s">
        <dc:Creator>%s</dc:Creator>
      </rdf:Description>
    </rdf:RDF>
    <element />
</metadata>
```

```
...
    input = StringIO.StringIO(TEST_RDF)
    filter_rdf(input, sys.stdout)
```

This module, when run as a main script, emits something like:

```
<?xml version="1.0" encoding="iso-8859-1"?>
<metadata xmlns:rdf="http://www.w3.org/1999/02/22-rdf-syntax-ns#"
          xmlns:dc="http://purl.org/dc/elements/1.1/">
  <title>  This is non-RDF content </title>
  <element></element>
</metadata>
```

Discussion

My motivation for originally writing this recipe came from processing files of metadata, containing RDF mixed with other elements. I wanted to generate a version of the metadata with the RDF filtered out.

The filter_rdf function does the job, reading XML input from the input stream and writing it to the output stream. The standard XMLGenerator class in xml.sax.saxutils is used to produce the output. Function filter_rdf internally uses a filtering class called RDFFilter, also shown in this recipe's Solution, pushing that filter on top of the XML parser to suppress elements and attributes belonging to the RDF_NS namespace.

Non-RDF elements contained within an RDF element are also removed. To modify this behavior, change the first line of the startElementNS method to use just if uri == RDF_NS as the guard.

This code doesn't delete the xmlns declaration for the RDF namespace; I'm willing to live with a little unnecessary but harmless cruft in the output rather than go to huge trouble to remove it.

See Also

Library Reference and *Python in a Nutshell* document the built-in XML support in the Python Standard Library.

12.10 Merging Continuous Text Events with a SAX Filter

Credit: Uche Ogbuji, James Kew, Peter Cogolo

Problem

A SAX parser can report contiguous text using multiple *characters events* (meaning, in practice, multiple calls to the characters method), and this multiplicity of events for a single text string may give problems to SAX handlers. You want to insert a filter into the SAX handler chain to ensure that each text node in the document is reported as a single SAX characters event (meaning, in practice, that it calls character just once).

Solution

Module `xml.sax.saxutils` in the standard Python library includes a class `XMLFilterBase` that we can subclass to implement any XML filter we may need:

```
from xml.sax.saxutils import XMLFilterBase
class text_normalize_filter(XMLFilterBase):
    """ SAX filter to ensure that contiguous text nodes are merged into one
    """
    def __init__(self, upstream, downstream):
        XMLFilterBase.__init__(self, upstream)
        self._downstream = downstream
        self._accumulator = [ ]
    def _complete_text_node(self):
        if self._accumulator:
            self._downstream.characters(''.join(self._accumulator))
            self._accumulator = [ ]
    def characters(self, text):
        self._accumulator.append(text)
    def ignorableWhitespace(self, ws):
        self._accumulator.append(text)
    def _wrap_complete(method_name):
        def method(self, *a, **k):
            self._complete_text_node( )
            getattr(self._downstream, method_name)(*a, **k)
        # 2.4 only: method.__name__ = method_name
        setattr(text_normalize_filter, method_name, method)
    for n in '''startElement startElementNS endElement endElementNS
                processingInstruction comment'''.split( ):
        _wrap_complete(n)
if __name__ == "__main__":
    import sys
    from xml import sax
    from xml.sax.saxutils import XMLGenerator
    parser = sax.make_parser( )
    # XMLGenerator is a special predefined SAX handler that merely writes
    # SAX events back into an XML document
    downstream_handler = XMLGenerator( )
    # upstream, the parser; downstream, the next handler in the chain
    filter_handler = text_normalize_filter(parser, downstream_handler)
    # The SAX filter base is designed so that the filter takes on much of the
    # interface of the parser itself, including the "parse" method
    filter_handler.parse(sys.argv[1])
```

Discussion

A SAX parser can report contiguous text using multiple characters events (meaning, in practice, multiple calls to the characters method of the downstream handler). In other words, given an XML document whose content is 'abc', the text could technically be reported as up to three character events: one for the 'a' character, one for the 'b', and a third for the 'c'. Such an extreme case of "fragmentation" of a text string into multiple events is unlikely in real life, but it is not impossible.

A typical reason that might cause a parser to report text nodes a bit at a time would be buffering of the XML input source. Most low-level parsers use a buffer of a certain number of characters that are read and parsed at a time. If a text node straddles such a buffer boundary, many parsers will just wrap up the current text event and start a new one to send characters from the next buffer. If you don't account for this behavior in your SAX handlers, you may run into very obscure and hard-to-reproduce bugs. Even if the parser you usually use does combine text nodes for you, you never know when you may want to run your code in a situation where a different parser is selected. You'd need to write logic to accommodate the possibility, which can be rather cumbersome when mixed into typical SAX-style state machine logic.

The class text_normalize_filter presented in this recipe ensures that all text events are reported to downstream SAX handlers in the contiguous manner that most developers would expect. In this recipe's example case, the filter would consolidate the three characters events into a single one for the entire text node 'abc'.

For more information on SAX filters in general, see my article "Tip: SAX filters for flexible processing," *http://www-106.ibm.com/ developerworks/xml/library/x-tipsaxflex.html*.

Python's XMLGenerator does not do anything with processing instructions, so, if you run the main code presented in this recipe on an XML document that uses them, you'll have a gap in the output, along with other minor deviations between input and output. Comments are similar but worse, because XMLFilterBase does not even filter them; if you do need to get comments, your test_normalize_filter class must multiply inherit from xml.sax.saxlib.LexicalHandler, as well as from xml.sax.saxutils.XMLFilterBase, and it must override the parse method as follows:

```
def parse(self, source):
    # force connection of self as the lexical handler
    self._parent.setProperty(property_lexical_handler, self)
    # Delegate to XMLFilterBase for the rest
    XMLFilterBase.parse(self, source)
```

This code is hairy enough, using the "internal" attribute self._parent, and the need to deal properly with XML comments is rare enough, to make this addition somewhat doubtful, which is why it is not part of this recipe's Solution.

If you need ease of chaining to other filters, you may prefer not to take both upstream and downstream parameters in __init__. In this case, keep the same signature as XMLFilterBase.__init__:

```
def __init__(self, parent):
    XMLFilterBase.__init__(self, parent)
    self._accumulator = [ ]
```

and change the _wrap_complete factory function so that the wrapper, rather than calling methods on the downstream handler directly, delegates to the default implementations in XMLFilterBase, which in turn call out to handlers that have been set on the filter with such methods as setContentHandler and the like:

```
def _wrap_complete(method_name):
    def method(self, *a, **k):
        self._complete_text_node( )
        getattr(XMLFilterBase, method_name)(self, *a, **k)
    # 2.4 only: method.__name__ = method_name
    setattr(text_normalize_filter, method_name, method)
```

This is slightly less convenient for the typical simple case, but it pays back this inconvenience by letting you easily chain filters:

```
parser = sax.make_parser( )
filtered_parser = text_normalise_filter(some_other_filter(parser))
```

as well as letting you use a filter in contexts that call the parse method on your behalf:

```
doc = xml.dom.minidom.parse(input_file, parser=filtered_parser)
```

See Also

Library Reference and *Python in a Nutshell* document the built-in XML support in the Python Standard Library.

12.11 Using MSHTML to Parse XML or HTML

Credit: Bill Bell

Problem

Your Python application, running on Windows, needs to use the Microsoft MSHTML COM component, which is also the parser that Microsoft Internet Explorer uses to parse HTML and XML web pages.

Solution

As usual, PyWin32 lets our Python code access COM quite simply:

```
from win32com.client import Dispatch
html = Dispatch('htmlfile')    # the disguise for MSHTML as a COM server
html.writeln( "<html><header><title>A title</title>"
    "<meta name='a name' content='page description'></header>"
    "<body>This is some of it. <span>And this is the rest.</span>"
    "</body></html>" )
print "Title: %s" % (html.title,)
```

```
    print "Bag of words from body of the page: %s" % (html.body.innerText,)
    print "URL associated with the page: %s" % (html.url,)
    print "Display of name:content pairs from the metatags: "
    metas = html.getElementsByTagName("meta")
    for m in xrange(metas.length):
        print "\t%s: %s" % (metas[m].name, metas[m].content,)
```

Discussion

While Python offers many ways to parse HTML or XML, as long as you're running your programs only on Windows, MSHTML is very speedy and simple to use. As the recipe shows, you can simply use the writeln method of the COM object to feed the page into MSHTML and then you can use the methods and properties of the components to get at all kinds of aspects of the page's DOM. Of course, you can get the string of markup and text to feed into MSHTML in any way that suits your application, such as by using the Python Standard Library module urllib if you're getting a page from some URL.

Since the structure of the enriched DOM that MSHTML makes available is quite rich and complicated, I suggest you experiment with it in the PythonWin interactive environment that comes with PyWin32. The strength of PythonWin for such exploratory tasks is that it displays all of the properties and methods made available by each interface.

See Also

A detailed reference to MSHTML, albeit oriented to Visual Basic and C# users, can be found at *http://www.xaml.net/articles/type.asp?o=MSHTML*.

## CHAPTER 13

Network Programming

13.0 Introduction

Credit: Guido van Rossum, creator of Python

Network programming is one of my favorite Python applications. I wrote or started most of the network modules in the Python Standard Library, including the socket and select extension modules and most of the protocol client modules (such as ftplib). I also wrote a popular server framework module, SocketServer, and two web browsers in Python, the first predating Mosaic. Need I say more?

Python's roots lie in a distributed operating system, Amoeba, which I helped design and implement in the late 1980s. Python was originally intended to be the scripting language for Amoeba, since it turned out that the Unix shell, while ported to Amoeba, wasn't very useful for writing Amoeba system administration scripts. Of course, I designed Python to be platform independent from the start. Once Python was ported from Amoeba to Unix, I taught myself BSD socket programming by wrapping the socket primitives in a Python extension module and then experimenting with them using Python; this was one of the first extension modules.

This approach proved to be a great early testimony of Python's strengths. Writing socket code in C is tedious: the code necessary to do error checking on every call quickly overtakes the logic of the program. Quick: in which order should a server call accept, bind, connect, and listen? This is remarkably difficult to find out if all you have is a set of Unix manpages. In Python, you don't have to write separate error-handling code for each call, making the logic of the code stand out much clearer. You can also learn about sockets by experimenting in an interactive Python shell, where misconceptions about the proper order of calls and the argument values that each call requires are cleared up quickly through Python's immediate error messages.

Python has come a long way since those first days, and now few applications use the socket module directly; most use much higher-level modules such as urllib or smtplib, and third-party extensions such as the Twisted framework, whose popularity keeps growing. The examples in this chapter are a varied bunch: some construct and send complex email messages, while others dwell on lower-level issues such as tunneling. My favorite is recipe 13.11 "Detecting Inactive Computers," which implements PyHeartBeat: it's useful, it uses the socket module, and it's simple enough to be an educational example. I do note, with that mixture of pride and sadness that always accompanies a parent's observation of children growing up, that, since the *Python Cookbook*'s first edition, even PyHeartBeat has acquired an alternative server implementation based on Twisted!

Nevertheless, my own baby, the socket module itself, is still the foundation of all network operations in Python. It's a plain transliteration of the socket APIs—first introduced in BSD Unix and now widespread on all platforms—into the object-oriented paradigm. You create socket objects by calling the socket.socket factory function, then you call methods on these objects to perform typical low-level network operations. You don't have to worry about allocating and freeing memory for buffers and the like—Python handles that for you automatically. You express IP addresses as (host, port) pairs, in which host is a string in either dotted-quad ('1.2.3.4') or domain-name ('www.python.org') notation. As you can see, even low-level modules in Python aren't as low level as all that.

Despite the various conveniences, the socket module still exposes the actual underlying functionality of your operating system's network sockets. If you're at all familiar with sockets, you'll quickly get the hang of Python's socket module, using Python's own *Library Reference*. You'll then be able to play with sockets interactively in Python to become a socket expert, if that is what you want. The classic, highly recommended work on this subject is W. Richard Stevens, *UNIX Network Programming, Volume 1: Networking APIs - Sockets and XTI, 2d ed.* (Prentice-Hall). For many practical uses, however, higher-level modules will serve you better.

The Internet uses a sometimes dazzling variety of protocols and formats, and the Python Standard Library supports many of them. In the Python Standard Library, you will find dozens of modules dedicated to supporting specific Internet protocols (such as smtplib to support the SMTP protocol to send mail and nntplib to support the Network News Transfer Protocol (NNTP) to send and receive Network News). In addition, you'll find about as many modules that support specific Internet formats (such as htmllib to parse HTML data, the email package to parse and compose various formats related to email—including attachments and encoding).

I cannot even come close to doing justice to the powerful array of tools mentioned in this introduction, nor will you find all of these modules and packages used in this chapter, nor in this book, nor in most programming shops. You may never need to write any program that deals with Network News, for example; if that is the case, you don't need to study nntplib. But it is still reassuring to know it's there (part of the "batteries included" approach of the Python Standard Library).

Two higher-level modules that stand out from the crowd, however, are urllib and urllib2. Each of these two modules can deal with several protocols through the magic of URLs—those now-familiar strings, such as *http://www.python.org/ index.html*, that identify a protocol (such as *http*), a host and port (such as *www.python.org*, port 80 being the default for the HTTP protocol), and a specific resource at that address (such as */index.html*). urllib is very simple to use, but urllib2 is more powerful and extensible. HTTP is the most popular protocol for URLs, but these modules also support several others, such as FTP. In many cases, you'll be able to use these modules to write typical client-side scripts that interact with any of the supported protocols much quicker and with less effort than it might take with the various protocol-specific modules.

To illustrate, I'd like to conclude with a cookbook example of my own. It's similar to recipe 13.2 "Grabbing a Document from the Web," but, rather than a program fragment, it's a little script. I call it *wget.py* because it does everything for which I've ever needed wget. (In fact, I originally wrote this script on a system where wget wasn't installed but Python was; writing *wget.py* was a more effective use of my time than downloading and installing the real thing.)

```
import sys, urllib
def reporthook(*a): print a
for url in sys.argv[1:]:
    i = url.rfind('/')
    file = url[i+1:]
    print url, "->", file
    urllib.urlretrieve(url, file, reporthook)
```

Pass this script one or more URLs as command-line arguments; the script retrieves them into local files whose names match the last components of the URLs. The script also prints progress information of the form:

```
(block number, block size, total size)
```

Obviously, it's easy to improve on this script; but it's only seven lines, it's readable, and it works—and that's what's so cool about Python.

Another cool thing about Python is that you can incrementally improve a program like this, and after it's grown by two or three orders of magnitude, it's still readable, and it still works! To see what this particular example might evolve into, check out *Tools/webchecker/websucker.py* in the Python source distribution. Enjoy!

13.1 Passing Messages with Socket Datagrams

Credit: Jeff Bauer

Problem

You want to communicate small messages between machines on a network in a lightweight fashion, without needing absolute assurance of reliability.

Solution

This task is just what the UDP protocol is for, and Python makes it easy for you to access UDP via datagram sockets. You can write a UDP server script (*server.py*) as follows:

```
import socket
port = 8081
s = socket.socket(socket.AF_INET, socket.SOCK_DGRAM)
# Accept UDP datagrams, on the given port, from any sender
s.bind(("", port))
print "waiting on port:", port
while True:
    # Receive up to 1,024 bytes in a datagram
    data, addr = s.recvfrom(1024)
    print "Received:", data, "from", addr
```

You can write a corresponding UDP client script (*client.py*) as follows:

```
import socket
port = 8081
host = "localhost"
s = socket.socket(socket.AF_INET, socket.SOCK_DGRAM)
s.sendto("Holy Guido! It's working.", (host, port))
```

Discussion

Sending short text messages with socket datagrams is simple to implement and provides a lightweight message-passing idiom. Socket datagrams should not be used, however, when reliable delivery of data must be guaranteed. If the server isn't available, your message is lost. However, in many situations, you won't care whether the message gets lost, or, at least, you do not want to abort a program just because a message can't be delivered.

Note that the sender of a UDP datagram (the "client" in this example) does not bind the socket before calling the sendto method. On the other hand, to receive UDP datagrams, the socket does have to be bound before calling the recvfrom method.

Don't use this recipe's simple code to send large datagram messages, especially under Windows, which may not respect the buffer limit. To send larger messages, you may want to do something like this:

```
BUFSIZE = 1024
while msg:
    bytes_sent = s.sendto(msg[:BUFSIZE], (host, port))
    msg = msg[bytes_sent:]
```

The sendto method returns the number of bytes it has actually managed to send, so each time, you retry from the point where you left off, while ensuring that no more than BUFSIZE octets are sent in each datagram.

Note that with datagrams (UDP) you have no guarantee that all (or any) of the pieces that you send as separate datagrams arrive to the destination, nor that the pieces that do arrive are in the same order in which they were sent. If you need to worry about any of these reliability issues, you may be better off with a TCP connection, which gives you all of these assurances and handles many delicate behind-the-scenes aspects nicely on your behalf. Still, I often use socket datagrams for debugging, especially (but not exclusively) where an application spans more than one machine on the same, reliable local area network. The Python Standard Library's logging module also supports optional use of UDP for its logging output.

See Also

Recipe 13.11 "Detecting Inactive Computers" for a typical, useful application of UDP datagrams in network operations; documentation for the standard library modules socket and logging in the *Library Reference* and *Python in a Nutshell*.

13.2   Grabbing a Document from the Web

Credit: Gisle Aas, Magnus Bodin

Problem

You need to grab a document from a URL on the Web.

Solution

urllib.urlopen returns a file-like object, and you can call the read method on that object to get all of its contents:

```
from urllib import urlopen
doc = urlopen("http://www.python.org").read( )
print doc
```

Discussion

Once you obtain a file-like object from urlopen, you can read it all at once into one big string by calling its read method, as I do in this recipe. Alternatively, you can read the object as a list of lines by calling its readlines method, or, for special purposes, just get one line at a time by looping over the object in a for loop. In addition to these file-like operations, the object that urlopen returns offers a few other useful features. For example, the following snippet gives you the headers of the document:

```
doc = urlopen("http://www.python.org")
print doc.info( )
```

such as the Content-Type header (text/html in this case) that defines the MIME type of the document. doc.info returns a mimetools.Message instance, so you can access it in various ways besides printing it or otherwise transforming it into a string. For example, doc.info( ).getheader('Content-Type') returns the 'text/html' string. The maintype attribute of the `mimetools.Message` object is the `'text'` string, subtype is the `'html'` string, and type is also the `'text/html'` string. If you need to perform sophisticated analysis and processing, all the tools you need are right there. At the same time, if your needs are simpler, you can meet them in very simple ways, as this recipe shows.

If what you need to do with the document you grab from the Web is specifically to save it to a local file, `urllib.urlretrieve` is just what you need, as the "Introduction" to this chapter describes.

`urllib` implicitly supports the use of proxies (as long as the proxies do not require authentication: the current implementation of `urllib` does not support authentication-requiring proxies). Just set environment variable `HTTP_PROXY` to a URL, such as `'http://proxy.domain.com:8080'`, to use the proxy at that URL. If the environment variable `HTTP_PROXY` is not set, `urllib` may also look for the information in other platform-specific locations, such as the Windows registry if you're running under Windows.

If you have more advanced needs, such as using proxies that require authentication, you may use the more sophisticated `urllib2` module of the Python Standard Library, rather than simple module `urllib`. At *http://pydoc.org/2.3/urllib2.html*, you can find an example of how to use `urllib2` for the specific task of accessing the Internet through a proxy that does require authentication.

See Also

Documentation for the standard library modules `urllib`, `urllib2`, and `mimetools` in the *Library Reference* and *Python in a Nutshell*.

13.3 Filtering a List of FTP Sites

Credit: Mark Nenadov

Problem

Several of the FTP sites on your list of sites could be down at any time. You want to filter that list and obtain the list of those sites that are currently up.

Solution

Clearly, we first need a function to check whether one particular site is up:

```
import socket, ftplib
def isFTPSiteUp(site):
    try:
        ftplib.FTP(site).quit( )
    except socket.error:
        return False
    else:
        return True
```

Now, a simple list comprehension can perform the recipe's task, but we may as well wrap that list comprehension inside another function:

```
def filterFTPsites(sites):
    return [site for site in sites if isFTPSiteUp(site)]
```

Alternatively, `filter(isFTPSiteUp, sites)` returns exactly the same resulting list as the list comprehension.

Discussion

Lists of FTP sites are sometimes difficult to maintain, since sites may be closed or temporarily down for all sorts of reasons. The code in this recipe is simple and suitable, for example, for use inside a small interactive program that must let the user choose among FTP sites—we may as well not even present for choice those sites we know are down! If you run this code regularly a few times a day and append the results to a file, the results may also be a basis for long-term maintenance of a list of FTP sites. Any site that has been down for more than a certain number of days should probably be moved away from the main list and into a list of sites that may well have croaked.

Very similar ideas could be used to filter lists of sites that serve protocols other than FTP, by using, instead of standard Python library module `ftplib`, other such modules, such as `nntplib` for the NNTP protocol, `httplib` for the Hypertext Transport Protocol (HTTP), and so on.

When you're checking many FTP sites within one program run, it could be much faster to use multiple threads to check on multiple sites at once (so that the delays while waiting for the various sites to respond can overlap), or else use an asynchronous approach. The simple approach presented in this recipe is easiest to program and to understand, but for most real-life networking programs, you do want to enhance performance by using either multithreading or asynchronous approaches, as other recipes in this chapter demonstrate.

See Also

Documentation for the standard library modules socket, ftplib, nntplib, and httplib, and built-in function filter, in the *Library Reference* and *Python in a Nutshell*.

13.4 Getting Time from a Server via the SNTP Protocol

Credit: Simon Foster

Problem

You need to contact an SNTP (Simplified Network Time Protocol) server (which respects RFC 2030) to obtain the time of day as returned by that server.

Solution

SNTP is quite simple to implement, for example in a small script:

```
import socket, struct, sys, time
TIME1970 = 2208988800L                          # Thanks to F.Lundh
client = socket.socket(socket.AF_INET, socket.SOCK_DGRAM)
data = '\x1b' + 47 * '\0'
client.sendto(data, (sys.argv[1], 123))
data, address = client.recvfrom(1024)
if data:
    print 'Response received from:', address
    t = struct.unpack('!12I', data)[10]
    t -= TIME1970
    print '\tTime=%s' % time.ctime(t)
```

Discussion

An SNTP exchange begins with a client sending a 48-byte UDP datagram which starts with byte '\x1b'. The server answers with a 48-byte UDP datagram made up of twelve network-order longwords (4 bytes each). We can easily unpack the server's returned datagram into a tuple of ints, by using standard Python library module struct's unpack function. Then, for simplicity, we look only at the eleventh of those twelve longwords. That integer gives the time in seconds—but it measures time from an epoch that's different from the 1970-based one normally used in Python. The difference in epochs is easily fixed by subtracting the *magic number* (kindly supplied by F. Lundh) that is named TIME1970 in the recipe. After the subtraction, we have a time in seconds from the epoch that complies with Python's standard time module, and we can handle it with the functions in module time. In this recipe, we just display it on standard output as formatted by function time.ctime.

See Also

Documentation for the standard library modules socket, struct and time in the *Library Reference* and *Python in a Nutshell*; the SNTP protocol is defined in RFC 2030 (*http://www.ietf.org/rfc/rfc2030.txt*), and the richer NTP protocol is defined in RFC 1305 (*http://www.ietf.org/rfc/rfc1305.txt*); Chapter 3 for general issues dealing with time in Python.

13.5 Sending HTML Mail

Credit: Art Gillespie

Problem

You need to send HTML mail and accompany it with a plain text version of the message's contents, so that the email message is also readable by MUAs that are not HTML-capable.

Solution

Although the modern Python way to perform any mail manipulation is with the standard Python library email package, the functionality we need for this recipe is also supplied by the MimeWriter and mimetools modules (which are also in the Python Standard Library). We can easily code a function that just accesses and uses that functionality:

```python
def createhtmlmail(subject, html, text=None):
    " Create a mime-message that will render as HTML or text, as appropriate"
    import MimeWriter, mimetools, cStringIO
    if text is None:
        # Produce an approximate textual rendering of the HTML string,
        # unless you have been given a better version as an argument
        import htmllib, formatter
        textout = cStringIO.StringIO( )
        formtext = formatter.AbstractFormatter(formatter.DumbWriter(textout))
        parser = htmllib.HTMLParser(formtext)
        parser.feed(html)
        parser.close( )
        text = textout.getvalue( )
        del textout, formtext, parser
    out = cStringIO.StringIO( )             # output buffer for our message
    htmlin = cStringIO.StringIO(html)       # input buffer for the HTML
    txtin = cStringIO.StringIO(text)        # input buffer for the plain text
    writer = MimeWriter.MimeWriter(out)
    # Set up some basic headers. Place subject here because smtplib.sendmail
    # expects it to be in the message, as relevant RFCs prescribe.
    writer.addheader("Subject", subject)
    writer.addheader("MIME-Version", "1.0")
    # Start the multipart section of the message.  Multipart/alternative seems
    # to work better on some MUAs than multipart/mixed.
    writer.startmultipartbody("alternative")
    writer.flushheaders( )
    # the plain-text section: just copied through, assuming iso-8859-1
    subpart = writer.nextpart( )
    pout = subpart.startbody("text/plain", [("charset", 'iso-8859-1')])
    pout.write(txtin.read( ))
    txtin.close( )
    # the HTML subpart of the message: quoted-printable, just in case
    subpart = writer.nextpart( )
    subpart.addheader("Content-Transfer-Encoding", "quoted-printable")
    pout = subpart.startbody("text/html", [("charset", 'us-ascii')])
    mimetools.encode(htmlin, pout, 'quoted-printable')
    htmlin.close( )
    # You're done; close your writer and return the message as a string
    writer.lastpart( )
    msg = out.getvalue( )
    out.close( )
    return msg
```

Discussion

This recipe's module is completed in the usual style with a few lines to ensure that, when run as a script, it runs a self-test by composing and sending a sample HTML mail:

```python
if __name__=="__main__":
    import smtplib
    f = open("newsletter.html", 'r')
    html = f.read()
    f.close()
    try:
        f = open("newsletter.txt", 'r')
        text = f.read()
    except IOError:
        text = None
    subject = "Today's Newsletter!"
    message = createhtmlmail(subject, html, text)
    server = smtplib.SMTP("localhost")
    server.sendmail('agillesp@i-noSPAMSUCKS.com',
        'agillesp@i-noSPAMSUCKS.com', message)
    server.quit()
```

Sending HTML mail is a popular concept, and (as long as you avoid sending it to newsgroups and open mailing lists) there's no reason your Python scripts shouldn't do it. When you do send HTML mail, never forget to embed a text-only version of your message along with the HTML version. Lots of folks still prefer character-mode mail readers (technically known as MUAs), and it makes no sense to alienate those users by sending mail that they can't conveniently read. This recipe shows how easy Python makes the task of sending an email in both HTML and text forms.

Ideally, your input will be a properly formatted text version of the message, as well as the HTML version. But, if you don't have such nice textual input, you can still prepare a text version on the fly starting from the HTML version; one way to prepare such text is shown in the recipe. Remember that htmllib has some limitations, so you may want to use alternative approaches, such as saving the HTML string to disk and then using:

```python
text = os.popen('lynx -dump %s' % tempfile).read()
```

or whatever works best for you. Alternatively, if all you have as input is plain text (following some specific conventions, such as empty lines to mark paragraphs and underlines for emphasis), you can parse the text and throw together some HTML markup on the fly.

The emails generated by this code have been successfully read on Outlook 2000, Eudora 4.2, Hotmail, and Netscape Mail. It's likely that they will work in other HTML-capable MUAs as well. Mutt has been used to test the acceptance of messages generated by this recipe in text-only MUAs. Again, other such MUAs can be expected to work just as acceptably.

See Also

Recipe 13.6 "Bundling Files in a MIME Message" shows how the email package in the Python Standard Library can also be used to compose a MIME multipart message; documentation in the *Library Reference* and *Python in a Nutshell* about the standard library package email, as well as modules mimetools, MimeWriter, htmllib, formatter, cStringIO, and smtplib; Henry Minsky's article about MIME (*http://www.arsdigita.com/asj/mime/*) for information on various issues related to sending HTML mail.

13.6 Bundling Files in a MIME Message

Credit: Matthew Dixon Cowles, Hans Fangohr, John Pywtorak

Problem

You want to create a multipart MIME (Multipurpose Internet Mail Extensions) message that includes all files in the current directory.

Solution

If you often deal with composing or parsing mail messages, or mail-like messages such as Usenet news posts, the Python Standard Library email package gives you very powerful tools to work with. Here is a module that uses email to solve the task posed in the "Problem":

```
#!/usr/bin/env python
import base64, quopri
import mimetypes, email.Generator, email.Message
import cStringIO, os
# sample addresses
toAddr = "example@example.com"
fromAddr = "example@example.com"
outputFile = "dirContentsMail"
def main( ):
    mainMsg = email.Message.Message( )
    mainMsg["To"] = toAddr
    mainMsg["From"] = fromAddr
    mainMsg["Subject"] = "Directory contents"
    mainMsg["Mime-version"] = "1.0"
    mainMsg["Content-type"] = "Multipart/mixed"
    mainMsg.preamble = "Mime message\n"
    mainMsg.epilogue = "" # to ensure that message ends with newline
    # Get names of plain files (not subdirectories or special files)
    fileNames = [f for f in os.listdir(os.curdir) if os.path.isfile(f)]
    for fileName in fileNames:
        contentType, ignored = mimetypes.guess_type(fileName)
        if contentType is None:    # If no guess, use generic opaque type
            contentType = "application/octet-stream"
        contentsEncoded = cStringIO.StringIO( )
```

```
        f = open(fileName, "rb")
        mainType = contentType[:contentType.find("/")]
        if mainType=="text":
            cte = "quoted-printable"
            quopri.encode(f, contentsEncoded, 1)   # 1 to also encode tabs
        else:
            cte = "base64"
            base64.encode(f, contentsEncoded)
        f.close()
        subMsg = email.Message.Message()
        subMsg.add_header("Content-type", contentType, name=fileName)
        subMsg.add_header("Content-transfer-encoding", cte)
        subMsg.set_payload(contentsEncoded.getvalue())
        contentsEncoded.close()
        mainMsg.attach(subMsg)
    f = open(outputFile, "wb")
    g = email.Generator.Generator(f)
    g.flatten(mainMsg)
    f.close()
    return None
if __name__=="__main__":
    main()
```

Discussion

The email package makes manipulating MIME messages a snap. The Python Standard Library also offers other older modules that can serve many of the same purposes, but I suggest you look into email as an alternative to all such other modules. email requires some study because it is a very functionally rich package, but it will amply repay the time you spend studying it.

MIME is the Internet standard for sending files and non-ASCII data by email. The standard is specified in RFCs 2045-2049. A few points are especially worth keeping in mind:

- The original specification for the format of an email (RFC 822) didn't allow for non-ASCII characters and had no provision for attaching or enclosing a file along with a text message. Therefore, not surprisingly, MIME messages are very common these days.

- Messages that follow the MIME standard are backward compatible with ordinary RFC 822 (now RFC 2822) messages. An old mail reader (technically, an MUA) that doesn't understand the MIME specification will probably not be able to display a MIME message in a way that's useful to the user, but the message will still be legal and therefore shouldn't cause unexpected behavior.

- An RFC 2822 message consists of a set of headers, a blank line, and a body. MIME handles attachments and other multipart documents by specifying a format for the message's body. In multipart MIME messages, the body is divided into submessages, each of which has a set of headers, a blank line, and a body.

Generally, each submessage is referred to as a MIME part, and parts may nest recursively.

- MIME parts (whether or not in a multipart message) that contain characters outside of the strict US-ASCII range are encoded as either base-64 or quoted-printable data, so that the resulting mail message contains only ordinary ASCII characters. Data can be encoded with either method, but, generally, only data that has few non-ASCII characters (basically text, possibly with a few extra characters outside of the ASCII range, such as national characters in Latin-1 and similar codes) is worth encoding as quoted-printable, because even without decoding it may be readable. If the data is essentially binary, with all bytes being equally likely, base-64 encoding is more compact.

Not surprisingly, given all of these issues, manipulating MIME messages is often considered to be a nuisance. In the old times, back before Python 2.2, the standard library's modules for dealing with MIME messages were quite useful but rather miscellaneous. In particular, putting MIME messages together and taking them apart required two distinct approaches. The email package, which was added in Python 2.2, unified and simplified these two related jobs.

See Also

Recipe 13.7 "Unpacking a Multipart MIME Message" shows how the email package can be used to unpack a MIME message; documentation for the standard library modules email, mimetypes, base64, quopri, and cStringIO in the *Library Reference* and *Python in a Nutshell*.

13.7   Unpacking a Multipart MIME Message

Credit: Matthew Cowles

Problem

You want to unpack a multipart MIME message.

Solution

The walk method of message objects generated by the email package makes this task really easy. Here is a script that uses email to solve the task posed in the "Problem":

```
import email.Parser
import os, sys
def main():
    if len(sys.argv) != 2:
        print "Usage: %s filename" % os.path.basename(sys.argv[0])
        sys.exit(1)
    mailFile = open(sys.argv[1], "rb")
    p = email.Parser.Parser()
```

```
        msg = p.parse(mailFile)
        mailFile.close( )
        partCounter = 1
        for part in msg.walk( ):
            if part.get_main_type( ) == "multipart":
                continue
            name = part.get_param("name")
            if name == None:
                name = "part-%i" % partCounter
            partCounter += 1
            # In real life, make sure that name is a reasonable filename
            # for your OS; otherwise, mangle that name until it is!
            f = open(name, "wb")
            f.write(part.get_payload(decode=1))
            f.close( )
            print name
if __name__=="__main__":
    main( )
```

Discussion

The email package makes parsing MIME messages reasonably easy. This recipe shows how to unbundle a MIME message with the email package by using the walk method of message objects.

You can create a message object in several ways. For example, you can instantiate the email.Message.Message class and build the message object's contents with calls to its methods. In this recipe, however, I need to read and analyze an existing message, so I work the other way around, calling the parse method of an email.Parser.Parser instance. The parse method takes as its only argument a file-like object (in the recipe, I pass it a real file object that I just opened for binary reading with the built-in open function) and returns a message object, on which you can call message object methods.

The walk method is a generator (i.e., it returns an iterator object on which you can loop with a for statement). You usually will use this method exactly as I use it in this recipe:

```
for part in msg.walk( ):
```

The iterator sequentially returns (depth-first, in case of nesting) the parts that make up the message. If the message is not a container of parts (i.e., has no attachments or alternates—message.is_multipart returns false), no problem: the walk method will then return an iterator with a single element—the message itself. In any case, each element of the iterator is also a message object (an instance of email.Message.Message), so you can call on it any of the methods that a message object supplies.

In a multipart message, parts with a type of 'multipart/something' (i.e., a main type of 'multipart') may be present. In this recipe, I skip them explicitly since they're just glue holding the true parts together. I use the get_main_type method to obtain the main type and check it for equality with 'multipart'; if equality holds, I skip this part and move to the next one with a continue statement. When I know I have a real part in hand, I locate its name (or synthesize one if it has no name), open that name as a file, and write the message's contents (also known as the message's *payload*), which I get by calling the get_payload method, into the file. I use the decode=1 argument to ensure that the payload is decoded back to a binary content (e.g., an image, a sound file, a movie) if needed, rather than remaining in text form. If the payload is not encoded, decode=1 is innocuous, so I don't have to check before I pass it.

See Also

Recipe 13.6 "Bundling Files in a MIME Message"; documentation for the standard library package email in the *Library Reference*.

13.8   Removing Attachments from an Email Message

Credit: Anthony Baxter

Problem

You're handling email in Python and need to remove from email messages any attachments that might be dangerous.

Solution

Regular expressions can help us identify dangerous content types and file extensions, and thus code a function to remove any potentially dangerous attachments:

```
ReplFormat = """
This message contained an attachment that was stripped out.
The filename was: %(filename)s,
The original type was: %(content_type)s
(and it had additional parameters of:
%(params)s)
"""

import re
BAD_CONTENT_RE = re.compile('application/(msword|msexcel)', re.I)
BAD_FILEEXT_RE = re.compile(r'(\.exe|\.zip|\.pif|\.scr|\.ps)$')
def sanitise(msg):
    ''' Strip out all potentially dangerous payloads from a message '''
    ct = msg.get_content_type( )
    fn = msg.get_filename( )
    if BAD_CONTENT_RE.search(ct) or (fn and BAD_FILEEXT_RE.search(fn)):
        # bad message-part, pull out info for reporting then destroy it
        # present the parameters to the content-type, list of key, value
        # pairs, as key=value forms joined by comma-space
```

```
params = msg.get_params()[1:]
params = ', '.join([ '='.join(p) for p in params ])
# put informative message text as new payload
replace = ReplFormat % dict(content_type=ct, filename=fn, params=params)
msg.set_payload(replace)
# now remove parameters and set contents in content-type header
for k, v in msg.get_params()[1:]:
    msg.del_param(k)
msg.set_type('text/plain')
# Also remove headers that make no sense without content-type
del msg['Content-Transfer-Encoding']
del msg['Content-Disposition']
    else:
        # Now we check for any sub-parts to the message
        if msg.is_multipart():
            # Call sanitise recursively on any subparts
            payload = [ sanitise(x) for x in msg.get_payload() ]
            # Replace the payload with our list of sanitised parts
            msg.set_payload(payload)
    # Return the sanitised message
    return msg
# Add a simple driver/example to show how to use this function
if __name__ == '__main__':
    import email, sys
    m = email.message_from_file(open(sys.argv[1]))
    print sanitise(m)
```

Discussion

This issue has come up a few times on the newsgroup *comp.lang.python*, so I decided to post a cookbook entry to show how easy it is to deal with this kind of task. Specifically, this recipe shows how to read in an email message, strip out any dangerous or suspicious attachments, and replace them with a harmless text message informing the user of the alterations that we're performed.

This kind of task is particularly important when end users are using something like Microsoft Outlook, which is targeted by harmful virus and worm messages (collectively known as *malware*) on a daily basis.

The email parser in Python 2.4 has been completely rewritten to be robust first, correct second. Prior to that version, the parser was written for correctness first. But focusing on correctness was a problem because many virus/worm messages and other malware routinely send email messages that are broken and nonconformant—malformed to the point that the old email parser chokes and dies. The new parser is designed to never actually break when reading a message. Instead, it tries its best to fix whatever it can fix in the message. (If you have a message that causes the parser to crash, please let us, the core Python developers, know. It's a bug, and we'll fix it. Please include a copy of the message that makes the parser crash, or else it's very unlikely that we can reproduce your problem!)

The recipe's code itself is fairly well commented and should be easy enough to follow. A mail message consists of one or more parts; each of these parts can contain nested parts. We call the `sanitise` function on the top-level `Message` object, and it calls itself recursively on the subobjects if and as needed.

The `sanitise` function first checks the `Content-Type` of the part, and if there's a filename, it also checks that filename's extension against a known-to-be-bad list. If the message part is bad, we replace the message itself with a short text description describing the now-removed part and clean out the headers that are relevant. We set this message part's `Content-Type` to `'text/plain'` and remove other headers related to the now-removed message.

Finally, we check whether the message is a multipart message. If so, it means the message has subparts, so we recursively call the `sanitise` function on each of them. We then replace the payload with our list of sanitized subparts.

If you're interested in working further on this recipe, the most important extra functionality, which is easy to add with a small amount of work, might be to store the attached file in some directory (instead of destroying all suspect attachments), and give the user a link to that file. Also consider extending the check in `sanitise` that filters dangerous attachments to have it verify more than just the content type and file extension; other headers may be able to carry known signs of worm or virus messages.

See Also

Documentation for the standard library modules `email` and `re` in the *Library Reference* and *Python in a Nutshell*.

13.9 Fixing Messages Parsed by Python 2.4 email.FeedParser

Credit: Matthew Cowles

Problem

You're using Python 2.4's new `email.FeedParser` module, but sometimes, when dealing with badly malformed incoming messages, that module produces message objects that are internally inconsistent (e.g., a message has a content-type header that says the message is multipart, but the body isn't), and you need to fix those inconsistencies.

Solution

Python 2.4's new standard library module `email.FeedParser` is very useful, but a little post-processing on the messages it returns can heuristically fix some inconsisten-

cies and make it even better. Here's a module containing a class and a few functions
to help with this task:

```python
import email, email.FeedParser
import re, sys, sgmllib
# what chars are non-Ascii, what max fraction of them can be in a text part
kGuessBinaryThreshold = 0.2
kGuessBinaryRE = re.compile("[\\0000-\\0025\\0200-\\0377]")
# what max fraction of HTML tags can be in a text (non-HTML) part
kGuessHTMLThreshold = 0.05
class Cleaner(sgmllib.SGMLParser):
    entitydefs = {"nbsp": " "}  # I'll break if I want to
    def __init__(self):
        sgmllib.SGMLParser.__init__(self)
        self.result = [ ]
    def do_p(self, *junk):
        self.result.append('\n')
    def do_br(self, *junk):
        self.result.append('\n')
    def handle_data(self, data):
        self.result.append(data)
    def cleaned_text(self):
        return ''.join(self.result)
def stripHTML(text):
    ''' return text, with HTML tags stripped '''
    c = Cleaner( )
    try:
        c.feed(text)
    except sgmllib.SGMLParseError:
        return text
    else:
        return c.cleaned_text( )
def guessIsBinary(text):
    ''' return whether we can heuristically guess 'text' is binary '''
    if not text: return False
    nMatches = float(len(kGuessBinaryRE.findall(text)))
    return nMatches/len(text) >= kGuessBinaryThreshold
def guessIsHTML(text):
    ''' return whether we can heuristically guess 'text' is HTML '''
    if not text: return False
    lt = len(text)
    textWithoutTags = stripHTML(text)
    tagsChars = float(lt-len(textWithoutTags))
    return tagsChars/lt >= kGuessHTMLThreshold
def getMungedMessage(openFile):
    openFile.seek(0)
    p = email.FeedParser.FeedParser( )
    p.feed(openFile.read( ))
    m = p.close( )
    # Fix up multipart content-type when message isn't multi-part
    if m.get_main_type( )=="multipart" and not m.is_multipart( ):
        t = m.get_payload(decode=1)
        if guessIsBinary(t):
            # Use generic "opaque" type
```

```
            m.set_type("application/octet-stream")
        elif guessIsHTML(t):
            m.set_type("text/html")
        else:
            m.set_type("text/plain")
    return m
```

Discussion

FeedParser is a new module in the Python 2.4 Standard Library's email package. The module's name comes from the fact that it maintains a buffer, so that you don't have to give it all the text at once. Possibly more interesting is that the module doesn't raise an error when called on malformed messages; instead, it tries to make some sense of them and return a useful email.Message object. That's useful because so much mail is spam and so much spam is malformed.

The other side of the coin, given that the heroic feed parser works on incorrect messages, is that you can get back from it an email.Message object that's internally inconsistent. This recipe tries to make sense of one kind of inconsistency: a message with a content-type header that says that the message is multipart, but the body isn't.

The heuristics that the recipe uses to guess at the correct content-type are inevitably messy. Still, better to have such messy heuristics in recipes, rather than embedded forever in the Python Standard Library.

See Also

Documentation for the standard library package email in the Python 2.4 *Library Reference*.

13.10 Inspecting a POP3 Mailbox Interactively

Credit: Xavier Defrang

Problem

You have a POP3 mailbox somewhere, perhaps on a slow connection, and need to examine messages and possibly mark them for deletion interactively.

Solution

The poplib module of the Python Standard Library lets you write a script to solve this task quite easily:

```
# Interactive script to clean POP3 mailboxes from malformed or too-large mails
#
# Iterates over nonretrieved mails, prints selected elements from the headers,
# prompts interactively about whether each message should be deleted
```

```
import sys, getpass, poplib, re
# Change according to your needs: POP host, userid, and password
POPHOST = "pop.domain.com"
POPUSER = "jdoe"
POPPASS = ""
# How many lines to retrieve from body, and which headers to retrieve
MAXLINES = 10
HEADERS = "From To Subject".split()
args = len(sys.argv)
if args>1: POPHOST = sys.argv[1]
if args>2: POPUSER = sys.argv[2]
if args>3: POPPASS = sys.argv[3]
if args>4: MAXLINES= int(sys.argv[4])
if args>5: HEADERS = sys.argv[5:]
# An RE to identify the headers you're actually interested in
rx_headers  = re.compile('|'.join(HEADERS), re.IGNORECASE)
try:
    # Connect to the POP server and identify the user
    pop = poplib.POP3(POPHOST)
    pop.user(POPUSER)
    # Authenticate user
    if not POPPASS or POPPASS=='=':
        # If no password was supplied, ask for the password
        POPPASS = getpass.getpass("Password for %s@%s:" % (POPUSER, POPHOST))
    pop.pass_(POPPASS)
    # Get and print some general information (msg_count, box_size)
    stat = pop.stat()
    print "Logged in as %s@%s" % (POPUSER, POPHOST)
    print "Status: %d message(s), %d bytes" % stat
    bye = False
    count_del = 0
    for msgnum in range(1, 1+stat[0]):
        # Retrieve headers
        response, lines, bytes = pop.top(msgnum, MAXLINES)
        # Print message info and headers you're interested in
        print "Message %d (%d bytes)" % (msgnum, bytes)
        print "-" * 30
        print "\n".join(filter(rx_headers.match, lines))
        print "-" * 30
        # Input loop
        while True:
            k = raw_input("(d=delete, s=skip, v=view, q=quit) What? ")
            k = k[:1].lower()
            if k == 'd':
                # Mark message for deletion
                k = raw_input("Delete message %d? (y/n) " % msgnum)
                if k in "yY":
                    pop.dele(msgnum)
                    print "Message %d marked for deletion" % msgnum
                    count_del += 1
                    break
            elif k == 's':
                print "Message %d left on server" % msgnum
                break
```

```
        elif k == 'v':
            print "-" * 30
            print "\n".join(lines)
            print "-" * 30
        elif k == 'q':
            bye = True
            break
    # Time to say goodbye?
    if bye:
        print "Bye"
        break
    # Summary
    print "Deleting %d message(s) in mailbox %s@%s" % (
        count_del, POPUSER, POPHOST)
    # Commit operations and disconnect from server
    print "Closing POP3 session"
    pop.quit()
except poplib.error_proto, detail:
    # Fancy error handling
    print "POP3 Protocol Error:", detail
```

Discussion

Sometimes your POP3 mailbox is behind a slow Internet link, and you don't want to
wait for that funny 10MB MPEG movie that you already received twice yesterday to
be fully downloaded before you can read your mail. Or maybe a peculiar malformed
message is hanging your MUA. Issues of this kind are best tackled interactively, but
you need a helpful script to let you examine data about each message and determine
which messages should be removed.

I used to deal with this kind of thing by telneting to the POP (Post Office Protocol)
server and trying to remember the POP3 protocol commands (while hoping that the
server implements the help command in particular). Nowadays, I use the script presented in this recipe to inspect my mailbox and do some cleaning. Basically, the
Python Standard Library POP3 module, poplib, remembers the protocol commands
on my behalf, and this script helps me use those commands appropriately.

The script in this recipe uses the poplib module to connect to your mailbox. It then
prompts you about what to do with each undelivered message. You can view the top
of the message, leave the message on the server, or mark the message for deletion.
No particular tricks or hacks are used in this piece of code: it's a simple example of
poplib usage. In addition to being practically useful in emergencies, it can show you
how poplib works. The poplib.POP3 call returns an object that is ready for connection to a POP3 server specified as its argument. We complete the connection by calling the user and pass_ methods to specify a user ID and password. Note the trailing
underscore in pass_: this method could not be called pass because that is a Python
keyword (the do-nothing statement), and by convention, such issues are often solved
by appending an underscore to the identifier.

After connection, we keep working with methods of the pop object. The stat method returns the number of messages and the total size of the mailbox in bytes. The top method takes a message-number argument and returns information about that message, as well as the message itself as a list of lines. (You can specify a second argument n to ensure that no more than n lines are returned.) The dele method also takes a message-number argument and deletes that message from the mailbox (without renumbering all other messages). When we're done, we call the quit method. If you're familiar with the POP3 protocol, you'll notice the close correspondence between these methods and the POP3 commands.

See Also

Documentation for the standard library modules poplib and getpass in the *Library Reference* and *Python in a Nutshell*; the POP protocol is described in RFC 1939 (*http://www.ietf.org/rfc/rfc1939.txt*).

13.11 Detecting Inactive Computers

Credit: Nicola Larosa

Problem

You need to monitor the working state of a number of computers connected to a TCP/IP network.

Solution

The key idea in this recipe is to have every computer periodically send a heartbeat UDP packet to a computer acting as the server for this heartbeat-monitoring service. The server keeps track of how much time has passed since each computer last sent a heartbeat and reports on computers that have been silent for too long.

Here is the "client" program, *HeartbeatClient.py*, which must run on every computer we need to monitor:

```
""" Heartbeat client, sends out a UDP packet periodically """
import socket, time
SERVER_IP = '192.168.0.15'; SERVER_PORT = 43278; BEAT_PERIOD = 5
print 'Sending heartbeat to IP %s , port %d' % (SERVER_IP, SERVER_PORT)
print 'press Ctrl-C to stop'
while True:
    hbSocket = socket.socket(socket.AF_INET, socket.SOCK_DGRAM)
    hbSocket.sendto('PyHB', (SERVER_IP, SERVER_PORT))
    if __debug__:
        print 'Time: %s' % time.ctime()
    time.sleep(BEAT_PERIOD)
```

The server program, which receives and keeps track of these "heartbeats", must run on the machine whose address is given as SERVER_IP in the "client" program. The server must support concurrency, since many heartbeats from different computers might arrive simultaneously. A server program has essentially two ways to support concurrency: multithreading, or asynchronous operation. Here is a multithreaded *ThreadedBeatServer.py*, using only modules from the Python Standard Library:

```python
""" Threaded heartbeat server """
import socket, threading, time
UDP_PORT = 43278; CHECK_PERIOD = 20; CHECK_TIMEOUT = 15
class Heartbeats(dict):
    """ Manage shared heartbeats dictionary with thread locking """
    def __init__(self):
        super(Heartbeats, self).__init__()
        self._lock = threading.Lock()
    def __setitem__(self, key, value):
        """ Create or update the dictionary entry for a client """
        self._lock.acquire()
        try:
            super(Heartbeats, self).__setitem__(key, value)
        finally:
            self._lock.release()
    def getSilent(self):
        """ Return a list of clients with heartbeat older than CHECK_TIMEOUT """
        limit = time.time() - CHECK_TIMEOUT
        self._lock.acquire()
        try:
            silent = [ip for (ip, ipTime) in self.items() if ipTime < limit]
        finally:
            self._lock.release()
        return silent
class Receiver(threading.Thread):
    """ Receive UDP packets and log them in the heartbeats dictionary """
    def __init__(self, goOnEvent, heartbeats):
        super(Receiver, self).__init__()
        self.goOnEvent = goOnEvent
        self.heartbeats = heartbeats
        self.recSocket = socket.socket(socket.AF_INET, socket.SOCK_DGRAM)
        self.recSocket.settimeout(CHECK_TIMEOUT)
        self.recSocket.bind(('', UDP_PORT))
    def run(self):
        while self.goOnEvent.isSet():
            try:
                data, addr = self.recSocket.recvfrom(5)
                if data == 'PyHB':
                    self.heartbeats[addr[0]] = time.time()
            except socket.timeout:
                pass
def main(num_receivers=3):
    receiverEvent = threading.Event()
    receiverEvent.set()
    heartbeats = Heartbeats()
    receivers = []
    for i in range(num_receivers):
        receiver = Receiver(goOnEvent=receiverEvent, heartbeats=heartbeats)
        receiver.start()
```

```
            receivers.append(receiver)
        print 'Threaded heartbeat server listening on port %d' % UDP_PORT
        print 'press Ctrl-C to stop'
        try:
            while True:
                silent = heartbeats.getSilent()
                print 'Silent clients: %s' % silent
                time.sleep(CHECK_PERIOD)
        except KeyboardInterrupt:
            print 'Exiting, please wait...'
            receiverEvent.clear()
            for receiver in receivers:
                receiver.join()
            print 'Finished.'
    if __name__ == '__main__':
        main()
```

As an alternative, here is an asynchronous *AsyncBeatServer.py* program based on the
powerful Twisted framework:

```
import time
from twisted.application import internet, service
from twisted.internet import protocol
from twisted.python import log
UDP_PORT = 43278; CHECK_PERIOD = 20; CHECK_TIMEOUT = 15
class Receiver(protocol.DatagramProtocol):
    """ Receive UDP packets and log them in the "client"s dictionary """
    def datagramReceived(self, data, (ip, port)):
        if data == 'PyHB':
            self.callback(ip)
class DetectorService(internet.TimerService):
    """ Detect clients not sending heartbeats for too long """
    def __init__(self):
        internet.TimerService.__init__(self, CHECK_PERIOD, self.detect)
        self.beats = {}
    def update(self, ip):
        self.beats[ip] = time.time()
    def detect(self):
        """ Log a list of clients with heartbeat older than CHECK_TIMEOUT """
        limit = time.time() - CHECK_TIMEOUT
        silent = [ip for (ip, ipTime) in self.beats.items() if ipTime < limit]
        log.msg('Silent clients: %s' % silent)
application = service.Application('Heartbeat')
# define and link the silent clients' detector service
detectorSvc = DetectorService()
detectorSvc.setServiceParent(application)
# create an instance of the Receiver protocol, and give it the callback
receiver = Receiver()
receiver.callback = detectorSvc.update
# define and link the UDP server service, passing the receiver in
udpServer = internet.UDPServer(UDP_PORT, receiver)
udpServer.setServiceParent(application)
# each service is started automatically by Twisted at launch time
log.msg('Asynchronous heartbeat server listening on port %d\n'
    'press Ctrl-C to stop\n' % UDP_PORT)
```

Discussion

When a number of computers are connected by a TCP/IP network, we are often interested in monitoring their working state. The client and server programs presented in this recipe help you detect when a computer stops working, while having minimal impact on network traffic and requiring very little setup. Note that this recipe does not monitor the working state of single, specific services running on a machine, just that of the TCP/IP stack and the underlying operating system and hardware components.

This PyHeartBeat approach is made up of two files: a client program, *HeartbeatClient.py*, sends UDP packets to the server, while a server program, either *ThreadedBeatServer.py* (using only modules from the Python Standard Library to implement a multithreaded approach) or *AsyncBeatServer.py* (implementing an asynchronous approach based on the powerful Twisted framework), runs on a central computer to listen for such packets and detect inactive clients. Client programs, running on any number of computers, periodically send UDP packets to the server program that runs on the central computer. The server program, in either version, dynamically builds a dictionary that stores the IP addresses of the "client" computers and the timestamp of the last packet received from each one. At the same time, the server program periodically checks the dictionary, checking whether any of the timestamps are older than a defined timeout, to identify clients that have been silent too long.

In this kind of application, there is no need to use reliable TCP connections since the loss of a packet now and then does not produce false alarms, as long as the server-checking timeout is kept suitably larger than the "client"-sending period. Since we may have hundreds of computers to monitor, it is best to keep the bandwidth used and the load on the server at a minimum: we do this by periodically sending a small UDP packet, instead of setting up a relatively expensive TCP connection per client.

The packets are sent from each client every 5 seconds, while the server checks the dictionary every 20 seconds, and the server's timeout defaults to 15 seconds. These parameters, along with the server IP number and port used, can be adapted to one's needs.

Threaded server

In the threaded server, a small number of worker threads listen to the UDP packets coming from the "client"s, while the main thread periodically checks the recorded heartbeats. The shared data structure, a dictionary, must be locked and released at each access, both while writing and reading, to avoid data corruption on concurrent access. Such data corruption would typically manifest itself as intermittent, time-dependent bugs that are difficult to reproduce, investigate, and correct.

A very sound alternative to such meticulous use of locking around access to a resource is to dedicate a specialized thread to be the only one interacting with the resource (in this case, the dictionary), while all other threads send work requests to the specialized thread with a Queue.Queue instance. A Queue-based approach is more scalable when per-resource locking gets too complicated to manage easily: Queue is less bug-prone and, in particular, avoids worries about deadlocks. See recipe 9.3 "Using a Queue.Queue as a Priority Queue," recipe 9.5 "Executing a Function in Parallel on Multiple Argument Sets," recipe 9.4 "Working with a Thread Pool," and recipe 11.9 "Combining GUIs and Asynchronous I/O with Threads" for more information about Queue and examples of using Queue to structure the architecture of a multithreaded program.

Asynchronous server

The Twisted server employs an asynchronous, event-driven model based on the Twisted framework (*http://www.twistedmatrix.com/*). The framework is built around a central "reactor" that dispatches events from a queue in a single thread, and monitors network and host resources. The user program is composed of short code fragments invoked by the reactor when dispatching the matching events. Such a working model guarantees that only one user code fragment is executing at any given time, eliminating at the root all problems of concurrent access to shared data structures. Asynchronous servers can provide excellent performance and scalability under very heavy loads, by avoiding the threading and locking overheads of multithreader servers.

The asynchronous server program presented in this recipe is composed of one application and two services, the UDPServer and the DetectorService, respectively. It is invoked at any command shell by means of the twistd command, with the following options:

```
$ twistd -ony AsyncBeatServer.py
```

The twistd command controls the reactor, and many other delicate facets of a server's operation, leaving the script it loads the sole responsibility of defining a global variable named application, implementing the needed services, and connecting the service objects to the application object.

Normally, twistd runs as a daemon and logs to a file (or to other logging facilities, depending on configuration options), but in this case, with the -ony flags, we're specifically asking twistd to run in the foreground and with logging to standard output, so we can better see what's going on. Note that the most popular file extension for scripts to be loaded by twistd is *.tac*, although in this recipe I have used the more generally familiar extension *.py*. The choice of file extension is just a convention, in this case: twistd can work with Python source files with any file extension, since you pass the full filename, extension included, as an explicit command-line argument anyway.

See Also

Documentation for the standard library modules socket, threading, Queue and time in the *Library Reference* and *Python in a Nutshell*; twisted is at *http://www.twistedmatrix.com*; Jeff Bauer has a related program, known as *Mr. Creosote* (*http://starship.python.net/crew/jbauer/creosote/*), using UDP for logging information; UDP is described in depth in W. Richard Stevens, *UNIX Network Programming, Volume 1: Networking APIs–Sockets and XTI*, 2d ed. (Prentice-Hall); for the truly curious, the UDP protocol is defined in the two-page RFC 768 (*http://www.ietf.org/rfc/rfc768.txt*), which, when compared with current RFCs, shows how much the Internet infrastructure has evolved in 20 years.

13.12 Monitoring a Network with HTTP

Credit: Magnus Lyckå

Problem

You want to implement special-purpose HTTP servers to enable you to monitor your network.

Solution

The Python Standard Library BaseHTTPServer module makes it easy to implement special-purpose HTTP servers. For example, here is a special-purpose HTTP server program that runs local commands on the server host to get the data for replies to each GET request:

```
import BaseHTTPServer, shutil, os
from cStringIO import StringIO
class MyHTTPRequestHandler(BaseHTTPServer.BaseHTTPRequestHandler):
    # HTTP paths we serve, and what commandline-commands we serve them with
    cmds = {'/ping': 'ping www.thinkware.se',
            '/netstat' : 'netstat -a',
            '/tracert': 'tracert www.thinkware.se',
            '/srvstats': 'net statistics server',
            '/wsstats': 'net statistics workstation',
            '/route' : 'route print',
            }
    def do_GET(self):
        """ Serve a GET request. """
        f = self.send_head( )
        if f:
            f = StringIO( )
            machine = os.popen('hostname').readlines( )[0]
            if self.path == '/':
                heading = "Select a command to run on %s" % (machine)
                body = (self.getMenu( ) +
                        "<p>The screen won't update until the selected "
```

```
                            "command has finished. Please be patient.")
            else:
                heading = "Execution of ``%s'' on %s" % (
                        self.cmds[self.path], machine)
                cmd = self.cmds[self.path]
                body = '<a href="/">Main Menu&lt;/a&gt;<pre>%s</pre>\n' % \
                        os.popen(cmd).read( )
                # Translation CP437 -> Latin 1 needed for Swedish Windows.
                body = body.decode('cp437').encode('latin1')
            f.write("<html><head><title>%s</title></head>\n" % heading)
            f.write('<body><H1>%s</H1>\n' % (heading))
            f.write(body)
            f.write('</body></html>\n')
            f.seek(0)
            self.copyfile(f, self.wfile)
            f.close( )
        return f
    def do_HEAD(self):
        """ Serve a HEAD request. """
        f = self.send_head( )
        if f:
            f.close( )
    def send_head(self):
        path = self.path
        if not path in ['/'] + self.cmds.keys( ):
            head = 'Command "%s" not found. Try one of these:<ul>' % path
            msg = head + self.getMenu( )
            self.send_error(404, msg)
            return None
        self.send_response(200)
        self.send_header("Content-type", 'text/html')
        self.end_headers( )
        f = StringIO( )
        f.write("A test %s\n" % self.path)
        f.seek(0)
        return f
    def getMenu(self):
        keys = self.cmds.keys( )
        keys.sort( )
        msg = [ ]
        for k in keys:
            msg.append('<li><a href="%s">%s => %s&lt;/a&gt;</li>' %(
                                k,  k,    self.cmds[k]))
        msg.append('</ul>')
        return "\n".join(msg)
    def copyfile(self, source, outputfile):
        shutil.copyfileobj(source, outputfile)
def main(HandlerClass = MyHTTPRequestHandler,
        ServerClass = BaseHTTPServer.HTTPServer):
    BaseHTTPServer.test(HandlerClass, ServerClass)
if __name__ == '__main__':
    main( )
```

Discussion

The Python Standard Library module BaseHTTPServer makes it easy to set up custom web servers on an internal network. This way, you can run commands on various machines by just visiting those servers with a browser. The code in this recipe is Windows-specific, indeed specific to the version of Windows normally run in Sweden, because it knows about code page 437 providing the encoding for the various commands' results. The commands themselves are Windows ones, but that's just as easy to customize for your own purposes as the encoding issue—for example, using traceroute (the Unix spelling of the command) instead of tracert (the way Windows spells it).

In this recipe, all substantial work is performed by external commands invoked by os.popen calls. Of course, it would be perfectly feasible to satisfy some or all of the requests by running actual Python code within the same process as the web server. We would normally not worry about concurrency issues for this kind of special-purpose, ad hoc, administrative server (unlike most web servers): the scenario it's intended to cover is one system administrator sitting at her system and visiting, with her browser, various machines on the network being administered/monitored—concurrency is not really needed. If your scenario is somewhat different so that you do need concurrency, then multithreading and asynchronous operations, shown in several other recipes, are your fundamental options.

See Also

Documentation for the standard library modules BaseHTTPServer, shutil, os, and cStringIO in the *Library Reference* and *Python in a Nutshell*.

13.13 Forwarding and Redirecting Network Ports

Credit: Simon Foster

Problem

You need to forward a network port to another host (*forwarding*), possibly to a different port number (*redirecting*).

Solution

Classes using the threading and socket modules can provide port forwarding and redirecting:

```
import sys, socket, time, threading
LOGGING = True
loglock = threading.Lock( )
def log(s, *a):
    if LOGGING:
```

```python
            loglock.acquire()
            try:
                print '%s:%s' % (time.ctime(), (s % a))
                sys.stdout.flush()
            finally:
                loglock.release()
class PipeThread(threading.Thread):
    pipes = []
    pipeslock = threading.Lock()
    def __init__(self, source, sink):
        Thread.__init__(self)
        self.source = source
        self.sink = sink
        log('Creating new pipe thread %s ( %s -> %s )',
            self, source.getpeername(), sink.getpeername())
        self.pipeslock.acquire()
        try: self.pipes.append(self)
        finally: self.pipeslock.release()
        self.pipeslock.acquire()
        try: pipes_now = len(self.pipes)
        finally: self.pipeslock.release()
        log('%s pipes now active', pipes_now)

    def run(self):
        while True:
            try:
                data = self.source.recv(1024)
                if not data: break
                self.sink.send(data)
            except:
                break
        log('%s terminating', self)
        self.pipeslock.acquire()
        try: self.pipes.remove(self)
        finally: self.pipeslock.release()
        self.pipeslock.acquire()
        try: pipes_left = len(self.pipes)
        finally: self.pipeslock.release()
        log('%s pipes still active', pipes_left)
class Pinhole(threading.Thread):
    def __init__(self, port, newhost, newport):
        Thread.__init__(self)
        log('Redirecting: localhost:%s -> %s:%s', port, newhost, newport)
        self.newhost = newhost
        self.newport = newport
        self.sock = socket.socket(socket.AF_INET, socket.SOCK_STREAM)
        self.sock.bind(('', port))
        self.sock.listen(5)
    def run(self):
        while True:
            newsock, address = self.sock.accept()
            log('Creating new session for %s:%s', *address)
            fwd = socket.socket(socket.AF_INET, socket.SOCK_STREAM)
            fwd.connect((self.newhost, self.newport))
```

```
        PipeThread(newsock, fwd).start( )
        PipeThread(fwd, newsock).start( )
```

A short ending to this *pinhole.py* module, with the usual guard to run this part only when pinhole is run as a main script rather than imported, lets us offer this recipe's functionality as a command-line script:

```
if __name__ == '__main__':
    print 'Starting Pinhole port forwarder/redirector'
    import sys
    # get the arguments, give help in case of errors
    try:
        port = int(sys.argv[1])
        newhost = sys.argv[2]
        try: newport = int(sys.argv[3])
        except IndexError: newport = port
    except (ValueError, IndexError):
        print 'Usage: %s port newhost [newport]' % sys.argv[0]
        sys.exit(1)
    # start operations
    sys.stdout = open('pinhole.log', 'w')
    Pinhole(port, newhost, newport).start( )
```

Discussion

Port forwarding and redirecting can often come in handy when you're operating a network, even a small one. Applications or other services, possibly not under your control, may be hardwired to connect to servers on certain addresses or ports; by interposing a forwarder and redirector, you can send such applications' connection requests onto any other host and/or port that suits you better.

The code in this recipe supplies two classes that liberally use threading to provide this functionality and a small "main script" at the end, with the usual if __name__ = = '__main__' guard, to deliver this functionality as a command-line script. For once, the small "main script" is not just for demonstration and testing purposes but is actually quite useful on its own. For example:

```
# python pinhole.py 80 webserver
```

forwards all incoming HTTP sessions on standard port 80 to host *webserver*;

```
# python pinhole.py 23 localhost 2323
```

redirects all incoming telnet sessions on standard port 23 to port 2323 on this same host (since *localhost* is the conventional hostname for "this host" in all TCP/IP implementations).

See Also

Documentation for the standard library modules socket and threading in the *Library Reference* and *Python in a Nutshell*.

13.14 Tunneling SSL Through a Proxy

Credit: John Nielsen

Problem

You need to tunnel SSL (Secure Socket Layer) communications through a proxy, but the Python Standard Library doesn't support that functionality out of the box.

Solution

We can code a generic proxy, defaulting to SSL but, in fact, good for all kinds of network protocols. Save the following code as module file *pytunnel.py* somewhere along your Python sys.path:

```
import threading, socket, traceback, sys, base64, time
def recv_all(the_socket, timeout=1):
    ''' receive all data available from the_socket, waiting no more than
        ``timeout'' seconds for new data to arrive; return data as string.'''
    # use non-blocking sockets
    the_socket.setblocking(0)
    total_data = [ ]
    begin = time.time( )
    while True:
        ''' loop until timeout '''
        if total_data and time.time( )-begin > timeout:
            break       # if you got some data, then break after timeout seconds
        elif time.time( )-begin > timeout*2:
            break       # if you got no data at all yet, wait a little longer
        try:
            data = the_socket.recv(4096)
            if data:
                total_data.append(data)
                begin = time.time( )        # reset start-of-wait time
            else:
                time.sleep(0.1)             # give data some time to arrive
        except:
            pass
    return ''.join(total_data)
class thread_it(threading.Thread):
    ''' thread instance to run a tunnel, or a tunnel-client '''
    done = False
    def __init__(self, tid='', proxy='', server='', tunnel_client='',
                 port=0, ip='', timeout=1):
        threading.Thread.__init__(self)
        self.tid = tid
        self.proxy = proxy
        self.port = port
        self.server = server
        self.tunnel_client = tunnel_client
        self.ip = ip; self._port = port
        self.data = {}      #   store data here to get later
```

```
            self.timeout = timeout
    def run(self):
        try:
            if self.proxy and self.server:
                ''' running tunnel operation, so bridge server <-> proxy '''
                new_socket = False
                while not thread_it.done:     # loop until termination
                    if not new_socket:
                        new_socket, address = self.server.accept()
                    else:
                        self.proxy.sendall(
                            recv_all(new_socket, timeout=self.timeout))
                        new_socket.sendall(
                            recv_all(self.proxy, timeout=self.timeout))
            elif self.tunnel_client:
                ''' running tunnel client, just mark down when it's done '''
                self.tunnel_client(self.ip, self.port)
                thread_it.done = True     # normal termination
        except Exception, error:
            print traceback.print_exc(sys.exc_info()), error
            thread_it.done = True          # orderly termination upon exception
class build(object):
    ''' build a tunnel object, ready to run two threads as needed '''
    def __init__(self, host='', port=443, proxy_host='', proxy_port=80,
                 proxy_user='', proxy_pass='', proxy_type='', timeout=1):
        self._port=port; self.host=host; self._phost=proxy_host
        self._puser=proxy_user; self._pport=proxy_port; self._ppass=proxy_pass
        self._ptype=proxy_type; self.ip='127.0.0.1'; self.timeout=timeout
        self._server, self.server_port = self.get_server()
    def get_proxy(self):
        if not self._ptype:
            proxy = socket.socket(socket.AF_INET, socket.SOCK_STREAM)
            proxy.connect((self._phost, self._pport))
            proxy_authorization = ''
            if self._puser:
                proxy_authorization = 'Proxy-authorization: Basic '+\
                    base64.encodestring(self._puser+':'+self._ppass
                                        ).strip()+'\r\n'
            proxy_connect = 'CONNECT %s:%sHTTP/1.0\r\n' % (
                             self.host, self._port)
            user_agent = 'User-Agent: pytunnel\r\n'
            proxy_pieces = proxy_connect+proxy_authorization+user_agent+'\r\n'
            proxy.sendall(proxy_pieces+'\r\n')
            response = recv_all(proxy, timeout=0.5)
            status = response.split(None, 1)[1]
            if int(status)/100 != 2:
                print 'error', response
                raise RuntimeError(status)
            return proxy
    def get_server(self):
        port = 2222
        server = socket.socket(socket.AF_INET, socket.SOCK_STREAM)
        server.bind(('localhost', port))
```

```
        server.listen(5)
        return server, port
    def run(self, func):
        Threads = [ ]
        Threads.append(thread_it(tid=0, proxy=self.get_proxy(),
                            server=self._server, timeout=self.timeout))
        Threads.append(thread_it(tid=1, tunnel_client=func, ip=self.ip,
                            port=self.server_port, timeout=0.5))
        for Thread in Threads:
            Thread.start( )
        for Thread in Threads:
            Thread.join( )
```

Discussion

Here is how you would typically use this pytunnel module in a small example script
that tunnels an SSL connection through a proxy:

```
import pytunnel, httplib
def tunnel_this(ip, port):
    conn = httplib.HTTPSConnection(ip, port=port)
    conn.putrequest('GET', '/')
    conn.endheaders( )
    response = conn.getresponse( )
    print response.read( )
tunnel = pytunnel.build(host='login.yahoo.com', proxy_host='h1',
                        proxy_user='u', proxy_pass='p')
tunnel.run(tunnel_this)
```

This example assumes you have a proxy server running on host h1, which is ready to
accept basic authentication for a proxy user named u with a proxy password of p.
Since it's unlikely that this is, in fact, your specific setup, you'll have to tweak these
parameters if you want to see an example of this recipe's code running. But you
understand the general idea: you instantiate class pytunnel.build, with all appropriate parameters passed with named-argument syntax, to build a tunnel object; then,
you call the tunnel object's method run, passing as its argument your function that
you want to be "tunneled" through the proxy. That function, in turn, receives as its
arguments an IP address and a port number, and can connect to that address and
port via SSL or any protocol implying SSL/TLS (Transport Layer Security), such as
HTTPS.

Internally, the tunnel object instantiates two threads that are instances of thread_it,
one to run the tunnel client function, the other to perform the tunneling operation
itself. The tunneling operation, in turn, is nothing more than an endless loop where
all data available are received from one party and resent to the other, and vice versa;
function recv_all deals with the task of receiving all available data, while the socket
method send_all does the sending. The thread_it instance which runs the tunneling
operation, therefore, does no more than an endless loop of just such calls.

The code shown in this recipe is still being actively developed at the time of writing. For the latest version, see *http://ftp.gnu.org/pub/savannah/files/pytunnel/pytunnel.py*. Another alternative worth considering for tunneling and forwarding is Twisted's simple proxy (*http://www.twistedmatrix.com/*), but I have not personally tried that one yet.

See Also

For SSL/TLS standards, *http://www.ietf.org/html.charters/tls-charter.html*; documentation for the standard library modules socket, threading and time in the *Library Reference* and *Python in a Nutshell*.

13.15 Implementing the Dynamic IP Protocol

Credit: Nicola Paolucci, Mark Rowe, Andrew Notspecified

Problem

You use a Dynamic DNS Service which accepts the GnuDIP protocol (like *yi.org*), and need a command-line script to update your IP which is recorded with that service.

Solution

The Twisted framework has plenty of power for all kinds of network tasks, so we can use it to write a script to implement GnuDIP:

```
import md5, sys
from twisted.internet import protocol, reactor
from twisted.protocols import basic
from twisted.python import usage
def hashPassword(password, salt):
    ''' compute and return MD5 hash for given password and `salt`. '''
    p1 = md5.md5(password).hexdigest() + '.' + salt.strip()
    return md5.md5(p1).hexdigest()
class DIPProtocol(basic.LineReceiver):
    """ Implementation of GnuDIP protocol(TCP) as described at:
    http://gnudip2.sourceforge.net/gnudip-www/latest/gnudip/html/protocol.html
    """
    delimiter = '\n'
    def connectionMade(self):
        ''' at connection, we start in state "expecting salt". '''
        basic.LineReceiver.connectionMade(self)
        self.expectingSalt = True
    def lineReceived(self, line):
        ''' we received a full line, either "salt" or normal response '''
        if self.expectingSalt:
            self.saltReceived(line)
            self.expectingSalt = False
        else:
```

```python
            self.responseReceived(line)
    def saltReceived(self, salt):
        """ Override this 'abstract method' """
        raise NotImplementedError
    def responseReceived(self, response):
        """ Override this 'abstract method' """
        raise NotImplementedError
class DIPUpdater(DIPProtocol):
    """ A simple class to update an IP, then disconnect. """
    def saltReceived(self, salt):
        ''' having received `salt', login to the DIP server '''
        password = self.factory.getPassword()
        username = self.factory.getUsername()
        domain = self.factory.getDomain()
        msg = '%s:%s:%s:2' % (username, hashPassword(password, salt), domain)
        self.sendLine(msg)
    def responseReceived(self, response):
        ''' response received: show errors if any, then disconnect. '''
        code = response.split(':', 1)[0]
        if code == '0':
            pass   # OK
        elif code == '1':
            print 'Authentication failed'
        else:
            print 'Unexpected response from server:', repr(response)
        self.transport.loseConnection()
class DIPClientFactory(protocol.ClientFactory):
    """ Factory used to instantiate DIP protocol instances with
        correct username, password and domain.
    """

    protocol = DIPUpdater
    # simply collect data for login and provide accessors to them
    def __init__(self, username, password, domain):
        self.u = username
        self.p = password
        self.d = domain
    def getUsername(self):
        return self.u
    def getPassword(self):
        return self.p
    def getDomain(self):
        return self.d
    def clientConnectionLost(self, connector, reason):
        ''' terminate script when we have disconnected '''
        reactor.stop()
    def clientConnectionFailed(self, connector, reason):
        ''' show error message in case of network problems '''
        print 'Connection failed. Reason:', reason
class Options(usage.Options):
    ''' parse options from commandline or config script '''
    optParameters = [['server', 's', 'gnudip2.yi.org', 'DIP Server'],
                     ['port', 'p', 3495, 'DIP Server  port'],
                     ['username', 'u', 'durdn', 'Username'],
                     ['password', 'w', None, 'Password'],
```

```
                        ['domain', 'd', 'durdn.yi.org', 'Domain']]
    if __name__ == '__main__':
        # running as main script: first, get all the needed options
        config = Options()
        try:
            config.parseOptions()
        except usage.UsageError, errortext:
            print '%s: %s' % (sys.argv[0], errortext)
            print '%s: Try --help for usage details.' % (sys.argv[0])
            sys.exit(1)
        server = config['server']
        port = int(config['port'])
        password = config['password']
        if not password:
            print 'Password not entered. Try --help for usage details.'
            sys.exit(1)
        # and now, start operations (via Twisted's ``reactor'')
        reactor.connectTCP(server, port,
                DIPClientFactory(config['username'], password, config['domain']))
        reactor.run()
```

Discussion

I wanted to use a Dynamic DNS Service called *yi.org*, but I did not like the option of installing the suggested small client application to update my IP address on my OpenBSD box. So I resorted to writing the script shown in this recipe. I put it into my *crontab* to keep my domain always up-to-date with my dynamic IP address at home.

This little script is now at version 0.4, and its development history is quite instructive. I thought that even the first version. 0.1, which I got working in a few minutes, effectively demonstrated the power of the Twisted framework in developing network applications, so I posted that version on the ActiveState cookbook site. Lo and behold—Mark first, then Andrew, showered me with helpful suggestions, and I repeatedly updated the script in response to their advice. So it now demonstrates even better, not just the power of Twisted, but more generally the power of collaborative development in an open-source or free-software community.

To give just one example: originally, I had overridden buildProtocol and passed the factory object to the protocol object explicitly. The factory object, in the Twisted framework architecture, is where shared state is kept (in this case, the username, password, and domain), so I had to ensure the protocol knew about the factory—I thought. It turns out that, exactly because just about every protocol needs to know about its factory object, Twisted takes care of it in its own default implementation of buildProtocol, making the factory object available as the factory attribute of every protocol object. So, my code, which duplicated Twisted's built-in functionality in this regard, was simply ripped out, and the recipe's code is simpler and better as a result.

Too often, software is presented as a finished and polished artifact, as if it sprang pristine and perfect like Athena from Zeus' forehead. This gives entirely the wrong impression to budding software developers, making them feel inadequate because *their* code isn't born perfect and fully developed. So, as a counterweight, I thought it important to present one little story about how software actually grows and develops!

One last detail: it's tempting to place methods `updateIP` and `removeIP` in the `DIPProtocol` class, to ease the writing of subclasses such as `DIPUpdater`. However, in my view, that would be an over-generalization, overkill for such a simple, lightweight recipe as Python and Twisted make this one. In practice we won't need all that many dynamic IP protocol subclasses, and if it turns out that we're wrong and we do, in fact, need them, hey, refactoring is clearly *not* a hard task with such a fluid, dynamic language and powerful frameworks to draw on. So, respect the prime directive: "do the simplest thing that can possibly work."

In a sense, the code in this recipe could be said to violate the prime directive, because it uses an elegant object-oriented architecture with an abstract base class, a concrete subclass to specialize it, and, in the factory class, accessor methods rather than simple attribute access for the login data (i.e., user, password, domain). All of these niceties are lifesavers in big programs, but they admittedly *could* be foregone for a program of only 120 lines (which would shrink a little further if it didn't use all these niceties). However, adopting a uniform style of program architecture, even for small programs, eases the refactoring task in those not-so-rare cases where a small program grows into a big one. So, I have deliberately developed the habit of always coding in such an "elegant OO way", and once the habit is acquired, I find that it enhances, rather than reduces, my productivity.

See Also

The GnuDIP protocol is specified at *http://gnudip2.sourceforge.net/gnudip-www/ latest/gnudip/html/protocol.html*; Twisted is at *http://www.twistedmatrix.com/*.

13.16 Connecting to IRC and Logging Messages to Disk

Credit: Gian Mario Tagliaretti, J P Calderone

Problem

You want to connect to an IRC (Internet Relay Chat) server, join a channel, and store private messages into a file on your hard disk for future reading.

Solution

The Twisted framework has excellent support for many network protocols, including IRC, so we can perform this recipe's task with a very simple script:

```
from twisted.internet import reactor, protocol
from twisted.protocols import irc
class LoggingIRCClient(irc.IRCClient):
    logfile = file('/tmp/msg.txt', 'a+')
    nickname = 'logging_bot'
    def signedOn(self):
        self.join('#test_py')
    def privmsg(self, user, channel, message):
        self.logfile.write(user.split('!')[0] + ' -> ' + message + '\n')
        self.logfile.flush()
def main():
    f = protocol.ReconnectingClientFactory()
    f.protocol = LoggingIRCClient
    reactor.connectTCP('irc.freenode.net', 6667, f)
    reactor.run()
if __name__ == '__main__':
    main()
```

Discussion

If, for some strange reason, you cannot use Twisted, then you can implement similar functionality from scratch based only on the Python Standard Library. Here's a reasonable approach—nowhere as simple, solid, and robust as, and lacking the beneficial performance of, Twisted, but nevertheless sort of workable:

```
import socket
SERVER = 'irc.freenode.net'
PORT = 6667
NICKNAME = 'logging_bot'
CHANNEL = '#test_py'
IRC = socket.socket(socket.AF_INET, socket.SOCK_STREAM)
def irc_conn():
    IRC.connect((SERVER, PORT))
def send_data(command):
    IRC.send(command + '\n')
def join(channel):
    send_data("JOIN %s" % channel)
def login(nickname, username='user', password=None,
          realname='Pythonist', hostname='Helena', servername='Server'):
    send_data("USER %s %s %s %s" %
              (username, hostname, servername, realname))
    send_data("NICK %s" % nickname)
irc_conn()
login(NICKNAME)
join(CHANNEL)
filetxt = open('/tmp/msg.txt', 'a+')
try:
    while True:
```

```
        buffer = IRC.recv(1024)
        msg = buffer.split( )
        if msg[0] == "PING":
            # answer PING with PONG, as RFC 1459 specifies
            send_data("PONG %s" % msg[1])
        if msg [1] == 'PRIVMSG' and msg[2] == NICKNAME:
            nick_name = msg[0][:msg[0].find("!")]
            message = ' '.join(msg[3:])
            filetxt.write(nick_name.lstrip(':') + ' -> ' +
                          message.lstrip(':') + '\n')
            filetxt.flush( )
finally:
    filetxt.close( )
```

For this roll-our-own reimplementation, we do need some understanding of the protocol's RFC, such as the need to answer a server's PING with a proper PONG to confirm that our connection is alive. In any case, since the code has already grown to over twice as much as Twisted requires, we've omitted niceties (which are very important for reliable unattended operation) such as automatic reconnection attempts when the connection drops, which Twisted gives us effortlessly via its protocol.ReconnectingClientFactory.

See Also

Documentation for the standard library module socket in the *Library Reference* and *Python in a Nutshell*; twisted is at *http://www.twistedmatrix.com*.

13.17 Accessing LDAP Servers

Credit: John Nielsen

Problem

You need to access an LDAP (Lightweight Directory Access Protocol) server from your Python programs.

Solution

The simplest solution is offered by the freely downloadable third-party extension ldap (*http://python-ldap.sourceforge.net*). This script shows a few LDAP operations with ldap:

```
try:
    path = 'cn=people,ou=office,o=company'
    l = ldap.open('hostname')
    # set which protocol to use, if you do not like the default
    l.protocol_version = ldap.VERSION2
    l.simple_bind('cn=root,ou=office,o=company','password')
    # search for surnames beginning with a
    # available options for how deep a search you want:
```

```
        # LDAP_SCOPE_BASE, LDAP_SCOPE_ONELEVEL,LDAP_SCOPE_SUBTREE,
        a = l.search_s(path, ldap.SCOPE_SUBTREE, 'sn='+'a*')
        # delete fred
        l.delete_s('cn=fred,'+path)
        # add barney
        # note: objectclass depends on the LDAP server
        user_info = {'uid':'barney123',
                     'givenname':'Barney',
                     'cn':'barney123',
                     'sn':'Smith',
                     'telephonenumber':'123-4567',
                     'facsimiletelephonenumber':'987-6543',
                     'objectclass':('Remote-Address','person', 'Top'),
                     'physicaldeliveryofficename':'Services',
                     'mail':'fred123@company.com',
                     'title':'programmer',
                     }
        id = 'cn=barney,'+path
        l.add_s(id, user_info.items())
    except ldap.LDAPError, error:
        print 'problem with ldap:', error
```

Discussion

The ldap module wraps the open source Openldap C API. However, with ldap, your Python program can talk to various versions of LDAP servers, as long as they're standards compliant, not just to Openldap servers.

The recipe shows a script with a few example uses of the ldap module. For simplicity, all the functions the recipe calls from the library are the '_s' versions (e.g., search_s): this means the functions are synchronous—that is, they wait for a response or an error code and don't return control to your program until either an error or a response appears from the server. Asynchronous programming is less elementary than synchronous, although it can often offer far better performance and scalability.

LDAP is widely used to keep and coordinate network-accessible information, particularly in large and geographically distributed organizations. Essentially, LDAP lets you organize information, search for it, create new items, and delete existing items. The ldap module lets your Python program perform the search, creation, and deletion functions.

See Also

http://python-ldap.sourceforge.net/docs.shtml for all the documentation about the ldap module and other relevant pointers.

CHAPTER 14

Web Programming

14.0   Introduction

Credit: Andy McKay

The Web has been a key technology for many years now, and it has become unusual to develop an application that doesn't involve some aspects of the Web. From showing a help file in a browser to using web services, the Web has become an integral part of most applications.

I came to Python through a rather tortuous path of ASP (Active Server Pages), then Perl, some Zope, and then Python. Looking back, it seems strange that I didn't find Python earlier, but the dominance of Perl and ASP (and later PHP) in this area makes it difficult for new developers to see the advantages of Python shining through all the other languages.

Unsurprisingly, Python is an excellent language for web development, and, as a *batteries included* language, Python comes with most of the modules you need. The relatively recent inclusion of xmlrpclib in the Python Standard Library is a reassuring indication that batteries continue to be added as the march of technology requires, making the standard libraries even more useful. One of the modules I often use is urllib, which demonstrates the power of a simple, well-designed module—saving a file from the Web in two lines (using urlretrieve) is easy. The cgi module is another example of a module that has enough functionality to work with, but not too much to make your scripts slow and bloated.

Compared to other languages, Python seems to have an unusually large number of application servers and templating languages. While it's easy to develop anything for the Web in Python "from scratch", it would be peculiar and unwise to do so without first looking at the application servers available. Rather than continually recreating dynamic pages and scripts, the community has taken on the task of building these application servers to allow other users to create the content in easy-to-use templating systems.

Zope is the most well-known product in this space and provides an object-oriented interface to web publishing. With features too numerous to mention, Zope allows a robust and powerful object-publishing environment. The new, revolutionary major release, Zope 3, makes Zope more Pythonic and powerful than ever. Quixote and WebWare are two other application servers with similar, highly modular designs. Any of these can be a real help to the overworked web developer who needs to reuse components and to give other users the ability to create web sites. The Twisted network-programming framework, increasingly acknowledged as the best-of-breed Python framework for asynchronous network programming, is also starting to expand into the web application server field, with its newer "Nevow" offshoot, which you'll also find used in some of the recipes in this chapter.

For all that, an application server is just too much at times, and a simple CGI script is really all you need. Indeed, the very first recipe, recipe 14.1 "Testing Whether CGI Is Working," demonstrates all the ingredients you need to make sure that your web server and Python CGI scripting setup are working correctly. Writing a CGI script doesn't get much simpler than this, although, as the recipe's discussion points out, you could use the cgi.test function to make it even shorter.

Another common web-related task is the parsing of HTML, either on your own site or on other web sites. Parsing HTML tags correctly is not as simple as many developers first think, as they optimistically assume a few regular expressions or string searches will see them through. However, we have decided to deal with such issues in other chapters, such as Chapter 1, *Text*, rather than in this one. After all, while HTML was born with and for the Web, these days HTML is also often used in other contexts, such as for distributing documentation. In any case, most web developers create more than just web pages, so, even if you, the reader, primarily identify as a web developer, and maybe turned to this chapter as your first one in the book, you definitely should peruse the rest of the book, too: many relevant, useful recipes in other chapters describe parsing XML, reading network resources, performing systems administration, dealing with images, and many great ideas about developing in Python, testing your programs, and debugging them!

14.1   Testing Whether CGI Is Working

Credit: Jeff Bauer, Carey Evans

Problem

You want a simple CGI (Common Gateway Interface) program to use as a starting point for your own CGI programming or to determine whether your setup is functioning properly.

Solution

The cgi module is normally used in Python CGI programming, but here we use only its escape function to ensure that the value of an environment variable doesn't accidentally look to the browser as HTML markup. We do all of the real work ourselves in the following script:

```
#!/usr/local/bin/python
print "Content-type: text/html"
print
print "<html><head><title>Situation snapshot</title></head><body><pre>"
import sys
sys.stderr = sys.stdout
import os
from cgi import escape
print "<strong>Python %s</strong>" % sys.version
keys = os.environ.keys()
keys.sort()
for k in keys:
    print "%s\t%s" % (escape(k), escape(os.environ[k]))
print "</pre></body></html>"
```

Discussion

CGI is a standard that specifies how a web server runs a separate program (often known as a CGI script) that generates a web page dynamically. The protocol specifies how the server provides input and environment data to the script and how the script generates output in return. You can use any language to write your CGI scripts, and Python is well suited for the task.

This recipe is a simple CGI program that takes no input and just displays the current version of Python and the environment values. CGI programmers should always have some simple code handy to drop into their *cgi-bin* directories. You should run this script before wasting time slogging through your Apache configuration files (or whatever other web server you want to use for CGI work). Of course, cgi.test does all this and more, but it may, in fact, do too much. It does so much, and so much is hidden inside cgi's innards, that it's hard to tweak it to reproduce any specific problems you may be encountering in true scripts. Tweaking the program in this recipe, on the other hand, is very easy, since it's such a simple program, and all the parts are exposed.

Besides, this little script is already quite instructive in its own way. The starting line, #!/usr/local/bin/python, must give the absolute path to the Python interpreter with which you want to run your CGI scripts, so you may need to edit it accordingly. A popular solution for non-CGI scripts is to have a first line (the so-called *shebang* line) that looks something like this:

```
#!/usr/bin/env python
```

However, this approach puts you at the mercy of the PATH environment setting, since it runs the first program named python that it finds on the PATH, and that may well not be what you want under CGI, where you don't fully control the environment. Incidentally, many web servers implement the shebang line even when running under non-Unix systems, so that, for CGI use specifically, it's not unusual to see Python scripts on Windows start with a first line such as:

```
#!c:/python23/python.exe
```

Another issue you may be contemplating is why the import statements are not right at the start of the script, as is the usual Python style, but are preceded by a few print statements. The reason is that import could fail if the Python installation is terribly misconfigured. In case of failure, Python emits diagnostics to standard error (which is typically directed to your web server logs, depending on how you set up and configured your web server), and nothing will go to standard output. The CGI standard demands that all output be on standard output, so we first ensure that a minimal quantity of output will display a result to a visiting browser. Then, assuming that import sys succeeds (if it fails, the whole Python installation is so badly broken that you can do very little about it!), we immediately perform the following assignment:

```
sys.stderr = sys.stdout
```

This assignment statement ensures that error output will go to standard output, so that you'll have a chance to see it in the visiting browser. You can perform other import operations or do further work in the script only when this is done. Another option makes getting tracebacks for errors in CGI scripts much simpler. Simply add the following at the start of your script:

```
import cgitb; cgitb.enable( )
```

and the standard Python library module cgitb takes care of whatever else is needed to get error tracebacks on the browser. However, as already stated, the point of this recipe is to show how everything is done, rather than just reusing prepackaged funcitonality.

One last reflection is that, in Python 2.4, instead of the three lines:

```
keys = os.environ.keys( )
keys.sort( )
for k in keys:
```

used in the recipe, you could use the single line:

```
for k in sorted(os.environ):
```

Unfortunately, since CGI scripts must often run in environments you do not control, I cannot suggest you code to a specific, recent version of Python in this particular case—particularly not a script such as this one, which is meant to let you examine and check out the exact circumstances under which your CGI runs.

Yet another consideration, not strictly related to Python, is that this script is coded to emit correct HTML. Just about all known browsers let you get away with skipping most of the HTML tags that this script outputs, but why skimp on correctness, relying on the browser to patch your holes? It costs little to emit correct HMTL, so you should get into the habit of doing things right, when the cost is so modest. (I wish more authors of web pages, and of programs producing web pages, shared this sentiment. If they did, there would be a lot less broken HTML out on the Web!)

See Also

Documentation on the cgi and cgitb standard library modules in the *Library Reference* and *Python in a Nutshell*; a basic introduction to the CGI protocol is available at *http://hoohoo.ncsa.uiuc.edu/cgi/overview.html*.

14.2 Handling URLs Within a CGI Script

Credit: Jürgen Hermann

Problem

You need to build URLs within a CGI script—for example, to send an HTTP redirection header.

Solution

To build a URL within a script, you need information such as the hostname and script name. According to the CGI standard, the web server sets up a lot of useful information in the process environment of a script before it runs the script itself. In a Python script, we can access the process environment as the dictionary os.environ, an attribute of the standard Python library os module, and through accesses to the process environment build our own module of useful helper functions:

```
import os, string
def isSSL():
    """ Return true if we are on an SSL (https) connection. """
    return os.environ.get('SSL_PROTOCOL', '') != ''
def getScriptname():
    """ Return the scriptname part of the URL ("/path/to/my.cgi"). """
    return os.environ.get('SCRIPT_NAME', '')
def getPathinfo():
    """ Return the remaining part of the URL. """
    pathinfo = os.environ.get('PATH_INFO', '')
    # Fix for a well-known bug in IIS/4.0
    if os.name == 'nt':
        scriptname = getScriptname()
        if pathinfo.startswith(scriptname):
            pathinfo = pathinfo[len(scriptname):]
    return pathinfo
def getQualifiedURL(uri=None):
```

```
    """ Return a full URL starting with schema, servername, and port.
        Specifying uri causes it to be appended to the server root URL
        (uri must then start with a slash).
    """
    schema, stdport = (('http', '80'), ('https', '443'))[isSSL()]
    host = os.environ.get('HTTP_HOST', '')
    if not host:
        host = os.environ.get('SERVER_NAME', 'localhost')
        port = os.environ.get('SERVER_PORT', '80')
        if port != stdport: host = host + ":" + port
    result = "%s://%s" % (schema, host)
    if uri: result = result + uri
    return result
def getBaseURL():
    """ Return a fully qualified URL to this script. """
    return getQualifiedURL(getScriptname())
```

Discussion

URLs can be manipulated in numerous ways, but many CGI scripts have common needs. This recipe collects a few typical high-level functional needs for URL synthesis from within CGI scripts. You should never hard-code hostnames or absolute paths in your scripts. Doing so makes it difficult to port the scripts elsewhere or rename a virtual host. The CGI environment has sufficient information available to avoid such hard-coding. By importing this recipe's code as a module, you can avoid duplicating code in your scripts to collect and use that information in typical ways.

The recipe works by accessing information in os.environ, the attribute of Python's standard os module that collects the process environment of the current process and lets your script access it as if it were a normal Python dictionary. In particular, os.environ has a get method, just like a normal dictionary does, that returns either the mapping for a given key or, if that key is missing, a default value that you supply in the call to get. This recipe performs all accesses through os.environ.get, thus ensuring sensible behavior even if the relevant environment variables have been left undefined by your web server (which should never happen—but not all web servers are free of bugs).

Among the functions presented in this recipe, getQualifiedURL is the one you'll use most often. It transforms a URI (Universal Resource Identifier) into a URL on the same host (and with the same schema) used by the CGI script that calls it. It gets the information from the environment variables HTTP_HOST, SERVER_NAME, and SERVER_PORT. Furthermore, it can handle secure (https) as well as normal (http) connections, and selects between the two by using the isSSL function, which is also part of this recipe.

Suppose you need to redirect a visiting browser to another location on this same host. Here's how you can use a function from this recipe, hard-coding only the redirect location on the host itself, but not the hostname, port, and normal or secure schema:

```
# example redirect header:
print "Location:", getQualifiedURL("/go/here")
```

See Also

Documentation on the os standard library module in the *Library Reference* and *Python in a Nutshell*; a basic introduction to the CGI protocol is available at *http://hoohoo.ncsa.uiuc.edu/cgi/overview.html*.

14.3   Uploading Files with CGI

Credit: Noah Spurrier, Georgy Pruss

Problem

You need to enable the visitors to your web site to upload files by means of a CGI script.

Solution

Net of any security checks, safeguards against denial of service (DOS) attacks, and the like, the task boils down to what's exemplified in the following CGI script:

```
#!/usr/local/bin/python
import cgi
import cgitb; cgitb.enable( )
import os, sys
try: import msvcrt              # are we on Windows?
except ImportError: pass        # nope, no problem
else:                           # yep, need to set I/O to binary mode
    for fd in (0, 1): msvcrt.setmode(fd, os.O_BINARY)
UPLOAD_DIR = "/tmp"
HTML_TEMPLATE = \
"""<!DOCTYPE HTML PUBLIC "-//W3C//DTD HTML 4.01 Transitional//EN">
<html><head><title>Upload Files</title>
</head><body><h1>Upload Files</h1>
<form action="%(SCRIPT_NAME)s" method="POST" enctype="multipart/form-data">
File name: <input name="file_1" type="file"><br>
File name: <input name="file_2" type="file"><br>
File name: <input name="file_3" type="file"><br>
<input name="submit" type="submit">
</form> </body> </html>"""
def print_html_form( ):
    """ print the form to stdout, with action set to this very script (a
        'self-posting form': script both displays AND processes the form)."""
    print "content-type: text/html; charset=iso-8859-1\n"
    print HTML_TEMPLATE % {'SCRIPT_NAME': os.environ['SCRIPT_NAME']}
def save_uploaded_file(form_field, upload_dir):
    """ Save to disk a file just uploaded, form_field being the name of the
        file input field on the form.  No-op if field or file is missing."""
    form = cgi.FieldStorage( )
```

```
    if not form.has_key(form_field): return
    fileitem = form[form_field]
    if not fileitem.file: return
    fout = open(os.path.join(upload_dir, fileitem.filename), 'wb')
    while True:
        chunk = fileitem.file.read(100000)
        if not chunk: break
        fout.write(chunk)
    fout.close( )
save_uploaded_file("file_1", UPLOAD_DIR)
save_uploaded_file("file_2", UPLOAD_DIR)
save_uploaded_file("file_3", UPLOAD_DIR)
print_html_form( )
```

Discussion

The CGI script shown in this recipe is very bare-bones, but it does get the job done. It's a self-posting script: it displays the upload form, and it processes the form when the user submits it, complete with any uploaded files. The script just saves files to an upload directory, which in the recipe is simply set to */tmp*.

The script as presented takes no precaution against DOS attacks, so a user could try to fill up your disk with endless uploads. If you deploy this script on a system that is accessible to the public, do add checks to limit the number and size of files written to disk, perhaps depending, also, on how much disk space is still available. A version that might perhaps be more to your liking can be found at *http://zxw.nm.ru/test_w_upload.py.htm*.

See Also

Documentation on the cgi, cgitb, and msvcrt standard library modules in the *Library Reference* and *Python in a Nutshell*.

14.4   Checking for a Web Page's Existence

Credit: James Thiele, Rogier Steehouder

Problem

You want to check whether an HTTP URL corresponds to an existing web page.

Solution

Using httplib allows you to easily check for a page's existence without actually downloading the page itself, just its headers. Here's a module implementing a function to perform this task:

```
    """
    httpExists.py
    A quick and dirty way to check whether a web file is there.
```

```
Usage:
>>> import httpExists
>>> httpExists.httpExists('http://www.python.org/')
True
>>> httpExists.httpExists('http://www.python.org/PenguinOnTheTelly')
Status 404 Not Found : http://www.python.org/PenguinOnTheTelly
False
"""
import httplib, urlparse
def httpExists(url):
    host, path = urlparse.urlsplit(url)[1:3]
    if ':' in host:
        # port specified, try to use it
        host, port = host.split(':', 1)
        try:
            port = int(port)
        except ValueError:
            print 'invalid port number %r' % (port,)
            return False
    else:
        # no port specified, use default port
        port = None
    try:
        connection = httplib.HTTPConnection(host, port=port)
        connection.request("HEAD", path)
        resp = connection.getresponse( )
        if resp.status == 200:       # normal 'found' status
            found = True
        elif resp.status == 302:      # recurse on temporary redirect
            found = httpExists(urlparse.urljoin(url,
                            resp.getheader('location', '')))
        else:                        # everything else -> not found
            print "Status %d %s : %s" % (resp.status, resp.reason, url)
            found = False
    except Exception, e:
        print e.__class__, e, url
        found = False
    return found
def _test( ):
    import doctest, httpExists
    return doctest.testmod(httpExists)
if __name__ == "__main__":
    _test( )
```

Discussion

While this recipe is very simple and runs quite fast (thanks to the ability to use the
HTTP command HEAD to get just the headers, not the body, of the page), it may be
too simplistic for your specific needs: the HTTP result codes you might need to deal
with may go beyond the simple 200 success code, and 302 temporary redirect, to
include permanent redirects, temporary inaccessibility, permission problems, and so on.

In my case, I needed to check the correctness of a huge number of mutual links among pages of a site generated by a complex web application on an intranet, so I knew I had the privilege of relying on a simple check for "200 or bust." At any rate, you can use this simple recipe as a starting point to which to add any refinements you determine you actually need.

See Also

Documentation on the urlparse and httplib standard library modules in the *Library Reference* and *Python in a Nutshell*.

14.5 Checking Content Type via HTTP

Credit: Bob Stockwell

Problem

You need to determine whether a URL, or an open file, obtained from urllib.open on a URL, is of a particular content type (such as 'text' for HTML or 'image' for GIF).

Solution

The content type of any resource can easily be checked through the pseudo-file that urllib.urlopen returns for the resource. Here is a function to show how to perform such checks:

```
import urllib
def isContentType(URLorFile, contentType='text'):
    """ Tells whether the URL (or pseudofile from urllib.urlopen) is of
        the required content type (default 'text').
    """
    try:
        if isinstance(URLorFile, str):
            thefile = urllib.urlopen(URLorFile)
        else:
            thefile = URLorFile
        result = thefile.info( ).getmaintype( ) == contentType.lower( )
        if thefile is not URLorFile:
            thefile.close( )
    except IOError:
        result = False    # if we couldn't open it, it's of _no_ type!
    return result
```

Discussion

For greater flexibility, this recipe accepts either the result of a previous call to urllib.urlopen, or a URL in string form. In the latter case, the Solution opens the URL with urllib and, at the end, closes the resulting pseudo-file again. If the attempt to open the URL fails, the recipe catches the IOError and returns a result of False, considering that a URL that cannot be opened is of no type at all, and therefore in particular is not of the type the caller was checking for. (Alternatively, you might prefer to propagate the exception; if that's what you want, remove the try and except clause headers and the result = False assignment that is the body of the except clause.)

Whether the pseudo-file was passed in or opened locally from a URL string, the info method of the pseudo-file gives as its result an instance of mimetools.Message (which doesn't mean you need to import mimetools yourself—urllib does all that's needed). On that object, we can call any of several methods to get the content type, depending on what exactly we want—gettype to get both main and subtype with a slash in between (as in 'text/plain'), getmaintype to get the main type (as in 'text'), or getsubtype to get the subtype (as in 'plain'). In this recipe, we want the main content type.

The string result from all of the type interrogation methods is always lowercase, so we take the precaution of calling the lower method on parameter contentType as well, before comparing for equality.

See Also

Documentation on the urllib and mimetools standard library modules in the *Library Reference* and *Python in a Nutshell*; a list of important content types is at *http://www.utoronto.ca/ian/books/html4ed/appb/mimetype.html*; a helpful explanation of the significance of content types at *http://ppewww.ph.gla.ac.uk/~flavell/www/content-type.html*.

14.6 Resuming the HTTP Download of a File

Credit: Chris Moffitt

Problem

You need to resume an HTTP download of a file that has been partially transferred.

Solution

Downloads of large files are sometimes interrupted. However, a good HTTP server that supports the Range header lets you resume the download from where it was interrupted. The standard Python module urllib lets you access this functionality almost seamlessly: you just have to add the required header and intercept the error code that the server sends to confirm that it will respond with a partial file. Here is a function, with a little helper class, to perform this task:

```
import urllib, os
class myURLOpener(urllib.FancyURLopener):
```

```
    """ Subclass to override err 206 (partial file being sent); okay for us """
    def http_error_206(self, url, fp, errcode, errmsg, headers, data=None):
        pass    # Ignore the expected "non-error" code
def getrest(dlFile, fromUrl, verbose=0):
    myUrlclass = myURLOpener( )
    if os.path.exists(dlFile):
        outputFile = open(dlFile, "ab")
        existSize = os.path.getsize(dlFile)
        # If the file exists, then download only the remainder
        myUrlclass.addheader("Range","bytes=%s-" % (existSize))
    else:
        outputFile = open(dlFile, "wb")
        existSize = 0
    webPage = myUrlclass.open(fromUrl)
    if verbose:
        for k, v in webPage.headers.items( ):
            print k, "=", v
    # If we already have the whole file, there is no need to download it again
    numBytes = 0
    webSize = int(webPage.headers['Content-Length'])
    if webSize == existSize:
        if verbose:
            print "File (%s) was already downloaded from URL (%s)" % (
                    dlFile, fromUrl)
    else:
        if verbose:
            print "Downloading %d more bytes" % (webSize-existSize)
        while True:
            data = webPage.read(8192)
            if not data:
                break
            outputFile.write(data)
            numBytes = numBytes + len(data)
    webPage.close( )
    outputFile.close( )
    if verbose:
        print "downloaded", numBytes, "bytes from", webPage.url
    return numbytes
```

Discussion

The HTTP Range header lets the web server know that you want only a certain range of data to be downloaded, and this recipe takes advantage of this header. Of course, the server needs to support the Range header, but since the header is part of the HTTP 1.1 specification, it's widely supported. This recipe has been tested with Apache 1.3 as the server, but I expect no problems with other reasonably modern servers.

The recipe lets urllib.FancyURLopener do all the hard work of adding a new header, as well as the normal handshaking. I had to subclass the standard class from urllib only to make it known that the error 206 is not really an error in this case—so you can proceed normally. In the function, I also perform extra checks to quit the download if I've already downloaded the entire file.

Check out HTTP 1.1 RFC (2616) to learn more about the meaning of the headers. You may find a header that is especially useful, and Python's urllib lets you send any header you want.

See Also

Documentation on the urllib standard library module in the *Library Reference* and *Python in a Nutshell*; the HTTP 1.1 RFC (*http://www.ietf.org/rfc/rfc2616.txt*).

14.7 Handling Cookies While Fetching Web Pages

Credit: Mike Foord, Nikos Kouremenos

Problem

You need to fetch web pages (or other resources from the web) that require you to handle cookies (e.g., save cookies you receive and also reload and send cookies you had previously received from the same site).

Solution

The Python 2.4 Standard Library provides a cookielib module exactly for this task. For Python 2.3, a third-party ClientCookie module works similarly. We can write our code to ensure usage of the best available cookie-handling module—including none at all, in which case our program will still run but without saving and resending cookies. (In some cases, this might still be OK, just maybe slower.) Here is a script to show how this concept works in practice:

```
import os.path, urllib2
from urllib2 import urlopen, Request
COOKIEFILE = 'cookies.lwp'  # "cookiejar" file for cookie saving/reloading
# first try getting the best possible solution, cookielib:
try:
    import cookielib
except ImportError:              # no cookielib, try ClientCookie instead
    cookielib = None
    try:
        import ClientCookie
    except ImportError:          # nope, no cookies today
        cj = None                # so, in particular, no cookie jar
    else:                        # using ClientCookie, prepare everything
        urlopen = ClientCookie.urlopen
        cj = ClientCookie.LWPCookieJar( )
        Request = ClientCookie.Request
else:                            # we do have cookielib, prepare the jar
```

```
        cj = cookielib.LWPCookieJar( )
    # Now load the cookies, if any, and build+install an opener using them
    if cj is not None:
        if os.path.isfile(COOKIEFILE):
            cj.load(COOKIEFILE)
        if cookielib:
            opener = urllib2.build_opener(urllib2.HTTPCookieProcessor(cj))
            urllib2.install_opener(opener)
        else:
            opener = ClientCookie.build_opener(ClientCookie.HTTPCookieProcessor(cj))
            ClientCookie.install_opener(opener)
    # for example, try a URL that sets a cookie
    theurl = 'http://www.diy.co.uk'
    txdata = None  # or, for POST instead of GET, txdata=urrlib.urlencode(somedict)
    txheaders = {'User-agent': 'Mozilla/4.0 (compatible; MSIE 5.5; Windows NT)'}
    try:
        req = Request(theurl, txdata, txheaders)  # create a request object
        handle = urlopen(req)                     # and open it
    except IOError, e:
        print 'Failed to open "%s".' % theurl
        if hasattr(e, 'code'):
            print 'Error code: %s.' % e.code
    else:
        print 'Here are the headers of the page:'
        print handle.info( )
    # you can also use handle.read( ) to get the page, handle.geturl( ) to get the
    # the true URL (could be different from `theurl' if there have been redirects)
    if cj is None:
        print "Sorry, no cookie jar, can't show you any cookies today"
    else:
        print 'Here are the cookies received so far:'
        for index, cookie in enumerate(cj):
            print index, ': ', cookie
        cj.save(COOKIEFILE)                       # save the cookies again
```

Discussion

The third-party module ClientCookie, available for download at *http://wwwsearch.sourceforge.net/ClientCookie/*, was so successful that, in Python 2.4, its functionality has been added to the Python Standard Library—specifically, the cookie-handling parts in the new module cookielib, the rest in the current version of urllib2.

So, you do need to be careful if you want your code to work just as well on any 2.4 installation (using the latest and greatest cookielib) or an installation of Python 2.3 with ClientCookie on top. As long as we're at it, we might as well handle running on a 2.3 installation that does *not* have ClientCookie—run anyway, just don't save and resend cookies when we lack library code to do so. On some sites, the inability to handle cookies will just be a bother and perhaps a performance hit due to the loss of session continuity, but the site will still work. Other sites, of course, will be completely unusable without cookies.

The recipe's code is an exercise in the careful management of an idiom that's an essential part of making your Python code portable among releases and installations, while ensuring minimal graceful degradation when third-party modules you'd like to use just aren't there. The idiom is known as *conditional import* and is expressed as follows:

```
try:
    import something
except ImportError:              # 'something' not available
    ...code to do without, degrading gracefully...
else:                            # 'something' IS available, hooray!
    ...code to run only when something is there...
# and then, go on with the rest of your program
...code able to run with or w/o `something'...
```

The use of "conditional import" is particularly delicate in this recipe because ClientCookie and cookielib aren't drop-in replacements for each other—therefore, careful management is indeed necessary. But, if you study this recipe, you will see that it is not rocket science—it just requires attention.

One key technique is to make double use of a small number of names as "flags", with value None when the object to which they would normally refer is not available. In this recipe, we do that for cookielib (which refers to the module of that name when there is one, and otherwise to None) and cj (which refers to a cookie-jar object when there is any, and otherwise to None). Even better, when feasible, is to assign names appropriately to refer to the best available object under the circumstances: the recipe does that for variables urlopen and Request. Note how crucial it is for this purpose that Python treats all objects as first class: urlopen is a function, Request is a class, cookielib (if any) a module, cj (if any) an instance object. The distinction, however, doesn't matter in the least: the name-object reference concept is exactly the same in every case, with total uniformity, simplicity, and power.

When either cookielib or ClientCookie is available, the cookies are saved in a file in cookie jar format (a useful plain-text format that is automatically handled by either module but can also be examined and modified with text editors and other programs). If the file already exists when the program runs, cookies are loaded from the file, ready to be sent back to the appropriate sites.

My reason for developing this code is that I'm developing a cgi-proxy, *approx.py* (*http://www.voidspace.org.uk/atlantibots/pythonutils.html#cgiproxy*), which needs to be able to handle cookies when feasible. To keep the proxy usable on various versions of Python, and ensure it degrades gracefully when no cookie-handling library is available, I needed to develop the carefully managed conditional imports that are shown in the recipe's Solution. I decided to share them in this recipe since, besides the importance of cookie handling, conditional imports are such a generally important Python idiom. Particularly when installing your code on a server you don't control, it is unfortunately quite common to have little say in which version of Python is running, nor in which third-party extensions are installed—exactly the kind of situation that requires the conditional import technique to ensure your code does the best it can under the circumstances.

See Also

Documentation on the cookielib and urllib2 standard library modules in the *Library Reference* for Python 2.4; ClientCookie is at *http://wwwsearch.sourceforge.net/ClientCookie/*.

14.8 Authenticating with a Proxy for HTTPS Navigation

Credit: John Nielsen

Problem

You need to use httplib for HTTPS navigation through a proxy that requires basic authentication, but httplib out of the box supports HTTPS only through proxies that do *not* require authentication.

Solution

Unfortunately, it takes a wafer-thin amount of trickery to achieve this recipe's task. Here is a script that is just tricky enough:

```
import httplib, base64, socket
# parameters for the script
user = 'proxy_login'; passwd = 'proxy_pass'
host = 'login.yahoo.com'; port = 443
phost = 'proxy_host'; pport = 80
# setup basic authentication
user_pass = base64.encodestring(user+':'+passwd)
proxy_authorization = 'Proxy-authorization: Basic '+user_pass+'\r\n'
proxy_connect = 'CONNECT %s:%s HTTP/1.0\r\n' % (host, port)
user_agent = 'User-Agent: python\r\n'
proxy_pieces = proxy_connect+proxy_authorization+user_agent+'\r\n'
# connect to the proxy
proxy_socket = socket.socket(socket.AF_INET, socket.SOCK_STREAM)
proxy_socket.connect((phost, pport))
proxy_socket.sendall(proxy_pieces+'\r\n')
response = proxy_socket.recv(8192)
status = response.split( )[1]
if status!='200':
    raise IOError, 'Connecting to proxy: status=%s' % status
# trivial setup for SSL socket
```

```
ssl = socket.ssl(proxy_socket, None, None)
sock = httplib.FakeSocket(proxy_socket, ssl)
# initialize httplib and replace the connection's socket with the SSL one
h = httplib.HTTPConnection('localhost')
h.sock = sock
# and finally, use the now-HTTPS httplib connection as you wish
h.request('GET', '/')
r = h.getresponse( )
print r.read( )
```

Discussion

HTTPS is essentially HTTP spoken on top of an SSL connection rather than a plain
socket. So, this recipe connects to the proxy with basic authentication at the very
lowest level of Python socket programming, wraps an SSL socket around the proxy
connection thus secured, and finally plays a little trick under httplib's nose to use
that laboriously constructed SSL socket in place of the plain socket in an
HTTPConnection instance. From that point onwards, you can use the normal httplib
approach as you wish.

See Also

Documentation on the socket and httplib standard library modules in the *Library
Reference* and *Python in a Nutshell*.

14.9   Running a Servlet with Jython

Credit: Brian Zhou

Problem

You need to code a servlet using Jython.

Solution

Java (and Jython) are most often deployed server-side, and thus servlets are a typical
way of deploying your code. Jython makes servlets very easy to use. Here is a tiny
"hello world" example servlet:

```
import java, javax, sys
class hello(javax.servlet.http.HttpServlet):
    def doGet(self, request, response):
        response.setContentType("text/html")
        out = response.getOutputStream( )
        print >>out, """<html>
<head><title>Hello World</title></head>
<body>Hello World from Jython Servlet at %s!
</body>
</html>
""" % (java.util.Date( ),)
```

```
out.close( )
return
```

Discussion

This recipe is no worse than a typical JSP (Java Server Page) (see *http://jywiki.sourceforge.net/index.php?JythonServlet* for setup instructions). Compare this recipe to the equivalent Java code: with Python, you're finished coding in the same time it takes to set up the framework in Java. Most of your setup work will be strictly related to Tomcat or whichever servlet container you use. The Jython-specific work is limited to copying *jython.jar* to the *WEB-INF/lib* subdirectory of your chosen serv-let context and editing *WEB-INF/web.xml* to add `<servlet>` and `<servlet-mapping>` tags so that `org.python.util.PyServlet` serves the **.py* `<url-pattern>`.

The key to this recipe (like most other Jython uses) is that your Jython scripts and modules can import and use Java packages and classes just as if the latter were Python code or extensions. In other words, all of the Java libraries that you could use with Java code are similarly usable with Python (i.e., Jython) code. This example servlet first uses the standard Java servlet `response` object to set the resulting page's content type (to `text/html`) and to get the output stream. Afterwards, it can `print` to the output stream, since the latter is a Python file-like object. To further show off your seamless access to the Java libraries, you can also use the `Date` class of the `java.util` package, incidentally demonstrating how it can be printed as a string from Jython.

See Also

Information on Java servlets at *http://java.sun.com/products/servlet/*; information on JythonServlet at *http://jywiki.sourceforge.net/index.php?JythonServlet*.

14.10 Finding an Internet Explorer Cookie

Credit: Andy McKay

Problem

You need to find a specific IE cookie.

Solution

Cookies that your browser has downloaded contain potentially useful information, so it's important to know how to get at them. With Internet Explorer (IE), one simple approach is to access the registry to find where the cookies are, then read them as files. Here is a module with the function you need for that purpose:

```
import re, os, glob
import win32api, win32con
def _getLocation():
```

```
    """ Examines the registry to find the cookie folder IE uses """
    key = r'Software\Microsoft\Windows\CurrentVersion\Explorer\Shell Folders'
    regkey = win32api.RegOpenKey(win32con.HKEY_CURRENT_USER, key, 0,
        win32con.KEY_ALL_ACCESS)
    num = win32api.RegQueryInfoKey(regkey)[1]
    for x in range(num):
        k = win32api.RegEnumValue(regkey, x)
        if k[0] == 'Cookies':
            return k[1]
def _getCookieFiles(location, name):
    """ Rummages through cookie folder, returns filenames including `name`.
    `name` is normally the domain, e.g 'activestate' to get cookies for
    activestate.com (also e.g. for activestate.foo.com, but you can
    filter out such accidental hits later). """
    filemask = os.path.join(location, '*%s*' % name)
    return glob.glob(filemask)
def _findCookie(filenames, cookie_re):
    """ Look through a group of files for a cookie that satisfies a
    given compiled RE, returning first such cookie found, or None. """
    for file in filenames:
        data = open(file, 'r').read()
        m = cookie_re.search(data)
        if m: return m.group(1)
def findIECookie(domain, cookie):
    """ Finds the cookie for a given domain from IE cookie files """
    try:
        l = _getLocation()
    except Exception, err:
        # Print a debug message
        print "Error pulling registry key:", err
        return None
    # Found the key; now find the files and look through them
    f = _getCookieFiles(l, domain)
    if f:
        cookie_re = re.compile('%s\n(.*?)\n' % cookie)
        return _findCookie(f, cookie_re)
    else:
        print "No cookies for domain (%s) found" % domain
        return None
if __name__=='__main__':
    print findIECookie(domain='kuro5hin', cookie='k5-new_session')
```

Discussion

While Netscape cookies are in a text file, IE keeps cookies as files in a directory, and you need to access the registry to find which directory that is. To access the Windows registry, this recipe uses the PyWin32 Windows-specific Python extensions; as an alternative, you could use the _winreg module that is part of Python's standard distribution for Windows. This recipe's code has been tested and works on IE 5 and 6.

In the recipe, the _getLocation function accesses the registry and finds and returns the directory that IE is using for cookie files. The _getCookieFiles function receives the directory as an argument and uses standard module `glob` to return all filenames in the directory whose names include a particular requested domain name. The `_findCookie` function opens and reads all such files in turn, until it finds one whose contents satisfy a compiled regular expression that the function receives as an argument. It then returns the substring of the file's contents corresponding to the first parenthesized group in the regular expression, or `None` when no satisfactory file is found. As the leading underscore in the names indicates, these are all internal functions, used only as implementation details of the only function this module is meant to expose, namely `findIECookie`, which uses the other functions to locate and return the value of a specific cookie for a given domain.

An alternative to this recipe would be to write a Python extension, or use `calldll` or `ctypes`, to access the `InternetGetCookie` API function in *Wininet.DLL*, as documented on MSDN (Microsoft Developer Network).

See Also

The Unofficial Cookie FAQ (*http://www.cookiecentral.com/faq/*) is chock-full of information on cookies; documentation for `win32api` and `win32con` in PyWin32 (*http://starship.python.net/crew/mhammond/win32/Downloads.html*) or ActivePython (*http://www.activestate.com/ActivePython/*); Windows API documentation available from Microsoft (*http://msdn.microsoft.com*); Mark Hammond and Andy Robinson, *Python Programming on Win32* (O'Reilly); `calldll` is available at Sam Rushing's page (*http://www.nightmare.com/~rushing/dynwin/*); `ctypes` is at *http://sourceforge.net/projects/ctypes*.

14.11 Generating OPML Files

Credit: Moshe Zadka, Premshree Pillai, Anna Martelli Ravenscroft

Problem

OPML (Outline Processor Markup Language) is a standard file format for sharing subscription lists used by RSS (Really Simple Syndication) feed readers and aggregators. You want to share your subscription list, but your blogging site provides only a FOAF (Friend-Of-A-Friend) page, not one in the standard OPML format.

Solution

Use `urllib2` to open and read the FOAF page and `xml.dom` to parse the data received; then, output the data in the proper OPML format to a file. For example, LiveJournal is a popular blogging site that provides FOAF pages; here's a module with the functions you need to turn those pages into OPML files:

```
#!/usr/bin/python
import sys
```

```
import urllib2
import HTMLParser
from xml.dom import minidom, Node
def getElements(node, uri, name):
    ''' recursively yield all elements w/given namespace URI and name '''
    if (node.nodeType==Node.ELEMENT_NODE and
        node.namespaceURI==uri and
        node.localName==name):
        yield node
    for node in node.childNodes:
        for node in getElements(node, uri, name):
            yield node
class LinkGetter(HTMLParser.HTMLParser):
    ''' HTML parser subclass which collecs attributes of link tags '''
    def __init__(self):
        HTMLParser.HTMLParser.__init__(self)
        self.links = [ ]
    def handle_starttag(self, tag, attrs):
        if tag == 'link':
            self.links.append(attrs)
def getRSS(page):
    ''' given a `page' URL, returns the HREF to the RSS link '''
    contents = urllib2.urlopen(page)
    lg = LinkGetter( )
    try:
        lg.feed(contents.read(1000))
    except HTMLParser.HTMLParserError:
        pass
    links = map(dict, lg.links)
    for link in links:
        if (link.get('rel')=='alternate' and
            link.get('type')=='application/rss+xml'):
            return link.get('href')
def getNicks(doc):
    ''' given an XML document's DOM, `doc', yields a triple of info for
        each contact: nickname, blog URL, RSS URL '''
    for element in getElements(doc, 'http://xmlns.com/foaf/0.1/', 'knows'):
        person, = getElements(element, 'http://xmlns.com/foaf/0.1/', 'Person')
        nick, = getElements(person, 'http://xmlns.com/foaf/0.1/', 'nick')
        text, = nick.childNodes
        nickText = text.toxml( )
        blog, = getElements(person, 'http://xmlns.com/foaf/0.1/', 'weblog')
        blogLocation = blog.getAttributeNS(
            'http://www.w3.org/1999/02/22-rdf-syntax-ns#', 'resource')
        rss = getRSS(blogLocation)
        if rss:
            yield nickText, blogLocation, rss
def nickToOPMLFragment((nick, blogLocation, rss)):
    ''' given a triple (nickname, blog URL, RSS URL), returns a string
        that's the proper OPML outline tag representing that info '''
    return '''
<outline text="%(nick)s"
         htmlUrl="%(blogLocation)s"
         type="rss"
```

```
                  xmlUrl="%(rss)s"/>
    ''' % dict(nick=nick, blogLocation=blogLocation, rss=rss)
def nicksToOPML(fout, nicks):
    ''' writes to file `fout' the OPML document representing the
        iterable of contact information `nicks' '''
    fout.write('''<?xml version="1.0" encoding="utf-8"?>
<opml version="1.0">
<head><title>Subscriptions</title></head>
<body><outline title="Subscriptions">
''')
    for nick in nicks:
        print nick
        fout.write(nickToOPMLFragment(nick))
    fout.write("</outline></body></opml>\n")
def docToOPML(fout, doc):
    ''' writes to file `fout' the OPLM for XML DOM `doc' '''
    nicksToOPML(fout, getNicks(doc))
def convertFOAFToOPML(foaf, opml):
    ''' given URL `foaf' to a FOAF page, writes its OPML equivalent to
        a file named by string `opml' '''
    f = urllib2.urlopen(foaf)
    doc = minidom.parse(f)
    docToOPML(file(opml, 'w'), doc)
def getLJUser(user):
    ''' writes an OPLM file `user'.opml for livejournal's FOAF page '''
    convertFOAFToOPML('http://www.livejournal.com/users/%s/data/foaf' % user,
                      user+".opml")
if __name__ == '__main__':
    # example, when this module is run as a main script
    getLJUser('moshez')
```

Discussion

RSS feeds have become extremely popular for reading news, blogs, wikis, and so on. OPML is one of the standard file formats used to share subscription lists among RSS fans. This recipe generates an OPML file that can be opened with any RSS reader. With an OPML file, you can share your favorite subscriptions with anyone you like, publish it to the Web, and so on.

getElements is a convenience function that gets written in almost every XML DOM-processing application. It recursively scans the document, finding nodes that satisfy certain criteria. This version of getElements is somewhat quick and dirty, but it is good enough for our purposes. getNicks is where the heart of the parsing brains lie. It calls getElements to look for "foaf:knows" nodes, and inside those, it looks for the "foaf:nick" element, which contains the LiveJournal nickname of the user, and uses a generator to yield the nicknames in this FOAF document.

Note an important idiom used four times in the body of getNicks:

```
name, = some iterable
```

The key is the comma after name, which turns the left-hand side of this assignment into a one-item tuple, making the assignment into what's technically known as an *unpacking assignment*. Unpacking assignments are of course very popular in Python (see recipe 19.4 "Unpacking a Few Items in a Multiple Assignment" for a technique to make them even more widely applicable) but normally with at least two names on the left of the assignment, such as:

```
aname, another = iterable yielding 2 items
```

The idiom used in getNicks has exactly the same function, but it demands that the iterable yield exactly *one* item (otherwise, Python raises a ValueError exception). Therefore, the idiom has the same semantics as:

```
_templist = some iterable
if len(_templist) != 1:
    raise ValueError, 'too many values to unpack'
name = _templist[0]
del _templist
```

Obviously, the name, = ... idiom is much cleaner and more compact than this equivalent snippet, which is worth keeping in mind for the next time you need to express the same semantics.

nicksToOPML, together with its helper function nickToOPMLFragment, generates the OPML, while docToOPML ties together getNicks and nicksToOPML into a FOAF->OPML convertor. saveUser is the main function, which actually interacts with the operating system (accessing the network to get the FOAF, and using a file to save the OPML).

The recipe has a specific function getLJUser(user) to work with the LiveJournal (*http://www.livejournal.com*) friends lists. However, the point is that the main convertFOAFToOPML function is general enough to use for other sites as well. The various helper functions can also come in handy in your own different but related tasks. For example, the getRSS function (with some aid from its helper class LinkGetter) finds and returns a link to the RSS feed (if one exists) for a given web site.

See Also

About OPML, *http://feeds.scripting.com/whatIsOpml*; for more on RSS readers, *http://blogspace.com/rss/readers*; for FOAF Vocabulary Specification, *http://xmlns.com/foaf/0.1/*.

14.12 Aggregating RSS Feeds

Credit: Valentino Volonghi, Peter Cogolo

Problem

You need to aggregate potentially very high numbers of RSS feeds, with top performance and scalability.

Solution

Parsing RSS feeds in Python is best done with Mark Pilgrim's Universal Feed Parser from *http://www.feedparser.org*, but aggregation requires a lot of network activity, in addition to parsing.

As for any network task demanding high performance, Twisted is a good starting point. Say that you have in *out.py* a module that binds a huge list of RSS feed names to a variable named rss_feed, each feed name represented as a tuple consisting of a URL and a description (e.g., you can download a module exactly like this from *http://xoomer.virgilio.it/dialtone/out.py*.). You can then build an aggregator server on top of that list, as follows:

```
#!/usr/bin/python
from twisted.internet import reactor, protocol, defer
from twisted.web import client
import feedparser, time, sys, cStringIO
from out import rss_feed as rss_feeds
DEFERRED_GROUPS = 60        # Number of simultaneous connections
INTER_QUERY_TIME = 300      # Max Age (in seconds) of each feed in the cache
TIMEOUT = 30                # Timeout in seconds for the web request
# dict cache's structure will be the following: { 'URL': (TIMESTAMP, value) }
cache = { }
class FeederProtocol(object):
    def __init__(self):
        self.parsed = 0
        self.error_list = [ ]
    def isCached(self, site):
        ''' do we have site's feed cached (from not too long ago)? '''
        # how long since we last cached it (if never cached, since Jan 1 1970)
        elapsed_time = time.time() - cache.get(site, (0, 0))[0]
        return elapsed_time < INTER_QUERY_TIME
    def gotError(self, traceback, extra_args):
        ''' an error has occurred, print traceback info then go on '''
        print traceback, extra_args
        self.error_list.append(extra_args)
    def getPageFromMemory(self, data, addr):
        ''' callback for a cached page: ignore data, get feed from cache '''
        return defer.succeed(cache[addr][1])
    def parseFeed(self, feed):
        ''' wrap feedparser.parse to parse a string '''
        try: feed+''
        except TypeError: feed = str(feed)
        return feedparser.parse(cStringIO.StringIO(feed))
    def memoize(self, feed, addr):
        ''' cache result from feedparser.parse, and pass it on '''
        cache[addr] = time.time(), feed
        return feed
    def workOnPage(self, parsed_feed, addr):
        ''' just provide some logged feedback on a channel feed '''
        chan = parsed_feed.get('channel', None)
```

```
            if chan:
                print chan.get('title', '(no channel title?)')
            return parsed_feed
        def stopWorking(self, data=None):
            ''' just for testing: we close after parsing a number of feeds.
                Override depending on protocol/interface you use to communicate
                with this RSS aggregator server.
            '''
            print "Closing connection number %d..." % self.parsed
            print "=-"*20
            self.parsed += 1
            print 'Parsed', self.parsed, 'of', self.END_VALUE
            if self.parsed >= self.END_VALUE:
                print "Closing all..."
                if self.error_list:
                    print 'Observed', len(self.error_list), 'errors'
                    for i in self.error_list:
                        print i
                reactor.stop()
        def getPage(self, data, args):
            return client.getPage(args, timeout=TIMEOUT)
        def printStatus(self, data=None):
            print "Starting feed group..."
        def start(self, data=None, standalone=True):
            d = defer.succeed(self.printStatus())
            for feed in data:
                if self.isCached(feed):
                    d.addCallback(self.getPageFromMemory, feed)
                    d.addErrback(self.gotError, (feed, 'getting from memory'))
                else:
                    # not cached, go and get it from the web directly
                    d.addCallback(self.getPage, feed)
                    d.addErrback(self.gotError, (feed, 'getting'))
                    # once gotten, parse the feed and diagnose possible errors
                    d.addCallback(self.parseFeed)
                    d.addErrback(self.gotError, (feed, 'parsing'))
                    # put the parsed structure in the cache and pass it on
                    d.addCallback(self.memoize, feed)
                    d.addErrback(self.gotError, (feed, 'memoizing'))
                # now one way or another we have the parsed structure, to
                # use or display in whatever way is most appropriate
                d.addCallback(self.workOnPage, feed)
                d.addErrback(self.gotError, (feed, 'working on page'))
                # for testing purposes only, stop working on each feed at once
                if standalone:
                    d.addCallback(self.stopWorking)
                    d.addErrback(self.gotError, (feed, 'while stopping'))
            if not standalone:
                return d
class FeederFactory(protocol.ClientFactory):
    protocol = FeederProtocol()
    def __init__(self, standalone=False):
        self.feeds = self.getFeeds()
        self.standalone = standalone
```

```
            self.protocol.factory = self
            self.protocol.END_VALUE = len(self.feeds) # this is just for testing
            if standalone:
                self.start(self.feeds)
        def start(self, addresses):
            # Divide into groups all the feeds to download
            if len(addresses) > DEFERRED_GROUPS:
                url_groups = [[ ] for x in xrange(DEFERRED_GROUPS)]
                for i, addr in enumerate(addresses):
                    url_groups[i%DEFERRED_GROUPS].append(addr[0])
            else:
                url_groups = [[addr[0]] for addr in addresses]
            for group in url_groups:
                if not self.standalone:
                    return self.protocol.start(group, self.standalone)
                else:
                    self.protocol.start(group, self.standalone)
        def getFeeds(self, where=None):
            # used for a complete refresh of the feeds, or for testing purposes
            if where is None:
                return rss_feeds
            return None
    if __name__=="__main__":
        f = FeederFactory(standalone=True)
        reactor.run( )
```

Discussion

RSS is a lightweight XML format designed for sharing headlines, news, blogs, and other web contents. Mark Pilgrim's Universal Feed Parser (*http:// www.feedparser.org*) does a great job of parsing "feeds" that can be in various dialects of RSS format into a uniform memory representation based on Python dictionaries. This recipe builds on top of feedparser to provide a full-featured RSS aggregator.

This recipe is scalable to very high numbers of feeds and is usable in multiclient environments. Both characteristics depend essentially on this recipe being built with the powerful Twisted framework for asynchronous network programming. A simple web interface built with Nevow (from *http://www.nevow.com*) is also part of the latest complete package for this aggregator, which you can download from my blog at *http://vvolonghi.blogspot.com/*.

An important characteristic of this recipe's code is that you can easily set the following operating parameters to improve performance:

- Number of parallel connections to use for feed downloading
- Timeout for each feed request
- Maximum age of a feed in the aggregator's cache

Being able to set these parameters helps you balance performance, network load, and load on the machine on which you're running the aggregator.

See Also

Universal Feed Parser is at *http://www.feedparser.org*; the latest version of this RSS aggregator is at *http://vvolonghi.blogspot.com/*; Twisted is at *http://twistedmatrix.com/*.

14.13 Turning Data into Web Pages Through Templates

Credit: Valentino Volonghi

Problem

You need to turn some Python data into web pages based on *templates*, meaning files or strings of HTML code in which the data gets suitably inserted.

Solution

Templating with Python can be accomplished in an incredible number of ways. but my favorite is Nevow.

The Nevow web toolkit works with the Twisted networking framework to provide excellent templating capabilities to web sites that are coded on the basis of Twisted's powerful asynchronous model. For example, here's one way to render a list of dictionaries into a web page according to a template, with Nevow and Twisted:

```
from twisted.application import service, internet
from nevow import rend, loaders, appserver
dct = [{'name':'Mark', 'surname':'White', 'age':'45'},
       {'name':'Valentino', 'surname':'Volonghi', 'age':'21'},
       {'name':'Peter', 'surname':'Parker', 'age':'Unknown'},
       ]
class Pg(rend.Page):
    docFactory = loaders.htmlstr("""
    <html><head><title>Names, Surnames and Ages</title></head>
        <body>
            <ul nevow:data="dct" nevow:render="sequence">
                <li nevow:pattern="item" nevow:render="mapping">
                    <span><nevow:slot name="name"/> </span>
                    <span><nevow:slot name="surname"/> </span>
                    <span><nevow:slot name="age"/></span>
                </li>
            </ul>
        </body>
    </html>
    """)
    def __init__(self, dct):
        self.data_dct = dct
```

```
        rend.Page.__init__(self)
    site = appserver.NevowSite( Pg(dct) )
    application = service.Application("example")
    internet.TCPServer(8080, site).setServiceParent(application)
```

Save this code to *nsa.tac*. Now, entering at a shell command prompt `twistd -noy`
`nsa.tac` serves up the data, formatted into HTML as the template specifies, as a tiny
web site. You can visit the site, at *http://localhost:8080*, by running a browser on the
same computer where the `twistd` command is running. On the command window
where `twistd` is running, you'll see a lot of information, roughly equivalent to a typical web server's log file.

Discussion

This recipe uses Twisted (*http://www.twistedmatrix.com*) for serving a little web site
built with Nevow (*http://nevow.com/*). Twisted is a large and powerful framework for
writing all kinds of Python programs that interact with the network (including, of
course, web servers). Nevow is a web application construction kit, normally used in
cooperation with a Twisted server but usable in other ways. For example, you could
write Nevow CGI scripts that can run with any web server. (Unfortunately, CGI
scripts' performance might prove unsatisfactory for many applications, while
Twisted's performance and scalability are outstanding.)

A vast range of choices is available for packages you can use to perform templating
with Python. You can look up some of them at *http://www.webwareforpython.org/
Papers/Templates/* (which lists a dozen packages suitable for use with the Webware
web development toolkit), and specific ones at *http://htmltmpl.sourceforge.net/*, *http:/
/freespace.virgin.net/hamish.sanderson/htmltemplate.html*, *http://aspn.activestate.com/
ASPN/Cookbook/Python/Recipe/52305*, *http://www.alcyone.com/pyos/empy/*, *http://
www.entrian.com/PyMeld/*... and many, *many* more besides. I definitely don't claim
to have thoroughly tried each and every one of these dozens of templating systems in
production situations, and I wonder whether anyone can truthfully make such a
claim! However, out of all I *have* tried, my favorite is Nevow.

Nevow builds web pages by working on the HTML DOM tree. Recipe 14.14 "Rendering Arbitrary Objects with Nevow" shows how you can build such a DOM tree
from within your program by using the `stan` subsystem of Nevow. This recipe shows
that you can also building a DOM tree from HTML source, known as a *template*. In
this case, for simplicity, we keep that template source in a string in our code, and
load the DOM for it by calling `loaders.htmlstr`; more commonly, we keep the template source in a separate *.html* file, and load the DOM for it by calling
`loaders.htmlfile`.

Examining the HTML string, you will notice it contains, besides standard HTML
tags and attributes, a few attributes and one tag from the `'nevow:'` namespace, such
as `'nevow:slot'`, `'nevow:data'` and `'nevow:render'`. These additions are in accord
with the HTML standards, and also, in practice, the additions work with all brows-

ers. They amount to Nevow defining its own small supplementary namespace, so that HTML templates can express directives to Nevow for building a dynamic page from the template together with data coming from Python code. Note that the attributes and tags in the 'nevow:' namespace do *not* remain in the HTML output from Nevow: you can verify that, as you visit the web page served by this recipe's script, by asking your browser to "view source". Nevertheless, it's important that template files are perfectly correct HTML: this means those files can be edited with all kinds of specialized HTML editor programs! So, like many other templating systems, Nevow chooses to have correct HTML as its input, as well as (of course) as its output.

The 'nevow:data' directive defines the source of the data for the page: in this case, we use the data_dct attribute of the Pg class instance which is building the page. The 'nevow:render' directive defines the method to use for rendering the data into HTML strings. In this case, we use two standard rendering methods supplied by Nevow itself: sequence, for rendering a sequence of items, such as a list, one after the other; and mapping, for rendering items of a mapping, such as a dictionary, based on the items' keys appearing as name attributes of nevow:slot tags. More generally, we could code our own rendering methods in any class that subclasses rend.Page.

After defining the Pg class, the recipe continues by building a site object, then an application object, then a TCP server on port 8080 using that site and application—all of this building makes up a common Twisted idiom. The source file *nsa.tac* into which you save the code from this recipe is not meant to be run with the usual python interpreter. Rather, you should run *nsa.tac* with the twistd command that you installed as part of Twisted's own installation procedure: twistd handles all the startup, daemonization, and logging issues, depending on the flags we pass to it. That is exactly why, by convention, one should normally use file extension *.tac*, rather than *.py*, for source files that are meant to be run with twistd, rather than directly with python—to avoid any confusion.

Given the experimental, toy-like nature of this recipe, you should pass the flags -noy, to ask twistd to run in the foreground and to "log" information to standard output rather than to some file. An even better idea is to read up on twistd in the Twisted documentation, to learn about all the options for the flags.

See Also

Twisted is at *http://www.twistedmatrix.com*; Nevow is at *http://nevow.com/*.

14.14 Rendering Arbitrary Objects with Nevow

Credit: Valentino Volonghi, Matt Goodall

Problem

You're writing a web application that uses the Twisted networking framework and the Nevow subsystem for web rendering. You need to be able to render some arbitrary Python objects to a web page.

Solution

Interfaces and adapters are the Twisted and Nevow approach to this task. Here is a toy example web server script to show how they work:

```
from twisted.application import internet, service
from nevow import appserver, compy, inevow, loaders, rend
from nevow import tags as T
# Define some simple classes to be the example's "application data"
class Person(object):
    def __init__(self, firstName, lastName, nickname):
        self.firstName = firstName
        self.lastName = lastName
        self.nickname = nickname
class Bookmark(object):
    def __init__(self, name, url):
        self.name = name
        self.url = url
# Adapter subclasses are the right way to join application data to the web:
class PersonView(compy.Adapter):
    """ Render a full view of a Person. """
    __implements__ = inevow.IRenderer
    attrs = 'firstName', 'lastName', 'nickname'
    def rend(self, data):
        return T.div(_class="View person") [
            T.p['Person'],
            T.dl[ [(T.dt[attr], T.dd[getattr(self.original, attr)])
                   for attr in self.attrs]
            ]
        ]
class BookmarkView(compy.Adapter):
    """ Render a full view of a Bookmark. """
    __implements__ = inevow.IRenderer
    attrs = 'name', 'url'
    def rend(self, data):
        return T.div(_class="View bookmark") [
            T.p['Bookmark'],
            T.dl[ [(T.dt[attr], T.dd[getattr(self.original, attr)])
                   for attr in self.attrs]
            ]
        ]
# register the rendering adapters (could be done from a config textfile)
compy.registerAdapter(PersonView, Person, inevow.IRenderer)
compy.registerAdapter(BookmarkView, Bookmark, inevow.IRenderer)
# some example data instances for the 'application'
objs = [
```

```
        Person('Valentino', 'Volonghi', 'dialtone'),
        Person('Matt', 'Goodall', 'mg'),
        Bookmark('Nevow', 'http://www.nevow.com'),
        Person('Alex', 'Martelli', 'aleax'),
        Bookmark('Alex', 'http://www.aleax.it/'),
        Bookmark('Twisted', 'http://twistedmatrix.com/'),
        Bookmark('Python', 'http://www.python.org'),
        ]
    # a simple Page that renders a list of objects
    class Page(rend.Page):
        def render_item(self, ctx, data):
            return inevow.IRenderer(data)
        docFactory = loaders.stan(
            T.html[
                T.body[
                    T.ul(data=objs, render=rend.sequence)[
                        T.li(pattern='item')[render_item],
                        ],
                    ],
                ]
            )
    # start this very-special-purpose tiny toy webserver:
    application = service.Application('irenderer')
    httpd = internet.TCPServer(8000, appserver.NevowSite(Page()))
    httpd.setServiceParent(application)
```

Discussion

This recipe's purpose is to provide an example of how to get Nevow to render instances of application classes directly to a web page. To supply this example, the recipe shows two classes, Person and Bookmark, whose instances contain information which, one can suppose, is coming from a database, or from a file, or from some other site on the web, wherever.

A key point is that the application classes do not get altered in any way to allow their instances to be rendered onto web pages: rather, *adaptation* is used to allow instances of such classes to be rendered through separate renderer-adapter classes.

We need two different adapters, one each for Person and Bookmark. We code the two adapters as classes PersonView and BookmarkView, each inheriting from compy.Adapter and overriding the rend method.

compy.Adapter is an abstract superclass intended just for this purpose: it accepts as its constructor argument an object that must be adapted to another interface, and holds that object as self.original for its subclasses' benefit. Each subclass asserts that it implements inevow.IRenderer by listing that interface in its class-level __implements__ attribute.

inevow.IRenderer is an interface that supplies a rend method. The Nevow rendering pipeline knows about IRenderer and calls the rend method of the interface to serialize objects to HTML. Objects that implement the interface (on their own behalf or as adapters of other objects) can directly become part of the rendering pipeline.

The two key statements of this recipe are the two calls to the `registerAdapter` function of Nevow's module compy:

```
compy.registerAdapter(PersonView, Person, inevow.IRenderer)
compy.registerAdapter(BookmarkView, Bookmark, inevow.IRenderer)
```

These calls tell Nevow that `PersonView` is the class to use to adapt any instance of `Person` to interface `IRenderer`, and similarly for `BookmarkView` and `Bookmark`. So, when the `IRenderer` interface is called with an instance p of `Person` as its argument, it automatically returns an adapter that is an instance of `PersonView` with p as its `self.original` (and, again, similarly for `Bookmark`).

Note how accurately this approach distributes appropriate knowledge to the various parts of the software and minimizes coupling among them while strengthening cohesion within each. Nevow itself has no built-in knowledge of any application class nor of any specific adapter: nor does it need any such knowledge. Nevow just specifies the `IRenderer` interface it needs for rendering and the `registerAdapter` function used to inform the framework about adaptation connections. Application-level classes neither have nor need any knowledge of the framework at all. Each adapter class knows about the application level class it's adapting, the interface it's implementing, and utilities such as the `Adapter` base class that the framework supplies (just to factor out a little repetitive coding that would be needed otherwise), and the tags mechanism. (The tags mechanism eases dynamic generation of HTML output. However, you could code adapters to return strings with HTML markup directly, if that suited the needs of your specific application better than the tags mechanism does.)

Finally, the recipe includes an example `Page` class which ties everything together—again, for convenience, using tags to generate the output. `Page` uses (explicitly) the `rend.sequence` renderer provided by Nevow to loop over a sequence and render each item, and (implicitly) the various adapters, by "casting" each item to the `IRenderer` interface. The recipe ends with three lines to build Twisted application and service objects and to put them together, so that running this recipe's script with Twisted's `twistd` general-purpose daemon provides a small demonstration one-page web site running on the local host at port 8000.

A more complete (and complicated) version of this recipe can be found as part of the Nevow 0.3 distribution, downloadable from *http://www.nevow.com*, as *examples/irenderer.tac*.

See Also

Nevow is at *http://www.nevow.com*; Twisted is at *http://twistedmatrix.com/*.

CHAPTER 15

Distributed Programming

15.0 Introduction

Credit: Jeremy Hylton, Google, Inc.

The recipes in this chapter describe simple techniques for using Python in distributed systems. Programming distributed systems is a difficult challenge, and recipes alone won't even come close to completely solving it. The recipes help you get programs on different computers talking to each other, so that you can start writing applications.

Remote Procedure Call (RPC) is an attractive approach to structuring a distributed system. The details of network communication are exposed through an interface that looks like normal procedure calls. When you call a function on a remote server, the RPC system is responsible for all the details of communication. It encodes the arguments so they can be passed over the network to the server, which might use different internal representations for the data. It invokes the right function on the remote machine and waits for a response.

The recipes in this chapter use three different systems that provide RPC interfaces—Common Object Request Broker Architecture (CORBA), Twisted's Perspective Broker (PB), and, in most recipes, XML-RPC. These systems are attractive because they make it easy to connect programs that can be running on different computers and might even be written in different languages. CORBA is a rather "heavyweight" protocol, very rich in functionality, with specialized and dedicated marshaling and transport layers (and much more besides). XML-RPC is a lightweight, simple-to-use protocol, which uses XML to marshal the call and its associated data, and HTTP for transport. Being simple and lightweight, XML-RPC is less functionally rich than CORBA. Both CORBA and XML-RPC are well-established standards, with implementations available for a wide variety of languages. In particular, XML-RPC is so simple and widespread that XML-RPC recipes take up half this chapter, a good, if rough, indication of how often Pythonistas are using it in preference to other distributed programming approaches.

PB is also "lightweight", while offering richer functionality than XML-RPC. However, PB is not a separate standard but a part of the Twisted framework, so PB implementations are currently limited to what Twisted itself provides and are mostly in Python. Perspective Broker is unusual among RPC systems because it openly exposes at application level the fact that network transactions are *asynchronous*, not *synchronous* like procedure calls within a single process. Therefore, in PB, the launching of a call to the remote procedure does not necessarily imply an immediate wait for the procedure's results; rather, the "result"s arrive "later" through a callback mechanism (specifically, Twisted's deferred objects). This asynchronous approach, which is the conceptual core of the Twisted framework, offers substantial advantages in terms of performance and scalability of the "result"ing network applications, but it may take some getting used to. Simon Foster's approach, shown in recipe, 15.7 "Using Twisted Perspective Broker," is a simple way to get started exploring Perspective Broker.

XML-RPC is well supported by the Python Standard Library, with the xmlrpclib module for writing XML-RPC clients and the SimpleXMLRPCServer module for writing XML-RPC servers. For Twisted, CORBA, and other RPC standards yet (such as the emerging SOAP—Simple Object Access Protocol—system), you need to install third-party extensions before you can get started. The recipes in this chapter include pointers to the software you need. Unfortunately, you will not find pointers specifically to SOAP resources for Python in the recipes: for such pointers, I suggest you check out *http://pywebsvcs.sourceforge.net/*.

The Python Standard Library also provides a set of modules for doing the lower-level work of network programming—socket, select, asyncore, and asynchat. The library also includes modules for marshaling data and sending it across sockets: struct, pickle, xdrlib. Chapter 13, *Network Programming*, includes recipes in which some of these modules are directly used, and Chapter 7, *Persistence and Databases*, contains recipes dealing with serialization and marshaling. These lower-level modules, in turn, provide the plumbing for many other higher-level modules that directly support a variety of standard network protocols. Jeff Bauer offers recipe 15.9 "Performing Remote Logins Using telnetlib," using the telnetlib module to send commands to remote machines via the Telnet protocol. Telnet is not a very secure protocol, and thus, except for use within well-protected LANs, has been largely supplanted by more secure protocols such as SSH (Secure Shell). Peter Cogolo and Anna Martelli Ravenscroft offer similar functionality to Bauer's, in recipe 15.10 "Performing Remote Logins with SSH," which uses SSH (via the third-party package paramiko) rather than Telnet.

Six of the recipes, just about half of the chapter, focus on XML-RPC. Rael Dornfest and Jeremy Hylton demonstrate how to write an XML-RPC client program that retrieves data from O'Reilly's Meerkat service. Recipe 15.1 "Making an XML-RPC Method Call" is only three lines long (including the import statement): indeed, this extreme conciseness is the recipe's main appeal.

Brian Quinlan and Jeff Bauer contribute two different recipes for constructing XML-RPC servers. Quinlan, in recipe 15.2 "Serving XML-RPC Requests," shows how to use the SimpleXMLRPCServer module from the Python Standard Library to handle incoming requests. Bauer's is recipe 15.3 "Using XML-RPC with Medusa." Medusa, like Twisted, is a framework for writing asynchronous network programs. In both cases, the libraries do most of the work; other than a few lines of initialization and registration, the server looks like normal Python code.

Christop Dietze (with contributions from Brian Quinlan and Jeff Bauer), in recipe 15.4 "Enabling an XML-RPC Server to Be Terminated Remotely," elaborates on the XML-RPC server theme by showing how to add the ability that enables remote clients to terminate the server cleanly. Rune Hansen, in recipe 15.5 "Implementing SimpleXMLRPCServer Niceties," shows how to add several minor but useful niceties to your XML-RPC servers.

Peter Arwanitis, in recipe 15.6 "Giving an XML-RPC Server a wxPython GUI," demonstrates how to implement an XML-RPC server with Twisted and, at the same time, give your server a GUI, thanks to the wxPython GUI framework.

A strong alternative to XML-based protocols is CORBA, an object-based RPC mechanism using its own protocol, IIOP (Internet Inter-Orb Protocol). CORBA is a mature technology compared to XML-RPC (or, even more, SOAP, which isn't used in any of these recipes—apparently, Pythonistas aren't doing all that much with SOAP yet). CORBA was introduced in 1991. The Python language binding was officially approved more recently, in February 2000, and several ORBs (Object Request Brokers—roughly, CORBA servers) support Python. Duncan Grisby, a researcher at AT&T Laboratories in Cambridge (U.K.), describes the basics of getting a CORBA client and server running in recipe 15.8 "Implementing a CORBA Server and Client," which uses omniORB, a free ORB, and the Python binding he wrote for it.

CORBA has a reputation for complexity, but Grisby's recipe makes it look straightforward. More steps are involved in the CORBA client than in the XML-RPC client example, but they are not difficult. To connect an XML-RPC client to a server, you just need a URL. To connect a CORBA client to a server, you need a URL—a special corbaloc URL—and you also need to know the server's interface. Of course, you need to know the interface regardless of protocol, but CORBA uses it explicitly. In general, CORBA offers more features than other distributed programming frameworks—interfaces, type checking, passing references to objects, and more. CORBA also supports just about every Python data type as argument or result.

Regardless of the protocols or systems you choose, the recipes in this chapter can help get you started. Inter-program communication is an important part of building a distributed system, but it's just one part. Once you have a client and server working, you'll find you have to deal with other interesting, challenging problems—error detection, concurrency, and security, to name a few. The recipes here won't solve those problems, but they will prevent you from getting caught up in unimportant details of the communication protocols. Rob Riggs in recipe 15.11 "Authenticating an SSL Client over HTTPS" presents a simple way to use HTTPS (as supported by the Python Standard Library module `httplib`) to authenticate SSL clients; Simon Foster's previously mentioned Perspective Broker recipe provides a way to implement one specific but frequent strategy for error detection and handling, namely periodically trying to reconnect to a server after a timeout or explicitly discovered network error.

15.1 Making an XML-RPC Method Call

Credit: Rael Dornfest, Jeremy Hylton

Problem

You need to make a method call to an XML-RPC server.

Solution

The `xmlrpclib` module makes writing XML-RPC clients very easy. For example, we can use XML-RPC to access O'Reilly's Meerkat server and get the five most recent items about Python:

```
from xmlrpclib import Server
server = Server("http://www.oreillynet.com/meerkat/xml-rpc/server.php")
print server.meerkat.getItems(
    {'search': '[Pp]ython', 'num_items': 5, 'descriptions': 0}
)
```

Discussion

XML-RPC is a simple, lightweight approach to distributed processing. `xmlrpclib`, which makes it easy to write XML-RPC clients in Python, is part of the Python Standard Library.

To use `xmlrpclib`, you first instantiate a proxy to the server, calling the `ServerProxy` class (also known by the name `Server`) and passing in the URL to which you want to connect. Then, on that proxy instance, you can access and call whatever methods the remote XML-RPC server supplies. In this case, you know that Meerkat supplies a `getItems` method, so you call the method of the same name on the server proxy instance. The proxy relays the call to the server, waits for the server to respond, and finally returns the call's results.

This recipe uses O'Reilly's Meerkat service, intended for syndication of contents such as news and product announcements. Specifically, the recipe queries Meerkat for the five most recent items mentioning either "Python" or "python". If you try this recipe, be warned that response times from Meerkat are variable, depending on the quality of your Internet connection, the time of day, and the level of traffic on the Internet. If the script takes a long time to answer, it doesn't mean you did something wrong—it just means you have to be patient!

Using `xmlrpclib` by passing raw dictionaries, as in this recipe's code, is quite workable but somewhat unPythonic. Here's an easy alternative that looks nicer:

```
from xmlrpclib import Server
server = Server("http://www.oreillynet.com/meerkat/xml-rpc/server.php")
class MeerkatQuery(object):
    def __init__(self, search, num_items=5, descriptions=0):
        self.search = search
        self.num_items = num_items
        self.descriptions = descriptions
q = MeerkatQuery("[Pp]ython")
print server.meerkat.getItems(q)
```

You can package the instance attributes and their default values in several different ways, but the main point of this variant is that, as the argument to the `getItems` method, an instance object with the right attributes works just as well as a dictionary object with the same information packaged as dictionary items.

See Also

The `xmlrpclib` module is part of the Python Standard Library and is well documented in its chapter of the *Library Reference* portion of Python's online documentation. Meerkat is at *http://www.oreillynet.com/meerkat/*.

15.2 Serving XML-RPC Requests

Credit: Brian Quinlan

Problem

You need to implement an XML-RPC server.

Solution

Module `SimpleXMLRPCServer`, which is part of the Python Standard Library, makes writing XML-RPC servers reasonably easy. Here's how you can write an XML-RPC server:

```
# Server code sxr_server.py
import SimpleXMLRPCServer
class StringFunctions(object):
    def __init__(self):
        # Make all the functions in Python's standard string module
        # available as 'python_string.func_name' for each func_name
        import string
        self.python_string = string
    def _privateFunction(self):
        # This function cannot be called directly through XML-RPC because
```

```
                # it starts with an underscore character '_', i.e., it's "private"
                return "you'll never get this result on the client"
        def chop_in_half(self, astr):
            return astr[:len(astr)/2]
        def repeat(self, astr, times):
            return astr * times
    if __name__=='__main__':
        server = SimpleXMLRPCServer.SimpleXMLRPCServer(("localhost", 8000))
        server.register_instance(StringFunctions())
        server.register_function(lambda astr: '_' + astr, '_string')
        server.serve_forever()
```

And here is a client script that accesses the server you just wrote:

```
# Client code sxr_client.py
import xmlrpclib
server = xmlrpclib.Server('http://localhost:8000')
print server.chop_in_half('I am a confident guy')
# emits: I am a con
print server.repeat('Repetition is the key to learning!\n', 5)
# emits 5 lines, all Repetition is the key to learning!
print server._string('<= underscore')
# emits _<= underscore
print server.python_string.join(['I', 'like it!'], " don't ")
# emits I don't like it!
print server._privateFunction()    # this will throw an exception
# terminates client script with traceback for xmlrpclib.Fault
```

Discussion

This recipe demonstrates the creation of a simple XML-RPC server using the
SimpleXMLRPCServer module of the standard Python library. The module contains a
class of the same name that listens for HTTP requests on a specified port and dispatches any XML-RPC calls to registered instances or registered functions. This
recipe demonstrates both usages. To create a server, we instantiate the
SimpleXMLRPCServer class, supplying the hostname and port for the server. Then, on
that instance, we call register_instance as many times as needed to make other
instances available as services. In addition, or as an alternative, we call register_
function to make functions similarly available as services. Once we have registered
all the instances and/or all the functions we want to expose, we call the serve_
forever method of the server instance, and our XML-RPC server is active. Yes, it is
really that simple. The only output on the shell prompt window on which you run
the server is one line of log information each time a client accesses the server; the
only way to terminate the server is to send it an interrupt, for example with a Ctrl-C
keystroke.

Registering functions (as opposed to an instance) is necessary when a function name
begins with an underscore (_) or contains characters not allowed in Python identifiers (e.g., accented letters, punctuation marks, etc.). Dotted names (e.g., python_
string.join) are correctly resolved for registered instances.

See Also

The SimpleXMLRPCServer module is part of the Python Standard Library and is documented in its chapter of the *Library Reference* portion of Python's online documentation.

15.3   Using XML-RPC with Medusa

Credit: Jeff Bauer

Problem

You need to establish a lightweight, highly scalable, distributed processing system and want to use the XML-RPC protocol.

Solution

Package medusa lets you implement lightweight, highly scalable, asynchronous (event-driven) network servers. An XML-RPC handler is included in the Medusa distribution. Here is how you can code an XML-RPC server with Medusa:

```
# xmlrpc_server.py
from socket import gethostname
from medusa.xmlrpc_handler import xmlrpc_handler
from medusa.http_server import http_server
from medusa import asyncore
class xmlrpc_server(xmlrpc_handler):
    # initialize and run the server
    def __init__(self, host=None, port=8182):
        if host is None:
            host = gethostname( )
        hs = http_server(host, port)
        hs.install_handler(self)
        asyncore.loop( )
    # an example of a method to be exposed via the XML-RPC protocol
    def add(self, op1, op2):
        return op1 + op2
    # the infrastructure ("plumbing") to expose methods
    def call(self, method, params):
        print "calling method: %s, params: %s" % (method, params)
        if method == 'add':
            return self.add(*params)
        return "method not found: %s" % method
if __name__ == '__main__':
    server = xmlrpc_server( )
```

And here is a client script that accesses the server you just wrote:

```
# xmlrpc_client.py
from socket import gethostname
from xmlrpclib import Transport, dumps
class xmlrpc_connection(object):
```

```
        def __init__(self, host=None, port=8182):
            if host is None:
                host = gethostname( )
            self.host = "%s:%s" % (host, port)
            self.transport = Transport( )
        def remote(self, method, params=( )):
            """ Invoke the server with the given method name and parameters.
                The return value is always a tuple. """
            return self.transport.request(self.host, '/RPC2',
                                          dumps(params, method))
    if __name__ == '__main__':
        connection = xmlrpc_connection( )
        answer, = connection.remote("add", (40, 2))
        print "The answer is:", answer
```

Discussion

This recipe demonstrates remote method calls between two machines (or two processes, even on the same machine) using the XML-RPC protocol and provides a complete example of working client/server code.

XML-RPC is one of the easiest ways to handle distributed processing tasks. There's no messing around with the low-level socket details, nor is it necessary to write an interface definition. The protocol is platform and language neutral. The XML-RPC specification can be found at *http://www.xml-rpc.com* and is well worth studying. It's nowhere as functionally rich as heavyweight stuff like CORBA, but, to compensate, it *is* much simpler!

To run this recipe's Solution, you must download the Medusa library from *http:// www.nightmare.com* (the Python Standard Library includes the asyncore and asynchat modules, originally from Medusa, but not the other parts of Medusa required for this recipe). With Medusa, you implement an XML-RPC server by subclassing the xmlrpc_handler class and passing an instance of your class to the install_handler method of an instance of http_server. HTTP is the transport-level protocol used by the XML-RPC standard, and http_server handles all transport-level issues on your behalf. You need to provide only the handler part, by customizing xmlrpc_handler through subclassing and method overriding. Specifically, you must override the call method, which the Medusa framework calls on your instance with the name of the XML-RPC method being called, along with its parameters, as arguments. This is exactly what we do in this recipe, in which we expose a single XML-RPC method named add which accepts two numeric parameters and returns their sum as the method's result.

This recipe's XML-RPC client uses xmlrpclib in a more sophisticated way than recipe 15.1 "Making an XML-RPC Method Call," by accessing the Transport class explicitly. In theory, this approach allows finer-grained control. However, this recipe does not exert that kind of control, and it's rarely required in XML-RPC clients that you actually deploy, anyway.

See Also

The xmlrpclib module is part of the Python Standard Library and is documented in a chapter of the *Library Reference* portion of Python's online documentation. Medusa is at *http://www.nightmare.com*.

15.4 Enabling an XML-RPC Server to Be Terminated Remotely

Credit: Christoph Dietze, Brian Quinlan, Jeff Bauer

Problem

You are coding an XML-RPC server, using the Python Standard Library's SimpleXMLRPCServer module, and you want to make it possible for a remote client to cause the XML-RPC server to exit cleanly.

Solution

You have to use your own request-handling loop (instead of the serve_forever method of SimpleXMLRPCServer) so that you can stop looping when appropriate. For example:

```
import SimpleXMLRPCServer
running = True
def finis( ):
    global running
    running = False
    return 1
server = SimpleXMLRPCServer.SimpleXMLRPCServer(('127.0.0.1', 8000))
server.register_function(finis)
while running:
    server.handle_request( )
```

Discussion

SimpleXMLRPCServer's serve_forever method, as its name implies, attempts to keep serving "forever"—that is, it keeps serving until the whole server process is killed. Sometimes, it's useful to allow remote clients to request a clean termination of a service by remotely calling a server-exposed function, and this recipe demonstrates the simplest way to allow this functionality.

The finis function (which gets exposed to remote clients via the register_function call) sets the global variable running to False (and then returns something that is not None because the XML-RPC protocol cannot deal with the None object). Using the while running loop, instead of a serve_forever call, then ensures that the server stops serving and terminates when the variable running becomes false.

If you prefer to subclass SimpleXMLRPCServer, you can obtain a similar effect by over-riding the serve_forever method: that is, instead of placing the simple while running: server.handle_request loop inline, you can code, for example (with the same function finis as in the recipe's Solution):

```
class MyServer(SimpleXMLRPCServer.SimpleXMLRPCServer):
    def serve_forever(self):
        while running:
            self.handle_request( )
server = MyServer(('127.0.0.1', 8000))
server.register_function(finis)
server.serve_forever( )
```

However, this alternative approach offers no special advantage (unless you have a fetish for being object oriented for no particular purpose), and, since this alternative approach is telling a little white lie (by using the name serve_forever for a method that does *not* keep serving "forever"!), the simpler approach in the recipe's Solution can definitely be recommended.

See Also

The SimpleXMLRPCServer module is part of the Python Standard Library and is docu-mented in a chapter of the *Library Reference* portion of Python's online documen-tation.

15.5 Implementing SimpleXMLRPCServer Niceties

Credit: Rune Hansen

Problem

You are coding XML-RPC servers with the Python Standard Library SimpleXMLRPCServer class and want to ensure you're using the simple but useful idi-oms that can ease your coding, or give your servers more flexibility at no substantial cost to you.

Solution

Here are a few tweaks I generally use, to enhance my servers' usability, when I'm developing servers based on SimpleXMLRPCServer:

```
# give the base class a short, readable nickname
from SimpleXMLRPCServer import SimpleXMLRPCServer as BaseServer
class Server(BaseServer):
    def __init__(self, host, port):
        # accept separate hostname and portnumber and group them
```

```
        BaseServer.__init__(self, (host, port))
    def server_bind(self):
        # allow fast restart of the server after it's killed
        import socket
        self.socket.setsockopt(socket.SOL_SOCKET, socket.SO_REUSEADDR, 1)
        BaseServer.server_bind(self)
    allowedClientHosts = '127.0.0.1', '192.168.0.15',
    def verify_request(self, request, client_address):
        # forbid requests except from specific client hosts
        return client_address[0] in self.allowedClientHosts
```

Discussion

The recipe begins with a statement of the form from module import name as nickname, a Python idiom that is often handy for importing something under a short and usable nickname. It's certainly miles better than having to repeatedly write SimpleXMLRPC-Server.SimpleXMLRPCServer after a simple import statement, or using the ill-advised construct from module import *, which mixes up all the namespaces and can often cause subtle and hard-to-find bugs.

The sole purpose of the __init__ statement of class Server is to accept host and port as separate parameters and group them into the required tuple. I find myself often writing such statements with the many Python functions and classes that require this *address tuple* grouping (your tastes, of course, may be different).

By default, a server socket belonging to a process that dies is kept busy for quite a while. Particularly during development, it is handy to kill such a process, edit the script, and restart immediately. For such an immediate restart to work, you must ensure the code of your server sets the SO_REUSEADDR option on the relevant socket, as the recipe's code does in its overridden method server_bind.

Last but not least, the recipe overrides verify_request in order to apply a simple check that refuses service except to requests coming from client hosts on a pre-defined list. This approach doesn't provide rock-solid security, but nevertheless, it is potentially useful. Again, it's particularly useful during development, to help avoid those cases where some other developer on the same LAN accidentally connects his client to the server I'm just developing, and we both experience puzzling problems until we figure out what's happened!

See Also

The SimpleXMLRPCServer module is part of the Python Standard Library and is documented in a chapter of the *Library Reference* portion of Python's online documentation.

15.6   Giving an XML-RPC Server a wxPython GUI

Credit: Peter Arwanitis, Alex Martelli

Problem

You are writing an XML-RPC server and want to add a GUI to it, or you're writing a GUI application that you want to be able to interact as an XML-RPC server too.

Solution

As long as you use Twisted for the network interaction, and wxPython for the GUI, this task is reasonably easy, since these packages can cooperate through the `twisted.internet.wxreactor` module. You do need to have specific incantations at the start of your program, as follows:

```
# To use wxPython and Twisted together, do the following, in exact order:
import wx
from twisted.internet import wxreactor
wxreactor.install( )
from twisted.internet import reactor
# Then, have whatever other imports as may be necessary to your program
from twisted.web import xmlrpc, server
class MyFrame(wx.Frame):
    ''' Main window for this wx application. '''
    def __init__(self, parent, ID, title, pos=wx.DefaultPosition,
                size=(200, 100), style=wx.DEFAULT_FRAME_STYLE):
        wx.Frame.__init__(self, parent, ID, title, pos, size, style)
        wx.EVT_CLOSE(self, self.OnCloseWindow)
    def OnCloseWindow(self, event):
        self.Destroy( )
        reactor.stop( )
class MyXMLRPCApp(wx.App, xmlrpc.XMLRPC):
    ''' We're a wx Application _AND_ an XML-RPC server too. '''
    def OnInit(self):
        ''' wx-related startup code: builds the GUI. '''
        self.frame = MyFrame(None, -1, 'Hello')
        self.frame.Show(True)
        self.SetTopWindow(self.frame)
        return True
    # methods exposed to XML-RPC clients:
    def xmlrpc_stop(self):
        """ Closes the wx application. """
        self.frame.Close( )
        return 'Shutdown initiated'
    def xmlrpc_title(self, x):
        """ Change the wx application's window's caption. """
        self.frame.SetTitle(x)
        return 'Title set to %r' % x
    def xmlrpc_add(self, x, y):
        """ Provide some computational services to clients. """
        return x + y
```

```
if __name__ == '__main__':
    # pass False to emit stdout/stderr to shell, not an additional wx window
    app = MyXMLRPCApp(False)
    # Make the wx application twisted-aware
    reactor.registerWxApp(app)
    # Make a XML-RPC Server listening to port 7080
    reactor.listenTCP(7080, server.Site(app))
    # Start both reactor parts (wx MainLoop and XML-RPC server)
    reactor.run()
```

Discussion

It is often useful to give an XML-RPC server a GUI, for example, to display the current status to an operator or administrator. Conversely, it is often useful to give a GUI application the ability to accept remote requests from other programs, and making the application an XML-RPC server is an excellent, simple way to accomplish that purpose.

Either way, if you use Twisted for the networking part, you're off to a good start, because Twisted offers specialized reactor implementations to ease cooperation with several GUI toolkits. In particular, this recipe shows how a Twisted-based XML-RPC server can sport a wxPython GUI thanks to the twisted.internet.wxreactor module.

To try this recipe, save the code from the "Solution" as a Python script and start it from a shell. If you run some kind of "personal firewall" that's normally set to impede TCP/IP communication between programs running on your machine, ensure it's set to let such communication happen on TCP port 7080. Then, from any interactive Python interpreter session on the same machine, do:

```
>>> import xmlrpclib
>>> s = xmlrpclib.ServerProxy('http://localhost:7080')
>>> s.add(23, 42)
65
>>> s.title('Changed Title')
Title set to 'Changed Title'
```

Observe that the title of the *wx* application's window has changed. Now, you can close the application, either by whatever GUI means you normally use on your platform (it is a totally cross-platform application, after all), or by calling s.stop() from the same Python interpreter interactive session that we just showed. You can also run such a client on any other machine, as long as it has open TCP/IP connectivity on port 7080 with the machine running the server. (In particular, make sure you open port 7080 on any firewall that would normally block that port, whether the firewall is on either of the machines, or on any other network apparatus that may lie between them.)

Both Twisted and wxPython, while already rich and solid frameworks, are still growing and changing, so it may be important to ensure you have the right releases installed properly on your machine. This recipe should run on any platform that is equipped with Python 2.3 or better, wxPython 2.4.2.4 or better, and Twisted 1.3.0

or better. Of course, we don't have access to every platform in the world, nor to all future releases of these tools, so we tested the recipe only under Windows/XP, Mac OS X 10.3.6, and Linux, with Python 2.3 and 2.4, wxPython 2.4.2.4, and some 2.5.x.y releases, and Twisted 1.3.0 specifically.

Since the recipe relies only on published, supported aspects of the various tools, one can hope that the recipe will also work elsewhere, and will work with future releases of the tools. However, if this recipe's approach does not prove satisfactory for your purposes, you may want to try a different approach based on threads, shown at *http://aspn.activestate.com/ASPN/Cookbook/Python/Recipe/286201*.

See Also

Twisted's home page is *http://www.twistedmatrix.com*; documentation on Twisted XML-RPC support is at *http://www.twistedmatrix.com/documents/current/howto/xmlrpc*; wxPython's home page is *http://www.wxpython.org*.

15.7 Using Twisted Perspective Broker

Credit: Simon Foster

Problem

You want to implement Python clients and servers for some distributed processing task, without repetitious "boilerplate" code, and with excellent performance and scalability characteristics.

Solution

Use the *Perspective Broker* (PB) subsystem of the *Twisted* framework. A PB server just subclasses the PB's Root class and adds remotely callable methods. Here is an example of a server script which adds just one remotely callable method, named Pong:

```
from twisted.spread import pb
from twisted.internet import reactor
PORT = 8992
class Ponger(pb.Root):
    def remote_Pong(self, ball):
        print 'CATCH', ball,
        ball += 1
        print 'THROW', ball
        return ball
reactor.listenTCP(PORT, pb.BrokerFactory(Ponger()))
reactor.run()
```

We could write an equally trivial script for the client side of the interaction, but let's instead have a rather feature-rich PB client, which deals with important issues often ignored in introductory examples of distributed programming, such as error handling:

```python
from twisted.spread import pb
from twisted.internet import reactor
import sys
PORT = 8992
DELAY        = 1
DOG_DELAY    = 2
RESTART_DELAY = 5
class Pinger(object):
    def __init__(self, host):
        self.ping = None
        self.host = host
        self.ball = 0
        self._start()
    def _start(self):
        print 'Waiting for Server', self.host
        dfr = pb.getObjectAt(self.host, PORT, 30)
        dfr.addCallbacks(self._gotRemote, self._remoteFail)
    def _gotRemote(self, remote):
        remote.notifyOnDisconnect(self._remoteFail)
        self.remote = remote
        self._ping()
    def _remoteFail(self, __):
        if self.ping:
            print 'ping failed, canceling and restarting'
            self.ping.cancel()
            self.ping = None
        self.restart = reactor.callLater(RESTART_DELAY, self._start)
    def _watchdog(self):
        print 'ping timed out, canceling and restarting'
        self._start()
    def _ping(self):
        self.dog = reactor.callLater(DOG_DELAY, self._watchdog)
        self.ball += 1
        print 'THROW', self.ball,
        dfr = self.remote.callRemote('Pong', self.ball)
        dfr.addCallbacks(self._pong, self._remoteFail)
    def _pong(self, ball):
        self.dog.cancel()
        print 'CATCH',  ball
        self.ball = ball
        self.ping = reactor.callLater(DELAY, self._ping)
if __name__ == '__main__':
    if len(sys.argv) != 2:
        print 'Usage: %s serverhost' % sys.argv[0]
        sys.exit(1)
    host = sys.argv[1]
    print 'Ping-pong client to host', host
    Pinger(host)
    reactor.run()
```

Discussion

Twisted is a framework for *asynchronous* (also known as *event-driven*) programming of network clients, servers, proxies, and so on. The asynchronous programming model (which Twisted implements through the Reactor Design Pattern embodied in the twisted.internet.reactor module) provides excellent performance and scalability characteristics for Twisted-based programs.

Twisted also includes many subsystems that offer your programs ready-to-go networking functionality. One of these subsystems, Perspective Broker (PB), is implemented in the twisted.spread.pb module. PB lets you code distributed-programming clients and servers, with an ease of use that's most clearly displayed in the server program at the start of this recipe's Solution. In just a few lines of code, the server class is able to expose remotely callable methods: all it takes is subclassing the Root class of the pb module and naming each remotely callable method with a prefix of remote_.

Most of the client code in this recipe is concerned with diagnosing and handling possible problems and errors with the connection to the server. Specifically, if the connection fails for any reason, including a timeout diagnosed by the watchdog timer that the client sets up each time it pings, the client attempts to reconnect to the server. If you kill the server, the client keeps trying to reconnect, periodically, until you restart the server.

Error-handling apart, the client is essentially as simple as the server. In the method _start, the client calls function getObjectAt of module twisted.spread.pb, which takes as its arguments the server's host, a port number, and a "time-out" delay in seconds. As usual in Python networking, the host can be either a network name, such as localhost, or a string representing an IP address, such as 127.0.0.1.

If no problems arise, getObjectAt returns an object that proxies for the remote PB server. The proxy object, in turn, has a callRemote method, which takes as its arguments the method name as a string, followed by any arguments you are passing to the remote method. callRemote returns a Twisted deferred object, the lynchpin of Twisted's style of asynchronous (event-driven) programming. Learning to use deferreds effectively is the fundamental step in learning to program with Twisted.

A deferred object represents an event that may occur in the future (the *success-case*) or may end in failure. Given a deferred, you can add callbacks to it for both success and failure cases. (You can also *chain* callbacks, a possibility that this recipe does not exploit.) When the deferred's event occurs, *Twisted* calls your "success-case" callback, passing as its argument the "result" of the deferred. Alternatively, if the deferred ends in failure, *Twisted* calls your *failure-case* callback, passing as its argument a failure object that wraps a Python exception object.

As you see in this recipe, despite deferreds' potentially rich and vast functionality, their use is really quite simple in most cases. For example, in the failure cases, the client in this recipe wants to retry connecting: therefore, method _remoteFail accepts the failure-object argument with an argument name of "two underscores" (__), a common Python convention that indicates the argument will be ignored.

See Also

The Twisted web site, at *http://www.twistedmatrix.com*, has abundant documentation about all of Twisted's elements and subsystems, including Perspective Broker and deferred objects.

15.8 Implementing a CORBA Server and Client

Credit: Duncan Grisby

Problem

You need to implement a CORBA server and client to distribute a processing task, such as the all-important network-centralized fortune-cookie distribution.

Solution

CORBA is a solid, rich, mature object-oriented RPC protocol, and several CORBA ORBs offer excellent Python support. This recipe requires multiple files. Here is the interface definition file, *fortune.idl*, coded in CORBA's own IDL (Interface Definition Language):

```
module Fortune {
    interface CookieServer {
        string get_cookie();
    };
};
```

This code is quite readable even if you've never seen CORBA's IDL before: it defines a module named Fortune, whose only contents is an interface named CookieServer, whose only contents is a function (method) named get_cookie, which takes no arguments and returns a string. This code says nothing at all about the *implementation*: IDL is a language for defining *interfaces*.

The server script is a simple Python program:

```
import sys, os
import CORBA, Fortune, Fortune__POA
FORTUNE_PATH = "/usr/games/fortune"
class CookieServer_i(Fortune__POA.CookieServer):
    def get_cookie(self):
        pipe   = os.popen(FORTUNE_PATH)
        cookie = pipe.read()
        if pipe.close():
            # An error occurred with the pipe
            cookie = "Oh dear, couldn't get a fortune\n"
        return cookie
```

```
orb = CORBA.ORB_init(sys.argv)
poa = orb.resolve_initial_references("RootPOA")
servant = CookieServer_i()
poa.activate_object(servant)
print orb.object_to_string(servant._this())
# see the Discussion session about what this print statement emits
poa._get_the_POAManager().activate()
orb.run()
```

And here's a demonstration of client code for this server, using a Python interactive command shell:

```
>>> import CORBA, Fortune
>>> orb = CORBA.ORB_init()
>>> o = orb.string_to_object(
...     "corbaloc::host.example.com/fortune")
>>> o = o._narrow(Fortune.CookieServer)
>>> print o.get_cookie()
```

Discussion

CORBA has a reputation for being hard to use, but it is really very easy, especially with Python. This example shows the complete CORBA implementation of a fortune-cookie server and its client. To run this example, you need a Python-compatible CORBA implementation (i.e., an ORB)—or, if you wish, two such ORBs, since you can use two different CORBA implementations, one for the client and one for the server, and let them interoperate with the CORBA IIOP inter-ORB protocol. Several free CORBA implementations, which fully support Python, are available for you to download and install. The Python language support is part of the CORBA standards, so, if a certain ORB supports Python at all, you can code your Python source for it in just the same way as you can code it for any other compliant ORB, be it free or commercial. In this recipe, we use the free ORB known as omniORB. With omniORB, you can use omniORBpy, which lets you develop CORBA applications from Python.

With most ORBs, you must convert the interface definition coded in IDL into Python declarations with an IDL compiler. For example, with omniORBpy:

```
omniidl -bpython fortune.idl
```

This creates Python modules named Fortune and Fortune__POA, in files *Fortune.py* and *Fortune_POA.py*, to be used by clients and servers, respectively.

In the server, we implement the CookieServer CORBA interface by importing Fortune__POA and subclassing the CookieServer class that the module exposes. Specifically, in our own subclass, we need to override the get_cookie method (i.e., implement the methods that the interface asserts we're implementing). Then, we start CORBA to get an orb instance, ask the ORB for a POA (Portable Object Adaptor), instantiate our own interface-implementing object, and pass it to the POA instance's activate_object method. Finally, we call the activate method on the POA manager and the run method on the ORB to start our service.

When you run the server, it prints out a long hex string, such as:

```
IOR:010000001d00000049444c3a466f7274756e652f436f6f6b69655365727665572
a312e3000000000010000000000000005c000000010102000d0000003135382e313234
2e36342e330000f90a07000000666f7274756e6565500020000000000000008000000010
00000005454441010000001c00000001000000010001000100000001000100105090010100
0100000009010100
```

Printing this string is the purpose of the object_to_string call that our recipe's server performs just before it activates and runs.

You have to pass this string value as the argument of the client's orb.string_to_object( ) call to contact your server. Such long hex strings may not be convenient to communicate to clients. To remedy this, it's easy to make your server support a simple corbaloc URL string, like the one used in the client example, but doing so involves omniORB-specific code that is not necessarily portable to other ORBs. (See the omniORBpy manual for details of corbaloc URL support.)

See Also

You can download omniORBpy, including its documentation, from *http://www.omniorb.org/omniORBpy/*.

15.9 Performing Remote Logins Using telnetlib

Credit: Jeff Bauer

Problem

You need to send commands to one or more logins that can be on a local machine, or a remote machine, and the Telnet protocol is acceptable.

Solution

Telnet is one of the oldest protocols in the TCP/IP stack, but it may still be serviceable (at least within an intranet that is well protected against sniffing and spoofing attacks). In any case, Python's standard module telnetlib supports Telnet quite well:

```
# auto_telnet.py - remote control via telnet
import os, sys, telnetlib
from getpass import getpass
class AutoTelnet(object):
    def __init__(self, user_list, cmd_list, **kw):
        # optional parameters are host, timeout in seconds, command
        # prompt to expect from the host on successful logins:
        self.host = kw.get('host', 'localhost')
```

```
                self.timeout = kw.get('timeout', 600)
                self.command_prompt = kw.get('command_prompt', "$ ")
                # collect passwords for each user, interactively
                self.passwd = {}
                for user in user_list:
                    self.passwd[user] = getpass("Enter user '%s' password: " % user)
                # instantiate Telnet proxy
                self.telnet = telnetlib.Telnet()
                for user in user_list:
                    # login with given host and user, and act appropriately
                    self.telnet.open(self.host)
                    ok = self.action(user, cmd_list)
                    if not ok:
                        print "Unable to process:", user
                    self.telnet.close()
            def action(self, user, cmd_list):
                # wait for a login prompt
                t = self.telnet
                t.write("\n")
                login_prompt = "login: "
                response = t.read_until(login_prompt, 5)
                if login_prompt in response:
                    print response
                else:
                    return 0
                # supply user and password for login
                t.write("%s\n" % user)
                password_prompt = "Password:"
                response = t.read_until(password_prompt, 3)
                if password_prompt in response:
                    print response
                else:
                    return 0
                t.write("%s\n" % self.passwd[user])
                # wait for command prompt to indicate successful login
                response = t.read_until(self.command_prompt, 5)
                if self.command_prompt not in response:
                    return 0
                # send each command and wait for command prompt after each
                for cmd in cmd_list:
                    t.write("%s\n" % cmd)
                    response = t.read_until(self.command_prompt, self.timeout)
                    if self.command_prompt not in response:
                        return 0
                    print response
                return 1
        if __name__ == '__main__':
            # code which runs as a main script, only
            basename = os.path.splitext(os.path.basename(sys.argv[0]))[0]
            logname = os.environ.get("LOGNAME", os.environ.get("USERNAME"))
            host = 'localhost'
            import getopt
            optlist, user_list = getopt.getopt(sys.argv[1:], 'c:f:h:')
            usage = """
```

```
        usage: %s [-h host] [-f cmdfile] [-c "command"] user1 user2 ...
            -c command
            -f command file
            -h host  (default: '%s')
        Example:  %s -c "echo $HOME" %s
        """ % (basename, host, basename, logname)
            if len(sys.argv) < 2:
                print usage
                sys.exit(1)
        cmd_list = [ ]
        for opt, optarg in optlist:
            if opt == '-f':
                for r in open(optarg):
                    if r.rstrip():
                        cmd_list.append(r)
            elif opt == '-c':
                command = optarg
                if command[0] == '"' and command[-1] == '"':
                    command = command[1:-1]
                cmd_list.append(command)
            elif opt == '-h':
                host = optarg
        autoTelnet = AutoTelnet(user_list, cmd_list, host=host)
```

Discussion

Python's telnetlib lets you easily automate access to Telnet servers, even from non-Unix machines. As a flexible alternative to the popen functions, which only run commands locally as the user that's running the script, telnetlib, which can work across an intranet and can login and run commands as different users, is a handy technique to have in your system administration toolbox.

Production code generally has to be made more robust, but this recipe should be enough to get you started in the right direction. The recipe's AutoTelnet class instantiates a single telnetlib.Telnet object and uses that single object in a loop over a list of users. For each user, the recipe calls the open method of the Telnet instance to open the connection to the specified host, runs a series of commands in AutoTelnet's action method, and finally calls the close method of the Telnet instance to terminate the connection.

AutoTelnet's action method is where the action is. All operations depend on two methods of the Telnet instance. The write method takes a single string argument and writes it to the connection. The read_until method takes two arguments, a string to wait for and a timeout in seconds, and returns a string with all the characters received from the connection until the timeout elapsed or the waited-for string occurred. action's code uses these two methods to wait for a login prompt and send the username; wait for a password prompt and send the password; and then, repeatedly, wait for a command prompt (typically from a Unix shell at the other end of the connection) and send the commands in the list sequentially (waiting for a command prompt again after sending each one).

One warning (which applies to *any* use of Telnet and some other old protocols): except when transmitting completely public data, not protected by passwords that might be of interest to intruders of ill will, do not run Telnet (or non-anonymous FTP, for that matter) on networks on which you are not *completely* sure that nobody is packet-sniffing, since these protocols date from an older, more trusting age. These protocols let passwords and everything else travel in the clear, open to any snooper. This issue is not Python specific; it applies to any implementation of these protocols, since it depends on the definition of the protocols themselves. Whether or not you use Python, be advised: if there is any risk that someone might be packet-sniffing, use SSH instead, as shown next in recipe 15.10 "Performing Remote Logins with SSH" so that no password ever travels on the network in the clear, and so that the connection stream itself gets encrypted.

See Also

Documentation on the standard library module telnetlib in the *Library Reference*; Recipe 15.10 "Performing Remote Logins with SSH."

15.10 Performing Remote Logins with SSH

Credit: Peter Cogolo, Anna Martelli Ravenscroft

Problem

You need to send commands, using the SSH protocol, to one or more logins that can be on a local machine or a remote machine.

Solution

SSH is a secure replacement for the old Telnet protocol. One way to use SSH from a Python program is with the third-party paramiko package:

```
# auto_ssh.py - remote control via ssh
import os, sys, paramiko
from getpass import getpass
paramiko.util.log_to_file('auto_ssh.log', 0)
def parse_user(user, default_host, default_port):
    ''' given name[@host[:port]], returns name, host, int(port),
        applying defaults for hose and/or port if necessary
    '''
    if '@' not in user:
        return user, default_host, default_port
    user, host = user.split('@', 1)
    if ':' in host:
        host, port = host.split(':', 1)
    else:
```

```
            port = default_port
        return user, host, int(port)
    def autoSsh(users, cmds, host='localhost', port=22, timeout=5.0,
               maxsize=2000, passwords=None):
        ''' run commands for given users, w/default host, port, and timeout,
            emitting to standard output all given commands and their
            responses (no more than 'maxsize' characters of each response).
        '''
        if passwords is None:
            passwords = {}
        for user in users:
            if user not in passwords:
                passwords[user] = getpass("Enter user '%s' password: " % user)
        for user in users:
            user, host, port = parse_user(user, default_host, default_port)
            try:
                transport = paramiko.Transport((host, port))
                transport.connect(username=user, password=passwords[user])
                channel = transport.open_session()
                if timeout: channel.settimeout(timeout)
                for cmd in cmd_list:
                    channel.exec_command(cmd)
                    response = channel.recv(max_size)
                    print 'CMD %r(%r) -> %s' % (cmd, user, response)
            except Exception, err:
                print "ERR: unable to process %r: %s" % (user, err)
    if __name__ == '__main__':
        logname = os.environ.get("LOGNAME", os.environ.get("USERNAME"))
        host = 'localhost'
        port = 22
        usage = """
usage: %s [-h host] [-p port] [-f cmdfile] [-c "command"] user1 user2 ...
    -c  command
    -f  command file
    -h  default host  (default: localhost)
    -p  default host  (default: 22)
Example:  %s -c "echo $HOME" %s
same as:  %s -c "echo $HOME" %s@localhost:22
""" % (sys.argv[0], sys.argv[0], logname, sys.argv[0], logname)
        import getopt
        optlist, user_list = getopt.getopt(sys.argv[1:], 'c:f:h:p:')
        if not user_list:
            print usage
            sys.exit(1)
        cmd_list = []
        for opt, optarg in optlist:
            if opt == '-f':
                for r in open(optarg, 'rU'):
                    if r.rstrip():
                        cmd_list.append(r)
            elif opt == '-c':
                command = optarg
                if command[0] == '"' and command[-1] == '"':
                    command = command[1:-1]
```

```
        cmd_list.append(command)
    elif opt == '-h':
        host = optarg
    elif opt == '-p':
        port = optarg
    else:
        print 'unknown option %r' % opt
        print usage
        sys.exit(1)
autoSsh(user_list, cmd_list, host=host, port=port)
```

Discussion

The third-party extension paramiko package lets you easily automate access to all sorts of SSH services, even from non-Unix machines. paramiko even lets you write your own SSH servers in Python. In this recipe, however, we use paramiko on the client side, as a more secure alternative to the similar use of telnetlib shown previously in recipe 15.9 "Performing Remote Logins Using telnetlib."

Production code generally has to be made more robust, but this recipe should be enough to get you started in the right direction. The recipe's autoSsh function first ensures it knows passwords for all the users (asking interactively for the passwords of users it doesn't know about). Then, it loops over all the users, parsing strings such as foo@bar:2222 to mean user foo at host bar, port 2222, and defaulting the host and port values, if necessary.

The loop body relies on two types of objects supplied by paramiko, Transport and Channel. The transport is constructed by giving it the (host, port) pair and then a connection is made with a username and password. (Alternatively, depending on the SSH server, one might connect using a private key, but this recipe uses just a password.) The channel is obtained from the transport, and the recipe then sets a timeout (by default, 6 seconds) to ensure that no long-term *hanging* occurs in case of problems with an SSH server or the network path to it. Finally, an inner loop over all commands sends each command, receives a response (up to a maximum length in bytes, 2000 by default), and prints the command and response.

See Also

paramiko's home page at *http://www.lag.net/~robey/paramiko/*; paramiko requires another third-party extension to Python, the Python Cryptography Toolkit, whose home page is at *http://www.amk.ca/python/code/crypto*; docs on SSH at *http://www.openssh.com/*, *http://www.ucolick.org/~sla/ssh/*, *http://kimmo.suominen.com/docs/ssh/*; Richard Silverman and Daniel J. Barrett, *SSH: The Secure Shell, The Definitive Guide* (O'Reilly); recipe 15.9 "Performing Remote Logins Using telnetlib."

SSH, the Secure Shell

The SSH protocol is secure, powerful, and flexible. No password ever travels on the network in the clear, and the connection stream itself gets encrypted. Besides single commands (as used in this recipe) and entire interactive shell sessions, SSH allows secure copying of files in either direction and secure remote tunneling of X11 GUI sessions and other TCP/IP-based network protocols. Moreover, unlike other secure transport-level protocols such as SSL/TLS, SSH does not require certificates signed by some kind of "central authority". You can learn more about SSH from the OpenSSH's web page at *http://www.openssh.com/*, Steve Allen's pages at *http://www.ucolick.org/~sla/ssh/*, and Kimmon Suominen's tutorial at *http://kimmo.suominen.com/docs/ssh/*—as well as from Richard Silverman and Daniel J. Barrett, *SSH: The Secure Shell, The Definitive Guide* (O'Reilly).

15.11 Authenticating an SSL Client over HTTPS

Credit: Rob Riggs

Problem

You want your Python application to check SSL client authentication, by delegating, over HTTPS, to an Apache server that is running mod_ssl.

Solution

The Apache web server has good support for SSL, and we can write a Python script to exploit that support to authenticate a client. For example:

```
import httplib
CERT_FILE = '/home/robr/mycert'
PKEY_FILE = '/home/robr/mycert'
HOSTNAME = 'localhost'
conn = httplib.HTTPSConnection(HOSTNAME,
        key_file = PKEY_FILE, cert_file = CERT_FILE)
conn.putrequest('GET', '/ssltest/')
conn.endheaders( )
response = conn.getresponse( )
print response.read( )
```

Discussion

The Solution code assumes that *mycert* is a certificate file formatted by PEM (Privacy-enhanced Electronic Mail), which includes both the public certificate and the private key. You can keep the public and private keys in separate files: you need to pass the names of the files in question as the values for the key_file and cert_file arguments of HTTPSConnection.

To safely perform SSL authentication, you will generally set up your own certification authority (CA). You do not want to enable a third-party organization to hand out all the "keys" to the locks that you put up to protect your security.

The Apache server installation that you use for this authentication needs to be configured to require SSL client authentication with the appropriate CA. My *httpd.conf* file contains the stanza:

```
SSLCACertificatePath /etc/httpd/conf/ssl.crt
SSLCACertificateFile /etc/httpd/conf/ssl.crt/myCA.crt
SSLVerifyClient      require
SSLVerifyDepth       2
SSLRequireSSL
```

The configuration of an Apache server cannot refer to more than one SSLCACertificateFile. You can put more than one CA certificate in that file, but doing so grants authentication to any client who has a certificate from any *one* of the certificate authorities you accept, which is unlikely to be what you want. Therefore, this recipe is fully applicable only when you can reasonably set up an Apache server to accept your own CA as the sole recognized one. In exchange for this modest inconvenience, however, you do get a handy and robust approach to client authentication between web-enabled applications, particularly good for SOAP or XML-RPC implementations, or custom applications that communicate via HTTP/HTTPS.

See Also

Descriptions of SSL and its use with Apache can be found at *http://httpd.apache.org/docs-2.0/ssl/ssl_howto.html* and *http://www.pseudonym.org/ssl/ssl_cook.html*. The httplib module is part of the Python Standard Library and is documented in a chapter of the *Library Reference* portion of Python's online documentation.

## CHAPTER 16

Programs About Programs

16.0 Introduction

Credit: Paul F. Dubois, Ph.D., Program for Climate Model Diagnosis and Intercomparison, Lawrence Livermore National Laboratory

This chapter was originally meant to cover mainly topics such as lexing, parsing, and code generation—the classic issues of *programs that are about programs*. It turns out, however, that Pythonistas did not post many recipes about such tasks, focusing more on highly Python-specific topics such as program introspection, dynamic importing, and generation of functions by closure. Many of those recipes, we decided, were more properly located in various other chapters—on shortcuts, debugging, object oriented programming, algorithms, metaprogramming, and specific areas such as the handling of text, files, and persistence Therefore, you will find those topics covered in other chapters. In this chapter, we included only those recipes that are still best described as *programs about programs*. Of these, probably the most important one is that about *currying*, the creation of new functions by predetermining some arguments of other functions.

This arrangement doesn't mean that the classic issues aren't important! Python has extensive facilities related to lexing and parsing, as well as a large number of user-contributed modules related to parsing standard languages, which reduces the need for doing your own programming. If Pythonistas are not using these tools, then, in this one area, they are doing more work than they need to. Lexing and parsing are among the most common of programming tasks, and as a result, both are the subject of much theory and much prior development. Therefore, in these areas more than most, you will often profit if you take the time to search for solutions before resorting to writing your own. This Introduction contains a general guide to solving some common problems in these categories to encourage reusing the wide base of excellent, solid code and theory in these fields.

Lexing

Lexing is the process of dividing an input stream into meaningful units, known as *tokens*, which are then processed. Lexing occurs in tasks such as data processing and in tools for inspecting and modifying text.

The regular expression facilities in Python are extensive and highly evolved, so your first consideration for a lexing task is often to determine whether it can be formulated using regular expressions. Also, see the next section about parsers for common languages and how to lex those languages.

The Python Standard Library tokenize module splits an input stream into Python-language tokens. Since Python's tokenization rules are similar to those of many other languages, this module may often be suitable for other tasks, perhaps with a modest amount of pre- and/or post-processing around tokenize's own operations. For more complex tokenization tasks, Plex, *http://nz.cosc.canterbury.ac.nz/~greg/python/Plex/*, can ease your efforts considerably.

At the other end of the lexing complexity spectrum, the built-in string method split can also be used for many simple cases. For example, consider a file consisting of colon-separated text fields, with one record per line. You can read a line from the file as follows:

```
fields = line.split(':')
```

This produces a list of the fields. At this point, if you want to eliminate spurious whitespace at the beginning and ends of the fields, you can remove it:

```
fields = [f.strip() for f in fields]
```

For example:

```
>>> x = "abc :def:ghi    : klm\n"
>>> fields = x.split(':')
>>> print fields
['abc ', 'def', 'ghi    ', ' klm\n']
>>> print [f.strip() for f in fields]
['abc', 'def', 'ghi', 'klm']
```

Do not elaborate on this example: do not try to over-enrich simple code to perform lexing and parsing tasks which are in fact quite hard to perform with generality, solidity, and good performance, and for which much excellent, reusable code exists. For parsing typical comma-separated values files, or files using other delimiters, study the standard Python library module csv. The ScientificPython package, *http://starship.python.net/~hinsen/ScientificPython/*, includes a module for reading and writing with Fortran-like formats, and other such precious I/O modules, in the Scientific.IO sub-package.

A common "gotcha" for beginners is that, while lexing and other text-parsing techniques can be used to read numerical data from a file, at the end of this stage, the entries are text strings, not numbers. The `int` and `float` built-in functions are frequently needed here, to turn each field from a string into a number:

```
>>> x = "1.2, 2.3, 4, 5.6"
>>> print [float(y.strip()) for y in x.split(',')]
[1.2, 2.2999999999999998, 4.0, 5.5999999999999996]
```

Parsing

Parsing refers to discovering semantic meaning from a series of tokens according to the rules of a grammar. Parsing tasks are quite ubiquitous. Programming tools may attempt to discover information about program texts or to modify such texts to fit a task. (Python's introspection capabilities come into play here, as we will discuss later.) *Little languages* is the generic name given to application-specific languages that serve as human-readable forms of computer input. Such languages can vary from simple lists of commands and arguments to full-blown languages.

The grammar in the previous lexing example was implicit: the data you need is organized as one line per record with the fields separated by a special character. The "parser" in that case was supplied by the programmer reading the lines from the file and applying the simple `split` method to obtain the information. This sort of input file can easily grow, leading to requests for a more elaborate form. For example, users may wish to use comments, blank lines, conditional statements, or alternate forms. While most such parsing can be handled with simple logic, at some point, it becomes so complicated that it is much more reliable to use a real grammar.

There is no hard-and-fast way to decide which part of the job is a lexing task and which belongs to the grammar. For example, comments can often be discarded in the lexing, but doing so is not wise in a program-transformation tool that must produce output containing the original comments.

Your strategy for parsing tasks can include:

- Using a parser for that language from the Python Standard Library.
- Using a parser from the user community. You can often find one by visiting the *Vaults of Parnassus* site, *http://www.vex.net/parnassus/*, or by searching the Python site, *http://www.python.org*.
- Generating a parser using a parser generator.
- Using Python itself as your input language.

A combination of approaches is often fruitful. For example, a simple parser can turn input into Python-language statements, which Python then executes in concert with a supporting package that you supply.

A number of parsers for specific languages exist in the standard library, and more are out there on the Web, supplied by the user community. In particular, the standard library includes parsing packages for XML, HTML, SGML, command-line arguments, configuration files, and for Python itself. For the now-ubiquitous task of parsing XML specifically, this cookbook includes a chapter—Chapter 14, specifically dedicated to XML.

You do not have to parse C to connect C routines to Python. Use SWIG (*http://www.swig.org*). Likewise, you do not need a Fortran parser to connect Fortran and Python. See the Numerical Python web page at *http://www.pfdubois.com/numpy/* for further information. Again, this cookbook includes a chapter, Chapter 17, *Extending and Embedding*, which is dedicated to these kind of tasks.

PLY, SPARK, and Other Python Parser Generators

PLY and SPARK are two rich, solid, and mature Python-based parser generators. That is, they take as their input some statements that describe the grammar to be parsed and generate the parser for you. To make a useful tool, you must add the semantic actions to be taken when a certain construct in the grammar is recognized.

PLY (*http://systems.cs.uchicago.edu/ply*) is a Python implementation of the popular Unix tool yacc. SPARK (*http://pages.cpcc.ucalgary-ca/~aycoch/spart/content.html*) parses a more general set of grammars than yacc. Both tools use Python introspection, including the idea of placing grammar rules in functions' docstrings.

Parser generators are one of the many application areas that may have even too many excellent tools, so that you may end up frustrated by having to pick just one. Besides SPARK and PLY, other Python tools in this field include TPG (Toy Parser Generator), DParser, PyParsing, kwParsing (or kyParsing), PyLR, Yapps, PyGgy, mx.Text-Tools and its SimpleParse frontend—too many to provide more than a bare mention of each, so, happy googling!

The chief problem in using any of these tools is that you need to educate yourself about grammars and learn to write them. A novice without any computer science background will encounter some difficulty except with very simple grammars. A lot of literature is available to teach you how to use yacc, and most of this knowledge will help you use SPARK and most of the others just as well.

If you are interested in this area, the penultimate reference is Alfred V. Aho, Ravi Sethi, and Jeffrey D. Ullman, *Compilers* (Addison-Wesley), affectionately known as "the Dragon Book" to generations of computer science majors.[*]

Using Python Itself as a Little Language

Python itself can be used to create many application-specific languages. By writing suitable classes, you can rapidly create a program that is easy to get running, yet is extensible later. Suppose I want a language to describe graphs. Nodes have names,

---

[*] I'd even call this book the ultimate reference, were it not for the fact that Donald Knuth continues to promise that the fifth volume (current ETA, the year 2010) of his epoch-making *The Art of Computer Programming* will be about this very subject.

and edges connect the nodes. I want a way to input such graphs, so that after reading the input I will have the data structures in Python that I need for any further processing. So, for example:

```
nodes = { }
def getnode(name):
    " Return the node with the given name, creating it if necessary. "
    if name in nodes:
        node = nodes[name]
    else:
        node = nodes[name] = node(name)
    return node
class node(object):
    " A node has a name and a list of edges emanating from it. "
    def __init__(self, name):
        self.name = name
        self.edgelist = [ ]
class edge(object):
    " An edge connects two nodes. "
    def __init__(self, name1, name2):
        self.nodes = getnode(name1), getnode(name2)
        for n in self.nodes:
            n.edgelist.append(self)
    def __repr__(self):
        return self.nodes[0].name + self.nodes[1].name
```

Using just these simple statements, I can now parse a list of edges that describe a graph, and afterwards, I will now have data structures that contain all my information. Here, I enter a graph with four edges and print the list of edges emanating from node 'A':

```
>>> edge('A', 'B')
>>> edge('B', 'C')
>>> edge('C', 'D')
>>> edge('C', 'A')
>>> print getnode('A').edgelist
[AB, CA]
```

Suppose that I now want a weighted graph. I could easily add a `weight=1.0` default argument to the edge constructor, and the old input would still work. Also, I could easily add error-checking logic to ensure that edge lists have no duplicates. Furthermore, I already have my node class and can start adding logic to it for any needed processing purposes, be it directly or by subclassing. I can easily turn the entries in the dictionary nodes into similarly named variables that are bound to the node objects. After adding a few more classes corresponding to other input I need, I am well on my way.

The advantage to this approach is clear. For example, the following is already handled correctly:

```
edge('A', 'B')
if 'X' in nodes:
```

```
        edge('X', 'A')
    def triangle(n1, n2, n3):
        edge(n1, n2)
        edge(n2, n3)
        edge(n3, n1)
    triangle('A','W','K')
    execfile('mygraph.txt')        # Read graph from a datafile
```

So I already have syntactic sugar, user-defined language extensions, and input from other files. The definitions usually go into a module, and the user simply import them. Had I written my own language, instead of reusing Python in this *little language* role, such accomplishments might be months away.

Introspection

Python programs have the ability to examine themselves; this set of facilities comes under the general title of introspection. For example, a Python function object knows a lot about itself, including the names of its arguments, and the docstring that was given when it was defined:

```
>>> def f(a, b):
        " Return the difference of a and b "
        return a-b
...
>>> dir(f)
['__call__', '__class__', '__delattr__', '__dict__', '__doc__',
'__get__', '__getattribute__', '__hash__', '__init__', '__module__',
'__name__', '__new__', '__reduce__', '__reduce_ex__', '__repr__',
'__setattr__', '__str__', 'func_closure', 'func_code', 'func_defaults',
'func_dict', 'func_doc', 'func_globals', 'func_name']
>>> f.func_name
'f'
>>> f.func_doc
'Return the difference of a and b'
>>> f.func_code
<code object f at 0175DDF0, file "<pyshell#18>", line 1>
>>> dir (f.func_code)
['__class__', '__cmp__', '__delattr__', '__doc__',
'__getattribute__', '__hash__', '__init__', '__new__', '__reduce__',
'__reduce_ex__', '__repr__', '__setattr__', '__str__', 'co_argcount',
'co_cellvars', 'co_code', 'co_consts', 'co_filename', 'co_firstlineno',
'co_flags', 'co_freevars', 'co_lnotab', 'co_name', 'co_names',
'co_nlocals', 'co_stacksize', 'co_varnames']
>>> f.func_code.co_names
('a', 'b')
```

SPARK and PLY make an interesting use of introspection. The grammar is entered as docstrings in the routines that take the semantic actions when those grammar constructs are recognized. (Hey, don't turn your head all the way around like that! Introspection has its limits.)

Introspection is very popular in the Python community, and you will find many examples of it in recipes in this book, both in this chapter and elsewhere. Even in this field, though, *always* remember the possibility of reuse! Standard library module inspect has a lot of solid, reusable inspection-related code. It's all pure Python code, and you can (and should) study the *inspect.py* source file in your Python library to see what "raw" facilities underlie inspect's elegant high-level functions—indeed, this suggestion generalizes: studying the standard library's sources is among the best things you can do to increment your Python knowledge and skill. But *reusing* the standard library's wealth of modules and packages is still best: any code you don't write is code you don't have to maintain, and solid, heavily tested code such as the code that you find in the standard library is very likely to have far fewer bugs than any newly developed code you might write yourself.

Python is the most powerful language that you can still read. The kinds of tasks discussed in this chapter help to show just how versatile and powerful it really is.

16.1 Verifying Whether a String Represents a Valid Number

Credit: Gyro Funch, Rogier Steehouder

Problem

You need to check whether a string read from a file or obtained from user input has a valid numeric format.

Solution

The simplest and most Pythonic approach is to "try and see":

```
def is_a_number(s):
    try: float(s)
    except ValueError: return False
    else: return True
```

Discussion

If you insist, you can also perform this task with a regular expression:

```
import re
num_re = re.compile(r'^[-+]?([0-9]+\.?[0-9]*|\.[0-9]+)([eE][-+]?[0-9]+)?$')
def is_a_number(s):
    return bool(num_re.match(s))
```

Having a regular expression to start from may be best if you need to be tolerant of certain specific variations, or to pick up numeric substrings from the middle of larger strings. But for the specific task posed as this recipe's Problem, it's simplest and best to "let Python do it!"

See Also

Documentation for the re module and the float built-in module in the *Library Reference* and *Python in a Nutshell*.

16.2   Importing a Dynamically Generated Module

Credit: Anders Hammarquist

Problem

You need to wrap code in either compiled or source form in a module, possibly adding it to sys.modules as well.

Solution

We build a new module object, optionally add it to sys.modules, and populate it with an exec statement:

```
import new
def importCode(code, name, add_to_sys_modules=False):
    """ code can be any object containing code: a string, a file object, or
        a compiled code object.  Returns a new module object initialized
        by dynamically importing the given code, and optionally adds it
        to sys.modules under the given name.
    """
    module = new.module(name)
    if add_to_sys_modules:
        import sys
        sys.modules[name] = module
    exec code in module.__dict__
    return module
```

Discussion

This recipe lets you import a module from code that is dynamically generated or obtained. My original intent for it was to import a module stored in a database, but it will work for modules from any source. Thanks to the flexibility of the exec statement, the importCode function can accept code in many forms: a string of source (which gets implicitly compiled on the fly), a file object (ditto), or a previously compiled code object.

The addition of the newly generated module to sys.modules is optional. You shouldn't normally do so for such dynamically obtained code, but there are exceptions—specifically, when import statements for the module's name are later executed, and it's important that they retrieve from sys.modules your dynamically generated module. If you want the sys.modules addition, it's best to perform it before the module's code body executes, just as normal import statements do, in case the code body relies on that normal behavior (which it usually doesn't, but it can't hurt to be prepared).

Note that the normal Python statement:

```
import foo
```

in simple cases (where no hooks, built-in modules, imports from zip files, etc., come into play!) is essentially equivalent to:

```
if 'foo' in sys.modules:
    foo = sys.modules['foo']
else:
    foofile = open("/path/to/foo.py")        # for some suitable /path/to/...
    foo = importCode(foofile, "foo", 1)
```

A toy example of using this recipe:

```
code = """
def testFunc():
    print "spam!"
class testClass(object):
    def testMethod(self):
        print "eggs!"
"""
m = importCode(code, "test")
m.testFunc()
o = m.testClass()
o.testMethod()
```

See Also

Sections on the import and exec statements in the *Language Reference*; documentation on the modules attribute of the sys standard library module and the new module in the *Library Reference*; *Python in a Nutshell* sections about both the language and library aspects.

16.3   Importing from a Module Whose Name Is Determined at Runtime

Credit: Jürgen Hermann

Problem

You need to import a name from a module, just as from module import name would do, but module and name are runtime-computed expressions. This need often arises, for example, when you want to support user-written plug-ins.

Solution

The __import__ built-in function lets you perform this task:

```
def importName(modulename, name):
    """ Import a named object from a module in the context of this function.
    """
    try:
        module = __import__(modulename, globals(), locals(), [name])
    except ImportError:
        return None
    return getattr(module, name)
```

Discussion

This recipe's function lets you perform the equivalent of from module import name, in which either or both module and name are dynamic values (i.e., expressions or variables) rather than constant strings. For example, this functionality can be used to implement a plug-in mechanism to extend an application with external modules that adhere to a common interface.

Some programmers' instinctive reaction to this task would be to use exec, but this instinct would be a pretty bad one. The exec statement is *too powerful*, and therefore is a last-ditch measure, to be used only when nothing else is available (which is almost never). It's just too easy to have horrid bugs and/or security weaknesses where exec is used. In almost all cases, there are better ways. This recipe shows one such way for an important problem.

For example, suppose you have, in a file named *MyApp/extensions/spam.py*, the following code:

```
class Handler(object):
    def handleSomething(self):
        print "spam!"
```

and, in a file named MyApp/extensions/eggs.py:

```
class Handler(object):
    def handleSomething(self):
        print "eggs!"
```

We must also suppose that the MyApp directory is in a directory on sys.path, and both it and the extensions subdirectory are identified as Python *packages* (meaning that each of them must contain a file, possibly empty, named *__init__.py*). Then, we can get and call both implementations with the following code:

```
for extname in 'spam', 'eggs':
    HandlerClass = importName("MyApp.extensions." + extname, "Handler")
    handler = HandlerClass()
    handler.handleSomething()
```

It's possible to remove the constraints about sys.path and *__init__.py*, and dynamically import from anywhere, with the imp standard module. However, imp is substantially harder to use than the __import__ built-in function, and you can generally arrange things to avoid imp's greater generality and difficulty.

The import pattern implemented by this recipe is used in MoinMoin (*http://moin.sourceforge.net/*) to load extensions implementing variations of a common interface, such as action, macro, and formatter.

See Also

Documentation on the __import__ and getattr built-ins in the *Library Reference* and *Python in a Nutshell*; MoinMoin is available at *http://moin.sourceforge.net*.

16.4 Associating Parameters with a Function (Currying)

Credit: Scott David Daniels, Nick Perkins, Alex Martelli, Ben Wolfson, Alex Naanou, David Abrahams, Tracy Ruggles

Problem

You need to wrap a function (or other callable) to get another callable with fewer formal arguments, keeping given values fixed for the other arguments (i.e., you need to *curry* a callable to make another).

Solution

Curry is not just a delightful spice used in Asian cuisine—it's also an important programming technique in Python and other languages:

```
def curry(f, *a, **kw):
    def curried(*more_a, **more_kw):
        return f(*(a+more_a), **dict(kw, **more_kw))
    return curried
```

Discussion

Popular in functional programming, *currying* is a way to bind some of a function's arguments and wait for the rest of them to show up later. Currying is named in honor of Haskell Curry, a mathematician who laid some of the cornerstones in the theory of formal systems and processes. Some pedants (and it must be grudgingly admitted they have a point) claim that the technique shown in this recipe should be called *partial application*, and that "currying" is something else. But whether they're right or wrong, in a book whose title claims it's a *cookbook*, the use of *curry* in a title was simply irresistible. Besides, the use of the verb *to curry* that this recipe supports *is* the most popular one among programmers.

The curry function defined in this recipe is invoked with a callable and some or all of the arguments to the callable. (Some people like to refer to functions that accept function objects as arguments, and return new function objects as results, as *higher-order* functions.) The curry function returns a closure curried that takes subsequent parameters as arguments and calls the original with all of those parameters. For example:

```
double = curry(operator.mul, 2)
triple = curry(operator.mul, 3)
```

To implement currying, the choice is among closures, classes with callable instances, and lambda forms. Closures are simplest and fastest, so that's what we use in this recipe.

A typical use of curry is to construct callback functions for GUI operations. When the operation does not merit a new function name, curry can be useful in creating these little functions. For example, this can be the case with commands for Tkinter buttons:

```
self.button = Button(frame, text='A', command=curry(transcript.append, 'A'))
```

Recipe 11.2 "Avoiding lambda in Writing Callback Functions" shows a specialized subset of "curry" functionality intended to produce callables that require no arguments, which are often needed for such GUI-callback usage. However, this recipe's curry function is vastly more flexible, without any substantial extra cost in either complexity or performance.

Currying can also be used interactively to make versions of your functions with debugging-appropriate defaults, or initial parameters filled in for your current case. For example, database debugging work might begin by setting:

```
Connect = curry(ODBC.Connect, dsn='MyDataSet')
```

Another example of the use of curry in debugging is to wrap methods:

```
def report(originalFunction, name, *args, **kw):
    print "%s(%s)"%(name, ', '.join(map(repr, args) +
                                    [k+'='+repr(kw[k]) for k in kw])
    result = originalFunction(*args, **kw)
    if result: print name, '==>', result
    return result
class Sink(object):
    def write(self, text): pass
dest = Sink()
dest.write = curry(report, dest.write, 'write')
print >>dest, 'this', 'is', 1, 'test'
```

If you are creating a function for regular use, the def fun form of function definition is more readable and more easily extended. As you can see from the implementation, no magic happens to specialize the function with the provided parameters. curry should be used when you feel the code is clearer with its use than without. Typically, this use will emphasize that you are only providing some pre-fixed parameters to a commonly used function, not providing any separate processing.

Currying also works well in creating a "lightweight subclass". You can curry the constructor of a class to give the illusion of a subclass:

```
BlueWindow = curry(Window, background="blue")
```

BlueWindow.__class__ is still Window, not a subclass, but if you're changing only default parameters, not behavior, currying is arguably more appropriate than subclassing anyway. And you can still pass additional parameters to the curried constructor.

Two decisions must be made when coding a curry implementation, since both positional and keyword arguments can come in two "waves"—some at currying time, some more at call time. The two decisions are: do the call-time positional arguments go before or after the currying-time ones? do the call-time keyword arguments override currying-time ones, or vice versa? If you study this recipe's Solution, you can see I've made these decisions in a specific way (the one that is most generally useful): call-time positional arguments *after* currying-time ones, call-time keyword arguments *overriding* currying-time ones. In some circles, this is referred to as *left-left partial application*. It's trivial to code other variations, such as *right-left partial application*:

```
def rcurry(f, *a, **kw):
    def curried(*more_a, **more_kw):
        return f(*(more_a+a), **dict(kw, **more_kw))
    return curried
```

As you can see, despite the grandiose-sounding terms, this is just a matter of concatenating more_a+a rather than the reverse; and similarly, for keyword arguments, you just need to call dict(more_kw, **kw) if you want currying-time keyword arguments to override call-time ones rather than vice versa.

If you wish, you could have the curried function carry a copy of the original function's docstring, or even (easy in Python 2.4, but feasible, with a call to new.function, even in 2.3—see the sidebar in recipe 20.1 "Getting Fresh Default Values at Each Function Call") a name that is somehow derived from the original function. However, I have chosen not to do so because the original name, and argument descriptions in the docstring, are probably not *appropriate for* the curried version. The task of constructing and documenting the actual signature of the curried version is also feasible (with a liberal application of the helper functions from standard library module inspect), but it's so disproportionate an effort, compared to curry's delightfully simple four lines of code (!), that I resolutely refuse to undertake it.

A special case, which may be worth keeping in mind, is when the callable you want to curry is a Python function (*not* a bound method, a C-coded function, a callable class instance, etc.), *and* all you need to curry is the *first* parameter. In this case, the function object's __get__ special method may be all you need. It takes an arbitrary argument and returns a bound-method object with the first parameter bound to that argument. For example:

```
>>> def f(adj, noun='world'):
...     return 'Goodbye, %s %s!' % (adj, noun)
```

```
...
>>> cf = f.__get__('cruel')
>>> print cf()
Goodbye, cruel world!
>>> cf
<bound method ?.f of 'cruel'>
>>> type(cf)
<type 'instancemethod'>
>>> cf.im_func
<function f at 0x402dba04>
>>> cf.im_self
'cruel'
```

See Also

Recipe 11.2 "Avoiding lambda in Writing Callback Functions" shows a specialized subset of the curry functionality that is specifically intended for GUI callbacks; docs for the inspect module and the dict built-in type in the *Library Reference* and *Python in a Nutshell*.

16.5 Composing Functions

Credit: Scott David Daniels

Problem

You need to construct a new function by composing existing functions (i.e., each call of the new function must call one existing function on its arguments, then another on the result of the first one).

Solution

Composition is a fundamental operation between functions and yields a new function as a result. The new function must call one existing function on its arguments, then another on the result of the first one. For example, a function that, given a string, returns a copy that is lowercase and does not have leading and trailing blanks, is the composition of the existing string.lower and string.strip functions. (In this case, it does not matter in which order the two existing functions are applied, but generally, it could be important.)

A *closure* (a nested function returned from another function) is often the best Pythonic approach to constructing new functions:

```
def compose(f, g, *args_for_f, **kwargs_for_f):
    ''' compose functions.  compose(f, g, x)(y) = f(g(y), x)) '''
    def fg(*args_for_g, **kwargs_for_g):
        return f(g(*args_for_g, **kwargs_for_g), *args_for_f, **kwargs_for_f)
    return fg
def mcompose(f, g, *args_for_f, **kwargs_for_f):
    ''' compose functions.  mcompose(f, g, x)(y) = f(*g(y), x)) '''
```

```
def fg(*args_for_g, **kwargs_for_g):
    mid = g(*args_for_g, **kwargs_for_g)
    if not isinstance(mid, tuple):
        mid = (mid,)
    return f(*(mid+args_for_f), **kwargs_for_f)
return fg
```

Discussion

The closures in this recipe show two styles of function composition. I separated mcompose and compose because I think of the two possible forms of function composition as being quite different, in mathematical terms. In practical terms, the difference shows only when the second function being composed, g, returns a tuple. The closure returned by compose passes the result of g as f's first argument anyway, while the closure returned by mcompose treats it as a tuple of arguments to pass along. Any extra arguments provided to either compose or mcompose are treated as extra arguments for f (there is no standard functional behavior to follow here):

```
compose(f, g, x)(y) = f(g(y), x)
mcompose(f, g, x)(y) = f(*g(y), x)
```

As in currying (see recipe 16.4 "Associating Parameters with a Function (Currying)"), this recipe's functions are for constructing functions from other functions. Your goal in so doing should be clarity, since no efficiency is gained by using these functional forms.

Here's a quick example for interactive use:

```
parts = compose(' '.join, dir)
```

When called on a module object, the callable we just bound to name parts gives you an easy-to-view string that lists the module's contents.

See Also

Recipe 16.4 "Associating Parameters with a Function (Currying)" for an example of "curry"ing (i.e., associating parameters with partially evaluated functions).

16.6 Colorizing Python Source Using the Built-in Tokenizer

Credit: Jürgen Hermann, Mike Brown

Problem

You need to convert Python source code into HTML markup, rendering comments, keywords, operators, and numeric and string literals in different colors.

Solution

tokenize.generate_tokens does most of the work. We just need to loop over all tokens it finds, to output them with appropriate colorization:

```python
""" MoinMoin - Python Source Parser """
import cgi, sys, cStringIO
import keyword, token, tokenize
# Python Source Parser (does highlighting into HTML)
_KEYWORD = token.NT_OFFSET + 1
_TEXT    = token.NT_OFFSET + 2
_colors = {
    token.NUMBER:       '#0080C0',
    token.OP:           '#0000C0',
    token.STRING:       '#004080',
    tokenize.COMMENT:   '#008000',
    token.NAME:         '#000000',
    token.ERRORTOKEN:   '#FF8080',
    _KEYWORD:           '#C00000',
    _TEXT:              '#000000',
}
class Parser(object):
    """ Send colorized Python source HTML to output file (normally stdout).
    """
    def __init__(self, raw, out=sys.stdout):
        """ Store the source text. """
        self.raw = raw.expandtabs().strip()
        self.out = out
    def format(self):
        """ Parse and send the colorized source to output. """
        # Store line offsets in self.lines
        self.lines = [0, 0]
        pos = 0
        while True:
            pos = self.raw.find('\n', pos) + 1
            if not pos: break
            self.lines.append(pos)
        self.lines.append(len(self.raw))
        # Parse the source and write it
        self.pos = 0
        text = cStringIO.StringIO(self.raw)
        self.out.write('<pre><font face="Lucida, Courier New">')
        try:
            for token in tokenize.generate_tokens(text.readline):
                # unpack the components of each token
                toktype, toktext, (srow, scol), (erow, ecol), line = token
                if False:  # You may enable this for debugging purposes only
                    print "type", toktype, token.tok_name[toktype],
                    print "text", toktext,
                    print "start", srow,scol, "end", erow,ecol, "<br>"
                # Calculate new positions
                oldpos = self.pos
```

```
                        newpos = self.lines[srow] + scol
                        self.pos = newpos + len(toktext)
                        # Handle newlines
                        if toktype in (token.NEWLINE, tokenize.NL):
                            self.out.write('\n')
                            continue
                        # Send the original whitespace, if needed
                        if newpos > oldpos:
                            self.out.write(self.raw[oldpos:newpos])
                        # Skip indenting tokens, since they're whitespace-only
                        if toktype in (token.INDENT, token.DEDENT):
                            self.pos = newpos
                            continue
                        # Map token type to a color group
                        if token.LPAR <= toktype <= token.OP:
                            toktype = token.OP
                        elif toktype == token.NAME and keyword.iskeyword(toktext):
                            toktype = _KEYWORD
                        color = _colors.get(toktype, _colors[_TEXT])
                        style = ''
                        if toktype == token.ERRORTOKEN:
                            style = ' style="border: solid 1.5pt #FF0000;"'
                        # Send text
                        self.out.write('<font color="%s"%s>' % (color, style))
                        self.out.write(cgi.escape(toktext))
                        self.out.write('</font>')
            except tokenize.TokenError, ex:
                msg = ex[0]
                line = ex[1][0]
                self.out.write("<h3>ERROR: %s</h3>%s\n" % (
                    msg, self.raw[self.lines[line]:]))
            self.out.write('</font></pre>')
    if __name__ == "__main__":
        print "Formatting..."
        # Open own source
        source = open('python.py').read()
        # Write colorized version to "python.html"
        Parser(source, open('python.html', 'wt')).format()
        # Load HTML page into browser
        import webbrowser
        webbrowser.open("python.html")
```

Discussion

This code is part of MoinMoin (see *http://moin.sourceforge.net/*) and shows how to use the built-in keyword, token, and tokenize modules to scan Python source code and re-emit it with appropriate color markup but no changes to its original formatting ("no changes" is the hard part!).

The Parser class' constructor saves the multiline string that is the Python source to colorize, and the file object, which is open for writing, where you want to output the colorized results. Then, the format method prepares a self.lines list that holds the offset (i.e., the index into the source string, self.raw) of each line's start.

format then loops over the result of generator tokenize.tokenize, unpacking each token tuple into items specifying the token type and starting and ending positions in the source (each expressed as line number and offset within the line). The body of the loop reconstructs the exact position within the original source code string self.raw, so it can emit exactly the same whitespace that was present in the original source. It then picks a color code from the _colors dictionary (which uses HTML color coding), with help from the keyword standard module to determine whether a NAME token is actually a Python keyword (to be output in a different color than that used for ordinary identifiers).

The test code at the bottom of the module formats the module itself and launches a browser with the result, using the standard Python library module webbrowser to enable you to see and enjoy the result in your favorite browser.

If you put this recipe's code into a module, you can then import the module and reuse its functionality in CGI scripts (using the PATH_TRANSLATED CGI environment variable to know what file to colorize), command-line tools (taking filenames as arguments), filters that colorize anything they get from standard input, and so on. See *http://skew.org/~mike/colorize.py* for versions that support several of these various possibilities.

With small changes, it's also easy to turn this recipe into an Apache handler, so your Apache web site can serve colorized *.py* files. Specifically, if you set up this script as a handler in Apache, then the file is served up as colorized HTML whenever a visitor to the site requests a *.py* file.

For the purpose of using this recipe as an Apache handler, you need to save the script as *colorize.cgi* (not *.py*, lest it confuses Apache), and add, to your *.htaccess* or *httpd.conf* Apache configuration files, the following lines:

```
AddHandler application/x-python .py
Action application/x-python /full/virtual/path/to/colorize.cgi
```

Also, make sure you have the Action module enabled in your *httpd.conf* Apache configuration file.

See Also

Documentation for the webbrowser, token, tokenize, and keyword modules in the *Library Reference* and *Python in a Nutshell*; the colorizer is available at *http://purl.net/wiki/python/MoinMoinColorizer*, as part of MoinMoin (*http://moin.sourceforge.net*), and, in a somewhat different variant, also at *http://skew.org/~mike/colorize.py*; the Apache web server is available and documented at *http://httpd.apache.org*.

16.7 Merging and Splitting Tokens

Credit: Peter Cogolo

Problem

You need to tokenize an input language whose tokens are almost the same as Python's, with a few exceptions that need token merging and splitting.

Solution

Standard library module tokenize is very handy; we need to wrap it with a generator to do the post-processing for a little splitting and merging of tokens. The merging requires the ability to "peek ahead" in an iterator. We can get that ability by wrapping any iterator into a small dedicated iterator class:

```
class peek_ahead(object):
    sentinel = object()
    def __init__(self, it):
        self._nit = iter(it).next
        self.preview = None
        self._step()
    def __iter__(self):
        return self
    def next(self):
        result = self._step()
        if result is self.sentinel: raise StopIteration
        else: return result
    def _step(self):
        result = self.preview
        try: self.preview = self._nit()
        except StopIteration: self.preview = self.sentinel
        return result
```

Armed with this tool, we can easily split and merge tokens. Say, for example, by the rules of the language we're lexing, that we must consider each of ':=' and ':+' to be a single token, but a floating-point token that is a '.' with digits on both sides, such as '31.17', must be given as a sequence of three tokens, '31', '.', '17' in this case. Here's how (using Python 2.4 code with comments on how to change it if you're stuck with version 2.3):

```
import tokenize, cStringIO
# in 2.3, also do 'from sets import Set as set'
mergers = {':' : set('=+'), }
def tokens_of(x):
    it = peek_ahead(toktuple[1] for toktuple in
        tokenize.generate_tokens(cStringIO.StringIO(x).readline)
        )
    # in 2.3, you need to add brackets [ ] around the arg to peek_ahead
    for tok in it:
        if it.preview in mergers.get(tok, ()):
            # merge with next token, as required
```

```
                yield tok+it.next( )
        elif tok[:1].isdigit( ) and '.' in tok:
            # split if digits on BOTH sides of the '.'
            before, after = tok.split('.', 1)
            if after:
                # both sides -> yield as 3 separate tokens
                yield before
                yield '.'
                yield after
            else:
                # nope -> yield as one token
                yield tok
        else:
            # not a merge or split case, just yield the token
            yield tok
```

Discussion

Here's an example of use of this recipe's code:

```
>>> x = 'p{z:=23,  w:+7}: m :+ 23.4'
>>> print ' / '.join(tokens_of(x))
p / { / z / := / 23 / , / w / :+ / 7 / } / : / m / :+ / 23 / . / 4 /
```

In this recipe, I yield tokens only as substrings of the string I'm lexing, rather than the whole tuple yielded by tokenize.generate_tokens, including such items as token position within the overall string (by line and column). If your needs are more sophisticated than mine, you should simply peek_ahead on whole token tuples (while I'm simplifying things by picking up just the substring, item 1, out of each token tuple, by passing to peek_ahead a generator expression), and compute start and end positions appropriately when splitting or merging. For example, if you're merging two adjacent tokens, the overall token has the same start position as the first, and the same end position as the second, of the two tokens you're merging.

The peek_ahead iterator wrapper class can often be useful in many kinds of lexing and parsing tasks, exactly because such tasks are well suited to operating on streams (which are well represented by iterators) but often require a level of peek-ahead and/or push-back ability. You can often get by with just one level; if you need more than one level, consider having your wrapper hold a container of peeked-ahead or pushed-back tokens. Python 2.4's collections.deque container implements a double-ended queue, which is particularly well suited for such tasks. For a more powerful look-ahead iterator wrapper, see recipe 19.18 "Looking Ahead into an Iterator."

See Also

Library Reference and *Python in a Nutshell* sections on the Python Standard Library modules tokenize and cStringIO; recipe 19.18 "Looking Ahead into an Iterator" for a more powerful look-ahead iterator wrapper.

16.8 Checking Whether a String Has Balanced Parentheses

Credit: Peter Cogolo

Problem

You need to check whether a certain string has balanced parentheses, but regular expressions are not powerful enough for this task.

Solution

We want a "true" parser to check a string for balanced parentheses, since parsing theory proves that a regular expression is not sufficient. Choosing one out of the many Python parser generators, we'll use David Beazley's classic but evergreen PLY:

```
# define token names, and a regular expression per each token
tokens = 'OPEN_PAREN', 'CLOS_PAREN', 'OTHR_CHARS'
t_OPEN_PAREN = r'\('
t_CLOS_PAREN = r'\)'
t_OTHR_CHARS = r'[^()]+'          # RE meaning: one or more non-parentheses
def t_error(t): t.skip(1)
# make the lexer (AKA tokenizer)
import lex
lexer = lex.lex(optimize=1)
# define syntax action-functions, with syntax rules in docstrings
def p_balanced(p):
    ''' balanced : balanced OPEN_PAREN balanced CLOS_PAREN balanced
                 | OTHR_CHARS
                 | '''
    if len(p) == 1:
        p[0] = ''
    elif len(p) == 2:
        p[0] = p[1]
    else:
        p[0] = p[1]+p[2]+p[3]+p[4]+p[5]
def p_error(p): pass
# make the parser (AKA scanner)
import yacc
parser = yacc.yacc( )
def has_balanced_parentheses(s):
    if not s: return True
    result = parser.parse(s, lexer=lexer)
    return s == result
```

Discussion

Here's an example of use of this recipe's code:

```
>> s = 'ba(be, bi(bo, bu))'
>> print s, is_balanced(s)
ba(be, bi(bo, bu)) True
```

```
>> s = 'ba(be, bi(bo), bu))'
>> print s, is_balanced(s)
ba(be, bi(bo), bu)) False
```

The first string has balanced parentheses, but the second one has an extra closed parenthesis; therefore, its parentheses are not balanced.

"How do I check a string for balanced parentheses?" is a frequently asked question about regular expressions. Programmers without a computer science background are often surprised to hear that regular expressions just aren't powerful enough for this apparently simple task and a more complete form of grammar is required. (Perl's *regular expressions plus arbitrary embedded expressions* kitchen sink *does* suffice—which just proves they aren't anywhere near "regular" expressions any more!)

For this very simplified parsing problem we're presenting, any real parser is over-kill—just loop over the string's characters, keeping a running count of the number of open and yet unclosed parentheses encountered at this point, and return False if the running count ever goes negative or doesn't go back down to exactly 0 at the end:

```
def has_bal_par(s):
    op = 0
    for c in s:
        if c=='(':
            op += 1
        elif c==')':
            if op == 0:
                return False
            op -= 1
    return op == 0
```

However, using a parser when you need to parse is still a better idea, in general, than hacking up special-purpose code such as this has_bal_par function. As soon as the problem gets extended a bit (and problems invariably *do* grow, in real life, in often unpredictable directions), a real parser can grow gracefully and proportionally with the problem, while ad hoc code often must be thrown away and completely rewritten.

All over the web, you can find oodles of Python packages that are suitable for lexing and parsing tasks. My favorite, out of all of them, is still good old PLY, David Beazley's Python Lexx and Yacc, which reproduces the familiar structure of Unix commands lexx and yacc while taking advantage of Python's extra power when compared to the C language that those Unix commands support.

You can find PLY at *http://www.dabeaz.com/ply/*. PLY is a pure Python package: download it (as a *.tgz* compressed archive file), decompress and unarchive it (all reasonable archiving tools now support this subtask on all platforms), open a command shell, cd into the directory into which you unarchived PLY, and run the usual python setup.py install, with the proper privileges to be able to write into your Python installation's *site-packages* directory (which privileges those are depends on how you installed Python, and on what platform you're running). Briefly, install it just as you would install any other pure Python package.

As you can see from this recipe, PLY is quite easy to use, if you know even just the fundamentals of lexing and parsing. First, you define your grammar's *tokens*—make a tuple or list of all their names (conventionally uppercase) bound to name tokens at your module's top level, define for each token a regular expression bound to name t_ token_name (again at the module's top level), import lex, and call lex.lex to build your tokenizer (lexer). Then, define your grammar's action functions (each of them carries the relevant syntax rule—*production*—in its docstring in BNF, Backus-Naur Form), import yacc, and call yacc.yacc to build your parser (scanner). To parse any string, call the parse method of your parser with the string as an argument.

All the action is in your grammar's action functions, as their name implies. Each action function receives as its single argument p a list of production elements corresponding to the production that has been matched to invoke that function; the action function's job is to put into p[0] whatever you need as "the result" of that syntax rule getting matched. In this recipe, we use as results the very strings we have been matching, so that function is_balanced just needs to check whether the whole string is matched by the parse operation.

When you run this script the first time, you will see a warning about a shift/reduce conflict. Don't worry: as any old hand at yacc can tell you, that's the yacc equivalent of a rite of passage. If you want to understand that message in depth, and maybe (if you're an ambitious person) even do something about it, open with your favorite browser the *doc/ply.html* file in the directory in which you unpacked PLY. That file contains a rather thorough documentation of PLY. As that file suggests, continue by studying the contents of the *examples* directory and then read a textbook about compilers—I suggest Dick Grune and Ceriel J.H. Jacobs, "Parsing Techniques, a Practical Guide." The first edition, at the time of this writing, is freely available for download as a PDF file from *http://www.cs.vu.nl/~dick/PTAPG.html*, and a second edition should be available in technical bookstores around the middle of 2005.

See Also

PLY web page at *http://www.dabeaz.com/ply/*; Dick Grune and Ceriel J.H. Jacobs, "Parsing Techniques, a Practical Guide," a PDF, downloadable from *http://www.cs.vu.nl/~dick/PTAPG.html*.

16.9 Simulating Enumerations in Python

Credit: Will Ware

Problem

You want to define an enumeration in the spirit of C's enum type.

Solution

Python's introspection facilities let you code a class that implements a version of enum, even though Python, as a language, does not support the enum construct:

```python
class EnumException(Exception):
    pass
class Enumeration(object):
    def __init__(self, name, enumList, valuesAreUnique=True):
        self.__doc__ = name
        self.lookup = lookup = { }
        self.reverseLookup = reverseLookup = { }
        i = 0
        for x in enumList:
            if type(x) is tuple:
                try:
                    x, i = x
                except ValueError:
                    raise EnumException, "tuple doesn't have 2 items: %r" % (x,)
            if type(x) is not str:
                raise EnumException, "enum name is not a string: %r" % (x,)
            if type(i) is not int:
                raise EnumException, "enum value is not an integer: %r" % (i,)
            if x in lookup:
                raise EnumException, "enum name is not unique: %r" % (x,)
            if valuesAreUnique and i in reverseLookup:
                raise EnumException, "enum value %r not unique for %r" % (i, x)
            lookup[x] = i
            reverseLookup[i] = x
            i = i + 1
    def __getattr__(self, attr):
        try: return self.lookup[attr]
        except KeyError: raise AttributeError, attr
    def whatis(self, value):
        return self.reverseLookup[value]
```

Discussion

In the C language, enum lets you declare several named constants, typically with unique values (although you can also explicitly arrange for a value to be duplicated under two different names), without necessarily specifying the actual values (except when you want it to). Despite the similarity in naming, C's enum and this recipe's Enumeration class have little to do with the Python built-in enumerate generator, which is used to loop on (index, item) pairs given an iterable—an entirely different issue!

Python has an accepted idiom that's fine for small numbers of constants:

```python
A, B, C, D = range(4)
```

However, this idiom doesn't scale well to large numbers of constants and doesn't allow you to specify values for some constants while leaving others to be determined automatically. This recipe provides for all these niceties and, optionally, also checks that all values (both the ones explicitly specified and the ones automatically determined) are unique. Enum values are attributes of an Enumeration class instance (Volkswagen.BEETLE, Volkswagen.PASSAT, etc.). A further feature, missing in C but really quite useful, is the ability to go from the value to the corresponding name inside the enumeration (the name you get can be somewhat arbitrary for those enumerations in which you don't constrain values to be unique).

This recipe's Enumeration class has an initializer that accepts a string argument to specify the enumeration's name and a sequence argument to specify the names of all values in the enumeration. Each item of the sequence argument can be a string (to specify that the value named is one more than the last value used) or else a tuple with two items (the string that is the value's name, then the value itself, which must be an integer). The code in this recipe relies heavily on strict type checking to determine which case applies, but the recipe's essence would not change by much if the checking was performed in a more lenient way (e.g., with the isinstance built-in function).

Each Enumeration instance has two dict attributes: self.lookup to map names to values and self.reverselookup to map values back to the corresponding names. The special method __getattr__ lets you use names with attribute syntax (e.x is mapped to e.lookup['x']), and the whatis method allows reverse lookups (i.e., find a name given a value) with similar ease.

Here's an example of how you can use this Enumeration class:

```
if __name__ == '__main__':
    import pprint
    Volkswagen = Enumeration("Volkswagen",
        ("JETTA", "RABBIT", "BEETLE", ("THING", 400), "PASSAT", "GOLF",
        ("CABRIO", 700), "EURO_VAN", "CLASSIC_BEETLE", "CLASSIC_VAN"
        ))
    Insect = Enumeration("Insect",
        ("ANT", "APHID", "BEE", "BEETLE", "BUTTERFLY", "MOTH", "HOUSEFLY",
        "WASP", "CICADA", "GRASSHOPPER", "COCKROACH", "DRAGONFLY"
        ))
    def whatkind(value, enum):
        return enum.__doc__ + "." + enum.whatis(value)
    class ThingWithKind(object):
        def __init__(self, kind):
            self.kind = kind
    car = ThingWithKind(Volkswagen.BEETLE)
    print whatkind(car.kind, Volkswagen)
# emits Volkswagen.BEETLE
    bug = ThingWithKind(Insect.BEETLE)
    print whatkind(bug.kind, Insect)
# emits Insect.BEETLE
    print car.__dict__
# emits {'kind': 2}
    print bug.__dict__
# emits {'kind': 3}
```

```
    pprint.pprint(Volkswagen.__dict__)
    pprint.pprint(Insect.__dict__)
# emits dozens of line showing off lookup and reverseLookup dictionaries
```

Note that the attributes of car and bug don't include any of the enum machinery because that machinery is held as class attributes, not as instance attributes. This means you can generate thousands of car and bug objects with reckless abandon, never worrying about wasting time or memory on redundant copies of the enum stuff.

See Also

Recipe 6.2 "Defining Constants" shows how to define constants in Python; documentation on the special method __getattr__ in the *Language Reference* and *Python in a Nutshell*.

16.10 Referring to a List Comprehension While Building It

Credit: Chris Perkins

Problem

You want to refer, from inside a list comprehension, to the same list object you're building. However, the object being built by the list comprehension doesn't have a name while you're building it.

Solution

Internally, the Python interpreter does create a "secret" name that exists only while a list comprehension is being built. In Python 2.3, that name is usually '_[1]' and refers to the bound method append of the list object we're building. We can use this secret name as a back door to refer to the list object as it gets built. For example, say we want to build a copy of a list but without duplicates:

```
>>> L = [1, 2, 2, 3, 3, 3]
>>> [x for x in L if x not in locals()['_[1]'].__self__]
[1, 2, 3]
```

Python 2.4 uses the same name to indicate the list object being built, rather than the bound-method access. In the case of nested list comprehensions, inner ones are named '_[2]', '_[3]', and so on, as nesting goes deeper. Clearly, all of these considerations are best wrapped up into a function:

```
import inspect
import sys
version_23 = sys.version_info < (2, 4)
def this_list():
    import sys
    d = inspect.currentframe(1).f_locals
```

```
nestlevel = 1
while '_[%d]' % nestlevel in d: nestlevel += 1
result = d['_[%d]' % (nestlevel - 1)]
if version_23: return result.__self__
else: return result
```

Using this function, we can make the preceding snippet more readable, as well as making it work properly in Python 2.4 as well as in version 2.3:

```
>>> [x for x in L if x not in this_list()]
[1, 2, 3]
```

Discussion

List comprehensions may look a little like magic, but the bytecode that Python generates for them is in fact quite mundane: create an empty list, give the empty list's bound-method append, a temporary name in the locals dictionary, append items one at a time, and then delete the name. All of this happens, conceptually, between the open square bracket ([) and the close square bracket (]), which enclose the list comprehension.

The temporary name that Python 2.3 assigns to the bound append method is '_[1]' (or '_[2]', etc., for nested list comprehensions). This name is deliberately chosen (to avoid accidental clashes) to *not* be a syntactically valid Python identifier, so we cannot refer to the bound method directly, by name. However, we *can* access it as locals()['_[1]']. Once we have a reference to the bound method object, we just use the bound method's __self__ attribute to get at the list object itself. In Python 2.4, the same name refers directly to the list object, rather than to its bound method, so we skip the last step.

Having a reference to the list object enables us to do all sorts of neat party tricks, such as performing if tests that involve looking at the items that have already been added to the list, or even modifying or deleting them. These capabilities are just what the doctor ordered for finding primes in a "one-liner", for example: for each odd number, we need to test whether it is divisible by any prime number less than or equal to the square root of the number being tested. Since we already have all the smaller primes stored and, with our new parlor trick, have access to them, this test is a breeze and requires no auxiliary storage:

```
import itertools
def primes_less_than(N):
    return [ p for p in itertools.chain([2], xrange(3,N,2))
                if 0 not in itertools.imap(
                    lambda x: p % x, itertools.takewhile(
                        lambda v: v*v <= p, this_list() ))]
```

The list comprehension that's the whole body of this function primes_less_than, while long enough not to fit into a single physical line, *is* all in a single logical line (indeed, it must be, since any list comprehension is a single expression), and therefore qualifies as a "one-liner" if you squint in just the right way.

This simple prime-finding algorithm is nowhere near as fast as the Sieve of Eratosthenes shown in recipe 18.10 "Computing Prime Numbers," but the ability to fit the entire algorithm inside a single expression is nevertheless kind of neat. Part of its neatness comes from the just-in-time evaluation that the functions from standard library module itertools perform so nicely.

Alas, this neat trick definitely *cannot* be recommended for production code. While it works in Python 2.3 and 2.4, it could easily break in future releases, since it depends on undocumented internals; for the same reason, it's unlikely to work properly on other implementations of the Python language, such as Jython or IronPython. So, I suggest you use it to impress friends, but for any real work, stick to clearer, faster, and solid good old for loops!

See Also

Documentation for bound methods, lists' append method, and the itertools module in the *Library Reference* and *Python in a Nutshell*.

16.11 Automating the py2exe Compilation of Scripts into Windows Executables

Credit: Alexander Semenov

Problem

You often use py2exe to build Windows *.exe* files from Python scripts, but you don't want to bother writing a *setup.py* build script for each and every such script.

Solution

distutils is a package in the standard Python library, ready to be imported from your Python code. py2exe is a third-party extension to distutils for the specific task of generating Windows executables from Python code: you must download and install py2exe separately, but once installed, it cooperates smoothly with the standard distutils. Thanks to these features, you can easily write Python scripts to automate distutils tasks (including py2exe tasks). For example:

```
from distutils.core import setup
import sys, os, py2exe
# the key trick with our arguments and Python's sys.path
name = sys.argv[1]
sys.argv[1] = 'py2exe'
sys.path.append(os.path.dirname(os.path.abspath(name)))
setup(name=name[:-3], scripts=[name])
```

Save this as *makexe.py* in the *Tools\Scripts* folder of your Python installation. (You should always add this folder to your Windows PATH because it contains many useful tools.) Now, from a Windows command prompt, you're able to cd to a directory where you have placed a script (say *C:\MyDir*), and there run, say:

```
C:\MyDir> makeexe.py myscript.py
```

and (assuming that you have a *myscript.py* script there, and *.py* among your Windows executable extensions, with association to the Python interpreter) py2exe prepares all the files you need for distributing your masterpiece (as a Windows executable and supporting DLLs), neatly arranged in folder *c:\MyDir\dist\myscript*.

Discussion

The distutils package is part of the Python Standard Library. It helps you prepare your Python modules and extensions for distribution, as well as letting you install such packages as distributed by others. py2exe is a freely downloadable third-party extension that works on top of distutils to help you build a Windows *.exe* file (and a set of supporting DLL files) from a Python-coded program, so that you can distribute your program in executable form to other Windows PCs that may not have Python installed; see *http://starship.python.net/crew/theller/py2exe/*, both to download py2exe and for detailed documentation of this useful tool.

Following the details given in the distutils (and py2exe) documentation, the canonical way to use distutils (including py2exe) is to write a script, conventionally always named *setup.py*, to perform all kinds of distutils tasks on your package. Normally, you write a *setup.py* for each package you distribute, placing it in the top directory of the package (known as the *distribution root* in distutils terminology).

However, there is nothing mandatory about the convention of writing a *setup.py* script per package. distutils and py2exe, after all, are written as modules to be imported from Python. So, you can, if you so choose, use all the power of Python to code scripts that help you perform distutils and py2exe tasks in whatever ways you find most convenient.

This recipe shows how I eliminate the need to write a separate *setup.py* script for each Python script that I convert to an executable with py2exe, and related issues such as the need to keep such scripts in dedicated "distribution root" directories. I suggest you name this recipe's script *makeexe.py*, but any name will do, as long as you avoid naming it *py2exe.py* (a natural enough temptation). (Naming it *py2exe.py* would break the script because the script must import py2exe, and if you named the script *py2exe.py* it would "import itself" instead!)

Place this script on any directory on your Windows PATH where you normally keep executable Python scripts. I suggest you use the *Tools\Scripts* folder of the Python distribution, a folder that contains several other useful scripts you'll want to have handy (have a look in that folder—it's worth your time). I'm not going to delve into the details of how to set and examine your Windows PATH, open a command prompt, make your Python scripts executable, and so on. Such system administration details differ slightly on each version of Windows, and you'll need to master them for any Windows version on which you want to perform significant programming, anyway.

Once you have implemented this Solution, you'll find that making your Python scripts into Windows executables has become so easy and so fast that soon you'll be distributing your neat and useful programs to friends and acquaintances right and left. You won't need to convince them to install the Python runtime files before they can install and run your programs, either! (Of course, in this way they *will* end up with what amounts to several copies of the runtime files, if they install several of your compiled programs—there is little you can do about that.)

See Also

The section "Distributing Python Modules" of the standard Python documentation set is still incomplete but a good source of information on the distutils package; *Python in a Nutshell* covers the essentials of the distutils package; py2exe is at *http://starship.python.net/crew/theller/py2exe/*.

16.12 Binding Main Script and Modules into One Executable on Unix

Credit: Joerg Raedler

Problem

You have a Python application composed of a main script and some additional modules. You want to bind the script and modules into one executable file, so that no installation procedure is necessary.

Solution

Prepare the following mixed sh/Python script and save it as file *zipheader.unix*:

```
#!/bin/sh
PYTHON=$(which python 2>/dev/null)
if [ x ! -x "x$PYTHON" ] ; then
    echo "python executable not found - cannot continue!"
    exit 1
fi
exec $PYTHON - $0 $@ << END_OF_PYTHON_CODE
import sys
version = sys.version_info[:2]
if version < (2, 3):
    print 'Sorry, need Python 2.3 or better; %s.%s is too old!' % version
sys.path.insert(0, sys.argv[1])
del sys.argv[0:2]
import main
```

```
main.main( )
END_OF_PYTHON_CODE
```

Make sure you have the Python bytecode files for the main script of your application (file *main.pyc*, containing a function named main, which starts the application when called without arguments) and any additional modules your application needs (e.g., files *spam.pyc* and *eggs.pyc*). Make a zip file out of them all:

```
$ zip myapp.zip main.pyc spam.pyc eggs.pyc
```

(If you prefer, you can build the zip file with an auxiliary Python program, of course.) Next, concatenate the "header" and the zip file, and make the resulting file executable:

```
$ cat zipheader.unix myapp.zip > myapp
$ chmod +x myapp
```

That's all! Your application is now contained in this executable file *myapp*. When *myapp* runs, the shell /bin/sh sets things up and replaces itself with the Python interpreter. The Python interpreter reopens the file as a zip file, skipping the "header" text, and finds all needed modules in the zip file itself.

Discussion

On Windows machines, you would normally use py2exe for similar tasks, as shown previously in recipe 16.11 "Automating the py2exe Compilation of Scripts into Windows Executables"; on Mac OS X, you would normally use py2app (although this recipe works just as well on Mac OS X as it does on any other Unix).

This recipe is particularly useful for Linux and other Unix variants that come with Python installed. By following the steps outlined in this recipe's Solution, you can distribute a Python application as a single, self-contained standalone executable file, which runs on any version of Unix, on any hardware platform—as long as your Python application does not need any C-coded extension modules beyond the ones that come with Python itself. When you do need more, you can use Python's own distutil package to perform more complicated packaging tasks. But for many simple Python applications and quite a few that aren't all that simple, this recipe can be very useful, since it results in a file that can just be run *as is*, without needing any kind of "installation" step!

The key idea of this recipe is to exploit Python's ability to import modules from a zip file, while skipping leading text that may precede the zip file itself. Here, as leading text, we use a small shell script that turns itself into a Python script, and within the same file continues with the zip file from which everything gets imported. The concept of importing from a zip file is described in recipe 2.9 "Reading Data from zip Files."

In the zip file, you may, if you wish, place Python source files (with extension *.py*), as well as compiled bytecode files (with extension *.pyc*); the latter option is often preferable because if you zip up source files, Python compiles them every time you run the application, slowing your application's startup. On the other hand, if you zip up compiled bytecode files, your application may be unable to run with versions of Python that are newer than the one you used to prepare the bytecode files, since binary compatibility of bytecode files is not guaranteed across Python releases. The best approach may be to place both sources and bytecodes in the zip file.

You may also choose to zip up *optimized* bytecode files (with extension *.pyo*)—if you do so, you need to add the flag -O right after the $PYTHON in the shell script in this recipe's Solution. Execution speed doesn't generally change much, but optimized execution skips assert statements, which may be important to you. Also, if you prepare the *.pyo* files by running Python with option -OO, all docstrings are eliminated, which may slightly reduce your application's size on disk (although docstrings tend to compress well, so that size advantage may be minor).

If you need help in finding all the modules that you need to place in the zip file, see the modulefinder module in the Python Standard Library. Unfortunately, no real documentation about it is available at the time of this writing, but just running (in version 2.3) something like:

```
$ python /usr/lib/python2.3/modulefinder.py main.py
```

should help (you may have to change the change the path to the *modulefinder.py* script, depending on your Python installation). With Python 2.4, you can just use the handy new -m switch:

```
$ python -mmodulefinder main.py
```

Python 2.4's -m switch lets you run as the main script any module that's on Python's sys.path—a very convenient little feature!

See Also

Recipe 16.11 "Automating the py2exe Compilation of Scripts into Windows Executables"; recipe 2.9 "Reading Data from zip Files"; the sources of modules modulefinder and zipimport (which are not yet documented in the *Library Reference* at the time of writing).

CHAPTER 17

Extending and Embedding

17.0 Introduction

Credit: David Beazley, University of Chicago

One of Python's most powerful features is its ability to be hooked to libraries and programs written in classic compiled languages such as C, C++, and Fortran. A large number of Python's built-in library modules are written as extension modules in C so that operating system services, networking functions, databases, and other features can be easily accessed from the interpreter. In addition, a number of application programmers write extensions in order to use Python as a framework for controlling large software packages coded in other languages.

The gory details of how Python interfaces with other languages can be found in various Python programming books, as well as online documentation at *www.python.org* (directory *Demo*, distributed as part of the Python source distribution, also contains several useful examples). However, the general approach revolves around the creation of special wrapper functions that hook into the interpreter. For example, if you had a C function like this:

```
int gcd(int x, int y) {
    int g = y;
    while (x > 0) {
        g = x;
        x = y % x;
        y = g;
    }
    return g;
}
```

and you wanted to access it from Python in a module named spam, you'd write some special wrapper code like this:

```
#include "Python.h"
extern int gcd(int, int);
PyObject *wrap_gcd(PyObject *self, PyObject *args) {
    int x, y, g;
```

```
        if(!PyArg_ParseTuple(args, "ii", &x, &y))
            return NULL;
        g = gcd(x, y);
        return Py_BuildValue("i", g);
    }
    /* List of all functions in the module */
    static PyMethodDef spammethods[ ] = {
        {"gcd", wrap_gcd, METH_VARARGS },
        { NULL, NULL }
    };
    /* Module initialization function */
    void initspam(void) {
        Py_InitModule("spam", spammethods);
    }
```

Once this code is compiled into an extension module, you can use the gcd function just as you would expect. For example:

```
>>> import spam
>>> spam.gcd(63,56)
7
>>> spam.gcd(71,89)
1
```

This short example extends in a natural way to larger programming libraries—each function that you want to access from Python simply gets its own wrapper.

Although writing simple extension functions is fairly straightforward, writing many wrappers quickly becomes tedious and prone to error if you are building anything of reasonable complexity. Therefore, a lot of programmers rely on automatic module building tools to simplify the process. Python is fortunate to have a variety of such tools, many of which are listed below:

bgen

bgen is a module-building tool that can be found in the *Tools* directory of a standard Python distribution. Maintained by Jack Jansen, it is used to generate many of the extension modules available in the Macintosh version of Python, but it is not Mac specific.

pyfort

pyfort is a tool developed by Paul Dubois that can be used to build extension modules for Fortran code. Details are available at the following web page: *http://pyfortran.sourceforge.net*.

f2py

f2py is a wrapper generator for creating extensions in Fortran 90/95 that has been developed by Pearu Peterson. Details are available at *http://cens.ioc.ee/projects/f2py2e/*.

SIP

SIP is a C++ module builder developed by Phil Thompson that creates wrappers for C++ classes. The system has most notably been used to create the PyQt and

PyKDE extension modules. More information can be found at *http://www.thekompany.com/projects/pykde*.

WrapPy

WrapPy is another C++ module builder that produces extension modules by reading C++ header files. It is developed by Greg Couch and is available at *http://www.cgl.ucsf.edu/home/gregc/wrappy/index.html*.

Boost Python Library

Boost Python Library, developed by David Abrahams, provides one of the most powerful and unusual C++ wrapping techniques. Classes are automatically wrapped into Python extensions by simply writing a few additional C++ classes that specify information about the extension module. More information is available at *http://www.boost.org/libs/python/doc/*.

SWIG

SWIG (Simplified Wrapper and Interface Generator) is an automatic extension-building tool that reads annotated C and C++ header files and produces extension modules for Python, Tcl, Perl, and a variety of other high-level languages such as Scheme, Ruby, Java, OCAML (Objective Caml), and C#. SWIG is able to wrap a large subset of C++ language features into a Python extension module. However, since I developed SWIG, I may be a little biased :-). In any event, further details are available at *http://www.swig.org*.

Pyrex

Pyrex is a language for writing Python extension modules, developed by Greg Ewing. The Pyrex language is a large subset of Python, with semantics slightly less fluidly dynamic than Python, and the addition of a few language constructs (particularly optional declarations of types of parameters and variables) that enables the Pyrex compiler to generate fast C code. Further details are available at *http://nz.cosc.canterbury.ac.nz/~greg/python/Pyrex/*.

Regardless of the approach used to build Python extension modules, certain important topics remain somewhat mysterious to many extension programmers. The recipes in this chapter describe some of the common problems and extension-building tricks that are rarely covered in the standard documentation or other Python books. Topics include interacting with threads, returning NULL values, accessing Python sequences and iterables, creating extension types, and debugging.

One recipe, in particular, highlights an especially important topic: you don't necessarily have to use other languages (even one as close to Python as Pyrex is) to write Python extensions to access functionality that's available through dynamically loaded libraries (*.DLLs* on Windows, *.sos* on Linux, *.dylib* on Mac OS X, etc.). It often may be sufficient to use existing third-party general-purpose extensions, such as the classic calldll or the newer ctypes packages, which enable you to wrap such dynamic libraries and make their functionality available to your Python programs, by writing just a little pure Python code.

17.1   Implementing a Simple Extension Type

Credit: Alex Martelli

Problem

You want to code and build a C extension type for Python with a minimal amount of hard work.

Solution

First of all, we need to create a *setup.py* file to use the distutils package to build and install our module:

```
from distutils.core import setup, Extension
setup(name = "elemlist",
      version = "1.0",
      maintainer = "Alex Martelli",
      maintainer_email = "amcx@aleax.it",
      description = "Sample, simple Python extension module",
      ext_modules = [Extension('elemlist',sources=['elemlist.c'])]
)
```

Then, we need a file *elemlist.c* with our module's source code:

```
#include "Python.h"
/* type-definition and utility-macros */
typedef struct {
    PyObject_HEAD
    PyObject *car, *cdr;
} cons_cell;
staticforward PyTypeObject cons_type;
/* a type-testing macro (we don't actually use it here) */
#define is_cons(v) ((v)->ob_type == &cons_type)
/* utility macros to access car and cdr, as either lvalues or rvalues */
#define carof(v) (((cons_cell*)(v))->car)
#define cdrof(v) (((cons_cell*)(v))->cdr)
/* ctor ("internal" factory-function) and dtor */
static cons_cell*
cons_new(PyObject *car, PyObject *cdr)
{
    cons_cell *cons = PyObject_New(cons_cell, &cons_type);
    if(cons) {
        cons->car = car; Py_INCREF(car); /* INCREF when holding a PyObject */
        cons->cdr = cdr; Py_INCREF(cdr); /* ditto */
    }
    return cons;
}
static void
cons_dealloc(cons_cell* cons)
{
    /* DECREF when releasing previously-held PyObject*'s */
    Py_DECREF(cons->car); Py_DECREF(cons->cdr);
```

```
        PyObject_Del(cons);
    }
    /* A minimal Python type-object */
    statichere PyTypeObject cons_type = {
        PyObject_HEAD_INIT(0)      /* initialize to 0 to ensure Win32 portability  */
        0,                         /* ob_size */
        "cons",                    /* tp_name */
        sizeof(cons_cell),         /* tp_basicsize */
        0,                         /* tp_itemsize */
        /* methods */
        (destructor)cons_dealloc, /* tp_dealloc */
        /* implied by ISO C: all zeros thereafter, i.e., no other method */
    };
    /* module-functions */
    static PyObject*
    cons(PyObject *self, PyObject *args)     /* the exposed factory-function */
    {
        PyObject *car, *cdr;
        if(!PyArg_ParseTuple(args, "OO", &car, &cdr))
            return 0;
        return (PyObject*)cons_new(car, cdr);
    }
    static PyObject*
    car(PyObject *self, PyObject *args)      /* car-accessor */
    {
        PyObject *cons;
        if(!PyArg_ParseTuple(args, "O!", &cons_type, &cons)) /* type-checked */
            return 0;
        return Py_BuildValue("O", carof(cons));
    }
    static PyObject*
    cdr(PyObject *self, PyObject *args)      /* cdr-accessor */
    {
        PyObject *cons;
        if(!PyArg_ParseTuple(args, "O!", &cons_type, &cons)) /* type-checked */
            return 0;
        return Py_BuildValue("O", cdrof(cons));
    }
    static PyObject*
    setcar(PyObject *self, PyObject *args)  /* car-setter */
    {
        PyObject *cons;
        PyObject *value;
        if(!PyArg_ParseTuple(args, "O!O", &cons_type, &cons, &value))
            return 0;
        Py_INCREF(value);
        Py_DECREF(carof(cons));
        carof(cons) = value;
        return Py_BuildValue("");
    }
    static PyObject*
    setcdr(PyObject *self, PyObject *args)  /* cdr-setter */
    {
        PyObject *cons;
```

```
        PyObject *value;
        if(!PyArg_ParseTuple(args, "O!O", &cons_type, &cons, &value))
            return 0;
        Py_INCREF(value);
        Py_DECREF(cdrof(cons));
        cdrof(cons) = value;
        return Py_BuildValue("");
}
static PyMethodDef elemlist_module_functions[ ] = {
        {"cons",   cons,   METH_VARARGS},
        {"car",    car,    METH_VARARGS},
        {"cdr",    cdr,    METH_VARARGS},
        {"setcar", setcar, METH_VARARGS},
        {"setcdr", setcdr, METH_VARARGS},
        {0, 0}
};
/* module entry-point (module-initialization) function */
void
initelemlist(void)
{
        /* Create the module, with its functions */
        PyObject *m = Py_InitModule("elemlist", elemlist_module_functions);
        /* Finish initializing the type-objects */
        cons_type.ob_type = &PyType_Type;
}
```

Discussion

C-coded Python extension types have an undeserved aura of mystery and difficulty.
Sure, it's a lot of work to implement every possible feature, but a minimal yet useful
type doesn't necessarily take all that much effort.

This module is roughly equivalent to the Python-coded module:

```
def cons(car, cdr): return car, cdr
def car(conscell): return conscell[0]
def cdr(conscell): return conscell[1]
def setcar(conscell, value): conscell[0] = value
def setcdr(conscell, value): conscell[1] = value
```

except that the C source is about 25 times larger, even excluding comments and
empty lines (and it is not much faster than the Python-coded version, either).

However, the point of this recipe is to demonstrate a minimal C-coded extension
type. I'm not even supplying object methods (except the indispensable destructor)
but, rather, I am providing module-level functions to build cons cells and to read and
write their car and cdr fields. This recipe also shows the utter simplicity of building a
C-coded extension module on any platform, thanks to the distutils package, which
does all of the hard work.

Lisp-savvy readers will have recognized from the names involved that this little
extension offers the core functionality to implement a Lisp-like linked list type—
using some NIL marker (e.g. None), by convention, as the cdr of the last cons-cell of a

list, and otherwise "consing up a list" by having every cdr be another cons-cell. You might easily *constrain* the cdr to be either None or another cons-cell, giving up on generality for a bit of extra error checking.

Because this recipe is meant as an introduction to writing extension modules in C for Python, here are the instructions for building this extension module, assuming you have a Windows machine with Python 2.3 and Microsoft Visual C++ 6 (or the free command-line equivalent that you can download from Microsoft's site as a part of their .NET Framework SDK). You can presumably translate mentally to other platforms such as Linux with *gcc*, Mac OS X with *gcc*, and so on. On the other hand, using different C compilers on Windows involves more work, and I'm not going to cover that here (see *http://sebsauvage.net/python/mingw.html*).

Here are the steps you should follow to build this recipe's extension:

1. Make a new directory—for example, *C:\Temp\EL*.
2. Open a command-prompt window, and go to the new directory.
3. In the new directory, create the files *setup.py* and *elemlist.c* with the contents of the recipe's text.
4. Run the following at the command prompt (assuming you've performed a standard Python 2.3 installation, so that your *python.exe* lives in *C:\Python23*):

   ```
   <m>C:\Temp\EL> C:\Python23\python setup.py install</m>
   ```

   This command will result in lots of output, which you should examine to check for problems. Presumably, all has gone well, and the new elemlist extension module has been built and installed.
5. Now try the extension by running the following at the DOS prompt:

   ```
   <m>C:\Temp\EL> C:\Python23\python</m>
   (snipped: various greeting messages from Python)
   >>> from elemlist import cons, car, cdr
   >>> a = cons(1, cons(2, cons(3, ())))
   >>> car(cdr(a))
   2
   >>>
   ```

There—your new extension module is installed and ready!

See Also

The *Extending and Embedding* manual is available as part of the standard Python documentation set at *http://www.python.org/doc/current/ext/ext.html*; the section "Distributing Python Modules" of the standard Python documentation set is still incomplete, but it's a reliable source of information on the distutils package. *Python in a Nutshell* covers the essentials of extending and embedding and of the distutils package.

17.2 Implementing a Simple Extension Type with Pyrex

Credit: Alex Martelli

Problem

You want to code and build an extension type for Python with a minimal amount of hard work.

Solution

The Pyrex language is the simplest and fastest way to build Python extensions. Once we have Pyrex installed, the next step is to create a *setup.py* file to use the distutils package to build and install our module:

```python
from distutils.core import setup, Extension
from Pyrex.Distutils import build_ext
setup(name = "elemlist",
      version = "1.0",
      maintainer = "Alex Martelli",
      maintainer_email = "amcx@aleax.it",
      description = "Simple Python extension module in Pyrex",
      ext_modules = [Extension('elemlist',sources=['elemlist.pyx'])],
      cmdclass = {'build_ext': build_ext},
)
```

Then, we need a file *elemlist.pyx* with our module's source code:

```python
cdef class cons:
    cdef public object car, cdr
    def __init__(self, car, cdr):
        self.car = car
        self.cdr = cdr
    def __repr__(self):
        return 'cons(%r, %r)' % (self.car, self.cdr)
```

Discussion

Pyrex is a language for writing Python extension modules. It was developed by Greg Ewing and is freely downloadable and installable. The Pyrex language is a large subset of Python, with the addition of a few language constructs to allow easy generation of fast C code. In this recipe, the only special Pyrex construct we use is the `cdef` statement, which lets us express C-level declarations.

This module is roughly equivalent to the Python-coded module:

```python
class cons(object):
    __slots__ = ('car', 'cdr')
    def __init__(self, car, cdr):
        self.car = car
        self.cdr = cdr
```

```
        def __repr__(self):
            return 'cons(%r, %r)' % (self.car, self.cdr)
```

As you see, Pyrex code is very similar to Python code. Pyrex code gets compiled into C, which in turn gets compiled to machine code, while Python code is compiled into bytecode instead. For such a simple type as cons, the Pyrex version is not much faster than the Python version, but a pure C version, such as the one that I demonstrated previously in recipe 17.1 "Implementing a Simple Extension Type," despite having 25 times as much code, wouldn't be any faster either.

Building a compiled extension module is just as simple when it's coded in Pyrex as when it's coded directly in C, thanks to the distutils package, which does all of the hard work. (You need to have Pyrex installed.) When you build a Pyrex-coded module, you may get warnings from your C compiler about symbols with names starting with __pyx or __pyx that are defined but not used, or declared but not defined. Do not let these warning messages worry you: your C compiler is running with the highest possible level of warnings, and the little anomalies it's warning about are just perfectly normal and innocuous artifacts in the C sources that Pyrex automatically generates. Pyrex is not quite finished yet (the Pyrex version at the time of writing is 0.9.3), so no attention has yet been spent on purely cosmetic warts. (By the time you read this, a mature version of Pyrex may have been released, with all i's dotted and all t's crossed. Nevertheless, I would recommend Pyrex even if the latest version still causes numerous warnings.)

Installing Pyrex

To use Pyrex, you need to download and install it (*http://nz.cosc.canterbury.ac.nz/~greg/python/Pyrex/*), and you also need to have a C compiler. Pyrex translates your *.pyx* source into C source and then uses your C compiler to make from that C source a machine-code Python extension module (a *.pyd* file on Windows, a *.so* file on Linux, a *.dynlib* file on the Mac, etc.). Installing Pyrex itself is a snap: unpack the *.tar.gz* file, cd with the shell of your choice into the directory thus made, and at the shell prompt type the usual command to install any Python module: python setup.py install. Just as for any other Python module, you may need "root" or "administrator" privileges to install Pyrex, depending on your platform and on the details of your Python installation. In the directory where you unpacked Pyrex's *.tar.gz* archive, you will also find abundant documentation and examples, particularly in subdirectories *Doc* and *Demos*.

See Also

Abundant documentation on Pyrex, as well as examples, can be found in the directory (and particularly in subdirectories *Doc* and *Demos*) where you unpacked Pyrex's *.tar.gz* file; essentially the same documentation can also be read online, starting from the Pyrex web site at *http://nz.cosc.canterbury.ac.nz/~greg/python/Pyrex/*.

17.3 Exposing a C++ Library to Python

Credit: Ralf W. Grosse-Kunstleve, David Abrahams

Problem

You want to use a C++ library in Python. For example, you might have a fast rational-numbers library, coded in C++, that you wish to wrap for use from Python.

Solution

Boost, *http://www.boost.org*, is a large free package with more than 50 fast and solid C++ libraries. Among those libraries, we find both *Boost.Rational*, a rational number library, and *Boost.Python*, which makes it easy to turn any other C++ library into a Python extension. So, we simply use the latter to wrap the former:

```cpp
#include <boost/python.hpp>
#include <boost/rational.hpp>
/* two specific conversion functions: rational to float and to str */
static double
as_float(boost::rational<int> const& self)
{
  return double(self.numerator()) / self.denominator();
}
static boost::python::object
as_str(boost::rational<int> const& self)
{
  using boost::python::str;
  if (self.denominator() == 1) return str(self.numerator());
  return str(self.numerator()) + "/" + str(self.denominator());
}
/* the 'rational' Python extension module, with just one class in it: */
BOOST_PYTHON_MODULE(rational)
{
  boost::python::class_<boost::rational<int> >("int")
    .def(boost::python::init<int, optional<int> >())
    .def("numerator", &boost::rational<int>::numerator)
    .def("denominator", &boost::rational<int>::denominator)
    .def("__float__", as_float)
    .def("__str__", as_str)
    .def(-self)
    .def(self + self)
    .def(self - self)
    .def(self * self)
    .def(self / self)
    .def(self + int())
    .def(self - int())
    .def(self * int())
    .def(self / int())
    .def(int() + self)
    .def(int() - self)
    .def(int() * self)
```

```
    .def(int( ) / self)
  ;
}
```

Discussion

Once you have built and installed the `rational` extension shown in this recipe's Solution, you can use it to perform simple, natural tasks, such as:

```
>>> import rational
>>> x = rational.int(1, 3)
>>> y = rational.int(-2, 4)
>>> print "x =", x
x = 1/3
>>> print "y =", y
y = -1/2
>>> print "x+y =", x+y
x+y = -1/6
>>> print "x*2 =", x * 2
x*2 = 2/3
>>> print "3/y =", 3 / y
3/y = -6
```

Compiling and linking Boost.Python extensions is supported by the Boost.Build tool; we do not cover that topic here. Extensive documentation is available online at the Boost site. Such tools as `make` and `SCons` are also popular for software compilation and linking tasks, including tasks that involve Boost.

The Solution's code shows off a few of Boost.Python's powerful features. Consider the snippet:

```
BOOST_PYTHON_MODULE(rational)
{
   class_<boost::rational<int> >("int")
   ...
```

The `BOOST_PYTHON_MODULE` macro takes a module name as a parameter, and a module body immediately afterwards within braces, and does all that's needed to make a module we can `import` from Python.

The `class_` template, instantiated with the `boost::rational` type as a parameter and "called" with the string argument `"int"`, does all we need to have as part of our module a Python-usable class, named `rational.int`, each of whose instances wraps an instance of the `boost::rational` class. The type `boost::rational` is itself a template, and we instantiate that template with `int` as a parameter, to use `int` as the type of each rational number's numerator and denominator.

If we stopped here, wrapping a C++ class in the `class_` template, and exposing the wrapper without adding any more to it, we'd have a rather empty type available on the Python side. It would have no constructor (save for the default argument-less one), no methods, and no attributes. To remedy this, the Solution code continues with several `.def(...)` calls, which are *chained*: each call enriches the object, and also returns it, so you can just string such calls one after the other. The methods we add with all those def calls include a constructor (which uses the init template), then a couple of ordinary methods that delegate to the methods of the same names in the wrapped class (accessors to the numerator and denominator parts of a rational number), and then a couple of type-conversion special methods for which we've previously coded corresponding functions (just before the BOOST_PYTHON_MODULE macro). Note, in particular, that the implementation of the as_str function is so concise because it makes full use of Boost.Python's object interface—it's almost like writing Python in C++.

The baker's dozen of `.def(...)` calls that begins with:

```
.def(-self)
```

and proceeds all the way to:

```
.def(int() / self)
```

exposes all the arithmetic special methods for our new rational.int class—unary minus (__neg__), and the four operations, each in three versions—between two instances of our class, and between such instances and ints on either side (__add__, __radd__, etc.). The magic is performed using *expression templates*, a technique originally developed for optimizing high-performance matrix algebra expressions. Boost.Python's use of expression templates has a different purpose, but it certainly comes in handy anyway!

A comprehensive rational number extension would require more functionality—comparison operators, __repr__, __hash__, support for pickling, and so on. A more complete implementation, one that is actively used in applications, can be found at *http://cvs.sourceforge.net/viewcvs.py/cctbx/boost_adaptbx/*, in the file *rational_ext.cpp*.

See Also

Boost's site is *http://www.boost.org*; the rational number library Boost.Rational, is at *http://www.boost.org/libs/rational*; Boost.Python is at *http://www.boost.org/libs/python*.

17.4 Calling Functions from a Windows DLL

Credit: Stefano Spinucci

Problem

You want to avoid writing a Python extension in C, by directly calling from Python functions that already exist in a Windows DLL.

Solution

The third-party ctypes extension makes this task pretty easy:

```
from ctypes import windll, c_int, c_string, byref
# load 'Ehllapi.dll' (from current dir), and function 'hllapi' from the DLL
Ehllap32 = windll.ehllapi
hllapi = Ehllap32.hllapi
# prepare the arguments with types and initial values
h_func = c_int(1)
h_text = c_string('A')
h_len = c_int(1)
h_ret = c_int(999)
# call the function
hllapi(byref(h_func), h_text, byref(h_len), byref(h_ret))
# print the resulting values of all arguments after the call
print h_func.value, h_text.value, h_len.value, h_ret.value
```

Discussion

I needed the code in this recipe specifically to call a C function whose prototype is:

```
void FAR PASCAL hllapi(int FAR *, char FAR *, int FAR *, int FAR *);
```

from a DLL named *Ehllapi.DLL* (an implementation of the IBM 3270 HLLAPI for an Italian 3270 terminal emulator, as it happens). Thomas Heller's ctypes extension, found at *http://sourceforge.net/projects/ctypes*, made the task very easy. In particular, ctypes makes mincemeat of problems related to representing function arguments that must belong to a certain C type and possibly get passed "by reference" (i.e., via a pointer).

In the past, I used another extension, known as calldll, which was (and still is) available from *http://www.nightmare.com/software.html*. While once very useful, calldll cannot rely on some of the modern techniques that ctypes uses internally, because these possibilities were introduced only in relatively recent versions of Python. calldll, using a single membuf Python type to represent all possible C types, tends to be much more cumbersome than ctypes when they are both used to perform the same tasks.

Judge for yourself: here is a working calldll version of the same script that I just showed how to code with ctypes:

```
import calldll, struct
# some helpful auxiliary functions
def myPrintLong(vVar):
    ''' print a long contained in a membuf '''
    print calldll.read_long(vVar.address())
def myPrintString(vVar):
    ''' print a string contained in a membuf '''
```

```
        a = calldll.read_string(vVar.address())
        print a, len(a)
def mySetLong(vMemBuf, vValueToSet):
        ''' set to an unsigned long the value of a membuf with len == 4 '''
        vMemBuf.write(struct.pack('L', vValueToSet))
def mySetString(vMemBuf, vValueToSet):
        ''' set to a string (with \0 terminator) the value of a membuf '''
        pack_format = "%ds" % 1+len(vValueToSet)          # +1 for the \0
        string_packed = struct.pack(pack_format, vValueToSet) # pack() adds the \0
        vMemBuf.write(string_packed)
# load 'Ehllapi.dll' (from current dir), and function 'hllapi' from the DLL
dll_handle = calldll.load_library ('.\\Ehllapi')
function_address = calldll.get_proc_address (dll_handle, 'HLLAPI')
# allocate and init three membufs with the size to hold an unsigned long
Lsize = struct.calcsize('L')
vFunction = calldll.membuf(Lsize)
mySetLong(vFunction, 1)
vTextLen = calldll.membuf(Lsize)
vResult = calldll.membuf(Lsize)
mySetLong(vResult, 1)
# allocate a membuf as large as the DLL requires; in this case, space
# for 24 x 80 characters + 1 for a \0 terminator
vText = calldll.membuf(1921)
# init the text and text-length variables based on string of interest
string_value_to_write = 'A'
mySetString(vText, string_value_to_write)
mySetLong(vTextLen, len(string_value_to_write))
# call the function, print the results, and clean up
calldll.call_foreign_function(function_address, 'llll', 'l',
    (vFunction.address(), vText.address(), vTextLen.address(), vResult.address()))
myPrintLong(vResult)
myPrintString(vText)
calldll.free_library(dll_handle)
```

To be honest, I can't quite be sure whether all of these gyrations are truly indispensable to making this calldll-based version work. Whenever I try to simplify this version a bit, something or other always breaks noisily, so I've stopped messing with it. One reason the ctypes-based version is cleaner and simpler is that ctypes has never given me trouble, so I've been encouraged to continue working on that version to improve it.

See Also

ctypes is at *http://sourceforge.net/projects/ctypes*; calldll is at *http://www.nightmare.com/software.html*.

17.5 Using SWIG-Generated Modules in a Multithreaded Environment

Credit: Joe VanAndel, Mark Hammond

Problem

You want to use SWIG-generated modules in a multithreaded environment; therefore, the C code in those modules must release the Python global interpreter lock (see the Introduction to Chapter 9 for more information about the global interpreter lock).

Solution

Use a typemap for SWIG, written by Mark Hammond, that was posted on comp.lang.python. It maps Win32 API functions that return BOOL to Python functions that return None and raise exceptions to diagnose errors. The wrapped function must set the standard Windows global LastError if it returns FALSE (indicating that it has detected an error). The wrapping function also automatically releases the Python global interpreter lock (GIL) for the duration of the wrapped function's execution, to allow free multithreading.

```
%typedef BOOL BOOLAPI
%typemap(python,except) BOOLAPI {
        Py_BEGIN_ALLOW_THREADS
        $function
          Py_END_ALLOW_THREADS
          if (!$source)  {
                $cleanup
                 return PyWin_SetAPIError("$name");
          }
}
```

Discussion

To use multiple threads effectively, you must release the Python GIL from your C-coded extension whenever it's safe to do so. The simplest way to do this with SWIG is to use an except directive, as shown in the recipe's typemap. Within the typemap, you can then use the normal Python C API's macros Py_BEGIN_ALLOW_THREADS and Py_END_ALLOW_THREADS (around the call to the wrapped function, indicated by the special SWIG directive $function) to release the GIL and acquire it again.

Another interesting effect of this simple typemap is that it turns the C-oriented error-return convention (returning FALSE and setting a global error indicator code) into a highly Pythonic convention (raising an exception).

See Also

SWIG and its typemaps are documented at *http://www.swig.org*; Windows API documentation on LastError is available from the Microsoft MSDN site at *http://msdn.microsoft.com*; Chapter 9 for general information on threads and particularly its Introduction for information on the GIL.

17.6 Translating a Python Sequence into a C Array with the PySequence_Fast Protocol

Credit: Luther Blissett

Problem

You have an existing C function that takes as an argument a C array of C-level values (e.g., doubles), and you want to wrap it into a Python-callable C extension that takes as an argument a Python sequence or iterator.

Solution

The easiest way to accept an arbitrary Python sequence (or any other iterable object) in the Python C API is with the PySequence_Fast function. It builds and returns a tuple when needed but returns only its argument (with the reference count incremented) when the argument is already a list or tuple:

```
#include <Python.h>
/* a preexisting C-level function you want to expose, e.g: */
static double total(double* data, int len)
{
    double total = 0.0;
    int i;
    for(i=0; i<len; ++i)
        total += data[i];
    return total;
}
/* here is how you expose it to Python code: */
static PyObject *totalDoubles(PyObject *self, PyObject *args)
{
    PyObject* seq;
    double *dbar;
    double result;
    int seqlen;
    int i;
    /* get one argument as a sequence */
    if(!PyArg_ParseTuple(args, "O", &seq))
        return 0;
    seq = PySequence_Fast(seq, "argument must be iterable");
    if(!seq)
        return 0;
```

```
    /* prepare data as an array of doubles */
    seqlen = PySequence_Fast_GET_SIZE(seq);
    dbar = malloc(seqlen*sizeof(double));
    if(!dbar) {
        Py_DECREF(seq);
        return PyErr_NoMemory();
    }
    for(i=0; i < seqlen; i++) {
        PyObject *fitem;
        PyObject *item = PySequence_Fast_GET_ITEM(seq, i);
        if(!item) {
            Py_DECREF(seq);
            free(dbar);
            return 0;
        }
        fitem = PyNumber_Float(item);
        if(!fitem) {
            Py_DECREF(seq);
            free(dbar);
            PyErr_SetString(PyExc_TypeError, "all items must be numbers");
            return 0;
        }
        dbar[i] = PyFloat_AS_DOUBLE(fitem);
        Py_DECREF(fitem);
    }
    /* clean up, compute, and return result */
    Py_DECREF(seq);
    result = total(dbar, seqlen);
    free(dbar);
    return Py_BuildValue("d", result);
}
static PyMethodDef totalMethods[ ] = {
    {"total", totalDoubles, METH_VARARGS, "Sum a sequence of numbers."},
    {0} /* sentinel */
};
void
inittotal(void)
{
    (void) Py_InitModule("total", totalMethods);
}
```

Discussion

The two best ways for your C-coded, Python-callable extension functions to accept
generic Python sequences as arguments are PySequence_Fast and PyObject_GetIter.
The latter, which I cover in the next recipe, can often save some memory, but it is
appropriate only when it's OK for the rest of your C code to get the items one at a
time, without knowing beforehand how many items there will be in total. You often
have preexisting C functions from an existing library that you want to expose to
Python code, and such functions may require C arrays as their input arguments.
Thus, this recipe shows how to build a C array (in this case, an array of double) from
a generic Python sequence (or other iterable) argument, so that you can pass the

---

array (and the integer that gives the array's length) to your existing C function (represented here, purely as an example, by the total function at the start of the recipe). (In the real world, you would use Python's built-in function sum for this specific functionality, rather than exposing any existing C function (but this *is* meant to be just an example!)

PySequence_Fast takes two arguments: a Python iterable object to be presented as a sequence, and a string to use as the error message in case the Python object cannot be presented as a sequence, in which case PySequence_Fast returns 0 (the C null pointer, NULL, an error indicator). If the Python object is already a list or tuple, PySequence_Fast returns the same object with the reference count increased by one. If the Python object is any other kind of sequence (or any iterator, or other iterable), PySequence_Fast builds and returns a new tuple with all items already in place. In any case, PySequence_Fast returns an object on which you can call PySequence_Fast_GET_SIZE to obtain the sequence length (as we do in the recipe, in order to malloc the appropriate amount of storage for the C array) and PySequence_Fast_GET_ITEM to get an item given a valid index (an int between 0, included, and the sequence length, excluded).

The recipe requires quite a bit of care (as is typical of all C-coded Python extensions, and more generally of any C code) to deal properly with memory issues and error conditions. For C-coded Python extensions, in particular, it's imperative that you know which Python C API functions return *new* references (which you must Py_DECREF when you are done with them) and which ones return *borrowed* references (which you must not Py_DECREF when you're done with them; on the contrary, you must Py_INCREF such a reference if you want to keep a copy for a longer time). In this specific case, you have to know the following (by reading the Python documentation):

- PyArg_ParseTuple produces borrowed references.
- PySequence_Fast returns a new reference.
- PySequence_Fast_GET_ITEM returns a borrowed reference.
- PyNumber_Float returns a new reference.

There is method to this madness, even though, as you start your career as a coder of C API Python extensions, you'll no doubt have to double-check each case carefully. Python's C API strives to return borrowed references (for the sake of the modest performance increase that they afford, by avoiding needless incrementing and decrementing of reference counts), when it *knows* it can always do so safely (i.e., it knows that the reference it is returning necessarily refers to an already existing object). However, Python's C API has to return a new reference when it's possible (or certain) that a new object may have to be created.

For example, in the preceding list, PyNumber_Float and PySequence_Fast may be able to return the same object they were given as an argument, but it's also quite possible that they may have to create a new object for this purpose, to ensure that the returned object has the correct type. Therefore, these two functions are specified as always returning new references. PyArg_ParseTuple and PySequence_Fast_GET_ITEM, on the other hand, always return references to objects that already exist elsewhere (as items in the arguments' tuple, or as items in the fast-sequence container, respectively). Therefore, these two functions can afford to return borrowed references and are thus specified as doing so.

One last note: in this recipe, as soon as we obtain an item from the fast-sequence container, we immediately try to transform it into a Python float object, and thus we have to deal with the possibility that the transformation will fail (e.g., if we're passed a sequence containing a string, a complex number, etc.). It is most often futile to first attempt a check (with PyNumber_Check) because the check might succeed, and the later transformation attempt might fail anyway (e.g., with a complex-number item). Therefore, it's better to attempt the transformation and deal with the resulting error, if any. This approach is yet another case of the common situation in which it's easier to get forgiveness than permission!

As usual, the best way to build this extension (assuming e.g., that you've saved the extension's source code as a file named *total.c*) is with the distutils package. Place a file named *setup.py* in the same directory as the C source:

```
from distutils.core import setup, Extension
setup(name="total", maintainer="Luther Blissett", maintainer_email=
    "situ@tioni.st", ext_modules=[Extension('total', sources=['total.c'])]
)
```

then build and install by running:

```
$ python setup.py install
```

An appealing aspect of this approach is that it works on any platform, assuming that you have access to the same C compiler used to build your version of Python, and permission to write on the *site-packages* directory where the resulting dynamically loaded library gets installed.

See Also

The *Extending and Embedding* manual is available as part of the standard Python documentation set at *http://www.python.org/doc/current/ext/ext.html*; documentation on the Python C API is at *http://www.python.org/doc/current/api/api.html*; the section "Distributing Python Modules" in the standard Python documentation set is still incomplete, but it's a good source of information on the distutils package; *Python in a Nutshell* covers the essentials of extending and embedding, of the Python C API, and of the distutils package.

17.7 Accessing a Python Sequence Item-by-Item with the Iterator Protocol

Credit: Luther Blissett

Problem

You want to write a Python-callable C extension that takes as an argument a Python sequence (or other iterable) and accesses it sequentially, one item at a time, requiring no extra storage.

Solution

If you can afford to access the sequence item-by-item, without knowing in advance the number of items it has, you can often save memory by using PyObject_GetIter instead of PySequence_Fast:

```c
#include <Python.h>
static PyObject *totalIter(PyObject *self, PyObject *args)
{
    PyObject* seq;
    PyObject* item;
    double result;
    /* get one argument as an iterator */
    if(!PyArg_ParseTuple(args, "O", &seq))
        return 0;
    seq = PyObject_GetIter(seq);
    if(!seq)
        return 0;
    /* process data sequentially */
    result = 0.0;
    while((item=PyIter_Next(seq))) {
        PyObject *fitem;
        fitem = PyNumber_Float(item);
        if(!fitem) {
            Py_DECREF(seq);
            Py_DECREF(item);
            PyErr_SetString(PyExc_TypeError, "all items must be numbers");
            return 0;
        }
        result += PyFloat_AS_DOUBLE(fitem);
        Py_DECREF(fitem);
        Py_DECREF(item);
    }
    /* clean up and return result */
    Py_DECREF(seq);
    return Py_BuildValue("d", result);
}
static PyMethodDef totitMethods[ ] = {
    {"totit", totalIter, METH_VARARGS, "Sum a sequence of numbers."},
    {0} /* sentinel */
};
```

```
void
inittotit(void)
{
    (void) Py_InitModule("totit", totitMethods);
}
```

Discussion

PyObject_GetIter is appropriate only when it's OK for the rest of your C code to get the items one at a time, without knowing in advance the number of items in total. When this condition is met, PyObject_GetIter gives you roughly the same performance as PySequence_Fast (if the input argument is a list or tuple), but it can save memory allocation, and therefore can run faster, if the input argument is an iterator or another kind of sequence or iterable. In this recipe's function, since we are just summing the items, it is indeed perfectly OK to get them one at a time, and we don't need to know in advance the total number; therefore, using PyObject_GetIter is preferable. (In the real world, you would use Python's built-in function sum for this specific functionality, rather than coding a dedicated C function, but then, this *is* meant to be just an example!)

PyObject_GetIter takes one argument: a Python object from which an iterator is desired (much like Python's iter built-in function). It either returns 0, indicating an error, or an iterator object, on which you can repeatedly call PyIter_Next to get the next item (or 0, NULL, which does not indicate an error, but rather indicates the end of the iteration). Both PyObject_GetIter and PyIter_Next return new references, so we must use Py_DECREF when we're done with the respective objects.

As usual, the best way to build this extension (assuming that you've saved it as a file named *totit.c*) is with the distutils package. Place in the same directory as the C source a file named *setup.py* such as:

```
from distutils.core import setup, Extension
setup(name="totit", maintainer="Luther Blissett", maintainer_email=
    "situ@tioni.st", ext_modules=[Extension('totit', sources=['totit.c'])]
)
```

then build and install by running:

```
$ python setup.py install
```

Part of the appeal of this approach is that it works on any platform, assuming that you have access to the same C compiler used to build your version of Python, and permission to write on the *site-packages* directory where the resulting dynamically loaded library gets installed.

Since Python extensions are often coded in C to maximize performance, it's interesting to measure performance compared to pure Python code dealing with the same task. A typical measurement setup might be a script such as the following *timon.py*:

```
import timeit, operator
from total import total
from totit import totit
```

```
def timo(fn, sq, init):
    T = timeit.Timer('timon.%s(%s)'%(fn,sq), 'import timon\n'+init)
    print ' %5.5s: %5.2f' % (fn, T.timeit(40000))
def totpy(x):
    result = 0.0
    for item in x: result += item
    return result
def totre(x):
    return reduce(operator.add, x, 0.0)
def totsu(x):
    return sum(x, 0.0)
if __name__ == '__main__':
    print 'on lists:'
    for f in 'totre totpy total totit totsu'.split():
        timo(f, 'seq', 'seq=range(2000)')
    print 'on iters:'
    for f in 'totre totpy total totit totsu'.split():
        timo(f, 'g()', 'def g():\n  for x in range(2000): yield x')
```

This script uses the timeit module of the Python Standard Library to measure accurately 40,000 calls to each function on 2,000-item lists and 2,000-item generators. The timeit.Timer constructor takes two string arguments: first the statement we're timing, then the setup statements that run before timing begins. Here, the statement we're timing calls functions in this module; therefore, the setup statements must import this module—which is why we add the import timon at the beginning of the setup statement string. I have also taken care to make all these functions strictly comparable, by having them all sum floats (not just ints). This purpose is the reason that I provide the explicit 0.0 initial arguments to built-in functions reduce and sum.

On my machine, running with the command-line switch -O so that Python can optimize operations a little bit, the timing results on Python 2.3 are:

```
<m>$ python -O timon.py</m>
on lists:
 totre: 136.04
 totpy: 118.18
 total: 56.61
 totit: 59.66
 totsu: 74.11
on iters:
 totre: 220.86
 totpy: 198.98
 total: 199.72
 totit: 201.70
 totsu: 157.44
```

As you can see, the most important optimization is to avoid the "attractive nuisance" of the reduce built-in function: even a pure Python loop is faster! When we're dealing with lists, the special-purpose C-coded extensions presented in the last two recipes are fastest; but when we're dealing with generators, the fastest solution is provided by the built-in function sum. In practice, one would always use sum for this functionality, rather than bothering to code or expose special-purpose C functions.

See Also

The *Extending and Embedding* manual is available as part of the standard Python documentation set at *http://www.python.org/doc/current/ext/ext.html*; documentation on the Python C API is at *http://www.python.org/doc/current/api/api.html*; the section "Distributing Python Modules" in the standard Python documentation set is still incomplete but is a good source of information on the distutils package; Chapter 19 of this book covers iterators and generators in pure Python terms; *Python in a Nutshell* covers the essentials of extending and embedding, of the Python C API, of the distutils package, and of iterators; Python's *Library Reference* covers the timeit module.

17.8 Returning None from a Python-Callable C Function

Credit: Alex Martelli

Problem

Your C-coded, Python-callable function in an extension module needs to return nothing in particular (i.e., a Python None), but it must, of course, do so without messing up reference counts.

Solution

Suppose we need an empty C-coded function, equivalent to Python:

```
def empty1(*args):
    pass
```

or, identically:

```
def empty2(*args):
    return None
```

Despite the simplicity of the task, there are right and wrong ways to perform it. The canonical solution is:

```
static PyObject*
empty3(PyObject* self, PyObject* args)
{
    Py_INCREF(Py_None);
    return Py_None;
}
```

and the simplest, but still correct way, is:

```
static PyObject*
empty4(PyObject* self, PyObject* args)
{
```

```
    return Py_BuildValue("");
}
```

Discussion

A function written in C for Python often needs to return nothing in particular. In Python terms, it must return None. Don't just code return Py_None; from C: that messes up reference counts! None—the Python object we must explicitly return from a Python-callable, C-coded function—is a normal Python object, subject to all normal reference count rules. One of these rules is that each function must Py_INCREF the Python object it returns.

A bare return Py_None; is a nasty lurking bug—a frequent beginner's error that messes up reference counts:

```
static PyObject*
empty5(PyObject* self, PyObject* args)
{
    return Py_None;          /* ***WRONG*** */
}
```

Either explicitly Py_INCREF the None object you're returning, or (a simpler approach, but one that costs a few machine cycles) delegate the work to the handy function Py_BuildValue, which can be used to handle just about all cases of returning values from C to Python, offering potential uniformity advantages. To have Py_BuildValue build a properly incref'd None on your behalf, call it with just one argument, an empty format string.

In Python 2.4, the C API has gained a new macro just for this purpose. If you're coding a C extension that supports only Python 2.4, you can write Py_RETURN_NONE; instead of the return statement, and the macro takes care of everything for you.

See Also

The *Extending and Embedding* manual is available as part of the standard Python documentation set at *http://www.python.org/doc/current/ext/ext.html*; documentation on the Python C API is at *http://www.python.org/doc/current/api/api.html*.

17.9 Debugging Dynamically Loaded C Extensions with gdb

Credit: Joe VanAndel, Michael Aivazis

Problem

A dynamically loaded C/C++ Python extension is giving you trouble on a Unix or Unix-like platform, and you want to use the interactive debugger *gdb* to determine what's wrong.

Solution

One way to determine the cause of core dumps or other serious trouble with a C Python extension is to compile the extension source with -g and then follow these steps. (You may also want to recompile any other extensions you use, such as Numeric, with -g, if you hadn't built them that way in the first place.)

```
<m>% gdb /usr/bin/python2.1</m>
(gdb) br _PyImport_LoadDynamicModule
(gdb) run    # start python
(gdb) cont   # repeat until your extension is loaded
(gdb) # you may need an import statement at python's >>> prompt
(gdb) finish # finish loading your extension module
(gdb) br wrap_myfunction  # break at the entry point in your code
(gdb) disable 1   # don't break for any more modules being loaded
(gdb) cont   # back to Python, run things normally from here
```

Discussion

If a dynamically loaded C/C++ extension is causing Python to core dump, or causing some other kind of serious trouble, this recipe can help you determine the root cause, by demonstrating a technique for debugging your extension using *gdb* (if you use Unix or some Unix-like platform, and *gdb* is your debugger of choice). The overall concept generalizes to other debuggers with abilities similar to *gdb*'s.

The main point of this recipe is that you cannot set a break on your function at the start, because your function lives in a dynamic library (shared object) that isn't initially loaded. However, you can break in the PyImport_LoadDynamicModule function, and eventually (when your module is finally being loaded) get control at the debugger prompt right after your module is in memory. You are then able, at last, to set the breakpoints you need.

This technique works. However, if you do this kind of thing often, the process of stepping through all the modules, as Python loads them at startup, can easily become tedious. A handier alternative, although more invasive, requires you to modify your Python sources and rebuild Python from them.

The key idea of this handier alternative is to add a do-nothing function somewhere in the body of code that Python loads immediately. Specifically, you can edit the *Modules/main.c* file, adding one new function:

```
void Py_DebugTrap(void) { }
```

In the extension you're debugging, you can now add a call to Py_DebugTrap( ) right where you want to break into the code. The Py_DebugTrap( ) symbol is immediately available when you start *gdb*, because the symbol lives in *main.c*. So you can immediately set a breakpoint there, as soon as you are at the *gdb* prompt, then continue. This approach even works in parallel under MPI (message passing interface).

See Also

The *gdb* online documentation (just type **help** at the *gdb* interactive prompt), manual pages, and online manual (*http://www.gnu.org/manual/gdb-4.17/gdb.html*).

17.10 Debugging Memory Problems

Credit: Will Ware

Problem

You're developing C extensions, and you experience memory problems. You suspect mismanagement of reference counts and want to check whether your C extension code is correctly managing reference counts.

Solution

To chase these problems in an optimal way, you need to alter Python's sources and rebuild Python. Specifically, add the following function in *Objects/object.c*, immediately before the _Py_PrintReferences function:

```
void
_Py_CountReferences(FILE *fp)
{
    int nr, no;
    PyObject *op;
    for (nr = no = 0, op = refchain._ob_next;
         op != &refchain;
         op = op->_ob_next, nr += op->ob_refcnt, no += 1)
    { }
    fprintf(fp, "%d refs (%d), %d objs\n", nr, _Py_RefTotal, no);
}
```

I place the following macros in my C extensions:

```
#if defined(Py_DEBUG) || defined(DEBUG)
extern void _Py_CountReferences(FILE*);
#define CURIOUS(x) { fprintf(stderr, __FILE__ ":%d ", __LINE__); x; }
#else
#define CURIOUS(x)
#endif
#define MARKER()        CURIOUS(fprintf(stderr, "\n"))
#define DESCRIBE(x)     CURIOUS(fprintf(stderr, "  " #x "=%d\n", x))
#define DESCRIBE_HEX(x) CURIOUS(fprintf(stderr, "  " #x "=%08x\n", x))
#define COUNTREFS()     CURIOUS(_Py_CountReferences(stderr))
```

To debug, I rebuild Python using make OPT="-DPy_DEBUG", which causes the code under Py_TRACE_REFS to be built. My own makefile for my extensions uses the same trick by including these lines:

```
debug:
        make clean; make OPT="-g -DPy_DEBUG" all
CFLAGS = $(OPT) -fpic -O2 -I/usr/local/include -I/usr/include/python2.3
```

Discussion

When I'm developing C extensions and running into memory problems, I find that the typical cause is mismanagement of reference counts, particularly misuse of Py_INCREF and Py_DECREF, as well as forgetfulness of the reference-count effects of functions like Py_BuildValue, PyArg_ParseTuple, and PyTuple/List_SetItem/GetItem. The Python sources offer help with this problem (search for Py_TRACE_REFS), and function sys.getrefcounts in the Python Standard Library is also helpful. Nevertheless, it's useful to add this recipe's function in *Objects/object.c* just before _Py_PrintReferences.

Unlike _Py_PrintReferences, this recipe's _Py_CountReferences function prints only the totals of all the refcounts and number of objects in the system, so it can be sensibly called, even in loops that repeat millions of times, while _Py_PrintReferences would print out way too much stuff to be useful. The information printed by _Py_CountReferences can help you identify errantly wandering Py_INCREFs and Py_DECREFs. _Py_CountReferences plays it safe by performing its own counts of objects references, which it prints side by side with the "official" count of references that Python itself maintains (when compiled for debugging) as global variable _Py_RefTotal. Should any discrepancy arise, you *know* something deeply wrong is going on.

When I suspect that one of my C-coded functions is responsible for memory problems, I liberally sprinkle the suspect function with calls to the COUNTREFS macro. Doing so allows me to keep track of exactly how many references are being created or destroyed as I go through my function. This information is particularly useful in tight loops, in which dumb mistakes can cause reference counts to grow ridiculously fast. Also, reference counts that shrink too fast (because of overzealous use of Py_DECREF) can cause core dumps because the memory for objects that should still exist has been reallocated for new objects.

See Also

The only documentation in this case is Python's own source code. Use the source, Luke!

## CHAPTER 18

Algorithms

18.0 Introduction

Credit: Tim Peters, PythonLabs

Algorithm research is what drew me to Python—and I fell in love. It wasn't love at first sight, but it was an attraction that grew into infatuation, which grew steadily into love. And that love shows no signs of fading. Why? I've worked in fields pushing the state of the art, and, in a paradoxical nutshell, Python code is easy to throw away!

When you're trying to solve a problem that may not have been solved before, you may have some intuitions about how to proceed, but you rarely know in advance exactly what needs to be done. The only way to proceed is to try things, many things, everything you can think of, just to see what happens. Python makes such exploration easier by minimizing the time and pain from conception to code: if your colleagues are using, for example, C or Java, it's not unusual for you to try (and discard) six different approaches in Python while they're still getting the bugs out of their first attempt.

In addition, you will have naturally grown classes and modules that capture key parts of the problem domain, simply because you find the need to keep reinventing them when starting over from scratch. I've used many languages in my computer career, and I know of none more productive than Python for prototyping. Best of all, while being an expert is often helpful, moderate skill in Python is much easier to obtain than for many other languages, yet much more productive for research and prototyping than merely moderate skill in any other language I've used. You don't have to be an expert to start!

So if you're in the research business—and every programmer who doesn't know everything occasionally is—you've got a nearly perfect language in Python. How then do you develop the intuitions that can generate a myriad of plausible approaches to try? Experience is the final answer, as we all get better at what we do often, but studying the myriad approaches other people have tried develops a firm base from which to explore. Toward that end, here are the most inspiring algorithm books I've read. They'll teach you possibilities you may never have discovered on your own:

John Bentley, *Programming Pearls and More Programming Pearls* (Addison-Wesley)
> Every programmer should read these books from cover to cover for sheer joy. The chapters are extended versions of a popular column Bentley wrote for the Communications of the Association for Computing Machinery (CACM). Each chapter is generally self-contained, covering one or two lovely (and often surprising, in the "Aha! why didn't I think of that?!" sense) techniques of real practical value.

Robert Sedgewick, *Algorithms in C++* or *Algorithms in C* (Addison-Wesley)
> These books cover the most important general algorithms, organized by problem domain, and provide brief but cogent explanations, along with working code. The books cover the same material; the difference is in which computer language is used for the code. I recommend the C++ book for Python programmers, because idiomatic Python is closer to C++ than to C. Sedgewick's use of C++ is generally simple and easily translated to equivalent Python. This is the first book to reach for when you need to tackle a new area quickly.

Donald Knuth, *The Art of Computer Programming*, series (Addison-Wesley)
> For experts (and those who aspire to expertise), this massive series in progress is the finest in-depth exposition of the state of the art. Nothing compares to its unique combination of breadth and depth, rigor, and historical perspective. Note that these books aren't meant to be read, they have to be actively studied, and many valuable insights are scattered in answers to the extensive exercises. While the books include detailed analysis, there's virtually no working code, except for programs written in assembly language for a hypothetical machine of archaic design (yes, it can be maddeningly obscure). It can be hard going at times, but few books so richly reward time invested.

To hone your skills, you can practice on an endless source of problems from the wonderful *On-Line Encyclopedia of Integer Sequences*, at *http://www.research.att.com/~njas/sequences/Seis.html*. When stress-testing upcoming Python releases, I sometimes pick a sequence at random from its list of sequences needing more terms and write a program to attempt an extension the sequence. Sometimes I'm able to extend a sequence that hasn't been augmented in years, in large part because Python has so many powerful features for rapid construction of new algorithms. Then the new terms are contributed to the database, where they benefit others. Give it a try! You may love it, but even if you hate it, you'll certainly find it challenging.

Timing and timeit.py

The first edition of this book contained a lengthy discussion of the difficulties in timing alternative approaches. Such difficulties include the fact that the resolution of time.time varies across platforms, and time.clock measures different things on different platforms (e.g., process CPU time on Linux systems, wall-clock time on Windows).

It may still be important for some to learn all those details, but Python 2.3 introduced a new timeit module, which captures best practice and is perfectly suited to timing small programs with a minimum of fuss and pitfalls. Everyone should learn how to use timeit, and basic usage is very easy to learn.

The simplest use of timeit is to pass one or more Python statements on the command line. Of course, shell syntax varies across platforms, so you may need to adjust these statements to the shell you use:

```
% python timeit.py "100 + 200"
10000000 loops, best of 3: 0.0932 usec per loop
% python timeit.py "100 - 200"
10000000 loops, best of 3: 0.0931 usec per loop
```

As expected, integer addition and subtraction are just about equally expensive. (Don't fall into the trap of attributing any significance to differences as tiny as this one!) timeit picks the best way of measuring time on your platform and runs your code in a loop. The module tries a few times first to determine how many iterations to use in the loop, aiming at a total loop time between 0.2 and 2 seconds. When it determines a suitable number of iterations for the loop, it then runs the loop three times, reports the shortest time, and computes the time per loop iteration. The iterations per loop, and number of loops to run, can be forced to specific values with command-line options. See the *Python Library Reference* for details. (It's part of Python's online documentation and probably also comes in some handy form with your version of Python.)

As always, you should keep your machine as quiet as possible when running timing tests. The primary reason timeit runs three repetitions of the loop and reports the minimum time is to guard against skewed results due to other machine activity. This is especially important when running snippets that do very little work, such as the preceding examples. In such cases, even just one unfortunate interruption can grossly increase the reported time. Even so, on my quiet machine, snippets that run this fast can still yield confusing results:

```
% python timeit.py "100 + 200; 100 - 200"
10000000 loops, best of 3: 0.151 usec per loop
% python timeit.py "100 + 200" "100 - 200"
10000000 loops, best of 3: 0.151 usec per loop
```

One correct conclusion is that modern Python no longer has a time penalty for writing two statements on two lines, instead of squashing them together on one line separated by a semicolon. Older Pythons generated a SET_LINENO opcode at the start of each logical line of code, and those opcodes consumed time to execute!

A more puzzling result is that adding and subtracting in one shot took 0.151 usec, but adding alone and subtracting alone took 0.0932 usec each. Why didn't we get 2*0.093 = 0.186 usec in the second experiment? The explanation is quite simple: timeit uses a fast iteration technique and doesn't try to subtract the iteration overhead from the reported results. When timing very fast snippets, this can be mildly disconcerting. Let's try to measure the overhead by timing a do-nothing statement:

```
% python timeit.py "pass"
10000000 loops, best of 3: 0.0203 usec per loop
```

While 0.02 usec is tiny, it's significant compared to the 0.093 usec reported for an integer add! Of course this effect diminishes to insignificance when timing more expensive operations:

```
% python timeit.py "100**100"
100000 loops, best of 3: 4.04 usec per loop
% python timeit.py "200**200"
100000 loops, best of 3: 9.03 usec per loop
% python timeit.py "100**100" "200**200"
100000 loops, best of 3: 13.1 usec per loop
```

Large integer exponentiation is much more expensive than adding small integers, and here the sum of the times for doing 100**100 and 200**200 in isolation is very close to the time for doing both at once.

The timeit module supports several other command-line options, and a programmatic interface too, but I'll defer to the *Python Library Reference* for that information. To start making productive use of timeit, the only other option you need to know about is the ability to pass "setup" statements on the command line. These statements execute once, outside the loop containing the code you're timing. For example, import statements are often used, as well as code that populates data structures. For example (assuming a backslash \ is your shell's way to indicate that a long logical line continues in the next physical line):

```
% python timeit.py -s "import random" \
    -s "x=range(100000); random.shuffle(x)" "sorted(x)"
10 loops, best of 3: 152 msec per loop
```

For each of the three loops, timeit constructed the randomly ordered array just once, then ran sorted(x) repeatedly inside the loop. This was so expensive that timeit ran only 10 iterations per loop and changed its reporting units from microseconds to milliseconds. (In Python 2.3, timeit always reported in microseconds, but in version 2.4, it tries to be more helpful by picking the appropriate reporting units.) This is very different from:

```
% python timeit.py "import random" \
    "x=range(100000); random.shuffle(x)" "sorted(x)"
10 loops, best of 3: 309 msec per loop
```

This snippet timed *all* the operations: importing `random`, building the list, randomly permuting the list, and sorting the list. This preparation code takes longer than sorting does! You may be surprised that we see from the reported times that it took at least as long to build and shuffle the list as it took to sort it. The first two operations take 0(n) time, but sorting random data takes 0(n log n) time; given this, how can this strange measurement be explained? Why didn't sorting take longer?

I won't explain that mystery here but will point out a more significant lesson: timing code *always* uncovers mysteries, and a timing tool as easy to use as `timeit` can be addictive. So be careful what you measure! Measuring itself will consume more of your time than you expect. As noted innumerable times by innumerable authors, the speed of most of your code doesn't matter at all. Find the 10% that consumes most of the time before worrying about any of it. When you find the true bottlenecks, `timeit` can help you measure the speed of alternatives objectively—and you may be surprised by what you find.

18.1 Removing Duplicates from a Sequence

Credit: Tim Peters

Problem

You have a sequence that may include duplicates, and you want to remove the duplicates in the fastest possible way, without knowing much about the properties of the items in the sequence. You do not care about the "or"der of items in the resulting sequence.

Solution

The key is to try several approaches, fastest first, and use try/except to handle the failing cases of the faster approaches by falling back to slower approaches. Here's a function that implements exactly this strategy:

```
# support 2.3 as well as 2.4
try: set
except NameError: from sets import Set as set
def unique(s):
    """ Return a list of the elements in s in arbitrary order, but without
        duplicates. """
    # Try using a set first, because it's the fastest and will usually work
    try:
        return list(set(s))
    except TypeError:
        pass  # Move on to the next method
    # Since you can't hash all elements, try sorting, to bring equal items
    # together and then weed them out in a single pass
    t = list(s)
    try:
```

```
        t.sort()
    except TypeError:
        del t   # Move on to the next method
    else:
        # the sort worked, so we're fine -- do the weeding
        return [x for i, x in enumerate(t) if not i or x != t[i-1]]
    # Brute force is all that's left
    u = [ ]
    for x in s:
        if x not in u:
            u.append(x)
    return u
```

Discussion

The purpose of this recipe's unique function is to take a sequence s as an argument and return a list of the items in s in arbitrary order, but without duplicates. For example, calling unique([1, 2, 3, 1, 2, 3]) returns an arbitrary permutation of [1, 2, 3], calling unique('abcabc') returns an arbitrary permutation of ['a', 'b', 'c'], and calling unique(([1, 2], [2, 3], [1, 2])) returns an arbitrary permutation of [[2, 3], [1, 2]].

The fastest way to remove duplicates from a sequence depends on fairly subtle properties of the sequence elements, such as whether they're hashable and whether they support full comparisons. The unique function shown in this recipe tries three methods, from fastest to slowest, letting runtime exceptions pick the best method for the sequence at hand.

For fastest speed, all sequence elements must be hashable. When they are, the unique function will usually work in linear time (i.e., $O(n)$, or directly proportional to the number of elements in the input, which is good and highly scalable performance behavior).

If it turns out that hashing the elements (e.g., using them as dictionary keys, or, as in this case, set elements) is not possible, the next best situation is when the elements enjoy a total ordering, meaning that each element can be compared to each other element with the < operator. If list(s).sort() doesn't raise a TypeError, we can assume that s' elements can be sorted and therefore enjoy a total ordering. Then unique will usually work in $O(n \log(n))$ time. Python lists' sort method is particularly efficient in the presence of partially ordered data (including, e.g., data with many duplicates), so the sorting approach may be more effective in Python than elsewhere.

If sorting also turns out to be impossible, the sequence items must at least support equality testing, or else the very concept of duplicates can't really be meaningful for them. In this case, unique works in quadratic time—that is, $O(n^2)$, meaning time proportional to the square of the number of elements in the input: not very scalable, but the least of all evils, given the sequence items' obviously peculiar nature (assuming we get all the way to this subcase).

This recipe is a pure example of how algorithm efficiency depends on the strength of the assumptions you can make about the data. You could split this recipe's function into three distinct functions and directly call the one that best meets your needs. In practice, however, the brute-force method is so slow for large sequences that nothing measurable is lost by simply letting the function as written try the faster methods first.

If you need to preserve the same order of items in the output sequence as in the input sequence, see recipe 18.2 "Removing Duplicates from a Sequence While Maintaining Sequence Order."

See Also

Recipe 18.2 "Removing Duplicates from a Sequence While Maintaining Sequence Order."

18.2   Removing Duplicates from a Sequence While Maintaining Sequence Order

Credit: Alex Martelli

Problem

You have a sequence that may include duplicates, and you want to remove the duplicates in the fastest possible way. Moreover, the output sequence must respect the item ordering of the input sequence.

Solution

The need to respect the item ordering of the input sequence means that picking unique items becomes a problem quite different from that explored previously in recipe 18.1 "Removing Duplicates from a Sequence." This requirement often arises in conjunction with a function f that defines an equivalence relation among items: x is equivalent to y if and only if f(x)==f(y). In this case, the task of removing duplicates may often be better described as picking the first representative of each resulting equivalence class. Here is a function to perform this task:

```
# support 2.3 as well as 2.4
try: set
except NameError: from sets import Set as set
# f defines an equivalence relation among items of sequence seq, and
# f(x) must be hashable for each item x of seq
def uniquer(seq, f=None):
    """ Keeps earliest occurring item of each f-defined equivalence class """
    if f is None:     # f's default is the identity function f(x) -> x
        def f(x): return x
    already_seen = set( )
```

```
    result = [ ]
    for item in seq:
        marker = f(item)
        if marker not in already_seen:
            already_seen.add(marker)
            result.append(item)
    return result
```

Discussion

The previous recipe 18.1 "Removing Duplicates from a Sequence" is applicable only if you are not concerned about item ordering or, in other words, if the sequences involved are meaningful only as the sets of their items, which is often the case. When sequential order is significant, a different approach is needed.

If the items are hashable, it's not hard to maintain sequence order, keeping only the first occurrence of each value. More generally, we may want uniqueness within equivalence classes, as shown in this recipe's Solution: the uniquer function accepts as an argument a function f that must return hashable objects, such that $f(x)==f(y)$ if and only if items x and y are equivalent. Identity (in the mathematical sense, not in the Python sense) is used as the default when no argument f is supplied. The added generality of allowing an f different from the identity function costs no added complication whatsoever.

If you need to keep the last occurrence, rather than the earliest occurrence, of an item in each equivalence class, the simplest approach is to reverse the input sequence (or, rather, a copy thereof into a local list, since the input might be immutable or at any rate not support reversing), then, after processing with uniquer, reverse the resulting list:

```
def uniquer_last(seq, f=None):
    seq = list(seq)
    seq.reverse()
    result = uniquer(seq, f)
    result.reverse()
    return result
```

In Python 2.4, instead of the first three statements of this version of uniquer_last, you could use the single statement:

```
result = uniquer(reversed(seq), f)
```

exploiting the new built-in reversed. However, this Python 2.4 version, while marginally faster, is less general, because it does require seq to be really a sequence, while the previously shown version (and the uniquer function in the "Solution") work with any *iterable* seq. For example:

```
somelines = uniquer_last(open('my.txt'), str.lower)
```

binds name somelines to the list of unique lines from text file *my.txt*, considering two lines equivalent if they're equal aside from uppercase and lowercase distinctions, picking the last occurring one from each set of equivalent lines, and preserving the order of the lines in the file (phew). If you used Python 2.4's built-in reversed, this latest snippet would not work, due to reversed's prerequisites.

If you must deal with nonhashable items, the simplest fallback approach is to use a set-like container that supports the add method and membership testing without requiring items to be hashable. Unfortunately, performance will be *much* worse than with a real set. Here's the simplest fallback implementation, which demands of items nothing but support for equality testing:

```
def uniquer_with_simplest_fallback(seq, f=None):
    if f is None:
        def f(x): return x
    already_seen = set()
    result = []
    for item in seq:
        marker = f(item)
        try:
            new_marker = marker not in already_seen
        except TypeError:
            class TotallyFakeSet(list):
                add = list.append
            already_seen = TotallyFakeSet(already_seen)
            new_marker = marker not in already_seen
        if new_marker:
            already_seen.add(marker)
            result.append(item)
    return result
```

A more refined approach would be to use two levels of fallback, the intermediate one based on sorting, as shown previously in recipe 18.1 "Removing Duplicates from a Sequence" testing in a sorted list can be performed efficiently by using the Python Standard Library module bisect.

However, remember that you can often use an f that gives you hashable markers for nonhashable items. The built-in function repr can often be useful for this purpose. For example:

```
lol = [ [1, 2], [ ], [1, 2], [3], [ ], [3, 4], [1, 2], [ ], [2, 1] ]
print uniquer(lol, repr)
# emits: [[1, 2], [ ], [3], [3, 4], [2, 1]]
```

While the items of lol are lists, and thus are not hashable, the built-in function repr produces representations of each of the items as a string, which *is* hashable. This enables use of the fast function uniquer. Unfortunately, repr is not useful for non-hashable items of other types, including dict and set. Because of the workings of hash-collision resolution, it's quite possible to have d1==d2 and yet repr(d1)!=repr(d2) for two dictionaries d1 and d2, depending on the exact sequences of adds that built each dict. Still, you may be able build your own repr-like function to work around these issues, depending on the exact nature of your data. Whether repr can help for instances of a certain user-defined type depends on how accurately and usefully that specific type defines special method __repr__, which repr calls.

The task of picking one representative item, out of all of those belonging to each equivalence class, can be generalized. Instead of the simple ideas of implicitly picking the first such item, or the last such item, we can choose among multiple items in the same equivalence class via an arbitrary *picking* function p that considers both the actual items and their indexes of occurrence. As long as function p can operate pairwise, the key idea is just to keep a dictionary that maps the marker of each equivalence class to the index and item of the representative so far picked for that class. At the end, we reconstruct sequence order by sorting on the indices:

```
def fancy_unique(seq, f, p):
    """ Keeps "best" item of each f-defined equivalence class, with
        picking function p doing pairwise choice of (index, item) """
    representative = {}
    for index, item in enumerate(seq):
        marker = f(item)
        if marker in representative:
            # It's NOT a problem to rebind index and item within the
            # for loop: the next leg of the loop does not use their binding
            index, item = p((index, item), representative[marker])
        representative[marker] = index, item
    # reconstruct sequence order by sorting on indices
    auxlist = representative.values()
    auxlist.sort()
    return [item for index, item in auxlist]
```

It's possible that the picking function cannot operate pairwise, but rather must be presented with the whole bunch of (index, item) pairs for each equivalence class in order to pick the best representative of that class (e.g., it may have to get the *median* of the items in each class as being the best representative of that class). Then we need one pass over the sequence to collect the bunches, followed by a pass over the bunches, to pick the representatives:

```
def fancier_uniquer(seq, f, p):
    """ Keeps "best" item of each f-defined equivalence class, with
        picking function p choosing appropriate (index, item) for each
        equivalence class from the list of all (index, item) pairs in
        that class """
    bunches = {}
    for index, item in enumerate(seq):
        marker = f(item)
        bunches.setdefault(marker, []).append((index, item))
    auxlist = [p(candidates) for candidates in bunches.values()]
    auxlist.sort()
    return [item for index, item in auxlist]
```

These fancy approaches that rely on a picking function are useful only for substantial equivalence functions, not for identity, so I removed f's default value from these versions.

An example of use for fancy_unique may help. Say we're given a list of words, and we need to get a sublist from it, respecting order, such that no two words on the sublist begin with the same letter. Out of all the words in the "or"iginal list that begin with each given letter, we need to keep the longest word and, in case of equal lengths, the word appearing later on the list. This sounds complicated, but with fancy_unique to help us, it's really not that bad:

```
def complicated_choice(words):
    def first_letter(aword):
        return aword[0].lower( )
    def prefer((indx1, word1), (indx2, word2)):
        if len(word2) > len(word1):
            return indx2, word2
        return indx1, word1
    return fancy_unique(words, first_letter, prefer)
```

The prefer nested function within complicated_choice is simplified because it knows fancy_unique always calls it with indx2<indx1. So, the older indx2, word2 pair must be returned only when word2 is longer than word1; otherwise, indx1, word1 is always the proper result. The automatic tuple unpacking in prefer's signature is debatable, stylewise, but I like it (it reminds me of SML or Haskell).

Out of all the general programming techniques presented in the various functions of this recipe, the idea of writing higher-order functions, which organize a computation and appropriately call back to functions that they receive as arguments, is easily the most precious and widely applicable concept. This idea is well worth keeping in mind in several circumstances—not just for old Haskell-heads, because it works just as well in Python.

See Also

Recipe 18.1 "Removing Duplicates from a Sequence."

18.3 Generating Random Samples with Replacement

Credit: Sean Ross

Problem

You need to generate random samples with replacement out of a "population" of items that are held in a sequence.

Solution

A generator for the purpose is quintessentially simple:

```
import random
def sample_wr(population, _choose=random.choice):
    while True: yield _choose(population)
```

Discussion

random.sample lets you do random sampling without replacement, and recipe 18.4 "Generating Random Samples Without Replacement," which follows, shows a generator to perform sampling without replacement with excellent memory-consumption characteristics. This recipe provides a generator for sampling *with* replacement, which is an even simpler task. Basically all the work gets delegated to random.choice. The sample_wr generator shown in this recipe is unbounded: used on its own, it will keep looping forever. To bound the output of an intrinsically unbounded generator, you can use it in a for statement that at some point executes a break, or use other techniques shown in recipe 19.2 "Building a List from Any Iterable."

For example, to make a random string of 50 lowercase ASCII letters:

```
import itertools
from string import ascii_lowercase
x = ''.join(itertools.slice(sample_wr(ascii_lowercase), 50))
```

string.ascii_lowercase is exactly the string 'abcdefghijklmnopqrstuvwxyz'. If you didn't have the sample_wr generator, the equivalent code might be something like:

```
from string import ascii_lowercase
from random import choice
x = ''.join([ random.choice(ascii_lowercase) for i in xrange(50) ])
```

So, the practical added-value of sample_wr is modest, when compared to other available building-blocks. It is, however, preferable to have such a fundamental concept of statistics as *sampling with replacement* embodied as its own function, rather than having to implement it with an explicit loop over random.choice each time it is needed.

See Also

Library Reference and *Python in a Nutshell* docs for module random.

18.4 Generating Random Samples Without Replacement

Credit: Raymond Hettinger

Problem

You need to generate random samples without replacement out of a "population" (the integers between 0 included and some n excluded), and you want better memory consumption characteristics than random.sample provides.

Solution

A generator for this purpose requires only constant memory and makes a small number of calls to random.random:

```
import random
def sample(n, r):
    " Generate r randomly chosen, sorted integers from [0,n) "
    rand = random.random
    pop = n
    for samp in xrange(r, 0, -1):
        cumprob = 1.0
        x = rand( )
        while x < cumprob:
            cumprob -= cumprob * samp / pop
            pop -= 1
        yield n-pop-1
```

Discussion

random.sample(xrange(10), 3) produces output statistically equal to list(sample(10, 3)) using this recipe's sample. Differently from random.sample(xrange(n), r), this recipe's sample(n, r) requires a bounded amount of memory (which does not grow with either r or n) and is guaranteed to make only r calls to random.random. Moreover, this recipe's sample yields the r numbers of the sample in sorted order, while random.sample returns them in random order—which may be insignificant or a crucial advantage one way or the other, depending on your application's needs. A definite advantage of random.sample is that its running time is O(r), while this recipe's sample function's running time is O(n).

This recipe was inspired by Knuth's *Algorithm S* in Donald E. Knuth, *The Art of Computer Programming, Volume 3, Seminumerical Algorithms*, in section 3.4.2. However, this recipe has one improvement over Knuth's algorithm: by tracking a cumulative probability for each selection, this recipe eliminates the need to make n calls to random.random.

A potential major improvement would be to find a direct formula giving the same result as the inner loop: given x, samp, and pop, compute the index of the first sample. Finding this formula would reduce the running time to O(r).

See Also

Library Reference and *Python in a Nutshell* docs about random.

18.5 Memoizing (Caching) the Return Values of Functions

Credit: Paul Moore, Mitch Chapman, Hannu Kankaanp

Problem

You have a pure function that is often called with the same arguments (particularly a recursive function) and is slow to compute its results. You want to find a simple way to gain substantial improvement in performance.

Solution

The key idea behind memoizing is to store a function's results in a dictionary, keyed by the arguments that produce each result. This approach makes sense only for a pure function (i.e., one that yields the same result when called more than once with the same arguments). It's easy to memoize a function by hand. For example, using the recursive Fibonacci function, here is a manually memoized function:

```
fib_memo = {}
def fib(n):
    if n < 2: return 1
    if n not in fib_memo:
        fib_memo[n] = fib(n-1) + fib(n-2)
    return fib_memo[n]
```

Having to code the memoization inside each function to be memoized is repetitive and degrades the function's readability. An alternative is to encapsulate the memoization mechanics into a closure:

```
def memoize(fn):
    memo = {}
    def memoizer(*param_tuple, **kwds_dict):
        # can't memoize if there are any named arguments
        if kwds_dict:
            return fn(*param_tuple, **kwds_dict)
        try:
            # try using the memo dict, or else update it
            try:
                return memo[param_tuple]
            except KeyError:
                memo[param_tuple] = result = fn(*param_tuple)
                return result
        except TypeError:
            # some mutable arguments, bypass memoizing
            return fn(*param_tuple)
    # 2.4 only: memoizer.__name__ = fn.__name__
    return memoizer
```

Using this memoize closure to memoize fib, the function definition becomes obvious, without caching boilerplate to obscure the algorithm. You must assign the memoize result to the same name, fib, as the recursive function; otherwise, the recursive calls bypass the memoizing:

```
def fib(n):
    if n < 2: return 1
    return fib(n-1) + fib(n-2)
fib = memoize(fib)
```

This latest snippet shows that memoize is meant to be used exactly as a Python 2.4 *decorator*, so in Python 2.4, you could use decorator syntax (instead of the explicit call to memoize):

```
@memoize
def fib(n):
    if n < 2: return 1
    return fib(n-1) + fib(n-2)
```

giving exactly the same semantics as the previous snippet.

Discussion

The memoize function is called with just one argument, a function f. It returns a closure memoizer that acts just like f but memoizes its arguments and result if the actual arguments to a call are hashable and positional. Calls with mutable or keyword arguments bypass the memoizing. If you're worried that such bypassing happens too often, making memoizing counterproductive, you should do a few dry runs that are representative of your intended production usage, with a closure that's modified to collect statistics. Then you can decide whether memoization is worth using for your specific application. Here's the modified memoize for this purpose:

```
def memoize(fn):
    memo = {}
    def memoizer(*param_tuple, **kwds_dict):
        if kwds_dict:
            memoizer.namedargs += 1
            return fn(*param_tuple, **kwds_dict)
        try:
            memoizer.cacheable += 1
            try:
                return memo[param_tuple]
            except KeyError:
                memoizer.misses += 1
                memo[param_tuple] = result = fn(*param_tuple)
                return result
        except TypeError:
            memoizer.cacheable -= 1
            memoizer.noncacheable += 1
            return fn(*param_tuple)
    memoizer.namedargs = memoizer.cacheable = memoizer.noncacheable = 0
    memoizer.misses = 0
    return memoizer
```

Functions to be memoized must be pure (i.e., they must have no side effects and must always return the same value whenever they are called with the same arguments). More significantly, memoize returns a closure that does not memoize calls that receive mutable arguments, such as len on a list, nor functions that receive named parameters.

memoize cannot really check the semantics of the functions you wrap. The notions of *same value* and *same arguments* are vaguely defined in many cases, so take care. memoize does try to field occasional calls with keyword and mutable arguments (with an interesting mix of checking and try/except), but performance will suffer unless such cases are rare. This is why it's worth having around a version of memoize that keeps counts of the various possibilities, so that you can check their rarity.

See Also

Recipe 20.4 "Caching Attribute Values" applies caching to class instances' attributes.

18.6 Implementing a FIFO Container

Credit: Sébastien Keim, Alex Martelli, Raymond Hettinger, Jeremy Fincher, Danny Yoo, Josiah Carlson

Problem

You need a container that allows element insertion and removal, in which the first element inserted is also the first to be removed (i.e., a first-in first-out, FIFO, queue).

Solution

We can subclass list to implement a Pythonic version of an idea found in Knuth's *Art of Computer Programming*: the frontlist/backlist approach to building a FIFO out of two one-way linked lists. Here's how:

```
class Fifo(list):
    def __init__(self):
        self.back = [ ]
        self.append = self.back.append
    def pop(self):
        if not self:
            self.back.reverse( )
            self[:] = self.back
            del self.back[:]
        return super(Fifo, self).pop( )
```

Discussion

Here is a usage example, protected by the usual guard so it runs only when the module executes as a main script rather than being imported:

```
if __name__ == '__main__':
    a = Fifo()
    a.append(10)
    a.append(20)
    print a.pop(),
    a.append(5)
    print a.pop(),
    print a.pop(),
    print
# emits: 10 20 5
```

The key idea in class Fifo is to have an auxiliary backlist, self.back, to which incoming items get appended. Outgoing items get popped from the frontlist, self. Each time the frontlist is exhausted, it gets replenished with the reversed contents of the backlist, and the backlist is emptied. The reversing and copying are O(n), where n is the number of items appended since the "front list" was last empty, but these operations are performed only once every n times, so the *amortized* cost of each call to pop is a constant—that is, O(1).

A simpler way to build a FIFO in Python is no doubt to just use a standard list's append and pop(0) methods—something like:

```
class FifoList(list):
    def pop(self):
        return super(FifoList, self).pop(0)
```

However, when using a list in this way, we need to keep in mind that pop(0) is O(n), where n is the current length of the list. O(1) performance can be ensured by building the FIFO in a slightly less intuitive way, on top of a dictionary:

```
class FifoDict(dict):
    def __init__(self):
        self.nextin = 0
        self.nextout = 0
    def append(self, data):
        self.nextin += 1
        self[self.nextin] = data
    def pop(self):
        self.nextout += 1
        return dict.pop(self, self.nextout)
```

In Python 2.4, we also have collections.deque, a double-ended queue type that also ensures O(1) performance when used as a FIFO (using its append and popleft methods):

```
import collections
class FifoDeque(collections.deque):
    pop = collections.deque.popleft
```

To choose among different implementations of the same interface, such as the various Fifo... classes shown in this recipe, the best approach often is to measure their performance on artificial benchmark examples that provide a reasonable simulation of the expected load in your application. I ran some such measurements on a somewhat slow laptop, with Python 2.4, using the `timeit` module from the Python Standard Library. For a total of 6,000 appends and pops, with a maximum length of 3,000, class `Fifo` takes about 62 milliseconds, class `FifoList` about 78, `FifoDict` about 137, and `FifoDeque` about 30. Making the problem exactly ten times bigger, we see the advantages of O(1) behavior (exhibited by all of these classes except `FifoList`). `Fifo` takes 0.62 seconds, `FifoList` 3.8, `FifoDict` 1.4, and `FifoDeque` 0.29. Clearly, in Python 2.4, `FifoDeque` is fastest as well as simplest; if your code has to support Python 2.3, the `Fifo` class shown in this recipe's Solution is best.

See Also

Library Reference and *Python in a Nutshell* docs for built-ins `list` and `dict`; *Library Reference* docs on modules collections (Python 2.4 only) and `timeit`. *Python in a Nutshell*'s chapter on optimization; Donald Knuth, *The Art Of Computer Programming* (exercise 14, section 2.2.1).

18.7 Caching Objects with a FIFO Pruning Strategy

Credit: David M. Wilson, Raymond Hettinger

Problem

You need to build a mapping to be used as a cache, holding up to a fixed number of previous entries and automatically discarding older entries.

Solution

A mapping can implement a relatively small number of core methods and rely on `UserDict.DictMixin` to provide all the other methods that make up the full official mapping interface. Here is a mapping class for FIFO caching, implemented with this "let `DictMixin` do it" strategy:

```
import UserDict
class FifoCache(object, UserDict.DictMixin):
    ''' A mapping that remembers the last `num_entries' items that were set '''
    def __init__(self, num_entries, dct=()):
        self.num_entries = num_entries
        self.dct = dict(dct)
        self.lst = [ ]
    def __repr__(self):
        return '%r(%r,%r)' % (
            self.__class__.__name__, self.num_entries, self.dct)
    def copy(self):
        return self.__class__(self.num_entries, self.dct)
    def keys(self):
        return list(self.lst)
    def __getitem__(self, key):
```

```
        return self.dct[key]
    def __setitem__(self, key, value):
        dct = self.dct
        lst = self.lst
        if key in dct:
            lst.remove(key)
        dct[key] = value
        lst.append(key)
        if len(lst) > self.num_entries:
            del dct[lst.pop(0)]
    def __delitem__(self, key):
        self.dct.pop(key)
        self.lst.remove(key)
    # a method explicitly defined only as an optimization
    def __contains__(self, item):
        return item in self.dct
    has_key = __contains__
```

Discussion

Here is a typical example of usage for this `FifoCache` class:

```
if __name__ == '__main__':
    f = FifoCache(num_entries=3)
    f["fly"] = "foo"
    f["moo"] = "two"
    f["bar"] = "baz"
    f["dave"] = "wilson"
    f["age"] = 20
    print f.keys( )
    # emits ['bar', 'dave', 'age']
```

For any case where you might use a dictionary object to cache expensive lookups, the `FifoCache` class shown in this recipe might be a safer alternative for use in long-running applications, whose caches might otherwise consume all system memory if left unchecked.

Thanks to `UserDict.DictMixin`, class `FifoCache` exhibits a full dictionary (i.e., mapping) interface: you can substitute an instance of `FifoCache` wherever you're using a dictionary (as long as you *do* want entries that were set "a long time ago" to drop out automatically to make space for newer ones).

In Python 2.4, you can get a faster version of `FifoCache` by setting `self.lst` to be an instance of `collections.deque` rather than a `list`, and using `self.lst.popleft( )` where this recipe's solution uses `self.lst.pop(0)`. Since the deque type does not have a remove method, you have to implement that with a little auxiliary function:

```
def remove_from_deque(d, x):
    for i, v in enumerate(d):
        if v == x:
            del d[i]
            return
    raise ValueError, '%r not in %r' % (x, d)
```

and use `remove_from_deque(self.lst, key)` where this recipe's Solution uses `self.list.remove(key)`. While, as always, you should measure how useful this optimization is in the context of your specific application, it's likely to be helpful when num_entries is high, since `self.lst.pop(0)` on a list `self.lst` is O(n), while `self.list.popleft()` on a deque `self.lst` is O(1). (`remove_from_deque`, like `list.remove`, is unfortunately and unavoidably O(n)).

FIFO is not the ideal policy for a cache's decision about what should "fall off"; a better one would be LRU (Least Recently Used). You can tweak this class' policy into LRU by subclassing and overriding:

```
class LRUCache(FifoCache):
    def __getitem__(self, key):
        if key in self.dct:
            self.lst.remove(key)
        else:
            raise KeyError
        self.lst.append(key)
        return self.dct[key]
```

This variant does ensure the use of the LRU policy without much extra code. Unfortunately, it makes every read access quite costly O(n), where n is the number of entries in the cache at that time), due to the need for the `self.lst.remove` call. Therefore, this recipe's official "Solution" uses the simpler implementation, even though FIFO is notoriously suboptimal as a cache replacement strategy.

See Also

Library Reference and *Python in a Nutshell* docs for module UserDict; recipe 5.14 "Enriching the Dictionary Type with Ratings Functionality" also uses UserDict.DictMixin to round up a mapping interface while coding a minimum of boilerplate.

18.8   Implementing a Bag (Multiset) Collection Type

Credit: Raymond Hettinger, Alex Martelli, Matt R

Problem

You need a set-like collection type that lets each element be in the set a number of times. In other words, you need a collection type of the kind that is known as multiset in C++ and SQL, and bag in Smalltalk, Objective C, and Haskell's Edison module.

Solution

We can implement bag as a class. We could restrict the implementation to language constructs that are present in Python 2.3 or are easy to emulate; however, such restrictions would give substantial inefficiencies or complications with comparison to a pure Python 2.4 implementation. So, here is a Python 2.4 implementation, with no attempt to support Python 2.3:

```python
from operator import itemgetter
from heapq import nlargest
class bag(object):
    def __init__(self, iterable=()):
        # start empty, then add the `iterable' if any
        self._data = {}
        self.update(iterable)
    def update(self, iterable):
        # update from an element->count mapping, or from any iterable
        if isinstance(iterable, dict):
            for elem, n in iterable.iteritems():
                self[elem] += n
        else:
            for elem in iterable:
                self[elem] += 1
    def __contains__(self, elem):
        # delegate membership test
        return elem in self._data
    def __getitem__(self, elem):
        # default all missing items to a count of 0
        return self._data.get(elem, 0)
    def __setitem__(self, elem, n):
        # setting an item to a count of 0 removes the item
        self._data[elem] = n
        if n == 0:
            del self._data[elem]
    def __delitem__(self, elem):
        # delegate to __setitem__ to allow deleting missing items
        self[elem] = 0
    def __len__(self):
        # length is computed on-the-fly
        return sum(self._data.itervalues())
    def __nonzero__(self):
        # avoid truth tests using __len__, as it's relatively slow
        return bool(self._data)
    def __eq__(self, other):
        # a bag can only equal another bag
        if not isinstance(other, bag):
            return False
        return self._data == other._data
    def __ne__(self, other):
        # a bag always differs from any non-bag
        return not (self == other)
    def __hash__(self):
        # a bag can't be a dict key nor an element in a set
```

```
            raise TypeError
    def __repr__(self):
        # typical string-representation
        return '%s(%r)' % (self.__class__.__name__, self._data)
    def copy(self):
        # make and return a shallow copy
        return self.__class__(self._data)
    __copy__ = copy # For the copy module
    def clear(self):
        # remove all items
        self._data.clear()
    def __iter__(self):
        # yield each element the # of times given by its count
        for elem, cnt in self._data.iteritems():
            for i in xrange(cnt):
                yield elem
    def iterunique(self):
        # yield each element only once
        return self._data.iterkeys()
    def itercounts(self):
        # yield element-count pairs
        return self._data.iteritems()
    def mostcommon(self, n=None):
        # return the n (default: all) most common elements, each as an
        # element-count pair, as a list sorted by descending counts
        if n is None:
            return sorted(self.itercounts(), key=itemgetter(1), reverse=True)
        it = enumerate(self.itercounts())
        nl = nlargest(n, ((cnt, i, elem) for (i, (elem, cnt)) in it))
        return [(elem, cnt) for cnt, i, elem in nl]
```

Discussion

Python offers several useful container classes, including built-in tuples, lists and
dicts, sets (in Python 2.4, sets are built-in; in Python 2.3, they're in module sets)—
which, unlike bags, can be seen as "holding only one instance" of each of their elements—and double-ended queues, deques (in Python 2.4 only, in module
collections). This abundance of container classes doesn't mean there is no use for
yet more. The bag, (i.e., multiset), presented in this recipe, is widely useful, since
counting the numbers of occurrences of different objects is a frequent task useful in
many applications. Rather than coding a bag each time you need such a container
(generally based on a dictionary mapping items to counts), it's better to design and
code it once, put it among one's utilities, and lobby for it to become part of the standard library for a future Python, such as 2.5 (which can be expected sometime in
2006 and will focus on enhancements to the standard library rather than to the core
language).

The API offered by the bag class presented in this recipe is largely based on indexing,
due to the strong analogy between a bag and a mapping of items to counts. For
example:

```
>>> b = bag('banana')
>>> b['a']
3
>>> b['a'] += 1
>>> b['a']
4
>>> del b['a']          # removes all 'a's from the bag
>>> b['a']
0
```

Items that are not in the bag can also be used as indices, giving a value (i.e., count) of 0; a lot of bag's convenience comes from this default. A bag also offers several ways to iterate on it (by unique elements; by elements, each repeated as many times as its count; by (element, count) pairs); and also supplies a handy method mostcommon to return (element, count) pairs sorted by descending count (all such pairs, or just the top n). An example use of mostcommon:

```
>>> bag(word for line in open('somefile.txt')
...      for word in line.split()).mostcommon(5)
[('to', 83), ('for', 71), ('the', 61), ('of', 53), ('and', 52)]
```

All design choices are tradeoffs. For some applications, it might be more convenient to have bag's API closer to set's rather than to dict's, with an add method, and binary operators, for example, to join two bags returning a new one (as list does with operator + and set does with the "or", vertical-bar operator |). In most cases, this would be overkill. After all, "a designer knows he has achieved perfection, not when there is nothing left to add, but when there is nothing left to take away" (Antoine de Saint-Exupéry). So, for example, to join two bags, getting a new one, without altering either input bag, code a little function using roughly the same update-based approach you would use with dicts, as follows:

```
def bagjoin(b1, b2):
    b = bag(b1)
    b.update(b2)
    return b
```

Just as would be the case for an analogous function joining dicts, this works, not only when b1 and b2 are bags, but also when they are other kinds of objects that can be passed to bag and bag.update—objects such as arbitrary iterables or mappings (generally dictionaries) from items to counts. Such polymorphism comes at negligible cost, and it's well worth preserving.

Although the crucial design choices in this recipe are those about bag's API, some implementation choices must be made as well. In this recipe's code, implementation choices are oriented towards simplicity. In particular, there is no attempt to allow this code to run on Python 2.3. This recipe is optimized for Python 2.4 because it is Python's current release and is likely to be used soon in lieu of Python 2.3, particularly among Pythonistas who are sensitive to performance issues, given the amount of highly successful effort that was devoted to optimizing version 2.4's performance. If Python 2.3 support was deemed necessary, it would be best implemented separately, rather than hobbling the primary 2.4 implementation with inefficiencies or complications.

See Also

Smalltalk's Bag class at *http://www.gnu.org/software/smalltalk/gst-manual/gst_49.html*; C++'s `std::multiset` template class at *http://gcc.gnu.org/onlinedocs/libstdc++/latest-doxygen/classstd_1_1multiset.html*.

18.9 Simulating the Ternary Operator in Python

Credit: Jürgen Hermann, Alex Martelli, Oliver Steele, Chris Perkins, Brent Burley, Lloyd Goldwasser, Doug Hudgeon

Problem

You want to express in Python the equivalent of C's so-called ternary operator ?:— as in `condition?iftrue:iffalse`).

Solution

There are many ways to skin a ternary operator. An explicit `if/else` is most Pythonic, although slightly verbose:

```
for i in range(1, 3):
    if i == 1:
        plural = ''
    else:
        plural = 's'
    print "The loop ran %d time%s" % (i, plural)
```

Indexing is more compact, and therefore useful, if using the `iftrue` and `iffalse` expressions has no side effects:

```
for i in range(1, 3):
    print "The loop ran %d time%s" % (i, ('', 's')[i != 1])
```

For the specific case of plurals, there's also a neat variant using slicing:

```
for i in range(1, 3):
    print "The loop ran %d time%s" % (i, "s"[i==1:])
```

Short-circuited logical expressions can deal correctly with side effects:

```
for i in range(1, 3):
    print "The loop ran %d time%s" % (i, i != 1 and 's' or '')
```

The output of each of these loops is:

```
The loop ran 1 time
The loop ran 2 times
```

However, beware: the short-circuit version (which is necessary when either or both of iftrue and iffalse have side effects) fails if "turned around":

```
for i in range(1, 3):
    print "The loop ran %d time%s" % (i, i == 1 and '' or 's')
```

Since '' evaluates as false, the would-be-ternary expression always evaluates to 's', so that this latest snippet outputs:

```
The loop ran 1 times
The loop ran 2 times
```

Therefore, in general, when iftrue and iffalse are unknown at coding time (and therefore either could have side effects or be false), we need more cumbersome constructs, such as:

```
for i in range(1, 3):
    print "The loop ran %d time%s" % (i, (i == 1 and [''] or ['s'])[0])
```

or:

```
for i in range(1, 3):
    print "The loop ran %d time%s" % (i, (lambda:'', lambda:'s')[i!=1]())
```

or even weirder variations:

```
for i in range(1, 3):
    print "The loop ran %d time%s" % (i, [i==1 and '', i!=1 and 's'][i!=1])
for i in range(1, 3):
    print "The loop ran %d time%s" % (i,
            (i==1 and (lambda:'') or (lambda:'s'))())
```

As you can see, good old if/else is starting to look pretty good when compared to these terse and complicated approaches.

And now for something completely different (for plurals only, again):

```
for i in range(1, 3):
    print "The loop ran %d time%s" % (i, 's'*(i!=1))
```

Discussion

Programmers coming to Python from C, C++, or Perl sometimes miss the so-called ternary operator (?:). The ternary operator is most often used for avoiding a few lines of code and a temporary variable for simple decisions, such as printing the plural form of words after a counter, as in this recipe's examples. In most cases, Python's preference for making things clear and explicit at the cost of some conciseness is an acceptable tradeoff, but one can sympathize with the withdrawal symptoms of ternary-operator addicts.

Nevertheless, 99.44 times out of 100, you're best off using a plain if/else statement. If you want your if/else to fit in an expression (so you can use that expression inside a lambda form, list comprehension, or generator expression), put it inside a named local function and use that function in the expression. For the remaining 56 cases out of 10,000, the idioms in this recipe might be useful. A typical case would be when you're transliterating from another language into Python and need to keep program structure as close as possible to the "or"iginal, as mentioned in recipe 4.19 "Assigning and Testing with One Statement."

There are several ways to get the ternary operator effect in Python, and this recipe presents a fair selection of the wide range of possibilities. Indexing and slicing are nice but don't apply to cases in which either or both of the iftrue and iffalse expressions may have side effects. If side effects are an issue, the short-circuiting nature of and/or can help, but this approach may run into trouble when iftrue and iffalse might be Python values that evaluate as false. To resolve both the side-effect and the might-be-false issues, two variants in this recipe mix indexing and function calling or a lambda form, and two more use even weirder mixtures of lambda and indexing and short circuiting.

If you're not worried about side effects, you could overload slicing syntax to express a ternary operator:

```python
class cond(object):
    def __getitem__(self, sl):
        if sl.start: return sl.stop
        else: return sl.step
cond = cond( )
```

After executing this snippet, you could code the example presented in this recipe's Solution as:

```python
for i in range(1, 3):
    print "The loop ran %d time%s" % (i, cond[i==1:'':'s'])
```

When you slice this cond object, iftrue and iffalse (masquerading as the stop and step attributes of the slice object) are both evaluated in any case, which is the reason this syntax is no use if you must worry about side effects. If you must have syntax sugar, using nullary lambdas may be the least of evils:

```python
def cond(test, when_true, when_false):
    if test:
        return when_true( )
    else:
        return when_false( )
```

to be used as, for example, print cond(x%2==0, lambda:x//2, lambda:3*x+1).

Note that the lack of a ternary operator in Python is not due to an oversight: it's a deliberate design decision, made after much debate pro and con. Therefore, you can be sure that Python will never "grow" a ternary operator. For many details about the various proposed syntax forms for a ternary operation, you can see the rejected PEP 308 at *http://www.python.org/peps/pep-0308.html*.

See Also

Recipe 4.19 "Assigning and Testing with One Statement."

18.10 Computing Prime Numbers

Credit: David Eppstein, Tim Peters, Alex Martelli, Wim Stolker, Kazuo Moriwaka, Hallvard Furuseth, Pierre Denis, Tobias Klausmann, David Lees, Raymond Hettinger

Problem

You need to compute an unbounded sequence of all primes, or the list of all primes that are less than a certain threshold.

Solution

To compute an unbounded sequence, a generator is the natural Pythonic approach, and the Sieve of Eratosthenes, using a dictionary as the supporting data structure, is the natural algorithm to use:

```
import itertools
def eratosthenes():
    '''Yields the sequence of prime numbers via the Sieve of Eratosthenes.'''
    D = {}  # map each composite integer to its first-found prime factor
    for q in itertools.count(2):       # q gets 2, 3, 4, 5, ... ad infinitum
        p = D.pop(q, None)
        if p is None:
            # q not a key in D, so q is prime, therefore, yield it
            yield q
            # mark q squared as not-prime (with q as first-found prime factor)
            D[q*q] = q
        else:
            # let x <- smallest (N*p)+q which wasn't yet known to be composite
            # we just learned x is composite, with p first-found prime factor,
            # since p is the first-found prime factor of q -- find and mark it
            x = p + q
            while x in D:
                x += p
            D[x] = p
```

Discussion

To compute all primes up to a predefined threshold, rather than an unbounded sequence, it's reasonable to wonder if it's possible to use a faster way than good old Eratosthenes, even in the smart variant shown as the "Solution". Here is a function that uses a few speed-favoring tricks, such as a hard-coded tuple of the first few primes:

```
def primes_less_than(N):
    # make `primes' a list of known primes < N
    primes = [x for x in (2, 3, 5, 7, 11, 13) if x < N]
    if N <= 17: return primes
    # candidate primes are all odd numbers less than N and over 15,
```

```
# not divisible by the first few known primes, in descending order
candidates = [x for x in xrange((N-2)|1, 15, -2)
                  if x % 3 and x % 5 and x % 7 and x % 11 and x % 13]
# make `top' the biggest number that we must check for compositeness
top = int(N ** 0.5)
while (top+1)*(top+1) <= N:
    top += 1
# main loop, weeding out non-primes among the remaining candidates
while True:
    # get the smallest candidate: it must be a prime
    p = candidates.pop()
    primes.append(p)
    if p > top:
        break
    # remove all candidates which are divisible by the newfound prime
    candidates = filter(p.__rmod__, candidates)
# all remaining candidates are prime, add them (in ascending order)
candidates.reverse()
primes.extend(candidates)
return primes
```

On a typical small task such as looping over all primes up to 8,192, eratosthenes (on an oldish 1.2 GHz Athlon PC, with Python 2.4) takes 22 milliseconds, while primes_less_than takes 9.7; so, the slight trickery and limitations of primes_less_than can pay for themselves quite handsomely if generating such primes is a bottleneck in your program. Be aware, however, that eratosthenes scales better. If you need all primes up to 199,999, eratosthenes will deliver them in 0.88 seconds, while primes_less_than takes 0.65.

Since primes_less_than's little speed-up tricks can help, it's natural to wonder whether a perhaps simpler trick can be retrofitted into eratosthenes as well. For example, we might simply avoid wasting work on a lot of *even* numbers, concentrating on odd numbers only, beyond the initial 2. In other words:

```
def erat2():
    D = {}
    yield 2
    for q in itertools.islice(itertools.count(3), 0, None, 2):
        p = D.pop(q, None)
        if p is None:
            D[q*q] = q
            yield q
        else:
            x = p + q
            while x in D or not (x&1):
                x += p
            D[x] = p
```

And indeed, erat2 takes 16 milliseconds, versus eratosthenes' 22, to get primes up to 8,192; 0.49 seconds, versus eratosthenes' 0.88, to get primes up to 199,999. In other words, erat2 scales just as well as eratosthenes and is always approximately 25% faster. Incidentally, if you're wondering whether it might be even faster to program at a slightly lower level, with q = 3 to start, a while True as the loop header, and a q += 2 at the end of the loop, don't worry—the slightly higher-level approach using itertools' count and islice functions is repeatedly approximately 4% faster. Other languages may impose a performance penalty for programming with higher abstraction, Python *rewards* you for doing that.

You might keep pushing the same idea yet further, avoiding multiples of 3 as well as even numbers, and so on. However, it would be an exercise in diminishing returns: greater and greater complication for smaller and smaller gain. It's better to quit while we're ahead!

If you're into one liners, you might want to study the following:

```
def primes_oneliner(N):
    aux = {}
    return [aux.setdefault(p, p) for p in range(2, N)
                if 0 not in [p%d for d in aux if p>=d+d]]
```

Be aware that one liners, even clever ones, are generally anything but speed demons! primes_oneliner takes 2.9 seconds to complete the same small task (computing primes up to 8,192) which, eratosthenes does in 22 milliseconds, and primes_less_than in 9.7—so, you're slowing things down by 130 to 300 times just for the fun of using a clever, opaque one liner, which is clearly not a sensible tradeoff. Clever one liners can be instructive but should almost never be used in production code, not just because they're terse and make maintenance harder than straightforward coding (which is by far the main reason), but also because of the speed penalties they may entail.

While prime numbers, and number theory more generally, used to be considered purely theoretical problems, nowadays they have plenty of practical applications, starting with cryptography.

See Also

To explore both number theory and its applications, the best book is probably Kenneth Rosen, *Elementary Number Theory and Its Applications* (Addison-Wesley); *http://www.utm.edu/research/primes/* for more information about prime numbers.

18.11 Formatting Integers as Binary Strings

Credit: Antti Kaihola, Scott David Daniels, W.J. van der Laan

Problem

You need to display non-negative integers in binary form—that is, you need to turn them into strings made up of the characters '0' and '1'.

Solution

The best approach, assuming you must perform this task on several numbers in the course of one run of your application, is to first prepare an auxiliary table, for example, with an auxiliary function:

```
def _bytes_to_bits():
    # prepare and return a list of the first 256 int as binary strings
    # start with table of the right length, filled with place-holders
    the_table = 256*[None]
    # we'll repeatedly need to loop on [7, 6, ..., 1, 0], make it once
    bits_per_byte = range(7, -1, -1)
    for n in xrange(256):
        # prepare the nth string: start with a list of 8 place-holders
        bits = 8*[None]
        for i in bits_per_byte:
            # get the i-th bit as a string, shift n right for next bit
            bits[i] = '01'[n&1]
            n >>= 1
        # join up the 8-character string of 0's and 1's into the table
        the_table[n] = ''.join(bits)
    return the_table
# rebind function's name to the table, function not needed any more
_bytes_to_bits = _bytes_to_bits()
```

and then use the auxiliary table to make a fast conversion function that works 8 bits
at a time:

```
def binary(n):
    # check precondition: only non-negative numbers supported
    assert n>=0
    # prepare the list of substrings 8 bits at a time
    bits = []
    while n:
        bits.append(_bytes_to_bit[n&255])
        n >>= 8
    # we need it left-to-right, thus the reverse
    bits.reverse()
    # strip leading '0's, but ensure at least one is left!
    return ''.join(bits).lstrip('0') or '0'
```

If you need to perform this task only a very small number of times in the course of
one run of your application, you might instead choose to perform the conversion
directly, bit by bit—it's easy, although somewhat slow. Just use the same approach
as binary, but 1 bit at a time instead of 8 bits at a time:

```
def binary_slow(n):
    assert n>=0
    bits = []
    while n:
        bits.append('01'[n&1])
        n >>= 1
    bits.reverse()
    return ''.join(bits) or '0'
```

Discussion

If you also need to display negative numbers, you can take two different roads. Either
do as the built-in functions hex and oct and prepend a minus sign to negative numbers:

```
def bin_with_sign(n):
    if n<0: return '-'+binary(-n)
    else: return binary(n)
```

or use *two's complement* notation, but in that case you need to know how many bits fit in a "word", because that's how two's complement is defined—in terms of fixed-length words:

```
def bin_twos_complement(n, bits_per_word=16):
    if n<0: n = (2<<bits_per_word) + n
    return binary(n)
```

Function `binary` produces just as many binary digits as each argument needs, avoiding leading `'0'`s (except the single zero digit needed to avoid displaying an empty string when n is 0). If instead you need to produce a fixed number of binary digits, you could ensure that at string level, which is particularly easy with Python 2.4:

```
def bin_fixed(n, bits_per_word=16):
    return bin_twos_complement(n, bits_per_word).rjust(bits_per_word, '0')
```

but is also quite feasible with Python 2.3 as well:

```
def bin_fixed_23(n, bits_per_word=16):
    result = bin_twos_complement(n, bits_per_word)
    return (('0'*bits_per_word)+result)[-bits_per_word:]
```

Alternatively, you could generalize some version of the auxiliary _bytes_to_bits function used in the "Solution", which is indeed oriented to producing fixed-length results. However, using the variable-length version, and a little string manipulation on top of it for the occasional need for fixed-length results, should be enough.

See Also

Library Reference and *Python in a Nutshell* docs for built-ins oct and hex; recipe 18.12 "Formatting Integers as Strings in Arbitrary Bases" for displaying integers in an arbitrary base.

18.12 Formatting Integers as Strings in Arbitrary Bases

Credit: Moon aka Sun, Raymond Hettinger

Problem

You need to display non-negative integers in arbitrary bases—that is, you need to turn them into strings made up of "digit" characters (which may include letters for bases that are > 10).

Solution

A function is clearly the right way to package the "Solution" to this task:

```
import string
def format(number, radix, digits=string.digits+string.ascii_lowercase):
    """ format the given integer `number' in the given `radix' using the given
        `digits' (default: digits and lowercase ascii letters) """
    if not 2 <= radix <= len(digits):
        raise ValueError, "radix must be in 2..%r, not %r" % (len(digits), radix)
    # build result as a list of "digit"s in natural order (least-significant digit
    # leftmost), at the end flip it around and join it up into a single string
    result = [ ]
    addon = result.append                       # extract bound-method once
    # compute 'sign' (empty for number>=0) and ensure number >= 0 thereafter
    sign = ''
    if number < 0:
        number = -number
        sign = '-'
    elif number == 0:
        sign = '0'
    _divmod = divmod                            # access to locals is faster
    while number:
        # like: rdigit = number % radix; number //= radix
        number, rdigit = _divmod(number, radix)
        # append appropriate string for the digit we just found
        addon(digits[rdigit])
    # append sign (if any), flip things around, and join up into a string
    addon(sign)
    result.reverse( )
    return ''.join(result)
```

Discussion

Here is a simple usage example, with the usual guard to let us append the example to the same module where we define function format. The usage example runs when the module is run as a main script but not when the module is imported:

```
if __name__ == '__main__':
    as_str = 'qwertyuioplkjhgfdsazxcvbnm0987654321'
    as_num = 79495849566202193863718934176854772085778985434624775545L
    num = int( as_str, 36 )
    assert num == as_num
    res = format( num, 36 )
    assert res == as_str
```

This usage example is designed to be totally quiet when everything works fine, emitting messages only in case of problems.

The code in this recipe is designed with careful attention to both generality and performance. The string of digits used by default is made up of all decimal digits followed by lowercase ASCII letters, allowing a radix of up to 36; however, you can pass any sequence of strings (rather than just a string, to be used as a sequence of characters), for example to support even larger bases. Performance is vastly enhanced, with respect to a naive approach to coding, by a few precautions taken in the code—in decreasing order of importance:

---

1. Building the result as a list and then using `''.join` to create a string containing all the list items. (The alternative of adding each item to a string, one at a time, would be much slower than the `''.join` approach.)

2. Building the result in natural order (least-significant digit leftmost) and flipping it around at the end. Inserting each digit at the front as it gets computed would be slow.

3. Extracting the bound method `result.append` into a local variable.

4. Giving a local name `_divmod` to the `divmod` buit-in.

Items 2 and 3 speed lookups that otherwise would extract a small extra price each time through the loop because lookup of local variables is measurably faster than lookup of built-ins and quite a bit faster than compound-name lookups such as `result.append`.

Here is an example of how you could use format with "digits" that are not single characters, but rather longer strings:

```
digs = [ d+'-' for d in
        'zero one two three four five six seven eight nine'.split() ]
print format(315, 10, digs).rstrip('-')
# emits: three-one-five
```

See Also

Library Reference and *Python in a Nutshell* docs for built-ins oct and hex; recipe 18.11 "Formatting Integers as Binary Strings" for displaying integers specifically in binary.

18.13 Converting Numbers to Rationals via Farey Fractions

Credit: Scott David Daniels

Problem

You have a number v (of almost any type) and need to find a rational number (in reduced form) that is as close to v as possible but with a denominator no larger than a prescribed value.

Solution

Farey fractions, whose crucial properties were studied by Augustin Louis Cauchy, are an excellent way to find rational approximations of floating-point values:

```
def farey(v, lim):
    """ No error checking on args.  lim = maximum denominator.
        Results are (numerator, denominator); (1, 0) is "infinity".
    """
    if v < 0:
```

```
        n, d = farey(-v, lim)
        return -n, d
    z = lim - lim     # Get a "0 of the right type" for denominator
    lower, upper = (z, z+1), (z+1, z)
    while True:
        mediant = (lower[0] + upper[0]), (lower[1] + upper[1])
        if v * mediant[1] > mediant[0]:
            if lim < mediant[1]:
                return upper
            lower = mediant
        elif v * mediant[1] == mediant[0]:
            if lim >= mediant[1]:
                return mediant
            if lower[1] < upper[1]:
                return lower
            return upper
        else:
            if lim < mediant[1]:
                return lower
            upper = mediant
```

For example:

```
import math
print farey(math.pi, 100)
# emits: (22, 7)
```

Discussion

The rationals resulting from the algorithm shown in this recipe are in reduced form (meaning that numerator and denominator are mutually prime), but the proof, which was given by Cauchy, is rather subtle (see *http://www.cut-the-knot.com/blue/Farey.html*).

You can use farey to compute odds from a probability, such as:

```
probability = 0.333
n, d = farey(probability, 100)
print "Odds are %d : %d" % (n, d-n)
# emits: Odds are 1 : 2
```

This recipe's algorithm is ideally suited for reimplementation in a lower-level language (e.g., C, or assembly, or, maybe best, Pyrex) if you use it heavily. Since the code uses only multiplication and addition, it can play optimally to hardware strengths.

If you are using this recipe in an environment where you call it with a lot of values near 0.0, 1.0, or 0.5 (or other simple fractions), you may find that the algorithm's convergence is too slow. You can improve convergence in a continued fraction style, by appending to the first if in the farey function:

```
if v < 0:
...
elif v < 0.5:
```

```
        n, d = farey((v-v+1)/v, lim)      # lim is wrong; decide what you want
        return d, n
    elif v > 1:
        intpart = floor(v)
        n, d = farey(v-intpart)
        return n+intpart*d, d
    ...
```

James Farey was an English geologist and surveyor who wrote a letter to the *Journal of Science* in 1816. In that letter he observed that, while reading a privately published list of the decimal equivalents of fractions, he had noticed an interesting fact. Consider the set of all the fractions with values between 0 and 1, reduced to the lowest terms, with denominators not exceeding some integer N. Arrange the set in order of magnitude to get a sequence. For example, for N equal to 5, the Farey sequence is:

```
0/1, 1/5, 1/4, 1/3, 2/5, 1/2, 3/5, 2/3, 3/4, 4/5, 1/1
```

For any three consecutive fractions in this sequence (e.g., A/B, C/D, E/F), the middle fraction (C/D), called the *mediant*, is equal to the ratio (A + E)/(B + F). I enjoy envisioning Mr. Farey sitting up late on a rainy English night, reading tables of decimal expansions of fractions by an oil lamp. Calculation has come a long way since his day, and I'm pleased to be able to benefit from his work.

See Also

Library Reference and *Python in a Nutshell* docs for built-in types int and long; *http://www.cut-the-knot.org/blue/Farey.shtml* for more information about the Farey Series.

18.14 Doing Arithmetic with Error Propagation

Credit: Mario Hilgemeier

Problem

You have numbers coming from measurements affected by known percentual uncertainties, and you want to perform arithmetic on these numbers while tracking the uncertainty in the results.

Solution

The simplest approach is to code a class that implements arithmetic operators applying the classical physicists' error-propagation formulas:

```python
import math
class Measurement(object):
    ''' models a measurement with % uncertainty, provides arithmetic '''
    def __init__(self, val, perc):
        self.val = val                          # central value
        self.perc = perc                        # % uncertainty
        self.abs = self.val * self.perc / 100.0 # absolute error
```

```
    def __repr__(self):
        return "Measurement(%r, %r)" % (self.val, self.perc)
    def __str__(self):
        return "%g+-%g%%" % (self.val, self.perc)
    def _addition_result(self, result, other_abs):
        new_perc = 100.0 * (math.hypot(self.abs, other_abs) / result)
        return Measurement(result, new_perc)
    def __add__(self, other):
        result = self.val + other.val
        return self._addition_result(result, other.abs)
    def __sub__(self, other):
        result = self.val - other.val
        return self._addition_result(result, other.abs)
    def _multiplication_result(self, result, other_perc):
        new_perc = math.hypot(self.perc, other_perc)
        return Measurement(result, new_perc)
    def __mul__(self, other):
        result = self.val * other.val
        return self._multiplication_result(result, other.perc)
    def __div__(self, other):
        result = self.val / other.val
        return self._multiplication_result(result, other.perc)
```

Discussion

Here is a typical example of use for this Measurement class:

```
m1 = Measurement(100.0, 5.5)    # measured value of 100.0 with 5.5% error
m2 = Measurement(50, 2)         # measured value of 50.0 with 2% error
print "m1 = ", m1
print "m2 = ", m2
print "m1 + m2 = ", m1 + m2
print "m1 - m2 = ", m1 - m2
print "m1 * m2 = ", m1 * m2
print "m1 / m2 = ", m1 / m2
print "(m1+m2) * (m1-m2) = ", (m1+m2) * (m1-m2)
print "(m1-m2) / (m1+m2) = ", (m1-m2) / (m1+m2)
# emits:
# m1 =   100+-5.5%
# m2 =   50+-2%
# m1 + m2 =   150+-3.72678%
# m1 - m2 =   50+-11.1803%
# m1 * m2 =   5000+-5.85235%
# m1 / m2 =   2+-5.85235%
# (m1+m2) * (m1-m2) =   7500+-11.7851%
# (m1-m2) / (m1+m2) =   0.333333+-11.7851%
```

What is commonly known as a *percentage error* is of course best described as a *percentage of uncertainty*. For example, when we state that some measured quantity is 100 with an error of 5.5% (or, equivalently, ± 5.5%), we mean that we know, with a reasonable level of confidence, that the quantity lies somewhere between 94.5 and 105.5. The error-propagation formulas are somewhat heuristic, rather than rigorous, but they're quite traditional and have proven over the centuries that they perform acceptably in most large computations in physics or engineering.

Class Measurement, as shown in this recipe, does not support arithmetic with floats—only arithmetic between instances of Measurement. For those rare occasions when I need, in such computations, numbers that are known "exactly", it is easiest to input them as "measurements with an error of 0%". For example, if I have measured some sphere's radius as 1 meter +- 3%, I can compute the sphere's volume (with the well-known formula, 4/3 pi times the cube of the radius) as follows:

```
r = Measurement(1, 3)
v = Measurement(4/3.0*math.pi, 0) * r * r * r
print v
# emits: 4.18879+-5.19615%
```

Avoiding *accidental* operations with floats that are presumed to be exact, but in fact are not, is quite helpful: this way, when I need to state that a certain number has 0 error, I'm reminded to consider whether things *are* truly that way. If your applications are different, so that you do need operations between measurements and exact floats all over the place, you can insert, as the first line of every one of the arithmetic special methods, the following statement:

```
if isinstance(other, float):
    other = Measurement(other, 0)
```

Alternatively, you could perform this coercion in a special method named __coerce__, but that approach is considered obsolete and is discouraged in modern Python. If you do perform the coercion in the various arithmetic special methods (__add__, __sub__, etc.), don't forget to also add the __radd__, etc, equivalents—after all, if you want to be able to code:

```
some_measurement * 2.0
```

you will no doubt also want to be able to code:

```
2.0 * some_measurement
```

and get exactly the same effects. For this purpose, in Python, your class needs to define the various __r... versions of the operator special methods. However, I'm not pursuing this line of reasoning further, because in most cases, you will be best served by *not* having the implicit ability to do arithmetic in an automatic way between measurements and floats—much like, with Python 2.4's decimal module, you can't implicitly do arithmetic in an automatic way between decimal numbers and floats.

See Also

Library Reference and *Python in a Nutshell* docs for module math.

18.15 Summing Numbers with Maximal Accuracy

Credit: Yaroslav Bulatov, Connelly Barnes

Problem

Due to the properties of floating point arithmetic, the simplest loop to sum a list of numbers (also embodied in the built-in sum function, as well as similar functions such as add.reduce in add-on modules such as Numeric and numarray) is not maximally accurate. You wish to minimize such numeric inaccuracy.

Solution

A careful and accurate algorithm, using and progressively accumulating partial sums (i.e., *partials*), can reduce inaccuracy:

```
import math
def sum_with_partials(arr):
    arr = list(arr)
    size = len(arr)
    iters = int(math.ceil(math.log(size) / math.log(2)))
    step = 1
    for itr in xrange(iters):
        for i in xrange(0, size-step, step+step):
            next_i = i+step
            arr[i] += arr[next_i]
        step += step
    return arr[0]
```

Discussion

Here is an example of the numeric behavior of this sum_with_partials function compared to that of the built-in sum:

```
if __name__ == '__main__':
    arr = [0.123456789012345]*10000000
    true_answer = arr[0] * len(arr)
    print '"True" result: %r' % true_answer
    sum_result = sum(arr)
    print '"sum"  result: %r' % sum_result
    sum_p_resu = sum_with_partials(arr)
    print 'sum_p. result: %r' % sum_p_resu
# emits:
# "True" result: 1234567.89012345
# "sum"  result: 1234567.8902233159
# sum_p. result: 1234567.89012345
```

As you can see, in this case, the built-in sum accumulated a relative error of almost 10^{-10} after summing 10 million floats all equal to each other (giving less than 11 digits of accuracy in the result), while sum_with_partials happens to be "perfect" for this case to within machine precision (15 digits of accuracy). Summing just a million copies rather than 10 million lowers sum's relative error only to a bit more than 10^{-11}.

The Trouble with Summations

How come a simple summing loop is less than maximally accurate? The root of the trouble is that summing two floating-point numbers of very different magnitudes loses accuracy. For example, suppose we used decimal floating-point numbers with a precision of four digits: then, summing 1.234 to 123.4 would give 124.6, "losing" 0.034 from the smaller number. Such artefacts are inevitable, as long as we have finite precision during our computations.

Now, imagine we're using a simple loop such as:

```
total = 0.0
for number in numbers:
    total += number
```

to sum a million numbers, all positive and of reasonably similar magnitudes. Built-in sum internally uses exactly this kind of simple loop. By the time we've summed, say, the first 100,000 numbers, the running total *has* become much larger than each new number we're adding to it. We have thus put ourselves in exactly the situation just shown to be problematic: after a while, we're systematically summing floating-point numbers of very different magnitudes, and thus systematically losing accuracy.

The partials algorithm shown in this recipe works by summing numbers two at a time—therefore, no major loss of accuracy occurs, since we're assuming that the numbers we start with are of reasonably similar magnitudes. So, after the first pass of the partials algorithm, we're left with half as many partials as the amount of numbers we started with. All the partials are of reasonably similar magnitudes, so we just iterate the same procedure: at each step, we keep halving the number of partials that are left, until we're down to just one number, the grand total, having lost along the way as little accuracy as feasible.

If you know that the input argument arr is a list, and you don't mind destroying that list as part of the summation, you can omit from the body of sum_with_partials the statement:

```
arr = list(arr)
```

and recover a little bit of performance. Without this small enhancement, on one slow laptop, summing a million floats with the built-in sum takes 360 milliseconds, while the more accurate function sum_with_partials shown in this recipe takes 1.8 seconds to perform the same task (a slowdown of five times). In theory, sum_with_partials should be asymptotically faster than built-in sum if you're doing unbounded-precision arithmetic (e.g., with Python's built-in longs or other unbounded-precision data types from such add-ons as gmpy, which you can download from *http://gmpy.sourceforge.net*). To sum a list of n elements with d digits of precision, in unbounded-precision exact arithmetic, sum takes O(n(d+logd)) time, while sum_with_ partials takes O(nd). However, I have not been able to observe that effect in empirical measurements.

Most of the time, you probably don't want to pay the price of slowing down a summation by five times in order to increase your digits of accuracy from 10 or 11 to 15. However, for those occasions in which this tradeoff is right for your applications, and you need to sum millions and millions of floating-point numbers, this recipe might well prove rather useful to you. Another simple way to increase accuracy, particularly when your input numbers are *not* necessarily all of similar magnitude, is to ensure the small-magnitude ones are summed first. This is particularly easy to code in Python 2.4, although it's inevitably O(n log n): just sum(sorted(data, key=abs)). Finally, if precision is *much* more important than speed, consider using decimal.Decimal (which lets you ask for as much precision as you're willing to wait for and is part of Python 2.4's standard library). Or you could use gmpy.mpf (which also allows any precision you require, may even be faster, but must be downloaded as part of gmpy from *http://gmpy.sourceforge.net*.)

See Also

Recipe 18.16 "Simulating Floating Point" shows how to use a bounded-precision simulation of floating point to estimate the accuracy of algorithms; *ftp://ftp.icsi.berkeley.edu/pub/theory/priest-thesis.ps.Z* for Douglas M. Priest's Ph.D. thesis *On Properties of Floating Point Arithmetics: Numerical Stability and the Cost of Accurate Computations*, covering this entire field with depth and rigor; gmpy is at *http://gmpy.sourceforge.net*.

18.16 Simulating Floating Point

Credit: Raymond Hettinger

Problem

You need to simulate floating-point arithmetic in software, either to show to students the details of the various classic problems with floating point (e.g., representation error, loss of precision, failure of distributive, commutative, and associative laws), or to explore the numerical robustness of alternative algorithms.

Solution

We can reproduce every floating-point operation, with explicitly bounded precision, by coding a Python class that overloads all the special methods used in arithmetic operators:

```
prec = 8                # number of decimal digits (must be under 15)
class F(object):
    def __init__(self, value, full=None):
        self.value = float('%.*e' % (prec-1, value))
```

```
        if full is None:
            full = self.value
        self.full = full
    def __str__(self):
        return str(self.value)
    def __repr__(self):
        return "F(%s, %r)" % (self, self.full)
    def error(self):
        ulp = float('1'+('%.4e' % self.value)[-5:]) * 10 ** (1-prec)
        return int(abs(self.value - self.full) / ulp)
    def __coerce__(self, other):
        if not isinstance(other, F):
            return (self, F(other))
        return (self, other)
    def __add__(self, other):
        return F(self.value + other.value, self.full + other.full)
    def __sub__(self, other):
        return F(self.value - other.value, self.full - other.full)
    def __mul__(self, other):
        return F(self.value * other.value, self.full * other.full)
    def __div__(self, other):
        return F(self.value / other.value, self.full / other.full)
    def __neg__(self):
        return F(-self.value, -self.full)
    def __abs__(self):
        return F(abs(self.value), abs(self.full))
    def __pow__(self, other):
        return F(pow(self.value, other.value), pow(self.full, other.full))
    def __cmp__(self, other):
        return cmp(self.value, other.value)
```

Discussion

The initializer of class F rounds the input value to the given precision (the global constant prec). This rounding produces what is known as *representation error* because the result is the nearest possible representable value for the specified number of digits. For instance, at three digits of precision, 3.527104 is stored as 3.53, so the representation error is 0.002896.

Since the underlying representation used in this recipe is Python's ordinary float, the simulation works only up to 15 digits (the typical limit for double-precision floating point). If you need more than 15 digits, you can use Python 2.4's decimal.Decimal type as the underlying representation. This way, you can get any precision you ask for, although the computation occurs in decimal rather than in binary. Alternatively, to get binary floating point with arbitrarily high precision, use the gmpy Python wrapper for the GMP (Gnu Multiple Precision) multiple-precision arithmetic library, specifically the gmpy.mpf type. One way or another, you need change only the two calls to float in this recipe's Solution into calls to Python 2.4's decimal.Decimal, or to gmpy.mpf (requesting the appropriate number of "digits" or bits), to use class F with higher precision than 15 digits. gmpy is at *http://gmpy.sourceforge.net*.

One key use of this recipe is to show to students the classic failure of associative, commutative, and distributive laws (Knuth, *The Art of Computer Programming*, vol. 2, pp. 214–15)—for example:

```
# Show failure of the associative law
u, v, w = F(11111113), F(-11111111), F(7.51111111)
assert (u+v)+w == 9.5111111
assert u+(v+w) == 10
# Show failure of the commutative law for addition
assert u+v+w != v+w+u
# Show failure of the distributive law
u, v, w = F(20000), F(-6), F(6.0000003)
assert u*v == -120000
assert u*w == 120000.01
assert v+w == .0000003
assert (u*v) + (u*w) == .01
assert u * (v+w) == .006
```

The other main way to use the code in this recipe is to compare the numerical accuracy of different algorithms that compute the same results. For example, we can compare the following three approaches to computing averages:

```
def avgsum(data):        # Sum all of the elements, then divide
    return sum(data, F(0)) / len(data)
def avgrun(data):        # Make small adjustments to a running mean
    m = data[0]
    k = 1
    for x in data[1:]:
        k += 1
        m += (x-m)/k     # Recurrence formula for mean
    return m
def avgrun_kahan(data): # Adjustment method with Kahan error correction term
    m = data[0]
    k = 1
    dm = 0
    for x in data[1:]:
        k += 1
        adjm = (x-m)/k - dm
        newm = m + adjm
        dm = (newm - m) - adjm
        m = newm
    return m
```

Here is a way to exercise these approaches and display their errors:

```
import random
prec = 5
data = [F(random.random( )*10-5) for i in xrange(1000)]
print '%s\t%s\t%s' %('Computed', 'ULP Error', 'Method')
print '%s\t%s\t%s' %('--------', '---------', '------')
for f in avgsum, avgrun, avgrun_kahan:
```

```
    result = f(data)
    print '%s\t%6d\t\t%s' % (result, result.error(), f.__name__)
print '\n%r\tbaseline average using full precision' % result.full
```

Here is typical output from this snippet (the exact numbers in play will be different each time you run it, since what we are summing are random numbers):

```
Computed         ULP Error      Method
--------         ---------      ------
-0.020086              15               avgsum
-0.020061               9               avgrun
-0.020072               1               avgrun_kahan
-0.020070327734999997       baseline average using full precision
```

The last example demonstrates how to extract a full-precision floating-point result from an instance of F, by using the full attribute of the instance. This example is helpful for running an algorithm to full precision, as a baseline for seeing the effects of using less precision.

The full-precision result excludes the representation error in the "or"iginal inputs. For example, with prec = 3 and d = F(3.8761) / F(2.7181), d.full is 1.4264705882352939, the same result as regular division would yield, starting from the nearest representable values, 3.88 / 2.72. This helpful choice isolates accumulated floating-point operation errors from the artifacts of the "or"iginal data entry. This separation is reasonable because real floating-point systems have to start with representable constants; however, if the "or"iginal representation error has to be tracked, you can do so by entering the number twice in the call to F—for example, use F(2.7181, 2.7181) rather than F(2.7181).

See Also

Recipe 18.15 "Summing Numbers with Maximal Accuracy" for algorithms for accurate sums; gmpy is at *http://gmpy.sourceforge.net*.

18.17 Computing the Convex Hulls and Diameters of 2D Point Sets

Credit: David Eppstein, Dinu Gherman

Problem

You have a list of 2D points, represented as pairs (x, y), and need to compute the convex hull (i.e., upper and lower chains of vertices) and the diameter (the two points farthest from each other).

Solution

We can easily compute the hulls by the classic *Graham's scan* algorithm, with sorting based on coordinates rather than radially. Here is a function to perform this task:

```
def orientation(p, q, r):
    ''' >0 if p-q-r are clockwise, <0 if counterclockwise, 0 if colinear. '''
    return (q[1]-p[1])*(r[0]-p[0]) - (q[0]-p[0])*(r[1]-p[1])
def hulls(Points):
    ' Graham scan to find upper and lower convex hulls of a set of 2D points '
    U = [ ]
    L = [ ]
    # the natural sort in Python is lexicographical, by coordinate
    Points.sort()
    for p in Points:
        while len(U) > 1 and orientation(U[-2], U[-1], p) <= 0:
            U.pop()
        while len(L) > 1 and orientation(L[-2], L[-1], p) >= 0:
            L.pop()
        U.append(p)
        L.append(p)
    return U, L
```

Given the hulls, the *rotating calipers* algorithm provides all pairs of points that are candidates to be set's diameter. Here is a function to embody this algorithm:

```
def rotatingCalipers(Points):
    ''' Given a list of 2d points, finds all ways of sandwiching the points
        between two parallel lines that touch one point each, and yields the
        sequence of pairs of points touched by each pair of lines. '''
    U, L = hulls(Points)
    i = 0
    j = len(L) - 1
    while i < len(U) - 1 or j > 0:
        yield U[i], L[j]
        # if all the way through one side of hull, advance the other side
        if i == len(U) - 1:
            j -= 1
        elif j == 0:
            i += 1
        # still points left on both lists, compare slopes of next hull edges
        # being careful to avoid divide-by-zero in slope calculation
        elif (U[i+1][1]-U[i][1]) * (L[j][0]-L[j-1][0]) > \
             (L[j][1]-L[j-1][1]) * (U[i+1][0]-U[i][0]):
            i += 1
        else: j -= 1
```

Given all the candidates, we need only to scan for the `max` on pairwise point-point distances of candidate pairs of points to get the diameter. Here is a function that performs exactly this task:

```
def diameter(Points):
    ''' Given a list of 2d points, returns the pair that's farthest apart. '''
    diam, pair = max( [((p[0]-q[0])**2 + (p[1]-q[1])**2, (p,q))
```

```
                    for p,q in rotatingCalipers(Points)] )
        return pair
```

Discussion

As function hulls shows, we can apply Graham's scan algorithm without needing an expensive radial sort as a preliminary step: Python's own built-in sort (which is *lexicographical*, meaning, in this case, by x coordinate first, and by y coordinate when the x coordinates of two points coincide) is sufficient.

From hulls, we get the upper and lower convex hulls as distinct lists, which, in turn, helps in the rotatingCalipers function: that function can maintain separate indices i and j on the lower and upper hulls and still be sure to yield all pairs of *sandwich boundary* points that are candidates to be the set's diameter. Given the sequence of candidate pairs, function diameter's task is quite simple—it boils down to one call to built-in max on a list comprehension (a generator expression would suffice in Python 2.4) that associates the pairwise point distance to each pair of candidate points. We use the *squared* distance, in fact. There's no reason to compute a costly square root to get the actual non-squared distance: we're comparing only distances, and for any non-negative x and y, x < y and sqrt(x) < sqrt(y) always have identical truth values. (In practice, however, using math.hypot(p[0]-q[0], p[1]-q[1]) in the list comprehension gives us just about the same performance.)

The computations in this recipe take care to handle tricky cases, such as pairs of points with the same x coordinate, multiple copies of the same point, colinear triples of points, and slope computations that, if not carefully handled, would produce a division by zero (i.e., again, pairs of points with the same x coordinate). The set of unit tests that carefully probe each of these corner cases is far longer than the code in the recipe itself, which is why it's not posted on this cookbook.

Some of the formulas become a little simpler and more readable when we represent points by complex numbers, rather than as pairs of reals:

```
def orientation(p, q, r):
    return ((q - p) * (r - p).conjugate()).imag
    ...
            # still points left on both lists, compare slopes of next hull edges
            # being careful to avoid divide-by-zero in slope calculation
            elif ((U[i+1] - U[i]) * (L[j] - L[j-1]).conjugate()).imag > 0:
                i += 1
            else: j -= 1
    ...
def diameter(Points):
    diam, pair = max([(abs(p-q), (p,q)) for p,q in rotatingCalipers(Points)])
    return pair
```

If we represent points by complex numbers, of course, we cannot just use Points.sort() any more because complex numbers cannot be compared. We need to "pay back" some of the simplification by coding our own sort, such as:

```
aux = [ (p.real, p.imag) for p in Points ]
aux.sort( )
Points[:] = [ complex(*p) for p in aux ]
del aux
```

or equivalently, in Python 2.4:

```
Points.sort(key=lambda p: p.real, p.imag)
```

Moreover, under the hood, a complex numbers–based version is doing more arithmetic: finding the real as well as imaginary components in the first and second formula, and doing an unnecessary square root in the third one. Nevertheless, performance as measured on my machine, despite this extra work, turns out to be slightly *better* with this latest snippet than with the "Solution"'s code. The reason I've not made the complex-numbers approach the "official" one, aside from the complication with sorting, is that you should not require familiarity with complex arithmetic just to understand geometrical computations.

If you're comfortable with complex numbers, don't mind the sorting issues, and have to perform many 2D geometrical computations, you should consider representing points as complex numbers and check whether this provides a performance boost, as well as overall simplification to your source code. Among other advantages, representing points as complex numbers lets you use the Numeric package to hold your data, saving much memory and possibly gaining even more performance, when compared to the natural alternative of representing points as (x, y) tuples holding two floats.

See Also

M. de Berg, M. van Kreveld, M. Overmars, and O. Schwarzkopf, *Computational Geometry: Algorithms and Applications*, 2nd ed. (Springer-Verlag).

## CHAPTER 19

Iterators and Generators

19.0 Introduction

Credit: Raymond Hettinger

> Lather, Rinse, Repeat
> —*Docs for my bottle of shampoo*

The Iterator Protocol

After namespaces, iterators and generators emerged as the next "honking great ideas" in Python. Since their introduction in Python 2.2, they have come to pervade and unify the language. They encourage a loosely coupled programming style that is simple to write, easy to read, flexible, and extendable.

Simply put, the iterator protocol has two halves, a producer and a consumer. An iterable object says, "I know how to supply data one element at a time," and the consumer says "please give me data one element at a time and say Stop when you're done."

The producer/consumer connection can appear in a number of guises. The simplest is where a function or constructor wraps around an iterable object. For example, sorted(set('simsalabim')) has the set constructor looping over the elements of the iterable string and a sorted function wrapping around the resulting iterable set object. replaceable literal

In addition to functions and constructors, regular Python statements can use the in operator to loop over iterable objects. for line in myfile: print line loops over lines of an iterable file object. Likewise, if token in sequence loops over elements of a sequence until it finds a match (or until it reaches the end with no matches).

Both guises of the consumer side of the iterator protocol use the protocol implicitly. In addition, an explicit form is more flexible but used less often. The iterator object is saved as a variable, it = iter(mystring). Then, the iterator's next method is called to retrieve a data element, elem = it.next( ). Such calls are usually wrapped in try/

except statements to catch the StopIteration exception that the iterator raises when the data stream is exhausted.

All of these approaches provide the full range of iterator benefits, including loose coupling and memory friendliness. The loose coupling is evident in the first example, where the independently created and maintained sorted function, set data type, and string objects were readily combined. The memory friendliness derives from the one-at-a-time structure of the iterator protocol. Programs using iterators are likely to be less resource intensive and more scalable than their list-based counterparts.

Iterators and Generators

An object that wants to be iterable should implement an __iter__ method, which returns an iterator object. Ideally, the iterator should be a distinct object from the iterable, to make it possible to have multiple iterators over the same iterable container. There are exceptions to this general recommendation: for example, a sequential file object does not readily lend itself to multiple iterations; therefore, it is more appropriate in this case to have the file object be its own iterator rather than return a separate iterator object; given any file instance f, indeed, iter(f) is f.

Any iterator object must implement a next method and an __iter__ method. The next method should raise StopIteration when the iteration is complete. Care should be taken that subsequent calls to next continue to raise StopIteration (once stopped, it stays stopped). The __iter__ method of an iterator object should always return the iterator itself (__iter__ is idempotent on iterators). This simplifies client code by allowing it to treat iterators and iterables the same way (i.e., both return an iterator in response to the iter function).

To be useful, most iterators have a stored state that enables them to return a new data element on each call. The previously described responsibilities and the need to have a stored state both suggest that classes are the way to create iterable objects. That approach is obvious, explicit, and rarely used (only two recipes in this chapter make any use of classes).

Instead of writing classes, two alternate approaches dominate. Starting with the observation that many functions and types both accept iterable inputs and return iterable outputs, an obvious approach is to link them together in a "pipes and filters" style to create new tools. For example, def uniq(seq): return sorted(set(seq)) is a way to create a new tool directly from existing functions and types. Like functional programming, the resulting code is terse, readable, trivial to debug, and often runs at the speed of compiled C code. The economy of this approach motivated the creation of an entire module of iterator building blocks, the itertools module. Indeed, many of the brilliant, effective recipes in this chapter make frequent use of itertools components.

If no combination of building blocks solves the problem, the next best approach is to write a generator. The recipe 19.1 "Writing a range-like Function with Float Increments" shows how trivially easy it is to write a generator. By introducing a yield keyword, the responsibilities of creating an iterator are handled automatically. The iterator objects obtained by calling a generator are distinct, save their state, have an idempotent __iter__ method, and have a next method that raises StopIteration when complete and stays stopped if called again afterwards. Python internally takes care of all of these details. Because of generators' compelling simplicity, most of the recipes in this chapter make use of generators.

Starting with version 2.4, Python continued its evolution toward using iterators everywhere by introducing generator expressions (*genexps* for short). Genexps can be likened to a memory-efficient, scalable form of list comprehensions. Simply by replacing brackets with parentheses, an expression will yield one element at a time rather than filling memory all at once. Used correctly (i.e., in a context where they are consumed immediately, one item at a time), genexps can offer remarkable clarity and economy: sum(x*x for x in xrange(10)) is a great way to express the sum of the squares of the first ten natural numbers.

Thinking Out of the Box

Paradoxically, the simpler and more general an idea, the more likely that people will find extraordinary and unexpected ways of using it. Here is a brief sampling of the ways that iterators and generators have been pushed to their outer limits.

Observing that the yield keyword has the unique capability of stopping execution, saving state, and later resuming, it is not surprising that techniques have been discovered for using generators to simulate co-routines and continuations. The core idea is to implement each routine as a generator and having a *dispatch* function launch the routines in orderly succession. Whenever a task switch is needed, the routines yield back to the dispatcher, which then launches or resumes the next routine by calling its next method. Small complications are involved for startup, termination, and data sharing, but they each are solvable without much ado and present fewer challenges than equivalent thread-based solutions. See recipe 9.8 "Multitasking Cooperatively Without Threads" for an example.

Observing that some tools can be both producers and consumers, it is natural to want to stack them together like pipes and filters. While that analogy can lead to useful decoupling, be aware that underlying models are different. Iterators do not run independently from start to finish; instead, an outermost layer is always in control, requesting data elements one at a time, so that nothing runs until the outer layer starts making requests.

When stacking tools together (as in the first example with sorted, set, and a string), the code takes on the appearance of a functional programming language. The resemblance is not shallow: iterators do fulfill some of the promise of lazy languages. So, it is natural to borrow some of the most successful techniques from those languages, such as Haskell and SML.

One such technique is to write innermost iterators to yield infinite streams and concentrate the control logic in an outermost driver function. For instance, in numerical programming, write a generator that yields successively better approximations to a desired result and call it from a function that stops whenever two successive approximations fall within a tolerance value. Separating the control logic from the calculation decouples the two, making them easier to write, test, and debug, and makes them more reusable in other contexts.

Odds and Ends

Here are some instructive snippets. Consider each of them carefully, study how they work, and you'll be well on your way towards understanding how best to link iterators together to solve practical problems. Each of the following lines is independent from the "other"s:

```
result = dict(enumerate(myseq))
result = set(word for line in page for word in line.split())
def dotproduct(v1, v2): return sum(itertools.imap(operator.mul, v1, v2))
def dotproduct(v1, v2): return sum(x*y for x,y in itertools.izip(v1, v2))
randgen = itertools.starmap(random.random, itertools.repeat(()))
randgen = iter(random.random, -1.0)
```

The idea for restartable iterators surfaces every so often and then drowns in quicksand. sys.stdin is a plain example of an iterable that cannot logically be restarted unless an entire session is saved in memory. A craving for restartability should be taken as a cue that a list might well be a more appropriate data structure.

Just because iterators cannot be restarted doesn't mean they cannot be abandoned in mid-stream. The lazy, just-in-time style of production is a key feature of iterators. Take advantage of it. That's why the for statement supports a break keyword, after all.

The core itertools and their derivatives (see the recipes in the itertools docs that are part of the Python *Library Reference*) all run at nearly the speed of compiled code. When Python 2.4 introduced a native set data type, I timed it against the pure-Python version, *sets.py*, and learned that some of the set logic (intersection, union, etc.) achieved only a two to one increase in speed. The reason was that *sets.py* used itertools, and itertools performance was exceptional. So, when performance is an issue, consider an itertools solution before turning to more labor-intensive optimizations or native language extensions.

19.1 Writing a range-like Function with Float Increments

Credit: Dinu Gherman, Paul Winkler, Stephen Levings

Problem

You need an arithmetic progression, like the built-in xrange but with float values (xrange works only on integers).

Solution

Although float arithmetic progressions are not available as built-ins, it's easy to code a generator to supply them:

```
import itertools
def frange(start, end=None, inc=1.0):
    "An xrange-like generator which yields float values"
    # imitate range/xrange strange assignment of argument meanings
    if end is None:
        end = start + 0.0      # Ensure a float value for 'end'
        start = 0.0
    assert inc                 # sanity check
    for i in itertools.count():
        next = start + i * inc
        if (inc>0.0 and next>=end) or (inc<0.0 and next<=end):
            break
        yield next
```

Discussion

Sadly missing in the Python Standard Library, the generator in this recipe lets you use arithmetic progressions, similarly to the built-in xrange but with float values.

Many theoretical restrictions apply, but this generator is more useful in practice than in theory. People who work with floating-point numbers all the time tell many war stories about billion-dollar projects that failed because someone did not take into consideration the strange things that modern hardware can do, at times, when comparing floating-point numbers. But for pedestrian cases, simple approaches like this recipe generally work.

This observation by no means implies that you can afford to ignore the fundamentals of numerical analysis, if your programs need to do anything at all with floating-point numbers! For example, in this recipe, we rely on a single multiplication and one addition to compute each item, to avoid accumulating error by repeated additions. Precision would suffer in a potentially dangerous way if we "simplified" the first statement in the loop body to something like:

```
next += inc
```

as might appear very tempting, were it not for those numerical analysis considerations.

One variation you may want to consider is based on pre-computing the number of
items that make up the bounded arithmetic progression:

```
import math
def frange1(start, end=None, inc=1.0):
    if end == None:
        end = start + 0.0      # Ensure a float value for 'end'
        start = 0.0
    nitems = int(math.ceil((end-start)/inc))
    for i in xrange(nitems):
        yield start + i * inc
```

This frange1 version may or may not be faster than the frange version shown in the
solution; if the speed of this particular generator is crucial to your programs, it's best
to try both versions and measure resulting times. In my limited benchmarking, on
most of the hardware I have at hand, frange1 does appear to be consistently faster.

Talking about speed—believe it or not, looping with for i in itertools.count( ) is
measurably *faster* than apparently obvious lower-level alternatives such as:

```
i = 0
while True:
    ...loop body unchanged...
    yield next
    i += 1
```

Do consider using itertools any time you want speed, and you may be in for more
of these pleasant surprises.

If you work with floating-point numbers, you should definitely take a look at Numeric
and other third-party extension packages that make Python such a powerful language for floating-point computations. For example, with Numeric, you could code
something like:

```
import math, Numeric
def frange2(start, end=None, inc=1.0, typecode=None):
    if end == None:
        end = start + 0.0      # Ensure a float value for 'end'
        start = 0.0
    nitems = math.ceil((end-start)/inc)
    return Numeric.arange(nitems) * inc + start
```

This one is *definitely* going to be faster than both frange and frange1 if you need to
collect all of the progression's items into a sequence.

See Also

Documentation for the xrange built-in function, and the itertools and math modules, in the *Library Reference*; Numeric Python (*http://www.pfdubois.com/numpy/*).

19.2 Building a List from Any Iterable

Credit: Tom Good, Steve Alexander

Problem

You have an iterable object x (it might be a sequence or any other kind of object on which you can iterate, such as an iterator, a `file`, a `dict`) and need a `list` object y, with the same items as x and in the same order.

Solution

When you know that iterable object x is bounded (so that, e.g., a loop `for item in x` would surely terminate), building the list object you require is trivial:

```
y = list(x)
```

However, when you know that x is unbounded, or when you are not sure, then you must ensure termination before you call `list`. In particular, if you want to make a list with no more than n items from x, then standard library module `itertools`' function `islice` does exactly what you need:

```
import itertools
y = list(itertools.islice(x, N))
```

Discussion

Python's generators, iterators, and sundry other iterables, are a wondrous thing, as this entire chapter strives to point out. The powerful and generic concept of *iterable* is a great way to represent all sort of sequences, including unbounded ones, in ways that can potentially save you huge (and even infinite!) amounts of memory. With the standard library module `itertools`, generators you can code yourself, and, in Python 2.4, generator expressions, you can perform many manipulations on completely general iterables.

However, once in a while, you need to build a good old-fashioned full-fledged `list` object from such a generic iterable. For example, building a list is the simplest way to sort or reverse the items in the iterable, and lists have many other useful methods you may want to apply. As long as you know for sure that the iterable is *bounded* (i.e., has a finite number of items), just call `list` with the iterable as the argument, as the "Solution" points out. In particular, avoid the goofiness of misusing a list comprehension such as `[i for i in x]`, when `list(x)` is faster, cleaner, *and* more readable!

Calling `list` won't help if you're dealing with an *unbounded* iterable. The need to ensure that some iterable x is bounded also arises in many other contexts, besides that of calling `list(x)`: all "accumulator" functions (`sum(x)`, `max(x)`, etc.) intrinsically need a bounded-iterable argument, and so does a statement such as `for i in x` (unless you have appropriate conditional breaks within the loop's body), a test such as `if i in x`, and so on.

If, as is frequently the case, all you want is to ensure that no more than n items of iterable x are taken, then `itertools.islice`, as shown in the "Solution", does just what you need. The `islice` function of the standard library `itertools` module offers many other possibilities (essentially equivalent to the various possibilities that slicing offers on sequences), but out of all of them, the simple "truncation" functionality (i.e., take no more than n items) is by far the most frequently used. The programming language Haskell, from which Python took many of the ideas underlying its list comprehensions and generator expression functionalities, has a built-in take function to cater to this rather frequent need, and `itertools.islice` is most often used as an equivalent to Haskell's built-in take.

In some cases, you cannot specify a maximum number of items, but you *are* able to specify a generic condition that you know will eventually be satisfied by the items of iterable x and can terminate the proceedings. `itertools.takewhile` lets you deal with such cases in a very general way, since it accepts the controlling predicate as a callable argument. For example:

```
y = list(itertools.takewhile((11).__cmp__, x))
```

binds name y to a new list made up of the sequence of items in iterable x up to, but not including, the first one that equals 11. (The reason we need to code (11).__cmp__ with parentheses is a somewhat subtle one: if we wrote 11.__cmp__ *without* parentheses, Python would parse 11. as a floating-point literal, and the entire construct would be syntactically invalid. The parentheses are included to force the tokenization we *mean*, with 11 as an integer literal and the period indicating an access to its attribute, in this case, bound method __cmp__.)

For the special and frequent case in which the terminating condition is the equality of an item to some given value, a useful alternative is to use the two-arguments variant of the built-in function `iter`:

```
y = list(iter(iter(x).next, 11))
```

Here, the `iter(x)` call (which is innocuous if x is already an iterator) gives us an object on which we can surely access callable (bound method) next—which is necessary, because `iter` in its two-arguments form requires a callable as its first argument. The second argument is the *sentinel* value, meaning the value that terminates the iteration as soon as an item equal to it appears. For example, if x were a sequence with items 1, 6, 3, 5, 7, 11, 2, 9, . . , y would now be the list [1, 6, 3, 5, 7]. (The sentinel value itself is excluded: from the beginning, included, to the end, excluded, is the normal Python convention for just about all loops, implicit or explicit.)

See Also

Library Reference documentation on built-ins `list` and `iter`, and module `itertools`.

19.3 Generating the Fibonacci Sequence

Credit: Tom Good, Leandro Mariano Lopez

Problem

You want an unbounded generator that yields, one item at a time, the entire (infinite) sequence of Fibonacci numbers.

Solution

Generators are particularly suitable for implementing infinite sequences, given their intrinsically "lazy evaluation" semantics:

```
def fib():
    ''' Unbounded generator for Fibonacci numbers '''
    x, y = 0, 1
    while True:
        yield x
        x, y = y, x + y
if __name__ == "__main__":
    import itertools
    print list(itertools.islice(fib(), 10))
# outputs: [0, 1, 1, 2, 3, 5, 8, 13, 21, 34]
```

Discussion

Generators make it quite easy to work with unbounded (infinite) sequences. In this recipe, we show a generator that produces all of the (infinitely many) Fibonacci numbers one after the "other". (If you want the variant in which the sequence starts with 1, 1, 2, . . . , rather than the one, implemented here, which starts with 0, 1, 1, . . . , just interchange the two statements in the loop's body.)

It's worth reflecting on why a generator is so perfectly suitable for implementing an unbounded sequence and letting you work with it. Syntactically, a generator is "just" a function containing the keyword yield. When you call a generator, however, the function body does not yet execute. Rather, calling the generator gives you a special anonymous iterator object that wraps the function's body, the function's local variables (including arguments, which, for any function, are local variables that happen to be initialized by the caller), and the current point of execution, which is initially the start of the function.

When you call this anonymous iterator object's next method, the function body executes up to the next yield statement. yield's argument is returned as the result of the iterator's next method, and the function is "frozen", with its execution state intact. When you call next again on the same iterator object, the function "thaws" and continues from where it left off, again up to the next yield statement.

If the function body "falls off the end", or executes a return, the iterator object raises StopIteration to indicate the end of the sequence. But, of course, if the sequence that the generator is producing is not bounded, the iterator never raises StopIteration. That's okay, as long as you don't rely on such an exception as the only way to terminate a loop. In this recipe, for example, the anonymous iterator object is passed as an argument to itertools.islice: as shown in recipe 19.2 "Building a List from Any Iterable," islice is the most typical way in which an unbounded iterator is made finite (truncated at an externally imposed boundary).

The main point to retain is that it's all right to have infinite sequences represented by generators, since generators are computed lazily (in other words, each item gets computed just in time, when required), as long as some control structure ensures that only a finite number of items are required from the generator. The answer to our curiosity as to why generators are so excellently suitable for this use is in the anonymous iterator object which a generator returns when we call it: that anonymous iterator wraps some code (the generator's function body) and some state (the function's local variables, and, crucially, the point at which the function's execution is to resume) in just the way that's most convenient for the computation of most sequences, be they bounded or unbounded.

Leonardo Pisano (meaning "from Pisa"), most often called Leonardo Bigollo (the traveler or "the good for nothing") during his lifetime in the 12th and 13th centuries, and occasionally Leonardo Fibonacci (for his connection to the Bonacci family), must look down with considerable pride from his place in the mathematicians' Empyreon. Although his most notable contributions were the introduction of decimal notation (arabic numerals) in the West, and the codification of the rules for double-entry bookkeeping, these monumental achievements are not usually connected to his name. The one that is, however—from the third problem in his *Liber Abaci*, which he originally expressed in terms of a rabbit-raising farm—still provides interesting applications for the distant successors of the abacus, modern computers.

See Also

Recipe 19.2 "Building a List from Any Iterable," shows how to make bounded iterators from unbounded (or "potentially unbounded") ones.

19.4 Unpacking a Few Items in a Multiple Assignment

Credit: Brett Cannon, Oren Tirosh, Alex Martelli

Problem

Python's multiple unpacking assignment is very handy when you are unpacking all the items from a sequence and binding each to a name. However, you often need to unpack (and bind to names) only some items from the "front" of a sequence, and bind another name to "the rest" of the sequence (the part you didn't unpack).

Solution

A generator provides an elegant solution to this problem:

```
def peel(iterable, arg_cnt=1):
    """ Yield each of the first arg_cnt items of the iterable, then
        finally an iterator for the rest of the iterable. """
    iterator = iter(iterable)
    for num in xrange(arg_cnt):
        yield iterator.next()
    yield iterator
if __name__ == '__main__':
    t5 = range(1, 6)
    a, b, c = peel(t5, 2)
    print a, b, list(c)
# emits: 1 2 [3, 4, 5]
```

Discussion

Python supports the handy idea of multiple unpacking assignment. Say that t5 is any sequence of five items. Then, you can code:

```
a, b, c, d, e = t5
```

to bind a name to each item of t5.

However, you often do not know (nor care) exactly how many items a certain sequence t holds: you want to bind (say) two names, one to each of the first two items, and a third name to "the rest" of t (this requirement does imply that t must hold *at least* two items). If you know that t is a "proper" sequence, with support for slicing, not just an arbitrary iterable, you can code:

```
a, b = t[:2]
c = t[2:]
```

but this is nowhere as elegant or handy as the multiple unpacking assignment. Moreover, if you are not certain about the nature of t (i.e., if t can be any iterable, not necessarily supporting slice syntax), the task becomes more cumbersome:

```
c = iter(t5)
a = c.next()
b = c.next()
```

Given these issues, the Python Development mailing list* once discussed a new syntax for generalized multiple unpacking assignment, such that:

```
a, b, *c = t
```

* The Python Development mailing list is the list on which all discussion regarding the development of Python itself is held; see *http://mail.python.org/pipermail/python-dev/2002-November/030380.html* for this specific subject.

would perform exactly this task—bind names a and b to the first two items of t and name c to "the rest".

I didn't like the idea of making the Python language bigger by adding this extra functionality to assignment statements, so I came up with this recipe's generator. This generator provides this functionality fully and without any need to add any new syntax to Python.

Just one caveat: you must make sure that you pass the arg_cnt argument properly. If you pass a wrong value for arg_cnt, or if the sequence you pass to peel is shorter than arg_cnt, you get an exception at runtime. But then, you also get a Python exception at runtime if you try to perform a multiple assignment and the number of names you have on the left of the = sign is not identical to the number of items of the sequence you have on the right. Therefore, this recipe isn't any different from normal, multiple unpacking assignment in this respect. If you think it is important to relax some parts of this requirement, see recipe 19.5 "Automatically Unpacking the Needed Number of Items."

See Also

Language Reference and *Python in a Nutshell* about multiple unpacking assignments; recipe 19.5 "Automatically Unpacking the Needed Number of Items.

19.5 Automatically Unpacking the Needed Number of Items

Credit: Sami Hangaslammi, Peter Cogolo

Problem

You want to unpack (and bind to names) some items from the "front" of a sequence and bind another name to "the rest" of the sequence (the part you didn't unpack). You want to obtain the number of items to unpack automatically, based on how many names are on the left of the = sign in a multiple unpacking assignment.

Solution

The previous approach in recipe 19.4 "Unpacking a Few Items in a Multiple Assignment" is clean and elegant, but you have to "manually" pass the number of items to unpack. If you're willing to stoop to a little black magic, peering into stack frames and bytecodes, you may be able to bypass that requirement:

```
import inspect, opcode
def how_many_unpacked():
    f = inspect.currentframe().f_back.f_back
```

```
        if ord(f.f_code.co_code[f.f_lasti]) == opcode.opmap['UNPACK_SEQUENCE']:
            return ord(f.f_code.co_code[f.f_lasti+1])
        raise ValueError, "Must be a generator on RHS of a multiple assignment!"
    def unpack(iterable):
        iterator = iter(iterable)
        for num in xrange(how_many_unpacked()-1):
            yield iterator.next()
        yield iterator
    if __name__ == '__main__':
        t5 = range(1, 6)
        a, b, c = unpack(t5)
        print a, b, list(c)
```

Discussion

While arguably spiffy, this recipe is a bit fragile, as you could well expect from a function relying on introspection on bytecode: while the recipe works in Python 2.3 and 2.4, any future release of Python might easily generate bytecode for a multiple unpacking assignment in a somewhat different way, and thus break the recipe.

Moreover, as presented, the recipe relies on how_many_unpacked being called specifically from a generator; if you call it from an ordinary function, it does not work, since in that case the UNPACK_SEQUENCE bytecode in the caller's caller happens to fall at offset f.f_lasti+3 instead of f.f_lasti.

For example, the following code doesn't work with the recipe's Solution because enumfunc is an ordinary function, not a generator:

```
def enumfunc():
    return xrange(how_many_unpacked())
a, b, c, d, e = enumfunc()
```

However, the following code does work:

```
def enumgen():
    for x in xrange(how_many_unpacked()): yield x
a, b, c, d, e = enumgen()
```

because enumgen *is* a generator.

In other words, this recipe is a hack—arguably a *neat* hack (to the point that one of the editors of this Cookbook successfully lobbied the "other" two and managed to obtain the recipe's inclusion in this volume), but, nevertheless, a hack. Therefore, you probably do not want to *use* this approach in "production code", meaning code that must stay around for a long time and will be maintained across future versions of Python.

Nevertheless, you *could* make how_many_unpacked work in both contexts by making it a little bit more complicated:

```
def how_many_unpacked():
    f = inspect.currentframe().f_back.f_back
    bytecode = f.f_code.co_code
```

```
ups_code = opcode.opmap['UNPACK_SEQUENCE']
if ord(bytecode[f.f_lasti]) == ups_code:
    return ord(bytecode[f.f_lasti+1])
elif ord(bytecode[f.f_lasti+3]) == ups_code:
    return ord(bytecode[f.f_lasti+4])
else:
    raise ValueError, "Must be on the RHS of a multiple assignment!"
```

With this more complicated variant, how_many_unpacked would work when called from either a generator or an ordinary function. However, I recommend sticking with the simpler version presented in this recipe's Solution, and calling how_many_unpacked only from the given unpack generator, or a few other specific generators.

Even such a limited use can be considered debatable, since most Pythonistas prefer clarity and simplicity to the risky kind of "convenience" that can be obtained by such shortcuts. After all, this recipe's only advantage, in comparison to recipe 19.4 "Unpacking a Few Items in a Multiple Assignment," is that you save yourself the trouble of passing to unpack the number of items required, which is nice, but clearly, not all that crucial."

See Also

Recipe 19.4 "Unpacking a Few Items in a Multiple Assignment"; *Language Reference* and *Python in a Nutshell* about multiple unpacking assignments; *Library Reference* and *Python in a Nutshell* about library modules inspect and opcode.

19.6 Dividing an Iterable into n Slices of Stride n

Credit: Gyro Funch, Alex Martelli

Problem

You have an iterable p and need to get the n non-overlapping extended slices of stride n, which, if the iterable was a sequence supporting extended slicing, would be p[0::n], p[1::n], and so on up to p[n-1::n].

Solution

While extended slicing would return sequences of the same type we start with, it's much more sensible to specify a strider function that, instead, solves this problem by returning a list of lists:

```
def strider(p, n):
    """ Split an iterable p into a list of n sublists, repeatedly taking
        the next element of p and adding it to the next sublist.  Example:
        >>> strider('abcde', 3)
        [['a', 'd'], ['b', 'e'], ['c']]
        In other words, strider's result is equal to:
            [list(p[i::n]) for i in xrange(n)]
```

```
        if iterable p is a sequence supporting extended-slicing syntax.
    """
    # First, prepare the result, a list of n separate lists
    result = [ [] for x in xrange(n) ]
    # Loop over the input, appending each item to one of
    # result's lists, in "round robin" fashion
    for i, item in enumerate(p):
        result[i % n].append(item)
    return result
```

Discussion

The function in this recipe takes an iterable p and pulls it apart into a user-defined number n of pieces (specifically, function strider returns a list of sublists), distributing p's items into what would be the n extended slices of stride n if p were a sequence.

If we were willing to sacrifice generality, forcing argument p to be a sequence supporting extended slicing, rather than a generic iterable, we could use a very different approach, as the docstring of strider indicates:

```
def strider1(p, n):
    return [list(p[i::n]) for i in xrange(n)]
```

Depending on our exact needs, with such a strong constraint on p, we might omit the list call to make each subsequence into a list, and/or code a generator to avoid consuming extra memory to materialize the whole list of results at once:

```
def strider2(p, n):
    for i in xrange(n):
        yield p[i::n]
```

or, equivalently:

```
import itertools
def strider3(p, n):
    return itertools.imap(lambda i: p[i::n], xrange(n))
```

or, in Python 2.4, with a generator expression:

```
def strider4(p, n):
    return (p[i::n] for i in xrange(n))
```

However, none of these alternatives accepts a generic iterable as p—each demands a full-fledged sequence.

Back to this recipe's exact specs, the best way to enhance the recipe is to recode it to avoid low-level fiddling with indices. While doing arithmetic on indices is conceptually quite simple, it can get messy and indeed is notoriously error prone. We can do better by a generous application of module itertools from the Python Standard Library:

```
import itertools
def strider5(p, n):
    result = [ [] for x in itertools.repeat(0, n) ]
    resiter = itertools.cycle(result)
    for item, sublist in itertools.izip(p, resiter):
```

```
            sublist.append(item)
    return result
```

This strider5 version uses three functions from module itertools—all of the functions in module itertools return iterable objects, and, as we see in this case, their results are therefore typically used in for loops. Function repeat yields an object, repeatedly, a given number of times, and here we use it instead of the built-in function xxrange to control the list comprehension that builds the initial value for result. Function cycle takes an iterable object and returns an iterator that walks over that iterable object repeatedly and cyclically—in other words, cycle performs exactly the round-robin effect that we need in this recipe. Function izip is essentially like the built-in function zip, except that it returns an iterator and thus avoids the memory-consumption overhead that zip incurs by building its whole result list in memory at once.

This version achieves deep elegance and conceptual simplicity (although you may need to gain some familiarity with itertools before you agree that this version is simple!) by foregoing all index arithmetic and leaving all of the handling of the round-robin issues to itertools.cycle. resiter, per se, is a nonterminating iterator, but the function deals effortlessly with that. Specifically, since we use resiter together with p as arguments to izip, termination is assured (assuming, of course, that p does terminate!) by the semantics of izip, which, just like built-in function zip, stops iterating as soon as any one of its arguments is exhausted.

See Also

The itertools module is part of the Python Standard Library and is documented in the *Library Reference* portion of Python's online documentation; the *Library Reference* and *Python in a Nutshell* docs about the built-ins zip and xrange, and extended-form slicing of sequences.

19.7 Looping on a Sequence by Overlapping Windows

Credit: Peter Cogolo, Steven Bethard, Ian Bicking

Problem

You have an iterable s and need to make another iterable whose items are sublists (i.e., *sliding windows*), each of the same given length, over s' items, with successive windows overlapping by a specified amount.

Solution

We can combine built-in function iter and function islice from the standard library module itertools to code a generator to solve our problem:

```
import itertools
def windows(iterable, length=2, overlap=0):
    it = iter(iterable)
    results = list(itertools.islice(it, length))
    while len(results) == length:
        yield results
        results = results[length-overlap:]
        results.extend(itertools.islice(it, length-overlap))
    if results:
        yield results
if __name__ == '__main__':
    seq = 'foobarbazer'
    for length in (3, 4):
        for overlap in (0, 1):
            print '%d %d: %s' % (length, overlap,
                        map(''.join, windows(seq, length, overlap)))
```

This module, when run as a main script, emits:

```
3 0: ['foo', 'bar', 'baz', 'er']
3 1: ['foo', 'oba', 'arb', 'baz', 'zer', 'r']
4 0: ['foob', 'arba', 'zer']
4 1: ['foob', 'barb', 'baze', 'er']
```

When you know you don't need any overlap, a fast and concise alternative is available:

```
def chop(iterable, length=2):
    return itertools.izip(*(iter(iterable),)*length)
```

The body of this concise alternative may be a bit confusing until you realize that the two occurrences of the asterisk (*) there play different roles: the first one is part of a *args syntax form (passing the elements of a sequence as separate positional arguments), the second one indicates that a sequence (the Singleton tuple (iter(iterable),) must be repeated length times.

Discussion

In many cases, we need a sequence of sub-sequences of a given length, and we have to start with a "flat" iterable. For example, we can build a dictionary with given keys and values by calling dict with a sequence of two-item sequences—but what if we start with a "flat" sequence where keys and values just alternate? The function windows in this recipe meets this need:

```
the_dict = dict(windows(flat_alternating_keys_and_values))
```

Or, say we have an iterable whose items are the amounts of sales on each day. To turn it into an iterable whose items are the amounts of sales in each week (seven days):

```
weekly_sales = itertools.imap(sum, windows(daily_sales, 7))
```

The two use cases just presented are examples of how windows can be useful when called without overlap (in other words, with an overlap argument of 0, its default value), so the alternative chop function also presented in the recipe would be just as good (and faster). However, overlap is often useful when you deal with iterables that are signals, or time series. For example, if you have a function average such as:

```
def average(sequence):
    return sum(sequence)/float(len(sequence))
```

then you can apply a simple low-pass filter to a signal:

```
filtered = itertools.imap(average, windows(raw_signal, 5, 2))
```

or get the moving average daily sales from the iterable of daily sales:

```
mvavg_daily_sales = itertools.imap(average, windows(daily_sales, 7, 6))
```

The implementation of the windows generator in this recipe is quite straightforward, if you're familiar with itertools.islice (and you should be, if you deal with iterables!). For the first "window", we must clearly fill list results with the appropriate number of items (islice does that for us). At each subsequent step, we must throw away a certain number of items from the "front" of results (we do that conveniently by list slicing, since results is, indeed, a list) and replenish the same number at the back (we do that by calling the extend method of results, with islice providing the needed "new" items). That number, as a little reasoning shows, is exactly that given by the expression length-overlap. The loop terminates, if ever, only when results cannot be entirely replenished. (The loop never executes if results cannot even be filled entirely in the first place.)

When the loop terminates, we may be left with a "tail" in results, a "last window" that is shorter than length. What to do in that case depends on your application's exact needs. The recipe, as given above, just yields the shorter window as the last item of the generator, which is what we'd probably want in all of the previously mentioned use cases. In other cases, we might want to drop the last, too-short window (just omit the last two statements in function windows as given in the recipe), raise an exception (when we know that such a situation should never occur), or pad the last window to the required length with a pad value such as None, by changing the last two statements in function windows to something like:

```
if result:
    result.extend(itertools.repeat(None, length-len(result)))
    yield result
```

One important implementation detail: function windows, as coded in the recipe, yields a new list object at each step. It takes some time to generate all of these objects. In some cases, it may be convenient to the caller to know that each object it gets is a separate and independent list. Such knowledge enables the caller to store or modify the objects it gets, without having to make explicit copies. However, none of the use cases we discussed gets any benefit from this feature. So, you could optimize, by yielding the same list object every time. If you want that optimization, just change the statement:

```
results = results[length-overlap:]
```

into:

```
del results[:length-overlap]
```

If you're applying this optimization, and you're using Python 2.4, you should also consider using the new type collections.deque instead of list. In order to do so, you need to add the statement:

```
import collections
```

at the start of your code, change the only occurrence of list in the recipe into collections.queue, and further change the updating of results to avoid slicing, using, instead:

```
for i in xrange(length-overlap): results.popleft()
```

If your windows are long, and if they overlap substantially, using deque instead of list might give you better performance, since deque is optimized to support adding and removing items at *either* end, while lists, being compact arrays in memory, are inherently slow (specifically, O(n) for a list of length n) when you add or remove items at the beginning.

When you want windows of some length n that overlap specifically by n-1 items, function itertools.tee, new in Python 2.4, offers an elegant alternative approach. Say that you want to look at each item of the iterable, with access to a few neighboring items and some padding at both ends, so that you get just as many windows as there are items in the iterable. In Python 2.4, you could then code:

```
import itertools as IT
def windowed(iterable, pre=1, post=1, padding=None):
    # tee-off one iterator for each index in the window
    copies = IT.tee(iterable, pre + 1 + post)
    pre_copies, copy, post_copies = copies[:pre], copies[pre], copies[pre+1:]
    # iterators before the element have their start filled in with the
    # padding value.  no need to slice off the ends, izip will do that.
    pre_copies = [IT.chain(IT.repeat(padding, pre - i), itr)
                    for i, itr in enumerate(pre_copies)]
    # iterators after the element have their starts sliced off and their
    # end filled in with the padding value, endlessly repeated.
    post_copies = [IT.chain(IT.islice(itr, i + 1, None), IT.repeat(padding))
                    for i, itr in enumerate(post_copies)]
    # zip the elements with their preceding and following elements
    return IT.izip(*(pre_copies + [copy] + post_copies))
```

For example:

```
>>> print list(windowed(xrange(4), 1, 2, 'x'))
[('x', 0, 1, 2), (0, 1, 2, 3), (1, 2, 3, 'x'), (2, 3, 'x', 'x')]
```

If you use Python 2.4 and want this flavor of "sliding windows" over the iterable, with specified "padding" at both ends, you might prefer this `windowed` function to the recipe's `windows` generator.

See Also

Library Reference documentation on built-in `iter` and module `itertools`.

19.8 Looping Through Multiple Iterables in Parallel

Credit: Andy McKay, Hamish Lawson, Corey Coughlin

Problem

You need to loop through every item of multiple iterables in parallel, meaning that you first want to get a tuple with all of the first items of each iterable, next, a tuple with all of the "second items", and so forth.

Solution

Say you have two iterables (lists, in this case) such as:

```
a = ['a1', 'a2', 'a3']
b = ['b1', 'b2']
```

If you want to loop "in parallel" over them, the most general and effective approach is:

```
import itertools
for x, y in itertools.izip(a, b):
    print x, y
```

This snippet outputs two lines:

```
a1 b1
a2 b2
```

Discussion

The most general and effective way to loop "in parallel" over multiple iterables is to use function `izip` of standard library module `itertools`, as shown in the "Solution". The built-in function `zip` is an alternative that is almost as good:

```
for x, y in zip(a, b):
    print x, y
```

However, `zip` has one downside that can hurt your performance if you're dealing with long sequences: it builds the list of tuples in memory all at once (preparing and returning a list), while you need only one tuple at a time for pure looping purposes.

Both zip and `itertools.izip`, when you iterate in parallel over iterables of different lengths, stop as soon as the "shortest" such iterable is exhausted. This approach to termination is normally what you want. For example, it lets you have one or more non-terminating iterable in the zipping, as long as at least one of the iterables does terminate—or (in the case of `izip`, only) as long as you use some control structure, such as a conditional break within a `for` statement, to ensure you always require a finite number of items and do not loop endlessly.

In some cases, when iterating in parallel over iterables of different lengths, you may want shorter iterables to be conceptually "padded" with None up to the length of the longest iterable in the zipping. For this special need, you can use the built-in function map with a first argument of None:

```
for x, y in map(None, a, b):
    print x, y
```

map, like zip, builds and returns a whole list. If that is a problem, you can reproduce map's pad with None's behavior by coding your own generator. Coding your own generator is also a good approach when you need to pad shorter iterables with some value that is different from None.

If you need to deal only with specifically two sequences, your iterator's code can be quite straightforward and linear:

```
import itertools
def par_two(a, b, padding_item=None):
    a, b = iter(a), iter(b)
    # first, deal with both iterables via izip until one is exhausted:
    for x in itertools.izip(a, b):
        yield x
    # only one of the following two loops, at most, will execute, since
    # either a or b (or both!) are exhausted at this point:
    for x in a:
        yield x, padding_item
    for x in b:
        yield padding_item, x
```

Alternatively, you can code a more general function, one that is able to deal with any number of sequences:

```
import itertools
def par_loop(padding_item, *sequences):
    iterators = map(iter, sequences)
    num_remaining = len(iterators)
    result = [padding_item] * num_remaining
    while num_remaining:
        for i, it in enumerate(iterators):
            try:
                result[i] = it.next()
            except StopIteration:
                iterators[i] = itertools.repeat(padding_item)
                num_remaining -= 1
```

```
            result[i] = padding_item
        if num_remaining:
            yield tuple(result)
```

Here's an example of use for generator par_loop:

```
print map(''.join, par_loop('x', 'foo', 'zapper', 'ui'))
# emits: ['fzu', 'oai', 'opx', 'xpx', 'xex', 'zrx']
```

Both par_two and par_loop start by calling the built-in function iter on all of their arguments and thereafter use the resulting iterators. This is important, because the functions rely on the *state* that these iterators maintain. The key idea in par_loop is to keep count of the number of iterators as yet unexhausted, and replace each exhausted iterator with a nonterminating iterator that yields the padding_item ceaselessly; num_remaining counts unexhausted iterators, and both the yield statement and the continuation of the while loop are conditional on *some* iterators being as yet unexhausted.

Alternatively, if you know in advance which iterable is the longest one, you can wrap every other iterable x as itertools.chain(iter(x), itertools.repeat(padding)) and then call itertools.izip. You can't do this wrapping on *all* iterables because the resulting iterators are nonterminating—if you izip iterators that are all nonterminating, izip itself cannot terminate! Here, for example, is a version that works as intended only when the longest (but terminating!) iterable is the very first one:

```
import itertools
def par_longest_first(padding_item, *sequences):
    iterators = map(iter, sequences)
    for i, it in enumerate(iterators):
        if not i: continue
        iterators[i] = itertools.chain(it, itertools.repeat(padding_item))
    return itertools.izip(iterators)
```

See Also

The itertools module is part of the Python Standard Library and is documented in the *Library Reference* portion of Python's online documentation; the *Library Reference* and *Python in a Nutshell* docs about built-ins zip, iter, and map.

19.9 Looping Through the Cross-Product of Multiple Iterables

Credit: Attila Vàsàrhelyi, Raymond Hettinger, Steven Taschuk

Problem

You need to loop through every item of multiple iterables cross-productwise, meaning that you first want to get the first item of the first iterable paired with all the others, next, the second item of the first iterable paired with all the others, and so forth.

Solution

Say you have two iterables (lists, in this case) such as:

```
a = ['a1', 'a2', 'a3']
b = ['b1', 'b2']
```

If you want to loop over their cross-product, the simplest approach is often just a couple of nested for loops:

```
for x in a:
    for y in b:
        print x, y
```

This snippet's output is six lines:

```
a1 b1
a1 b2
a2 b1
a2 b2
a3 b1
a3 b2
```

However, in many cases, you'd rather get all items in the "cross-product" of multiple iterables as a single, linear sequence, suitable for using in a single for or for passing onwards to other sequence manipulation functions, such as those supplied by itertools. For such needs, you may put the nested fors in a list comprehension:

```
for x, y in [(x,y) for x in a for y in b]:
    print x, y
```

Discussion

A list comprehension lets you easily generate (as a single, linear sequence) all the pairings of several iterables (also known as the *cross-product*, *product set*, or *Cartesian product* of these iterables). However, the number of items in such a cross-product is the arithmetic product (multiplication) of the lengths of all the iterables involved, a number that may easily get quite large. A list comprehension, by definition, builds the entire list at once, which means that it may consume substantial amounts of memory. Also, you get to start iterating only when the whole cross-product list is entirely built.

Python 2.4 offers one obvious way to solve this problem: the newly introduced construct of *generator expressions*:

```
for x, y in ((x,y) for x in a for y in b): print x, y
```

A generator expression looks just like a list comprehension, except that it uses parentheses rather than brackets: it returns an iterator, suitable for looping on, rather than building and returning a list. Thus, a generator expression can save substantial amounts of memory, if you are iterating over a very long sequence. Also, you start executing the loop's body very soon, since each successive element gets generated iteratively, before each iteration of the loop's body. If your loop's body contains conditional breaks, so that execution terminates as soon as some conditions are met, using a generator expression rather than a list comprehension can mean a potentially substantial improvement in performance.

If you need to support Python 2.3, and yet you want to achieve the kind of advantages that generator expressions can afford over list comprehensions, the best approach may be to code your own generator. This is quite simple if you only need to deal with a known number of sequences, such as two:

```
def cross_two(a, b):
    for x in a:
        for y in b:
            yield a, b
```

Dealing with an arbitrary number of sequences is a bit more complicated, but not terribly so, particularly if we use recursion to help:

```
def cross_loop(*sequences):
    if sequences:
        for x in sequences[0]:
            for y in cross_loop(sequences[1:]):
                yield (x,) + y
    else:
        yield ()
```

We can also do it without recursion. It's not hard if we're willing to build the entire result list in memory at once before returning it, just as a list comprehension would:

```
def cross_list(*sequences):
    result = [[ ]]
    for seq in sequences:
        result = [sublist+[item] for sublist in result for item in seq]
    return result
```

Alternatively, you can return map(tuple, result) if you need to ensure that each item of the sequence you return is a tuple, not a list.

Recursion-free iterative (incremental) generation of the "cross-product" sequence is also feasible, even though it's nowhere as simple as either the recursive or the nonincremental versions:

```
def cross(*sequences):
    # visualize an odometer, with "wheels" displaying "digits"...:
    wheels = map(iter, sequences)
    digits = [it.next() for it in wheels]
    while True:
        yield tuple(digits)
        for i in range(len(digits)-1, -1, -1):
            try:
                digits[i] = wheels[i].next()
                break
            except StopIteration:
                wheels[i] = iter(sequences[i])
                digits[i] = wheels[i].next()
        else:
            break
```

In Python 2.4, you might express the for statement more clearly as for i in reversed(range(len(digits))).

To repeat, it is important to remember that all of these solutions should be considered only if you *do* have the problem—that is, if and only if you do need to view all items in the "cross-product" of multiple iterables as a single, linear sequence. Many cases have no such requirement, and simply coding multiple nested for loops inline is quite acceptable, simpler, and more readable. In many cases, getting all items in the "cross-product" as a single sequence is preferable, so it's worth knowing how to do that. However, do keep in mind that simplicity is an important virtue, and do not lose sight of it in pursuit of a cool (but complicated) solution. All the cool tools, constructs, and library modules that Python offers exist strictly to serve *you*, to let you build and maintain your applications with minimal effort. Don't go out of your way to use the new shiny tools if you can solve your application's problems with less effort in simpler ways!

See Also

The *Library Reference* and *Python in a Nutshell* docs about built-ins iter, enumerate, map, and (Python 2.4 only) reversed; the *Language Reference* and *Python in a Nutshell* docs about list comprehensions and (Python 2.4 only) generator expressions.

19.10 Reading a Text File by Paragraphs

Credit: Alex Martelli, Magnus Lie Hetland, Terry Reedy

Problem

You need to read a text file (or any other iterable whose items are lines of text) paragraph by paragraph, where a "paragraph" is defined as a sequence of nonwhite lines (i.e., paragraphs are separated by lines made up exclusively of whitespace).

Solution

A generator is quite suitable for bunching up lines this way:

```
def paragraphs(lines, is_separator=str.isspace, joiner=''.join):
    paragraph = [ ]
    for line in lines:
        if is_separator(line):
            if paragraph:
                yield joiner(paragraph)
                paragraph = [ ]
        else:
            paragraph.append(line)
    if paragraph:
        yield joiner(paragraph)
if __name__ == '__main__':
```

```
text = 'a first\nparagraph\n\nand a\nsecond one\n\n'
for p in paragraphs(text.splitlines(True)): print repr(p)
```

Discussion

Python doesn't directly support paragraph-oriented file reading, but it's not hard to add such functionality. We define a "paragraph" as the string formed by joining a nonempty sequence of nonseparator lines, separated from any adjoining paragraphs by nonempty sequences of separator lines. A separator line is one that satisfies the predicate passed in as argument is_separator. (A *predicate* is a function whose result is taken as a logical truth value, and we say a *predicate* is *satisfied* when the predicate returns a result that is true.) By default, a line is a separator if it is made up entirely of whitespace characters (e.g., space, tab, newline, etc.).

The recipe's code is quite straightforward. The state of the generator during iteration is entirely held in local variable paragraph, a list to which we append the nonseparator lines that make up the current paragraph. Whenever we meet a separator in the body of the for statement, we test if paragraph to check whether the list is currently empty. If the list is empty, we're already skipping a run of separators and need do nothing special to handle the current separator line. If the list is not empty, we've just met a separator line that terminates the current paragraph, so we must join up the list, yield the resulting paragraph string, and then set the list back to empty.

This recipe implements a special case of sequence adaptation by bunching: an underlying iterable is "bunched up" into another iterable with "bigger" items. Python's generators let you express sequence adaptation tasks very directly and linearly. By passing as arguments, with reasonable default values, the is_separator predicate, and the joiner callable that determines what happens to each "bigger item" when we're done bunching it up, we achieve a satisfactory amount of generality without any extra complexity. To see this, consider a snippet such as:

```
import operator
numbers = [1, 2, 3, 0, 0, 6, 5, 3, 0, 12]
bunch_up = paragraphs
for s in bunch_up(numbers, operator.not_, sum): print 'S', s
for l in bunch_up(numbers, bool, len): print 'L', l
```

In this snippet, we use the paragraphs generator (under the name of bunch_up, which is clearer in this context) to get the sums of "runs" of nonzero numbers separated by runs of zeros, then the lengths of the runs of zeros—applications that, at first sight, might appear to be quite different from the recipe's stated purpose. That's the magic of abstraction: when appropriately and tastefully applied, it can easily turn the solution of a problem into a family of solutions for many other apparently unrelated problems.

An elementary issue, but a crucial one for getting good performance in the "main" use case of this recipe, is that the paragraphs' generator builds up each resulting paragraph as a list of strings, then concatenates all strings in the list with ''.join to

---

obtain each result it yields. An alternate approach, where a large string is built up as a string, by repeated application of += or +, is never the right approach in Python: it is both slow and clumsy. Good Pythonic style absolutely *demands* that we use a list as the intermediate accumulator, whenever we are building a long string by concatenating a number of smaller ones. Python 2.4 has diminished the performance penalty of the wrong approach. For example, to join a list of 52 one-character strings into a 52-character string on my machine, Python 2.3 takes 14.2 microseconds with the right approach, 73.6 with the wrong one; but Python 2.4 takes 12.7 microseconds with the right approach, 41.6 with the wrong one, so the penalty in this case has decreased from over five times to over three. Nevertheless, there is no reason to choose to pay such a performance penalty without any returns, even the lower penalty that Python 2.4 manages to extract!

Python 2.4 offers a new itertools.groupby function that is quite suitable for sequence-bunching tasks. Using it, we could express the paragraphs' generator in a really tight and concise way:

```
from itertools import groupby
def paragraphs(lines, is_separator=str.isspace, joiner=''.join):
    for separator_group, lineiter in groupby(lines, key=is_separator):
        if not separator_group:
            yield joiner(lineiter)
```

itertools.groupby, like SQL's GROUP BY clause, which inspired it, is not exactly trivial use, but it can be quite useful indeed for sequence-bunching tasks once you have mastered it thoroughly.

See Also

Recipe 19.11 "Reading Lines with Continuation Characters"; Chapter 1 for general issues about handling text; Chapter 2 for general issues about handling files; recipe 19.21 "Computing a Summary Report with itertools.groupby"; *Library Reference* documentation on Python 2.4's itertools.groupby.

19.11 Reading Lines with Continuation Characters

Credit: Alex Martelli

Problem

You have a file that includes long logical lines split over two or more physical lines, with backslashes to indicate that a continuation line follows. You want to process a sequence of logical lines, "rejoining" those split lines.

Solution

As usual, our first idea for a problem involving sequences should be a generator:

```python
def logical_lines(physical_lines, joiner=''.join):
    logical_line = [ ]
    for line in physical_lines:
        stripped = line.rstrip()
        if stripped.endswith('\\'):
            # a line which continues w/the next physical line
            logical_line.append(stripped[:-1])
        else:
            # a line which does not continue, end of logical line
            logical_line.append(line)
            yield joiner(logical_line)
            logical_line = [ ]
    if logical_line:
        # end of sequence implies end of last logical line
        yield joiner(logical_line)
if __name__=='__main__':
    text = 'some\\\n', 'lines\\\n', 'get\n', 'joined\\\n', 'up\n'
    for line in text:
        print 'P:', repr(line)
    for line in logical_lines(text, ' '.join):
        print 'L:', repr(line)
```

When run as a main script, this code emits:

```
<c>P: 'some\\\n'
P: 'lines\\\n'
P: 'get\n'
P: 'joined\\\n'
P: 'up\n'
L: 'some lines get\n'
L: 'joined up\n'</c>
```

Discussion

This problem is about sequence-bunching, just like the previous recipe 19.10 "Reading a Text File by Paragraphs." It is therefore not surprising that this recipe, like the previous, is a generator (with an internal structure quite similar to the one in the "other" recipe): today, in Python, sequences are often processed most simply and effectively by means of generators.

In this recipe, the generator can encompass just a small amount of generality without introducing extra complexity. Determining whether a line is a continuation line, and of how to proceed when it is, is slightly too idiosyncratic to generalize in a simple and transparent way. I have therefore chosen to code that functionality inline, in the body of the logical_lines generator, rather than "factoring it out" into separate callables. Remember, generality is good, but simplicity is even more important. However, I have kept the simple and transparent generality obtained by passing the joiner function as an argument, and the snippet of code under the if __name__

==`'__main__'` test demonstrates how we may want to use that generality, for example, to join continuation lines with a space rather than with an empty string.

If you are certain that the file you're processing is sufficiently small to fit comfortably in your computer's memory, with room to spare for processing, *and* you don't need the feature (offered in the version of `logical_lines` shown in the "Solution") of ignoring whitespace to the right of a terminating \\, a solution using a plain function rather than a generator is simpler than the one shown in this recipe's Solution:

```
def logical_lines(physical_lines, joiner=''.join, separator=''):
    return joiner(physical_lines).replace('\\\n', separator).splitlines(True)
```

In this variant, we join all of the physical lines into one long string, then we replace the "canceled" line ends (line ends immediately preceded by a backslash) with nothing (or any other separator we're requested to use), and finally split the resulting long string back into lines (keeping the line ends—that's what the `True` argument to method `splitlines` is for). This approach is a very different one from that suggested in this recipe but possibly worthwhile, if `physical_lines` is small enough that you can afford the memory for it. I prefer the "Solution"'s approach because giving semantic significance to trailing whitespace is a poor user interface design choice.

See Also

Recipe 19.10 "Reading a Text File by Paragraphs"; *Perl Cookbook* recipe 8.1; Chapter 1 for general issues about handling text; Chapter 2 for general issues about handling files.

19.12 Iterating on a Stream of Data Blocks as a Stream of Lines

Credit: Scott David Daniels, Peter Cogolo

Problem

You want to loop over all lines of a stream, but the stream arrives as a sequence of data blocks of arbitrary size (e.g., from a network socket).

Solution

We need to code a generator that gets blocks and yields lines:

```
def ilines(source_iterable, eol='\r\n', out_eol='\n'):
    tail = ''
    for block in source_iterable:
        pieces = (tail+block).split(eol)
        tail = pieces.pop()
        for line in pieces:
            yield line + out_eol
    if tail:
        yield tail
```

```
    if __name__ == '__main__':
        s = 'one\r\ntwo\r,\nthree,four,five\r\n,six,\r\nseven\r\nlast'.split(',')
        for line in ilines(s): print repr(line)
```

When run as a main script, this code emits:

```
'one\n'
'two\n'
'threefourfive\n'
'six\n'
'seven\n'
'last'
```

Discussion

Many data sources produce their data in fits and starts—sockets, RSS feeds, the results of expanding compressed text, and (at its heart) most I/O. The data often doesn't arrive at convenient boundaries, but you nevertheless want to consume it in logical units. For text, the logical units are often lines.

This recipe shows generator ilines, a simple way to consume a source_iterable, which yields blocks of data, producing an iterator that yields lines of text instead. ilines is vastly simplified by assuming that lines are separated, on input, by a known end-of-line (EOL) string—by default '\r\n', which is the standard EOL marker in most Internet protocols. ilines' implementation is further simplified by taking a high-level approach, relying on the split method of Python's string types to do most of the work. This basically leaves ilines with the single task of "buffering" data between successive input blocks, on all occasions when a line starts in one block and ends in a following one (including those occasions in which block boundaries "split" an EOL marker).

ilines easily accomplishes its buffering task through its local variable tail, which starts empty and, at each leg of the loop, holds that which followed the latest EOL marker seen so far. When tail+block ends with an EOL marker, the expression (tail+block).split(eol) produces a list whose last item is an empty string (''), exactly what we need; otherwise, the last item of the list is that which followed the last EOL, which *again* is exactly what we need.

Python's built-in file objects are even more powerful than ilines, since they support a *universal newlines* reading mode (mode 'U'), which is able to recognize and deal with all common EOL markers (even when different markers are mixed within the same stream!). However, ilines is more flexible, since you may apply it in many situations where you have a stream of arbitrary blocks of text and want to process it as a stream of lines, with a known EOL marker.

See Also

Library Reference and *Python in a Nutshell* docs about built-in file objects; Chapter 2 for general issues about handling files.

19.13 Fetching Large Record Sets from a Database with a Generator

Credit: Christopher Prinos

Problem

You want to fetch a result set from a database (using the Python DB API) and easily iterate over each record in the result set. However, you don't want to use the DB cursor's method fetchall: it could consume a lot of memory and would force you to wait until the whole result set comes back before you can start iterating.

Solution

A generator is the ideal solution to this problem:

```
def fetchsome(cursor, arraysize=1000):
    ''' A generator that simplifies the use of fetchmany '''
    while True:
        results = cursor.fetchmany(arraysize)
        if not results: break
        for result in results:
            yield result
```

Discussion

In applications that use the Python DB API, you often see code that goes somewhat like (where cursor is a DB API cursor object):

```
cursor.execute('select * from HUGE_TABLE')
for result in cursor.fetchall():
    doSomethingWith(result)
```

This simple approach is "just" fine, as long as fetchall returns a small result set, but it does not work very well if the query result is very large. A large result set can take a long time to return. Also, cursor.fetchall() needs to allocate enough memory to store the entire result set in memory at once. Further, with this simple approach, the doSomethingWith function isn't going to get called until the entire query's result finishes coming over from the database to our program.

An alternative approach is to rely on the cursor.fetchone method:

```
for result in iter(cursor.fetchone, None):
    doSomethingWith(result)
```

However, this alternative approach does not allow the database to optimize the fetching process: most databases can exhibit better efficiency when returning multiple records for a single query, rather than returning records one at a time as fetchone requires.

To let your applications obtain greater efficiency than fetchone allows, without the risks of unbounded memory consumption and delay connected to the use of fetchall, Python's DB API's cursors also have a fetchmany method. However, the direct use of fetchmany makes your iterations somewhat more complicated than the simple for statements such as those just shown. For example:

```
while True:
    results = cursor.fetchmany(1000)
    if not results: break
    for result in results:
        doSomethingWith(result)
```

Python's generators are a great way to encapsulate complicated iteration logic so that application code can just about always loop with simple for statements. With this recipe's fetchsome generator, you get the same efficiencies and safeguards as with the native use of the fetchmany method in the preceding snippet but with the same crystal-clear simplicity as in the snippets that used either fetchall or fetchone, namely:

```
for result in fetchsome(cursor):
    doSomethingWith(result)
```

By default, fetchsome fetches up to 1,000 records at a time, but you can change that number, depending on your requirements. Optimal values can depend on schema, database type, choice of Python DB API module. In general, you're best advised to experiment with a few different values in your specific settings if you need to optimize this specific aspect. (Such experimentation is often a good idea for any optimization task.)

This recipe is clearly an example of a more general case: a *subsequence unbuncher* generator that you can use when you have a sequence of subsequences (each subsequence being obtained through some call, and the end of the whole sequence being indicated by an empty subsequence) and want to flatten it into a simple, linear sequence of items. You can think of this unbunching task as the reverse of the sequence-bunching tasks covered earlier in recipe 19.10 "Reading a Text File by Paragraphs" and recipe 19.11 "Reading Lines with Continuation Characters," or as a simpler variant of the sequence-flattening task covered in recipe 4.6 "Flattening a Nested Sequence." A generator for unbunching might be:

```
def unbunch(next_subseq, *args):
    ''' un-bunch a sequence of subsequences into a linear sequence '''
    while True:
        subseq = next_subseq(*args)
        if not subseq: break
        for item in subseq:
            yield item
```

As you can see, the structure of unbunch is basically identical to that of the recipe's fetchsome. Usage would also be just about the same:

```
for result in unbunch(cursor.fetchmany, 1000):
    doSomethingWith(result)
```

However, while it is important and instructive to consider this kind of generalization, when you're writing applications you're often better off using specific generators that directly deal with your application's specific needs. In this case, for example, calling `fetchsome(cursor)` is more obvious and direct than calling `unbunch(cursor.fetchmany, 1000)`, and `fetchsome` usefully hides the usage of `fetchmany` as well as the specific choice of 1,000 as the subsequence size to fetch at each step.

See Also

Recipe 19.10 "Reading a Text File by Paragraphs"; recipe 19.11 "Reading Lines with Continuation Characters"; recipe 4.6 "Flattening a Nested Sequence"; Python's DB API is covered in Chapter 7 and in *Python in a Nutshell*.

19.14 Merging Sorted Sequences

Credit: Sébastien Keim, Raymond Hettinger, Danny Yoo

Problem

You have several sorted sequences (iterables) and need to iterate on the overall sorted sequence that results from "merging" these sequences.

Solution

A generator is clearly the right tool for the job, in the general case (i.e., when you might not have enough memory to comfortably hold all the sequences). Implementing the generator is made easy by the standard library module heapq, which supplies functions to implement the "heap" approach to priority queues:

```
import heapq
def merge(*subsequences):
    # prepare a priority queue whose items are pairs of the form
    # (current-value, iterator), one each per (non-empty) subsequence
    heap = [ ]
    for subseq in subsequences:
        iterator = iter(subseq)
        for current_value in iterator:
            # subseq is not empty, therefore add this subseq's pair
            # (current-value, iterator) to the list
            heap.append((current_value, iterator))
            break
    # make the priority queue into a heap
    heapq.heapify(heap)
    while heap:
        # get and yield lowest current value (and corresponding iterator)
        current_value, iterator = heap[0]
```

```
        yield current_value
        for current_value in iterator:
            # subseq is not finished, therefore add this subseq's pair
            # (current-value, iterator) back into the priority queue
            heapq.heapreplace(heap, (current_value, iterator))
            break
        else:
            # subseq has been exhausted, therefore remove it from the queue
            heapq.heappop(heap)
```

Discussion

The need for "merging" sorted subsequences into a larger sorted sequence is reason-ably frequent. If the amount of data is small enough to fit entirely in memory with-out problems, then the best approach is to build a list by concatenating all subsequences, then sort the list:

```
def smallmerge(*subsequences):
    result = [ ]
    for subseq in subsequences: result.extend(subseq)
    result.sort()
    return result
```

The sort method of list objects is based on a sophisticated *natural merge* algorithm, able to take advantage of existing sorted subsequences in the list you're sorting; therefore, this approach is quite fast, as well as simple (and general, since this approach's correctness does *not* depend on all subsequences being already sorted). If you can choose this approach, it has many other advantages. For example, smallmerge works fine even if one of the subsequences isn't perfectly sorted to start with; and in Python 2.4, you may add a generic keywords argument **kwds to smallmerge and pass it right along to the result.sort( ) step, to achieve the flexibil-ity afforded in that version by the cmp=, key=, and reverse= arguments to list's sort method.

However, you sometimes deal with large sequences, which might not comfortably fit in memory all at the same time (e.g., your sequences might come from files on disk, or be computed on the fly, item by item, by other generators). When this happens, this recipe's generator will enable you to perform your sequence merging while con-suming a very moderate amount of extra memory (dependent only on the number of subsequences, not on the number of items in the subsequences).

The recipe's implementation uses a classic sequence-merging algorithm based on a priority queue, which, in turn, lets it take advantage of the useful heapq module in the Python Standard Library. heapq offers functions to implement a priority queue through the data structure known as a *heap*.

A *heap* is any list H such that, for any valid index 0<=i<len(H), H[i]<=H[2*i+1], and H[i]<=H[2*i+2] (if 2*i+1 and 2*i+2 are also valid indices into H). This *heap property* is fast to establish on an arbitrary list (function heapify does that) and very fast to re-establish after altering or removing the smallest item (and functions heapreplace and heappop do that). The smallest item is always H[0] (it's easy to see that the "heap" property implies this), and being able to find the smallest item instantly makes heaps an excellent implementation of priority queues.

In this recipe, we use as items in the "heap" a "pair" (i.e., two-items tuple) for each subsequence that is not yet exhausted (i.e., each subsequence through which we have not yet fully iterated). As its first item, each pair has the "current item" in the corresponding subsequence and, as its second item, an iterator over that subsequence. At each iteration step, we yield the smallest "current item", then we advance the corresponding iterator and re-establish the "heap" property; when an iterator is exhausted, we remove the corresponding pair from the "heap" (so that, clearly, we're finished when the "heap" is emptied). Note the idiom that we use to advance an iterator by one step, dealing with the possibility that the iterator is exhausted:

```
for current_value in iterator:
    # if we get here the iterator was not empty, current_value was
    # its first value, and the iterator has been advanced one step
    ...use pair (current_value, iterator)...
    # we break at once as we only wanted the first item of iterator
    break
else:
    # if we get here the break did not execute, so the iterator
    # was empty (exhausted)
    # deal with the case of iterator being exhausted...
```

We use this idiom twice in the recipe, although in the first of the two uses we do not need the else clause since we can simply ignore iterators that are immediately exhausted (they correspond to empty subsequences, which can be ignored for merging purposes).

If you find this idiom confusing or tricky (because it uses a for statement whose body immediately breaks—i.e., a statement that looks like a loop but is not really a loop because it never executes more than once!), you may prefer a different approach:

```
try:
    current_value = iterator.next( )
except StopIteration:
    # if we get here the iterator was empty (exhausted)
    # deal with the case of iterator being exhausted...
else:
    # if we get here the iterator was not empty, current_value was
    # its first value, and the iterator has been advanced one step
    # use pair (current_value, iterator)...
```

I slightly prefer the idiom using for; in my view, it gains in clarity by putting the normal case (i.e., an unexhausted iterator) first and the rare case (an exhausted iterator) later. A variant of the try/except idiom that has the same property is:

```
try:
    current_value = iterator.next( )
    # if we get here the iterator was not empty, current_value was
    # its first value, and the iterator has been advanced one step
```

```
    # use pair (current_value, iterator)...
except StopIteration:
    # if we get here the iterator was empty (exhausted)
    # deal with the case of iterator being exhausted...
```

However, I somewhat dislike this variant (even though it's quite OK for the two specific uses of this recipe) because it crucially depends on the code indicated as "use pair" *never* raising a StopIteration exception. As a general principle, it's best to use a try clause's body that is as small as possible—just the smallest fragment that you *do* expect to possibly raise the exception you're catching in the following handlers (except clauses), *not* the follow-on code that must execute only if the exception was not raised. The follow-on code goes in the else clause of the try statement, in properly defensive Pythonic coding style. In any case, as long as you are fully aware of the tradeoffs in clarity and defensiveness between these three roughly equivalent idioms, you're welcome to develop your own distinctive Pythonic style and, in particular, to choose freely among them!

If you do choose either of the idioms that explicitly call iterator.next( ), a further "refinement" (i.e., a tiny optimization) is to keep as the second item of each pair, rather than the iterator object, the bound-method iterator.next directly, ready for you to call. This optimization is not really tricky at all (it *is* quite common in Python to stash away bound methods and other such callables), but it may nevertheless result in code of somewhat lower readability. Once again, the choice is up to you!

See Also

Chapter 5 for general issues about sorting and recipe 5.7 "Keeping a Sequence Ordered as Items Are Added" and recipe 5.8 "Getting the First Few Smallest Items of a Sequence" about heapq specifically; *Library Reference* and *Python in a Nutshell* documentation on module heapq and lists' sort method; Robert Sedgewick, *Algorithms* (Addison-Wesley) (heaps are covered starting on p. 178 in the 2d edition); *heapq.py* in the Python sources contains an interesting discussion of heaps.

19.15 Generating Permutations, Combinations, and Selections

Credit: Ulrich Hoffmann, Guy Argo, Danny Yoo, Carl Bray, Doug Zongker, Gagan Saksena, Robin Houston, Michael Davies

Problem

You need to iterate on the permutations, combinations, or selections of a sequence. The fundamental rules of combinatorial arithmetic indicate that the length of these derived sequences are very large even if the starting sequence is of moderate size: for example, there are over 6 billion permutations of a sequence of length 13. So you definitely do not want to compute (and keep in memory) all items in a derived sequence before you start iterating,

---

Solution

Generators enable you to compute needed objects one by one as you iterate on them. The loop inevitably takes a long time if there are vast numbers of such objects and you really need to examine each one. But at least you do not waste memory storing all of them at once:

```python
def _combinators(_handle, items, n):
    ''' factored-out common structure of all following combinators '''
    if n==0:
        yield [ ]
        return
    for i, item in enumerate(items):
        this_one = [ item ]
        for cc in _combinators(_handle, _handle(items, i), n-1):
            yield this_one + cc
def combinations(items, n):
    ''' take n distinct items, order matters '''
    def skipIthItem(items, i):
        return items[:i] + items[i+1:]
    return _combinators(skipIthItem, items, n)
def uniqueCombinations(items, n):
    ''' take n distinct items, order is irrelevant '''
    def afterIthItem(items, i):
        return items[i+1:]
    return _combinators(afterIthItem, items, n)
def selections(items, n):
    ''' take n (not necessarily distinct) items, order matters '''
    def keepAllItems(items, i):
        return items
    return _combinators(keepAllItems, items, n)
def permutations(items):
    ''' take all items, order matters '''
    return combinations(items, len(items))
if __name__=="__main__":
    print "Permutations of 'bar'"
    print map(''.join, permutations('bar'))
# emits ['bar', 'bra', 'abr', 'arb', 'rba', 'rab']
    print "Combinations of 2 letters from 'bar'"
    print map(''.join, combinations('bar', 2))
# emits ['ba', 'br', 'ab', 'ar', 'rb', 'ra']
    print "Unique Combinations of 2 letters from 'bar'"
    print map(''.join, uniqueCombinations('bar', 2))
# emits ['ba', 'br', 'ar']
    print "Selections of 2 letters from 'bar'"
    print map(''.join, selections('bar', 2))
# emits ['bb', 'ba', 'br', 'ab', 'aa', 'ar', 'rb', 'ra', 'rr']
```

Discussion

The generators in this recipe accept any sequence as the items argument and always yield lists of length n, where n is the second argument to the generator (permutations accepts only one argument, and n is by definition equal to len(items)).

You can modify the recipe so the generators yield tuples (or instances of another sequence type), instead of lists, by changing two lines of code in _combinators. The yield [ ] must become yield ( ) (more generally, this statement must yield the empty sequence of any sequence type you wish to use), and name this_one must be bound to the Singleton sequence of any sequence type you wish to use. For example, to yield tuples, change the statement that assigns to name this_one into:

```
this_one = items[i],
```

(A subtle, often-forgotten point of Python syntax is that the *comma* identifies the right side of the assignment as a tuple. Placing parentheses around the right-hand side would be both insufficient and superfluous.)

Another way to modify this recipe is to have the generators yield sequences of the same type as argument items. (As long as this type is indeed a sequence: specifically, it must support slicing, as well as the use of the plus sign, +, for concatenation). If that is what you want, change the yield of the empty sequence into:

```
yield items[:0]
```

and change the assignment to name this_one into:

```
this_one = items[i:i+1]
```

The definition of *distinct items* for this recipe's purposes is: "items that occur at different indices in the input sequence." If your input sequence has duplicates (i.e., the same item occurring at multiple indices), none of the functions in this recipe will care about removing them: rather, all functions will treat the duplicates as "distinct items" for all purposes.

See Also

Recipe 19.16 "Generating the Partitions of an Integer" for another combinatorics building block; recipe 18.1 "Removing Duplicates from a Sequence" and recipe 18.2 "Removing Duplicates from a Sequence While Maintaining Sequence Order."

19.16 Generating the Partitions of an Integer

Credit: David Eppstein, Jan Van lent, George Yoshida

Problem

You want to generate all *partitions* of a given positive integer, that is, all the ways in which that integer can be represented as a sum of positive integers (for example, the partitions of 4 are 1+1+1+1, 1+1+2, 2+2, 1+3, and 4).

Solution

A recursive generator offers the simplest approach for this task, as is often the case with combinatorial computations:

```
def partitions(n):
    # base case of the recursion: zero is the sum of the empty tuple
    if n == 0:
        yield ()
        return
    # modify the partitions of n-1 to form the partitions of n
    for p in partitions(n-1):
        yield (1,) + p
        if p and (len(p) < 2 or p[1] > p[0]):
            yield (p[0] + 1,) + p[1:]
```

Discussion

Partitions, like permutations, combinations and selections, are among the most basic primitives of combinatorial arithmetic. In other words, such constructs, besides being useful on their own, are building blocks for generating other kinds of combinatorial objects.

This recipe works along classic recursive lines. If you have a partition of a positive integer n, you can reduce it to a partition of n-1 in a canonical way by subtracting one from the smallest item in the partition. For example, you can build partitions of 5 from partitions of 6 by such transformation steps as 1+2+3 => 2+3, 2+4 => 1+4, and so forth. The algorithm in this recipe reverses the process: for each partition p of n-1, the algorithm finds the partitions of n that would be reduced to p by this canonical transformation step. Therefore, each partition p of n is output exactly once, at the step when we are considering the partition p1 of n-1 to which p canonically reduces.

Be warned: the number of partitions of n grows fast when n itself grows. Ramanujan's upper bound for the number of partitions of a positive integer k is:

```
int(exp(pi*sqrt(2.0*k/3.0))/(4.0*k*sqrt(3.0)))
```

(where names exp, pi and sqrt are all taken from module math, in Python terms). For example, the number 200 has about 4,100 billion partitions.

This recipe generates each partition as a tuple of integers in ascending order. If it's handier for your application to deal with partitions as tuples of integers in *descending* order, you need only change the body of the for loop in the recipe to:

```
yield p + (1,)
if p and (len(p) < 2 or p[-2] > p[-1]):
    yield p[:-1] + (p[-1] + 1,)
```

Creating a new tuple per item in the output stream, as this recipe does, may result in performance issues, if you're dealing with a very large n. One way to optimize this aspect would be to return lists instead of tuples, and specifically to return the *same* list object at each step (with the descending-order modification, and append and pop operations rather than list concatenation):

```
def partfast(n):
    # base case of the recursion: zero is the sum of the empty tuple
    if n == 0:
```

```
      yield [ ]
      return
   # modify the partitions of n-1 to form the partitions of n
   for p in partfast(n-1):
      p.append(1)
      yield p
      p.pop( )
      if p and (len(p) < 2 or p[-2] > p[-1]):
         p[-1] += 1
         yield p
```

This optimization is not worth the bother—not so much because of the modest extra complication in partfast's own code, but mostly because yielding the same list object at each step means that code *using* partfast must take precautions. For example, list(partfast(4)) is a potentially surprising list of five empty sublists, while list(partitions(4)) is exactly the expected list of the five partitions of the number 4.

On the "other" hand, a different approach using an auxiliary parameter can actually produce a simplification for the descending-order case:

```
def partitions_descending(num, lt=num):
   if not num: yield ()
   for i in xrange(min(num, lt), 0, -1):
      for parts in partitions_descending(num-i, i):
         yield (i,) + parts
```

This code is simpler than the variant given in the recipe and could be made even clearer in Python 2.4 by changing its outer loop into:

```
   for i in reversed(xrange(1, min(num, lt)-1)):
```

See Also

Recipe 19.15 "Generating Permutations, Combinations, and Selections" for more combinatorics building blocks.

19.17 Duplicating an Iterator

Credit: Heiko Wundram, Raymond Hettinger

Problem

You have an iterator (or other iterable) object x, and need to iterate twice over x's sequence of values.

Solution

In Python 2.4, solving this problem is the job of function tee in the standard library module itertools:

```
   import itertools
   x1, x2 = itertools.tee(x)
   # you can now iterate on x1 and x2 separately
```

In Python 2.3, you can code tee yourself:

```
import itertools
def tee(iterable):
    def yield_with_cache(next, cache={ }):
        pop = cache.pop
        for i in itertools.count( ):
            try:
                yield pop(i)
            except KeyError:
                cache[i] = next( )
                yield cache[i]
    it = iter(iterable)
    return yield_with_cache(it.next), yield_with_cache(it.next)
```

Discussion

The need to iterate repeatedly over the same sequence of values is a reasonably common one. If you know that the sequence comes from a list, or some other container that intrinsically lets you iterate over its items repeatedly, then you simply perform the iteration twice. However, sometimes your sequence may come from a generator, a sequential file (which might, e.g., wrap a stream of data coming from a network socket—data that you can read only once), or some other iterator that is not intrinsically re-iterable. Even then, in some cases, the best approach is the simplest one— first save the data into a list in memory, then repeatedly iterate over that list:

```
saved_x = list(x)
for item in saved_x: do_something(item)
for item in saved_x: do_something_else(item)
```

The simple approach of first saving all data from the iterator into a list is not feasible for an infinite sequence x, and may not be optimal if x is very large and your separate iterations over it never get far out-of-step from each other. In these cases, the tee function shown in this recipe can help. For example, say that the items of x are either numbers or operators (the latter being represented as strings such as '+', '*', etc.). Whenever you encounter an operator, you must output the result of applying that operator to all numbers immediately preceding it (since the last operator). Using tee, you could code:

```
def is_operator(item):
    return isinstance(item, str)
def operate(x):
    x1, x2 = tee(iter(x))
    while True:
        for item in x1:
            if is_operator(item): break
        else:
            # we get here when there are no more operators in the input
            # stream, thus the operate function is entirely done
            return
        if item == '+':
            total = 0
            for item in x2:
                if is_operator(item): break
```

```
                total += item
            yield total
        elif item == '*':
            total = 1
            for item in x2:
                if is_operator(item): break
                total *= item
            yield total
```

This kind of "look-ahead" usage is pretty typical of many of the common use cases of tee. Even in this case, you might choose the alternative approach of accumulating items in a list:

```
def operate_with_auxiliary_list(x):
    aux = [ ]
    for item in x:
        if is_operator(item):
            if item == '+':
                yield sum(aux)
            elif item == '*':
                total = 1
                for item in aux:
                    total *= item
                yield total
            aux = [ ]
        else:
            aux.append(item)
```

Having tee available lets you freely choose between these different styles of look-ahead processing.

Function itertools.tee as implemented in Python 2.4 is faster and more general than the pure Python version given in this recipe for version 2.3 usage. However, the pure Python version is quite instructive and deserves study for the sake of the techniques it demonstrates, even if you're lucky enough to be using Python 2.4 and therefore don't need to use this pure Python version of tee.

In the pure Python version of tee, the nested generator yield_with_cache makes use of the fact (which some consider a "wart" in Python but is actually quite useful) that the default values of arguments get computed just once, at the time the def statement executes. Thus, both calls to the nested generator in the return statement of tee implicitly share the same initially empty dict as the value of the cache argument.

itertools.count returns non-negative integers, 0 and up, one at a time. yield_with_cache uses each of these integers as a key into the cache dictionary. The call to pop(i) (the argument of the yield statement in the try clause) simultaneously returns and removes the entry corresponding to key i, *if* that entry was present—that is, in this case, if the "other" instance of the generator had already reached that point in the iteration (and cached the item for our benefit). Otherwise, the except clause executes, computes the item (by calling the object bound to name next, which in this case is the next bound method of an iterator over the iterable object, which tee is duplicating), and caches the item (for the "other" instance's future benefit) before yielding it.

So, in practice, cache is being used as a FIFO queue. Indeed, were it not for the fact that we don't need a pure-Python tee in Python 2.4, we could code an equivalent implementation of it in Python 2.4 using the new type deque in standard library module collections:

```
import collections
def tee_just_an_example(iterable):
    def yield_with_cache(it, cache=collections.deque):
        while True:
            if cache:
                yield cache.popleft( )
            else:
                result = it.next( )
                cache.append(result)
                yield result
    it = iter(iterable)
    return yield_with_cache(it), yield_with_cache(it)
```

This latest version is meant purely as an illustrative example, and therefore, it's simplified by not using any of the bound-method extraction idioms shown in the version in the "Solution" (which *is* intended for "production" use in Python 2.3).

Once you've called tee on an iterator, you should no longer use the original iterator anywhere else; otherwise, the iterator could advance without the knowledge of the tee-generated objects, and those objects would then "get out of sync" with the original. Be warned that tee requires auxiliary storage that is proportional to how much the two tee-generated objects get "apart" from each other in their separate iterations. In general, if one iterator is going to walk over most or all of the data from the original before the "other" one starts advancing, you should consider using list instead of tee. Both of these caveats apply to the itertools.tee function of Python 2.4 just as well as they apply to the pure Python versions of tee presented in this recipe. One more caveat: again both for the versions in this recipe, and the itertools.tee function in Python 2.4, there is no guarantee of thread safety: to access the tee'd iterators from different threads, you need to guard those iterators with a single lock!

See Also

The itertools module is part of the Python Standard Library and is documented in the *Library Reference* portion of Python's online documentation; recipe 19.2 "Building a List from Any Iterable" shows how to turn an iterator into a list.

19.18 Looking Ahead into an Iterator

Credit: Steven Bethard, Peter Otten

Problem

You are using an iterator for some task such as parsing, which requires you to be able to "look ahead" at the next item the iterator is going to yield, without disturbing the iterator state.

Solution

The best solution is to wrap your original iterator into a suitable class, such as the following one (Python 2.4-only):

```
import collections
class peekable(object):
    """ An iterator that supports a peek operation.  Example usage:
    >>> p = peekable(range(4))
    >>> p.peek()
    0
    >>> p.next(1)
    [0]
    >>> p.peek(3)
    [1, 2, 3]
    >>> p.next(2)
    [1, 2]
    >>> p.peek(2)
    Traceback (most recent call last):
      ...
    StopIteration
    >>> p.peek(1)
    [3]
    >>> p.next(2)
    Traceback (most recent call last):
      ...
    StopIteration
    >>> p.next()
    3
    """
    def __init__(self, iterable):
        self._iterable = iter(iterable)
        self._cache = collections.deque()
    def __iter__(self):
        return self
    def _fillcache(self, n):
        if n is None:
            n = 1
        while len(self._cache) < n:
            self._cache.append(self._iterable.next())
    def next(self, n=None):
        self._fillcache(n)
        if n is None:
            result = self._cache.popleft()
        else:
            result = [self._cache.popleft() for i in range(n)]
        return result
    def peek(self, n=None):
        self._fillcache(n)
        if n is None:
            result = self._cache[0]
        else:
            result = [self._cache[i] for i in range(n)]
        return result
```

Discussion

Many iterator-related tasks, such as parsing, require the ability to "peek ahead" (once or a few times) into the sequence of items that an iterator is yielding, in a way that does not alter the iterator's observable state. One approach is to use the new Python 2.4 function iterator.tee to get two independent copies of the iterator, one to be advanced for peeking purposes and the "other" one to be used as the "main" iterator. It's actually handier to wrap the incoming iterator once for all, at the start, with the class peekable presented in this recipe; afterwards, a peek method, which is safe and effective, can be counted on. A little added sweetener is the ability to call peek (and, as long as we're at it, the standard next method too) with a specific number argument n, to request a list of the next n items of the iterator (without disturbing the iterator's state when you call peek(n), with iterator state advancement when you call next(n)—just like for normal calls without arguments to the same methods).

The obvious idea used in this recipe for implementing peekable is to have it keep a cache of peeked-ahead arguments. Since the cache must grow at the tail and get consumed from the end, a natural choice is to make the cache a collections.deque, a new type introduced in Python 2.4. However, if you need this code to run under version 2.3 as well, make self._cache a list instead—you only need to change method next's body a little bit, making it:

```
if n is None:
    result = self._cache.pop(0)
else:
    result, self_cache = self._cache[:n], self._cache[n:]
```

As long as you're caching only one or just a few items of lookahead at a time, performance won't suffer much by making self._cache a list rather than a deque.

An interesting characteristic of the peekable class presented in this recipe is that, if you request too many items from the iterator, you get a StopIteration exception but that does not throw away the last few values of the iterator. For example, if p is an instance of peekable with just three items left, when you call p.next(5), you get a StopIteration exception. You can later call p.next(3) and get the list of the last three items.

A subtle point is that the n argument to methods peek and next defaults to None, not to 1. This gives you two distinct ways to peek at a single item: the default way, calling p.peek( ), just gives you that item, while calling p.peek(1) gives you a list with that single item in it. This behavior is quite consistent with the way p.peek behaves when called with different arguments: any call p.peek(n) with any non-negative integer n returns a list with n items (or raises StopIteration if p has fewer than n items left). This approach even supports calls such as p.next(0), which in practice always returns an empty list [ ] without advancing the iterator's state. Typically, you just call p.peek( ), without arguments, and get one look-ahead item without problems.

As an implementation detail, note that the docstring of the class peekable presented in this recipe is essentially made up of examples of use with expected results. Besides being faster to write, and arguably to read for an experienced Pythonista, this style of docstring is perfect for use with the Python Standard Library module doctest.

See Also

collections.deque and doctest in the *Python Library Reference* (for Python 2.4).

19.19 Simplifying Queue-Consumer Threads

Credit: Jimmy Retzlaff, Paul Moore

Problem

You want to code a consumer thread which gets work requests off a queue one at a time, processes each work request, and eventually stops, and you want to code it in the simplest possible way.

Solution

This task is an excellent use case for the good old *Sentinel* idiom. The producer thread, when it's done putting actual work requests on the queue, must finally put a *sentinel* value, that is, a value that is different from any possible work request. Schematically, the producer thread will do something like:

```
for input_item in stuff_needing_work:
    work_request = make_work_request(input_item)
    queue.put(work_request)
queue.put(sentinel)
```

where sentinel must be a "well-known value", different from any work_request object that might be put on the queue in the first phase.

The consumer thread can then exploit the built-in function iter:

```
for work_request in iter(queue.get, sentinel):
    process_work_request(work_request)
cleanup_and_terminate( )
```

Discussion

Were it not for built-in function iter, the consumer thread would have to use a slightly less simple and elegant structure, such as:

```
while True:
    work_request = queue.get( )
    if work_request == sentinel:
        break
    process_work_request(work_request)
cleanup_and_terminate( )
```

However, the *Sentinel* idiom is so useful and important that Python directly supports it with built-in function iter. When you call iter with just one argument, that argument must be an iterable object, and iter returns an iterator for it. But when you call iter with two arguments, the first one must be a callable which can be called without arguments, and the second one is an arbitrary value known as the *sentinel*. In the two-argument case, iter repeatedly calls the first argument. As long as each call returns a value !=sentinel, that value becomes an item in the iteration; as soon as a call returns a value ==sentinel, the iteration stops.

If you had to code this yourself as a generator, you could write:

```
def iter_sentinel(a_callable, the_sentinel):
    while True:
        item = a_callable()
        if item == the_sentinel: break
        yield item
```

But the point of this recipe is that you don't have to code even this simple generator: just use the power that Python gives you as part of the functionality of the built-in function iter!

Incidentally, Python offers many ways to make *sentinel* values—meaning values that compare equal only to themselves. The simplest and most direct way, and therefore the one I suggest you always use for this specific purpose, is:

```
sentinel = object()
```

See Also

Documentation for iter in the *Library Reference* and *Python in a Nutshell*.

19.20 Running an Iterator in Another Thread

Credit: Garth Kidd

Problem

You want to run the code of a generator (or any other iterator) in its own separate thread, so that the iterator's code won't block your main thread even if it contains time-consuming operations, such as blocking calls to the operating system.

Solution

This task is best tackled by wrapping a subclass of threading.Thread around the iterator:

```
import sys, threading
class SpawnedGenerator(threading.Thread):
    def __init__(self, iterable, queueSize=0):
        threading.Thread.__init__(self)
```

```
        self.iterable = iterable
        self.queueSize = queueSize
    def stop(self):
        "Ask iteration to stop as soon as feasible"
        self.stopRequested = True
    def run(self):
        "Thread.start runs this code in another, new thread"
        put = self.queue.put
        try:
            next = iter(self.iterable).next
            while True:
                # report each result, propagate StopIteration
                put((False, next()))
                if self.stopRequested:
                    raise StopIteration
        except:
            # report any exception back to main thread and finish
            put((True, sys.exc_info()))
    def execute(self):
        "Yield the results that the "other", new thread is obtaining"
        self.queue = Queue.Queue(self.queueSize)
        get = self.queue.get
        self.stopRequested = False
        self.start()                    # executes self.run() in other thread
        while True:
            iterationDone, item = get()
            if iterationDone: break
            yield item
        # propagate any exception (unless it's just a StopIteration)
        exc_type, exc_value, traceback = item
        if not isinstance(exc_type, StopIteration):
            raise exc_type, exc_value, traceback
    def __iter__(self):
        "Return an iterator for our executed self"
        return iter(self.execute())
```

Discussion

Generators (and other iterators) are a great way to package the logic that controls an iteration and obtains the next value to feed into a loop's body. The code of a generator (and, equivalently, the code of the next method of another kind of iterator) usually runs in the same thread as the code that's iterating on it. The "calling" code can therefore *block*, each time around the loop, while waiting for the generator's code to do its job.

Sometimes, you want to use a generator (or other kind of iterator) in a "non-blocking" way, which means you need to arrange things so that the generator's body runs in a new, separate thread. This recipe shows a class which supplies exactly this kind of functionality: this recipe's SpawnedGenerator class subclasses threading.Thread and uses Thread's start/run mechanism to ensure the generator's body always executes in a separate thread from that of the calling code.

All communication between the two threads occurs through a single instance of the Queue.Queue class (held through a local-variable bound method in each of the communicating methods: the generator named execute that runs in the calling thread and the method named run that runs in a separate thread). The "calling" code may also call method stop on the SpawnedGenerator instance to ask for the iteration to stop as soon as feasible. Optionally, you may also specify a queue size when you instantiate SpawnedGenerator, if you want to limit how far ahead of the calling thread the spawned thread can get.

The main use case for this recipe is for wrapping iterators that make blocking calls to the operating system (e.g., walking a directory tree), when you need to use such iterators in an application where the "main" thread cannot be allowed to block for a long time. The typical examples of applications whose main thread must not block are event-driven applications, a description that applies to applications with a GUI, as well as to networking applications built on asynchronous frameworks, such as Twisted or the asyncore module of the Python Standard Library.

See Also

Library Reference and *Python in a Nutshell* docs about modules threading and asyncore; Twisted is at *http://www.twistedmatrix.com/*; Chapter 9 for general issues about threading; Chapter 11 for general issues about user interfaces; Chapter 13 and Chapter 14 for general issues about network and web programming, including asynchronous approaches to such programs.

19.21 Computing a Summary Report with itertools.groupby

Credit: Paul Moore, Raymond Hettinger

Problem

You have a list of data grouped by a key value, typically read from a spreadsheet or the like, and want to generate a summary of that information for reporting purposes.

Solution

The itertools.groupby function introduced in Python 2.4 helps with this task:

```
from itertools import groupby
from operator import itemgetter
def summary(data, key=itemgetter(0), field=itemgetter(1)):
    """ Summarise the given data (a sequence of rows), grouped by the
        given key (default: the first item of each row), giving totals
        of the given field (default: the second item of each row).
        The key and field arguments should be functions which, given a
        data record, return the relevant value.
```

```
    """
    for k, group in groupby(data, key):
        yield k, sum(field(row) for row in group)
if __name__ == "__main__":
    # Example: given a sequence of sales data for city within region,
    # _sorted on region_, produce a sales report by region
    sales = [('Scotland', 'Edinburgh', 20000),
             ('Scotland', 'Glasgow', 12500),
             ('Wales', 'Cardiff', 29700),
             ('Wales', 'Bangor', 12800),
             ('England', 'London', 90000),
             ('England', 'Manchester', 45600),
             ('England', 'Liverpool', 29700)]
    for region, total in summary(sales, field=itemgetter(2)):
        print "%10s: %d" % (region, total)
```

Discussion

In many situations, data is available in tabular form, with the information naturally grouped by a subset of the data values (e.g., recordsets obtained from database queries and data read from spreadsheets—typically with the csv module of the Python Standard Library). It is often useful to be able to produce summaries of the detail data.

The new groupby function (added in Python 2.4 to the itertools module of the Python Standard Library) is designed exactly for the purpose of handling such grouped data. It takes as arguments an iterator, whose items are to be thought of as records, along with a function to extract the *key* value from each record. itertools.groupby yields each distinct key from the iterator in turn, each along with a new iterator that runs through the data values associated with that key.

The groupby function is often used to generate summary totals for a dataset. The summary function defined in this recipe shows one simple way of doing this. For a summary report, two extraction functions are required: one function to extract the key, which is the function that you pass to the groupby function, and another function to extract the values to be summarized. The recipe uses another innovation of Python 2.4 for these purposes: the operator.itemgetter higher-order function: called with an index i as its argument. itemgetter produces a function f such that f(x) extracts the ith item from x, operating just like an *indexing* x[i].

The input records must be sorted by the given key; if you're uncertain about that condition, you can use groubpy(sorted(data, key=key), key) to ensure it, exploiting the built-in function sorted, also new in Python 2.4. It's quite convenient that the same key-extraction function can be passed to both sorted and groupby in this idiom. The groupby function itself does not sort its input, which gains extra flexibility that may come in handy—although most of the time you will want to use groupby only on sorted data. See recipe 19.10 "Reading a Text File by Paragraphs" for a case in which it's quite handy to use groupby on *non*sorted data.

For example, if the sales data was in a CSV file *sales.csv*, the usage example in the recipe's if __name__ == '__main__' section might become:

```
import csv
sales = sorted(cvs.reader(open('sales.csv', 'rb')),
               key=itemgetter(1))
for region, total in summary(sales, field=itemgetter(2)):
    print "%10s: %d" % (region, total)
```

Overall, this recipe provides a vivid illustration of how the new Python 2.4 features work well together: in addition to the groupby function, the operator.itemgetter used to provide field extraction functions, and the potential use of the built-in function sorted, the recipe also uses a generator expression as the argument to the sum built-in function. If you need to implement this recipe's functionality in Python 2.3, you can start by implementing your own approximate version of groupby, for example as follows:

```
class groupby(dict):
    def __init__(self, seq, key):
        for value in seq:
            k = key(value)
            self.setdefault(k, [ ]).append(value)
    __iter__ = dict.iteritems
```

This version doesn't include all the features of Python 2.4's groupby, but it's very simple and may be sufficient for your purposes. Similarly, you can write your own simplified versions of functions itemgetter and sorted, such as:

```
def itemgetter(i):
    def getter(x): return x[i]
    return getter
def sorted(seq, key):
    aux = [(key(x), i, x) for i, x in enumerate(seq)]
    aux.sort()
    return [x for k, i, x in aux]
```

As for the generator expression, you can simply use a list comprehension in its place—just call sum([field(row) for row in group]) where the recipe has the same call without the additional square brackets, [ ]. Each of these substitutions will cost a little performance, but, overall, you can build the same functionality in Python 2.3 as you can in version 2.4—the latter just is slicker, simpler, faster, neater!

See Also

itertools.groupy, operator.itemgetter, sorted, and csv in the *Library Reference* (for Python 2.4).

## CHAPTER 20

Descriptors, Decorators, and Metaclasses

20.0 Introduction

Credit: Raymond Hettinger

> I had my power drill slung low on my toolbelt and I said, "Go ahead, honey. Break something."

—*Tim Allen*
> *on the challenges of figuring out what*
> *to do with a new set of general-purpose tools*

This chapter is last because it deals with issues that look or sound difficult, although they really aren't. It is about Python's power tools.

Though easy to use, the power tools can be considered advanced for several reasons. First, the need for them rarely arises in simple programs. Second, most involve introspection, wrapping, and forwarding techniques available only in a dynamic language like Python. Third, the tools seem advanced because when you learn them, you also develop a deep understanding of how Python works internally.

Last, as with the power tools in your garage, it is easy to get carried away and create a gory mess. Accordingly, to ward off small children, the tools were given scary names such as *descriptors*, *decorators*, and *metaclasses* (such names as *pangalaticgarglebaster* were considered a bit too long).

Because these tools are so general purpose, it can be a challenge to figure out what to do with them. Rather that resorting to Tim Allen's tactics, study the recipes in this chapter: they will give you all the practice you need. And, as Tim Peters once pointed out, it can be difficult to devise new uses from scratch, but when a real problem demands a power tool, you'll know it when you need it.

Descriptors

The concept of *descriptors* is easy enough. Whenever an attribute is looked up, an action takes place. By default, the action is a get, set, or delete. However, someday you'll be working on an application with some subtle need and wish that more complex actions could be programmed. Perhaps you would like to create a log entry every time a certain attribute is accessed. Perhaps you would like to redirect a method lookup to another method. The solution is to write a function with the needed action and then specify that it be run whenever the attribute is accessed. An object with such functions is called a *descriptor* (just to make it sound harder than it really is).

While the concept of a descriptor is straightforward, there seems to be no limit to what can be done with them. Descriptors underlie Python's implementation of methods, bound methods, super, property, classmethod, and staticmethod. Learning about the various applications of descriptors is key to mastering the language.

The recipes in this chapter show how to put descriptors straight to work. However, if you want the full details behind the descriptor protocol or want to know exactly how descriptors are used to implement super, property, and the like, see my paper on the subject at *http://users.rcn.com/python/download/Descriptor.htm*.

Decorators

Decorators are even simpler than descriptors. Writing myfunc=wrapper(myfunc) was the common way to modify or log something about another function, which took place somewhere after myfunc was defined. Starting with Python 2.4, we now write @wrapper just before the def statement that performs the definition of myfunc. Common examples include @staticmethod and @classmethod. Unlike Java declarations, these wrappers are higher-order functions that can modify the original function or take some other action. Their uses are limitless. Some ideas that have been advanced include @make_constants for bytecode optimization, @atexit to register a function to be run before Python exits, @synchronized to automatically add mutual exclusion locking to a function or method, and @log to create a log entry every time a function is called. Such wrapper functions are called *decorators* (not an especially intimidating name but cryptic enough to ward off evil spirits).

Metaclasses

The concept of a *metaclass* sounds strange only because it is so familiar. Whenever you write a class definition, a mechanism uses the name, bases, and class dictionary to create a class object. For old-style classes that mechanism is types.ClassType. For new-style classes, the mechanism is just type. The former implements the familiar actions of a classic class, including attribute lookup and showing the name of the class when repr is called. The latter adds a few bells and whistles including support for __slots__ and __getattribute__. If only that mechanism were programmable, what you could do in Python would be limitless. Well, the mechanism *is* programmable, and, of course, it has an intimidating name, *metaclasses*.

The recipes in this chapter show that writing metaclasses can be straightforward. Most metaclasses subclass type and simply extend or override the desired behavior. Some are as simple as altering the class dictionary and then forwarding the arguments to type to finish the job.

For instance, say that you would like to automatically generate getter methods for all the private variables listed in slots. Just define a metaclass M that looks up __slots__ in the mapping, scans for variable names starting with an underscore, creates an accessor method for each, and adds the new methods to the class dictionary:

```
class M(type):
    def __new__(cls, name, bases, classdict):
        for attr in classdict.get('__slots__', ()):
            if attr.startswith('_'):
                def getter(self, attr=attr):
                    return getattr(self, attr)
                # 2.4 only: getter.__name__ = 'get' + attr[1:]
                classdict['get' + attr[1:]] = getter
        return type.__new__(cls, name, bases, classdict)
```

Apply the new metaclass to every class where you want automatically created accessor functions:

```
class Point(object):
    __metaclass__ = M
    __slots__ = ['_x', '_y']
```

If you now print dir(Point), you will see the two accessor methods as if you had written them out the long way:

```
class Point(object):
    __slots__ = ['_x', '_y']
    def getx(self):
        return self._x
    def gety(self):
        return self._y
```

In both cases, among the output of the print statement, you will see the names 'getx' and 'gety'.

20.1 Getting Fresh Default Values at Each Function Call

Credit: Sean Ross

Problem

Python computes the default values for a function's optional arguments just once, when the function's def statement executes. However, for some of your functions, you'd like to ensure that the default values are *fresh* ones (i.e., new and independent copies) each time a function gets called.

Solution

A Python 2.4 decorator offers an elegant solution, and, with a slightly less terse syntax, it's a solution you can apply in version 2.3 too:

```
import copy
def freshdefaults(f):
    "a decorator to wrap f and keep its default values fresh between calls"
    fdefaults = f.func_defaults
    def refresher(*args, **kwds):
        f.func_defaults = copy.deepcopy(fdefaults)
        return f(*args, **kwds)
    # in 2.4, only: refresher.__name__ = f.__name__
    return refresher
# usage as a decorator, in python 2.4:
@freshdefaults
def packitem(item, pkg=[ ]):
    pkg.append(item)
    return pkg
# usage in python 2.3: after the function definition, explicitly assign:
# f = freshdefaults(f)
```

Discussion

A function's default values are evaluated once, and only once, at the time the function is defined (i.e., when the def statement executes). Beginning Python programmers are sometimes surprised by this fact; they try to use mutable default values and yet expect that the values will somehow be regenerated afresh each time they're needed.

Recommended Python practice is to not use mutable default values. Instead, you should use idioms such as:

```
def packitem(item, pkg=None):
    if pkg is None:
        pkg = [ ]
    pkg.append(item)
    return pkg
```

The freshdefaults decorator presented in this recipe provides another way to accomplish the same task. It eliminates the need to set as your default value anything but the value you intend that optional argument to have by default. In particular, you don't have to use None as the default value, rather than (say) square brackets [ ], as you do in the recommended idiom.

freshdefaults also removes the need to test each argument against the stand-in value (e.g., None) before assigning the intended value: this could be an important simplification in your code, where your functions need to have several optional arguments with mutable default values, as long as all of those default values can be deep-copied.

On the other hand, the implementation of freshdefaults needs several reasonably advanced concepts: decorators, closures, function attributes, and deep copying. All in all, this implementation is no doubt more difficult to explain to beginning Python programmers than the recommended idiom. Therefore, this recipe cannot really be recommended to beginners. However, advanced Pythonistas may find it useful.

See Also

Python *Language Reference* documentation about decorators; *Python Language Reference* and *Python in a Nutshell* documentation about closures and function attributes; *Python Library Reference* and *Python in a Nutshell* documentation about standard library module copy, specifically function deepcopy.

20.2 Coding Properties as Nested Functions

Credit: Sean Ross, David Niergarth, Holger Krekel

Problem

You want to code properties without cluttering up your class namespace with accessor methods that are not called directly.

Solution

Functions nested within another function are quite handy for this task:

```
import math
class Rectangle(object):
    def __init__(self, x, y):
        self.y = x
        self.y = y
    def area():
        doc = "Area of the rectangle"
        def fget(self):
            return self.x * self.y
        def fset(self, value):
            ratio = math.sqrt((1.0*value)/self.area)
            self.x *= ratio
            self.y *= ratio
        return locals()
    area = property(**area())
```

Discussion

The standard idiom used to create a property starts with defining in the class body several accessor methods (e.g., getter, setter, deleter), often with boilerplate-like method names such as setThis, getThat, or delTheother. More often than not, such

If an outer function just returns an inner function (often a closure), the name of the returned function object is fixed, which can be confusing when the name is shown during introspection or debugging:

```
>>> def make_adder(addend):
...     def adder(augend): return augend+addend
...     return adder
...
>>> plus100 = make_adder(100)
>>> plus_23 = make_adder(23)
>>> print plus100(1000), plus_23(1000)
1100 1023
>>> print plus100, plus_23
<function adder at 0x386530> <function adder at 0x3825f0>
```

As you see, the functionality of plus100 and plus_23 is correct (they add 100 and 23 to their argument, respectively). Confusingly, however, their names are both 'adder', even though they are different functions. In Python 2.4, you can solve the problem by setting the __name__ attribute of the inner function right after the end of the inner function's def statement, and before the return statement from the outer function:

```
def make_adder(addend):
    def adder(augend):
        return augend+addend
    adder.__name__ = 'add_%s' % (addend,)
    return adder
```

With this change in make_adder, the previous snippet would now produce more useful output:

```
>>> print plus100, plus_23
<function add_100 at 0x386530> <function add_23 at 0x3825f0>
```

Unfortunately, in Python 2.3, you cannot assign to the __name__ attribute of a function object; in that release, the attribute is read-only. If you want to obtain the same effect in Python 2.3, you must follow a more roundabout route, making and returning a new function object that differs from the other only in name:

```
import new
def make_adder(addend):
    def adder(augend): return augend+addend
    return new.function(adder.func_code, adder.func_globals, 'add_%s' %
(addend,),
                        adder.func_defaults, adder.func_closure)
```

accessors are not required except inside the property itself; sometimes (rarely) programmers even remember to del them to clean up the class namespace after building the property instance.

The idiom suggested in this recipe avoids cluttering up the class namespace at all. Just write in the class body a function with the same name you intend to give to the property. Inside that function, define appropriate nested functions, which *must* be named exactly fget, fset, fdel, and assign an appropriate docstring named doc. Have the outer function return a dictionary whose entries have exactly those names, and no others: returning the locals() dictionary will work, as long as your outer function has no other local variables at that point. If you do have other names in addition to the fixed ones, you might want to code your return statement, for example, as:

```
return sub_dict(locals(), 'doc fget fset fdel'.split())
```

using the sub_dict function shown in recipe 4.13 "Extracting a Subset of a Dictionary." Any other way to subset a dictionary will work just as well.

Finally, the call to property uses the ** notation to expand a mapping into named arguments, and the assignment rebinds the name to the resulting property instance, so that the class namespace is left pristine.

As you can see from the example in this recipe's Solution, you don't have to define *all* of the four key names: you may, and should, omit some of them if a particular property forbids the corresponding operation. In particular, the area function in the solution does not define fdel because the resulting area attribute must be not deletable.

In Python 2.4, you can define a simple custom decorator to make this recipe's suggested idiom even spiffier:

```
def nested_property(c):
    return property(**c())
```

With this little helper at hand, you can replace the explicit assignment of the property to the attribute name with the decorator syntax:

```
@nested_property
def area():
    doc = "Area of the rectangle"
    def fget(self):
    the area function remains the same
```

In Python 2.4, having a decorator line @deco right before a def name statement is equivalent to having, right after the def statement's body, an assignment name = deco(name). A mere difference of syntax sugar, but it's useful: anybody reading the source code of the class knows up front that the function or method you're def'ing is meant to get decorated in a certain way, not to get used exactly as coded. With the Python 2.3 syntax, somebody reading in haste might possibly miss the assignment statement that comes *after* the def.

Returning locals works only if your outer function has no other local variables besides fget, fset, fdel, and doc. An alternative idiom to avoid this restriction is to move the call to property *inside* the outer function:

```
def area():
    what_is_area = "Area of the rectangle"
    def compute_area(self):
```

```
            return self.x * self.y
        def scale_both_sides(self, value):
            ratio = math.sqrt((1.0*value)/self.area)
            self.x *= ratio
            self.y *= ratio
        return property(compute_area, scale_both_sides, None, what_is_area)
    area = area()
```

As you see, this alternative idiom enables us to give different names to the getter and setter accessors, which is not a big deal because, as mentioned previously, accessors are often named in uninformative ways such as getThis and setThat anyway. But, if your opinion differs, you may prefer this idiom, or its slight variant based on having the outer function return a tuple of values for property's argument rather than a dict. In other words, the variant obtained by changing the last two statements of this latest snippet to:

```
        return compute_area, scale_both_sides, None, what_is_area
    area = property(*area())
```

See Also

Library Reference and *Python in a Nutshell* docs on built-in functions property and locals.

20.3 Aliasing Attribute Values

Credit: Denis S. Otkidach

Problem

You want to use an attribute name as an alias for another one, either just as a default value (when the attribute was not explicitly set), or with full setting and deleting abilities too.

Solution

Custom descriptors are the right tools for this task:

```
class DefaultAlias(object):
    ''' unless explicitly assigned, this attribute aliases to another. '''
    def __init__(self, name):
        self.name = name
    def __get__(self, inst, cls):
        if inst is None:
            # attribute accessed on class, return `self' descriptor
            return self
        return getattr(inst, self.name)
class Alias(DefaultAlias):
    ''' this attribute unconditionally aliases to another. '''
    def __set__(self, inst, value):
        setattr(inst, self.name, value)
```

```
    def __delete__(self, inst):
        delattr(inst, self.name)
```

Discussion

Your class instances sometimes have attributes whose default value must be the same as the current value of other attributes but may be set and deleted independently. For such requirements, custom descriptor DefaultAlias, as presented in this recipe's Solution, is just the ticket. Here is a toy example:

```
class Book(object):
    def __init__(self, title, shortTitle=None):
        self.title = title
        if shortTitle is not None:
            self.shortTitle = shortTitle
    shortTitle = DefaultAlias('title')
b = Book('The Life and Opinions of Tristram Shandy, Gent.')
print b.shortTitle
# emits: The Life and Opinions of Tristram Shandy, Gent.
b.shortTitle = "Tristram Shandy"
print b.shortTitle
# emits: Tristram Shandy
del b.shortTitle
print b.shortTitle
# emits: The Life and Opinions of Tristram Shandy, Gent.
```

DefaultAlias is *not* what is technically known as a *data descriptor* class because it has no __set__ method. In practice, this means that, when we assign a value to an instance attribute whose name is defined in the class as a DefaultAlias, the instance records the attribute normally, and the instance attribute *shadows* the class attribute. This is exactly what's happening in this snippet after we explicitly assign to b.shortTitle—when we del b.shortTitle, we remove the *per-instance* attribute, uncovering the per-class one again.

Custom descriptor class Alias is a simple variant of class DefaultAlias, easily obtained by inheritance. Alias aliases one attribute to another, not just upon accesses to the attribute's value (as DefaultAlias would do), but also upon all operations of value setting and deletion. It easily achieves this by being a "data descriptor" class, which means that it does have a __set__ method. Therefore, any assignment to an instance attribute whose name is defined in the class as an Alias gets intercepted by Alias' __set__ method. (Alias also defines a __delete__ method, to obtain exactly the same effect upon attribute deletion.)

Alias can be quite useful when you want to evolve a class, which you made publicly available in a previous version, to use more appropriate names for methods and other attributes, while still keeping the old names available for backwards compatibility.

For this specific use, you may even want a version that emits a warning when the old name is used:

```
import warnings
class OldAlias(Alias):
    def _warn(self):
        warnings.warn('use %r, not %r' % (self.name, self.oldname),
                        DeprecationWarning, stacklevel=3)
    def __init__(self, name, oldname):
        super(OldAlias, self).__init__(name)
        self.oldname = oldname
    def __get__(self, inst, cls):
        self._warn()
        return super(OldAlias, self).__get__(inst, cls)
    def __set__(self, inst, value):
        self._warn()
        return super(OldAlias, self).__set__(inst, value)
    def __delete__(self, inst):
        self._warn()
        return super(OldAlias, self).__delete__(inst)
```

Here is a toy example of using OldAlias:

```
class NiceClass(object):
    def __init__(self, name):
        self.nice_new_name = name
    bad_old_name = OldAlias('nice_new_name', 'bad_old_name')
```

Old code using this class may still refer to the instance attribute as bad_old_name, preserving backwards compatibility; when that happens, though, a warning message is presented about the deprecation, encouraging the old code's author to upgrade the code to use nice_new_name instead. The normal mechanisms of the warnings module of the Python Standard Library ensure that, by default, such warnings are output only once per occurrence and per run of a program, not repeatedly. For example, the snippet:

```
x = NiceClass(23)
for y in range(4):
    print x.bad_old_name
    x.bad_old_name += 100
```

emits:

```
xxx.py:64: DeprecationWarning: use 'nice_new_name', not 'bad_old_name'
  print x.bad_old_name
23
xxx.py:65: DeprecationWarning: use 'nice_new_name', not 'bad_old_name'
  x.bad_old_name += 100
123
223
323
```

The warning is printed once per line using the bad old name, not repeated again and again as the for loop iterates.

See Also

Custom descriptors are best documented on Raymond Hettinger's web page: *http://users.rcn.com/python/download/Descriptor.htm*; *Library Reference* and *Python in a Nutshell* docs about the warnings module.

20.4 Caching Attribute Values

Credit: Denis S. Otkidach

Problem

You want to be able to compute attribute values, either per instance or per class, on demand, with automatic caching.

Solution

Custom descriptors are the right tools for this task:

```
class CachedAttribute(object):
    ''' Computes attribute value and caches it in the instance. '''
    def __init__(self, method, name=None):
        # record the unbound-method and the name
        self.method = method
        self.name = name or method.__name__
    def __get__(self, inst, cls):
        if inst is None:
            # instance attribute accessed on class, return self
            return self
        # compute, cache and return the instance's attribute value
        result = self.method(inst)
        setattr(inst, self.name, result)
        return result
class CachedClassAttribute(CachedAttribute):
    ''' Computes attribute value and caches it in the class. '''
    def __get__(self, inst, cls):
        # just delegate to CachedAttribute, with 'cls' as ``instance''
        return super(CachedClassAttribute, self).__get__(cls, cls)
```

Discussion

If your class instances have attributes that must be computed on demand but don't generally change after they're first computed, custom descriptor CachedAttribute as presented in this recipe is just the ticket. Here is a toy example of use (with Python 2.4 syntax):

```
class MyObject(object):
    def __init__(self, n):
        self.n = n
    @CachedAttribute
    def square(self):
```

```
            return self.n * self.n
m = MyObject(23)
print vars(m)                          # 'square' not there yet
# emits: {'n': 23}
print m.square                         # ...so it gets computed
# emits: 529
print vars(m)                          # 'square' IS there now
# emits: {'square': 529, 'n': 23}
del m.square                           # flushing the cache
print vars(m)                          # 'square' removed
# emits: {'n': 23}
m.n = 42
print vars(m)
# emits: {'n': 42}              # still no 'square'
print m.square                         # ...so gets recomputed
# emits: 1764
print vars(m)                          # 'square' IS there again
# emits: {'square': 1764, 'n': 23}
```

As you see, after the first access to m.square, the square attribute is cached in instance m, so it will not get recomputed for that instance. If you need to flush the cache, for example, to change m.n, so that m.square will get recomputed if it is ever accessed again, just del m.square. Remember, attributes can be removed in Python! To use this code in Python 2.3, remove the decorator syntax @CachedAttribute and insert instead an assignment square = CachedAttribute(square) *after* the end of the def statement for method square.

Custom descriptor CachedClassAttribute is just a simple variant of CachedAttribute, easily obtained by inheritance: it computes the value by calling a method on the class rather than the instance, and it caches the result on the class, too. This may help when all instances of the class need to see the same cached value. CachedClassAttribute is mostly meant for cases in which you do not need to flush the cache because its __get__ method usually wipes away the instance descriptor itself:

```
class MyClass(object):
    class_attr = 23
    @CachedClassAttribute
    def square(cls):
        return cls.class_attr * cls.class_attr
x = MyClass()
y = MyClass()
print x.square
# emits: 529
print y.square
# emits: 529
del MyClass.square
print x.square          # raises an AttributeError exception
```

However, when you do need a cached class attribute with the ability to occasionally flush it, you can still get it with a little trick. To implement this snippet so it works as intended, just add the statement:

```
class MyClass(MyClass): pass
```

right after the end of the `class MyClass` statement and before generating any instance of MyClass. Now, two class objects are named MyClass, a hidden "base" one that always holds the custom descriptor instance, and an outer "subclass" one that is used for everything else, including making instances and holding the cached value if any. Whether this trick is a reasonable one or whether it's too cute and clever for its own good, is a judgment call you can make for yourself! Perhaps it would be clearer to name the base class MyClassBase and use `class MyClass(MyClassBase)`, rather than use the same name for both classes; the mechanism would work in exactly the same fashion, since it is not dependent on the names of classes.

See Also

Custom descriptors are best documented at Raymond Hettinger's web page: *http://users.rcn.com/python/download/Descriptor.htm.*

20.5 Using One Method as Accessor for Multiple Attributes

Credit: Raymond Hettinger

Problem

Python's built-in property descriptor is quite handy but only as long as you want to use a separate method as the accessor of each attribute you make into a property. In certain cases, you prefer to use the same method to access several different attributes, and property does not support that mode of operation.

Solution

We need to code our own custom descriptor, which gets the attribute name in `__init__`, saves it, and passes it on to the accessors. For convenience, we also provide useful defaults for the various accessors. You can still pass in None explicitly if you want to forbid certain kinds of access but the default is to allow it freely.

```
class CommonProperty(object):
    def __init__(self, realname, fget=getattr, fset=setattr, fdel=delattr,
                 doc=None):
        self.realname = realname
        self.fget = fget
        self.fset = fset
        self.fdel = fdel
        self.__doc__ = doc or ""
```

```
    def __get__(self, obj, objtype=None):
        if obj is None:
            return self
        if self.fget is None:
            raise AttributeError, "can't get attribute"
        return self.fget(obj, self.realname)
    def __set__(self, obj, value):
        if self.fset is None:
            raise AttributeError, "can't set attribute"
        self.fset(obj, self.realname, value)
    def __delete__(self, obj):
        if self.fdel is None:
            raise AttributeError, "can't delete attribute"
        self.fdel(obj, self.realname, value)
```

Discussion

Here is a simple example of using this CommonProperty custom descriptor:

```
class Rectangle(object):
    def __init__(self, x, y):
        self._x = x                    # don't trigger _setSide prematurely
        self.y = y                     # now trigger it, so area gets computed
    def _setSide(self, attrname, value):
        setattr(self, attrname, value)
        self.area = self._x * self._y
    x = CommonProperty('_x', fset=_setSide, fdel=None)
    y = CommonProperty('_y', fset=_setSide, fdel=None)
```

The idea of this Rectangle class is that attributes x and y may be freely accessed but never deleted; when either of these attributes is set, the area attribute must be recomputed at once. You could alternatively recompute the area on the fly each time it's accessed, using a simple property for the purpose; however, if area is accessed often and sides are changed rarely, the architecture of this simple example obviously can be preferable.

In this simple example of CommonProperty use, we just need to be careful on the very first attribute setting in __init__: if we carelessly used self.x = x, that would trigger the call to _setSide, which, in turn, would try to use self._y before the _y attribute is set.

Another issue worthy of mention is that if any one or more of the fget, fset, or fdel arguments to CommonProperty is defaulted, the realname argument must be *different* from the attribute name to which the CommonProperty instance is assigned; otherwise, unbounded recursion would occur on trying the corresponding operation (in practice, you'd get a RecursionLimitExceeded exception).

See Also

The *Library Reference* and *Python in a Nutshell* documentation for built-ins getattr, setattr, delattr, and property.

20.6 Adding Functionality to a Class by Wrapping a Method

Credit: Ken Seehof, Holger Krekel

Problem

You need to add functionality to an existing class, without changing the source code for that class, and inheritance is not applicable (since it would make a new class, rather than changing the existing one). Specifically, you need to enrich a method of the class, adding some extra functionality "around" that of the existing method.

Solution

Adding completely new methods (and other attributes) to an existing `class` object is quite simple, since the built-in function `setattr` does essentially all the work. We need to "decorate" an existing method to add to its functionality. To achieve this, we can build the new replacement method as a closure. The best architecture is to define general-purpose wrapper and unwrapper functions, such as:

```python
import inspect
def wrapfunc(obj, name, processor, avoid_doublewrap=True):
    """ patch obj.<name> so that calling it actually calls, instead,
            processor(original_callable, *args, **kwargs)
    """
    # get the callable at obj.<name>
    call = getattr(obj, name)
    # optionally avoid multiple identical wrappings
    if avoid_doublewrap and getattr(call, 'processor', None) is processor:
        return
    # get underlying function (if any), and anyway def the wrapper closure
    original_callable = getattr(call, 'im_func', call)
    def wrappedfunc(*args, **kwargs):
        return processor(original_callable, *args, **kwargs)
    # set attributes, for future unwrapping and to avoid double-wrapping
    wrappedfunc.original = call
    wrappedfunc.processor = processor
    # 2.4 only: wrappedfunc.__name__ = getattr(call, '__name__', name)
    # rewrap staticmethod and classmethod specifically (iff obj is a class)
    if inspect.isclass(obj):
        if hasattr(call, 'im_self'):
            if call.im_self:
                wrappedfunc = classmethod(wrappedfunc)
        else:
            wrappedfunc = staticmethod(wrappedfunc)
    # finally, install the wrapper closure as requested
    setattr(obj, name, wrappedfunc)
def unwrapfunc(obj, name):
    ''' undo the effects of wrapfunc(obj, name, processor) '''
    setattr(obj, name, getattr(obj, name).original)
```

This approach to wrapping is carefully coded to work just as well on ordinary functions (when obj is a module) as on methods of all kinds (e.g., bound methods, when obj is an instance; unbound, class, and static methods, when obj is a class). This method doesn't work when obj is a built-in type, though, because built-ins are immutable.

For example, suppose we want to have "tracing" prints of all that happens whenever a particular method is called. Using the general-purpose wrapfunc function just shown, we could code:

```
def tracing_processor(original_callable, *args, **kwargs):
    r_name = getattr(original_callable, '__name__', '<unknown>')
    r_args = map(repr, args)
    r_args.extend(['%s=%r' % x for x in kwargs.iteritems()])
    print "begin call to %s(%s)" % (r_name, ", ".join(r_args))
    try:
        result = call(*args, **kwargs)
    except:
        print "EXCEPTION in call to %s" %(r_name,)
        raise
    else:
        print "call to %s result: %r" %(r_name, result)
        return result
def add_tracing_prints_to_method(class_object, method_name):
    wrapfunc(class_object, method_name, tracing_processor)
```

Discussion

This recipe's task occurs fairly often when you're trying to modify the behavior of a standard or third-party Python module, since editing the source of the module itself is undesirable. In particular, this recipe can be handy for debugging, since the example function add_tracing_prints_to_method presented in the "Solution" lets you see on standard output all details of calls to a method you want to watch, without modifying the library module, and without requiring interactive access to the Python session in which the calls occur.

You can also use this recipe's approach on a larger scale. For example, say that a library that you imported has a long series of methods that return numeric error codes. You could wrap each of them inside an enhanced wrapper method, which raises an exception when the error code from the original method indicates an error condition. Again, a key issue is not having to modify the library's own code. However, methodical application of wrappers when building a subclass is also a way to avoid repetitive code (i.e., boilerplate). For example, recipe 5.12 "Performing Frequent Membership Tests on a Sequence" and recipe 1.24 "Making Some Strings Case-Insensitive" might be recoded to take advantage of the general wrapfunc presented in this recipe.

Particularly when "wrapping on a large scale", it is important to be able to "unwrap" methods back to their normal state, which is why this recipe's Solution also includes an unwrapfunc function. It may also be handy to avoid accidentally wrapping the same method in the same way twice, which is why wrapfunc supports the optional parameter avoid_doublewrap, defaulting to True, to avoid such double wrapping. (Unfortunately, classmethod and staticmethod do not support per-instance attributes, so the avoidance of double wrapping, as well as the ability to "unwrap", cannot be guaranteed in all cases.)

You can wrap the same method multiple times with different processors. However, unwrapping must proceed last-in, first-out; as coded, this recipe does not support the ability to remove a wrapper from "somewhere in the middle" of a chain of several wrappers. A related limitation of this recipe as coded is that double wrapping is not detected when another unrelated wrapping occurred in the meantime. (We don't even try to detect what we might call "deep double wrapping.")

If you need "generalized unwrapping", you can extend unwrap_func to return the processor it has removed; then you can obtain generalized unwrapping by unwrapping all the way, recording a list of the processors that you removed, and then pruning that list of processors and rewrapping. Similarly, generalized detection of "deep" double wrapping could be implemented based on this same idea.

Another generalization, to fully support staticmethod and classmethod, is to use a global dict, rather than per-instance attributes, for the original and processor values; functions, bound and unbound methods, as well as class methods and static methods, can all be used as keys into such a dictionary. Doing so obviates the issue with the inability to set per-instance attributes on class methods and static methods. However, each of these generalizations can be somewhat complicated, so we are not pursuing them further here.

Once you have coded some processors with the signature and semantics required by this recipe's wrapfunc, you can also use such processors more directly (in cases where modifying the source is OK) with a Python 2.4 decorator, as follows:

```
def processedby(processor):
    """ decorator to wrap the processor around a function. """
    def processedfunc(func):
        def wrappedfunc(*args, **kwargs):
            return processor(func, *args, **kwargs)
        return wrappedfunc
    return processedfunc
```

For example, to wrap this recipe's tracing_processor around a certain method at the time the class statement executes, in Python 2.4, you can code:

```
class SomeClass(object):
    @processedby(tracing_processor)
    def amethod(self, s):
        return 'Hello, ' + s
```

See Also

Recipe 5.12 "Performing Frequent Membership Tests on a Sequence" and recipe 1.24 "Making Some Strings Case-Insensitive" provide examples of the methodical application of wrappers to build a subclass to avoid boilerplate; *Library Reference* and *Python in a Nutshell* docs on built-in functions getattr and setattr and module inspect.

20.7 Adding Functionality to a Class by Enriching All Methods

Credit: Stephan Diehl, Robert E. Brewer

Problem

You need to add functionality to an existing class without changing the source code for that class. Specifically, you need to enrich all methods of the class, adding some extra functionality "around" that of the existing methods.

Solution

Recipe 20.6 "Adding Functionality to a Class by Wrapping a Method" previously showed a way to solve this task for one method by writing a closure that builds and applies a wrapper, exemplified by function add_tracing_prints_to_method in that recipe's Solution. This recipe generalizes that one, wrapping methods throughout a class or hierarchy, directly or via a custom metaclass.

Module inspect lets you easily find all methods of an existing class, so you can systematically wrap them all:

```python
import inspect
def add_tracing_prints_to_all_methods(class_object):
    for method_name, v in inspect.getmembers(class_object, inspect.ismethod):
        add_tracing_prints_to_method(class_object, method_name)
```

If you need to ensure that such wrapping applies to all methods of all classes in a whole hierarchy, the simplest way may be to insert a custom metaclass at the root of the hierarchy, so that all classes in the hierarchy will get that same metaclass. This insertion does normally need a minimum of "invasiveness"—placing a single statement

```python
    __metaclass__ = MetaTracer
```

in the body of that root class. Custom metaclass MetaTracer is, however, quite easy to write:

```python
class MetaTracer(type):
    def __init__(cls, n, b, d):
        super(MetaTracer, cls).__init__(n, b, d)
        add_tracing_prints_to_all_methods(cls)
```

Even such minimal invasiveness sometimes is unacceptable, or you need a more dynamic way to wrap all methods in a hierarchy. Then, as long as the root class of the hierarchy is new-style, you can arrange to get function add_tracing_prints_to_all_methods dynamically called on all classes in the hierarchy:

```
def add_tracing_prints_to_all_descendants(class_object):
    add_tracing_prints_to_all_methods(class_object)
    for s in class_object.__subclasses__():
        add_tracing_prints_to_all_descendants(s)
```

The inverse function unwrapfunc, in recipe 20.6 "Adding Functionality to a Class by Wrapping a Method," may also be similarly applied to all methods of a class and all classes of a hierarchy.

Discussion

We could code just about all functionality of such a powerful function as add_tracing_prints_to_all_descendants in the function's own body. However, it would not be a great idea to bunch up such diverse functionality inside a single function. Instead, we carefully split the functionality among the various separate functions presented in this recipe and previously in recipe 20.6 "Adding Functionality to a Class by Wrapping a Method." By this careful factorization, we obtain maximum reusability without code duplication: we have separate functions to dynamically add and remove wrapping from a single method, an entire class, and a whole hierarchy of classes; each of these functions appropriately uses the simpler ones. And for cases in which we can afford a tiny amount of "invasiveness" and want the convenience of automatically applying the wrapping to all methods of classes descended from a certain root, we can use a tiny custom metaclass.

add_tracing_prints_to_all_descendants cannot apply to old-style classes. This limitation is inherent in the old-style object model and is one of the several reasons you should always use new-style classes in new code you write: classic classes exist only to ensure compatibility in legacy programs. Besides the problem with classic classes, however, there's another issue with the structure of add_tracing_prints_to_all_descendants: in cases of multiple inheritance, the function will repeatedly visit some classes.

Since the method-wrapping function is carefully designed to avoid double wrapping, such multiple visits are not a serious problem, costing just a little avoidable overhead, which is why the function was acceptable for inclusion in the "Solution". In other cases in which we want to operate on all descendants of a certain root class, however, multiple visits might be unacceptable. Moreover, it is clearly not optimal to entwine the functionality of getting all descendants with that of applying one particular operation to each of them. The best idea is clearly to factor out the recursive structure into a generator, which can avoid duplicating visits with the memo idiom:

```
def all_descendants(class_object, _memo=None):
    if _memo is None:
```

```
    _memo = { }
elif class_object in _memo:
    return
yield class_object
for subclass in class_object.__subclasses__():
    for descendant in all_descendants(subclass, _memo):
        yield descendant
```

Adding tracing prints to all descendants now simplifies to:

```
def add_tracing_prints_to_all_descendants(class_object):
    for c in all_descendants(class_object):
        add_tracing_prints_to_all_methods(c)
```

In Python, whenever you find yourself with an iteration structure of any complexity, or recursion, it's always worthwhile to check whether it's feasible to factor out the iterative or recursive control structure into a separate, reusable generator, so that all iterations of that form can become simple for statements. Such separation of concerns can offer important simplifications and make code more maintainable.

See Also

Recipe 20.6 "Adding Functionality to a Class by Wrapping a Method" for details on how each method gets wrapped; *Library Reference* and *Python in a Nutshell* docs on module inspect and the __subclasses__ special method of new-style classes.

20.8   Adding a Method to a Class Instance at Runtime

Credit: Moshe Zadka

Problem

During debugging, you want to identify certain specific instance objects so that print statements display more information when applied to those specific objects.

Solution

The print statement implicitly calls the special method __str__ of the class of each object you're printing. Therefore, to ensure that printing certain objects displays more information, we need to give those objects new classes whose __str__ special methods are suitably modified. For example:

```
def add_method_to_objects_class(object, method, name=None):
    if name is None:
        name = method.func_name
    class newclass(object.__class__):
        pass
    setattr(newclass, name, method)
    object.__class__ = newclass
```

```
import inspect
def _rich_str(self):
    pieces = [ ]
    for name, value in inspect.getmembers(self):
        # don't display specials
        if name.startswith('__') and name.endswith('__'):
            continue
        # don't display the object's own methods
        if inspect.ismethod(value) and value.im_self is self:
            continue
        pieces.extend((name.ljust(15), '\t', str(value), '\n'))
    return ''.join(pieces)
def set_rich_str(obj, on=True):
    def isrich( ):
        return getattr(obj.__class__.__str__, 'im_func', None) is _rich_str
    if on:
        if not isrich( ):
            add_method_to_objects_class(obj, _rich_str, '__str__')
        assert isrich( )
    else:
        if not isrich( ):
            return
        bases = obj.__class__.__bases__
        assert len(bases) == 1
        obj.__class__ = bases[0]
        assert not isrich( )
```

Discussion

Here is a sample use of this recipe's set_rich_str function, guarded in the usual way:

```
if __name__ == '__main__':            # usual guard for example usage
    class Foo(object):
        def __init__(self, x=23, y=42):
            self.x, self.y = x, y
    f = Foo( )
    print f
    # emits: <__main__.Foo object at 0x38f770>
    set_rich_str(f)
    print f
    # emits:
    # x              23
    # y              42
    set_rich_str(f, on=False)
    print f
    # emits: <__main__.Foo object at 0x38f770>
```

In old versions of Python (and in Python 2.3 and 2.4, for backwards compatibility on instances of classic classes), intrinsic lookup of special methods (such as the intrinsic lookup for __str__ in a print statement) started on the instance. In today's Python, in the new object model that is recommended for all new code, the intrinsic lookup starts on the instance's class, bypassing names set in the instance's own __dict__. This innovation has many advantages, but, at a first superficial look, it may also

---

seem to have one substantial disadvantage: namely, to make it impossible to solve this recipe's Problem in the general case (i.e., for instances that might belong to either classic or new-style classes).

Fortunately, that superficial impression is not correct, thanks to Python's power of introspection and dynamism. This recipe's function add_method_to_objects_class shows how to change special methods on a given object obj's class, without affecting other "sibling" objects (i.e., other instances of the same class as obj's): very simply, start by changing the obj's class—that is, by setting obj.__class__ to a newly made class object (which inherits from the original class of obj, so that anything we don't explicitly modify remains unchanged). Once you've done that, you can then alter the newly made class object to your heart's contents.

Function _rich_str shows how you can use introspection to display a lot of information about a specific instance. Specifically, we display every attribute of the instance that doesn't have a special name (starting and ending with two underscores), except the instances' own bound methods. Function set_rich_str shows how to set the __str__ special method of an instance's class to either "rich" (the _rich_str function we just mentioned) or "normal" (the __str__ method the object's original class is coded to supply). To make the object's __str__ rich, set_rich_str uses add_method_to_objects_class to set __str__ to _rich_str. When the object goes back to "normal", set_rich_str sets the object's __class__ back to its original value (which is preserved as the only base class when the object is set to use _rich_str).

See Also

Recipe 20.6 "Adding Functionality to a Class by Wrapping a Method" and recipe 20.7 "Adding Functionality to a Class by Enriching All Methods" for other cases in which a class' methods are modified; documentation on the inspect standard library module in the *Library Reference*.

20.9 Checking Whether Interfaces Are Implemented

Credit: Raymond Hettinger

Problem

You want to ensure that the classes you define implement the interfaces that they claim to implement.

Solution

Python does not have a formal concept of "interface", but we can easily represent interfaces by means of "skeleton" classes such as:

```python
class IMinimalMapping(object):
    def __getitem__(self, key): pass
    def __setitem__(self, key, value): pass
    def __delitem__(self, key): pass
    def __contains__(self, key): pass
import UserDict
class IFullMapping(IMinimalMapping, UserDict.DictMixin):
    def keys(self): pass
class IMinimalSequence(object):
    def __len__(self): pass
    def __getitem__(self, index): pass
class ICallable(object):
    def __call__(self, *args): pass
```

We follow the natural convention that any class can *represent* an interface: the interface is the set of methods and other attributes of the class. We can say that a class C *implements* an interface i if C has all the methods and other attributes of i (and, possibly, additional ones).

We can now define a simple custom metaclass that checks whether classes implement all the interfaces they claim to implement:

```python
# ensure we use the best available 'set' type with name 'set'
try:
    set
except NameError:
    from sets import Set as set
# a custom exception class that we raise to signal violations
class InterfaceOmission(TypeError):
    pass
class MetaInterfaceChecker(type):
    ''' the interface-checking custom metaclass '''
    def __init__(cls, classname, bases, classdict):
        super(MetaInterfaceChecker, cls).__init__(classname, bases, classdict)
        cls_defines = set(dir(cls))
        for interface in cls.__implements__:
            itf_requires = set(dir(interface))
            if not itf_requires.issubset(cls_defines):
                raise InterfaceOmission, list(itf_requires - cls_defines)
```

Any class that uses MetaInterfaceChecker as its metaclass must expose a class attribute __implements__, an iterable whose items are the interfaces the class claims to implement. The metaclass checks the claim, raising an InterfaceOmission exception if the claim is false.

Discussion

Here's an example class using the `MetaInterfaceChecker` custom metaclass:

```
class Skidoo(object):
    ''' a mapping which claims to contain all keys, each with a value
        of 23; item setting and deletion are no-ops; you can also call
        an instance with arbitrary positional args, result is 23. '''
    __metaclass__ = MetaInterfaceChecker
    __implements__ = IMinimalMapping, ICallable
    def __getitem__(self, key): return 23
    def __setitem__(self, key, value): pass
    def __delitem__(self, key): pass
    def __contains__(self, key): return True
    def __call__(self, *args): return 23
sk = Skidoo()
```

Any code dealing with an instance of such a class can choose to check whether it can rely on certain interfaces:

```
def use(sk):
    if IMinimalMapping in sk.__implements__:
    ...code using 'sk[...]' and/or 'x in sk'...
```

You can, if you want, provide much fancier and more thorough checks, for example by using functions from standard library module inspect to check that the attributes being exposed and required are methods with compatible signatures. However, this simple recipe does show how to automate the simplest kind of checks for interface compliance.

See Also

Library Reference and *Python in a Nutshell* docs about module sets, (in Python 2.4 only) the set built-in, custom metaclasses, the inspect module.

20.10 Using __new__ and __init__ Appropriately in Custom Metaclasses

Credit: Michele Simionato, Stephan Diehl, Alex Martelli

Problem

You are writing a custom metaclass, and you are not sure which tasks your metaclass should perform in its __new__ method, and which ones it should perform in its __init__ method instead.

Solution

Any preliminary processing that your custom metaclass performs on the name, bases, or dict of the class being built, can affect the way in which the class object gets built only if it occurs in the metaclass' __new__ method, *before* your code calls the metaclass' superclass' __new__. For example, that's the only time when you can usefully affect the new class' __slots__, if any:

```
class MetaEnsure_foo(type):
    def __new__(mcl, cname, cbases, cdict):
        # ensure instances of the new class can have a '_foo' attribute
        if '__slots__' in cdict and '_foo' not in cdict['__slots__']:
            cdict['__slots__'] = tuple(cdict['__slots__']) + ('_foo',)
        return super(MetaEnsure_foo, mcl).__new__(mcl, cname, cbases, cdict)
```

Metaclass method __init__ is generally the most appropriate one for any changes that your custom metaclass makes to the class object *after* the class object is built—for example, continuing the example code for metaclass MetaEnsure_foo:

```
    def __init__(cls, cname, cbases, cdict):
        super(MetaEnsure_foo, cls).__init__(cls, cname, cbases, cdict)
        cls._foo = 23
```

Discussion

The custom metaclass MetaEnsure_foo performs a definitely "toy" task presented strictly as an example: if the class object being built defines a __slots__ attribute (to save memory), MetaEnsure_foo ensures that the class object includes a slot _foo, so that instances of that class can have an attribute thus named. Further, the custom metaclass sets an attribute with name _foo and value 23 on each new class object. The point of the recipe isn't really this toy task, but rather, a clarification on how __new__ and __init__ methods of a custom metaclass are best coded, and which tasks are most appropriate for each.

Whenever you instantiate any class x (whether x is a custom metaclass or an ordinary class) with or without arguments (we can employ the usual Python notation *a, **k to mean arbitrary positional and named arguments), Python internally performs the equivalent of the following snippet of code:

```
    new_thing = X.__new__(X, *a, **k)
    if isinstance(new_thing, X):
        X.__init__(new_thing, *a, **k)
```

The new_thing thus built and initialized is the result of instantiating x. If x is a custom metaclass, in particular, this snippet occurs at the end of the execution of a class statement, and the arguments (all positional) are the name, bases, and dictionary of the new class that is being built.

So, your custom metaclass' __new__ method is the code that has dibs—it executes first. That's the moment in which you can adjust the name, bases, and dictionary that you receive as arguments, to affect the way the new class object is built. Most characteristics of the class object, but not all, can also be changed later. An example of an attribute that you have to set *before* building the class object is __slots__. Once the class object is built, the slots, if any, are defined, and any further change to __slots__ has no effect.

The custom metaclass in this recipe carefully uses super to delegate work to its superclass, rather than carelessly calling type.__new__ or type.__init__ directly: the latter usage would be a subtle mistake, impeding the proper working of multiple inheritance among metaclasses. Further, this recipe is careful in naming the first parameters to both methods: cls to mean an ordinary class (the object that is the first argument to a custom metaclass' __init__), mcl to mean a metaclass (the object that is the first argument to a custom metaclass' __new__). The common usage of self should be reserved to mean normal instances, not classes nor metaclasses, and therefore it doesn't normally occur in the body of a custom metaclass. All of these names are a matter of mere convention, but using appropriate conventions promotes clarity, and this use of cls and mcl was blessed by Guido van Rossum himself, albeit only verbally.

The usage distinction between __new__ and __init__ that this recipe advocates for custom metaclasses is basically the same criterion that *any* class should always follow: use __new__ when you must, only for jobs that cannot be done later; use __init__ for all jobs that can be left until __init__ time. Following these conventions makes life easiest for anybody who must tweak your custom metaclass or make it work well in a multiple inheritance situation, and thus enhances the reusability of your code. __new__ should contain only the *essence* of your metaclass: stuff that anybody using your metaclass in any way at all *must* surely want (or else he wouldn't be using your metaclass!) because it's stuff that's not easy to tweak, modify, or override. __init__ is "softer", so most of what your metaclass is doing to the class objects you generate, should be there, exactly because it will be easier for reusers to tweak or avoid.

See Also

Library Reference and *Python in a Nutshell* docs on built-ins super and __slots__, and special methods __init__ and __new__.

20.11 Allowing Chaining of Mutating List Methods

Credit: Stephan Diehl, Alex Martelli

Problem

The methods of the list type that mutate a list object in place—methods such as append and sort—return None. To call a series of such methods, you therefore need to use a series of statements. You would like those methods to return self to enable you to *chain* a series of calls within a single expression.

Solution

A custom metaclass can offer an elegant approach to this task:

```
def makeChainable(func):
    ''' wrapp a method returning None into one returning self '''
    def chainableWrapper(self, *args, **kwds):
        func(self, *args, **kwds)
        return self
    # 2.4 only: chainableWrapper.__name__ = func.__name__
    return chainableWrapper
class MetaChainable(type):
    def __new__(mcl, cName, cBases, cDict):
        # get the "real" base class, then wrap its mutators into the cDict
        for base in cBases:
            if not isinstance(base, MetaChainable):
                for mutator in cDict['__mutators__']:
                    if mutator not in cDict:
                        cDict[mutator] = makeChainable(getattr(base, mutator))
                break
        # delegate the rest to built-in 'type'
        return super(MetaChainable, mcl).__new__(mcl, cName, cBases, cDict)
class Chainable: __metaclass__ = MetaChainable
if __name__ == '__main__':
    # example usage
    class chainablelist(Chainable, list):
        __mutators__ = 'sort reverse append extend insert'.split()
    print ''.join(chainablelist('hello').extend('ciao').sort().reverse())
# emits: oolliheca
```

Discussion

Mutator methods of mutable objects such as lists and dictionaries work in place, mutating the object they're called on, and return None. One reason for this behavior is to avoid confusing programmers who might otherwise think such methods build and return new objects. Returning None also prevents you from *chaining* a sequence of mutator calls, which some Python gurus consider bad style because it can lead to very dense code that may be hard to read.

Some programmers, however, occasionally prefer the chained-calls, dense-code style. This style is particularly useful in such contexts as lambda forms and list comprehensions. In these contexts, the ability to perform actions within an expression, rather than in statements, can be crucial. This recipe shows one way you can tweak mutators' return values to allow chaining. Using a custom metaclass means the runtime overhead of introspection is paid only rarely, at class-creation time, rather than repeatedly. If runtime overhead is not a problem for your application, it may be simpler for you to use a delegating wrapper idiom that was posted to comp.lang.python by Jacek Generowicz:

```
class chainable(object):
    def __init__(self, obj):
```

```
        self.obj = obj
    def __iter__(self):
        return iter(self.obj)
    def __getattr__(self, name):
        def proxy(*args, **kwds):
            result = getattr(self.obj, name)(*args, **kwds)
            if result is None: return self
            else: return result
        # 2.4 only: proxy.__name__ = name
        return proxy
```

The use of this wrapper is quite similar to that of classes obtained by the custom metaclass presented in this recipe's Solution—for example:

```
print ''.join(chainable(list('hello')).extend('ciao').sort().reverse())
# emits: oolliheca
```

See Also

Library Reference and Python in a Nutshell docs on built-in type list and special methods __new__ and __getattr__.

20.12 Using Cooperative Supercalls with Terser Syntax

Credit: Michele Simionato, Gonçalo Rodrigues

Problem

You like the cooperative style of multiple-inheritance coding supported by the super built-in, but you wish you could use that style in a more terse and direct way.

Solution

A custom metaclass lets us selectively wrap the methods exposed by a class. Specifically, if the second argument of a method is named super, then that argument gets bound to the appropriate instance of the built-in super:

```
import inspect
def second_arg(func):
    args = inspect.getargspec(func)[0]
    try: return args[1]
    except IndexError: return None
def super_wrapper(cls, func):
    def wrapper(self, *args, **kw):
        return func(self, super(cls, self), *args, **kw)
    # 2.4 only: wrapper.__name__ = func.__name__
    return wrapper
class MetaCooperative(type):
    def __init__(cls, name, bases, dic):
```

```
        super(MetaCooperative, cls).__init__(cls, name, bases, dic)
        for attr_name, func in dic.iteritems():
            if inspect.isfunction(func) and second_arg(func) == "super":
                setattr(cls, attr_name, super_wrapper(cls, func))
class Cooperative:
    __metaclass__ = MetaCooperative
```

Discussion

Here is a usage example of the custom metaclass presented in this recipe's Solution, in a typical toy case of "diamond-shaped" inheritance:

```
if __name__ == "__main__":
    class B(Cooperative):
        def say(self):
            print "B",
    class C(B):
        def say(self, super):
            super.say()
            print "C",
    class D(B):
        def say(self, super):
            super.say()
            print "D",
    class CD(C, D):
        def say(self, super):
            super.say()
            print '!'
    CD().say()
    # emits: B D C !
```

Methods that want to access the super-instance just need to use super as the name of their second argument; the metaclass then arranges to wrap those methods so that the super-instance gets synthesized and passed in as the second argument, as needed.

In other words, when a class cls, whose metaclass is MetaCooperative, has methods whose second argument is named super, then, in those methods, any call of the form super.something(*args, **kw) is a shortcut for super(cls, self).something(*args, **kw). This approach avoids the need to pass the class object as an argument to the built-in super.

Class cls may also perfectly well have other methods that do not follow this convention, and in those methods, it may use the built-in super in the usual way: all it takes for any method to be "normal" is to *not* use super as the name of its second argument, surely not a major restriction. This recipe offers nicer syntax sugar for the common case of cooperative supercalls, where the first argument to super is the current class—nothing more.

See Also

Library Reference and *Python in a Nutshell* docs on module inspect and the super built-in.

20.13 Initializing Instance Attributes Without Using __init__

Credit: Dan Perl, Shalabh Chaturvedi

Problem

Your classes need to initialize some instance attributes when they generate new instances. If you do the initialization, as normal, in the __init__ method of your classes, then, when anybody subclasses your classes, they must remember to invoke your classes' __init__ methods. Your classes often get subclassed by beginners who forget this elementary requirement, and you're getting tired of the resulting support requests. You'd like an approach that beginners subclassing your classes are less likely to mess up.

Solution

Beginners are unlikely to have heard of the __new__ method, so you can place your initialization there, instead of in __init__:

```python
# a couple of classes that you write:
class super1(object):
    def __new__(cls, *args, **kwargs):
        obj = super(super1, cls).__new__(cls, *args, **kwargs)
        obj.attr1 = [ ]
        return obj
    def __str__(self):
        show_attr = [ ]
        for attr, value in sorted(self.__dict__.iteritems()):
            show_attr.append('%s:%r' % (attr, value))
        return '%s with %s' % (self.__class__.__name__,
                               ', '.join(show_attr))
class super2(object):
    def __new__(cls, *args, **kwargs):
        obj = super(super2, cls).__new__(cls, *args, **kwargs)
        obj.attr2 = { }
        return obj
# typical beginners' code, inheriting your classes but forgetting to
# call its superclasses' __init__ methods
class derived(super1, super2):
    def __init__(self):
        self.attr1.append(111)
        self.attr3 = ( )
# despite the typical beginner's error, you won't get support calls:
```

```
d = derived( )
print d
# emits: derived with attr1:[111], attr2:{}, attr3:()
```

Discussion

One of Python's strengths is that it does very little *magic behind the curtains*—close to nothing, actually. If you know Python in sufficient depth, you know that essentially all internal mechanisms are clearly documented and exposed. This strength, however, means that you yourself must do some things that other languages do *magically*, such as prefixing self. to methods and attributes of the current object and explicitly calling the __init__ methods of your superclasses in the __init__ method of your own class.

Unfortunately, Python beginners, particularly if they first learned from other languages where they're used to such implicit and magical behavior, can take some time adapting to this brave new world where, if you want something done, you do it. Eventually, they learn. Until they have learned, at times it seems that their favorite pastime is filling my mailbox with help requests, in tones ranging from the humble to the arrogant and angry, complaining that "my classes don't work." Almost invariably, this complaint means they're inheriting from my classes, which are meant to ease such tasks as displaying GUIs and communicating on the Internet, and they have forgotten to call my classes' __init__ methods from the __init__ methods of subclasses they have coded.

To deal with this annoyance, I devised the simple solution shown in this recipe. Beginners generally don't know about the __new__ method, and what they don't know, they cannot mess up. If they *do* know enough to override __new__, you can hope they also know enough to do a properly cooperative supercall using the super built-in, rather than crudely bypassing your code by directly calling object.__new__. Well, hope springs eternal, or so they say. Truth be told, my hopes lie in beginners' total, blissful ignorance about __new__—and this theory seems to work because I don't get those kind of help requests any more. The help requests I now receive seem concerned more with how to actually use my classes, rather than displaying fundamental ignorance of Python.

If you work with more advanced but equally perverse beginners, ones quite able to mess up __new__, you should consider giving your classes a custom metaclass that, in its __call__ (which executes at class instantiation time), calls a special hidden method on your classes to enable you to do your initializations anyway. That approach should hold you in good stead—at least until the beginners start learning about metaclasses. Of course, "it is impossible to make anything foolproof, because fools are so ingenious" (Roger Berg). Nevertheless, see recipe 20.14 "Automatic Initialization of Instance Attributes" for other approaches that avoid __init__ for attribute initialization needs.

See Also

Library Reference and *Python in a Nutshell* documentation on special methods
__init__ and __new__, and built-in super; recipe 20.14 "Automatic Initialization of
Instance Attributes."

20.14 Automatic Initialization of Instance Attributes

Credit: Sébastien Keim, Troy Melhase, Peter Cogolo

Problem

You want to set some attributes to constant values, during object initialization, without forcing your subclasses to call your __init__ method.

Solution

For constant values of immutable types, you can just set them in the class. For example, instead of the natural looking:

```
class counter(object):
    def __init__(self):
        self.count = 0
    def increase(self, addend=1):
        self.count += addend
```

you can code:

```
class counter(object):
    count = 0
    def increase(self, addend=1):
        self.count += addend
```

This style works because self.count += addend, when self.count belongs to an immutable type, is exactly equivalent to self.count = self.count + addend. The first time this code executes for a particular instance self, self.count is not yet initialized as a per-instance attribute, so the per-class attribute is used, on the *right* of the equal sign (=); but the per-instance attribute is nevertheless the one assigned to (on the *left* of the sign). Any further use, once the per-instance attribute has been initialized in this way, gets or sets the per-instance attribute.

This style does *not* work for values of mutable types, such as lists or dictionaries. Coding this way would then result in all instances of the class sharing the *same* mutable-type object as their attribute. However, a custom descriptor works fine:

```
class auto_attr(object):
    def __init__(self, name, factory, *a, **k):
        self.data = name, factory, a, k
    def __get__(self, obj, clas=None):
```

```
        name, factory, a, k = self.data
        setattr(obj, name, factory(*a, **k))
        return getattr(obj, name)
```

With class auto_attr at hand, you can now code, for example:

```
class recorder(object):
    count = 0
    events = auto_attr('events', list)
    def record(self, event):
        self.count += 1
        self.events.append((self.count, event))
```

Discussion

The simple and standard approach of defining constant initial values of attributes by setting them as class attributes is just fine, as long as we're talking about constants of immutable types, such as numbers or strings. In such cases, it does no harm for all instances of the class to share the same initial-value object for such attributes, and, when you do such operations as self.count += 1, you intrinsically rebind the specific, per-instance value of the attribute, without affecting the attributes of other instances.

However, when you want an attribute to have an initial value of a *mutable* type, such as a list or a dictionary, you need a little bit more—such as the auto_attr custom descriptor type in this recipe. Each instance of auto_attr needs to know to what attribute name it's being bound, so we pass that name as the first argument when we instantiate auto_attr. Then, we have the factory, a callable that will produce the desired initial value when called (often factory will be a type object, such as list or dict); and finally optional positional and keyword arguments to be passed when factory gets called.

The first time you access an attribute named name on a given instance obj, Python finds in obj's class the descriptor (an instance of auto_attr) and calls the descriptor's method __get__, with obj as an argument. auto_attr's __get__ calls the factory and sets the result under the right name as an instance attribute, so that any further access to the attribute of that name in the instance gets the actual value.

In other words, the descriptor is designed to *hide itself* when it's first accessed on each instance, to get out of the way from further accesses to the attribute of the same name on that same instance. For this purpose, it's absolutely crucial that auto_attr is technically a *non*data descriptor class, meaning it doesn't define a __set__ method. As a consequence, an attribute of the same name may be set in the instance: the per-instance attribute overrides (i.e., takes precedence over) the per-class attribute (i.e., the instance of a nondata descriptor class).

You can regard this recipe's approach as "just-in-time generation" of instance attributes, the first time a certain attribute gets accessed on a certain instance. Beyond allowing attribute initialization to occur without an __init__ method, this approach may therefore be useful as an optimization: consider it when each instance has a potentially large set of attributes, maybe costly to initialize, and most of the attributes may end up never being accessed on each given instance.

It is somewhat unfortunate that this recipe requires you to pass to auto_attr the name of the attribute it's getting bound to; unfortunately, auto_attr has no way to find out for itself. However, if you're willing to add a custom metaclass to the mix, you can fix this little inconvenience, too, as follows:

```
class smart_attr(object):
    name = None
    def __init__(self, factory, *a, **k):
        self.creation_data = factory, a, k
    def __get__(self, obj, clas=None):
        if self.name is None:
            raise RuntimeError, ("class %r uses a smart_attr, so its "
                "metaclass should be MetaSmart, but is %r instead" %
                (clas, type(clas)))
        factory, a, k = self.creation_data
        setattr(obj, name, factory(*a, **k))
        return getattr(obj, name)
class MetaSmart(type):
    def __new__(mcl, clasname, bases, clasdict):
        # set all names for smart_attr attributes
        for k, v in clasdict.iteritems():
            if isinstance(v, smart_attr):
                v.name = k
        # delegate the rest to the supermetaclass
        return super(MetaSmart, mcl).__new__(mcl, clasname, bases, clasdict)
# let's let any class use our custom metaclass by inheriting from smart_object
class smart_object:
    __metaclass__ = MetaSmart
```

Using this variant, you could code:

```
class recorder(smart_object):
    count = 0
    events = smart_attr(list)
    def record(self, event):
        self.count += 1
        self.events.append((self.count, event))
```

Once you start considering custom metaclasses, you have more options for this recipe's task, automatic initialization of instance attributes. While a custom descriptor remains the best approach when you *do* want "just-in-time" generation of initial values, if you prefer to generate all the initial values at the time the instance is being initialized, then you can use a simple placeholder instead of smart_attr, and do more work in the metaclass:

```
class attr(object):
    def __init__(self, factory, *a, **k):
        self.creation_data = factory, a, k
import inspect
def is_attr(member):
```

```
        return isinstance(member, attr)
    class MetaAuto(type):
        def __call__(cls, *a, **k):
            obj = super(MetaAuto, cls).__call__(*a, **k)
            # set all values for 'attr' attributes
            for n, v in inspect.getmembers(cls, is_attr):
                factory, a, k = v.creation_data
                setattr(obj, n, factory(*a, **k))
            return obj
    # lets' let any class use our custom metaclass by inheriting from auto_object
    class auto_object:
        __metaclass__ = MetaAuto
```

Code using this more concise variant looks just about the same as with the previous one:

```
    class recorder(auto_object):
        count = 0
        events = attr(list)
        def record(self, event):
            self.count += 1
            self.events.append((self.count, event))
```

See Also

Recipe 20.13 "Initializing Instance Attributes Without Using __init__" for another approach that avoids __init__ for attribute initialization needs; *Library Reference* and *Python in a Nutshell* docs on special method __init__, and built-ins super and setattr.

20.15 Upgrading Class Instances Automatically on reload

Credit: Michael Hudson, Peter Cogolo

Problem

You are developing a Python module that defines a class, and you're trying things out in the interactive interpreter. Each time you reload the module, you have to ensure that existing instances are updated to instances of the new, rather than the old class.

Solution

First, we define a custom metaclass, which ensures its classes keep track of all their existing instances:

```
    import weakref
    class MetaInstanceTracker(type):
        ''' a metaclass which ensures its classes keep track of their instances '''
```

```
    def __init__(cls, name, bases, ns):
        super(MetaInstanceTracker, cls).__init__(name, bases, ns)
        # new class cls starts with no instances
        cls.__instance_refs__ = [ ]
    def __instances__(cls):
        ''' return all instances of cls which are still alive '''
        # get ref and obj for refs that are still alive
        instances = [(r, r()) for r in cls.__instance_refs__ if r() is not None]
        # record the still-alive references back into the class
        cls.__instance_refs__ = [r for (r, o) in instances]
        # return the instances which are still alive
        return [o for (r, o) in instances]
    def __call__(cls, *args, **kw):
        ''' generate an instance, and record it (with a weak reference) '''
        instance = super(MetaInstanceTracker, cls).__call__(*args, **kw)
        # record a ref to the instance before returning the instance
        cls.__instance_refs__.append(weakref.ref(instance))
        return instance
class InstanceTracker:
    ''' any class may subclass this one, to keep track of its instances '''
    __metaclass__ = MetaInstanceTracker
```

Now, we can subclass MetaInstanceTracker to obtain another custom metaclass, which, on top of the instance-tracking functionality, implements the auto-upgrading functionality required by this recipe's Problem:

```
import inspect
class MetaAutoReloader(MetaInstanceTracker):
    ''' a metaclass which, when one of its classes is re-built, updates all
        instances and subclasses of the previous version to the new one '''
    def __init__(cls, name, bases, ns):
        # the new class may optionally define an __update__ method
        updater = ns.pop('__update__', None)
        super(MetaInstanceTracker, cls).__init__(name, bases, ns)
        # inspect locals & globals in the stackframe of our caller
        f = inspect.currentframe().f_back
        for d in (f.f_locals, f.f_globals):
            if name in d:
                # found the name as a variable is it the old class
                old_class = d[name]
                if not isinstance(old_class, mcl):
                    # no, keep trying
                    continue
                # found the old class: update its existing instances
                for instance in old_class.__instances__():
                    instance.__class__ = cls
                    if updater: updater(instance)
                    cls.__instance_refs__.append(weakref.ref(instance))
                # also update the old class's subclasses
                for subclass in old_class.__subclasses__():
                    bases = list(subclass.__bases__)
                    bases[bases.index(old_class)] = cls
                    subclass.__bases__ = tuple(bases)
                break
```

```
            return cls
    class AutoReloader:
        ''' any class may subclass this one, to get automatic updates '''
        __metaclass__ = MetaAutoReloader
```

Here is a usage example:

```
# an 'old class'
class Bar(AutoReloader):
    def __init__(self, what=23):
        self.old_attribute = what
# a subclass of the old class
class Baz(Bar):
    pass
# instances of the old class & of its subclass
b = Bar()
b2 = Baz()
# we rebuild the class (normally via 'reload', but, here, in-line!):
class Bar(AutoReloader):
    def __init__(self, what=42):
        self.new_attribute = what+100
    def __update__(self):
        # compute new attribute from old ones, then delete old ones
        self.new_attribute = self.old_attribute+100
        del self.old_attribute
    def meth(self, arg):
        # add a new method which wasn't in the old class
        print arg, self.new_attribute
if __name__ == '__main__':
    # now b is "upgraded" to the new Bar class, so we can call 'meth':
    b.meth(1)
    # emits: 1 123
    # subclass Baz is also upgraded, both for existing instances...:
    b2.meth(2)
    # emits: 2 123
    # ...and for new ones:
    Baz().meth(3)
    # emits: 3 142
```

Discussion

You're probably familiar with the problem this recipe is meant to address. The scenario is that you're editing a Python module with your favorite text editor. Let's say at some point, your module *mod.py* looks like this:

```
class Foo(object):
    def meth1(self, arg):
        print arg
```

In another window, you have an interactive interpreter running to test your code:

```
>>> import mod
>>> f = mod.Foo()
>>> f.meth1(1)
1
```

and it seems to be working. Now you edit *mod.py* to add another method:

```
class Foo(object):
    def meth1(self, arg):
        print arg
    def meth2(self, arg):
        print -arg
```

Head back to the test session:

```
>>> reload(mod)
module 'mod' from 'mod.pyc'
>>> f.meth2(2)
Traceback (most recent call last):
  File "&lt;stdin&gt;", line 1, in ?
AttributeError: 'Foo' object has no attribute 'meth2'
```

Argh! You forgot that f was an instance of the *old* mod.Foo!

You can do two things about this situation. After reloading, either regenerate the instance:

```
>>> f = mod.Foo()
>>> f.meth2(2)
-2
```

or manually assign to f.__class__:

```
>>> f.__class__ = mod.Foo
>>> f.meth2(2)
-2
```

Regenerating works well in simple situations but can become very tedious. Assigning to the class can be automated, which is what this recipe is all about.

Class MetaInstanceTracker is a metaclass that tracks instances of its instances. As metaclasses go, it isn't too complicated. New classes of this metatype get an extra __instance_refs__ class variable (which is used to store weak references to instances) and an __instances__ class method (which strips out dead references from the __instance_refs__ list and returns real references to the still live instances). Each time a class whose metatype is MetaInstanceTracker gets instantiated, a weak reference to the instance is appended to the class' __instance_refs__ list.

When the definition of a class of metatype MetaAutoReloader executes, the namespace of the definition is examined to determine whether a class of the same name already exists. If it does, then it is assumed that this is a class *redefinition*, instead of a class definition, and all instances of the *old* class are updated to the *new* class. (MetaAutoReloader inherits from MetaInstanceTracker, so such instances can easily be found). All direct subclasses, found through the old class' intrinsic __subclasses__ class method, then get their __bases__ tuples rebuilt with the same change.

The new class definition can optionally include a method __update__, whose job is to update the state (meaning the set of attributes) of each instance, as the instance's class transitions from the old version of the class to the new one. The usage example in this recipe's Solution presents a case in which one attribute has changed name and is computed by different rules, as you can tell by observing the way the __init__ methods of the old and new versions are coded; in this case, the job of __update__ is to compute the new attribute based on the value of the old one, then del the old attribute for tidiness.

This recipe's code should probably do more thorough error checking; Net of error-checking issues, this recipe can also supply some fundamental tools to start solving a problem that is substantially harder than the one explained in this recipe's Problem statement: automatically upgrade classes in a long-running application, without needing to stop and restart that application.

Doing automatic upgrading in production code is more difficult than doing it during development because many more issues must be monitored. For example, you may need a form of locking to ensure the application is in a quiescent state while a number of classes get upgraded, since you probably don't want to have the application answering requests in the middle of the upgrading procedure, with some classes or instances already upgraded and others still in their old versions. You also often encounter issues of persistent storage because the application probably needs to update whatever persistent storage it keeps from old to new versions when it upgrades classes. And those are just two examples. Nevertheless, the key component of such on-the-fly upgrading, which has to do with updating instances and sub-classes of old classes to new ones, can be tackled with the tools shown in this recipe.

See Also

Docs for the built-in function reload in the *Library Reference* and *Python in a Nutshell*.

20.16 Binding Constants at Compile Time

Credit: Raymond Hettinger, Skip Montanaro

Problem

Runtime lookup of global and built-in names is slower than lookup of local names. So, you would like to bind constant global and built-in names into local constant names at compile time.

Solution

To perform this task, we must examine and rewrite bytecodes in the function's code object. First, we get three names from the standard library module opcode, so we can operate symbolically on bytecodes, and define two auxiliary functions for bytecode operations:

```
from opcode import opmap, HAVE_ARGUMENT, EXTENDED_ARG
globals().update(opmap)
def _insert_constant(value, i, code, constants):
    ''' insert LOAD_CONST for value at code[i:i+3].  Reuse an existing
        constant if values coincide, otherwise append new value to the
        list of constants; return index of the value in constants. '''
    for pos, v in enumerate(constants):
        if v is value: break
    else:
        pos = len(constants)
        constants.append(value)
    code[i] = LOAD_CONST
    code[i+1] = pos & 0xFF
    code[i+2] = pos >> 8
    return pos
def _arg_at(i, code):
    ''' return argument number of the opcode at code[i] '''
    return code[i+1] | (code[i+2] << 8)
```

Next comes the workhorse, the internal function that does all the binding and folding work:

```
def _make_constants(f, builtin_only=False, stoplist=(), verbose=False):
    # bail out at once, innocuously, if we're in Jython, IronPython, etc
    try: co = f.func_code
    except AttributeError: return f
    # we'll modify the bytecodes and consts, so make lists of them
    newcode = map(ord, co.co_code)
    codelen = len(newcode)
    newconsts = list(co.co_consts)
    names = co.co_names
    # Depending on whether we're binding only builtins, or ordinary globals
    # too, we build dictionary 'env' to look up name->value mappings, and we
    # build set 'stoplist' to selectively override and cancel such lookups
    import __builtin__
    env = vars(__builtin__).copy()
    if builtin_only:
        stoplist = set(stoplist)
        stoplist.update(f.func_globals)
    else:
        env.update(f.func_globals)
    # First pass converts global lookups into lookups of constants
    i = 0
    while i < codelen:
        opcode = newcode[i]
        # bail out in difficult cases: optimize common cases only
        if opcode in (EXTENDED_ARG, STORE_GLOBAL):
            return f
        if opcode == LOAD_GLOBAL:
            oparg = _arg_at(i, newcode)
            name = names[oparg]
```

```
                if name in env and name not in stoplist:
                    # get the constant index to use instead
                    pos = _insert_constant(env[name], i, newcode, newconsts)
                    if verbose: print '%r -> %r[%d]' % (name, newconsts[pos], pos)
            # move accurately to the next bytecode, skipping arg if any
            i += 1
            if opcode >= HAVE_ARGUMENT:
                i += 2
    # Second pass folds tuples of constants and constant attribute lookups
    i = 0
    while i < codelen:
        newtuple = [ ]
        while newcode[i] == LOAD_CONST:
            oparg = _arg_at(i, newcode)
            newtuple.append(newconsts[oparg])
            i += 3
        opcode = newcode[i]
        if not newtuple:
            i += 1
            if opcode >= HAVE_ARGUMENT:
                i += 2
            continue
        if opcode == LOAD_ATTR:
            obj = newtuple[-1]
            oparg = _arg_at(i, newcode)
            name = names[oparg]
            try:
                value = getattr(obj, name)
            except AttributeError:
                continue
            deletions = 1
        elif opcode == BUILD_TUPLE:
            oparg = _arg_at(i, newcode)
            if oparg != len(newtuple):
                continue
            deletions = len(newtuple)
            value = tuple(newtuple)
        else:
            continue
        reljump = deletions * 3
        newcode[i-reljump] = JUMP_FORWARD
        newcode[i-reljump+1] = (reljump-3) & 0xFF
        newcode[i-reljump+2] = (reljump-3) >> 8
        pos = _insert_constant(value, i, newcode, newconsts)
        if verbose: print "new folded constant: %r[%d]" % (value, pos)
        i += 3
    codestr = ''.join(map(chr, newcode))
    codeobj = type(co)(co.co_argcount, co.co_nlocals, co.co_stacksize,
                co.co_flags, codestr, tuple(newconsts), co.co_names,
                co.co_varnames, co.co_filename, co.co_name,
                co.co_firstlineno, co.co_lnotab, co.co_freevars,
                co.co_cellvars)
    return type(f)(codeobj, f.func_globals, f.func_name, f.func_defaults,
                f.func_closure)
```

Finally, we use _make_constants to optimize itself and its auxiliary function, and define the functions that are meant to be called from outside this module to perform the optimizations that this module supplies:

```
# optimize thyself!
_insert_constant = _make_constants(_insert_constant)
_make_constants = _make_constants(_make_constants)
import types
@_make_constants
def bind_all(mc, builtin_only=False, stoplist=(), verbose=False):
    """ Recursively apply constant binding to functions in a module or class.
    """
    try:
        d = vars(mc)
    except TypeError:
        return
    for k, v in d.items():
        if type(v) is types.FunctionType:
            newv = _make_constants(v, builtin_only, stoplist,  verbose)
            setattr(mc, k, newv)
        elif type(v) in (type, types.ClassType):
            bind_all(v, builtin_only, stoplist, verbose)
@_make_constants
def make_constants(builtin_only=False, stoplist=[ ], verbose=False):
    """ Call this metadecorator to obtain a decorator which optimizes
        global references by constant binding on a specific function.
    """
    if type(builtin_only) == type(types.FunctionType):
        raise ValueError, 'must CALL, not just MENTION, make_constants'
    return lambda f: _make_constants(f, builtin_only, stoplist, verbose)
```

Discussion

Assuming you have saved the code in this recipe's Solution as module *optimize.py* somewhere on your Python sys.path, the following example demonstrates how to use the make_constants *decorator with arguments* (i.e., metadecorator) to optimize a function—in this case, a reimplementation of random.sample:

```
import random
import optimize
@optimize.make_constants(verbose=True)
def sample(population, k):
    " Choose `k' unique random elements from a `population' sequence. "
    if not isinstance(population, (list, tuple, str)):
        raise TypeError('Cannot handle type', type(population))
    n = len(population)
    if not 0 <= k <= n:
        raise ValueError, "sample larger than population"
    result = [None] * k
    pool = list(population)
    for i in xrange(k):              # invariant:  non-selected at [0,n-i)
        j = int(random.random( ) * (n-i))
        result[i] = pool[j]
```

```
        pool[j] = pool[n-i-1]    # move non-selected item into vacancy
    return result
```

Importing this module emits the following output. (Some details, such as the
addresses and paths, will, of course, vary.)

```
'isinstance' -> <built-in function isinstance>[6]
'list' -> <type 'list'>[7]
'tuple' -> <type 'tuple'>[8]
'str' -> <type 'str'>[9]
'TypeError' -> <class exceptions.TypeError at 0x402952cc>[10]
'type' -> <type 'type'>[11]
'len' -> <built-in function len>[12]
'ValueError' -> <class exceptions.ValueError at 0x40295adc>[13]
'list' -> <type 'list'>[7]
'xrange' -> <type 'xrange'>[14]
'int' -> <type 'int'>[15]
'random' -> <module 'random' from '/usr/local/lib/python2.4/random.pyc'>[16]
new folded constant: (<type 'list'>, <type 'tuple'>, <type 'str'>)[17]
new folded constant: <built-in method random of Random object at 0x819853c>[18]
```

On my machine, *with* the decorator optimize.make_constants as shown in this snippet, sample(range(1000), 100) takes 287 microseconds; *without* the decorator (and
thus with the usual bytecode that the Python 2.4 compiler produces), the same operation takes 333 microseconds. Thus, using the decorator improves performance by
approximately 14% in this example—and it does so while allowing your own functions' source code to remain pristine, without any optimization-induced obfuscation. On functions making use of more constant names within loops, the
performance benefit of using this recipe's decorator can be correspondingly greater.

A common and important technique for manual optimization of a Python function,
once that function is shown by profiling to be a bottleneck of program performance,
is to ensure that all global and built-in name lookups are turned into lookups of local
names. In the source of functions that have been thus optimized, you see strange
arguments with default values, such as _len=len, and the body of the function uses
this local name _len to refer to the built-in function len. This kind of optimization is
worthwhile because lookup of local names is much faster than lookup of global and
built-in names. However, functions thus optimized can become cluttered and less
readable. Moreover, optimizing by hand can be tedious and error prone.

This recipe automates this important optimization technique: by just mentioning a
decorator before the def statement, you get all the constant bindings and foldings,
while leaving the function source uncluttered, readable, and maintainable. After
binding globals to constants, the decorator makes a second pass and folds constant
attribute lookups and tuples of constants. Constant attribute lookups often occur
when you use a function or other attribute from an imported module, such as the use
of random.random in the sample function in the example snippet. Tuples of constants
commonly occur in for loops and conditionals using the in operator, such as for x
in ('a', 'b', 'c'). The best way to appreciate the bytecode transformations

performed by the decorator in this recipe is to run "dis.dis(sample)" and view the disassembly into bytecodes, both with and without the decorator.

If you want to optimize every function and method in a module, you can call optimize.bind_all(sys.modules[__name__]) as the last instruction in the module's body, before the tests. To optimize every method in a class, you can call optimize.bind_all(theclass) just after the end of the body of the class theclass statement. Such wholesale optimization is handy (it does not require you to deal with any details) but generally not the best approach. It's best to bind, selectively, only functions whose speed is important. Functions that particularly benefit from constant-binding optimizations are those that refer to many global and built-in names, particularly with references in loops.

To ensure that the constant-binding optimizations do not alter the behavior of your code, apply them only where dynamic updates of globals are not desired (i.e., the globals do not change). In more dynamic environments, a more conservative approach is to pass argument builtin_only as True, so that only the built-ins get optimized (built-ins include functions such as len, exceptions such as IndexError, and such constants as True or False). Alternatively, you can pass a sequence of names as the stoplist argument, to tell the binding optimization functions to leave unchanged any reference to those names.

While this recipe is meant for use with Python 2.4, you can also use this approach in Python 2.3, with a few obvious caveats. In particular, in version 2.3, you cannot use the new 2.4 @decorator syntax. Therefore, to use in Python 2.3, you'll have to tweak the recipe's code a little, to expose _make_constants directly, without a leading underscore, and use f=make_constants(f) in your code, right after the end of the body of the def f statement. However, if you are interested in optimization, you should consider moving to Python 2.4 anyway: Python 2.4 is very compatible with Python 2.3, with just a few useful additions, and version 2.4 is generally measurably faster than Python 2.3.

See Also

Library Reference and *Python in a Nutshell* docs on the opcode module.

20.17 Solving Metaclass Conflicts

Credit: Michele Simionato, David Mertz, Phillip J. Eby, Alex Martelli, Anna Martelli Ravenscroft

Problem

You need to multiply inherit from several classes that may come from several metaclasses, so you need to generate automatically a custom metaclass to solve any possible metaclass conflicts.

Solution

First of all, given a sequence of metaclasses, we want to filter out "redundant" ones—those that are already implied by others, being duplicates or superclasses. This job nicely factors into a general-purpose generator yielding the unique, nonredundant items of an iterable, and a function using inspect.getmro to make the set of all superclasses of the given classes (since superclasses are redundant):

```
# support 2.3, too
try: set
except NameError: from sets import Set as set
# support classic classes, to some extent
import types
def uniques(sequence, skipset):
    for item in sequence:
        if item not in skipset:
            yield item
            skipset.add(item)
import inspect
def remove_redundant(classes):
    redundant = set([types.ClassType])    # turn old-style classes to new
    for c in classes:
        redundant.update(inspect.getmro(c)[1:])
    return tuple(uniques(classes, redundant))
```

Using the remove_redundant function, we can generate a metaclass that can resolve metatype conflicts (given a sequence of base classes, and other metaclasses to inject both before and after those implied by the base classes). It's important to avoid generating more than one metaclass to solve the same potential conflicts, so we also keep a "memoization" mapping:

```
memoized_metaclasses_map = { }
def _get_noconflict_metaclass(bases, left_metas, right_metas):
    # make tuple of needed metaclasses in specified order
    metas = left_metas + tuple(map(type, bases)) + right_metas
    needed_metas = remove_redundant(metas)
    # return existing confict-solving meta, if any
    try: return memoized_metaclasses_map[needed_metas]
    except KeyError: pass
    # compute, memoize and return needed conflict-solving meta
    if not needed_metas:         # whee, a trivial case, happy us
        meta = type
    elif len(needed_metas) == 1: # another trivial case
        meta = needed_metas[0]
    else:                        # nontrivial, darn, gotta work...
        # ward against non-type root metatypes
        for m in needed_metas:
            if not issubclass(m, type):
                raise TypeError( 'Non-type root metatype %r' % m)
        metaname = '_' + ''.join([m.__name__ for m in needed_metas])
        meta = classmaker()(metaname, needed_metas, { })
    memoized_metaclasses_map[needed_metas] = meta
    return meta
```

```
def classmaker(left_metas=(), right_metas=()):
    def make_class(name, bases, adict):
        metaclass = _get_noconflict_metaclass(bases, left_metas, right_metas)
        return metaclass(name, bases, adict)
    return make_class
```

The internal _get_noconflict_metaclass function, which returns (and, if needed, builds) the conflict-resolution metaclass, and the public classmaker closure must be mutually recursive for a rather subtle reason. If _get_noconflict_metaclass just built the metaclass with the reasonably common idiom:

```
meta = type(metaname, needed_metas, {})
```

it would work in all ordinary cases, but it might get into trouble when the meta-classes involved have custom metaclasses themselves! Just like "little fleas have lesser fleas," so, potentially, metaclasses can have meta-metaclasses, and so on—fortu-nately *not* "ad infinitum," pace Augustus De Morgan, so the mutual recursion does eventually terminate.

The recipe offers minimal support for old-style (i.e., classic) classes, with the simple expedient of initializing the set redundant to contain the metaclass of old-style classes, types.ClassType. In practice, this recipe imposes automatic conversion to new-style classes. Trying to offer more support than this for classic classes, which are after all a mere legacy feature, would be overkill, given the confused and confusing situation of metaclass use for old-style classes.

In all of our code outside of this *noconflict.py* module, we will only use noconflict.classmaker, optionally passing it metaclasses we want to inject, left and right, to obtain a callable that we can then use just like a metaclass to build new class objects given names, bases, and dictionary, but with the assurance that metatype conflicts cannot occur. Phew. Now *that* was worth it, wasn't it?!

Discussion

Here is the simplest case in which a metatype conflict can occur: multiply inheriting from two classes with independent metaclasses. In a pedagogically simplified toy-level example, that could be, say:

```
>>> class Meta_A(type): pass
...
>>> class Meta_B(type): pass
...
>>> class A: __metaclass__ = Meta_A
...
>>> class B: __metaclass__ = Meta_B
...
>>> class C(A, B): pass
Traceback (most recent call last):
  File "<stdin>", line 1, in ?
TypeError: Error when calling the metaclass bases
    metaclass conflict: the metaclass of a derived class must be a
```

```
(non-strict) subclass of the metaclasses of all its bases
>>>
```

A class normally inherits its metaclass from its bases, but when the bases have distinct metaclasses, the metatype constraint that Python expresses so tersely in this error message applies. So, we need to build a new metaclass, say Meta_C, which inherits from both Meta_A and Meta_B. For a demonstration of this need, see the book that's so aptly considered the bible of metaclasses: Ira R. Forman and Scott H. Danforth, *Putting Metaclasses to Work: A New Dimension in Object-Oriented Programming* (Addison-Wesley).

Python does not do magic: it does not automatically create the required Meta_C. Rather, Python raises a TypeError to ensure that the programmer is aware of the problem. In simple cases, the programmer can solve the metatype conflict by hand, as follows:

```
>>> class Meta_C(Meta_A, Meta_B): pass
>>> class C(A, B): __metaclass__ = Meta_C
```

In this case, everything works smoothly.

The key point of this recipe is to show an automatic way to resolve metatype conflicts, rather than having to do it by hand every time. Having saved all the code from this recipe's Solution into *noconflict.py* somewhere along your Python sys.path, you can make class C with automatic conflict resolution, as follows:

```
>>> import noconflict
>>> class C(A, B): __metaclass__ = noconflict.classmaker()
```

The call to the noconflict.classmaker closure returns a function that, when Python calls it, obtains the proper metaclass and uses it to build the class object. It cannot yet return the metaclass itself, but that's OK—you *can* assign anything you want to the __metaclass__ attribute of your class, as long as it's callable with the (name, bases, dict) arguments and nicely builds the class object. Once again, Python's signature-based polymorphism serves us well and unobtrusively.

Automating the resolution of the metatype conflict has many pluses, even in simple cases. Thanks to the "memoizing" technique used in *noconflict.py*, the same conflict-resolving metaclass is used for any occurrence of a given sequence of conflicting metaclasses. Moreover, with this approach you may also explicitly inject other metaclasses, beyond those you get from your base classes, and again you can avoid conflicts. Consider:

```
>>> class D(A): __metaclass__ = Meta_B
Traceback (most recent call last):
  File "<stdin>", line 1, in ?
TypeError: Error when calling the metaclass bases
    metaclass conflict: the metaclass of a derived class must be a
(non-strict) subclass of the metaclasses of all its bases
```

This metatype conflict is resolved just as easily as the former one:

```
>>> class D(A): __metaclass__ = noconflict.classmaker((Meta_B,))
```

The code presented in this recipe's Solution takes pains to avoid any subclassing that is not strictly necessary, and it also uses mutual recursion to avoid any meta-level of meta-meta-type conflicts. You might never meet higher-order-meta conflicts anyway, but if you adopt the code presented in this recipe, you need not even worry about them.

Thanks to David Mertz for help in polishing the original version of the code. This version has benefited immensely from discussions with Phillip J. Eby. Alex Martelli and Anna Martelli Ravenscroft did their best to make the recipe's code and discussion as explicit and understandable as they could. The functionality in this recipe is not absolutely complete: for example, it supports old-style classes only in a rather backhanded way, and it does not really cover such exotica as nontype metatype roots (such as Zope 2's old ExtensionClass). These limitations are there primarily to keep this recipe as understandable as possible. You may find a more complete implementation of metatype conflict resolution at Phillip J. Eby's PEAK site, *http://peak.telecommunity.com/*, in the peak.util.Meta module of the PEAK framework.

See Also

Ira R. Forman and Scott H. Danforth, *Putting Metaclasses to Work: A New Dimension in Object-Oriented Programming* (Addison-Wesley); Michele Simionato's essay, "Method Resolution Order," *http://www.python.org/2.3/mro.html*.

Index

We'd like to hear your suggestions for improving our indexes. Send email to *index@oreilly.com*.

asynchat module, 559
asyncore module, 559
    performance benefits, 356
atomic operations, 357
attachments, removing from email
        messages, 499–501
attributes
    adding to classes, 240
    checking objects for, 266–269
    hiding those supplied by delegate, 247
    named, tuple items accessible as, 250–252
    restricting setting in classes, 240
    settings for
        restricting in classes, 240
        __setattr__ method, 237
authentication
    HTTPS navigation through proxies, 541
    remote logins
        SSH, 579–581
        Telnet, 576–579
    SSL client over HTTPS, 582
    via POP server, 397
automatic caching, 29, 656
automatic delegation, 248
    as alternative to inheritance, 244–247
    wrapping by, 246

B

backslash (\), 5, 58, 717
backups, 403
    versioning filenames, 105
backwards compatibility
    classic classes for new code
        development, 282
    inheritance in Python, 234
bag (multiset), 662–666
basestring type, 9
Berkeley DB (Berkeley database), persisting
        data with, 307–309
big-O analysis and notation, 199
binary data, sending to Windows standard
        output, 82
binary files
    randomly reading bytes from, 74
    sequentially reading bytes from, 59, 66
binary large objects (BLOBs), 290
binary mode versus text mode (files), 59
binary search algorithm, 211
binary strings, formatting integers as, 671–675
binding attributes of instance objects, 230
bisect (binary search), 211

bisect_right function, 211
bits, printing integer as string of, 683
BLOBs (binary large objects), 290
    storing in
        MySQL, 312
        PostgreSQL, 313
        SQLite, 315
Borg class, 276
    avoiding Singleton Design Pattern
        with, 273–277
Borg design nonpattern, alternative to, 275
bound methods, 42
    held by objects, pickling, 300–302
    maintaining references to without
        inhibiting garbage collection, 256
    weak references to, 258
bounded precision, 113
bsddb package, 307–309
bsddb3 package, 307–309
building
    C extensions, 619–622
        with Pyrex, 623–624
    classes via metaclasses, 236
    dictionaries, 166–169
    empty class instance, 254
    list comprehensions, 609–611
    lists, 7, 151, 155
    modules, tools for, 617
__builtin__ module, 188
built-in type, inheriting, 235
bytecodes, multiple, 357
bytes, as distinguished from characters, 1
    CRC-64 computation on stream
        of, 107–109
    extracting from strings, 28
    randomly reading from binary file, 74
    sequentially reading from binary file, 66
    sequentially reading from binary files, 59
bytestrings, 45

C

C extensions
    building, 619–622
        with Pyrex, 623–624
    debugging, 639
C++ library, using in Python, 625–627
C programming language
    coding Python extensions, 357
    cPickle as built-in module for
        storing/retrieving data, 290
        (see also cPickle module)

DB API modules, single parameter passing
        style across various, 323–325
db_row (Python Database Row
        Module), 320
DDList class, 429
deadlocks, 376
    avoiding by nonblocking output and error
        streams, 386–388
debug mode, tracing
        expressions/comments, 339–342
debugging, 332–354
    C extensions, 639
    disabling conditions and loops, 333
    exception handling, 337–339
    garbage collection, 336, 337
    property function, 253
    starting debugger automatically after
        uncaught exception, 345–348
    threads in processes, 363
    tracebacks, 342–345
    unit tests
        checking values against, 352–354
        running automatically, 348
        running simply, 346
decimal module, 113–116, 135–141
decimal numeric data type, 113
decorate-sort-undecorate (DSU), 190
decorators, 740–787
    altering code objects in, 778
__deepcopy__ method, 256
def statement, defining methods with, 231
default values/bounds, using with
        tkSimpleDialog functions, 427
__delattr__ method, 245
delegation, 233
    flexibility of, 246
    in proxies, 247–250
    (see also automatic delegation)
description attribute, 316
    cursors, 321
descriptors, 740–787
design patterns, 269–278
    Adapter, 88
    Monostate, 276
    Null Object, 277–280
    object-oriented, 230
    Reactor, 570–573
    Singleton, 230, 271–277
    State, 269–271

Strategy, 270
Template Method, 226, 233
design tools, relational database design in
        appropriate for, 289
dict (built-in type), 167
    fromkeys classmethod, 176
dictionaries
    adding entries to, 165
    building, 166–169
    chaining lookups, 242
    dispatching methods/functions with, 175
    enriching type of, with rating
        functionality, 222–226
    extracting subsets from, 170
    finding unions/intersections of, 176
    getting values from, 163
    inverting, 171
    keys in (see dictionary keys)
    mapping column names to index
        values, 316
    sorting, 195
    using for search tasks, 190
    (see also mappings)
dictionary keys
    associating multiple values to, 173
    avoiding quoting in dictionary
        building, 166
directories
    computing relative path, 96
    finding files in, 91–96
    sharing on Windows, 414
    trees (see directory trees)
directory trees
    changing file extensions in, 90
    walking, 88
dispatching
    generators as co-routines, 691
    methods via dictionaries, 175
distributed programming, 558–583
    error handling in, 571
distutils package, 611
division, true versus truncating, 26
DLLs (dynamic link libraries), Windows
    calling functions from, 627–629
    registering/unregistering, 411
docstrings, 351
doctest module, 222, 333
DOM (Document Object Model), 464
drag-and-drop reordering, adding to a
        Tkinter listbox, 428

X

xdrlib module, 559

XML

accessing structural data in
human-readable form, 290
encoding Unicode for, 49
using MSHTML to parse, 483

XML documents

converting into tree of Python
objects, 471–473
counting tags in, 467
extracting text from, 468
validating, 477

XML processing, 463–484

autodetecting XML encoding, 469–471
checking XML well formedness, 465
eror handling in, 477
filtering elements/attributes of
namespace, 478–480
parsing Microsoft Excel XML, 475
removing whitespace-only text nodes from
DOM node subtree, 474

XML tags, counting number of "element"s in
XML document, 467
XML validation, 466
XMLFilterBase class, 481
XMLGenerator class, 480
XML-RPC, 464, 558

enabling remote termination, 566
method calls to, 561
serving requests to, 562
using with Medusa, 564

xmlrpclib module, 559
xml.sax.saxutils module, 481
xproperty function, 253

Z

zip, 167
zip files

handling inside strings, 79
reading data from, 77

zipfile module, 77
Z-Object Database (ZODB), 290
ZODB (Z-Object Database), 290
Zope, 527

About the Editors

Alex Martelli spent eight years with IBM Research, winning three Outstanding Technical Achievement Awards. He then spent 13 years as a senior software consultant at think3 Inc., developing libraries, network protocols, GUI engines, event frameworks, and web access frontends. He has also taught programming languages, development methods, and numerical computing at Ferrara University and other venues. He's a C++ MVP for Brainbench and a member of the Python Software Foundation. He currently works as a freelance consultant from his home in Italy.

Alex's proudest achievement is the publication of two articles in *The Bridge World* (January/February 2000) that were hailed as giant steps toward solving issues that had haunted contract bridge theoreticians for decades.

Anna Martelli Ravenscroft has a background in training and mentoring, particularly in office technologies. She discovered Python in 2002 and has since used it in various ways in her work and daily life. She has presented talks on various Python topics at EuroPython, PyCon, and OSCON, and chaired the Lightning Talks track at several conferences. Anna lives with her husband, Alex Martelli, and hopes to get through the red tape necessary for her two children to live with them. Her interests include reading, blogging, and weight lifting (not all at the same time).

David Ascher is the lead for Python projects at ActiveState, including Komodo, ActiveState's integrated development environment written mostly in Python. David has taught courses about Python for corporations, in universities, and at conferences. He also organized the Python track at the 1999 and 2000 O'Reilly Open Source Conventions and was the program chair for the 10th International Python Conference. In addition, he cowrote *Learning Python* and serves as a director of the Python Software Foundation. David holds a B.S. in physics and a Ph.D. in cognitive science, both from Brown University.

Colophon

Our look is the result of reader comments, our own experimentation, and feedback from distribution channels. Distinctive covers complement our distinctive approach to technical topics, breathing personality and life into potentially dry subjects.

The animal on the cover of *Python Cookbook*, Second Edition is a springhaas (*Pedetes capensis*), also known as a spring hare. Springhaas are not hares at all, but rather the only member of the family *Pedetidae* in the order *Rodentia*. They are not marsupials, but they are vaguely kangaroo-like, with small front legs, powerful hind legs designed for hopping, jumping, and leaping, and long, strong, bushy (but not prehensile) tails they use for balance and as a brace when sitting. They grow to be about 14 to 18 inches long, with tails as long as their bodies, and can weigh approximately 8 pounds. Springhaas have rich, glossy, tawny, or golden-reddish coats with long, soft fur and white underbellies. Their heads are disproportionately large, and they have long ears (with a flap of skin at the base they can close to prevent sand from getting inside while they are digging) and large, dark brown eyes.

Springhaas mate throughout the year and have a gestation period of about 78 to 82 days. Females generally give birth to only one baby (which stays with its mother until it is approximately seven weeks old) per litter but have three or four litters each year. Babies are born with teeth and are fully furred, with their eyes closed and ears open.

Springhaas are terrestrial and well-adapted for digging, and they tend to spend their days in the small networks of their burrows and tunnels. They are nocturnal and primarily herbivorous, feeding on bulbs, roots, grains, and occasionally insects. While they are foraging, they move about on all fours, but they are able to move 10 to 25 feet in a single horizontal leap and are capable of quick getaways when frightened. Although they are often seen foraging in groups in the wild, they do not form an organized social unit and usually nest alone or in breeding pairs. Springhaas can live up to 15 years in captivity. They are found in Zaire, Kenya, and South Africa, in dry, desert, or semiarid areas, and they are a favorite and important food source in South Africa.

Darren Kelly was the production editor for *Python Cookbook*, Second Edition. Nancy Crumpton copyedited the book. Emily Quill and Claire Cloutier provided quality control. Nancy Crumpton provided production services and wrote the index.

Emma Colby designed the cover of this book, based on a series design by Edie Freedman. The cover image is from *Animal Creation: Mammalia*. Emma Colby produced the cover layout with QuarkXPress 4.1 using Adobe's ITC Garamond font.

David Futato designed the interior layout. This book was converted to FrameMaker 5.5.6 by Joe Wizda with a format conversion tool created by Erik Ray, Jason McIntosh, Neil Walls, and Mike Sierra that uses Perl and XML technologies. The text font is Linotype Birka; the heading font is Adobe Myriad Condensed; and the code font is LucasFont's TheSans Mono Condensed. This colophon was written by Rachel Wheeler.

Keep in touch with O'Reilly

1. Download examples from our books

To find example files for a book, go to:

www.oreilly.com/catalog

select the book, and follow the "Examples" link.

2. Register your O'Reilly books

Register your book at *register.oreilly.com*

Why register your books?
Once you've registered your O'Reilly books you can:

- Win O'Reilly books, T-shirts or discount coupons in our monthly drawing.
- Get special offers available only to registered O'Reilly customers.
- Get catalogs announcing new books (US and UK only).
- Get email notification of new editions of the O'Reilly books you own.

3. Join our email lists

Sign up to get topic-specific email announcements of new books and conferences, special offers, and O'Reilly Network technology newsletters at:

elists.oreilly.com

It's easy to customize your free elists subscription so you'll get exactly the O'Reilly news you want.

4. Get the latest news, tips, and tools

www.oreilly.com

- "Top 100 Sites on the Web"—PC Magazine
- CIO Magazine's Web Business 50 Awards

Our web site contains a library of comprehensive product information (including book excerpts and tables of contents), downloadable software, background articles, interviews with technology leaders, links to relevant sites, book cover art, and more.

5. Work for O'Reilly

Check out our web site for current employment opportunities:

jobs.oreilly.com

6. Contact us

O'Reilly Media
1005 Gravenstein Hwy North
Sebastopol, CA 95472 USA

TEL: 707-827-7000 or 800-998-9938
      (6am to 5pm PST)

FAX: 707-829-0104

order@oreilly.com
For answers to problems regarding your order or our products. To place a book order online, visit:

www.oreilly.com/order_new

catalog@oreilly.com
To request a copy of our latest catalog.

booktech@oreilly.com
For book content technical questions or corrections.

corporate@oreilly.com
For educational, library, government, and corporate sales.

proposals@oreilly.com
To submit new book proposals to our editors and product managers.

international@oreilly.com
For information about our international distributors or translation queries. For a list of our distributors outside of North America check out:

international.oreilly.com/distributors.html

adoption@oreilly.com
For information about academic use of O'Reilly books, visit:

academic.oreilly.com
